The Structure of CP and IP

OXFORD STUDIES IN COMPARATIVE SYNTAX
Richard Kayne, *General Editor*

The Structure of CP and IP

*The Cartography of
Syntactic Structures,
Volume 2*

Edited by
LUIGI RIZZI

UNIVERSITY PRESS

2004

OXFORD
UNIVERSITY PRESS

Oxford   New York
Auckland   Bangkok   Buenos Aires   Cape Town   Chennai
Dar es Salaam   Delhi   Hong Kong   Istanbul   Karachi   Kolkata
Kuala Lumpur   Madrid   Melbourne   Mexico City   Mumbai   Nairobi
São Paulo   Shanghai   Taipei   Tokyo   Toronto

Copyright © 2004 by Oxford University Press, Inc.

Published by Oxford University Press, Inc.
198 Madison Avenue, New York, New York, 10016

www.oup.com

Oxford is a registered trademark of Oxford University Press

Library of Congress Cataloging-in-Publication Data
The structure of CP and IP / edited by Luigi Rizzi.
    p. cm.—(Oxford studies in comparative syntax) (The cartography
of syntactic structures ; v. 2)
Includes bibliographical references and index.
ISBN 0-19-515948-9; ISBN 0-19-515949-7 (pbk.)
1. Grammar, Comparative and general—Clauses.   2. Grammar,
Comparative and general—Inflection.   3. Generative grammar.
I. Rizzi, Luigi.   II. Series.   III. Series: The cartography
of syntactic structures ; v. 2

P297 .S77   2003
415—dc21   2002038159

9 8 7 6 5 4 3 2

Printed in the United States of America
on acid-free paper

Contents

Contributors

Adriana Belletti
University of Siena

Paola Beninca'
University of Padua

Valentina Bianchi
University of Siena

Anna Cardinaletti
University of Bologna and University
of Venice

Carlo Cecchetto
University of Milano-Bicocca

Alessandra Giorgi
University of Venice

M. Rita Manzini
University of Florence

Fabio Pianesi
ITC-IRST, Trento

Cecilia Poletto
University of Padua, CNR

Jean-Yves Pollock
University of Picardie, Amiens

Luigi Rizzi
University of Siena

Ian Roberts
Downing College, University of
Cambridge

Leonardo Savoia
University of Florence

Ur Shlonsky
University of Geneva

The Structure of CP and IP

On the Cartography of Syntactic Structures

LUIGI RIZZI

Syntactic structures are complex objects. Much theory-guided descriptive work on syntactic constituents over the 1980s and 1990s has shown that phrases and clauses have a richly articulated internal structure. As the empirical evidence of such complexity had been steadily accumulating, some researchers came to the conclusion that it was a worthwhile endeavor to study this rich domain on its own, and they set the goal of arriving at structural maps that could do justice to the complexity of syntactic structures.

This was the initial motivation of the cartographic projects that have come to the fore in the last few years. If the impulse that prompted these efforts has to do with the complexity and richness of the domain, an equally influential driving factor is the intuition of the fundamental uniformity and underlying simplicity of the basic constituents—the syntactic atoms. The tension between these two driving forces offers a useful vantage point to understand certain directions taken by the cartographic analyses and to place these studies within the broader context of current syntactic theory.

Here I illustrate some of the discoveries that are at the origins of the cartographic projects and provide certain guidelines that have directed these efforts. I will then discuss some of the results achieved and their possible influence on the general theory of syntax, with special reference to minimalism. An overview of the content of the different chapters will conclude this introduction.

1. Background

One of the backbones of cartographic research is the view that inflectional morphology is distributed in the syntax. This view originates from the analysis of the English inflectional system in *Syntactic Structures*. Chomsky (1957) showed that it was advantageous to analyze inflectional affixes as elements of the syntactic computation: assuming them to be subjected to certain syntactic processes (local movement) permitted a simple analysis of complex distributional dependencies in the English auxiliary system. This analysis suggested a fairly abstract view of syntactic representations: the atoms of syntactic computations can be elements that are not morphologically autonomous words; morphological well-formedness can be obtained by submitting such atoms to movement processes; an inflectional affix may occupy the same structural position that is expressed by an autonomous function word if different featural choices are made. These ideas had already been very influential in the early days of generative grammar, but their effect was multiplied when they were combined with two basic insights of X-bar theory: all syntactic atoms project a uniform subtree (Chomsky 1970), and functional elements are full-fledged syntactic atoms, capable of projecting their own phrasal categories (Chomsky 1986a). These considerations supported the conclusion that clauses should be formed by the articulation of lexical and functional elements, each projecting uniform subtrees according to the general laws of structure building.

The question then arose of the number and label of functional heads and projections constituting the structure of the clauses. Richly inflected languages provide direct morphological evidence illustrating the morphosyntactic components of the clause. If overt morphological richness is a superficial trait of variation and a fundamental assumption of uniformity is followed, as much work in Case theory suggests ever since Vergnaud (1982), then it is reasonable to expect that clauses should be formed by a constant system of functional heads in all languages, each projecting a subtree occurring in a fixed syntactic hierarchy, irrespective of the actual morphological manifestation of the head (as an affix, as an autonomous function word, or as nothing at all). If this is correct, it should be possible to detect the extra syntactic space determined by this richly articulated clausal structure even in languages in which the morphology does not provide direct evidence for the postulation of independent layers: layer detection may be provided by more indirect kinds of evidence, having to do with the need of syntactic positions to accommodate certain phrasal constituents (adverbials, etc.), to account for word order alternations through head movement and so on.

This is the line of reasoning that led from Chomsky's "affix hopping" to Emonds's (1978) comparative analysis of the position of the verb in French and English to Pollock's (1989) postulation of distinct affixal heads in the inflectional system. The latter reference, in particular, provided clear evidence that complex word order patterns could be reduced to uniform syntactic structures plus simple parameters having to do with the way in which affixation takes place. This provided a very appealing model for the cross-linguistic study of the clause, which gave rise to a phase of intense comparative research. Among other things, the detailed study of the ordering of adverbial positions started to bear very directly on the analysis of the basic clausal structure, a trend that culminated in Cinque's (1999) book, which fully integrated morphological, syntactic, and interpretive evidence in the exploration of the fine details of the clausal structure across languages. So the view that inflectional morphology is distributed in the syntax, combined with a host of uniformity assumptions (phrases are structured and ordered uniformly for lexical and functional heads across languages), paved the way to the articulated conception of syntactic structures that is assumed and validated by cartographic studies.

This view of the morphology-syntax interface bears primarily on the identification of head positions in the clausal and phrasal structure. Another important element of the background has to do directly with the positions occupied by phrases and the computations involved in phrasal movement. Traditional transformational analyses of movement processes divide phrasal movement into two types: substitution to a specifier (which, in turn, can be A or A') and phrasal adjunction. Earmarks of the latter were considered the apparent optionality and the correlated apparent lack of an explicit trigger: typical cases of phrasal adjunctions were considered various movements to the left periphery, argument and adverb preposing to a position in between the overt complementizer and the subject position (e.g., to derive *I think that yesterday, John went home* from *I think that John went home yesterday*), often analyzed as involving adjunction to IP. As of the late 1980s, economy principles started to acquire a central role in syntactic theory, leading to a conception of movement as a "last resort" operation, applicable only when necessary to warrant well-formedness (Chomsky 1986b); this and other related developments cast doubts on the possibility of truly optional movement.

The growing role of economy considerations within the minimalist program led researchers to pay more attention to the interpretive difference associated to preposing in terms of discourse-informational properties. Such more refined interpretive considerations invariably supported the view that no movement is really optional. So left peripheral movement is not free in that it goes with whatever additional interpretive properties are associated to left-peripheral positions (topicality, focus, etc.); but how is it formally triggered? As the triggering of phrasal movement is normally governed by heads, which attract phrases to local Spec positions, this naturally led to the postulation of special heads (often null, but sometimes morphologically overt; see, e.g., Aboh 1998) acting as attractors. These ideas crystallized in parallel with the proposal of restrictive frameworks of phrase structure, such as Kayne's (1994), which banned the possibility of phrasal adjunction (as an option formally distinct from specifier creation). The ban on phrasal adjunction as the result of movement was then extended to base-generated structures, with the major consequence of ruling out an adjunction analysis of adverbial positions in general (but see Chomsky 2004 for an analysis of relative clauses that assumes the possibility of base-generated phrasal adjunction). So these developments also offered formal support to the theory of adverbial positions in Cinque (1999), assuming adverbs to be licensed in specifier positions of dedicated heads of the inflectional system.

2. Cartography and minimalism

Cartographic projects have been developed in parallel with the development of minimalism, following partially independent trails. There are clear points of connection, such as the central role of economy considerations and the emphasis on the interfaces. There are also points of theoretical tension, at least at first sight. The cartographic projects underscore the richness and complexity of syntactic structures and try to provide realistic descriptions of this complexity. Minimalism tries to capture the fundamental empirical results of syntactic theory through a set of descriptive tools which is substantially impoverished with respect to previous versions of the Principles and Parameters framework. The apparent tension manifests itself very directly in the fact that syntactic representations in much minimalist literature (starting from Chomsky 1995, chap. 4, and much subsequent work) look somewhat simpler than the representations normally assumed some ten years ago, while cartographic representations (e.g., in Cinque 1999, 2002; Belletti 2004, and chapter 2 in this volume) look substantially enriched.

The tension is only apparent, though. The focus of much minimalist analysis on the "core categories" C, T, v, and V seems to be a matter of expository convenience, rather than a substantive hypothesis, and the possibility that each "core category" may, in fact, be shorthand for referring to a more articulated structural zone is explicitly acknowledged (e.g., in Chomsky 2001: n. 8; 2002). In fact, the only substantive reduction in the inventory of functional heads proposed in recent years in the minimalist literature is the ban on independent Agreement heads, on grounds that agreement features in the inflectional system are redundant, hence presumably uninterpretable; a syntactic head consisting uniquely of uninterpretable features could not subsist if uninterpretable features must disappear by LF.

The view that agreement features in the inflectional system are uninterpretable is not uncontroversial, and the theoretical arguments against the postulation of an independent Agr node leave room for a certain leeway (see Chomsky 2001, particularly n. 3, 12, 16). Nevertheless, the possibility that syntax may specify no independent Agr-type heads is per se not inconsistent with the cartographic work. Much of the work on the inflectional system is focused on the uncovering and identification of functional heads of mood, tense, aspect, voice, and heads with a clear interpretive content, which therefore uncontroversially pass the muster of minimalist analysis. Analyses based on the positional difference of an Agr head with respect to, say, T, or Asp (Pollock 1989; Belletti 1990, 2000; Guasti and Rizzi 2002) can be reanalyzed as showing that agreement of subjects and objects is checked in positions distinct from and higher than T or Asp; this state of affairs is naturally expressible in a richer system of heads such as Cinque (1999) without necessarily appealing to Agr. So the question of the independent existence of Agr as a syntactic atom is basically an empirical question having to do with the label of the categories carrying φ-features involved in agreement processes; this is a difficult question as questions involving choice of labels often are. Essentially the same considerations apply to the core cartographic work on the structure of the DP and the set of functional categories assumed there.

Consider now the system of functional heads proposed for the CP domain in Rizzi (1997, 2000) and subsequent work, including various chapters of the present volume. The two heads delimiting the C system have a clear interpretive import: Force expresses the illucutionary force (at least in main clauses), or the clausal type; Finiteness expresses a property related to Tense and Mood (in fact, it is identified with a mood-type head in some analyses; see chapter 7 in this volume). Both Topic and Focus are assumed to create a substructure that explicitly signals to the external systems certain interpretively relevant properties, along the following lines:

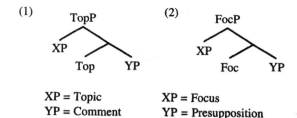

XP = Topic   XP = Focus
YP = Comment   YP = Presupposition

The specifier of the Top head is interpreted as the Topic, a kind of higher subject of predication assumed to be contextually familiar; its complement is interpreted as the Comment, a complex predicate predicated of the Topic. The specifier of the Foc head is interpreted as the Focus, and its complement as the Presupposition.

In this view, the syntactic computation hands over to the interpretive component representations transparently indicating dedicated positions for certain discourse functions (or other interpretively relevant properties, such as scope). Historically, this was the view underlying the assumption of special Criteria in the A-bar system (such as the Wh, or Q Criterion), formal principles triggering A-bar movement to ensure that an element with the appropriate featural specification will fill the positions dedicated to a particular interpretive property (the scope position of interrogative operators in the case at issue; Rizzi 1996).

The system of A-bar Criteria is akin to the system of inherent Case for argumental semantics in certain respects: the two systems transparently signal interpretive properties of the two basic kinds. Given the distinction in Chomsky (2004) between semantic properties associated with "external merge" (argumental and thematic structure) and semantic properties associated with "internal merge" (scope-discourse semantics)—the current variety of the classical divide between deep and surface semantics—inherent Case is to argumental semantics what the criterial features Top, Foc, Q, and so on are to scope-discourse semantics: they both signal syntactically (and sometimes also morphologically) certain positions dedicated to interpretive properties of the two kinds. From this viewpoint, Top, Foc and other left-peripheral heads don't seem to be less legitimate elements of minimalist syntactic computation than is inherent Case. Attempts to replace such labels with intepretively more neutral and opaque labels may not be more desirable than abandoning such labels as Instrumental, Benefactive, and Locative in favor of interpretively neutral labels in the system of inherent Case.

3. Local simplicity

One driving factor of the cartographic endeavor is a fundamental intuition of simplicity, which is clearly akin to core ideas of minimalism. Complex structures arise from the proliferation of extremely simple structural units: ideally, one structural unit (a head and the phrase it projects) is defined by a single syntactically relevant feature (again, we abstract away here from what the ultimate fate of Agr heads and projections may be; we also abstract away from the question of whether this fundamental biuniqueness extends to Spec Head relations—that is, if there is a single specifier per head or if multiple Spec's are allowed). Complex heads obviously exist, but they are not syntactic primitives: they can be assembled by the operation of head to head movement, the only device available to create conglomerates of syntactically relevant properties. Local simplicity is preserved by natural languages at the price of accepting a higher global complexity, through the proliferation of structural units.

The same intuition seems to underlie the teleological motivation of movement in the Minimalist Program. Movement exists, it is assumed, to allow elements to carry two types of interpretive properties: argumental and scope-discourse. Through movement, an element can occur in distinct positions specialized for the two kinds of interpretive properties (see, in particular, Chomsky 2000, 2002, 2004). But why couldn't languages attribute both kinds of interpretive properties to the same position, thus avoiding multiple occurrences of elements? Again, preservation of local simplicity seems to be the key factor: natural language design favors local attribution of single properties and is prepared to pay the price of multiplying the occurrences: recursion is cheap; local computation is expensive and to be reduced to the bare minimum.

What particular kind of simplicity natural language design chooses to favor is an empirical question. To quote Chomsky: "'Good design' conditions are in part a matter of empirical discovery, though within general guidelines of an aprioristic character, a familiar feature of rational inquiry. . . . Even the most extreme proponents of deductive reasoning from first principles, Descartes for example, held that experiment is critically necessary to discover which of the reasonable options was instantiated in the actual world" (Chomsky 2001: 1–2). In different domains, the empirical evidence seems to suggest that natural languages favor local simplicity, and accept paying the price of ending up with global representations involving such complex properties as multiple occurrences of elements (movement), along with a very rich articulation of functional structures.

4.   Contributions

In this section I highlight certain central ideas and analyses proposed in the different chapters by grouping them around three basic themes.

4.1.   The CP zone

The cartography of the CP zone is addressed directly in the chapters by Roberts (10), Beninca' and Poletto (3), and Poletto and Pollock (9); the chapters by Bianchi (4), Cecchetto (6), and Giorgi and Pianesi (7) address certain specific properties and computations relating to the CP zone.

Ian Roberts (chapter 9) deals with properties of the C-system in Celtic languages, in comparison with Germanic. Celtic languages tend to express the Fin head of the complementizer system, in that the element translated as *that* typically occurs after left peripheral elements, as the following Irish example shows, with the particle *go* occurring after the preposed adverbial:

(3) Is doíche [faoi cheann cúpla lá [go bhféadfaí imeacht]]
     is probable at-the-end-of couple day that could leave

This is a natural reinterpretation, within a richer theory of the left periphery, of the pattern analyzed by McCloskey (1996) in terms of PF cliticization of C to I across the left peripheral material. Straightforward evidence for the richer approach to C is provided by Welsh, Roberts argues, with the left peripheral field sandwiched in between the two C particles *mai* and *a*, arguably expressing Force and Fin:

(4)   dywedais i [*mai* 'r dynion fel arfer *a* [werthith y ci]]
        said I C the men as usual C will-sell the dog

The chapter then focuses on properties of the C system in Breton, in comparison with V-2 in Germanic. Long Verb Movement in Breton, with preposing of a lower verbal element to the left periphery across the higher zone of the inflectional system, is analyzed as involving a genuine violation of the Head Movement Constraint (rather than being a case of remnant VP movement), permitted by a suitable adaptation of the Relativized Minimality / Minimal Link Condition (Rizzi 1990; Chomsky 1995). An analysis of V-2, based on the idea that (unselected) Fin must be lexicalized in Celtic and Germanic, is outlined. This lexicalization may be achieved by special lexicalizing particles, as in Welsh, or by movement of the inflected verb, as in Germanic; in turn, the latter option involves the filling of Fin's specifier position.

Paola Beninca' and Cecilia Poletto's chapter (3) is a contribution to the cartographic study of the left periphery through a more fine-grained analysis of the form-function mapping concerning the left peripheral positions, with special reference to Italian and other Romance varieties. First, the authors suggest that the system of heads licensing discourse-related specifier positions disallows recursion (and multiple specifiers) of a single head. If this is correct, the proliferation of topics observed in Romance Clitic Left Dislocation constructions should, in fact, manifest different topic-like positions, each with certain specialized interpretive properties. Second, the authors argue that the different topic-like and focus-like positions postulated by their analysis are organized in distinct subfields, with the topic-like subfield higher than the focus-like subfield (this being a particular subcase of more general ordering restrictions between positions conveying old and new information). This hypothesis has the advantage of bringing Italian into line with the frequently observed pattern according to which topic strictly precedes left-peripheral focus (i.e., in systems like Hungarian: Brody 1995; Kiss 1987; Puskas 2000; and much related work). In contrast, as sentences with a left dislocated element following contrastive focus are acceptable in Italian (e.g., *Credo che domani, QUESTO, a Gianni, gli dovremmo dire* 'I believe that tomorrow, THIS, to Gianni we should say to him'; see Rizzi 1997: 295), the proposed reanalysis leads to the attempt to reanalyze such examples as not involving genuine Foc–Top configurations.

Cecilia Poletto and Jean-Yves Pollock (chapter 9) provide a comprehensive analysis of Wh constructions in French, Italian, and some Northern Italian dialects. Backbones of this analysis are the assumption of a structured left periphery, which, among other things, includes distinct positions that may be targeted by distinct Wh elements, and an extensive use of remnant movement, which subsumes effects more traditionally ascribed to covert movement and head movement. Particularly striking evidence in favor of distinct operator positions is provided by Northern Italian dialects like Bellunese, which allows multiple occurrences of (components of) certain Wh phrases in distinct positions:

(5) Cossa ha-lo fat che?
     'What has he done what?'

Building on previous work on this dialect, the authors motivate an analysis in which *che* and *cossa* occupy two distinct left-peripheral operator positions, with the rest of the IP remnant moved to a left peripheral position sandwiched in between. This analysis is extended to cover different cases of inversion in Romance (e.g., subject-clitic inversion, stylistic inversion) through the postulation of at least two topic-like positions in the intermediate Comp zone: the familiar Top position, which in this approach hosts the subject DP in stylistic inversion configurations, and a Ground position, which may attract remnant IPs that do not contain nonpronominal DPs.

Valentina Bianchi (chapter 4) addresses aspects of a major left peripheral construction, the relative clause. The main focus of the chapter is the typology of resumptive pronouns. Three kinds of resumptive pronouns are identified. First, optional resumptive pronouns, generally corresponding to argument DPs, as in the following example from Brazilian Portuguese:

(6) O livro che eu deixei (ele) aqui na mesa desapareceu.
     'The book that I left (it) here on the table disappeared.'

Second, obligatory resumptive pronouns, occurring within PPs or in other inherently Case-marked positions, as in the following example from Venetian, a Northern Italian dialect:

(7) Questo ze un argoment che no voio parlarghe *(ne).
     'This is a topic that I don't want to talk to him (about it).'

Third, resumptive pronouns rescuing island violations (e.g., in English: *The guy who I hate almost everything he does*).

Bianchi shows that the three types of resumptive pronouns give rise to distinct cross-linguistic generalizations as to their possible occurrence. The most interesting case is offered by optional resumptive pronouns, whose occurrence depends on certain interpretive properties of the relative clause: in some languages (e.g., certain Northern Italian dialects) they only occur in nonrestrictive relatives; in other languages (e.g., Brazilian Portuguese) they occur in nonrestrictive and specific restrictive relatives, but not in nonspecific restrictive relatives. Certain a priori imaginable distributions don't seem to be attested across languages: no language seems to allow optional resumptive pronouns in restrictive but not in nonrestrictive relatives, or in nonspecific restrictive relatives but not in specific restrictive relatives. This peculiar cross-linguistic distribution is explained by Bianchi by sharpening the theory of the LF representations of the different kinds of relatives, along lines that interact in important ways with the different properties of the three types of relatives with respect to the theory of reconstruction.

Carlo Cecchetto (chapter 6) addresses the question of the selective possibility of remnant movement. It is well known that a constituent from which a subconstituent has been extracted can undergo further movement in some cases (for instance, a VP from which the subject has been extracted can undergo topicalization: . . . *and [given t to Bill] it was t'*), but not in other cases; for instance, a constituent from which ClLD took place cannot undergo ClLD in Romance:

(8) *[*Di parlarle t*], credo che, [*a Maria*] non lo abbiano ancora deciso t'*.
     'To speak to her, I believe that, to Maria, they haven't decided it yet.'

Cecchetto's proposal is that what characterizes the second class of cases is that the relevant examples violate Chomsky's (2001) Phase Impenetrability Condition (PIC): the remnant constituent remains too deeply embedded to be successfully extracted at the relevant phase. Certain apparent cases of violation of PIC, such as the extraction of Wh arguments from weak islands, are explained by assuming a structured CP edge, in line with cartographic proposals.

Alessandra Giorgi and Fabio Pianesi (chapter 7) address the phenomenon of complementizer deletion in finite clauses in Italian, an option that differs from the much analyzed English equivalent, among other things, in that it is restricted to subjunctive environments. Rather then assuming an actual process of licensing of a zero complementizer (through deletion, base-generation of a null element or cliticization to the main verb, as in classical analyses of the English equivalent, from Kayne 1981 and Stowell 1981 to Pesetsky 1995), the authors propose that the CP system is not projected in the relevant structures, an option that can be expressed in the approach to the mapping from features to positions advocated in Giorgi and Pianesi (1997): in this system, distinct features can, in fact, coalesce to form single syntactic heads (see section 3), but this option is limited to the case in which specifiers are not activated. The authors then show that various formal and interpretive properties of the construction can be made to follow from the proposed analysis.

4.2. Clitics within the IP system

The remaining four chapters deal with different properties of the IP system. Manzini and Savoia (8) and Shlonsky (11) address the issues raised by cliticization within the cartographic study of the IP space.

Maria Rita Manzini and Leonardo Savoia (chapter 8) provide a comprehensive theory of clitic positions in Romance, based on comparative evidence originating mainly from the Italian dialects. This analysis is connected to an extensive survey that these authors have been conducting in recent years on the syntax of the Italian dialects. Clitic positions are assumed to be inherent components of the inflectional structure of the sentence and ordered according to a cross-linguistically stable hierarchy. Another guiding intuition that the authors borrow from Abney (1986) and Szabolcsi (1994) is that the sentence has a functional structure analogous to the one of the noun phrase, with the different clitic heads mirroring the order of elements in the functional nominal structure. This syntactic approach to cliticization is then compared with the morphological approaches involving templates and postsyntactic reorderings in the morphological component (Bonet 1995), as well as with the optimality theoretic approach advocated by Grimshaw (1997). The approach is then confronted with the empirical issues of cross-linguistic variation in clitic order (mainly Dat–Obj versus Obj–Dat). The various mutual exclusion patterns that several Romance varieties manifest and the appropriate way to express the relevant parametrization are discussed.

Ur Shlonsky (chapter 11) addresses another major aspect of the Romance clitic systems, the enclisis–proclisis alternation. The alternation manifests itself in different forms in Western Romance, where it gives rise to a complex pattern sensitive to the clause-initial element, and in other Romance varieties, where it is sensitive to finiteness. The author endorses the view that there are fundamental asymmetries between enclisis and proclisis. Enclisis arises when the verb adjoins to the functional head hosting the clitic; proclisis arises when the verb, in its movement in the inflectional space, does not cross over the clitic position, either because it stops at a lower functional head, or because the clitic itself adjoins to the complex created by verb movement: proclisis thus is a cover term for rather different structural configurations having in common the linear order clitic–verb. The proposed analysis assumes that the two configurations are normally mutually exclusive in that enclisis takes place whenever possible, and proclisis is the last resort case. The parametrisation required to express the observed patterns is then related to the position of the cliticization site with respect to the other components of the functional structure of the sentence.

4.3.   Subjects

Finally, the chapters by Belletti (2) and Cardinaletti (5) deal with the cartography of subject positions within the IP space.

Adriana Belletti's chapter (2) is, in fact, linked to both the IP and the CP domain. It proposes that the clausal structure contains a lower area peripheral to the argumental nucleus endowed with focus and topic positions, and thus analogous to the higher left peripheral domain. So-called free subject inversion in Italian and other Null Subject Languages involves movement of the subject to the low-focus position, whence the systematic focal character of postverbal subjects in Italian, shown by Weak-crossover effects and other diagnostics. That the inverted focal subject is not in the high left peripheral position is shown, among other things, by the fact that the position must be c-commanded by the IP internal negation, as shown by examples like the following:

(9)   Non me lo ha detto nessuno.
      'not said it to me anyone'

Here the negative quantifier *nessuno* requires c-command by *non*. Evidence of this kind argues against the possibility of movement of the subject to the left-peripheral focus position plus remnant movement of the IP. Other cases in which the subject (or any other constituent) is right-dislocated can be analyzed as involving movement to the Top position in the lower peripheral zone. If the lower part of the clause, the verb phrase, is endowed with a full-fledged periphery of discourse-related structural positions, it is tempting to capture the parallel with the higher left periphery by assuming that analogous discourse-related zones mark the edge of phases in Chomsky's (2001) sense.

Anna Cardinaletti's chapter (5) investigates the subject positions in the higher part of the IP space. Distributional evidence strongly suggests that referential subjects can occur in positions that are precluded to nonreferential subjects. For instance, in English, a referential subject can be separated from the inflected verb by a parenthetical expression, but a nonreferential subject cannot:

(10)   a. John, in my opinion, is a nice guy.
       b.*There, in my opinion, is hope.

Cardinaletti thus distinguishes a lower subject position, demanded by a purely structural need such as the satisfaction of the Case-agreement properties, which may be filled by an expletive, from a higher subject position, expressing the substantive subject-predicate relation, hence requiring a referential subject of which the predicate is predicated. Cardinaletti then argues that this higher subject position is to be kept distinct from the Topic position in the left periphery of the clause, which can host different types of topicalized arguments. Cardinaletti gives arguments that this positional difference also holds in Null Subject Languages, for which a total assimilation of preverbal subjects and topics has often been proposed. If the "subject of predication" position is more restricted than the Top position, it is not strictly limited to canonical DP subjects agreeing with the verbal inflection. It also is the position occupied by quirky subjects, predicative DPs in inverted copular constructions (Moro 1997) and inverted locatives, Cardinaletti argues.

Belletti's and Cardinaletti's chapters complement each other in drawing a partial map of the subject positions in the clause, with the identification of at least four positions, from lowest to highest: the thematic position in the VP, the VP-peripheral lower focus position, the EPP position, and the Subject of Predication position. Various types of comparative evidence considered in these chapters clearly hint at the conclusion that a more refined map would involve more positions—for instance, an IP medial position filled in VSO structures in the Romance languages allowing this word order, and possibly distinct positions for the checking of different ϕ-features.

To conclude, a word on the events that are at the source of the present volume. Two cartographic projects were funded by the Ministery of University and Research in Italy in 1997 and 1999, involving the Universities of Ferrara, Florence, Milan, Siena, and Venice; a third project connected to cartography is now being pursued. These projects generated a body of research that was presented in various formal and informal workshops and seminars. Some of the results are published in independent volumes of the Oxford Studies in Comparative Syntax of Oxford University Press, under the common heading *The Cartography of Syntactic Structures*: see Cinque 2002 and Belletti 2004. This volume represents the proceedings of the "Workshop on the Cartography of Syntactic Positions and Semantic Types" that took place at the Certosa di Pontignano (Siena), on November 25–26, 1999.

References

Abney, S. (1986) "The English Noun Phrase in its Sentential Aspects," Ph.D. diss., MIT, Cambridge.

Aboh, E. (1998) "From the Syntax of Gungbe to the Grammar of Gbe," Ph.D. diss., University of Geneva.

Belletti, A. (1990) *Generalized Verb Movement*. Turin: Rosenberg and Sellier.

Belletti, A. (2000) "(Past) Participle Agreement," in H. van Riemsdijk and M. Everaert (eds.), *SynCom: The Blackwell Companion to Syntax*. Oxford: Blackwell.

——— (ed.). (2004) *Structures and Beyond: The Cartography of Syntactic Structures*, vol. 3. New York: Oxford University Press.

Bonet, E. (1995) "Feature Structure of Romance Clitics." *Natural Language and Linguistic Theory* 13, 607–647.

Brody, M. (1995) "Focus and Checking Theory," in I. Kenesei (ed.) *Levels and Structures*. Approaches to Hungarian, no. 5. Szeged: JATE, 30–43.

Chomsky, N. (1957) *Syntactic Structures*. The Hague: Mouton.

Chomsky, N. (1970) "Remarks on Nominalization," in R. A. Jacobs and Rosenbaum P. S. (eds). *Readings in English Transformational Grammar*. Waltham, Mass: Ginn, 184–221.

——— (1986a) *Barriers*. Cambridge, Mass.: MIT Press.

——— (1986b) *Knowledge of Language*. New York: Praeger.

——— (1995) *The Minimalist Program*. Cambridge, Mass.: MIT Press.

——— (2000) "Minimalist Inquiries: The Framework," in R. Martin, D. Michaels, and J. Uriagereka (eds.) *Step by Step: Essays in Minimalist Syntax in Honor of Howard Lasnik*. Cambridge, Mass.: MIT Press, 89–155.

——— (2001) "Derivation by Phase," in M. Kenstowicz (ed.) *Ken Hale: A Life in Language*. Cambridge, Mass.: MIT Press, 1–52.

——— (2002) *On Language and Nature*. Cambridge: Cambridge University Press.

——— (2004) "Beyond Explanatory Adequacy," in A. Belletti (ed.) (2004).

Cinque, G. (1999) *Adverbs and Functional Heads*. New York: Oxford University Press.

——— (2002) *The Structure of DP and IP: The Cartography of Syntactic Structures, Vol. 1*. New York: Oxford University Press.

Emonds, J. (1978) "The verbal complex V'–V in French". *Linguistic Inquiry* 9, 151–175.

Giorgio, A., and Pianesi, F. (1997) *Tense and Aspect: From Semantics to Morphosyntax*. New York: Oxford University Press.

Grimshaw, J. (1997) "The Best Clitic: Constraint Conflict in Morphosyntax," in L. Haegeman, (ed.) *Elements of Grammar*. Dordrecht: Kluwer, 169–196.

Guasti, M. T., and L. Rizzi (2002) "Agreement and Tense as Distinct Syntactic Positions: Evidence from Acquisition," in G. Cinque, (ed.) *Functional Structure in DP and IP: The Cartography of Syntactic Structures*, Vol. 1. New York: Oxford University Press, 167–194.

Kayne, R. (1981) "ECP Extensions." *Linguistic Inquiry* 12, 93–133.

——— (1994) *The Antisymmetry of Syntax*. Cambridge, Mass.: MIT Press.

Kiss, K. É.(1987) *Configurationality in Hungarian*. Dordrecht: Reidel.

McCloskey, J. (1996) "On the Scope of Verb Movement in Irish." *Natural Language and Linguistic Theory* 14, 47–104.

Moro, A. (1997) *The Raising of Predicates: Predicative Noun Phrases and the Theory of Clause Structure*. Cambridge: Cambridge University Press.

Pesetsky, D. (1995) *Zero Syntax*. Cambridge, Mass.: MIT Press.

Pollock, J.-Y. (1989) "Verb Movement, Universal Grammar, and the Structure of IP." *Linguistic Inquiry* 20, 365–424.

Puskas, G. (2000) *Word Order in Hungarian*. Amsterdam: John Benjamins.

Rizzi, L. (1990) *Relativized Minimality*. Cambridge, Mass.: MIT Press.

——— (1996) "Residual Verb Second and the Wh Criterion," in A. Belletti and L. Rizzi, (eds.) *Parameters and Functional Heads*. New York: Oxford University Press, 63–90.

——— (1997) "The Fine Structure of the Left Periphery," in L. Haegeman (ed.) *Elements of Grammar*. Dordrecht, Kluwer, 281–337.

———— (2000) *Comparative Syntax and Language Acquisition*. London: Routledge.

Stowell, T. (1981) "Origins of Phrase Structure," Ph.D. diss., MIT, Cambridge, Mass.

Szabolcsi, A. (1994) "The Noun Phrase," in K. Kiss and F. Kiefer (eds.) *The Syntactic Structure of Hungarian* (Syntax and Semantics no. 27). New York, Academic Press, 179–274.

Vergnaud, J.-R. (1982) "Dépendances et niveaux de représentation en syntaxe," Thèse de doctorat d'état, Université de Paris VII.

2

Aspects of the Low IP Area

ADRIANA BELLETTI

This chapter reconsiders and develops a proposal presented in Belletti (2001). The discussion that follows leaves the core insight of the original proposal essentially unchanged, although some aspects of the implementation are revised in a way that leads to changes in some areas; the overall empirical coverage of the proposal itself is also widened.

Recent studies on the cartography of the left periphery of the clause, started with Rizzi (1997) and subsequent work (Poletto 2000; Beninca' 2001; Beninca' and Poletto [chapter 3 in this volume], and Poletto and Pollock [chapter 9 in this volume] and references cited therein), have come to the conclusion that the clause (IP, henceforth for simplicity) external area, traditionally labeled CP, is indeed a much richer and articulated space than traditionally assumed. Several dedicated positions split the single head C, including positions indicating the Force of the following clause and its Fin(itness). As extensively discussed in Rizzi (1997) and related work, between Force and Fin various other CP internal positions are identified: crucially a Focus position surrounded by (possibly iterated) Topic positions. Processes of Focalization and Topicalization are thus analyzed as involving movement of a phrase to the dedicated position in the left periphery.[1] In this view, the different interpretations of the peripheral constituent, either as a topic or as a focus with respect to the following sentence, are automatic reflexes of the derived configuration. Under the general idea that a relation which closely recalls an agreement relation, and which is often as-similated to it, is established between the head of a phrase and the constituent filling its Spec,[2] a focus head and the phrase in its specifier will share the focus feature; an identical relation will account for the topic interpretation of a phrase in the specifier of the topic projection.

These by now fairly standard assumptions provide a very simple and straight-forward way of expressing the mechanisms granting the possible different interpre-tations related to different configurations. The interpretation as focus or topic of an element in the left periphery is an automatic consequence of the element's filling the specifier of different heads. A simple conclusion of the sort could not be as easily drawn in a CP projection not internally analyzed and split in the different positions discussed in the references quoted. The relation between syntax and the interpreta-tive interface (LF) is expressed in an optimally simple way: the interpretation is read off the syntactic configuration. The same analysis should also lead to an equally simple way to express the relation of the syntactic configuration with the phonetic/phono-logical interface. In particular, as far as the stress contour of a clause and its overall intonation are concerned, they should be directly determined from the syntactic con-figuration. Typically, a focused constituent in the left periphery is contrastively stressed; a topicalized phrase in the peripheral position is associated with a special downgrading intonation:

(1)   a. A GIANNI ho dato il libro (non a Piero).
          to Gianni I have given the book (not to Piero)
      b. A Gianni, (gli) ho dato il libro.
          to Gianni (I) to him (cl) have given the book

Both intonations should be directly read off the different syntactic positions the phrases occupy in the CP area.

The proposal developed here analyses the fine-grained structural cartography of the clause's (IP) internal low area. It will be suggested that the area immediately above VP displays a significant resemblance to the left periphery of the clause, the so-called CP area just discussed. In particular, a clause-internal Focus position, sur-rounded by Topic positions, is identified in the low part of the clause.[3] Partly differ-ent intonations are associated with these positions, as opposed to the parallel positions in the left periphery. Different interpretations are also associated with the positions of what we may call the "clause-internal periphery" as opposed to those in the clause-external one. Both the interpretations and the related intonations are thus linked to properties of the configuration. Without attempting a systematic investigation of the various detectable differences between the left peripheral positions and the clause-internal parallel periphery but just pointing out some of the crucial ones, in what follows I concentrate on the properties of the clause-internal focus, with some refer-ence to the clause-internal topic.[4]

Before entering the close empirical investigation, one further general question should be raised. If the conclusion of the proposal to be presented here is on the right track, a significantly parallel configuration introduces the verb phrase and the IP. As-suming that this sort of duplication is justified on empirical grounds, the question as to why such a parallelism should exist arises. Although a definite answer to this at present relatively complex question cannot be produced, it is worth pointing out that similar conclusions, differently phrased and in different perspectives, have already been reached. Most recently, Chomsky (2001) has precisely singled out CP and complete verb phrases (vP in his terminology) as "(strong) phases" in the sense of the recent version of the MP—that is, syntactic units that share a certain amount of independence (and which are transmitted to the interface systems). According to our proposal, CP and the verb phrase (vP or VP) would be parallel in that vP/VP has a CP-like periphery. Furthermore, various proposals have appeared ultimately attributing to vP/VP a periphery resembling that of the clause. The idea has led to the assimilation of the vP/VP of the clause to the general format of small clauses, some of them VP small clauses. In this type of approach, small clauses are analyzed as full clauses (Starke 1995; Sportiche 1995), including a peripheral C projection. The proposal presented here can be seen as a contribution within this same line of approach to clause structure, providing a more finely grained design of the assumed vP/VP periphery.

1. Position of postverbal subjects

Let us briefly review the fundamental data arguing for the plausibility of the proposal that a clause-internal focus position is present in the VP area.[5]

Subject inversion is a widespread phenomenon in Romance. The topic has been extensively addressed, with the general conclusion that so-called Free Subject Inversion is a fundamental property of Null Subject languages somehow linked to the possibility of leaving the preverbal subject position phonetically unrealized.[6] Among the Romance languages, French has a special status in that it does not display the phenomenon of free subject inversion, a consequence of its non-Null Subject nature. Indeed, the kind of inversion structures allowed in French—the so-called Stylistic Inversion (SI) structures (Kayne and Pollock 1978, 2001)—have very different properties from those found in Null Subject Romance languages: descriptively, they require a "trigger" for inversion (wh, subjunctive), while no overt trigger is required in the case of Free Inversion (whence, the characterization as "free," FI). Basing my discussion mainly on Italian as far as FI is concerned,[7] the following contrasts arise with French:

(2)   a. Ha parlato Gianni.
         has spoken Gianni
      b. E' partito Gianni.
         is left Gianni
      c. *A parlé Jean.
         has spoken Jean
      d. *Est parti Jean.
         is left Jean
      e. Le jour où a parlé/est parti Jean.
         the day when has spoken/is left Jean
      f. Il faut que parle/parte Jean.
         it is necessary that speak/leave (subj.) Jean
      g. Il giorno in cui ha parlato/è partito Gianni.
         the day in which has spoken/is left Gianni
      h. E' necessario che parli/parta Gianni.
         it is necessary that speak/leave (subj.) Gianni

The fact that examples (2)g and h are possible in French as well, as in examples (2)e and f, whereas examples (2) a and b are also perfectly well formed in Italian but are excluded in French, as shown in examples (2)c and d, strongly indicates the different nature of the two inversion processes, SI and FI. The word by word parallelism of (2)e and f and (2)g and h must be considered epiphenomenal: the Italian structures in (2)g and h plausibly involve the same "inversion"[8] process that is at work in (2)a and b, which is different from the one at work in (2)e and f. In their recent analysis of SI, Kayne and Pollock (2001) have crucially characterized the phenomenon as involving the high, clause-external periphery of the clause. Briefly put: the subject is moved out of the clause[9] to a position within the left periphery; the remnant IP is subsequently moved past the subject into a higher position of the left periphery. One crucial feature of this analysis is that the subject is very high in the clause structure. A natural way to characterize the difference between SI and FI would then consist in assuming that the postverbal subject is not high in FI. As in traditional accounts, we could reach the conclusion that FI is indeed a clause-internal phenomenon.

According to this (rather traditional) hypothesis, the same order VS can be thought of as being obtained in two very different ways in the two processes: either through IP-remnant movement as for SI or through movement of the verb over the subject as for FI.[10] I assume that this characterization is fundamentally on the right track. As a general guideline, I adopt the restrictive working hypothesis that remnant-type movements be limited to those cases in which interpretive (or intonational) factors seem to call for them. I assume that, although not always explicitly discussed in these terms in Kayne and Pollock (2001), this should be taken to be the case for SI in the frame of their analysis. However, a remnant-type analysis is not justified for FI in the general case. The next step is then to determine how internal to IP the postverbal subject is.

1.1. Postverbal S is low in the clause structure

The distributional evidence concerning the respective location of the subject and adverbs which are located in a very low position in the clause structure, according to Cinque's (1999) hierarchy, as discussed in Belletti (2001) and also pointed out in Cardinaletti (2001), points to the conclusion that the postverbal subject is very low in the clause as it follows low adverbs. Consider the contrasts in (3) in this perspective:

(3) a. ?Capirà completamente Maria.
         will understand completely Maria
     b. ?Spiegherà completamente Maria al direttore.
         will explain completely Maria to the director
     c. ?Capirà/spiegherà bene Maria (al direttore).
         will understand/explain well Maria (to the director)
     d. Capirà/spiegherà tutto Maria (al direttore).
         will understand/explain everything Maria (to the director)

(4) a. *Capirà/spiegherà Maria completamente (al direttore).
         will understand/explain Maria completely (to the director)
     b. *Capirà/spiegherà Maria bene (al direttore).
         will understand/explain Maria well (to the director)
     c. *Capirà/spiegherà Maria tutto (al direttore).
         will understand Maria everything

Notice incidentally that similar data have been discussed also for Icelandic in Bobaljik and Jonas (1996), example (21), giving opposite results:

(5) það luku sennilega *einhverjir studentar* alveg verkefninu
    there finished probably some students completely the assignment

(6) *það luku sennilega alveg *einhverjir studentar* verkefninu
    there finished probably completely some students the assignment

The contrast between (3)–(4) and (5)–(6) suggests that a further, higher position is available for subjects in Icelandic, but not in Italian.

Note that no special intonation is associated with the sentences in (3). This will always be the case in the examples to be discussed here, unless explicitly indicated. The examples in (3)b, c, and d, where the postverbal subject is followed by a PP complement (see section 3.1 on this possibility) are particularly significant in that they indicate that even lower portions of the clause can be present following the subject (i.e., a PP complement).[11] Given the guidelines indicated here, as there do not seem to be reasons to admit a complex derivation including remnant movement steps, I assume that these steps are not implemented in the derivation of these sentences. Whence the significance of these cases.[12]

A closer discussion of the lack of the "?" in example (3)d is also relevant in this connection. Suppose that the "?" in (3)a, b, and c is due to some interference effect between the adverb and the postverbal subject, which should ideally immediately follow the verb. The perfect status of (3)d is an indication that no interference operates here. The relevant notion characterizing the disturbing proximity between the adverb and the postverbal subject must be hierarchical, as all the examples are alike from the linear point of view (see Rizzi 1996 for a proposal). As *tutto* is supposed to move in the clause leaving its original location,[13] contrary to adverbs, it can be assumed that precisely this movement is responsible for the establishment of the relevant necessary distance between *tutto* and the postverbal subject. Notice now that, were the Vadv/tuttoS order to be obtained through remnant movement of the relevant portion of the IP,[14] leaving the subject behind, there would be no way to capture the relevant hierarchical distinction between the adverbs and *tutto*, which are both equally included in the remnant moved portion.[15]

From the preceding considerations, we can conclude that paradigms (3) and (4) indicate that the subject is low in the clause structure.

1.2. Postverbal S and extraction

If we abstract away from the case of postverbal subjects of unaccusatives,[16] it appears that the postverbal subject is not a felicitous extraction domain. Both *ne* cliticization and wh-extraction are less than perfect, as illustrated in (7):

(7) a. Ha telefonato il direttore del giornale al presidente.
        has phoned the director of the newspaper to the president
     b. ?? Il giornale di cui ha telefonato il direttore al presidente.
        the newspaper of which phoned the director to the president
     c. ?? Ne ha telefonato il direttore al presidente.
        of it has phoned the director to the president

    d. ?? Ne hanno telefonato molti al presidente.
        of them have phoned many to the president

If we put together the observations of the preceding section and the shape of paradigm (7), we can conclude that the low position of the subject is not an extraction domain, as extraction gives rise to CED-type effects.[17]

    Kayne and Pollock (2001) point out a distinction as for extractability from the postverbal subject in French SI. While extraction of *en* appears to be impossible, *combien* extraction gives better results:

(8) a. *Le jour où en ont téléphoné trois. (K&P (19a))
       the day when of them (cl) have called three
    b. ?*Le jour où en sont partis trois. (K&P (19c))
       the day when of them (cl) are left three
    c. *Le criminel qu'en ont comdamné trois. (K&P (21))
       the criminal that of (them) have condemned three
    d. Combien ont téléphoné de linguistes? (K&P (29a))
       how many have called of linguists
    e. Combien sont partis de linguistes? (K&P (29b))
       how many are left of linguists

    Their interpretation of the contrast is in terms of c-command. The IP preceding the subject is moved past it through remnant movement. In the resulting configuration, *en* does not c-command its trace within the subject from which it has been extracted; hence, a violation of proper binding is created. No equivalent violation is created in the case of *combien* extraction via wh-movement as the wh-quantifier is further raised to the appropriate high position in the CP where wh-phrases normally end up. From there, it c-commands its trace as required. As no contrast is displayed in the Italian examples between *en* extraction and wh-extraction, this is an indication that a similar analysis should not be extended to the FI structures.[18] The conclusion must be that the position occupied by the postverbal subject in FI is not a felicitous extraction domain altogether. If the proposal that follows is on the right track, a natural reason can be provided for that, as such a position is identified with the Specifier of a Focus phrase,[19] not an argument position in the sense relevant for CED.[20] I now turn to the core of this proposal.

2. The interpretation of the postverbal subject in FI

Here I briefly review the fundamental paradigm leading to the proposal. Question-answer pairs like the following indicate that the postverbal subject can be interpreted as new information focus:

(9) a. Chi è partito / ha parlato?
       who has left / has spoken
    b. E' partito / ha parlato Gianni.
       has left / has spoken Gianni
    c. #Gianni è partito / ha parlato.
       Gianni has left / has spoken

However, with the appropriate intonation and in the appropriate pragmatic conditions, a postverbal subject can also receive the topic (given information) interpretation:

(10)   a. Che cosa ha poi fatto Gianni?
          What has Gianni finally done?
       b. Ha parlato, Gianni.
          He has spoken, Gianni.

In what follows I will mainly concentrate my attention on the new information focus interpretation, keeping the possibility of exchanges like the one in (10) in mind, as they can provide a direct indication of the fine configuration of the low IP internal area under discussion (see section 5 for more on that).

It is very clear from the contrast between (9)b and c that the postverbal and the preverbal positions[21] have a very different informational content: only the former can carry new information. The postverbal subject is also informationally new when the whole clause is new information. Example (9)b is also an appropriate answer to a general question like (11), while (9)c would not be, unless some presupposition is held by the speaker concerning the subject:

(11)   Che cosa è successo?
       What happened?

Let us concentrate our attention on the case of the so-called narrow new information focus reading of sentences like (9)b.[22]

According to the general guidelines assumed in this work, the focus interpretation of the postverbal subject should optimally come out of the syntactic configuration in which the subject DP is inserted. As I have shown that the subject is low in the clause structure, this naturally leads to the proposal that it should fill a low Focus position (or Topic; see following section 5).[23] This, in turn, argues in favor of the existence of such a position clause internally.

To make the point stronger, a possible alternative should be considered, in line with the following assumed guidelines: the postverbal subject fills a Focus position indeed, but this position is not clause internal; rather, this position should be identified with the left peripheral one already proposed and independently justified in the literature. According to this alternative, the subject is actually very high in the clause structure, and the portion of the clause preceding it is even higher. Within this analysis, FI would look much more akin to SI than we have hypothesized so far. The following section closely discusses, and dismisses on empirical grounds, this alternative, which the data discussed in section 1 already put into question.

2.1.   The subject is not high in FI

We saw in section 1 that the distribution of low adverbs leads to the conclusion that S is low in FI. We also noticed some properties (extraction) that differentiate SI and FI. We now look at other differentiating behaviors of SI and FI that appear to be naturally derived if the postverbal subject is thought of as being high in the former case but low in the latter. Consider the following contrasts:

(12) a. Non ho ho incontrato che (i/dei) linguisti.
          I have 'not' seen 'that' (the/some) linguists

      b. Non hanno parlato che (i/dei) linguisti.
          have 'not' spoken 'that' (the/some) linguists

      c.*(Che) (i/dei) linguisti non hanno parlato[24]
          ('that') (the/some) linguists 'not' have spoken

(13) a. Non conosco alcun linguista.[25]
          I do not know any linguist.

      b. Non parlerà alcun linguista.
          will not speak any linguist

      c.*Alcun linguista non parlerà.
          Any linguist will not speak.

(14) a. Non ho visto nessuno.
          (I) have not seen nobody.

      b. Non ha parlato nessuno.
          has not spoken nobody

      c.*Nessuno non ha parlato.
          nobody has not spoken

In all these examples, the postverbal noun phrase is an NPI element that needs to be licensed by the negative marker *non*. Suppose that licensing is obtained through c-command: in all of the b examples, the postverbal subject behaves like the direct object of the a examples and differently from the corresponding preverbal subject of the c examples. This strongly suggests that the necessary c-command relation is established in the b examples as it is in the a examples. In turn, this suggests that the b sentences should not be analyzed as involving a high subject and a higher remnant IP. If that were the case, the relevant c-command relation could not be established, and the resulting sentences should be as ungrammatical as those involving a preverbal subject are.[26] Indeed, precisely paradigms with this type of distribution of judgements are discussed by Kayne and Pollock and are used as an argument in favor of their analysis of SI in terms of remnant movement of IP past the high subject. The relevant examples that they discuss in this connection are reproduced in (15):

(15) a. Jean a peu vu de linguistes.
          Jean few saw of linguists

      b.*De linguistes ont peu vu Jean.
          of linguists have few seen Jean

      c.*Le jour où ont peu téléphoné de linguistes.
          the day where have few phoned of linguists

      d. Il n'a pas vu de linguistes.
          he has not seen of linguists

      e.*De linguistes ne sont pas venus.
          Of linguists are not come

      f.*Le jour où ne sont pas venus de linguistes.
          the day where are not come of linguists

If *peu* and *pas* are taken to be the licensor of the polarity noun phrase introduced by *de*, lack of c-command can be held as the responsible factor ruling out the *de-*

phrase from the preverbal subject position. Similarly, lack of c-command could account for the same impossibility in (15)c and f, which involve SI. This sort of paradigm is then used by Kayne and Pollock as a substantial argument in favor of their analysis of SI.

The shape of the Italian paradigm remains unchanged if the relevant examples are made equally complex, as in the SI cases:

(16) a. Il giorno in cui non hanno parlato che (i/dei) linguisti.
          the day when have not spoken that (the/some) linguists
      b. Il fatto di cui non parlerà alcun linguista.
          the fact of which will not speak any linguist
      c. Il momento in cui non ha parlato nessuno.
          the moment in which has not spoken nobody

The postverbal subject of FI is then not a high subject. If it is correct to assume that it fills a Focus position, this position cannot be the high, left peripheral one.[27]

2.2.   The postverbal subject does not fill the left peripheral focus

Furthermore, the identification of the focus position of postverbal subjects with the left peripheral one does not seem justified on empirical grounds if the kind of focal interpretation is considered in more detail. In Italian, the peripheral focus position is systematically associated with a contrastive/corrective interpretation and carries a special stress, as mentioned in connection with (1). No equivalent interpretation or intonation is necessarily associated with a postverbal subject. Although, as noted earlier, the postverbal subject is the carrier of new information, the peripheral focus position cannot be associated with simple new information:

(17) a. Chi è partito / ha parlato?
          Who has left / has spoken?
      b. (*) GIANNI è partito / ha parlato.
          GIANNI has left / has spoken.

(18) a. Che cosa hai letto?
          What have you read?
      b. (*) Il LIBRO ho letto (non il giornale).
          THE BOOK I have read, not the newspaper.

Examples (17)b and (18)b are not appropriate answers to genuine questions of information. Contrast or correction is necessarily implied. It would be difficult to understand why the opposite should hold for postverbal subjects.[28] From this it is legitimate to conclude that the focus position hosting the postverbal subject cannot be the same as the one located in the left periphery. Rather, it must be a clause-internal position, and the VS order is not obtained through a remnant topicalization process that moves a portion of IP over a left peripheral high subject. I maintain that an analysis along these lines could hold for SI, as in Kayne and Pollock, but not for FI.[29]

The most direct way to phrase the proposal is in term of a diagram like (19)a, which postulates the presence of the clause-internal focus position right above the VP. This is too simple a version of the proposal, though, and it must be enriched to allow for topic-like positions to also be present in the low, clause-internal domain. In this way the possible topic interpretation of postverbal subjects illustrated by sentences like (10)b will be directly captured. This leads to the version in (19)b, which assumes a strict parallelism between the clause-internal vP/VP periphery and the clause-external one in the CP left periphery, mentioned at the outset:

(19)   a. FocusP   b. TopP

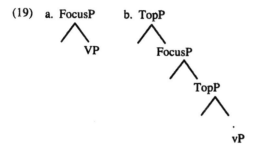

2.3.   Why is S focus (or topic) in FI?

We have established that S typically is new information focus in FI, and we have made the hypothesis that this is a consequence of S filling a clause-internal focus position where it is interpreted. The question then is, what forces S to be in focus? Or, put differently, why is S necessarily focalized in FI?

In Belletti (2001) I related that to Case: if Case is only assigned locally, there is no available Case assigner for S in the lower portion of the clause. S moves to Focus in order to be licensed by a feature different from Case—namely, Focus. But, the hypothesis of allowing Focus to play a role comparable to Case can look as a weakening of the general approach, as it is not obvious what Case and Focus should have in common to allow them to play an essentially equivalent role.[30] Moreover, in recent versions of MP, Chomsky has made the proposal that Case assignment can be a nonlocal process and that Case can also be available at a distance, with the (agreeing) Case assigning head looking for its Case assignee target also in a nonlocal domain. If some process of the sort has to be admitted, we should look for a different reason to account for the focalized nature of the postverbal subject.

I would like to speculate that this effect may be ultimately related to economy considerations. Let us ask, what would fill the preverbal subject position in FI structures; namely, what would satisfy EPP? I will assume that, as in traditional accounts, the preverbal subject position is filled by a nonovert expletive *pro*, the associate of the postverbal subject:

pro ha parlato Gianni
    has spoken Gianni

No expletive is present in structures that contain a preverbal subject, as the EPP is satisfied by the lexical subject in those structures. Hence, FI structures contain one element more than do the structures that contain a preverbal subject. Suppose that a kind of economy principle drives the selection of the initial Lexical Array (LA; Chomsky 2000) to the effect that an LA bigger in size is to be chosen only for some "purpose," or, to put it in Chomsky's terms, only if this choice has a reflex on the outcome. Focalization could precisely be one such reflex. It can be assumed that exactly the same ultimate reason is responsible for the topic interpretation of the postverbal subject as well.[31] If this line of interpretation is on the right track, focalization (or topic interpretation) of the postverbal subject could be derived without having to admit any special licensing property for the focus (or topic) feature, comparable to Case.[32] I tentatively make this assumption here.

3.   On VSXP

3.1.   VSO and VSPP

A fairly clear contrast can be detected with VSXP word order according to whether what follows S is a direct object or a PP. The following examples (discussed in part in the references quoted) illustrate the contrast:

(20)   a. (?)Ha telefonato Maria al giornale.
           has phoned Maria to the newspaper
       b. *Ha comprato Maria il giornale.
           has bought Maria the newspaper
       c. (?)Ha parlato uno studente col direttore.
           has spoken a student to the director
       d. *Ha corrotto uno studente il direttore.
           has bribed a student the director
       e. (?)Ha sparato il bandito al carabiniere.
           has shot the gangster at the policeman
       f. *Ha colpito il bandito il carabiniere.
           has hit the gangster the policeman
       g. (?)Ha telefonato il direttore del giornale al presidente.
           has phoned the director of the newspaper to the president
       h. *Ha incontrato il direttore del giornale il presidente.
           has met the director of the newspaper the president

The sentences in (20) should be pronounced with continuous intonation, with no special break between S and the following complement. When a break intervenes, the picture changes in a way discussed in section 3.2.

The crucial difference between a direct object and a prepositional object is that the former is a DP while the latter is a PP. DPs need Case, while PPs do not.[33] Rather, it is the DP embedded within the PP which needs Case and such Case is provided or checked within the PP, due to the presence of P. A Case-related account thus suggests itself, which I will phrase in the following terms. Assume that the direct object must be associated with a relevant Case assigning/checking head. Assume this Case-related head[34] is located outside vP/VP in a position higher than the Focus projection hosting the postverbal subject. This is the crucial factor ruling out VSO: the relation of O with the Case-assigning/checking head cannot be established due to the intervention of S, ultimately, due to RM.[35] Consider the simplified representation in (21) illustrating this point:

(21)

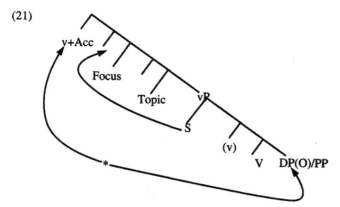

As no relation external to vP is required for PPs, no RM violation is brought about by the presence of a PP following the postverbal S.

Two further considerations have to be made, before moving to the discussion of VS#O (# is an intonational break). The VSPP sequences in (20) appear to be optimally appropriate in situations where the whole VP is taken to be new information focus. The most direct way to characterize this interpretation within the guidelines assumed so far would be to assume that it is actually the whole verb phrase, rather than just the subject, that moves to the specifier of the Focus phrase. We leave this as an open possibility. If this hypothesis is adopted, nothing changes in the proposed account for the different status of VSPP versus VSO, as all the relevant hierarchical relations involved remain unchanged.[36] Note that PP can also be topic in sentences displaying the VSPP order. This would be the case in a sentence like (22)b as an answer to (22)a, which is normally associated with a downgrading intonation on the PP:

(22)   a. Chi ha sparato al carabiniere?
         b. Ha sparato il bandito al carabiniere.

In these sentences only the subject should fill the Focus position.

As a last remark, something should also be said on the mild (the question mark in parentheses) degradation attributed to the VSPP examples in (20). The less than perfect status of these examples could be related to a tendency to have a narrow focus interpretation of the postverbal subject; hence, a preference to have it in the last position.[37] The tendency is not respected in the relevant examples in (20), whence their less than perfect status. Still, no grammatical principle is violated, so these sentences are acceptable.

3.2.   VS#O

Judgments change according to whether a pause intervenes between S and O, when O is a direct object. Consider the following two possible sentences:

(23) a. L'ha comprato Maria, il giornale.
          it(cl) bought Maria the newspaper
      b. Ha comprato Maria, il giornale.
          has bought Maria the newspaper

Example (23)a is a case of clitic right dislocation; (23)b is a case of so-called
emarginazione—"marginalization"—in the sense of Antinucci and Cinque (1977).

After the pause, indicated in both cases by the comma, a downgrading intonation characterizes the pronunciation of the following direct object. Although apparently very similar, the two structures can be considered to differ significantly. The
distinction, which only manifests itself in few special contexts, has been brought to
light in Cardinaletti (2001) and Frascarelli (2000). Consider the following question-
answer pairs:

(24) A. Chi ha comprato il giornale?
          Who bought the newspaper?
      B. a. L'ha comprato Maria, il giornale.
              it(cl) bought Maria the newspaper
          b.*Ha comprato MARIA, il giornale.
              has bought MARIA the newspaper

The postverbal subject is necessarily contrastively focused in the case of *emarginazione* ((24)Bb), while it is not necessarily so in the case of right dislocation ((24)Ba).
This explains why a sentence like (24)Ba can be a felicitous answer to the question
of information in (24)A, while (24)Bb cannot. Example (24)Bb essentially reproduces the judgment reported in (17)–(18). The following account can be provided
for the distinction.

Consider the analysis of (24)Ba first. Following Cecchetto (1999), I assume
that the right dislocated phrase fills a clause-internal low topic position; the clitic
is raised to the appropriate clitic position in the higher portion of the clause, leaving behind the topicalized object, with a stranding type of derivation that assimi-
lates these structures to clitic-doubling structures in most important respects.[38] Given
the shape of the vP/VP periphery assumed here, this amounts to claiming that the
right dislocated phrase fills the low topic position below the clause-internal focus.
We can assume that the necessary Case requirements are fulfilled by the clitic in
these structures.[39] Hence, there is no need to directly associate the topicalized direct object with the Case head located above the Focus projection. The postverbal
subject fills the low focus position, accounting for its possible interpretation as new
information focus.

Let us elaborate more on how the clitic fulfills Case requirements in (24)Ba. As
the clitic moves to the (Specifier of the) Case projection, it ends up in a position higher
than the position filled by S. In this position no interference by S occurs; hence, accusative can be correctly assigned, or checked.[40] Lack of a clitic would leave the direct
object as the only element to fulfill Case requirements, with O in VP and lower than
S; there is no way to avoid the interference by S. The structure is consequently impossible, as we saw VSO structures are in general. The following schema summarizes the two different situations:

(21')

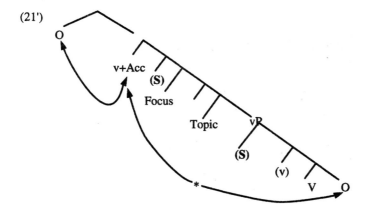

Given the very different status of (24)Ba and (24)Bb, an analysis along the lines just proposed is not to be extended to (24)Bb. In fact, an analysis along these lines could not be extended to (24)Bb, given the analysis just developed. Lack of the clitic in (24)Bb indicates that the object has to be related to its Case-assigning head directly, without the mediation of the clitic. Hence, the structure is impossible as VSO usually is, as discussed. The presence of a pause in VS#O should not make any difference. The fact that the same word order is in fact (only) acceptable with an interpretation of the subject as contrastive focus rather than new information focus indicates that a different structure and derivation should be associated with this interpretation/intonation.

Let us make the restrictive hypothesis that the contrastive focus interpretation is available in the left peripheral focus position and, in fact, this interpretation is available only in that position. If this is the case, the contrastive focus interpretation indicates that the element carrying it is located in the high left peripheral focus position. This means that the postverbal subject should fill the peripheral focus position in (24)Bb, and this has a direct consequence for the object. We can think that movement of the subject to the clause-external focus position frees the object to establish the appropriate relation with the VP external Case-assigning head. Schematically, if in (24)Ba the order of the relevant projections is the one indicated in (25), with S intervening between the object Case-assigning head and O itself, in (24)Bb the order is the one indicated in (26), where S does not create any intervention effect, it being much higher in the structure:

(25)   ... v+Acc ... [$_{Focus}$ (S)] ... [$_{Topic}$ (O)] ... [$_{vP}$ (S) ... (O)][41]

(26)   ... [$_{Focus}$ S] ... [$_{IP}$ ... v+Acc ... [$_{Focus}$] ... [$_{Topic}$] ... [$_{vP}$ ... (O)]]

If this is the correct hypothesis, the natural analysis of sentences like (24)Bb must imply that other topicalization processes are at work to reach the final word order: topicalization of the direct object into the peripheral topic position located below the focus projection (Rizzi 1997), and remnant topicalization of the remaining portion of the IP past the peripheral focalized subject and topicalized direct object:

(27)   ... [[$_{IPk}$ e$_i$ ha comprato e$_j$]Top [[MARIA] Foc] [[il giornale] Top] ... IP$_k$[42]

3.2.1.   A follow-up on VS#O

Given the described analysis of the "emarginazione" cases of VS#O, a natural question to ask is what would happen if the IP remnant movement part of the derivation did not take place.[43]

It appears that sentences resulting from this kind of derivation are relatively acceptable:[44]

(28)   a. ?MARIA, quel giornale, ha comprato.
          Maria that newspaper has bought
       b. ?QUEI RAGAZZI, Maria, hanno criticato.
          those boys Maria have criticized
       c. ?IL RESPONSABILE, le soluzioni, troverà.
          the responsible the solutions will find

We can assume that the same procedures involved in the derivation of the "emarginazione" "VS#O" cases would extend to (28), modulo absence of the IP remnant movement step.

Direct objects are not normally allowed to be topic, without a clitic being present in the following clause. Well-known contrasts like the one in (29) are easily detectable, however:

(29)   a. Il discorso, (Gianni) lo leggerà (Gianni) (a tutti).
          the discourse, (G.) it-cl will read (G.) (to everybody)
       b.*Il discorso, (Gianni) leggerà (Gianni) (a tutti).
          the discourse, (G.) will read (G.) (to everybody)

As the constituents in parentheses indicate, their presence and location appear to be irrelevant: the source of the contrast in (29)—in particular, the ungrammaticality of (29)b—is solely to be identified in the absence of the clitic. Suppose that necessity of the clitic here is due to the fact that the empty position to which the topicalized phrase should be linked would not otherwise have a precise status (an assumption often made).[45] The fact that the clitic can be missing in (28) is further indication that the possibility comes as a by-product of the clause external focalization of the subject. Indeed, the phenomenon appears to be more general, as the possibility is also manifested if another constituent, different from the subject, is focalized, as indicated in (30)a, which contrasts with (30)b:

(30)   a. A GIANNI, il libro, ho dato.
          to Gianni the book I have given
       b.*Il libro ho dato a Gianni.[46]
          The book I have given to Gianni.

We can conclude that O can be topicalized without presence of the clitic only if another constituent is simultaneously focalized in the left periphery. We leave open for the time being a precise analysis as to exactly what kind of parasitic use of focalization the topicalized object is allowed to make, this crucially depending on what the exact explanation for the impossibility of (29)b turns out to be, one option being the one alluded to above (and note 45). We just note here that the equivalent of the *emarginazione* VS#O type sentences not involving the remnant step seems indeed to be possible, as one would expect. Also, in all the possible cases, O is adequately Case-licensed IP internally due to lack of intervention of S. Lack of intervention is brought about by focalization of S in (28) and by movement of (null subject *pro*) S to the preverbal subject position in cases like (30).

The kind of parasitic use of focalization that a topicalized direct object seems to be able to make, which we just discussed and which allows it to appear without a clitic in the following sentence, seems to be constrained in a precise manner: it is available only in the respective order illustrated in (28) and (30) with the focused phrase preceding the topic phrase. The opposite order gives impossible results. Compare (28) and (30) with (31):

(31)   a. *Quel giornale, MARIA, ha comprato.
          that newspaper Maria has bought
       b. *Maria, QUEI RAGAZZI, hanno criticato.
          Maria those boys have criticized
       c. *Le soluzioni, IL RESPONSABILE, troverà.
          the solutions the responsible will find
       d. *Il libro, a GIANNI, ho dato.
          the book to Gianni I have given

We can describe the different status by observing that only a topic in a complement-like relation with focus can take advantage of the presence of focus in the structure. If topic has focus as a complement, the same advantage cannot be taken. I leave open further elaborations on this point.[47]

3.2.2.   VSO, S pronoun

A systematic class of "exceptions" to the general ban against VSO in Italian is provided by cases in which S corresponds to a personal pronoun. Consider in this respect the contrast in (32):

(32)   a. Di quel cassetto ho io le chiavi.
          of that drawer have I the keys
       b. *?Di quel cassetto ha Maria le chiavi.[48]
          of that drawer has Maria the keys

While the sentence in (32)b can only be rescued with a special contrastive or corrective intonation/interpretation on the postverbal subject "Maria," no similar special intonation/interpretation needs to be associated with the pronoun in (32)a. The contrast between the personal pronoun and the lexical noun phrase suggests that pronouns should avail themselves of a further position in the postverbal domain, which is excluded for lexical noun phrases. This further subject position should be higher than the one filled by the lexical noun phrase and such that it would not interfere in the Case assignment of the direct object.

Converging evidence is provided by the contrasts in (33). While a lexical postverbal subject noun phrase must follow low adverbs, a postverbal pronominal subject must precede them:

(33)   a. Di questo mi informerò io bene.
          of this will inform myself I well

b. *?Di questo si informerà Maria bene.
   of this will inform herself Maria well
c. Spiegherà lei completamente al direttore.
   will explain she completely to the director
d. *?Spiegherà Maria completamente al direttore. (cf. (3)).
   will explain M. completely to the director

Notice that if a low adverb precedes the postverbal pronominal subject, the latter necessarily receives a special contrastive or corrective interpretation ((34)a). This suggests that, in this case, the postverbal subject fills the higher focus position, and the sentence is associated with a very different representation involving remnant movement of the clause above the postverbal subject, as in the preceding analysis of (24)Bb.

The contrast in interpretation in (34) indicates that, contrary to the postverbal pronominal subject, the postverbal lexical subject can remain clause-internal, thus not requiring any contrastive/corrective interpretation, as assumed so far:

(34) a. Di questo mi informerò bene io (non tu / ... non importa che lo facciano altri).
         of this will inform myself well I (not you/ . . . it doesn't matter that other people
         do it)
      b. Di questo si informerà bene Maria.
         of this will inform herself well Maria

3.3.   VSO, VSPP: FI versus SI

In concluding this discussion, it is worth pointing out that a contrast in acceptability in VSXP structures seems to be detectable in French SI as well, with VSPP judged more acceptable than the excluded VSO. For instance, Kayne and Pollock (2001) quote pairs like the following:

(35) a. Qu'a dit Jean à Marie?   (K&P (133))
         what said Jean to Marie
      b. *A qui a dit Jean tout celà?
         to whom has said Jean all that

Although similar at first sight to the contrasts presented in (20), it is fairly clear from Kayne and Pollock's discussion that the similarity of the two paradigms in the two languages should not be taken as an indication that the processes involved in the derivation of SI and FI should ultimately be the same. The most significant indication that this would not be the right approach is provided by the fact that the VSPP order of Italian does not appear to be subject to the numerous constraints the equivalent order appears to be subject to in French. An illustration of that is provided by the fact that no so-called counterdefiniteness requirement constrains the nature of the PP in the VSPP order of Italian, as it does in French (36a--f in Kayne and Pollock 2001: (140)a,b, quoted from Cornulier 1974):

(36) a. (?) Sta parlando Maria a qualcuno.
         is talking Maria to somebody
      b. (?) Sta parlando Maria a Jean-Jacques.
         is talking Maria to Jean-Jacques

    c. *Sta salutando Maria qualcuno.
      is greeting Maria somebody
    d. *Sta salutando Maria Jean-Jacques.
      is greeting Maria Jean-Jacques
    e. ?*Qu'a avoué Pierre à quelqu'un?
      what has confessed Pierre to somebody
    f. Qu'a avoué Pierre à Jean-Jacques?
      what has confessed Pierre to Jean-Jacques

Furthermore, Kayne and Pollock remind the observation in Kampers-Mahne (1998) that VSPP is actually impossible in the structures where SI is induced by the presence of the subjunctive mood:

(37) *Il faut que le dise Jean à Marie
      it is necessary that it(cl) say (subj.) Jean to Marie

VSPP in Italian FI does not make any such distinction:

(38) a. E' necessario che lo dica Gianni a Maria.
        (it) is necessary the it(cl) say(subj.) G. to M.
     b. Mi sembrava che lo stesse dicendo Gianni a qualcuno.
        (it) seemed to me that was(subjunctive) saying it(cl) G. to somebody

The order VSPP is equally possible in both cases.[49]

3.4. On VSO in other Romance languages

As has been described in the literature (Zubizarreta 1998; Ordoñez 1997; Motapanyane 1995), VSO (where O is a direct object) is a possible word order in various Romance languages, not requiring any special stress or intonation associated to the sequence. I repeat below some examples from the reference quoted:

(39) a. Todos los días compra Juan el diario. (Zubizarreta 1998)
       every day buys Juan the newspaper
     b. Espero que te devuelva Juan el libro. (Ordóñez 1997)
       I hope that cl-you return Juan the book
       'I hope that Juan returns the book to you.'
     c. O invita cam des Ion pe fata acesta. (Motapanyane 1995)
       her invites quite often Ion 'pe' girl the-that
       'Ion invites that girl quite often.'

But why should it be so? Why should there be such a difference between Italian (and Catalan; see Picallo 1998) on the one side and Spanish and Romanian on the other, limiting the domain of investigation to (some of) Romance?

    There are two possible approaches to this problem: (a) the languages allowing VSO avail themselves of a further subject position, higher in the structure than the Focus (or Topic) position hosting the postverbal subject in Italian and such that it would not interfere with Case assignment of the object; (b) the languages allowing VSO avail themselves of a further way to Case mark the direct object, allowing it to remain VP internal, with no need to be associated to the VP external Case position, thus reducing VSO to the same status as VSPP in Italian.

In favor of the first approach, which is the one adopted, with differences, in the references quoted and in Belletti (2001) among others, is the observation that a similar higher subject position seems available in other languages anyway—for example, Icelandic (see (5) and (6) above), and, possibly, in Italian as well, but there limited to hosting subject pronouns only, as in the discussion in section 3.2.2. In favor of the second alternative, the following consideration is given: There appears to be a correlation between availability of VSO and existence of a special Case marking of direct objects in the same set of languages involving a preposition under certain conditions (e.g., animacy of the object in Spanish; see Torrego 1998, from which I draw the examples in (40)). The preposition is also visible in object Clitic doubling constructions also possible in both Spanish and Romanian, in Romance:

(40)   a. Ana saludò a uno amigo.
          Ana greeted to a friend
       b. Juan lo visitò al chico.
          Juan visited to the boy[50]

The hypothesis could then be that, at least in VSO, there can be recourse to an "abstract" version of the preposition for Case marking the direct object.

   Of course, the next step should be a thorough investigation of the conditions under which the abstract preposition should be licensed. I leave the two alternatives open here at this rather speculative stage, noticing that the correlation between possibility of VSO and existence of a preposition available to Case mark the direct object appears to hold beyond the Romance domain as it is also found in other languages as well, such as modern Greek.[51]

4.   On VOS

To the extent that VOS sequences are possible in Italian, they are only marginally so and appear to allow for only a special interpretation. To be able to have sentences like the following (41), the VO sequence must be given in the immediate context: that is, it must be topic:

(41)   a. ??Capirà il problema Gianni.
          will understand the problem Gianni
       b. ??Ha chiamato Maria Gianni.
          has called Maria Gianni
       c. ??Ha letto il romanzo Gianni.
          has read the novel Gianni

For instance, a sentence like (41)a could constitute a possible answer to (42):

(42)   Chi capirà il problema?
       Who will understand the problem?

   In (41)a, the given part of the VP, VO, is repeated word by word. Of course, there are other more natural ways to answer (42). In the by far most natural answer to (42), the direct object is not fully repeated but is rather pronominalized, as in (43)a;

(43)b and c are the respective more natural answers than (41)b and c to the relevant parallel questions:

(43) a. Lo capirà Gianni.
          it will understand Gianni
      b. L'ha chiamata Gianni.
          her has called Gianni
      c. L'ha letto Gianni.
          it has read Gianni

We can account for the difference between the relatively strong marginality of (41) and the full acceptability of (43) in the following terms. Suppose that O is not allowed to remain in the position where it checks its Case. O can transit through (the Spec of) the Case position, but must void it.[52] This leads us to conclude that VOS is impossible in Italian. I assume that this is the right idealization of the data. If O can empty the Case position, the structure is rescued, though: this is precisely what cliticization does. Whence, the full acceptability of (43).

But why is it that VOS, although highly marginal, is not fully ungrammatical, then? It is clear, for instance, that VOS is felt as more acceptable than VSO by Italian speakers. Suppose that, as suggested by the interpretation, VOS can be given an analysis such that no violation of grammatical principles is involved. According to this analysis, the constituent containing the VO sequence is interpreted as topic. Assume for concreteness that it fills the low topic position right above the clause-internal focus. S fills the low new information focus position. To the extent that they are considered acceptable, these sentences would then illustrate an instance of clause-internal remnant topicalization.[53] We can speculate that this analysis is felt as somehow more costly than the more straightforward one whereby O is pronominalized and then cliticized. Whence, the nonperfect status of the sentences in (41).[54]

As an independent indication that this might be the correct approach to the problem, the more "prototypical" the situation illustrated by the VO sequence is, the better the status of VOS becomes. For instance, sentences like the following (44) can often be heard in live radio broadcasting of soccer games, where VO expresses a typical situation in the games and counts as if it were taken from a given list of possibilities:

(44) Protegge l'uscita del portiere il terzino sinistro.
       protects the coming out of the goal keeper the left back

Another case where VOS is fully acceptable, and which does not involve pronominalization of O, is the one given in sentences like (3)d, repeated in (45), where O is the quantifier *tutto*:

(45) Capirà tutto Maria.
       will understand everything Maria

As noted in connection with the discussion of paradigm (3), the quantifier *tutto* moves in syntax to a position high enough to enable it not to give rise to the same interference effect that low adverbs give rise to, which leads to the marginal flavor of VAdvS.

The perfect status of (45) as opposed to the usually impossible VOS indicates that *tutto* should be located in a different position than the position a normal direct object would fill in VOS. As a possible way of characterizing the difference, we can assume that *tutto* is not in the object Case position. Possibly, *tutto* never ends up in this position altogether, as its quantifier status does not impose Case requirements on it. If the problem posed by VOS is linked to the impossibility of filling the object Case position, as we are assuming, we understand why *tutto* should not cause any similar problem. Moreover, the perfect status of "V tutto S" as opposed to the impossibility of VOS is further indication that the relevant ordering constraints do not involve any linear requirement. Furthermore, no topic-like interpretation is necessarily attributed to VO, O = *tutto*, as expected under the adopted analysis.

4.1. More on [VO] remnant topicalization

The postverbal subject in VOS is not c-commanded by the material contained within the remnant phrase. This leads us to expect that if some c-command relation is required to hold between O and S, this should not be possible. Indeed, it appears that binding relations cannot hold between O and S in VOS. Consider the following question-answer pair, necessary to provide a somewhat natural context for (the limited availability of) VOS in (46)b:

(46) a. Chi ha salutato Gianni?
         Who greeted Gianni?
      b.*Hanno salutato Gianni$_i$ i propri$_i$ genitori.[55]
         greeted(pl) Gianni his own parents

The opposite direction of binding significantly improves the judgment:

(47) a. Chi ha salutato i propri genitori?
         Who greeted his own parents?
      b. Ha salutato i propri$_i$ genitori Gianni$_i$.
         greeted (sing) his own parents Gianni.
      c. Chi ha baciato la propria moglie?
         Who kissed his own wife?
      d. Hanno baciato la propria$_i$ moglie tutti i candidati$_i$.
         have kissed (pl) their own wife all the candidates

The acceptability of binding in (47)b and d, can be assumed to be obtained through reconstruction of the remnant VO, with O interpreted in its base position where it is c-commanded by S.

The relative acceptability of the various answers to the questions in (48) following (granted the usual marginality of VOS) may appear as problematic, at least at first glance:

(48) a. Chi ha detto la verità?
         Who has said the truth?
      a. Che cosa/chi ha espresso la verità?
         What/who has expressed the truth?

(49) a. Non hanno detto la verità che due studenti.
         have "not" said the truth "that" two students
      b. Non ha detto la verità nessuno.
         has not said the truth nobody

c. Non ha espresso la verità alcunché/alcun ministro.
   has not expressed the truth anything/any minister

If *non*, the licensor of the polarity expression in the postverbal subject position, is contained within the remnant-moved VO sequence, the sentences in (49) should be impossible. But they are perfectly acceptable. How can this be? Suppose that, in fact, *non* is not contained within the remnant-moved [VO] constituent, but that it is outside the topicalized constituent, in a position from where it does c-command the postverbal subject. Indeed, this is directly suggested by the fact that the negation is attached to the auxiliary and not to the lexical verb. In the assumed analysis of VOS as involving remnant topicalization of the [VO] constituent, the verb involved in the process is the lexical verb; the auxiliary must be higher in the clause. The negation should then be at least as high as the auxiliary to which it is attached. This is schematically indicated in the simplified representation (50):

(50)   ... [$_{IP}$ non+hanno [$_{TOP}$ [$_{VP}$ e$_i$ detto la verità]$_j$ Top [$_{FOC}$ [che due studenti]$_i$ Foc Top
       [VP$_j$]]]] ...

Hence, the (marginal, as always for VOS) acceptability of (49) is not problematic for our general assumed account of the (marginal) VOS word order.

It is interesting that a contrastive focus interpretation/intonation on the postverbal subject in sentences like (49) leads to an even stronger marginality than the one normally associated with VOS. This is coherent with the restrictive assumption that contrastive focus is only established in the left peripheral focus position and not in the clause-internal one, which is reserved for new information focus only. If the postverbal subject fills the left peripheral focus position when it is contrastively focused or stressed, then the remnant portion of the clause to be topicalized must contain the whole clause itself (with the subject trace); this, in turn, implies that the negation should be contained within the remnant topicalized portion, whence, c-command would not hold between *non* and the polarity phrase in the postverbal subject. Indeed, it appears that it is not possible to associate the relevant interpretation/intonation to the following sentences in (51)B and D:[56]

(51) A. Hanno detto la verità tutti i partecipanti.
         have said the truth all the participants
      B. 1.*? No, non hanno detto la verità CHE GLI STUDENTI.
            no have "not" said the truth "that" the students
         2.*? No, non ha detto la verità NESSUNO.
            no has not said the truth nobody
      C. Ha espresso la verità quel comportamento/quel ministro.
         has expressed the truth that behavior/that minister
      D.*?No, non ha espresso la verità ALCUNCHE'/ALCUN MINISTRO
         no, has not said the truth anything/any minister

Sentences word by word identical to (51)B and D—for example, (49)—can be (marginally, as always with VOS) acceptable in the context of (51)A and C, but the intonation involved is not the contrastive one suggested by use of the capital letters on the postverbal subject in (51)B and D. In those cases, the whole sentence might count as a correction, and the postverbal subject is not contrastively stressed or focused.[57] It is only in the latter interpretation/intonation that the sentences in (51)B and D are judged as very strange—indeed, impossible. This is further illustrated by pairs like the following, which explicitly indicate the strong marginality arising if contrast/correction is exclusively put on the postverbal S:

(52) a. Ha detto la verità GIANNI (non Mario).
         has said the truth Gianni (not Mario)
      b.*?Non hanno detto la verità CHE GLI STUDENTI (non i professori).
         have "not" said the truth "that" the students (not the professors)
      c.*?Non ha detto la verità NESSUNO (non Gianni).
         has not said the truth nobody (not Gianni)

As a final remark on this point, we note that if we take the negative quantifier *nessuno* in the preverbal subject position where *non* licensing is not required in Italian as *non* does not show up altogether, and we associate it with contrastive focus intonation/interpretation, the resulting sentence is perfectly acceptable, as (53)b illustrates in the following:

(53) a. Tutti hanno detto la verità.
         Everybody has said the truth.
      b. No, NESSUNO ha detto la verità (non tutti).
         No, nobody has said the truth (not everybody).

This indicates that there is nothing intrinsically wrong with this particular intonation/interpretation, but that the problem in (52)c is indeed structural in nature.

5. Postverbal S can also be Topic

As we have assumed that a low topic position is available below the clause-internal focus one, nothing in principle should prevent a postverbal subject to fill the topic position in some cases. This possibility is available, as already illustrated in (10), and it is the only available one in some contexts. These contexts are the wh-interrogatives, which will be discussed in section 5.1.

Let us first consider some further examples of simple declaratives in which postverbal S appears to be a low topic, a possibility left open by the proposed account. As also suggested by the downgrading intonation on postverbal S, the most suitable analysis of the examples b and d of the exchange in (54), has the subject as a topic. This would precisely be the low topic in question:

(54) a. Che cosa ha poi fatto Gianni per quella questione?
         what has then done Gianni for that matter
      b. Sì, sì ha poi parlato, Gianni, al direttore.
         yes yes has then spoken Gianni to the director
      c. Che cosa farà Gianni?
         what will do Gianni
      d. Partirà, Gianni.
         will leave Gianni

The PP "al direttore" in (54)b is a further topic. It is known from the left periphery that topics can be iterated. There wouldn't be any reason for this not to happen for clause-internal topics as well.

5.1. Postverbal subjects in wh-interrogatives

We start by noting that wh-interrogatives allow—and, in fact, require—that the subject be postverbal. Contrasts like the following are well known and widely discussed in the literature:

(55) a. Che cosa ha detto Gianni?
       what has said Gianni
    b.*Che cosa Gianni ha detto?
       what Gianni has said

Without trying to provide an account for the reason(s) why the subject could not be preverbal in these interrogatives,[58] let us try to determine where it is found when it is in the postverbal position.

We start by noting that wh-interrogatives are systematically incompatible with left peripheral focalization. The ill-formedness of the sentences in (56), shaped on similar ones discussed in Rizzi (1997), illustrate this point:

(56) a.*Che cosa A GIANNI hai detto?
       what TO GIANNI have you said
    b.*A GIANNI che cosa hai detto?
       TO GIANNI what have you said?

This kind of ill-formedness is interpreted by Rizzi to be due to the fact that wh-words end up into the specifier of the peripheral focus position. This position being unique, it cannot contain both a contrastively focused phrase and the wh-word. Assuming this to be the right approach, we could suppose that since in the approach developed here the postverbal subject is located in a different clause-internal focus position, no incompatibility should be expected between wh-interrogatives and clause-internal focalization. It could then be assumed that there is no particular issue raised by wh-interrogatives and that the postverbal subject of interrogatives like (55)a could be a postverbal focalized subject. The situation does not appear to be that simple, however.

The next observation to make is that focalization appears to be a process normally affecting one single constituent per clause.[59] For instance, no more than one constituent can undergo focalization in the left periphery:

(57) *A GIANNI MARIA ho presentato.
     to Gianni Maria (I) have introduced

This impossibility could be traced back once again to the fact that there is only one focus position in the left periphery. The problem seems to be more general, though. It appears that left peripheral focalization is also not compatible with clause-internal focalization. It does not seem to be possible to associate the right interpretation/intonation to sentences like the following, with the left peripheral phrase contrastively focused and the direct object in (58)a and the postverbal subject in (58)b interpreted as new information focus (underscored, for clarity); the sentences are excluded under this interpretation:

(58) a. *A GIANNI ho regalato un libro
         to Gianni (I) have given a book
      b. *UN LIBRO ha letto Gianni
         a book has read Gianni

The shape of paradigms (56), (57), and (58) suggests that a constraint is operative to the effect that a sentence can contain only one focused element, but this constraint does not seem to make a distinction as to the kind of focus in question, as (58) reveals.[60] If this is the case, wh-interrogatives containing a postverbal subject are unlikely to be analyzed as involving a focalized postverbal subject and a wh-word in the left peripheral focus position; they would constitute an isolated exception to the set of the paradigms in (56), (57), and (58). I conclude that, in fact, the postverbal subject of wh-interrogatives fills the low topic, not the low focus, position. This possibility is made available by the analysis proposed and is used in other cases as well as those illustrated in (54) and (10).

Further independent indication that this hypothesis is on the right track is provided by data from some northern Italian dialects. In these dialects (Fiorentino and Trentino) a particular subject clitic (F) or no clitic at all (T) appear in inversion structures in declarative clauses. The data are taken from Brandi and Cordin (1981):

(59) a. Gl'è venuto le su' sorelle. (F)
         it+has come his sisters
      b. E' vegnù le so' sorele. (T)
         has come his sisters

In wh-interrogatives the subject must be in a postverbal position, much as in standard Italian, but a different clitic from the one that shows up signaling inversion in declarative clauses appears in these cases. The subject clitic appearing in wh-interrogatives is the one found in right dislocation. Consider (60) and (61) in this respect (from Brandi and Cordin 1981: 15a,b, 74, 75):

(60) a. Quando l'è venuta la Maria? (F)
         when she+has come the Maria
      b. Icché l'ha portato la Maria?
         what she+has brought the Maria
      c. *Icché gl'ha portato la Maria?
         what it+has brought the Maria

(61) a. Quando è la vegnuda la Maria? (T)
         when has-she come the Maria
      b. Cosa ha la portà la Maria?
         what has-she brought the Maria
      c. *Cosa ha portà la Maria?
         what has brought the Maria

These data are perfectly coherent with the analysis proposed above: the right dislocated subject of (60) and (61) fills the low topic position, as in the analysis developed for standard Italian both for subject inversion in wh-interrogatives and for right dislocation more generally. The interesting aspect of these data from the dialects is that the nature of the position occupied by the postverbal subject is revealed and made visible by the nature of the subject clitic (F) or by its very presence (T).

A last piece of evidence that the postverbal subject is not a focalized subject but rather a topic in wh-interrogatives comes from contrasts like the one in (62) involving weak crossover configurations:

(62)   a.*?Attualmente, in un suo$_i$ appartamento vive Gianni$_i$.
           at present in one his apartment lives Gianni
        b. Attualmente, in quale suo$_i$ appartamento vive Gianni$_i$?
           at present in which his apartment lives Gianni?

Example (62)a shows that a WCO violation is induced by a postverbal subject in declarative clauses, while no such violation is induced by a postverbal subject in a wh-interrogative. For reasons that I will not develop here, focus is known to give rise to WCO violations. Thus, the impossibility of (62)a can be seen as a typical WCO violation induced by focus, as the postverbal subject fills the clause-internal focus position according to our analysis.[61] The fact that no comparable violation is at work in the wh-interrogative (62)b is a further indication that the postverbal subject in these interrogatives is not focalized. The status of sentences like (62)b is perfectly compatible with the proposed analysis that the postverbal S is in topic position in wh-interrogatives and the contrast between (62)a and (62)b indirectly supports the overall approach.[62]

6.   Concluding remarks

The main purpose of this essay has been the identification of different positions in the low IP area surrounding the VP. These positions appear to be related to different types of interpretations and their associated intonations. The aim has been internal to the cartographic perspective presented at the outset. The main empirical domain analyzed has been the one concerning the distribution of postverbal subjects; however, the aim of this work has not been that of providing a systematic and comprehensive analysis of subject inversion structures. Several issues related to VS structures have not been touched upon, and they are central for a detailed account of this complex phenomenology. Two of them are dealt with in some detail in Belletti (2001): the integration within the proposed clause structure and the assumed processes of clause internal focalization/topicalization of structures containing unaccusative verbs; the availability of nominative Case for postverbal subjects. For a discussion of these issues, see the reference quoted.[63]

The evidence presented here strongly indicates that the low IP vP/VP-periphery is plausibly rich in the positions made available. These positions appear to be tightly connected with discourse-related interpretations of Focus and Topic in a way that is significantly parallel to the positions available in the clause-external (left) periphery.

Notes

1. With "topicalization" of an element, I refer here to the process through which that element is dealt with as a/the "topic" of discourse, the "given" information. In the literature the term "topicalization" often indicates the process that here we refer to as "focalization": the singling out of an element of the clause as the "new" or "contrastive" information. This terminological distinction should be kept in mind to avoid potential confusion.

I make use of the labels Focus and Topic here as commonly done in the current literature, but these labels are just a first approximation to a more adequate way of expressing aspects of the relation between discourse and syntactic configuration. The issue of the appropriateness of the labels arises here in a way comparable to the similar issue concerning the appropriateness of labels for Th-roles. In both cases, appropriateness concerns the expression of the relation between formal syntax and the interpretive interface.

2. I am using the term Spec in a traditional fashion incorporating classical X' terminology. The proposal to be developed here can also be phrased in a bare phrase structure frame.

3. See also Brody (1990) and the references quoted earlier. For a first formulation of a similar proposal assuming the presence of a clause internal focus position, see Belletti and Shlonsky (1995); see also Ndayiragije (1999) and Jayaseelan (2001).

4. As for the topic interpretation, it is conceivable that it is uniform in both peripheries and is assimilated to "given," "known," "nonfocus" interpretation. Although the notion "topic" no doubt requires further refinements on both semantic and pragmatic grounds (see Buring 1995), in what follows I am going to assume the general interpretation mentioned as "given" information.

5. Throughout this work the term "postverbal" is used in purely descriptive terms to refer to a subject that appears after the verb. Most of the data in this section concerning Italian are presented in more detail in Belletti (2001).

6. The literature is extensive in GB. See, among others, Burzio (1986), Rizzi (1982), and the references cited therein.

7. Given the subtlety of some of the data discussed in this work, I am sure to control for the relevant pragmatic and intonational variables involved only in Italian. Given the appropriate intonation and pragmatic situations assumed throughout, the conclusions to be reached should extend to the Romance area more generally. See Costa (2000) for a recent discussion of closely resembling data. The label FI is used here in pretheoretical terms to distinguish this type of subject inversion from French SI; as we will see, inversion structures containing a postverbal subject in FI correspond to peculiar interpretations, distinct to those of structures containing a preverbal subject. In this respect "inversion" is not at all "free" but is only compatible with the interpretations to be discussed later in this chapter.

8. On the potentially misleading effect of the term "inversion," see Belletti (2001).

9. A silent doubling subject clitic remains inside the IP, thus accounting for the "stylistically" rather marked status of the construction.

10. This characterization, which needs further qualification, creates the expectation that other XP complements may be allowed to intervene between the verb and the postverbal subject in SI but not as easily in FI. The question is complex, but, as the discussion in Kayne and Pollock (2001) suggests, this could only be a partially correct conclusion, as VOS and VPPS seem possible orders in French SI, at different levels of acceptability and with constraints regarding the interpretation of the object (preferably idiomatic). However, as discussed in section 4 (see also the previous quoted work of mine), VO/PPS is not possible in Italian FI unless the VO sequence receives a particular topic-like interpretation/intonation, which we will precisely interpret as involving the topicalization of a remnant constituent, although to a clause-internal rather than to a clause-external position.

11. On the impossibility for a direct object to follow the postverbal subject, see section 3.

12. As discussed in more detail later in this chapter, the external Focus position, which one might want to suggest to be the position hosting the postverbal subject (combined with IP remnant movement), appears to always carry a corrective or contrastive interpretation or intonation that is completely absent in the examples discussed in (3)–(4), as noted in the text. This strongly suggests that an analysis with the postverbal subject located in the left peripheral position and movement of the remnant IP across it is not revealing and should be dismissed for these cases of subject inversion. I limit this kind of analysis to those cases in which the postverbal subject is indeed contrastively or correctively focused, which also display various differentiating behaviors with respect to the noncontrastively or noncorrectively focused postverbal subject under analysis here. See sections 2.1, 2.2, and 4.1 in particular.

13. See Nicolis (2000) for recent discussion.

14. Or of the whole IP, if S had moved out of the IP as in French SI, according to Kayne and Pollock (2001).

15. In other words, movement of *tutto* puts it further away from the position of the postverbal subject, while "low adverbs" remain closer to it, with V in its final functional position in both cases. This hierarchical distinction would be lost under a remnant movement analysis. A reviewer claims that French SI appears to give rise to contrasts analogous to those in (3)–(4); if this is so, it might shed doubts on the overall analysis of SI as involving movement of the remnant IP across the left peripheral subject, developed by Kayne and Pollock. Since they do not explicitly discuss this point, I assume that their analysis of French SI can be maintained, pending further evidence.

16. On which, see Belletti (2001); see also Saccon (1993) and Pinto (1994).

17. Extraction remains bad with wh-interrogatives (actually worse than with relatives):

(i) *?Di che cosa/di quale giornale ha telefonato il direttore al presidente?
Of what/of what journal has telephoned the director to the president

As I argue in section 5, the postverbal subject fills a different position in wh-interrogatives than in declaratives. The evidence indicates that both positions are impossible or very marginal extraction domains.

One could try to relate the general impossibility of extraction out of a postverbal subject to the same impossibility of extraction out of the preverbal subject position, an instance of the operation of a "leftness constraint." To obtain the desired word order, however, such a reductionist approach—potentially attractive and taken for instance in Longobardi (1998)— would necessarily require the postulation of a derivation that includes a wider use of remnant movement than the one admitted here, given the adopted guidelines. Moreover, extraction appears to be worse when it takes place from the preverbal subject position than from the postverbal one. We could use diacritics ranging from * to ??/?*. Thus, if (ii) is a clear *, (iii) and the examples in the text can be judged as slightly more acceptable:

(ii) *La ragazza di cui il fratello ha telefonato alle 5.
the girl of whom the brother called at 5

(iii) ??La ragazza di cui ha telefonato il fratello alle 5.
the girl of whom called the brother at 5

See Belletti and Rizzi (1988) for a possible account phrased in terms of CED/subjacency and differences in the number of crossed barriers in the two extraction sites.

Such a distinction could not be easily expressed within the reductionist approach that identifies the extraction site in the two cases. I do not attempt a precise update of the mentioned previous account for the distinction here.

18. Kayne and Pollock (2001) point out that not all cases of wh-extraction are equally well-formed for different speakers, but they assume that essentially wh-extraction should be considered possible.

19. This is true in some of the most typical cases discussed here and in previous work. But see later in this chapter for cases in which the postverbal subject receives the topic (given, old information) interpretation. As for the possibility of extraction, no difference seems to be detectable as to whether the postverbal subject is focus or topic. See also note 17.

20. The A versus A' distinction is probably not refined enough to provide an adequate characterization of the notion relevant for CED. For the sake of this discussion, the matter is simplified in the text and is left open here.

In those cases in which V (or part of the clause containing V as in remnant type derivations; see section 4) is in focus or topic, the clause-internal focus and topic positions must be considered transparent domains for extraction of V to undertake morphological checking. See also Belletti (2001).

21. For the sake of simplicity, I disregard here the important conclusions reached in Cardinaletti (1997 and chapter 5 in this volume) that there is more than a single preverbal subject position in the clause.

22. The focalized status of the postverbal subject is further indicated by pairs like the following, also pointed out and discussed in some detail in Belletti (2001). See also Moro (1997) for a detailed discussion of (ii).

(i) a. (Pronto, chi parla?)
(Hello, who speaks?)

b. Parla Gianni.
speaks Gianni

c. *Gianni parla.
Gianni speaks.

(ii) a. (Chi è?)
(Who is (there)?)

b. 1 Sono io.
am I = it's me.

2 Sono Gianni
am Gianni = It's Gianni.

3 E' Gianni.
It's Gianni.

c. *Io/Gianni sono/è.
I/Gianni am/is.

23. A possible alternative according to which the postverbal subject remains in its original position internal to the verb phrase, assumed for instance in Cardinaletti (2001), is not viable within the guidelines adopted here according to which (both) the interpretation (and the intonation) should optimally be read off the syntactic configuration directly.

24. In these non . . . che sequences, the total omission of the article is more or less felicitous, depending on conditions yet to be understood and properly described. Although interesting in itself, I will not undertake a systematic description here, which will take the discussion too far afield. Kayne and Pollock (2001) seem to implicitly assume that the French ne . . . que construction is not submitted to the same kind of c-command requirement of ne over the que phrase that we are proposing for Italian. They allow for an extension of their analysis of SI to cases like the following (their examples (175) and (176)):

(i) Ne sont venus que Jean et Marie.
     are not come that Jean and Marie

(ii) Ne sont venus qu'eux.
      are not come that they

However, we think that c-command can still be taken to be the relevant notion here and that the facts in (i)–(ii) call for a better explanation. As they also indicate, these instances of SI are very peculiar and demand readjustments in their system anyway.

25. Similar facts hold with the NPI "alcunché":

(i) a. Questi esperimenti non mostrano alcunche'.
         These experiments do not show anything.
     b. Da questi sperimenti non risulta alcunche'.
         from these experiments does not follow anything
     c. *Alcunche' (non) risulta da questi esperimenti.
         anything does not follow from these experiments

In these cases and, more generally, with indefinite subjects of unaccusative verbs, the subject is likely to remain VP internal (Belletti 1988, 2001).

26. Note furthermore that, as is well known, the negative marker *non* normally disappears when *nessuno* is a preverbal subject in Italian:

(i) Nessuno (*non) ha parlato.
     Nobody has (*not) spoken.

With the described analysis it would not be obvious how to force presence of *non* when the subject appears in the postverbal position, in fact, a concealed preverbal position which normally excludes the presence of *non*.

27. A reviewer points out that paradigms similar to (12)–(14) hold in French SI as well. If this is the case, it is an open question how the analysis of SI proposed by Kayne and Pollock could analyze them in a way coherent with the interpretation provided for the relevance of the examples in (15). Possibly, not all cases of SI should be uniformly analyzed as involving IP remnant movement to the left periphery, as I am assuming following Kayne and Pollock's proposal. I leave the question open, once again pending further evidence on the relevant SI data.

28. It is also difficult to understand the interpretation associated with VOS structures, which is reviewed in section 4. See Kiss (1998) for a clear distinction of the two types of focuses.

29. One might suggest that, contrary to the text proposal, a new information Focus position could also be available in the left periphery and that whenever it is activated, remnant IP movement is always required. In this view, one should also explain why this should be the case for new information Focus but not for contrastive/corrective Focus. How could the relevant distinction be expressed? Moreover, all the evidence discussed in the text pointing to the "low" location of the postverbal subject in FI would be lost under any approach locating the postverbal subject in a "high" position, in the left periphery.

30. It is possible that those languages with a particular focus particle might make the relation between Focus and Case look more plausibly strict.

31. If one were to assume that once the preverbal subject is interpreted as a topic (Solà 1992 and Ordoñez 1997 on Spanish), it fills an external topic position, here, too, the reflex on the outcome would be a special interpretation. On preverbal subject positions, see Cardinaletti, chapter 5 in this volume. See also note 40 for a possible alternative.

32. For reasons of space, I do not address the Case issue on the postverbal subject here. See Belletti (2001 and 2003) for a proposal.

33. Clauses behave essentially like PPs: the order VSCP appears to be possible although with some complications hinted at in Belletti (2001) and which I will not further discuss here:

(i)   ha detto la mamma di andare a letto
      has said mom to go to bed

(ii) ha detto la mamma che ha telefonato Gianni
      has said mom that has telephoned Gianni

34. This Case-related head is identifiable with the original AgrO head of Chomsky (1993). In the implementation proposed in the text, it is assumed that the Case feature has to be related to small "v", the head only present in transitive (and intrasitive) VPs (not in unaccusatives). In (21) this is obtained through movement of small "v" to Acc.

35. The argument is a fortiori valid if S were to remain in VP. The relation between the Case-assigning/checking head and O is the Agree relation of Chomsky (2001, 2002).

36. If the whole VP is in focus, the fact that *ne* extraction out of S remains systematically impossible in VSPP suggests that location in focus remains responsible for this anyway, independently of whether a larger constituent than S is located in Focus.

37. This could possibly be related to the fact that, in this way, S could be stressed through the Nuclear Stress Rule, allowing it to carry the prominence that seems to fit well with focus (usually interpreted as the result of a focus alignment operation; see Cinque 1993, the important work by Zubizarreta 1998 in this perspective, and current unpublished work by Guasti and Nespor). With PP following S and being also interpreted as part of the new information focus, prominence must be spread in a way which is felt less than perfect.

38. See Cecchetto (1999) for convincing evidence that the topic position involved in right dislocation is indeed low in the clause structure. On the possibly "extended" analysis of doubling structures, see Belletti (2003).

39. I assume that RM is not violated by the movement of the clitic to the appropriate Case/head projection.

Assume that movement of S to Focus frees O, here the clitic, to move outside VP without RM being violated. On the intermediate VOS stage involved in this type of derivation, I assume that it is admitted as movement of the clitic continues. The assumption here is that if O does not move outside VP (and then further up), the Agree relation with the v+Acc head cannot be properly established if S intervenes, as in the discussion of (21). See following section 4 for more on VOS.

Past participle agreement holds in these structures ((24)Ba), as in the general case. This further suggests that the first portion of the movement of the clitic to the Case-assigning head is performed as XP-movement (a widely assumed hypothesis—see Belletti 1999, and the references cited there).

Finally, if sentences like (i) (discussed in Belletti 2001: n. 21) could have a derivation involving, (clause-internal) remnant topicalization of V+O to the Topic position above the Focus phrase followed by movement of the clitic projection (producing no violation of RM, as discussed in the reference quoted), the same derivation could not extend to (ii) (equivalent to (24)b in the text) as the topicalized direct object follows the new information postverbal subject:

(i)   L'ha comprato Maria.
      it(cl) bought Maria

(ii) L'ha comprato Maria, il giornale.
      it(cl) bought Maria, the newspaper

Thus a different derivation must also be allowed along the lines suggested above, with movement of the clitic projection directly starting out of the topicalized direct object, below the focalized subject, with no remnant VO topicalization stage involved in this case.

40. We can assume that it is sufficient that one of the two elements involved in the doubling construction (the clitic) fills a Case position for the structure to be well formed. (For more on doubling see Belletti (2003)).

41. The notation (S) and (O) is simply meant to indicate that the intervention of S is obtained independently of whether the position relevant to determine it is the VP base position or the derived clause-internal focus position.

42. With the relevant intonation, sentences with the VSO order containing a contrastively focalized S and a topicalized O do not easily admit an NPI subject of the type illustrated in (12), as expected under the proposed analysis:

> (i)   ?*non hanno detto che (i/ dei) LINGUISTI la verità
>   have "not" said the truth "that" (the/some) linguists the truth

The judgment improves if the object is right dislocated and a clitic is present, as expected:

> (ii) non l'hanno detta che (i/dei) linguisti, la verità
>   it(cl) have "not" said "that" (the/some) linguists the truth

As is clear from the proposed account, I agree with Cardinaletti's (2001) insight that Right dislocation and *emarginazione* should be given a different analysis, but the way to set the distinction is different. According to Cardinaletti (2001) the direct object remains in the VP internal position when it is "marginalized" and does not fill a topic position, while it does fill such a position in right dislocation. According to the analysis proposed here, in both cases the direct object fills a topic position, although a different one in the two cases (the clause internal one in (24)Ba and the peripheral one in (24)Bb).

43. It would seem that the interpretation probably does not force this step, as IP would be interpreted as topic also in situ. The plausible assumption seems to be that the topic interpretation can either be read off the structure or come from a negative definition: "nonfocus." See also Rizzi (1997).

44. Such sentences are slightly more marginal than the sentences analyzed as (26) (whence the "?"), a fact which I leave unexplained for now.

45. Presumably, it would be a variable. As the topicalized phrase is not an operator, it would not qualify as an adequate binder for it. Whence the impossibility. The fact that a real operator cannot be a topic either (to be contrasted with *NESSUNO ho visto*, where the operator is in focus) could receive different accounts:

> (i)   *Nessuno ho visto.
>   nobody I have seen

See Cinque (1990). Descriptively, we can state that there seems to be an intrinsic incompatibility between the operator status and the topic position.

46. Of course the perfect sentence (i) is a regular instance of left peripheral focalization, which, as such, never requires a clitic.

> (i)   IL LIBRO ho dato a Gianni.
>   The book I have given to Gianni.

47. One possibility could be to say that the special topic construction we are dealing with is, in fact, selected by focus (Luigi Rizzi, personal communication). Alternatively, if the role of focus in licensing the low topic consists in making the operator-vbl interpretation available for the topic (normally excluded, see preceding note 45), it could be tempting to say that in the excluded Topic-Focus order, Focus would interfere in establishing the relevant relation between topic and the IP internal vbl. No interference arises with the other order, Focus-Topic.

48. Similar contrasts are also presented in Beninca' (1988) and Cecchetto (1999).

49. It could be that the partial similarity of the Italian and French paradigms reflects the operation of an ultimately similar constraint. I do not pursue this question further here. See Alexiadou and Anagnostopoulou (2001) for recent discussion, which also gives a central role to Case.

50. As also discussed in Torrego (1998), the doubling clitic only shows up in the dative in Peninsular Spanish.

51. Thanks to A. Roussou for pointing this out to me.

52. This could be due to the fact that Italian is not an Object shift language, although the object shift position is probably not to be identified with the object Case position. On the necessity to empty the object Case position, see Belletti (1999). See the recent discussion in Chomsky (2000, 2001) in connection with the analysis of Object shift.

53. See Belletti (2001) for further elaboration on this point. In what follows I eliminate the "??" diacritics on VOS for the ease of the discussion. It should be kept in mind though, and it will be stressed throughout the text, that VOS is systematically marginal in status, as discussed here.

54. This could be due to the fact that the remnant type process involved is used here as a kind of "parasitic" salvaging strategy.

55. Cardinaletti (2001) agrees on the ungrammaticality of (46)b in the text, while finding the following (i) grammatical (see also Ordoñez 1998 on Spanish), with the anaphor more deeply embedded:

> (i) Ha visitato Gianni un collega della propria moglie.

Cardinaletti suggests that, for yet to be understood reasons, embedding the reflexive anaphor improves the judgment. We believe that when the grammatical functions of the two nominals are clearly differentiated through agreement, further embedding of the anaphor does not produce any real amelioration:

> (ii) *Hanno salutato Gianni i genitori della propria moglie.

Similar data hold for quantifier binding:

> (iii) *Hanno salutato ogni ragazzo i suoi genitori.

56. Of course, if contrastive focus could also be clause internal, we would not necessarily expect any degradation in (51) as opposed to (49). This constitutes further indication that contrastive focus is limited to the left peripheral area.

57. I will not make any concrete hypothesis as to what the correct analysis of a corrective clause should be. I assume that hierarchical relations are preserved in this kind of clauses as in simple declaratives.

58. See Rizzi (1996) and the references cited there; see also Poletto (2000).

59. This may possibly concern the whole clause.

60. This suggests that the core notion of focus is one and the same for both kinds of focuses identified. See Rooth (1992) for a formalization of what might be taken to be the core semantics of (any) focus. Answers to multiple questions are usually brought up as examples of sentences containing multiple foci. However, this is probably an oversimplification and, possibly, a not refined enough view of the interpretation of this kind of pairs. A detailed discussion of this topic would take us too far afield. I postpone to other work in progress a closer discussion of multiple question-answer pairs. For now, I just assume that the case of multiple questions can be put on the side and that real cases of multiple foci do not exist.

61. Any kind of focus induces WCO violations, so there is no difference in status depending on whether the focalized element is either contrastively focused or is new information focus, as the postverbal subject in (51)a(i) is equally impossible:

> (i) *?Attualmente in un suo$_i$ appartamento vive GIANNI$_i$.
>   at present in his own apartment lives Gianni

62. In a sentence like (i) with the focus of new information on the verb and the postverbal S interpreted as topic, no WCO appears to arise:

(i) Attualmente, nel suo$_i$ appartamento *dorme*, Gianni$_i$.
    at present, in his own apartment sleeps Gianni

63. The Case issue is also taken up in Belletti (2003) within the larger context of the analysis of doubling structures.

References

Alexiadou, A., and E. Anagnostopoulou (2001) "The Subject-in-situ Generalization and the Role of Case in Driving Computations." *Linguistic Inquiry* 32, 193–231.

Antinucci, F., and G. Cinque (1977) "Sull'ordine delle parole in italiano: l'emarginazione." *Studi di grammatica italiana* 6, 121–146.

Belletti, A. (1988) "The Case of Unaccusatives." *Linguistic Inquiry* 19, 1–34.

——— (1999) "Italian/Romance Clitics: Structure and Derivation," in H. van Riemsdijk (ed.) *Clitics in the Languages of Europe*. Berlin: de Gruyter, 543–579.

——— (2001) "Inversion as Focalization," in Hulk A., and J. Y. Pollock (eds.) *Subject Inversion in Romance and the Theory of Universal Grammar*. New York: Oxford University Press, 60–90.

——— (2003) "Extended Doubling." Unpublished ms., Università di Siena.

Belletti, A., and L. Rizzi (1988) "Psych Verbs and Th-Theory." *Natural Language and Linguistic Theory* 63, 291–352.

Belletti, A., and U. Shlonsky (1995) "The Order of Verbal Complements: A Comparative Study." *Natural Language and Linguistic Theory* 13, 489–526.

Beninca', P. (1988) "L'ordine degli elementi della frase e le costruzioni marcate," in L. Renzi (ed.), *Grande grammatica italiana di consultazione*, vol. 1. Bologna: Il Mulino, 129–194.

——— (2001) "Syntactic Focus and Intonational Focus in the Left Periphery," in G. Cinque and G. Salvi, (eds.) *Current Studies in Italian Syntax Offered to Lorenzo Renzi*. Amsterdam: North Holland, 39–64.

Bobaljik, J., and D. Jonas (1996) "Subject Positions and the Roles of TP." *Linguistic Inquiry* 27, 195–236.

Brandi, L., and P. Cordin (1981) "Dialetti e italiano: un confronto sul parametro del soggetto nullo." *Rivista di Grammatica Generativa* 6, 33–87.

Brody, M. (1990) "Some Remarks on the Focus Field in Hungarian." *UCL Working Papers* 2, 201–225.

Buring, D. (1995) "The Great Scope of Inversion Conspiracy." *Linguistic and Philosophy*.

Burzio, L. (1986) *Italian Syntax*. Dordrecht: Reidel.

Cardinaletti, A. (1997) "Subjects and Clause Structure," in L. Haegeman (ed.) *The New Comparative Syntax*. New York: Longman, 33–63.

——— (2001) "A second thought on *emarginazione*: Destressing vs 'Right Dislocation,'" in G. Cinque & G. P. Salvi (eds.) *Current Studies in Italian Syntax: Essays Offered to Lorenzo Renzi*. Amsterdam: North Holland, 117–135.

Cecchetto, C. (1999) "A Comparative Analysis of Left and Right Dislocation in Romance." *Studia Linguistica*, 53.1, 40–67.

Chomsky, N. (1993) "A Minimalist Program for Linguistic Theory," in K. Hale and S. J. Keyser (eds.) *The View from Building 20*. Cambridge, Mass.: MIT Press, 1–52.

——— (2000) "Minimalist Inquiries: The Framework," in R. Martin, D. Michaels, and J. Uriagereka (eds.) *Step by Step: Essays in Minimalist Syntax in Honor of Howard Lasnik*. Cambridge, Mass.: MIT Press, 89–155.

——— (2001) "Derivation by Phase," in M. Kenstowicz (ed.) *Ken Hale: A Life in Language*. Cambridge Mass.: MIT Press, 1–52.

———— (2003) "Beyond Explanatory Adequacy," in A. Belletti (ed.) *Structures and Beyond.* New York: Oxford University Press.

Cinque, G. (1990) *Types of A' Dependencies.* Cambridge, Mass.: MIT Press.

———— (1993) "A Null Theory of Phrase and Compound Stress." *Linguistic Inquiry* 24, 239–298.

———— (1999). *Adverbs and Functional Heads.* New York: Oxford University Press.

Cornulier, B. (1974) "Pourquoi et l'inversion du sujet non clitique," in C. Rohrer and N. Ruwet (eds.) *Actes du colloque Franco-Allemand de grammaire transformationelle,* vol. 1. Tubingen: Niemeyer, 139–163.

Costa, J. (2000) "Focus in situ: Evidence from Portuguese." *Probus* 12.2, 187–228.

Frascarelli, M. (2000) *The Syntax-Phonology Interface in Focus and Topic Constructions in Italian.* Dordrecht: Kluwer.

Jayaseelan, K. A. (2001) "IP-Internal Topic and Focus Phrases." *Studia Linguistica* 55.1, 39–75.

Kampers-Manhe, B. (1998) "'Je veux que parte Paul': A Neglected Construction," in A. Schwegler, B. Tranel, and M. Uribe-Extebarria (eds.) *Romance Linguistics: Theoretical Perspectives.* Amsterdam: John Benjamins, 129–141.

Kayne, R., and J. Y. Pollock (1978) "Stylistic Inversion, Successive Cyclicity, and Move NP in French." *Linguistic Inquiry* 9: 595–621.

———— (2001) "New Thoughts on Stylistic Inversion," in A. Hulk and J. Y. Pollock (eds.) *Subject Inversion in Romance and the Theory of Universal Grammar.* New York: Oxford University Press, 107–162.

Kiss, K. E. (1998) "Identificational Focus versus Information Focus." *Language* 74.2, 245–273.

Longobardi, G. (1998) "Two Types of 'Postverbal' Subjects in Italian." Unpublished ms., University of Trieste.

Moro, A. (1997) *The Raising of Predicates.* Cambridge: Cambridge University Press.

Motapanyane, V. (1995) *Theoretical Implications of Complementation in Romanian.* Padua: Unipress.

Nicolis, M. (2000) "'L-tous, Restructuring, and Quantifier Climbing." *Rivista di grammatica generativa* 26, 63–84.

Ndayiragije, J. (1999) "Checking Economy." *Linguistic Inquiry* 30.3, 399–444.

Ordoñez, F. (1997) "Word Order and Clause Structure in Spanish and Other Romance Languages," Ph.D. diss., City University of New York.

———— (1998) "Postverbal Asymmentries in Spanish." *Natural Language and Linguistic Theory* 16.2, 313–346.

Picallo, C. (1998) "On the Extended Projection Principle and Null Expletive Subjects." *Probus* 10, 219–241.

Pinto, M. (1994) "Subjects in Italian: Distribution and Interpretation," in R. Bok-Bennema and C. Cremers (eds.) *Linguistics in the Netherlands.* Amsterdam: John Benjamins.

Poletto, C. (2000) *The Higher Functional Field: Evidence from Northern Italian Dialects.* New York: Oxford University Press.

Rizzi, L. (1982) *Issues in Italian Syntax.* Dordrecht: Foris.

———— (1996) "Residual Verb Second and the *Wh*-Criterion," in A. Belletti and L. Rizzi (eds.) *Parameters and Functional Heads.* New York: Oxford University Press, 63–90.

———— (1997) "The Fine Structure of the Left Periphery," in L. Haegeman (ed.) *Elements of Grammar.* Dordrecht: Kluwer, 281–337.

Rooth, M. (1992) "A Theory of Focus Interpretation." *Natural Language Semantics* 1, 75–116

Saccon, G. (1993) "Post-verbal Subjects, Ph.D. diss., Harvard University.

Solà, J. (1992) "Agreement and Subjects," Ph.D. diss., Universitat Autonòma, Barcelona.

Sportiche, D. (1995) "French Predicate Clitics and Clause Structure," in A. Cardinaletti and M. T. Guasti (eds.) *Small Clauses* (Syntax and Semantics no. 28). New York: Academic Press, 287–324.

Starke, M. (1995) "On the Format of Small Clauses," in A. Cardinaletti and M. T. Guasti (eds.) *Small Clauses* (Syntax and Semantics no. 28). New York: Academic Press, 237–269.

Torrego, E. (1998) *The Dependecies of Objects*. Cambridge Mass.: MIT Press.

Zubizarreta, M. L. (1998) *Prosody, Focus and Word Order*. Cambridge, Mass.: MIT Press.

3

Topic, Focus, and V2

Defining the CP Sublayers

PAOLA BENINCA' AND CECILIA POLETTO

In this chapter we intend to contribute to the cartography of the CP layer and give a more detailed analysis of the portion of the CP structure that encodes distinctions between theme and rheme, exploiting data from standard Italian and nonstandard varieties. We interpret the cartographic program as an inquiry aiming at localizing functional projections and reconstructing a "fine structure." There is no limit, in our view, as to how many of these projections there will ultimately be, provided that there is a syntactic and semantic justification for them.

Cinque (1999), introducing his complex proposal concerning the mapping of IP structure, pointed out that it is necessary to begin by making assumptions that limit the range of variables to control; he made the very reasonable assumption that adverbs do not have to move in order to check features (they only move in marked constructions—for example, when focalized). The left periphery is a field to which elements are moved and, presumably also, within which they are moved. We then have to make assumptions of a different kind to render the task of localizing the positions related to pragmatics a feasible one. One assumption that seems natural to us, and possibly valid even beyond the immediate scope of this article, is that there is a one-to-one relation between position and function: in our case between each pragmatic interpretation and a syntactic position in CP. This means that recursion of a projection is not admitted.

Our analysis concentrates on the syntactic projections that have been defined as Topic and Focus in Rizzi's (1997) work on the split CP. We address two properties of the structure in (1).

The first property is CP recursion. Rizzi hypothesizes that Topic is a set of recursive projections (he indicates recursion with an asterisk), occurring both higher and lower than a single Focus projection:

(1)   Topic* FocusP Topic*

We claim that recursion is not an option. Neither of the two fields we examine here is recursive in the sense that there is a virtually infinite set of totally identical Topic phrases or Focus phrases. We claim that the asterisks in (1) indicate a finite set of distinct FPs, each of which can be labeled on the basis of the type of element it can host. We show that each projection has different semantic properties and can host a single XP. Both fields contain a limited set of FPs, each selecting a particular type of elements to express different semantics.

The second property is the Topic projection lower than Focus. We show that the projections lower than Topic all have the syntactic characteristics of focused elements—that is, they behave as operators. This conclusion lets us identify two different fields in CP: a higher Topic field hosting nonoperator elements, and a lower Focus field hosting operator-like elements.[1]

The chapter is organized as follows. We begin by presenting Beninca"s (2001) arguments, which show that the elements located lower than a contrastively stressed XP are not lower Topics but are themselves Focus. We will show that their trace behaves as a variable, as it is sensitive to weak crossover, while the empty category related to Topics does not. Hence, (a) there is no Topic projection (or set of projections) lower than Focus, and the only possible set of positions for Topics is higher than Focus; (b) Focus is not a single projection but is itself a set of projections. In other words, in the portion of the CP layer that we are considering, there are two "fields"—namely, two sets of contiguous and semantically related projections: one for Topics and the other for Focus projections. In the spirit of what we have pointed out above, we exploit the evidence in favor of an ordering of elements with different pragmatic functions in this area, and we examine the two fields in detail, sketching a first approximation of their internal "cartography." What distinguishes the Topic field from the Focus field in general is the fact that TopPs are connected with a clitic or a *pro* in the sentence, while FocPs are moved to CP and leave a variable. These conclusions are reached mainly on the basis of data from Italian.

In section 2, we concentrate on Contrastive Focus (CF). On the basis of data from a V2 Romance variety, Rhaeto-Romance, it appears that Focus can be split into (a) at least two contrastive Focus projections, depending on the type of elements contrasted (adverbs or DPs), and (b) at least one FocusP that is not marked for contrastiveness but just as "relevant information." We call it Informational Focus (IF). We consider data of standard and nonstandard Italian varieties and compare them with Old Italian data on Informational Focus. We claim that one difference between Old and Modern Italian syntax is in the accessibility of the Informational Focus, which was freely accessible in main clauses in Old Italian, while in Modern Italian it is only accessible under some conditions.

Sections 3 and 4 deal with the internal makeup of the Left Dislocation (LD) positions. It has been repeatedly observed that in Italian an indefinite number of topics can be permutated in the left periphery, apparently without any consequence for the pragmatic interpretation. Following the tradition initiated by Cinque (1977), and developed in Beninca' (1988) and Cinque (1990), we provide six empirical tests to distinguish between two types of thematized elements, which we refer to as Hanging Topics and Left Dislocated elements. We then discuss the position of Scene Setting adverbs and isolate the lowest position inside the Topic field to which a "List Interpretation" is assigned. We then present some hypotheses on the ordering of Left Dislocated elements.

Section 5 includes a speculation of the semantic characterization of these projections and the way they are layered.[2]

In this essay, we restrict our analysis to declarative clauses, although we occasionally make reference to other sentence types as interrogative or relative clauses when they become relevant for the syntactic tests we use.

1.   LD only occurs above FocusP

In this section we address the question of whether it is really necessary to admit that TopP can appear in two different positions in CP. Strictly related to this question is the shape of FocusP: Is it a single projection or a field hosting more than one element?

As mentioned, Rizzi (1997) proposes the following structure for the Topic/Focus portion of the CP structure:

(2)   C . . . (TOP*) (FOC) (TOP*)

In what follows we show that the lower Topic position(s) is not Topic at all, but an extension of the Focus field. Consider the following pair:

(3)a.*A GIANNI, un libro di poesie, lo regalerete.
      TO GIANNI a book of poems you will give it
   b. Un libro di poesie, A GIANNI, lo regalerete.
      a book of poems TO GIANNI, you will give it
      'You will give a book of poems to Gianni.'

Here the only possible order between the contrastively focalized PP *a Gianni* 'to John' and the Topic DP *un libro di poesie* 'a book of poems' is Topic Focus. The opposite order is strongly ungrammatical.

Suppose that what the contrast in (3) shows is precisely that no Topic position is available lower than Focus, as the ungrammaticality of (3a) suggests. The ordering of the Topic/Focus portion of the CP layer would thus be the one illustrated in (4):

(4)   [TopicP [FocusP [IP]]]

If we make this assumption, we are left with the problem of explaining sentences like (5) adapted from Rizzi (1997). We will argue that this is only apparent evidence in favor of LD on the right of Focus:

(5)   a. QUESTO a Gianni, domani, gli dovremmo dire!
         this to Gianni tomorrow to-him should tell
         'Tomorrow we should tell this to Gianni.'

    b. A Gianni, QUESTO, domani gli dovremmo dire!
       to Gianni this tomorrow to-him should tell
    c. A Gianni, domani, QUESTO gli dovremmo dire!
       to Gianni, tomorrow this to-him should tell

A sentence like (5c) does not constitute a problem for structure (4), as we could ana-lyze both the DP *a Gianni* 'to John' and the adverb *domani* 'tomorrow' as LD ele-ments occurring in front of the focalized pronoun *questo* 'this one'. In (5b) the element occurring after the focalized pronoun, and considered by Rizzi an instance of LD Topic, is a temporal adverb. It can be shown that adverbs have to be kept distinct from DPs and PPs because they can occupy a lower position occurring at the IP edge. The Paduan examples constitute evidence in favor of this claim:

(6)   a. Mario (l) compra na casa.
      Mario (he) buys a house
      'Mario is going to buy a house.'
    b. Mario, na casa, no*(l) la compra.
      Mario, a house not (he) it will buy
      'Mario is not going to buy a house.'
    c. Mario, de so sorela, *(el) ghe ne parla sempre.
      Mario, of his sister (he) of-her speaks always
      'Mario always talks about his sister.'
    d. Mario doman compra na casa.[3]
      Mario tomorrow buys a house
      'Mario is going to buy a house tomorrow.'
    e. Mario doman l compra na casa.
      Mario tomorrow he buys a house

In (6a) the subject clitic resuming the subject DP is apparently optional. If an LD object intervenes between the subject DP and the verb, as in (6b) and (6c), forc-ing an analysis of LD for the subject too, then the clitic becomes obligatory. Hence, the optionality of the subject clitic in (6a) corresponds to two different structures: if the subject clitic is not present, the subject DP occupies its usual preverbal position; if the subject clitic is present, the subject DP is left dislocated. This structurally nonambiguous sequence can be used as a test for determining the position of preverbal adverbs. If an adverb intervening between the subject DP and the inflected verb forces the presence of a subject clitic, as a left-dislocated objects does, this means that the only possible position for the adverb in a sentence like (5b) is an LD position, as is the case for objects. On the contrary, if an adverb intervening between the subject DP and the inflected verb does not force the presence of a subject clitic, the subject DP can be analyzed as remaining in its usual preverbal position and is not left dislocated.

The grammaticality of a sentence like (6d) shows that this is indeed the case: the adverb can occupy a position lower than the usual subject position, which is, in turn, lower than LD positions occupied by objects in (6b and c) and by the subject when the subject clitic is present. Hence, adverbials such as *tomorrow* cannot be used as a test for determining the presence or the absence of a lower LD position, as they are themselves structurally ambiguous between a Topic and a post-subject position. Therefore, we claim that sentences like (5b) are not relevant for deciding between structure (2) and (4), as the adverb is in the lower position. As for (5a) we point out the following:

>   a. Dative clitics are not as reliable as object clitics as a test for LD, as the following example shows:

(7)   Gliel'ho detto a Gianni.
       to him-it have told to Gianni
       'I told this to Gianni.'

Here the dative *a Gianni* is doubled by the clitic *gli*, even though the dative has not moved from its argument position;

>   b. Intonation is not a crucial test for determining the position of an XP: an intonationally focalized element can syntactically be an LD. The following examples are a dialogue: speaker A produces a left-dislocated object in the embedded clause; speaker B contradicts the assertion with a different LD object, which is intonationally focalized, but syntactically an LD, as the resumptive object clitic shows:

(8)   A: Mi ha detto che il tappeto, lo compra l'anno prossimo.
          'He has told me that the carpet he will buy *it* next year.'
       B: No, ti sbagli, IL DIVANO *lo* compra l'anno prossimo.
          'No, you are wrong, THE SOFA he will buy *it* next year.'

Given the evidence in (8), we will henceforth not consider intonation as a reliable test distinguishing between focalized and left-dislocated elements. The fact that a Topic can be intonationally stressed, as (8) shows, suggests the other logical option—namely, that focalized elements do not necessarily have to be intonationally stressed. Separating the intonational level from the syntactic one does not only account for (8), which is completely unexpected if we accept the equation: intonationally stressed = syntactically focalized. It also accounts for the behavior of these elements with respect to weak crossover. It is well known (see, among others, Chomsky 1981 and Cinque 1990) that the so-called weak crossover constraint is in fact a test that singles out variable-operator structures. As a result, only focalized XPs appear to be related to a variable inside the clause.

A structure like (9a) is grammatical with the interpretation in which *Gianni* is the object in Topic and *suo* corefers with *Gianni*. On the contrary, (9b), in which the object is focused, is ungrammatical, displaying the weak crossover effect.[4]

(9)   a. Gianni$_i$, suo$_i$ padre l$_i$'ha licenziato   (LD)
          Gianni $_i$ his$_i$ father has fired him$_i$
          'Gianni has been fired by his own father.'
       b. *GIANNI, suo$_i$ padre ha licenziato   (Focus)
          GIANNI, his$_i$ father has fired t$_i$

Notice that (9b) is possible if *suo padre* 'his father' is interpreted as the direct object and *Gianni* as the subject; if *suo padre* is the direct object, *suo* is correctly bound by a c-commanding antecedent, the sentence internal position of the focalized element in SpecIP. Weak crossover can be used as a test to distinguish between Topic and Focus elements in other cases. Note that Topics, even if intonationally focalized, always escape the weak crossover restriction:

(10) A: Mario$_i$, suo$_i$ padre non lo vede mai.
         Mario, his father never sees him
         'His father never sees Mario.'

     B: No, GIANNI $_i$, suo$_i$ padre non lo vede mai.
         no Gianni his father never sees him
         'No, his father never sees Gianni.'

In fact, as we argue later, in (10B) we have a constituent *Gianni* that still behaves syntactically as a Topic, and not as a Focus, although it is intonationally focalized.

Let us now examine cases parallel to (5a) on the basis of the test of weak crossover and see if the XP located after the intonationally focused XP, which in Rizzi's analysis is a lower Topic, behaves as a syntactic Topic or Focus. If it is a lower Topic, it should be insensitive to weak crossover; if it is a Focus, it will obey the weak crossover restriction:

(11)   a.*A MARIA, Giorgio$_i$, sua$_i$ madre presenterà.[5]
          to Maria Giorgio his mother will introduce
          'His mother will introduce Giorgio to Maria.'
       b.*A MARIA$_i$, Giorgio, sua$_i$ madre presenterà.
          to Maria Giorgio her mother will introduce
          'Her mother will introduce Giorgio to Maria.'
       c.*A MARIA, Giorgio, sua madre lo presenterà.
          to Maria Giorgio his mother will introduce him

Examples (11a) and (11b) show that both XPs *a Maria* and *Giorgio*, which are on the left of the subject *sua madre*, have to be distinct in reference from the pronoun *sua*. Hence, they both behave as Foci, and not as Topics. Independent evidence that they are both focalized is given by the fact that there cannot be a resumptive clitic in these structures (cf. (11c) and (3a)).

Since the second element is not intonationally marked as prominent in any way, we will assume that more than one element can be in the Focus field, but just one is intonationally focalized. Moreover, we will assume that the one that is intonationally marked is the highest one of the Focus field. We come back to this fact in section 2.

The sequence in (5a) is thus not to be interpreted as [Topic Focus Topic] but as [Topic Focus1 Focus2]. Thus, on the basis of the weak crossover test, we claim that Focus can also host more than one element, each with a peculiar function that we just begin to explore and characterize here. Hence, FocP is not a single XP but a "field," as Topic is (cf. Brody 1990 on Hungarian).

2.   The internal makeup of the focus field

Up to now we have concentrated on the interplay of Topic and Focus and shown that

1. There is no Topic projection lower than Focus.
2. What is apparently a Topic projection lower than FocusP has been shown to have the movement properties of focalized constituents.

Next we provide additional evidence for the hypothesis that Focus is to be conceived as a "field"—namely, a structural portion of the CP layer where contiguous projections encode different types of focalized elements. To do this we shift the language under examination and turn our attention to nonstandard Italian varieties. We first point out some properties of regional Southern Italian, where one of the typical properties of V2 Medieval Romance appears to some extent maintained. Informational Focus is found in all of these varieties in sentence initial position, as the following examples show (12a and b are from Beninca' 1994):

(12)   a. *Ço* dis-el plusor fiade.   (Old Venetian)
          this said he many times
          'He said this many times.'
       b. *Una fertra* fei lo reis Salomon.   (Old Piedmontese)
          a sedan chair made King Salomon
          'King Salomon made a sedan chair.'

(13)   a. *Un libro* comprasti?   (Sicilian)
          a book bought
          'Did you buy a book?'
      a'. Hai comprato *un libro*?   (Northern Italian)
          have bought a book
          'Did you buy a book?'

(14)   a. *Antonio* sono.   (Sicilian)
          Antonio am
          'It's Antonio.'
      a'. Sono *Antonio*.
          am Antonio
          'It's Antonio.'

On the minimal assumption that the inflected verb in the Southern Italian dialects raises at least to AgrS, we can analyze elements in first position in sentences like (12) as occurring inside the CP layer. Therefore, Informational Focus is indeed syntactically encoded in the CP domain. We comment further on these aspects in section 2.2.

2.1.   Contrastive and Informational Focus in Rhaeto-Romance

Independent evidence for the assumption of a low Comp position signaling IFoc comes from the Rhaeto-Romance dialect of S. Leonardo, a V2 variety spoken in the Dolomites. This dialect displays a sentence particle signaling that the whole sentence is totally new information intended as the introduction of a new context (see Poletto and Zanuttini 2000). In sentences like (15a), *pa* conveys the meaning of totally new information and can be uttered only in such a context.[6] This is not the case for the neutral sentence in (15b):

(15)   a. Al ploi *pa*.
          SCL rains *pa*
          'It is raining.'
       b. Al ploi.
          SCL rains

    c. Ci bel c al è pa!
       how nice that SCL is *pa*
       'How nice it is!'
    d. Ci bel c al é!
       how nice that SCL is

The same context restriction is found in exclamative clauses like (15c) and (15d). A sentence like (15c) can only be uttered when it is new information, while (15d) is neutral in this respect. As expected by the fact that *pa* signals that the whole sentence is new, it is incompatible with contexts that entail a presupposition, such as presuppositional negative or affirmative elements as the following (cf. Cinque 1976 on presuppositional negation *mica* in standard Italian):

(16)   a.*I n mangi *pa min* tres soni.
        SCL neg eat *pa* neg always potatoes
        'I do not always eat potatoes.'
     b.*E k i l a *pa* fat.
        yes that SCL have *pa* done
        'Sure, I did it.'

Poletto and Zanuttini (2000) show that the position of *pa* is the Spec of a low Comp projection, located lower than Contrastive Focus. *Pa* occurs after the inflected verb, which is expected given the fact that Central Rhaeto-Romance is a V2 language (see later); the following characteristics are worth noting: (a) *pa* appears higher than all adverbials located in the IP field (according to Cinque's 1999 hierarchy), as shown in (17); (b) it is higher than a subject in a subject-verb inversion context (cf. (18a)); (c) it is incompatible with lower complementizers such as the interrogative *s* "if" in embedded questions, as shown by the ungrammaticality of (18b):

(17)   a. Al a *pa d sigy* mangé. (S. Leonardo)
       SCL have *pa* of sure eaten
       'He has surely eaten.'
     b.*Al a *d sigy pa* mangé.
       SCL has of sure *pa* eaten
     c. Al a *pa magari* bel mangé.
       SCL has *pa* perhaps already eaten
       'Perhaps he has already eaten.'
     d.*Al a *magari pa* bel mangé.

(18)   a. Inier a *pa* Giani mangé la ciara.
       yesterday has *pa* Giani eaten the meat
       'Yesterday Giani ate meat.'
     b.*A i m a domané *s* al n fus *pa* bel.
       SCL SCL me asked if SCL neg was *pa* nice
       'He asked me whether it was nice.'

Moreover, the same dialect provides evidence for assuming that even Contrastive Focus is not to be conceived of as a single projection.

Examples (19) and (20) illustrate the typical V2 pattern: when an element precedes the inflected verb, the subject is inverted as in (19), and it is not possible to

have two constituents in preverbal position, as the ungrammaticality of (19c) and
(20) shows:

(19)   a. T vas gonoot a ciasa sua.   (S. Leonardo)
           you go often at home his
           'You often visit him.'
       b. Gonoot vas-t a ciasa sua.
           often go-you at home his
       c. *Gonoot t vas a ciasa sua.
           often you go at home his

(20)   a. *Da trai l liber ti a-i de a Giani.
           sometimes the book to-him have-I given to Giani
       b. *L liber da trai ti a-i de a Giani.
           the book sometimes have-I given to Giani

This is true even for Left-Dislocated items, as the ungrammaticality of (21a) shows:[7]

(21)   *Giani, duman l vaiges-t
        Giani tomorrow him see-you
        Giani, you will seen him tomorrow

Once we have stated the V2 character of this dialect, we focus on the analysis of main
versus embedded V2. This dialect is neither a "generalized V2" language (as Yiddish
or Icelandic) nor a "restricted V2 language" (as German, Dutch, and Mainland Scandinavian). It tolerates embedded V2 in all declarative sentences (though embedded V2
is excluded from all wh-contexts as relatives, embedded interrogatives, etc.), and the
type of element found in first position depends on the selecting verb: that is, among
the adverbials that can be placed in first position in a main clause, some are sensitive to
the main verb once they are placed in an embedded V2 structure.[8] While in main clauses
a bigger class of adverbials can be found in first position, in embedded clauses the class
of adverbials that can be found in first position depends on the selecting verb. Complements of bridge verbs display (as in many Germanic languages) essentially the same
possibilities found in main clauses. If a non-bridge verb is selected, the class of adverbials
that can be found in first position is more limited:

(22)   a. Al m a dit c d sigy mang-ela a ciasa.   (Bridge V)
           he to-me has said that for sure eats-she at home
           'He told me that he is surely going to eat at home.'
       b. *Al s cruzie c d sigy mang-la a ciasa.   (Non-bridge V)
           he is worried that for sure eats-she at home

The same contrast is found when the element in first position is an object:

(23)   a. Al m a dit c L GIAT a-al odù.
           he me has told that the cat has-he seen
           'He told that he has seen the cat.'
       b. *Al s cruzie c L GIAT a-al odù
           he is worried that the cat has-he seen

This is not true for certain quantificational adverbs like the temporal ones:

(24)   a. Al m a dit c DA TRAI l a-al odù.
           he me has told that sometimes him has-he seen
           'He told that he saw him sometimes.'

b. Al s cruzie c DA TRAI l a-al odù.
he is worried that sometimes him has-he seen
'He is worried because he saw him sometimes.'

The descriptive generalization is that only focalized circumstantial and quantificational adverbs are insensitive to the class of the selecting verb, while other adverbs and objects can be contrastively focalized only when the selecting verb belongs to the bridge class.

There is a unitary way to analyze the contrasts between (22a)/(23a) versus (22b)/(23b) and (22b)/(23b) versus (24b). On the basis of the analysis of bridge verbs, which are usually claimed to have one additional CP layer, we propose that these contrasts have to be analyzed as follows: bridge verbs select a "full CP layer" with all CP projections available; nonbridge verbs select only a smaller portion of the whole CP-structure, pruning the CP projections where objects and some adverbial classes are assigned contrastive Focus, while permitting the lower CPs to be filled.

All the elements in (22), (23), and (24) are interpreted as contrastively focalized; hence, if what we have assumed so far is correct, there must be at least two Contrastive Focus projections available in the CP structure: one hosting adverbs or objects, and one devoted to circumstantial and quantificational adverbs. The Focus field can thus be conceived as in (25):

(25) [Contr. CP1 adverbs/objects [Contr.CP2 circum./quant. adverbs [Informational CP]]]

In structure (25) Informational Focus is placed lower than both Contrastive Focus1 and 2 because the verb always raises higher than this projection in V2 contexts, occurring obligatorily to the left of the new information particle *pa* while it does not raise higher than the other two projections, as it occurs to the right of both focalized circumstantial and quantificational adverbs and other adverbs and objects.

2.2. Contrastive and Informational Focus in standard Italian

With structure (25) in mind, let us now go back to the cases discussed in the preceding section in which another XP occurs lower than Contrastive Focus in Italian:[9]

(26) A GIORGIO, questo libro, devi dare
TO GIORGIO this book you must give
'You must give this book to Giorgio.'

In section 1 we have shown that intonation is not in itself a test for determining whether an element is a Focus or a Topic, as higher Topics can also bear contrastive intonation, still maintaining the syntactic properties of non-operator elements (resumptive clitic, insensitivity to weak crossover). Likewise, elements that are not intonationally marked as Contrastive Focus can still be inside the Focus field. On the basis of a syntactic test as weak crossover, we have claimed in section 1 that the element located lower than Contrastive Focus still has the properties of an operator-moved element located inside the Focus field and not of a lower Topic.

Following this line of reasoning, we might analyze *questo libro* in (27) as an Informational Focus, similar to the one used in Southern Italian or medieval Romance. But sentences corresponding to (14) (here repeated in (27)) are ungrammatical in standard Italian, unless intonationally and pragmatically contrasted:

(27) a.*Antonio sono.
        Antonio am.
      b.*Una portantina fece re Salomone.
        a sedan chair made King Salomon

This difficulty can be dealt with assuming that in standard Italian the IF position is not accessible unless the Focus field has already been activated by a Contrastive Focus, while this would not be necessary in the Southern Italian varieties. More generally, we could say that the Focus field as such is only activated in standard Italian by explicitly marked elements; in this perspective, we can relate Contrastive Focus, which is signaled in Italian by a special intonation, with another interesting Italian construction that involves a Focus-like anteposition without intonational contrast: it is the so-called Anaphoric Anteposition (AA; see Beninca' 1988: 141), exemplified in (28a and b)

(28) a. Mi ha detto di portargli un libro e *un libro* gli ho portato.
          me has said to bring-him a book and a book I him have brought
          'They told me that I should bring them a book and I did it.'
      b. Le stesse cose ha detto ieri il fratello.
          the same things said the brother too
          'His/her brother said the same thing yesterday.'
      c. E questo farà anche lui.
          and this will-do also he
          'He will do the same.'

This construction appears to be another case where the Focus field needs a special context in order to be activated: in (28a) the context is given by a textual repetition of the element, in (28b and c) the anaphora is lexical ('the same', 'another', 'this', etc., often accompanied by a textual anaphoric adverb in the body of the sentence, such as *anche* 'too', solo 'only', etc.). It is interesting that a lexical or pronominal subject cannot appear between the anteposed element and the inflected verb, as they have to be adjacent, as shown in (29):

(29) *Le stesse cose il fratello ha detto ieri.
        the same things the brother said yesterday

This suggests that in the AA construction the inflected verb is in a head whose Spec is not appropriate for a DP or an NP subject. Similar effects are found with other types of A' movements, such as Focus movements, interrogatives, and exclamatives. The effect is stronger in main interrogative clauses than in other constructions. The reason why preverbal subjects are not totally excluded in some cases could be that subjects apparently following a contrastive Focus in SpecAgr position are in fact in IF. Once this phenomenon is better understood, we will have at our disposal a new test to identify A'-moved elements.[10]

Another case of movement to CP concerns indefinite quantifiers (see Beninca' 1988: 142):

(30) Qualcosa farò.
        something I-will do
        'I will do something.'

Again, we can interpret this one as a case of movement to Focus field of a marked element. In the perspective we are sketching concerning Focus, Italian would differ from a V2 language not in the path of the inflected verb in V2 contexts but simply in restricting the V2 contexts and requiring specific features on a nominal element to move it to CP, while a V2 language always has to move something to CP.[11]

Coming back to the question of the type of Focus projection hosting the DP *questo libro* 'this book' in (26), we have shown, on the basis of Rhaeto-Romance, that Contrastive Focus itself has to be split into at least two positions. This would lead us to hypothesize that the DP *questo libro* in (26) is not Informational Focus but a secondary Contrastive Focus position.[12] In this sense, we can further reflect on the semantics of sentences like (26): here the Focus is not on the first element *a Giorgio* itself, but on the relation between *a Giorgio* and *questo libro*, with respect to the predicate: this is the information to be contrasted with the preceding context. Moreover, as Federico Damonte (personal communication) has interestingly pointed out to us, the structure exemplified in (26) is perfectly good if both elements are arguments of the verb, but it is very bad if only one is an argument and the other is a so-called adjunct, as shown by the following contrast:

(31)   a. GIORGIO, di questo, ha parlato.
          GIORGIO of this has spoken
          'Giorgio spoke about this.'
       b.* GIORGIO, per questo, ha parlato.
          GIORGIO for this has spoken

For the moment, we will leave the matter of the exact label of this lower Focus position open, as it requires more specific research.

Summarizing, we have shown that nonstandard Italian varieties display Informational Focus positions lower than the Contrastive Focus position, and that Contrastive Focus is a subfield in itself. The structure of the Focus field we have evidence for is the one in (25), repeated here as (32):

(32)   [Contr. CP1 adverbs/objects [Contr.CP2 circum/quant adverbs [Informational CP]]]

More research is needed to enrich the cartography of the Focus field we have just begun to sketch, in particular trying to better understand the similarities between the different constructions involving movement of an element to CP in the Focus field.

3.   The internal makeup of the Topic field

We now concentrate on the Topic field and give a first approximation of its hierarchical structure. All the elements in the Topic field share at least two properties: (a) they are not related to a variable in the clause, differently from elements belonging to the Focus field; and (b) they are all "known information" in some sense.

The constituents that appear in this area with the "overall" characteristics of Topics, on a more careful examination show clearly distinct properties of a syntactic nature; this makes it possible to distinguish between two subfields of the Topic field: Hanging Topic and Left Dislocation.

3.1. Two types of thematized arguments

Hanging Topic (HT) and Left Dislocation (LD) differ for a number of syntactic properties as already noted by Cinque (1982) and Beninca' (1988). We sum them up in what follows. The first test that distinguishes between the two constructions is Case: LD elements maintain the preposition of the internal elements they correspond to, but HTs can only be DPs:

(33) a. Mario, non ne parla più nessuno.
         Mario not of-him talks anymore nobody
         'Mario, nobody talks of him anymore.'
      b. Di Mario, non (ne) parla più nessuno.
         of Mario not (of-him) talks anymore nobody
         'Of Mario, nobody talks of him anymore.'

(34) a. Mario, gli amici gli hanno fatto un brutto scherzo.
         Mario the friends to-him have done a bad joke
         'Mario, his friends played a bad joke on him.'
      b. A Mario, gli amici (gli) hanno fatto un brutto scherzo.
         to Mario the friends to-him have done a bad joke

Examples (33b) and (34b) are cases of LD, as the preposition occurs in front of the LD element; (33a) and (34a), where no preposition is realized, are cases of HT.

We can now use the first test to single out the two types of thematizations and show their different syntactic properties. First of all, there can be more than one LD element, while only a single HT position per clause is available:

(35) a.*Gianni, questo libro, non ne hanno parlato a lui.
         Gianni this book they of-it haven't talked to him
      b. A Gianni, di questo libro, non gliene hanno mai parlato.
         to Gianni of this book they of it haven't talked to him
         'They did not talk to Gianni about this book.'

Example (35a) is a case of double HT (as the lack of prepositions on the two Topics indicates), and it is ungrammatical. When the two prepositions are present, the two Topics are LDs, and the sentence is possible (35b).

The third difference concerns the necessity of a resumptive element corresponding to the Topic. LD elements require a resumptive pronoun only when they correspond to direct or partitive objects; the clitic is optional in the other cases (impossible if the type of argument has no appropriate clitic). If present, the clitic agrees with the Topic in gender, number, and Case. HTs always require a resumptive pronoun expressing the type of argument: this pronoun only agrees with the HT in number and gender, not in Case.

(36) a.*Mario, non parla più nessuno.
         Mario not talks anymore nobody
      b. Di Mario, non parla più nessuno.
         of Mario not talks anymore nobody
         'Mario, nobody talks of him anymore.'
      c. Mario, non ne parla più nessuno.
         Mario not of-him talks anymore nobody
         'Mario, nobody talks of him anymore.'

The contrast shows that the left-dislocated PP in (36b) can occur without any resumptive pronoun, while the HT DP in (36a) is ungrammatical if no resumptive pronoun is present in the clause (cf. (36c).

The fourth test concerns the type of resumptive element that can be used for LD and HT. The copy of the HT can also be a tonic pronoun or an epithet, while the copy of a LD can only be a clitic:

(37) a. Mario, non darò più soldi a quell'imbecille.
         Mario not will give anymore money to that idiot
         'Mario, I won't give more money to that idiot.'
      b.*A Mario, non darò più soldi a quell'imbecille.
         to Mario, not will give more money to that idiot

Note also that the two types of thematizations can cooccur: the order is fixed, and it is HT-LD. In an embedded declarative clause the complementizer is located between the two Topics:

(38) a. Giorgio, ai nostri amici, non parlo mai di lui.
         Giorgio to the our friends not talk never of him
         'Giorgio, to our friends, I never talk of him.'
      b.*Ai nostri amici, Giorgio, non parlo mai di lui.
         to our friends Giorgio not talk never of him

Example (38a) represents the order HT-LD, as only the second Topic is a PP, although they both correspond to PP arguments. Example (38b), which displays the reverse order, is ungrammatical.

(39) a.*Sono certa, di questo libro, che non (ne) abbia mai parlato nessuno.
         I am certain of this book that not (of-it) has ever spoken nobody
      b. Sono certa, questo libro, che non ne abbia mai parlato nessuno.[13]
         I am certain this book that not (of-it) has ever spoken nobody
         'I am sure that nobody has ever talked about this book.'
      c. Sono certa che, di questo libro, non ne abbia mai parlato nessuno.
         I am certain that of this book not (of-it) has ever spoken nobody
      d. ??Sono certa che, questo libro, non ne abbia mai parlato nessuno.[14]
         I am certain that this book not (of-it) has ever spoken nobody

Example (39a) is a case of LD, as the presence of the preposition shows. The only grammatical order between the complementizer and this type of thematized elements is *che*-XP, as the contrast between (39a) and (39c) shows. HT only allows the opposite order, as in the pair (39b) and (39d). The tests illustrated by (38) and (39) show that the order inside the Topic field of the CP layer is the one sketched in (40):

(40) [HT [che [LD [LD . . . [IP]]]]]

Moreover, HT is restricted in some types of embedded clauses. In relative clauses, for example, HTs are not possible, neither before nor after the relative pronoun:

(41) a.*Una persona che questo libro non ne parlerà mai.
         a person that this book not of-it will talk never
      b.*Una persona questo libro che non ne parlerà mai.
         a person this book that not of-it will talk never

The corresponding sentences with LD are perfect if the order relative pronoun–LD is chosen:

(42) a. Una persona che di questo libro non ne parlerà mai.
          a person that of this book not of-it will talk never
          'a person who will never talk about this book'
      b.*Una persona di questo libro che non ne parlerà mai.
          a person of this book that not of-it will talk never

On the basis of the tests discussed so far, we conclude that Hanging Topic has to be kept distinct from Left Dislocation and that it occurs in a unique FP located above LD, as illustrated in (40).

3.2.   A position for Scene Setting adverbs

There is additional evidence that HT is not the only type of element that has to be separated from LD. Scene Setting adverbials also occupy a very high position, probably located immediately lower than HT but still higher than LD. This is immediately visible in a language like the V2 Rhaeto-Romance variety examined in section 2. In main clauses, the class of Scene Setting adverbs can be intonationally focalized or not:

(43) a. DUMAN va-al a Venezia.
          TOMORROW goes-he to Venice
          'He is going to Venice tomorrow.'
      b. Duman va-al a Venezia.
          tomorrow goes-he to Venice

In the spirit or what we said so far, we might hypothesize that the two occurrences of the temporal adverb *duman* in (43a) and (43b) are not located in the same position: in (43a) the adverb is contrastively focalized, but in (43b) it is not. However, in our view intonation is not sufficient for determining syntactic structure; we present another test that discriminates between two possible structures for these adverbs when they occur as the first element of the clause. As discussed, Rhaeto-Romance tolerates embedded V2 of different types depending on the selecting verb. Even the more liberal class of selecting verbs, namely bridge verbs, does not tolerate a nonfocalized Scene Setting adverb in first position of an embedded V2 clause:

(44) a. Al m a dit c DUMAN va-al a Venezia.
          he me has told that tomorrow goes-he to Venice
          'He told me that he is going to Venice tomorrow.'
      b.*Al m a dit c duman va-al a Venezia.
          he me has told that tomorrow goes-he to Venice

The contrast between (43b) and (44b), compared with the lack of contrast between (43a) and (44a), shows that the positions of focalized and nonfocalized adverbs must be different. In a split CP perspective, we can hypothesize that embedded V2 never has a position for Scene Setting, which is only available in root contexts. This also makes sense from the semantic point of view, as "setting the scene" is an operation done at the beginning of the utterance, not in an embedded context. The property of being confined to root contexts recalls the distribution of HTs, which are ungrammatical in embedded clauses in French, for example (see note 3 for Italian). We can hypothesize that standard Italian has a Scene Setting position, too, in cases like (45):

(45) Domani Gianni lo vedo.
      tomorrow Gianni I will see him
      'Tomorrow I will see Gianni.'

Although standard Italian surely admits pre-subject temporal adverbs, it does not provide a clear test for an independent Scene Setting position, as the temporal adverb in (45) can also be analyzed as a left-dislocated element.[15]
    What can be shown on the basis of Italian data is that there is no Scene Setting position higher than Hanging Topic, as the ungrammaticality of (46b and c) testifies:

(46) a. Mario, nel 1999, gli hanno dato il premio Nobel.
         Mario in the 1999 to-him have given the Prize Nobel
      b. ??Nel 1999, Mario, gli hanno dato il premio Nobel.
         in the 1999 Mario to-him have given the Prize Nobel
      c. *Sul giornale Mario ne hanno parlato malissimo.
         on the newspaper Mario of him have spoken very badly

    A temporal adverb can indeed be located after a HT, but—as in (45)—it is indistinguishable from a Left Dislocated one. Hence, we will leave the matter of an independent Scene Setting position open. We simply point out that, if we are on the right track and the Scene Setting position has to be distinguished from the HP position for DPs (which would be a welcome result in a split-CP theory), we have to further split the Topic subfield into two portions: a Frame subfield and the LD subfield.

3.3. A position for Listed XPs

The Topic sublayer can be further split. If semantics is taken into account, it is possible to single out specialized subfields on the left of Focus. Well-known semantic differences in the interpretation of LD can be taken to reflect syntactic differences: let us examine the case of the contrast within a given set—namely, the case in which two elements belonging to the same list of already known items are contrasted. We can call this particular interpretation "List Interpretation" (LI).[16] To be clear, we add a context to our examples:

CONTEXT: a farm producing a set of goods that are known to the people involved in the conversation.
(47) a. La frutta la regaliamo, la verdura la vendiamo.
         the fruit it give for free the vegetables it sell
         'We give fruit for free, while we sell the vegetables.'
      b. La frutta la regaliamo e la verdura la vendiamo.
         the fruit it give for free and the vegetables it sell
      c. La frutta la regaliamo, invece la verdura la vendiamo.
         the fruit it give for free while the vegetables it sell

Here the two elements *la frutta* and *la verdura* are singled out from a list and attributed different predicates. The two sentences can also be conjoined by the conjunction *e* 'and', as in (43b) or by *invece* "while".

Various tests can be applied for isolating the relevant interpretation. The first one results from the substitution of the two items with 'the former–the latter', as shown in (48):

(48)   La prima la vendiamo, la seconda la regaliamo.
     the first it sell, the second it give for free
     'We sell the former, we give the latter for free.'

The second concerns Right dislocation. The RD position is only compatible with the "pure" thematization and not with the LI type of themathization. Whatever the analysis of RD is, the contrast in (49) shows that LI has to be distinguished from the more usual type of Left Dislocation:

(49)   a.   La frutta la regaliamo, la verdura la vendiamo.
        the fruit it give for free the vegetables it sell
        'We give fruit for free, while we sell vegetables.'
    b.*La regaliamo, la frutta e la vendiamo, la verdura.
        it give for free the fruit and it sell the vegetables
       *La regaliamo, la prima e la vendiamo, la seconda.
       it give for free the former and it sell the latter

In our view, the ungrammaticality of RD in LI is the consequence of a more general restriction: RD can only be a Theme, not a Topic. We call Theme an LD element that can be recovered from the immediate context. We call Topic an element that is present in the shared knowledge of the speaker and the hearer but is not accessible in the immediate context so that it cannot be recovered. Consider the following examples of a dialogue:

(50)   A: Hai visto i miei occhiali?
        have seen the my glasses
        'Did you see my glasses?'
    B: I tuoi occhiali, li ho messi sul tavolo.
        the your glasses, them have put on-the table
        'I put your glasses on the table.'
    B': Li ho messi sul tavolo.
        them have put on-the table
        'I put them on the table.'
    B": Li ho messi sul tavolo, i tuoi occhiali.
        them have put on-the table, the your glasses
        'I put your glasses on the table.'
    B''': I tuoi occhiali, li ho messi sul tavolo, i tuoi occhiali.[17]
        the your glasses, them have put on-the table, the your glasses

A sentence like (50B) is felicitous independently from the context: if there is a context like (50A), the LD object is interpreted as a Theme; if it is uttered without any available context, the LD element is interpreted as a Topic. A sentence like (50B') can only be uttered if there is a preceding context similar to (50A); if there is no preceding context, it is infelicitous, as there is no way to recover the Topic corresponding to the resumptive pronoun. Tentatively, we propose that RD is a copying process of an LD element, which can be either phonetically realized, as in (50B'''), or empty, as in (50B'').

We can infer that the copied LD element can only be a Theme and not a Topic from the fact that both B'' and B''' require a context like (50A), and are infelicitous if (50A) is missing.

On the basis of what we said so far, we can consider another interesting variant of the combination between the LI interpretation and RD, which we have shown to be ungrammatical in examples like (49). If the first item of the list is a RD and the second is on the left, the sentence is well-formed (cf. (51a)). This challenges our hypothesis that RD and LI are not compatible and leaves us without an explanation for the ungrammaticality of (49b,c) and (51b):

(51)   a. La regaliamo, la frutta, e la verdura la vendiamo.
          it give for free the fruit and the vegetables it sell
          'We give fruit for free, while we sell vegetables.'
       b.*La frutta, la regaliamo e la vendiamo, la verdura.
          the fruit it give for free and it sell the vegetables

But, if we apply the substitution test with 'the former–the latter' on (51a) and insert the specific lexical items that single out the LI construction, we obtain (52), which is ungrammatical:

(52) *La regaliamo, la prima e la seconda, la vendiamo.
       it give for free the first and the second it sell
       'We give the former for free, while we sell the latter.'

Therefore, we conclude that (51a) is only an apparent counterexample to the generalization that LI and RD are incompatible.

The fact that RD cannot be a Topic was first noted by Beninca' (1988) on the basis of sentences like the following:

(53)   a. Il vino lo porto io, la torta la porti tu.
          the wine it take I, the cake it take you
          'You take the wine, I'll take the cake.'
       b.*Lo porto io il vino, la porti tu la torta.
          it take I the wine it take you the cake

Now we can better characterize what kind of construction these sentences are: they are a special case of LI, where two lists are paired. This can be shown by the usual substitution test:

(54)   a. Il primo lo porto io, la seconda la porti tu.
          the first it take I the second it take you
          'I take the first, you take the second.'
       b. Il vino lo porta il primo, la torta la porta il secondo.
          the wine it takes the first the cake it takes the second
          'The former takes the wine, the latter takes the cake.'
       c. L'uno porta il primo, l'altro porta la seconda.
          the one takes the first the other takes the second

      d. Il primo porta l'una, il secondo porta l'altra.
        the first take the one the second takes the other

Both the elements on the left and the element in postverbal position can be substituted by 'the former–the latter', as shown in (54a, b, c, and d).

    This construction uses the LI in the left periphery as well as the in situ list, which is in general independently possible:[18]

(55) a. Regaliamo la frutta e vendiamo la verdura.
        give for free the fruit and sell the vegetables
        'We give the fruit for free and sell the vegetables.'
     b. Regaliamo la prima e vendiamo la seconda.
        give for free the first and sell the second
        'We give the first for free and sell the second.'

    In the spirit of what we have proposed above, we will assume that the construction we have characterized as LI corresponds to a syntactic position in the left periphery; now we have to determine the precise position of this FP in the CP domain. A thematized argument or adverbial can be found on the left of LI elements, as the sentences in (56) illustrate:

(56) a. Agli amici, la prima la vendiamo, la seconda la regaliamo.
        to the friends the first it sell the second it give for free
        'We sell the first to the friends and give them the second for free.'
     b. Agli amici, la frutta la vendiamo, invece la verdura la regaliamo.
        to the friends the fruit it sell while the vegetables it give for free
        'We sell fruit to the friends, while we give them vegetables for free.'
     c. Di storia, ai primi ne parliamo, coi secondi ne discutiamo.
        of history to the first of it speak with the second of it discuss
        'We speak of history with the former, while we discuss it with the latter.'

Interestingly, from the semantic point of view, the thematized element occurring on the left of LI seems to be interpreted only as the Topic of the sentence, not necessarily as a Theme. Although this function is the same as that attributed to the Hanging Topic discussed in the preceding section, the syntactic behavior of this kind of Topic is the one of a normal left-dislocated element (for instance, it copies the preposition, it can be embedded, and it does not always need to be doubled by a clitic, contrary to HT).

    Hence, we define the position(s) before LI as LDTopics, in order to distinguish them from HT, but we would like to have a more solid empirical basis to be able to make further, finer distinctions. Therefore, for the moment, we leave the matter at this point, proposing the following section of CP structure:

(57) [LD [LI [Focus . . .]]]

This is already a welcome result, it seems to us; if we are on the right track, the apparent recursion of the FPs will in the end disappear.

    We have shown that it is possible to find different positions, which are specialized for a particular interpretation. A lot of work remains to be done in this domain, especially concerning syntactic tests, which should go hand in hand with the interpretative differences we have described.

4. Conclusions

The cartographic project that aims to analyze the fine structure of the CP domain is based on the fundamental idea that the number of FPs present in the syntactic structure is finite and that each syntactic projection has its own special syntactic and semantic properties. In such a framework, it seems to us, there is no space for recursion. In this chapter we have begun to trace a map of the so-called Topic/Focus elements, which does not involve recursion of any FP.

We can now sum up some possible lines of research deriving from the analysis presented in this work and speculate about some general properties that seem to partially depend on nonsyntactic factors. We claim here that the CP portion hosting Topic and Focus elements can be split into two parts: a Topic field located higher than a Focus field. The Topic field can be further split into Frame and LD, as shown in the structure in (58):

(58)   [H. T [Scene Sett. [LD. [LI
        |_____FRAME_____||THEME_____|
        [$_{CONTR. CP1}$ adv/obj, [$_{CONTR.CP2}$ circ.adv. [$_{INFORM. CP}$]]]]]]]
        |_____FOCUS_____|

Such a complex structure has two interesting properties, the first of which is most probably universal, while the second might be language-specific. The first property concerns the relation between the semantics and the layering of the FPs involved: the highest projections are those that are already part of the information shared by the speaker and the hearer; the lower ones proceed toward new information. If we are right in our analysis of the Topic/Focus elements, the encoding of informational relations in the syntax of the left periphery follows a very precise semantic path.[19] This property does not only hold the layering of the three subfields—Frame, Thematization, and Focus—but possibly also inside each field. Considering the Focus layer, we have localized Informational Focus in the lowest of the FPs, while Contrastive Focus (which selects an element inside a given set and excludes all others) is higher: this can be seen as representing a progression toward simple "new information." In the same way, List Interpretation, which deals with a given set, follows the introduction of a theme. Moreover, the same "progression toward new information" is also found in an unmarked sentence, as has been shown by Antinucci and Cinque (1977) with data from a language like Italian, where the free word order permits one to test more clearly the meaning of some restrictions.[20]

A second interesting aspect concerns the layering of the elements that correspond to "given information"—namely, Themes and Frame. The highest of the two subfields is the one that contains more salient information from the informational point of view: Frame is higher than Themes because it is the FP giving information about the main Topic and the "where and when" of the sentence. We will not enter a detailed analysis of why this is so, but it seems clear to us that the layering of the projections as illustrated in (52) must derive from the fact it is the interface between syntax and pragmatics, the locus where informational characteristics of pragmatic relevance receive a syntactic encoding. Moreover, it is a well-known fact that the basic organization of information goes precisely from given to new. Thus, the reason why the left periphery of declarative clauses is built up in this way has to do primarily with pragmatic factors, just like the layering of the internal IP structure has to be reduced primarily to semantics. This is also coherent with Cinque's (1999) view that structure is part of the biological endowment.

The second property mentioned above concerns the operator-move procedure, which is available only to the XPs occupying the lowest of the three subfields: in standard Italian operator-movement stops at the highest Focus projection (as the test of weak crossover shows), while all the Frame and Theme XPs use a different strategy (either "merge" or a distinct type of "move"). We do not know whether other languages have different properties and display operator-movement also for Themes and Frames, or whether the point where operator-movement stops in Italian is a universal fact. Nevertheless, V2 might provide evidence in favor of one of these two options.

Notes

We would like to thank Guglielmo Cinque, Federico Damonte, Lidia Lonzi, Hans-Georg Obenauer, Luigi Rizzi, Laura Sgarioto, Margarita Suñer, Christina Tortora, and Raffaella Zanuttini. For the concerns of the Italian academy, Paola Beninca' takes responsibility for sections 1, 2, 2.2, and 3.1, and Cecilia Poletto for sections 2.1, 3.2, 3.3, and 4.

1. We do not intend to make any specific claim about the way the focused and topicalized elements are related to the empty category inside the clause. As for focused elements, it might be the case that the link between the variable and the focused XP is established by means of a null operator in some SpecC position. As for Topics, the relation between the null category and the Topic might be one of movement (as proposed by Cecchetto 1999, 2000) or the Topic might be merged directly inside the CP (as proposed in Cinque 1990). We do not intend to enter into this discussion and will simply make the claim that the two subfields we examine in this work have to be differently characterized with respect to the nature of the empty category they are related to inside the clause.

2. It would be interesting and important to check the possible overlapping of the projections we are going to illustrate in this paper and the results of recent research concerning pragmatic and syntactic properties of different types of 'fronting' in other languages: see, for example, Gyuris (2001), Lipták (2001) on Hungarian, Gregory and Michaelis (2001) on English, and others.

3. Consider the following example:

(i) *Mario doman ga dito che el compra na casa.
     Mario tomorrow has said that he buys a house

In both sentences a resumptive subject clitic is necessary: this means that the adverb position at the IP border is only available for an adverb specifying the time of the event in the same sentence, and nothing can move into this position from another sentence.

4. Note that the presence or absence of the clitic has no effect on the weak crossover restriction:

(i) Di Gianni$_i$, suoi padre non parla mai.
     of Gianni his father not talks never
     'His father never talks about Gianni.'

Example (i) contains a PP-Topic, which does not require a clitic, and nevertheless no weak crossover effect arises.

5. Note that this sentence has to be carefully contrasted with a parallel version without a possessive binding the focalized object:

(i)   ?A MARIA, Giorgio, mia madre presenterà.
      TO MARIA Giorgio my mother will-introduce

(ii) ?A MARIA, Giorgio$_j$, sua$_i$ madre presenterà.
      TO MARIA Giorgio his mother will-introduce

To evaluate this difference, we have to factor out the resistance against preverbal subjects in these structures (see example (29)).

6. The context given by the informants is the following: the speaker is looking out of the window while the hearer is not. This cannot occur when they are both looking out of the window.

7. Recall that, this variety being a V2 language, the adverb *duman* in a main clause such as (21a) is in a Spec of a CP projection (as is currently assumed for Germanic V2 languages as well); the position is then different from the one that has been identified for parallel sentences in Italian and Paduan (see (6) above).

Note that Left Dislocation is grammatical in interrogative clauses, as (i) shows:

(i)   Giani, inier, ci a-al pa fat?
      Giani yesterday what has-he interrogative marker done
      'What has Giani done yesterday?'

For a detailed analysis of this asymmetry, see Poletto (2000).

8. Even if the V2 linear constraint is respected, there is a class of adverbs (which cuts across modal, temporal, and locative adverbials) that cannot occur in first position:

(i)   a.*Bel a-i mangè.
         already have-I eaten
         'I have already eaten.'
      b.*Tosc vagne-l.
         soon comes-he
         'He is coming soon.'

The reason these adverbs cannot occur in first position might have to do with different factors, which we will not analyze here any deeper.

9. In this work we do not consider the position of wh-elements, which might well be distinct from the position of both contrastive and informational Focus.

10. See also the (severe, for some speakers) marginality of sentences like (ii) with respect to sentences like (i):

(i)   A MARIA questo devi dire.
      TO MARIA this have-to say
      'You have to say this TO MARIA.'

(ii) */? A MARIA questo Mario deve dire.
      TO MARIA this Mario has to say
      'Mario has to say this TO MARIA.'

Interestingly, a subject pronoun is more acceptable:

(iii) A MARIA, questo io devo dire.
      TO MARIA this I have to say
      'I have to say this TO MARIA.'

On the basis of Rizzi's (p.c.) judgments and comments, we could conclude that the different status of sentence (ii) can be traced back to the existence of two distinct grammars. The first one deals with Focus as it does with wh-movement, then it does not tolerate preverbal subjects when a focalized constituent is moved to the left. The second one marginally admits preverbal subjects when a focalized constituent is moved to Focus. This difference might depend on verb movement to the C domain.

11. A second difference between V2 languages and Italian is that V2 languages also require verb movement when Topic positions are occupied, which is not the case of Italian. Hence, Italian V2 is restricted to interrogatives and Focus movement.

12. It is important to stress that this secondary position cannot be singled out for a contrast, as the following examples show:

> (i) A GIORGIO, il tuo libro devi dare (non a Mario/* non il tuo articolo).
> to Giorgio your book (you) have to give (not to Mario/not your article)

> (ii) A GIORGIO IL TUO LIBRO devi dare (non a Mario il tuo articolo).
> to Giorgio your book (you) have to give (not to Mario your article)

13. Some speakers find embedded HT difficult to accept. This might be due to the semantics of this projection, which defines the "frame" the sentence refers to. In this sense its typical activation is in a main clause (cf. the scene setting position discussed in section 3.2). For those speakers who accept embedded HT, judgments vary depending on the selecting verb. In our view, this suggests that different verbs can select different portions of the CP complex domain.

14. This sentence is not completely ungrammatical; one possibility that comes to mind is that in Italian it is marginally possible to generate a complementizer higher than HT.

15. It has to be emphasized that Italian does not show any main versus embedded asymmetry with respect to scene setting adverbs; this is expected, since HT is also possible in embedded clauses.

16. This class of Topics possibly corresponds to what has been named Contrastive Topic by some linguists; see, for example, Ambar (1988).

17. A sentence like (50B''') differs from (50B'') in signaling that speaker B is annoyed by the question uttered in (50A) by the first speaker

18. We suspect that the postverbal list position in (53), (54), and (55) is parasitic on postverbal informational focus, which is in general allowed in Italian. This is shown by the fact that ergative postverbal subjects, which are not necessarily focus but can be part of presentational sentences, are not allowed in the in situ list construction:

> (i)   ?*Arriva il primo e parte il secondo.
> arrives the first and leaves the second

We will not further develop this point.

19. See, among many others, Firbas (1964), Gruppo di Padova (1974), Lonzi (1974), Calabrese (1980), and Prince (1981).

20. As L. Rizzi pointed out to us, this does not seem to hold in interrogative structures, where a wh-item like *perché* 'why' can be followed by LD. It is clear that (at least wh-) interrogative clauses exploit additional projections of the left periphery; see Poletto (2000) and Poletto and Pollock (chapter 9 in this volume) for details. Moreover, wh-items are not always located in the same position: this is evident in rhetorical questions, where the wh-item occurs in a higher position with respect to true questions (cf. Obenauer and Poletto 1999). The same can be argued on the basis of phenomena in exclamative clauses (as shown by Beninca' 2001) and for interrogatives with a special entailment (cf. Munaro and Obenauer 1999).

References

Ambar, M. (1988) *Para uma sintaxe da inversão sujeito-verbo em português*. Lisbon: Estudos Lingüìsticos.
Antinucci, F., and G. Cinque (1977) "Sull'ordine delle parole in italiano: l'emarginazione." *Studi di Grammatica Italiana* 6, 121–146.

Beninca', P. (1988) "L'ordine degli elementi della frase e le costruzioni marcate," in L. Renzi (ed.) *Grande grammatica italiana di consultazione.* Bologna: Il Mulino, vol. 1, 129–194.

———— (1994) *La variatione sintattica.* Bologna: Il Mulino.

———— (2001) "Syntactic Focus and Intonational Focus in the Left Periphery," in G. Cinque and G. Salvi (eds.) *Current Studies in Italian Syntax Offered to Lorenzo Renzi.* Amsterdam: Elsevier, 39–64.

Brody, M. (1990) "Remarks on the Order of Elements in the Hungarian Focus Field," in I. Kenesei (ed.) *Approaches to Hungarian,* Vol. 3: *Structures and Arguments.* Szeged: Jate, 95–121.

Calabrese, A. (1980) "Sui pronomi atoni e tonici dell'italiano." *Rivista di Grammatica Generativa* 5, 65–116.

Cecchetto, C. (1999) "A Comparative Analysis of Left and Right Dislocation in Romance." *Studia Linguistica* 53, 40–67.

———— (2000) "Doubling Structures and Reconstruction." *Probus* 12, 93–126.

Chomsky, N. (1981) *Lectures on Government and Binding.* Dordrecht: Foris.

Cinque, G. (1976) "Mica." *Annali della Facoltà di Lettere e Filosofia dell'Università di Padova* 1, 101–112.

———— (1977) "The Movement Nature of Left Dislocation." *Linguistic Inquiry* 8, 397–412.

———— (1982) "Topic Constructions in Some European Languages and Connectedness," in K. Ehlich and H. van Riemsdijk (eds.) *Connectedness in Sentence, Text and Discourse.* Tilburg: Tilburg, University, 7–41.

———— (1990) *Types of A-bar Dependencies.* Cambridge, Mass.: MIT Press.

———— (1999) *Adverbs and Functional Heads.* New York: Oxford University Press.

Firbas, J. (1964) "On Defining the Theme in Functional Sentence Analysis." *Travaux Linguistiques de Prague* 1, 267–380.

Gregory, M. L., and L. A. Michaelis (2001) "Topicalization and Left-Dislocation: A Functional Opposition Revisited." *Journal of Pragmatics* 33, 1665–1706.

Gruppo di Padova (1974) "L'ordine dei sintagmi nella frase," in M. Medici and A. Sangregorio (eds.) *Fenomeni morfologici e sintattici dell'italiano contemporaneo.* Atti del 7. Congresso della Società di Linguistica Italiana, 3 vols., Rome: Bulzoni, vol. 1, 147–161.

Gyuris, B. (2001) "Contrastive Topics and Alternatives." Paper presented at the Fifth International Conference on the Structure of Hungarian, Budapest, May 2001.

Lipták, A. (2001) *On the Syntax of Wh-Items in Hungarian.* Utrecht: LOT.

Lonzi, L. (1974) "L'articolazione presupposizione-asserzione e l'ordine V-S in italiano," in M. Medici and A. Sangregorio (eds.) *Fenomeni morfologici e sintattici dell'italiano contemporaneo.* Atti del 7. Congresso della Società di Linguistica Italiana, 3 vols., Rome: Bulzoni, vol. 1, 197–215.

Munaro, N., and H-G. Obenauer (1999) "Underspecified wh-Phrases in Pseudo-interrogatives." Unpublished ms., CNRS Paris-St. Denis / CNR Padua.

Obenauer, H-G., and C. Poletto (1999) "Rhetorical Wh-Phrases in the Left Periphery of the Sentence." *Venice Working Papers in Linguistics* (University of Venice).

Poletto, C. (2000) *The Higher Functional Field.* New York: Oxford University Press.

Poletto, C., and R. Zanuttini (2000) "Marking New Information in the Left Periphery: The Case of *pa* in Central Rhaeto-Romance." Talk delivered at the "VI Giornata di Dialettologia," University of Padua.

Prince, E. F. (1981) "Topicalization, Focus-Movement and Yiddish-Movement: A Pragmatic Differentiation," in *Proceedings of the Seventh Annual Meeting of the Berkeley Linguistic Society.* Berkeley: University of Berkeley, 243–264.

Rizzi, L. (1997) "The Fine Structure of the Left Periphery," in L. Haegeman, (ed.) *Elements of Grammar: Handbook of Generative Syntax,* Dordrecht: Kluwer, 281–337.

4

Resumptive Relatives
and LF Chains

VALENTINA BIANCHI

Many languages use resumptive relativization as a normal strategy alongside "gap" relativization. An important question is under which conditions either strategy is adopted. Recent research has concentrated mainly on the distribution of resumptive pronouns along the NP Accessibility Hierarchy proposed by Keenan and Comrie (1977): it has been pointed out that cross-linguistically, gap relativization tends to occur in the highest positions of the hierarchy,[1] whereas resumptive pronouns tend to be obligatory in the lower oblique positions.[2] In some languages, however, the two strategies seem to freely alternate in the subject and direct object position.[3]

In this chapter I will investigate another largely overlooked factor that bears on the distribution of resumptive pronouns: the type of the relative clause,[4] and more specifically, the nature of the LF chain that is involved in the various relative clause types.

In my analysis, I distinguish three types of resumptive pronouns:

1. Optional resumptive pronouns occurring in DP argument positions

    (1) O livro que eu deixei (*ele*) aqui na mesa desapareceu.   (Brazilian Portuguese)
         the book that I left (it) here on-the table disappeared

2. Obligatory resumptive pronouns occurring within PPs or in possessive position

    (2) O sobrinho que a Maria va deixar todo o dinheiro dela pra *(*ele*).   (Brazilian Portuguese)
         the nephew that Maria will leave all the money of-her to *(him)

3. Intrusive pronouns rescuing island violations

    (3) the guy who I hate almost everything *he* does

I show that, in the first case, the alternation between a gap and a resumptive pronoun varies cross-linguistically as a function of the type of relative clause. I adopt the three-way typology proposed by Grosu and Landman (1998), which distinguishes nonrestrictive, restrictive, and maximalizing relatives. On the basis of this typology, I propose an empirical generalization on the distribution of optional resumptive pronouns, and I account for it in terms of the nature of the LF chain involved in the three relative clause types, building on a proposal by Rizzi (2000) (sections 1–4).

I then show that obligatory resumptive pronouns of class (b) are insensitive to the type of relative clause, and they are realized for syntactic reasons independent of the nature of the LF chain (section 5). In contrast, intrusive pronouns of type (c) seem to be restricted to just one type of LF chain (section 6). I argue that in all three cases, resumptive pronouns are not independent lexical items merged in the argument position, but they are the spell-out of the referential index on the lowest link of the chain. The conditions under which this spell-out occurs are different in the three cases, giving rise to the typology just outlined.

1. A typology of relative clauses

Relative clauses are traditionally distinguished between nonrestrictive and restrictive. The former do not contribute to determining the reference of the "head" that they modify, because they fall outside the restrictive term of its determiner:

(4)   Mary knows few boys, who enjoy knitting → Mary knows few boys.

On the contrary, restrictive relatives are included in the restrictive term of the determiner and therefore contribute to determining the denotation of the whole DP:

(5)   Mary knows few boys who enjoy knitting — / → Mary knows few boys.

Syntactically, the difference can be minimally characterized in the following way: assuming that the restrictive term of a determiner corresponds to its c-command domain in LF, only restrictive relatives, but not nonrestrictives, are c-commanded by the determiner of the "head" at LF. Most of the existing analyses incorporate this hypothesis.[5]

A third type of relative clause has been identified by Carlson (1977), who calls it "amount relative." This type is superficially similar to the restrictive relative, but it is semantically distinct in that the head and the relative clause jointly denote not a set of individuals but a set of amounts. This interpretation emerges most clearly in examples like (6), in which the DP modified by the relative denotes an abstract quantity of wine, rather than a concrete quantity:

(6)   It will take us three days to drink the wine that John drank that night.

Carlson points out that the DP has to denote the *maximal* amount of wine that John drank. This semantic feature is reflected in a specific restriction: the head of an amount relative can only be introduced by a universal or definite determiner, but not by a weak determiner.

Building on this insight, Grosu and Landman (1998) propose that amount relatives are characterized by two semantic operations: first, the head is interpreted within the relative clause and a lambda operator binds a degree variable within it;[6] second, an operation of maximalization applies at the CP level. As a result, the relative CP denotes the maximal degree or amount that satisfies the property described within the CP; the external determiner of the head must preserve maximalization. Under this analysis, the LF representation of (6) will be something like (7):

(7)

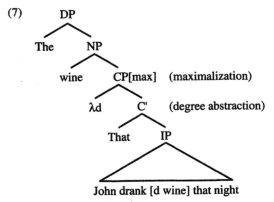

Grosu and Landman (1998) argue that amount relatives actually belong in a wider class of *maximalizing* relatives, which are characterized by the application of maximalization at the CP level. Another member in this class is the free relative, exemplified in (8):

(8)   a. [What you gave to Mary] was an expensive object.
      b. [Whatever you give to Mary] is expensive.

Both in the definite interpretation (8a) and in the universal interpretation (8b), the free relative denotes a maximal set of individuals.

I cannot go into the details of Grosu and Landman's proposal here. For the present purposes, it is sufficient to sketch out the basic properties of the three relative clause types that they identify: in nonrestrictive relatives, the head is denotationally independent of the relative clause; in restrictive relatives, the head and the relative CP denote two sets whose intersection constitutes the restrictive term of the determiner; finally, in maximalizing relatives the head is interpreted CP-internally. I will show that this typology constitutes an important dimension of cross-linguistic variation in the distribution of resumptive pronouns.

2. Optional resumptive pronouns and relative clause types

Let us consider first optional resumptive pronouns (type (a)), which alternate with a gap in the subject[7] and direct object position. It can be shown that their distribution is cross-linguistically sensitive to the type of the relative clause.[8] In particular, I have found out two distinct patterns.

1. In certain Northern Italian dialects like Venetian, Paduan, and Bergamasco,[9] optional resumptive pronouns can only appear in nonrestrictive relatives (a), whereas they are excluded from restrictive (b) and maximalizing (c–e) relatives:

(9)   a. Me fradeo Giorgio, che ti (? *o*) conossi anche ti, el ze partio par la
          merica.   (Venetian)
          my brother G. that you (him) know you too he has left for America
      b. El fio che ti (**o*) ga conossuo ieri el ze meo fradeo.
          the boy that you (him) have met yesterday he is my brother
      c. Me dispiase de tuto el tempo che (***lo*) go perso par gnente.
          to-me regrets of all the time that (it) [I] have wasted for nothing
      d. No ti sa quanti schei che el ze riusio a tirar(***li*) su sto ano.
          not you know how much money that he has managed to earn (it) up this year
      e. Go ciamà chi che ti me gavevi domandà de ciamar(**lo*).
          [I] have called who that you me had asked to call (him).

(10) a. 'Stó estìt che, che a' m' *l*'à prestàt mé sorèla, al ma sta benisem.   (Bergamasco)
          this dress here, that CL to-me it has lended my sister it me suits very well
      b. Ol liber che (?? *l*') ìe lassàt che söl tàol l'é sparìt.
          the book that (it) [I] had left here on the table it has disappeared
      c. Al ma dispiàs de töt ol tép che (?? *l*')ó perdìt.
          CL me regrets of all the time that (it) [I] have wasted
      d. Tó imaginèt gnàc i solcc che i à guadagnàt ist'ann!
          you imagine not-even the money that they have earned this year
      e. O avertìt chi (che) düsìe averti(* *l*).
          [I] have advised whom (that) [I] had to-advise (him)

2. In colloquial Italian,[10] Hebrew, Brazilian Portuguese, Spanish,[11] Irish, and
presumably also Swiss German,[12] resumptive pronouns are allowed both in nonrestrictive (a) and in restrictive (b) relatives, but not in maximalizing ones (c–e).

(11) a. Ha-bendod Sel-i, Se rina 'ohevet ('*oto*), haya baxur nexmad.   (Hebrew)
          the-cousin of-mine that Rina loves him was guy nice
      b. Ha-'iS Se rina 'ohevet ('*oto*) haya ha-bendod Sel-i.
          the-man that Rina loves him was the-cousin of-mine
      c. 'Animicta 'er 'alha-zman Se-bizbazti (*'*oto*).
          I sorry about the-time that-[I] wasted (it)
      d. 'Samtiba-kis 'et kolha-kesef Se-yakoltila-sim (*'*oto*).
          [I] put in-the-pocket ACC all the-money that [I] could put (it)
      e. Kaniti 'et ma Se-ra'it (*'*oto*).   (from Borer 1984: 239)
          [I] bought ACC what that-[you]-saw (it)

(12) a. Estes livros, que você pode achar (*eles*) em qualquer livraria, . . .   (Brazilian
          Portuguese)
          those books that you can find (them) in any bookshop . . .
      b. O livro que eu deixei (*ele*) aqui na mesa desapareceu.
          the book that I left (it) here on-the table disappeared
      c. Eu acho maus todo o tempo que eu desperdico (?* *ele*).
          I regret all the time that I waste (it)
      d. Você não imagina o dinheiro que eu ganhei (?* *ele*) esse ano!
          you not imagine the money that I earned (it) this year
      e. Eu avisei quem eu devia avisar (* *ele*).
          I advised whom I had to advise (him)

(13) a. Tháinig an saighdiúir eile, nach bhfaca mé roihme *é*, aníos chugainn.   (Irish)
          came the soldier other C+NEG saw I before him, up to-us

    b. An ghirseach ar ghoid na síogaí *í*.
       the girl COMP stole the fairies her
    c. Tá óth liom an méid ama a chuir mé amú (* *é*).
       is regret with-me the quantity time-GEN *a* put I out (it)
    d. Ní fhéadfá a shamhlú an méid airgid a shaoithraigh mé (* *é*).
       not [you]can imagine the quantity money-GEN *a* earned I (it)

Although the sample of languages that I have considered is very small, there seem to be some significant gaps. First, I have not found any language that allows for optional resumptive pronouns in maximalizing relatives.[13] Second, I have not found any language that allows for resumptive pronouns in restrictive relatives but not in nonrestrictive ones. These data suggest the implicational scale represented in (14).

(14)   appositive > restrictive > maximalizing relative

        ⌊—type I—⌋   ⌋
          ⌊————type II————⌋

In principle, this implicational scale would allow for a third language type, with optional resumptive pronouns in all the three relative clause types; however, it predicts that there should exist no language allowing resumptive pronouns in a given relative clause type but not in the higher one(s) on the scale. I tentatively propose (14) as an empirical generalization, to be further tested against a larger sample of languages in future research.[14]

As a first step toward an account of (14), it is necessary to syntactically characterize the three relative clause types so as to understand which factor is responsible for the implicational relations that it expresses. In the following sections, I propose that the relevant factor can be identified by inspecting the different LF representations of the three structures.

3.   A syntactic characterization of the three relative clause types

3.1.   Reconstruction effects

Starting from Chomsky (1995: 202ff.), reconstruction effects are considered a reliable diagnostic for LF configurations. Chomsky adopts the copy theory of traces and argues that reconstruction effects are determined by the computation of an operator-variable chain in which the restrictive term of an operator phrase may be visible either in the peripheral operator position (giving rise to restricted quantification) or in the argument position (giving rise to nonrestricted quantification) (cf. Heycock 1995: 560–561).

Chomsky's proposal has been pursued in many studies, which have shown that the simple version of the copy theory of traces cannot be maintained: as a matter of fact, one and the same A' structure may give rise to contradictory reconstruction effects for different phenomena. Many different approaches to this reconstruction paradox have already been proposed (see, as a representative sample, Epstein et al. 1998: chap. 2; Fox 2000; Rizzi 2000; Safir 1999; Sauerland 1998). A full discussion of these issues would exceed the limits of this essay; my discussion of reconstruction effects will be instrumental to giving a syntactic characterization of the three relative clause types in terms of different LF structures.

In fact, the three relative clause types show different reconstruction patterns for the head. Following Rizzi (2000), I focus here on three types of reconstruction effects: scope assignment,[15] anaphor binding,[16] and Principle C effects.

Before testing these phenomena, some remarks on Principle C effects are in order. Safir (1999) argues that the suspension of Principle C effects in an A' chain does not constitute evidence for antireconstruction (i.e., deletion of the lower copy). The alleviation of Principle C effects is instead due to an operation of 'vehicle change', which turns the R-expression in the lower copy into a coindexed pronoun, subject to Principle B.[17] This operation is blocked only if the R-expression is embedded in certain noun complements, for reasons that are not entirely clear (Safir 1999: 608–611).[18]

Safir also argues that in restrictive and nonrestrictive relatives Principle C effects are completely missing, even for the subset of noun complements that show them in wh-operator constructions.[19] As for restrictive relatives, however, the data are not clear-cut.[20] Bianchi (1999: 112–115) shows that in Italian there is a systematic contrast between a weak/null pronoun and a full pronoun: the former seems to be sensitive to reconstruction of the relative head, giving rise to a disjoint reference effect (15), whereas the latter does not (16):

(15)   *Questi sono i pettegolezzi su Gianni$_i$ che *pro*$_i$ ha sentito *t*.
these are the gossips about Gianni that (he) has heard

(16)   ?Questi sono i pettegolezzi su Gianni$_i$ che lui$_i$ ha sentito *t*.
these are the gossips about Gianni that he has heard

Since the nature of this contrast is unclear, the evaluation of Principle C effects in restrictives is somewhat arbitrary. Bianchi (1999: 114) considers (16) an exception and analyses (15) as a Principle C effect under reconstruction. However, Solan (1984) suggests that full (stressed) pronouns are used to pick out an "unexpected" antecedent. It is possible to speculate that in (15) coreference is excluded not because of reconstruction but because the R-expression *Gianni* embedded in the relative head represents a discourse referent that is not sufficiently prominent as an antecedent for the null pronoun.[21] Here I tentatively adopt this second view, taking (16) to show the lack of a Principle C effect. More precisely, I show in the following discussion that it is necessary to distinguish nonspecific from specific restrictive relatives: only the former show real Principle C effects.[22] Furthermore, I concur with Safir's claim that the lack of a Principle C effect in specific restrictive relatives does not imply the deletion of the lower copy (see the discussion around (27)).[23]

After this necessary digression, let us consider the relevant reconstruction effects in the three relative clause types. Starting from maximalizing relatives, we observe the following pattern: (a) scope assignment under reconstruction, (b) anaphor binding under recontruction only in the lowest chain position, and (c) Principle C effects:

(17)   a. *Pro* calcoleremo il tempo che ciascuno di noi ha dedicato *t* a questo progetto.
(we) will calculate the (amount of) time that each of us has devoted to this project

b. *Pro* sapessi i pettegolezzi su se stesso$_i$/?* se stessa$_k$ che Maria$_k$ dice [*t* che Gianni$_i$ ha sentito *t* alla festa]!
could (you) know the gossips on himself/herself that Maria says that Gianni has heard at the party

c. *Se tu immaginassi i pettegolezzi su Gianni$_i$ che lui$_i$/*pro*$_i$ può aver sentito *t* alla festa, capiresti perché sono preoccupata.
'If you could imagine the gossip on Gianni$_i$ that he$_i$ may have heard at the party, you would understand my being concerned.'

In (17a), there is a different amount of time for each of us: this means that the head [*time*] is interpreted in the scope of the universal subject of the maximalizing relative clause. In (17b), the anaphor embedded in the head can only be bound by the subject of the most deeply embedded clause *Gianni* and not by the higher subject *Maria*: this shows that the head is obligatorily reconstructed in the lowest position and is not visible in the intermediate Comp position for anaphor binding. Finally, in (17c) the subject of the relative clause (whether null or a full pronoun) cannot corefer with the R-expression *Gianni* embedded in the head. This seems to be a Principle C effect, suggesting that the head is obligatorily reconstructed in the lowest position of the chain.[24]

As for restrictive relatives, it is necessary to distinguish two possible interpretations. If the head requires a nonspecific interpretation, the pattern is as in (17). This is the case if the head is the object of a quasi-idiomatic expression (18), or of a creation verb (19):[25]

(18) a. L' immagine di sé$_i$ che ognuno$_i$ cerca di trasmettere *t* agli altri.
the image of himself that everyone tries to convey to other people

b. L'immagine di sé$_{i/*k}$ che Maria$_k$ dice [*t* che Gianni$_i$ cerca di trasmettere *t* agli altri].
the image of him/herself that Maria says that Gianni tries to convey to other people

c. *L' immagine di Gianni$_i$ che lui/*pro*$_i$ cerca di trasmettere *t* agli altri.
the image of Gianni that (he) tries to convey to other people

(19) a. Il bilancio della propria$_i$ vita che ognuno$_i$ ha fatto *t*.
the evaluation of his own life that everyone has made

b. Il bilancio della propria$_{i/*k}$ vita che Maria$_k$ dice [*t* che Gianni$_i$ ha fatto *t*].
the evaluation of his/*her own life that Maria says that Gianni has made

c. *Il bilancio della vita di Gianni$_i$ che lui/*pro*$_i$ ha fatto *t* in quell'occasione.
the evaluation of the life of Gianni that he has made on that occasion

When the head does not require a nonspecific interpretation, a different pattern emerges: (a) wide scope or narrow scope under reconstruction, (b) anaphor binding under reconstruction in all the chain positions, and (c) no sharp Principle C effects:

(20) a. *Pro* ho avvertito i due pazienti che ogni medico visiterà *t* domani.
(I) advised the two patients that every doctor will examine tomorrow

b. *Pro* mi hanno riferito i pettegolezzi su se stesso$_i$/se stessa$_k$ che Maria$_k$ dice [*t* che Gianni$_i$ ha sentito *t* alla festa].
(they) have reported to me the gossips on himself/herself that Maria says that Gianni has heard at the party

c. Mi hanno riferito i pettegolezzi su Gianni$_i$ che *pro*$_i$/?lui$_i$ può aver sentito *t* alla festa.
they reported to me the gossips on Gianni that he may have heard at the party

In (20a), *two patients* may have wide or narrow scope with respect to the universally quantified subject of the relative clause—that is, there may be exactly two patients who must be examined by every doctor, or there may be two different patients for every doctor.[26] In (20b), the anaphor can be bound by the higher or the lower subject in the relative clause. In (20c), a full subject pronoun may corefer with the R-expression embedded in the head: I tentatively take this as evidence that there is no Principle C effect under reconstruction (recall the discussion around (15)–(16)).

Finally, nonrestrictive relatives show a third pattern: (a) no scope assignment under reconstruction, (b) no anaphor binding under reconstruction, and (c) no Principle C effects—that is, no reconstruction effects at all.[27]

(21) a. *Pro ho telefonato ai due pazienti cardiopatici, che ogni medico visiterà t domani.*
      (I) phoned to the two cardiopath patients that every doctor will examine tomorrow

      b. *Maria$_i$ mi ha riferito [quei pettegolezzi su se stessa$_i$ / se stesso$_{*j}$], per i quali, a quanto pare, Gianni$_j$ si è offeso t.*
      Maria$_i$ has reported to me those gossips on herself/himself by which apparently Gianni was offended

      c. *[Questi pettegolezzi su Gianni], che lui$_i$/pro$_i$ può aver sentito, sono privi di fondamento.*
      these gossips on Gianni$_i$ which he may have heard are groundless

In a nonrestrictive relative, the head is by definition denotationally independent of the relative clause. In fact, the subject of the relative clause cannot take scope over the head (21a), nor can it bind an anaphor within it (21b); finally, no Principle C effect arises in (21c), even with a null subject pronoun.[28] In short, nonrestrictive relatives show no reconstruction effects at all.

3.2.   The raising analysis of relatives

As mentioned, Chomsky's (1995) analysis of reconstruction is based on the copy theory of traces. Thus, the reconstruction of the head of relative clauses may be considered an argument in support of a raising analysis, in which the head raises directly from the relativization site.[29]

I will assume for the present purposes the following version of the raising analysis:[30] the relative clause is selected by an external Determiner; the relative head is a DP consisting of a relative Determiner and an NP, which raises from the argument position to a peripheral position of the clause, immediately adjacent to the external Determiner. More specifically, assuming Rizzi's (1997) split CP system, the relative DP moves to the Spec of the Force projection, whose head is the declarative complementizer (Engl. *that*; Ital. *che*); this position is above the Topic and Focus projections:

(22) [$_{DP}$ the [$_{FP}$[$_{DP}$ which book]$_i$ [that [$_{TopP}$ for my son [I would never buy <[$_{DP}$ which book]$_i$>]]]]]

The *that*-relative results from phonetic deletion of the relative Determiner. In Bianchi (1999: chap. 3) it is argued that this obtains by abstract incorporation of the relative Determiner to the external Determiner selecting the relative clause;[31] in virtue of this incorporation, the external Determiner acquires the φ-features of the relative head. The wh-relative featuring an overt relative determiner is discussed in section 3.3.2.[32]

I will not work out a compositional semantic interpretation of the raising structure (22).[33] Following Reinhart (1987) and Bianchi (1999: 80–86), I assume that the relative DP is interpreted as a Heimian indefinite, denoting a restricted free variable that ultimately gets bound by the external Determiner. This means that the relative Determiner has no quantificational force of its own. More specifically, I assume that the relative Determiner introduces the variable and the NP complement restricts its range.

Note that in this approach, the A' chain of the relative clause is constituted by identical copies of the head raised to Spec,FP. It is then possible to reduce the reconstruction patterns observed in (17)–(21) to an elaboration of the copy theory of traces. This task is undertaken in the following discussion.

3.3.   LF chains

To characterize the LF structures of the various relative clause types, I adopt and extend the theory of LF chains proposed by Rizzi (2000). On this theory, a wh-movement chain can be modified by applying a deletion operation to parts of the chain links, so as to separate the operator from its restrictive term.[34]

3.3.1.   Nonspecific and maximalizing relatives

The first possibility is to delete the restrictive term from the peripheral operator position and from any other intermediate chain link, except for the lowest one: this is shown in (23b), where the deleted material is struck through. As a result, the trace in the base position is no longer c-commanded by any higher copy and it gets "shrunk,"— that is, it becomes fully visible in the LF representation, since it becomes the head of the resulting one-membered chain (23c). (By convention, the shrunk material is outside the angled brackets.)

(23)   a.   [How many books] did you buy <how many books> → (deletion)
      b.   [How many ~~books~~] did you buy <how many books> → (trace shrinking)
      c.   [How many] did you buy <how many> books

This process yields a *nonspecific chain*, in which the reconstructed restrictive term receives a nonspecific interpretation.[35]

I propose that both maximalizing and nonspecific restrictive relatives involve a nonspecific LF chain.[36] However, since I have assumed that the relative D° has no quantificational force, there seems to be no reason for it to stay in the left periphery at LF. Accordingly, I assume that the whole relative DP undergoes reconstruction and is interpreted in the base position as a free variable: a nonindividual variable in amount relatives, and a (nonrestricted) individual variable in nonspecific restrictive relatives like (18)–(19).

After shrinking, the lowest chain link is fully visible in LF, and it shows the full range of reconstruction effects. First, it is assigned narrow scope with respect to a QP internal to the relative clause (24a). Second, if it contains an anaphor, the latter must be bound by the closest c-commanding DP (24b). Finally, if the shrunk chain link contains an R-expression, the latter is visible for Principle C (24c).[37]

(24) a. [$_{DP}$ il [$_{CP}$ ~~tempo~~]$_i$ [che ciascuno di noi ha dedicato tempo$_i$ a questo progetto]]]

b. [$_{DP}$ i [$_{CP}$ [~~pettegolezzi su di sé~~] che Maria$_j$ dice [$_{CP}$ <~~pettegolezzi su di sé~~$_{*j}$> che Gianni$_i$ ha sentito pettegolezzi su di sé$_i$ alla festa]]]

c.*[$_{DP}$ i [$_{CP}$ [~~pettegolezzi su Gianni~~$_i$] che *pro*$_i$ può aver sentito pettegolezzi su Gianni$_i$ alla festa]]

3.3.2. Specific restrictive relatives

The second possibility is not to reconstruct the restrictive term to the base position. Rizzi (2000) argues, contrary to Chomsky (1993), that in this case the lower chain links are not deleted; all the copies are preserved, but they are not shrunk (see also Fox 2000 and Sauerland 1998):

(25) [How many books] did you buy <how many books>

This accounts for the partial reconstruction pattern of the specific LF chain. As noted by several authors, the lower chain links are not visible for Principle C effects (e.g., Heycock 1995); however, they are visible for anaphor binding. As for scope reconstruction, I will assume, following Rizzi (2000), that a non-shrunk trace is invisible for scope assignment. This hypothesis is justified by the observation that extraction from a weak island blocks scope reconstruction, forcing a wide scope reading of the extracted phrase (cf. Longobardi 1986; Cinque 1990; Frampton 1991):

(26) a. Quanti pazienti pensi [che ogni medico abbia visitato *t*]?   (∀>wh)
      how many patients (you) think that every doctor has examined

b. Quanti pazienti non sai [se ogni medico abbia visitato *t*]?   (* ∀>wh)
      how many patients (you) not know whether every doctor has examined

Since on Rizzi's analysis only a specific chain can cross a weak island, the lack of ambiguity of (26b) suggests that the specific chain disallows scope assignment under reconstruction.[38]

I wish to propose that this type of LF chain is instantiated in specific restrictive relatives like (20). The LF representations are as in (27):

(27) a. [$_{DP}$ i [$_{GrPP}$ [due pazienti]$_i$ [$_{FP}$ che ogni medico visiterà <due pazienti>$_i$ domani]]]

b. [$_{DP}$ i [$_{GrPP}$ pettegolezzi su di sé] [$_{FP}$ che Maria$_j$ dice [$_{FP}$ <pettegolezzi su di sé$_j$> che Gianni$_i$ ha sentito <pettegolezzi su di sé$_i$ >]]]]

c. ?Mi hanno riferito [$_{DPi}$ [$_{GrP}$ [pettegolezzi su Gianni$_i$] [$_{FP}$ che lui$_i$ può aver sentito <pettegolezzi su Gianni$_i$> alla festa]]]

Consider first (27b–c). In (27b), by hypothesis all the chain links are preserved: although they are not shrunk, the anaphor they contain is visible for binding, yielding multiple binding options.[39] On the contrary, in (27c) the lowest occurrence of the R-expression in the non-shrunk trace seems not to be visible for Principle C. Thus, here, too, we find an asymmetry between anaphors and R-expressions occurring in nonshrunk traces.

In the present context, it is possible to account for this asymmetry by refining the notion of binding index, a refinement that falls out naturally from the copy theory of traces. In (27c), for instance, the referential index appears both on the highest occurrence of the R-expression and on the copy-occurrence. The copy-occurrence is not shrunk, and it is licensed by being chain-connected to the higher one. Let us represent the highest independent occurrence of the index as a superscript and the dependent copy-occurrence as a subscript.[40] Example (27c) then corresponds to the abstract configuration (28):

(28)   . . . R-expression^i . . . *pro*^{i} . . . <R-expression$_i$ >

On the other hand, we can represent the referential index of an anaphor as an intrinsically dependent index, which is licensed by being bound by the independent index of an antecedent. Example (27b) will then correspond to the abstract structure (29):

(29)   [. . . anaphor . . .] . . . Maria^j . . . <. . . anaphor$_j$ . . .> . . . Gianni^i . . . <. . . anaphor$_i$ . . .>

We can now account for the apparent invisibility of the lower occurrence of the R-expression in (28) on the basis of the following assumption:

(30)   Only independent indices are subject to Principle C.

This accounts for the observed reconstruction asymmetry.[41]

As for (27a), I have assumed with Rizzi (2000) that the lowest nonshrunk trace is not visible for scope assignment; therefore, the specific LF chain only yields wide scope of the relative head. The available narrow scope interpretation must then be reduced to an alternative LF representation, featuring a nonspecific LF chain.

The derivation of the specific LF chain proposed by Rizzi (2000) is actually more complex. According to Rizzi, the restrictive term cannot be licensed in the operator position itself, but it must be licensed by covert movement to the Spec of a Topic-like projection above the operator projection, whereby it receives a presuppositional interpretation (31b):

(31)   a. [How many books] did you buy <how many books> → restrictive term to TopP
       b. [books] Top [how many <books>] did you buy <how many books>

From the perspective of the split CP hypothesis, it would be interesting to determine the exact position of these projections. Here specificity amounts to the presupposition or familiarity of the restrictive term of the DP, as proposed in Enç (1991). (See section 4.1 here for more discussion.) It is possible to speculate that the peripheral projection hosting presupposed material is above the Force projection, which encodes the assertive force, and also above the Interrogative projection of Rizzi (1999), which encodes the question operator. For concreteness, let us label this presuppositional projection "Ground Phrase."[42] We thus arrive at the following (minimal) structure of the Comp system:

(32)   [$_{GP}$ Ground [$_{FP}$ Force [$_{TopP}$ Top* [$_{IntP}$ Int [$_{FocP}$ Foc . . . [IP]]]]]]

Rizzi's hypothesis paves the way to an interesting analysis of the English (non-pied-piping) restrictive wh-relative, exemplified in (33):

(33)   the book which I consulted

Various authors have argued that the restrictive wh-relative necessarily involves a specific interpretation of the relative head, contrary to the that-relative, which allows for nonspecific and amount interpretations. For instance, Carlson (1977) argues that amount relatives can only be introduced by *that*, not by *which*:[43]

(34) a. I took with me every book that there was on the table.
      b. # I took with me every book which there was on the table.

Lee (2001: 324–325) points out that restrictive wh-relatives do not allow for narrow scope of the head with respect to a quantifier internal to the relative clause:[44]

(35) a. We're looking for [someone that *t* knows every application]   (some > every, every > some)
      b. We're looking for [someone who *t* knows every application]   (some > every, * every > some)

Furthermore, there is no infinitival wh-relative:

(36) *I'm looking for [some rich girl whom to marry]

This is coherent with the observation that infinitival relatives always force a nonspecific (nonpresuppositional) interpretation of the head.[45]

However, specificity seems not to be intrinsic to the wh-determiner itself. For instance, in a pied-piping relative the relative determiner appears overtly but does not force a specific interpretation of the head:

(37) a. I'm looking for somebody [with whom to discuss my problems]
      b. the way in which every actor should move t on the scene   (every > way)

To account for the specificity of the wh-relative, I now elaborate on the analysis proposed in Bianchi (1999: 188–194),[46] where it is argued, *pace* Kayne (1994: 87–90), that the wh-relative cannot be derived from a structure like (22), repeated here as (38a), by moving the NP to the Spec of the relative DP, as in (38b), because the latter position is unavailable for nonoperator phrases (cf. Szabolcsi 1994):

(38) a. [$_{DP}$ the [$_{FP}$[$_{DP}$ which book]$_i$ [that I bought <[$_{DP}$ which book]$_i$>]]]
      b. [$_{DP}$ the [$_{FP}$[$_{DP}$ book [which <book>]] $_i$ [(that) I bought <[$_{DP}$ which book]$_i$>]]]

Instead, a raising derivation is proposed which involves two distinct layers of the Comp system: the relative DP moves to the lower Spec, and then the internal NP is extracted and moves to the higher Spec, "stranding" the relative determiner in the lower Spec, as shown in (39). (For the time being, I use the generic labels C_1 and C_2 for the two Comp layers.)

(39) [$_{DP}$ the [$_{C1P}$ [$_{NP}$ book] C_1 [$_{C2P}$ [$_{DP}$ which <book>] C_2 [I bought <which book>]]]]

Note that the CP-internal derivation is parallel to that proposed by Rizzi (2000) for the specific LF chain, with the (nontrivial) difference that here movement of the NP is overt. We can then hypothesize that the wh-relative overtly shows that structure of a specific LF chain: the relative DP targets Spec, ForceP, and then the NP moves to Spec,GrP, when it is assigned a specific or presuppositional interpretation:[47]

(40) [$_{DP}$ the [$_{GrP}$ [$_{NP}$ book] Ground [$_{FP}$ [$_{DP}$ which <book>] (that) [I bought <which book>]]]]

From this perspective, the reason the wh-relative has only a specific interpretation is that its derivation necessarily involves two distinct Spec positions and, crucially, the

Ground Phrase layer above the Force Phrase. The impossibility of an infinitival wh-relative like (36) may follow from the plausible assumption that infinitival clauses have a defective Comp system, which, in particular, lacks the Ground Phrase.

On the contrary, pied-piping wh-relatives like (37) do not induce a specific interpretation of the head because their derivation does not need to involve the Ground layer. The NP constituent is allowed to raise to the Spec of the pied-piped PP, which itself occurs in Spec,Force Phrase (cf. Bianchi 1999: 169):

(41) $[_{DP}$ the $[_{FP}$ $[_{PP}$ way [in $[_{DP}$ which <way>] $]_i$ [(that) they should move <in which way$_i$>]]]]

This analysis yields a straightforward positional encoding of the semantic property of specificity, which will play a crucial role in the following discussion.[48] However, for the time being it can only be assumed as a working hypothesis, awaiting further independent confirmation.

3.3.3.   Nonrestrictive relatives

Let us finally turn to nonrestrictive relatives. We have seen in (21) that these do not show any reconstruction effects, and this leaves us without direct support for a raising analysis. One could assume, then, that nonrestrictive relatives have a completely different, nonraising derivation: that is, they contain a relative operator coindexed with a syntactically independent head.[49] Under such an analysis, the chain links within the relative clause will not share the internal structure of the head, and the lack of reconstruction effects falls out automatically.

The same result can actually be achieved by adopting the raising analysis of nonrestrictives proposed by Kayne (1994: 110–115). In his approach, after raising of the relative DP to the left periphery, the IP subconstituent of the relative clause moves covertly out of the scope of the external D° in LF (Kayne assumes that it moves to Spec,DP):

(42) $[_{DP}$ $[_{IP}$ ogni medico visiterà <i due pazienti cardiopatici> domani] [i $[_{CP}$ [due pazienti cardiopatici] [C° t_{IP}]]]]

Consider the status of the LF chain after IP movement has taken place. Because the lower chain link(s) contained in the raised IP are no longer in the scope of the external D°, they cannot be interpreted as variables bound by it. Suppose that in this configuration the internal structure of the lower link(s) get deleted. What remains is an empty category with no internal structure, which only shares the referential index of the relative head:

(43) $[_{IP}$ ogni medico visiterà e_i domani] . . . $[_{DP}$ i $[_{CP}$ [due pazienti cardiopatici]$_i$ C° t_{IP}]]

The empty chain link in (43) is equivalent to a definite anaphoric pronoun.[50] Accordingly, I will call this third type of LF chain a *pronominal chain*.[51] This constitutes an extension of Rizzi's (2000) typology.

This proposal also accounts for the complete lack of reconstruction of the head. Since the lower chain link is definite and anaphoric, no scope interaction will be possible. Furthermore, since its internal structure is deleted, it does not contain any occurrence of the anaphor or R-expression embedded in the head: accordingly, we find neither anaphor binding nor Principle C effects under reconstruction.

A further interesting consequence of this approach is that an LF chain cannot be simultaneously pronominal and nonspecific. The reason is that in a pronominal chain, the restrictive term is deleted in all the chain links except for the highest one; conversely, in a nonspecific chain, the restrictive term is deleted in all the chain links except for the lowest one. Therefore, if both deletion processes apply to the same LF chain, the restrictive term will be completely and unrecoverably deleted from all the chain links. We can then draw the conclusion that in pronominal chains, too, the highest chain link must be licensed in Spec, Ground Phrase.

3.4.   A restatement of the empirical generalization

Let us now go back to the empirical generalization (14), repeated here:

(14)   appositive > restrictive > maximalizing relative

└─type I─┘
└────────type II────────┘

On the basis of the preceding proposal, the generalization can be rephrased as in (44):

(44)   pronominal > specific > nonspecific chain link

└─type I─┘
└────────type II────────┘

There is an interesting discrepancy between (14) and (44): the nonspecific chain is found not only in maximalizing relatives, but also in nonspecific restrictive relatives like (18)–(19). Thus, (44) predicts that nonspecific restrictive relatives pattern with maximalizing ones, with respect to the distribution of resumptive pronouns (see section 4.4).

At this point, the reader will have an obvious objection in mind. I have reduced the reconstruction patterns of the three relative clause types to different LF chains, on the basis of the copy theory of traces and of the raising analysis of relative clauses. But how can all this be reconciled with the existence of *resumptive* relative clauses? The occurrence of a resumptive pronoun seems incompatible with the raising analysis: either the relativization site is filled by a resumptive pronoun in the base, or it is filled by the head to be raised, but it cannot be filled by both.[52] The next section is devoted to the solution of this apparent paradox.

4.   Deriving the empirical generalization

4.1.   Specificity and definiteness

The next step of my argument is a characterization of the links of the three LF chains in terms of different referential indices. My proposal is based on Enç's (1991) theory of specificity and definiteness, which I will now briefly summarize.

On this theory, each DP[53] bears two indices: the first one denotes the discourse referent of the whole DP, and the second one denotes a discourse referent in which the referent of DP is included:

(45) Every $[_{DP}\, a]_{<i,j>}$ is interpreted as (x_i) and
        $x_i \subseteq x_j$ if $DP_{<i,j>}$ is plural
        $\{x_i\} \subseteq x_j$ if $DP_{<i,j>}$ is singular.

Each index bears a definiteness feature. If it is definite, it is subject to the Familiarity Condition (Heim 1982): the referent that it points to must be familiar—that is, it must have been previously introduced in the discourse. If, instead, the index is indefinite, it is subject to the Novelty Condition: it must introduce a new discourse referent. The core of Enç's proposal is summarized in the following definitions:

(46) a. A DP is definite iff its first index is definite.
        b. A DP is specific iff its second index is definite.

Briefly put: if a DP is specific, its denotation is not familiar but it is included in a familiar discourse referent. An important consequence of this proposal is that definiteness implies specificity; since identity of referents entails inclusion, if the first index is definite the second one is, too (cf. Enç 1991: 9).

The links in the three LF chains can now be characterized as bearing different referential indices:

(47) Nonspecific link: $DP_{<i,j>}$ with i = [–def], j = [–def]
        Specific link: $DP_{<i,j>}$ with i = [–def], j = [+def]
        Pronominal link: $DP_{<i,j>}$ with i = [+def], j = [+def]

These definiteness features are actually semantic properties; however, they strictly correlate with certain aspects of the proposed LF configurations. To see this, let us reconsider the three LF chains, schematically represented in (48)–(50).[54]

(48) $[_{FP}\, DP_i\, [_{IP} \ldots <DP_i>]\,] \rightarrow [_{FP}\, e\, [_{IP} \ldots DP_i]\,]$ (Nonspecific chain)

(49) $[_{GrP}\, DP_i \ldots [_{IP} \ldots <DP_i>]\,]$ (Specific chain)

(50) $[_{GrP}\, DP_i\, [_{IP} \ldots <DP_i>]\,] \rightarrow [_{IP} \ldots e_i] \ldots [_{GrP}\, DP_i\, t_{IP}]$ (Pronominal chain)

By inspecting these abstract representations, we can find the following correspondences. The definiteness of the second index correlates with the status of the highest chain link:

1. A [– definite] second index corresponds to a "shrunk" chain link—that is, the highest link of the chain is in the argument position (48).
2. A [+ definite] second index corresponds to the highest link being licensed in Spec,GrP (49)–(50).

The definiteness of the first index instead correlates with the nature of the lowest chain link:

3. When the chain's tail has internal structure, it is interpreted as a (restricted) variable, and it does not denote a fixed discourse referent. This corresponds to a [– definite] first index (48)–(49).

4. On the contrary, in the pronominal chain (50), the lowest link in the argument position has no visible internal structure, since deletion has applied. The empty category is interpreted as a definite pronoun anaphoric to the highest link, which denotes a fixed discourse referent; this corresponds to a [+ definite] first index.

5. As discussed, a [+ definite] first index cannot cooccur with a [– definite] second index, because this would entail the unrecoverable deletion of the NP restriction from all the chain links.

On these grounds, I propose that the definiteness features associated to the two referential indices are not (necessarily) lexically specified on the relative D°, but they can be directly read off the LF configurations by the semantic module.

4.2.   On the structure of the referential index

At this point, it is natural to conceive of the referential index of a DP as a *feature structure*, which subsumes Enç's first and second indices. I also crucially adopt Pollard and Sag's (1994: 24–26) proposal that the referential index contains the ϕ-features of gender, number, and person. I assume that the Case feature is also included in the ϕ-features structure.[55] This gives us the (minimal) feature structure in (51).

(51)

$$
\begin{bmatrix}
\text{first} & i \\
\text{second} & j \\
\text{phi} & \begin{bmatrix}
\text{per} & \{1\text{st}, 2\text{nd}, 3\text{rd}\} \\
\text{num} & \{\text{sing}, \text{plur}\} \\
\text{gend} & \{m, f, n\} \\
\text{Case} & \{\text{structural}, \text{inherent}\}
\end{bmatrix}
\end{bmatrix}
$$

4.3.   An account of the empirical generalization

With this background, we can formulate the core hypothesis as follows:

(52)   An optional resumptive pronoun is the spell-out of the referential index on the chain's tail.

In other terms, the resumptive pronoun is not an independent lexical item in the initial numeration, but it is the spell-out of a substructure of the copy-trace.[56] Thus, the realization of a resumptive pronoun is consistent with a raising derivation.

The cross-linguistic variation in the distribution of optional resumptive pronouns observed in section 3 can now be reduced to the hypothesis that in each language a certain type of referential index is spelled out. Recall the characterization of the chain links proposed in (47), repeated here:

(47)   Nonspecific link: $DP_{<i,j>}$ with $i = [-\text{def}]$, $j = [-\text{def}]$
         Specific link: $DP_{<i,j>}$ with $i = [-\text{def}]$, $j = [+\text{def}]$
         Pronominal link: $DP_{<i,j>}$ with $i = [+\text{def}]$, $j = [+\text{def}]$

1. In type I languages, resumptive pronouns lexicalize a referential index whose first element is definite. This is the case in pronominal chains (i.e., in non-restrictive relatives).[57]

2. In type II languages, resumptive pronouns lexicalize a referential index whose second element is definite. This is the case both in pronominal and in specific chains (i.e., in nonrestrictive and specific restrictive relatives).

If we conceive of the definiteness associated to each index as a privative opposition (cf. Bianchi 1999: 82), the characterization of the chain links will then be as follows (Ø represents underspecification):

(53) Nonspecific link: $DP_{<i,j>}$ with i = Ø, j = Ø
      Specific link: $DP_{<i,j>}$ with i = Ø, j = [+def]
      Pronominal link: $DP_{<i,j>}$ with i = [+def], j = [+def]

From this perspective, the distribution of optional resumptive pronouns varies from the more restrictive type I languages, in which they spell out a maximally specified referential index, to the more liberal type II languages, in which they spell out a fully or partially specified referential index.

I have to leave open the question of whether there exist languages of a third type, in which an optional resumptive pronoun may be lexicalized also on the tail of a nonspecific chain.[58] In such languages the optional resumptive pronouns would be insensitive to any value of specificity and definiteness; they would merely spell-out the φ-feature substructure.

In this approach PF rules spell out a certain type of referential index on the chain links, but the type of the referential index is read off the LF configuration. This is inconsistent with Chomsky's (1995) minimalist architecture, in which PF and LF are independent branches of the derivation. I return to this issue in section 7.1.

4.4.   Nonspecific restrictive relatives

As mentioned, the restated empirical generalization (44) predicts that nonspecific restrictive relatives (featuring a nonspecific chain) pattern with maximalizing relatives in the distribution of optional resumptive pronouns. In particular, we expect a discrimination to emerge in type II languages, which allow resumptive pronouns in pronominal and specific chains but not in nonspecific ones.

This prediction seems to be borne out: in these languages the realization of an optional resumptive pronoun disambiguates a restrictive relative, forcing the specific interpretation. This is clear in contexts in which the relative head can, in principle, have wide or narrow scope with regard to a clause-internal quantifier. The optional resumptive pronoun forces wide scope, which corresponds to a specific LF chain (see the discussion around (26)).

(54) los tres estudiantes que cada profesor debe entrevistar*los*   (* ∀>3) (Spanish; Suñer 1998: 358)
      the three students that every professor must interview-them

(55) a. Eu telefonei pros dois pacientes que cada medico vai visitar *t* amanha.   (?? ∀>2)
         I phoned to-the two patients that every doctor will examine tomorrow

b. Eu telefonei pros dois pacientes que cada medico vai visitar *eles* amanha.   (* ∀>2)
(Brazilian Portuguese)
I phoned to-the two patients that every doctor will examine them tomorrow

(56)   BevakaSa taxin reSima Sel ha-holim Se-kol rofe bodek *'otam*.   (* ∀>∃)   (Hebrew;
U. Shlonsky, p.c.)
please prepare a list of the-patients that-every doctor examines them

(57)   %i due pazienti che ogni medico dovrebbe visitar*li*   (* ∀>2)   (colloquial Italian)
the two patients that every doctor should examine-them

A second relevant context has been pointed out by Cristina Figueiredo and Carlos Mioto (personal communication): a resumptive pronoun is impossible when the head requires a generic interpretation, as in (58a) and (59a):

(58)   a. Um medico que (* *ele*) ganha muito dinheiro não pode ser honesto.   (Brazilian Portuguese)
a doctor that he earns a lot of money cannot be honest
b. Eu conheco um medico que *ele* ganha muito dinheiro.
I know a doctor that he earns a lot of money

(59)   a. Un doctor que (* *él*) gana mucho dinero no puede ser honesto.   (Spanish;
M. Suñer, p.c.)
a doctor that he earns a lot of money cannot be honest
b. ?Yo conozco un doctor que *él* gana mucho dinero.
I know a doctor that he earns a lot of money

A third case of nonspecific interpretation is the *de dicto* interpretation of the relative head in intensional contexts. Doron (1982: 25) and Sells (1987a: 287–292) argue that in Hebrew restrictive relatives, a resumptive pronoun forces a *de re* interpretation of the head.[59]

(60)   Dani yimca 'et ha-iSa Se hu mexapes (*ota*).
Dani will find ACC the-woman that he seeks (her)

(61)   Todo hombre encontrará (a) la mujer que *la* busca.   (Spanish; Suñer 1998: 357)
every man will-find (*a*) the woman that her seeks

In all of these examples (54)–(61), the realization of a resumptive pronoun disambiguates a restrictive relative by indicating a specific LF chain, as predicted by generalization (44). As a matter of fact, one of the factors that strongly favors the appearance of a resumptive pronoun in a restrictive relative is the presence of a modal or quantificational element (Bernini 1989: 94): the resumptive pronoun marks the specific LF chain, excluding the alternative nonspecific chain that leads to narrow scope of the head.[60]

4.5.   Fronting of resumptive pronouns

In this approach, resumptive pronouns are analyzed as the spell-out of the referential index on the tail of the LF chain, that is, in the variable position. However, in some languages—as, for example, Hebrew—the resumptive pronoun can be fronted to a clause-initial position (see Demirdache 1997 for extensive discussion):

(62)   ha-'iS Se-'*oto* ra'iti
     the-man that-him (I)-saw

Following Shlonsky (1992: n. 2), I assume that the resumptive pronoun in (62) appears in a Topic position. According to Rizzi (1997), this is the Specifier of a Topic head below the declarative complementizer. My approach commits me to the claim that in (62) the referential index has been spelled out on the intermediate chain link in Spec,TopP.

Let us suppose that the relative head has raised through Spec,TopP. This step is only licensed if the head agrees with Top° for the feature [+topic]. However, the head must raise further to Spec,FP in order to check the features of the external D°. In the resulting structure, Spec,TopP contains a copy-trace of the head:

(63) $[_{DP}$ D° $[_{FP}$ DP$_{REL}$ Force° $[_{TopP}$ <DP$_{REL}$> [Top° $[_{IP}$ ... <DP$_{REL}$> ...]]]]]

I tentatively propose that it is possible to spell out the referential index on the intermediate trace in order to explicitly mark the topical status of the relative head—that is, the fact that the Topic Criterion is satisfied in the LF representation.

4.6.   Summary

To conclude this section, let me summarize the main points of the analysis that I have developed so far for optional resumptive pronouns:

- The cross-linguistic distribution of optional resumptive pronouns is sensitive to the type of the relative clause, suggesting the implicational scale (14).
- The three relative clause types can be characterized in terms of different LF chains. In maximalizing and nonspecific restrictive relatives, all the links except for the lowest one are deleted, yielding a nonspecific chain with full reconstruction of the relative head. In restrictive relatives, all the chain links are preserved, yielding a specific chain. Finally, in nonrestrictive relatives, all the chain links except for the highest one lose their internal structure and are interpreted as anaphoric pronouns, yielding a pronominal chain with full antireconstruction of the head. The empirical generalization (14) can thus be rephrased in terms of LF chains (44).
- The links in the three LF chains differ in the status of their referential indices, as defined by Enç (1991) and Kiss (1993). In nonspecific chains, neither element of the referential index is definite; in specific chains, only the second element is definite; in pronominal chains, both elements are definite.
- Optional resumptive pronouns are not independent lexical items merged in the argument position, but they are the spell-out of the referential index on the lowest chain link. The conditions under which this spell-out may occur vary cross-linguistically. Type I languages spell out only a referential index whose first element is definite, whereas type II languages may spell out the chain links whose second element is definite (independently of the nature of the first index).

- As predicted by (44), in type II languages the realization of an optional resumptive pronoun disambiguates a restrictive relative, indicating that it contains a specific LF chain.

This concludes my discussion of optional resumptive pronouns. In the next section, I turn to obligatory resumptive pronouns and I argue that they are spelled out under completely different conditions.

5. Obligatory resumptive pronouns

Obligatory resumptive pronouns appear in possessor position or as prepositional objects—both positions from which movement is excluded (in the relevant languages), so that they do not alternate with a gap.[61]

(64) o sobrinho que a Maria va deixar todo o dinheiro dela pra *(ele) (Brazilian Portuguese)
the nephew that Maria will leave all the money of-her to *(him)

These resumptive pronouns are insensitive to the type of the relative clause. In type I languages, they can appear in restrictive relatives, contrary to optional pronouns.

(65) Questo ze un argomento che no voio parlarghe*(ne). (Venetian)
this is a topic that (I) not want to-talk-to-him-(about-it)

(66) Gh'ó de laà fò la padèla che gh'ó facc indà dét ol brasàt. (Bergamasco)
(I) have to clean out the pan that (I) in-it have made cook within the meat

In type II languages, they can appear in maximalizing relatives and in nonspecific restrictive relatives, contrary to optional pronouns:

(67) a. ?Você não imagina as meninas que ele namorou com elas! (Brazilian Portuguese)
you not imagine the girls that he flirted with them
b. Eu vou falar com quem você falou com ele ontem.
I will speak with whom you spoke with him yesterday
c. João vai encontrar certamente a mulher rica que ele quer casar com ela. (? de dicto)
João will find surely the rich woman that he wants to marry with her
d. Precisa escrever em uma agenda os pacientes que cada médico trata deles. (? ∀>∃)
(it) is-necessary to write in a list the patients that every doctor treats of them

(68) a. los tres estudiantes que cada profesor les debe dar tarea extra[62] (∀>3) (Spanish)
the three students that every professor to-them mut give extra exercise
b. los tres estudiantes que cada profesor debe hablar con ellos (? ∀>3)
the three students that every professor must speak with them

(69) a. 'Ata lo yaxol le-ta'er 'et ha-mekomot Se hu biker *(ba-hem). (Hebrew)
you not can to-describe ACC the-places that he visited (in them)
b. 'Ani 'azmin 'et mi Se dibarta *('it-o) 'etmol.[63]
I will invite ACC who-that (you) talked (to-him) yesterday
c. Dani betax yimca 'et ha-'iSa ha-'aSira Se-hu roce lixyot 'ita.
d. certainly will-find ACC the-woman the-rich that-he wishes to live with-her (?? de dicto)[64]

(70)   a. Sin aN dtig liom labhairt *air*.
        that C can to-me speak[-fin] on-it
        'That's all I can talk about.'
    b. an buaireamh uilig aN ndeachaigh sé *fríd*   (Irish; James McCloskey, p.c.)
        the trouble all C went he through-it
        'all the trouble that he went through'

I conclude that the spell-out of obligatory resumptive pronouns is insensitive to the nature of the LF chain, but it is forced by an independent requirement. To see what this requirement may be, let us reconsider one aspect of the raising analysis. The relative clauses in (64)–(70) correspond to the structure (71), in which the preposition has not been pied piped by the relative head, but it has been stranded in the base position (cf. Suñer 1998: 361–362):

(71)   [$_{DP}$ the [$_{FP}$ [$_{DP}$ D° trouble] [that he went [$_{PP}$ through <[$_{DP}$ D° trouble]>]]]]

Note that the head originates in a position where inherent Case is assigned by the preposition. After raising to Spec,FP, the head is attracted to the Case of the external Determiner: this is visible in languages with morphological Case, as, for example, Polish (cf. Borsley 1997; Bianchi 1999: 94). As a result, the inherent Case originally assigned to the head is not spelled out in Spec,FP. The obligatory spell-out of the resumptive pronoun may then be determined by the following requirement:

(72)   Inherent Case must be spelled out.

Condition (72) has been independently adopted by Pesetsky (1998: 367–377), quoting Broihier (1995), in the analysis of certain relativization facts of Russian and Polish. The Polish data are particularly interesting because they feature obligatory resumptive pronouns. In Polish, when the relativized position bears nominative or accusative Case, a resumptive pronoun is impossible (73a);[65] on the contrary, a resumptive pronoun is obligatory if an oblique position bearing inherent Case is relativized (73b):

(73)   a. Ten samochód, co Janek (*go) widzial-wczoraj, zniknal.   (Polish)
       the car-nom that Janek it-ACC saw yesterday disappeared
    b. On spotkal- studenta co *(mu) on dal- piatke.
       he met student that him-DAT he gave good mark

In the optimality approach reported by Pesetsky, oblique Cases are visible for the Recoverability condition, hence they block the application of the lower ranked principle Silent-*t*, which bans the pronounciation of copy-traces.

The deep reason for this asymmetry between inherent and structural Cases remains to be accounted for; however, there is some independent evidence in support of (72), which I briefly summarize here.[66]

   1. In Latin and Ancient Greek, relative pronouns can be attracted to the Case of the external Determiner if they bear a structural Case; they cannot be attracted if they bear inherent Cases (see Bianchi 1999: 94–96; Harbert 1982/3).
   2. In Bavarian, relative pronouns bearing structural Case can be deleted; those bearing inherent Case can be deleted only if the external D° bears the same inherent Case (see Bayer 1984; Bianchi 1999: 172–174).

3. Similarly, in colloquial registers of Russian, relative pronouns can be deleted only if they bear structural Case (Pesetsky 1998: 369).
4. In Russian, within a DP bearing structural Case, a numeral Determiner assigns genitive to its NP complement; but if the whole DP is assigned inherent Case, the latter supersedes the Genitive assigned by the Determiner (see Babby 1987).

On the basis of this evidence, I adopt (72). I conclude that obligatory resumptive pronouns are the spell-out of the ϕ-feature substructure on the tail of the chain, forced by condition (72).

6. Intrusive pronouns

Lastly, let us consider "intrusive" pronouns that rescue island violations. (I consider only strong islands here.)

(74) a. the guy who I hate almost everything *he* does   (Kroch 1981)
      b. that asshole X, who I loathe and despise the ground *he* walks on   (Prince 1990: 483)

According to the standard view, intrusive pronouns can survive within islands because they are not connected to the antecedent via movement but by a representational binding relation: namely, the head is directly merged in its surface position and binds the pronoun merged in the argument position (see, in particular, Cinque 1990: chap. 3). This conception of intrusive pronouns is crucially based on the distinction between derivational and representational binding (see Safir 1996) and on the assumption that only derivational binding obeys island conditions (see section 7.2 for more discussion).

The resulting representational chain qualifies as a pronominal chain in the typology proposed above: the link in the argument position is not a copy of the head but only shares its referential index. We therefore expect the complete lack of reconstruction effects. This seems to be correct, as shown in (75):

(75) a. il test che ogni studente è stato bocciato [perché non *l*'ha superato]   (* $\forall > \exists$)
      the test that every student has been flunked because (he) not it-has passed
      b. *l'unico dei propri$_i$ parenti che ce ne siamo andati [senza che Gianni$_i$ lo salutasse]
      the only one of his own relatives that we went away without that Gianni him greeted
      c. i pettegolezzi su Gianni$_i$ che *pro*$_i$ / lui$_i$ si è offeso [per PRO$_i$ aver*li* sentiti]
      the gossip about Gianni that (he) took offense at having them heard

Thus, the theory of LF chains proposed in this chapter is consistent with the standard analysis of intrusive pronouns: these instantiate a representational pronominal chain and, as such, fail to give rise to any reconstruction effects.

The distinction between true resumption (representational binding) and apparent resumption (movement derivation) has been independently suggested by Aoun et al. (2001) in their discussion of Lebanese Arabic.[67] It is impossible here to fully compare the two proposals, but as far as I can see, they seem to converge on the core empirical generalizations.

7. Some theoretical issues

Before concluding this chapter, I wish to briefly discuss some theoretical issues that arise in connection with the spell-out analysis of resumptive relatives.

7.1. The PF and LF interface

In the approach presented here, optional resumptive pronouns are the spell-out of a certain type of referential index (definite or specific, in Enç's 1991 theory). I have suggested that the type of the referential index can be directly read off the LF representation, by inspecting the internal structure of the LF chain links. This implies that spell-out applies to a syntactic representation in which the chain types have already been differentiated—namely, it applies to the output of LF. Consequently, there must be a single syntactic representation that interfaces with both the morphophonological component and the semantic component. This conception of the architecture of the language system, which abandons the T-model of the Principle and Parameters Theory and of the Minimalist framework, has been independently proposed by Brody (1995) and Groat and O'Neil (1996).[68]

Furthermore, spell-out rules must be able to target a specific subset of the information contained within a syntactic object (namely its referential index). This is also required in Pesetsky's analysis, in which resumptive pronouns are a minimal pronounciation "of some, but not all the *nodes* of the trace" (Pesetsky 1998: 366; minimality of pronounciation is not made explicit). Similarly, in Suñer's approach, resumptive pronouns are the spell-out of an in situ relative pronoun manipulated by PF "only to the extent of disregarding its Operator feature while preserving all other intrinsic features" (Suñer 1998: 356). Here I have proposed a way of implementing this partial spell-out, by conceiving of syntactic objects as feature *structures*, in the technical sense defined in unification-based theories.[69]

Other issues arise with respect to the interface with the semantic component. My proposal is based on the assumption of the copy-trace analysis of reconstruction effects.[70] However, a number of recent papers have called into question the assumption that the LF representation is sufficient to capture all binding phenomena. For instance, Jackendoff (1992) and Culicover and Jackendoff (1995) argue that binding relations are based on Conceptual Structure representations which are not necessarily isomorphic to the output of the syntactic component. From a different perspective, Heycock and Kroch (1999: 388–394) argue that connectedness effects cannot be properly captured by means of a syntactic level of LF, but only in a semantic component that takes surface syntactic forms as input and interprets them dynamically in the discourse context.

If one adopts this perspective, it is certainly possible to characterize the three relative clause types in terms of distinct semantic representations without having recourse to different LF chains. This is obviously incompatible with the spell-out theory of resumptive pronouns proposed here. As far as I can see, the only alternative is to assume that resumptive pronouns are merged in the argument position and impose semantic constraints on their antecedents (cf. Sharvit 1999); it remains to be seen how such an approach can account for the fact that in one and the same language obligatory resumptive pronouns do not share the constraints imposed by optional pronouns with regard to the three relative clause types.

7.2. Derivations versus representation

In the preceding discussion, I formulated my analysis within a derivational framework in which movement creates a chain of copy-traces of the moved phrase, and subsequent LF rules manipulate the internal structure of the chain links. One advantage of the spell-out analysis for a derivational framework is that it never requires the comparison of two derivations with two different initial numerations (one including the pronoun, the other not): therefore, it avoids transderivational computation (cf. n. 3) .

However, I wish to stress that the spell-out analysis is actually neutral with respect to the derivational versus representational architecture of the theory. If we adopt a representational framework, the question of base generation versus movement does not even arise; the three chain types are simply distinguished on the basis of the amount of internal structure that their links share.

Whichever perspective one adopts, I believe that the main point remains unaffected: resumptive pronouns may correspond to different types of chain links, both cross-linguistically (type I vs. type II language) and intra-linguistically (optional vs. obligatory vs. intrusive resumptive pronouns).

7.3. Postal's (1994) typology of extractions

Postal (1994) has proposed a typology of extractions that mirrors the three-way distinction adopted here for relative clauses. On Postal's analysis, the three extraction types are distinguished by the obligatoriness, optionality, or impossibility of a null resumptive pronoun in the extraction site. Although it is impossible here to fully discuss his proposal, I would like to suggest that a substantial part of his evidence can be reinterpreted in terms of the LF chains I discussed earlier.

The starting point of Postal's argument is a very striking constraint that had never been systematically investigated before: certain types of extraction are excluded if the extraction site occurs in a (wide) *anti-pronominal context*—namely, a context that excludes definite pronouns. Postal distinguishes two classes of extractions on the basis of their sensitivity to anti-pronominal contexts, as reported in table 4.1. B-extractions

Table 4.1.   Two Clases of Extraction Proposed
by Postal

B-extractions	A-extractions
Topicalization	Questions
Nonrestrictive relatives	*Restrictive relatives*
Clefting	Pseudoclefting
Parasitic gaps	Negative preposing
COD constructions	Comparatives
	Free relatives

are barred from anti-pronominal contexts, whereas A-extractions are allowed. Note that nonrestrictive relatives fall into class B, whereas restrictive and free relatives fall into class A.

The anti-pronominal contexts identified by Postal are listed in (76)–(87): the (a) examples involve A-extractions, and the (b) examples, B-extractions.

(76) Existential *there*
    a. [No such chemicals] did he know that there were *e* in the bottle.
    b.*[Such chemicals], he knew that there were *e* in the bottle.

(77) Change of color contexts
    a. [What color] did he paint the car *e*?
    b.*[Green], he never painted the car *e*.

(78) Name positions
    a. [What] did they name him *e*?
    b.*[Raphael], I wouldn't name anybody *e*.

(79) Inalienable possession
    a. [What part of the body] did they touch him on *e*?
    b.*[His ear], they never touched him on *e*.

(80) Predicate nominals
    a. [What] are you going to become *e*?
    b.*[That kind of surgeon], Frank never became *e*.

(81) Bare DP adverbials
    a. [What way] does Harry talk *e* ?
    b.*[That way], Harry often talks *e*.

(82) Temporal DPs
    a. [How much time] did Frank stay *e* in Ireland?
    b.*[That much time], Frank could never stay *e* in Ireland.

(83) Idiomatic DPs
    a. [How much headway] did they make *e* on the job?
    b.*[That much headway], I am sure they made *e* on the job.

(84) *Be born in (a country)*
    a. [What country] was Ed born in *e*?
    b.*[Argentina], our president is said to have been born in *e*.

(85) PP extraposition
    a. [No such scurrilous review e_1]$_2$ did they publish e_2 [of his book]$_1$.
    b.*[Such a scurrilous review e_1]$_2$ they published e_2 last year [of his book]$_1$.

(86) Infinitival extraposition
    a. [No wish e_1]$_2$ did I perceive e_2 in Sylvia [to retire]$_1$.
    b.*[A definite wish e_1]$_2$ I did not perceive e_2 in Sylvia [to retire]$_1$.

(87) "Shifting" of an exceptive phrase
    a. [What e_1]$_2$ did he hand e_2 to Rita [other than the gun]$_1$?
    b.*[Something dangerous e_1]$_2$, he might have handed e_2 to Rita [other than the gun].

Since anti-pronominal contexts exclude definite pronouns, it is natural to assume that in B-dependencies the extraction site has pronominal properties. Postal proposes that B-dependencies have a phonetically null resumptive pronoun in the extraction site, which he analyzes as a weak definite pronoun.

In the second part of his article, Postal points out a further differentiation among A-extractions, which emerges with respect to their sensitivity to weak islands. A subset of A_1-extractions can cross weak islands, like B-extractions, whereas the complementary subset of A_2-extractions cannot (see table 4.2).

Interestingly, here a difference emerges between restrictive relatives (A_1) and free relatives (A_2). The contrast in extraction from a weak island is illustrated in (88):

(88) a. the pilots who we asked them [whether you had contacted e]
      b.*whatever pilots we asked them [whether you had contacted e]

A further crucial observation is that even A_1-dependencies cannot cross a weak island if the extraction site is anti-pronominal. Example (89) exemplifies the existential *there* context:[71]

(89) *How many bags do you wonder [whether I think [there are e on the table]]?

This observation leads Postal to conclude that the successful extraction from a weak island in (88a) involves a null resumptive pronoun. Since the anti-pronominal context in (89) bars the resumptive pronoun, extraction from the weak island is impossible.[72] The contrast between A_1 and A_2 extractions in (88) follows from the hypothesis that A_1-extractions optionally allow for a resumptive pronoun, whereas A_2-extractions forbid it. This yields the three-way typology schematically reported in table 4.3.

In the case of relative clauses, we can see that Postal's typology exactly matches the three LF chain types discussed here. Suppose that we generalize this conclusion in the folllowing way:

(90) a. A_2-extractions = nonspecific LF chains
      b. A_1-extractions = nonspecific or specific LF chains
      c. B-extractions = pronominal LF chain

The equivalence in (90a) is directly supported by the facts concerning the sensitivity to weak islands. Recall that A_2-extractions are always blocked by weak islands: this is a crucial property of nonspecific chains in Rizzi's (2000) analysis (see n. 37).

From the present perspective, (89) is excluded because a specific chain is required to cross the weak island, but the existential *there* context requires a nonspe-

Table 4.2. Differentiation among A-extractions
Proposed by Postal

A_1-extractions (not blocked by weak islands)	A_2-extractions (blocked by weak islands)
Questions	Comparatives
Restrictive relatives	Free relatives
Pseudocleft	"No matter wh"
Negative preposing	

Table 4.3.   Typology of Extractions Proposed by Postal

A_2-extractions (* RP)	A_1-extractions (optional RP)	B-extractions (obligatory RP)
Comparative	Questions	Parasitic gaps
Free relative	Restrictive relative	Nonrestrictive relative
No matter wh	Pseudocleft	Cleft
	Negative preposing	Topicalization
		COD

cific chain link. I would like to consider to what extent this approach can be generalized to the other anti-pronominal contexts, by exploring the following conjecture:

(91)   Postal's anti-pronominal contexts are anti-specific (and sometimes anti-referential).

Starting from existential *there*, it has been argued that it requires a weak DP (in the sense of Milsark 1977; Barwise and Cooper 1981; and Heim 1987). Crucially, the DP cannot be associated with any existential presupposition: in our terms, this means that it requires a nonspecific indefinite DP, and it is only compatible with a nonspecific LF chain. It follows that both specific chains (= subset of A_1) and pronominal chains (=B) are excluded.

As for the extraposition of PPs and infinitival clauses, Guéron (1980: 650–655) argues that extraposition is allowed only from DPs that do not bear an existential presupposition: in our terms, these are DPs that give rise to a nonspecific LF chain.

Finally, the inalienable possession construction involves obligatory binding of the possessor position inside the possessed DP (akin to the so-called sloppy identity):

(92)   They touched him$_i$ [on the e_i/ his$_i$ ear].

In the analysis proposed by Vergnaud and Zubizarreta (1992: 638ff.), the possessed DP is not independently referential. Suppose that the obligatory binding relation requires full reconstruction of the possessed DP in the base position: it follows that only a nonspecific LF chain is possible.

A further subset of anti-pronominal contexts includes measuring temporal DP, idiomatic DPs, and predicate nominals. All of these can be roughly characterized as "nonreferential" in the sense of Rizzi (1990: chap. 3): they fail to denote individuals participating in the event. According to Rizzi, they lack a referential θ-role and a referential index. More specifically, measuring DPs and idiomatic DPs[73] can only denote abstract quantities, whereas predicate nominals denote qualities: in neither case can their denotation bear an inclusion relation to a previously established discourse referent. Thus, they cannot be specific in Enç's sense, but they can only give rise to a nonspecific LF chain.

A last subset of cases includes bare DP adverbials, color DPs and naming DPs. In Rizzi's (1990) approach, these too are characterized as nonargumental and hence nonreferential; yet they may correspond to specific and even definite DPs. This suggests that "argumenthood" plays a crucial role after all, independently of specificity and definiteness. I have nothing interesting to suggest on this score.

Although this discussion is far from conclusive, it suggests that a reanalysis of Postal's evidence along the lines of (91) may be worth pursuing. I leave this point open for future research.

8. Concluding remarks

In this chapter I have proposed an analysis of resumptive pronouns according to which they are not lexical items inserted in the initial numeration, but they are the spell-out of the referential index on one of the chain links (usually the tail). This spell-out may take place under different conditions, giving rise to an intralinguistic typology of resumptive pronouns (optional, obligatory, and intrusive) and to cross-linguistic variation in the distribution of optional resumptive pronouns.

My analysis rests on the assumption of the copy-trace approach to reconstruction and on a specific conception of the interface of the syntactic component with the morphophonological component of the language faculty. Both of these assumptions have wide implications and may eventually turn out to be incorrect. Nevertheless, I believe that the empirical evidence presented here substantially corroborates the distinction between three types of A' chains independently proposed by other authors.

Notes

The empirical generalization presented here and the first insight into a possible account of it emerged during my stay at the Universidade Federal de Santa Catarina (Florianópolis) in August 1997. I am indebted to Cristina Figueiredo and Carlos Mioto for inviting me there; I greatly benefitted from the very stimulating environment at UFSC. I also wish to thank many other people both for insightful suggestions and for empirical data: Cecilia Poletto on Venetian/Paduan; Fabrizio and Mario Rota on Bergamasco; again, Cristina Figueiredo and Carlos Mioto on Brazilian Portuguese; Ur Shlonsky on Hebrew; Vittorio di Tomaso and Barbara Gili on Turinese; Margarita Suñer on Spanish; Alain Rouveret and Ian Roberts on Welsh; Paolo Acquaviva and James McCloskey on Irish. Thanks also to Alex Grosu for making me acquainted with his and Landman's analysis of relative clause types, and for subsequent discussion; to Luigi Rizzi, for many important suggestions; and to the audiences at the 25th Incontro di Grammatica Generativa (Siena, February 1999) and at the Workshop on the Cartography of Syntactic Positions and Semantic Types (Pontignano, November 1999), in particular, to Richard Kayne and Ur Shlonsky.

After this essay was completed, I came across a number of important contributions on the syntax and semantics of LF chains, in particular Cresti (2000), Fox (2000), and Sauerland (1998); unfortunately, it is impossible for me to compare my proposal to these within the limits of this essay.

1. Cinque (1981) argues against the NP Accessibility Hierarchy: he shows that in Italian bare NP adverbials (which are quite low in the hierarchy) pattern with subject and direct object DPs in allowing gap relativization, as opposed to PP adverbials. This suggests that the crucial factor is DP versus PP relativization. A similar point is made by Cennamo (1997: 197) on the basis of dialectal data.

2. See Suñer (1998) for a recent general overview.

3. Shlonsky (1992) argues that this alternation is only apparently free: resumptive pronouns are actually a last resort, and they are realized when the language selects a special [+Agr] complementizer whose Spec qualifies as an A position; movement to this Spec is only possible from the local subject position, whereas movement from any other position is blocked by Relativized Minimality. Resumptive pronouns appear only as a last resort in the positions below the local subject whenever the [+Agr] complementizer is selected; they never appear in the highest subject position because in that case the movement derivation converges. One problem with this account is that it requires an evaluation of global economy (see Chomsky 1998: 12 ff.; Collins 1997; Johnson and Lappin 1997: 278–313 for relevant discussion). There is also a more technical problem: if resumptive pronouns are included in the initial numeration, and if the numeration is the reference set that identifies the set of alternative derivations that can be compared (Chomsky 1995: 227), then the movement versus resumption derivations cannot even be compared. See also Aoun et al. (2001).

4. The different distribution of resumptive pronouns in restrictive versus nonrestrictive relatives in Italian dialects is systematically investigated in Cennamo (1997). A related but distinct phenomenon that shows the same sensitivity is clitic doubling, as argued by Suñer (1988) for Spanish; see also Beninca' and Vanelli (1982) and Suñer (1992) on subject clitics in some Northern Italian dialects.

5. See Grosu (2000) for a different view, in which relative clause types are not distinguished configurationally but on the basis of the interpretable features of the C head.

Nonrestrictive relatives are often assimilated to parenthetical clauses because they contribute backgrounded information about the referentially independent "head" (cf. Emonds 1979 and Safir 1986 for two implementations of this idea). See Bianchi (1999: 131–136) for a general overview.

6. Amount relatives also allow for the "identity of substance" reading, in which the CP denotation is converted from a maximal set of degrees to a maximal set of individuals. Grosu and Landman define the degree function as mapping a plural individual into a triple consisting of the cardinality, the sortal predicate, and the plural individual; the third element of the triple is exploited to derive the identity of substance reading.

7. In languages like Hebrew, Arabic, and Irish, resumptive pronouns are barred from the highest subject position of a relative clause. For various analyses of this "highest subject restriction," see McCloskey (1990), Shlonsky (1992), and Demirdache (1997).

8. The small sample of languages that I have considered includes the following: colloquial Italian, South American Spanish, Venetian, Paduan, Bergamasco, Torinese, Brazilian Portuguese, Hebrew, Welsh (Rouveret 1990), Irish, Swiss German (van Riemsdijk 1989), and Yiddish (Prince 1990). I am reporting the dialectal data in the written form that my informants provided.

9. According to Cennamo (1997: 191), Bergamasco optionally allows for resumptive pronouns in restrictives. It must be acknowledged that in the Bergamo area there is actually a constellation of dialects, so that Cennamo's data may have been drawn from a dialect different from my informants'. Cennamo also found that in Torinese resumptive pronouns are optionally possible in nonrestrictives and are impossible in restrictives, whereas my own two informants rejected resumptive pronouns in all relative clause types. Furthermore, according to Cennamo, resumptive pronouns are obligatory in nonrestrictives and are impossible in restrictives in some Ligurian and Piedmontese varieties; I have been unable to check these data, which are anyway consistent with the generalization in (14).

10. Bernini (1989: 93–95). My own variety of colloquial Italian follows the pattern in (9)–(10). According to Cennamo (1997: 196), the Nuorese dialect optionally allows for direct object resumptive pronouns both in nonrestrictives and in restrictives. I have been unable so far to check the data for maximalizing relatives.

11. M. Suñer, personal communication (South American Spanish varieties):

(i) Estoy de acuerdo con tu papà, que siempre *él* dice que ...
[I] am in agreement with your father, that always he says that . . .

(ii) Conozco a un tipo que *él* me aconseja a mí.
[I] know *a* a guy that he me-CL gives-advice to me

(iii) Siento todo el tiempo que (**lo*) gaste.
[I] regret all the time that it-CL [I] wasted

(iv) Aconsejé a quien (**lo*) tenía que aconsejar.
I advised *a* whom him-CL [I] had to advise

12. Van Riemsdijk (1989) reports that in Swiss German optional resumptive pronouns appear in restrictive relatives but not in free relatives (he doesn't discuss appositive relatives). The resumptive pronoun is obligatorily deleted when it occurs in the local subject and direct object positions.

13. However, Prince (1990: 493) claims that in Yiddish there may be a resumptive pronoun related to a nonspecific head (her examples (14a) and (15)).

14. In Welsh, indirect relativization featuring a resumptive pronoun or clitic is always in complementary distribution with regard to direct relativization, featuring a gap (Rouveret 1990, 1999): from the present perspective, the indirect strategy involves obligatory or intrusive pronouns (see sections 5–6 later in this chapter). The status of Welsh indirect relatives cannot be adequately dealt with here.

15. There exists an alternative analysis of scope assignment under reconstruction that does not have recourse to copy-traces—namely, the functional dependency approach (see Sharvit 1999 for an application to resumptive relatives). I do not try to compare the two approaches here.

16. Safir (1999: 594–596) argues that English *self*-anaphors are no test for reconstruction effects, since they can function logophorically in the sense of Reinhart and Reuland (1993). However, in Italian "logophoric" *self*-elements are morphologically distinct from true *self*-anaphors, at least in the third person: that is, they are composed by the pronoun *lui/lei/loro* plus *stesso/stessi* 'self', whereas the real *self*-anaphor is composed by *sé* plus *stesso/stessi* (Bianchi 1999: 115–117). The following examples also feature the anaphors *sé* and *proprio* 'his/her own', which are ambiguous between a short- and long-distance binding behavior; LD binding is considered logophoric by Sells (1987b: 475–476).

17. This operation is proposed for independent reasons by Fiengo and May (1994).

18. For indepedent reasons, Safir maintains Lebeaux's "late-insertion" analysis for adjunct PPs, whereby they are directly adjoined to the head of the A'-chain and have no copy in the lower chain. In the following examples I test R-expressions embedded in noun complements, and I use parallel examples for the three relative clause types.

19. Safir quotes Munn (1994: 402–403), but Munn points out that Principle C effects do arise if the head is an idiom chunk; see example (18) here.

20. Cf. Safir's note 11 and Schachter (1973).

21. As noted by L. Rizzi (personal communication), that reconstruction may not be the relevant factor in (15) is also suggested by a similar asymmetry between null and overt subject pronouns with "scene setting" adjuncts, which presumably don't have any clause-internal position to reconstruct:

(i) Nell'ultima foto di Maria$_i$, *pro$_i$/lei$_i$ sorride.
in the last photo of Maria (she) smiles

22. In Bianchi (1999: 109–115) I failed to distinguish restrictive from maximalizing relatives, and nonspecific from specific restrictives.

23. Safir (1999: 601–604) argues that a real test for presence of the lower copy is constituted by secondary crossover effects. These show a contrast between QPs embedded in adjunct PPs, which fail to reconstruct à la Lebeaux, and QPs in possessor or complement position, which do reconstruct giving rise to secondary crossover. These reconstruction effects also emerge in nonrestrictive relatives (cf. his (37)–(38)); but his examples involve reconstruction of pied piped material, rather than of the relative head. See Bianchi (1999: 126–127) and Munn (1994: 403) for evidence that pied piped material is obligatorily reconstructed.

24. Safir (1999: n. 22) suggests that in (i) coreference is allowed, though he admits that the judgment is difficult:

(i)   the number of pictures of Diana$_i$ that she$_i$ thought there were t in the envelope

Heycock (1995: n. 13) suggests that *of*-phrases in *picture* NPs can be ambiguous between complement and adjunct status.

25. One possible objection is that in (18) the head may contain a PRO controlled by the subject of the relative clause; this would account for anaphor binding in (18a and b) and for the Principle C effect in (18c) without actual reconstruction of the head:

(i)   the [PRO$_i$ image of himself$_i$] that everyone$_i$/Gianni$_i$ tries to convey

(ii)   *the [PRO$_i$ image of Gianni$_i$] that *pro$_i$* tries to convey

It is never possible to realize an overt possessive (**his image of himself*), which suggests that there is no thematic role for the postulated PRO.

26. When the numeral is not preceded by the definite determiner, it has obligatorily wide scope. See Bianchi (1999: 46), Bhatt (2000: 60), and Zamparelli (1997): the common insight is that in thus case, the numeral fills or licenses the external D° position, and hence cannot reconstruct.

27. See Bianchi (1999: 109–129) for a more extensive discussion.

28. The fact that the *null* subject pronoun allows coreference in (21c), as opposed to (20c), remains to be accounted for. It may be related to the fact that the head in which the R-expression is included typically denotes an independently familiar discourse referent (cf. Safir 1999: 613), and the nonrestrictive clause is backgrounded, which makes the information structure very different from that of (20c).

29. See, among others, Schachter (1973); Kayne (1994: 87); Munn (1994: 402); Bianchi (1999: chap. 4); and Safir (1999: 611–614). For the contrary view, see, among others, Cresti (2000), Citko (2000), and Platzack (2000). From now on, the copy-trace will be indicated between angled brackets.

30. See Kayne (1994: chap. 8) and Bianchi (1999).

31. See Pesetsky (1998) for a different approach.

32. The so-called *that*-deletion relative seems to involve a layer of the CP system lower than Force Phrase, and it disallows Topic and Focus phrases; see Bianchi (1999: 175–188).

33. See Grosu (2000) and Sauerland (1998) for two detailed proposals. Sauerland's proposal converges with mine on the core hypothesis that restrictive relative clauses allow for two different LF structures—one involving full reconstruction of the head, and the other not. Sauerland implements this distinction in terms of a "raising" versus "matching" derivation (Sauerland 1998: 62–90).

34. The operator may bind either a degree/amount variable (e.g., in *how-many* phrases) or an individual variable (e.g., in *which* phrases).

35. On the nonspecific interpretation of reconstructed wh-phrases, see Heycock (1995). On the semantic interpretation of reconstructed A' chains, see especially Sauerland (1998) and Ruys (2000).

36. Amount wh-phrases allow for both a nonspecific and a specific interpretation (Frampton 1991; Kroch 1981; Heycock 1995: 559; Kiss 1993: 91, 93; Rizzi 2000). For unclear reasons, amount/degree relatives seem to allow for only a nonspecific interpretation of the head.

37. Rizzi (2000) discusses the fact that nonspecific chains cannot cross weak islands (cf. Frampton 1991). This also holds for maximalizing and nonspecific restrictive relatives:

> (i)   ?*Non ti immagini il tempo che nessuno ha dedicato *t* al progetto!
>   (you) cannot imagine the (amount of) time that nobody has devoted to the project
>
> (ii)   ?*l'immagine di sé che non so a chi Gianni voglia trasmettere
>   the image of himself that (I) do not know to whom Gianni wants to convey

On Rizzi's account, this follows from the trace shrinking mechanism illustrated in (23): the NP restriction is deleted from the highest chain link(s) and shrunk in the lowest one; this yields a non-DP dependency, which cannot cross a weak island—for example, the negative island:

> (iii) *$[_{DP}$ D° ~~NP~~$]_i$ . . . not . . . $[_{DP}$ <D°> NP]

I have assumed that in both maximalizing and nonspecific relative clauses the whole DP head undergoes reconstruction because the relative D° has no quantificational force. This yields the LF representation (iv):

> (iv) $[_{DP}$ D° $[_{CP}$ ~~[DP D_REL NP]~~ [not . . . $[_{DP}$ D_REL NP]]]]

Nevertheless, in (iv) the reconstructed relative DP has to be bound by the external D° at LF for the structure to be interpretable. I tentatively propose that this binding relation is equivalent to the D°–NP relation in (iii) in essential respects, and therefore it, too, is blocked by an intervening weak island boundary.

38. One problem with this hypothesis is that a specific wh-operator should always have wide scope. This is apparently contradicted by an example like (i), where a specific wh-phrase raised to the local Comp can be interpreted in the scope of the universal QP subject, yielding a pair-list reading:

> (i)   Quanti dei libri in programma ha letto *t* ogni studente?   ($\forall$ > wh)
>   how many of-the books in (the) list has read every student
>   'How many of the assigned books did every student read?'

The wide scope of the QP subject in (i) may perhaps be obtained via LF movement of the QP to a position above the Comp layer that hosts the wh-operator.

39. As pointed out by Safir (1999: 595), this account of multiple binding options implies that there is successive cyclic movement even out of a weak island, as in (i):

> (i)   [I pettegolezzi su se stesso$_i$/se stessa$_k$ che Maria$_k$ non sa [<pettegolezzi su se stessa$_k$> da chi Gianni$_i$ abbia sentito <pettegolezzi su se stesso$_i$>]] sono molto offensivi.
>   the gossips about himself/herself that Maria doesn't know from whom Gianni has heard are very offensive

This may be accommodated in the split CP system, assuming that the interrogative phrase in the embedded clause is in the IntP layer, whereas the relative head uses Spec, Force Phrase as an escape hatch.

40. See Fiengo and May (1994: 47ff.) on the distinction between independent and dependent indices.

41. This proposal is somewhat similar to Safir's (1999) "vehicle change" approach, but unlike the latter, it is crucially sensitive to the shrunk/nonshrunk trace opposition. Like Safir's proposal, it does not account for the residual cases of Principle C effects under reconstruction for certain noun complements in specific chains. See Sauerland (1988: chap. 2) for an alternative approach.

This proposal may also be extended to account for antireconstruction effects in A chains, assuming that the copy-occurrences of an R-expression in an A chain also bear dependent indices (see Fox 1999: 192 for recent discussion in a minimalist setting):

(i)   [Every argument that John$_i$ is a genius] seems to him$_i$ <[every argument that John$_i$ is a genius]> to be flawless.

42. The Ground Phrase proposed here is similar to the analogous projection proposed by Poletto and Pollock (chapter 9 in this volume) in that it hosts familiar or "known" material; it differs in that it is here located above the Force Phrase (like the "Frame field" of Beninca' and Poletto (in chapter 3, in this volume), rather than immediately below it, as Poletto and Pollock propose. Perhaps the two proposals can be made compatible; see note 47.

43. However, Heim (1987: 36–37) notes some dialectal variation in this respect; see also Bianchi (1999: n. 3 to chap. 3). The restrictive wh-relative pertains to the formal register, and this fact may influence native speakers' judgments.

44. Åfarli (1994) and Platzack (2000) argue that the wh-relative disallows for anaphor binding under reconstruction of the head. These judgments are doubtful, however (see Bianchi 1999: 71–74).

45. An apparent counterexample to the specificity of the wh-relative is constituted by the possibility of extraposing it, as in (i). Guéron (1980) argues that only non-presuppositional noun phrases allow for extraposition (see also section 7.3).

(i)   I met a man yesterday who I knew in high school.

This issue deserves further investigation, which I cannot undertake here.

46. Alternatively, various authors have argued that the wh-relative involves a non-raising derivation: cf. Åfarli (1994) and Lee (2001).

47. The assumption that the relative DP moves to Spec,FP in the derivation of (40) is motivated by the observation that the relative wh-determiner precedes topics and preposed negative phrases (cf. Bianchi 1999: chap. 6 for discussion). Alternatively, the relative DP could move to some other projection below the Ground Phrase but above TopP (which would be compatible with the system of projections of Poletto and Pollock (in chapter 9 of this volume); I leave this possibility open here. The analysis in (40) requires a revision of the approach proposed in Bianchi (1999) for cross-linguistic variation in the occurrence of wh-versus *that*-relatives, a task that exceeds the limits of the present discussion.

48. See also Beghelli and Stowell's (1997) "Ref Phrase."

49. See Åfarli (1994), Bianchi (1999: chap. 4), and Safir (1999: 613–614) for discussion.

50. The deletion of the lower chain links bears some resemblance to Safir's (1996: 323) resumption conversion rule, which turns a trace into a resumptive pronoun in LF.

L. Rizzi (personal communication) asks whether the A' chain in non-restrictive relatives could be taken to involve a base-generated empty resumptive pronoun and an operator directly merged in Spec,CP. This view is incompatible with Cinque's (1990: 106–108) evidence, which suggests that nonrestrictive relatives are derived by successive cyclic A' movement.

51. I have here revised the analysis proposed in Bianchi (1999: 146–153).

52. Cf. Demirdache (1997: 220–222).

53. NP in Enç (1991). I adopt here the DP hypothesis, and I revise Enç's definitions accordingly.

54. Alternatively, it is possible to assume that the definiteness features are lexically specified on the relative D° and trigger the derivation of the appropriate LF chain. In fact, in some languages specificity is lexically encoded in two different forms of the relative determiner: for example, Hungarian *amit* versus *amelyk* (cf. Szamosi 1976; Horvath 1986: 44ff.). In many languages however, the distinction is not morphologically manifested on the relative determiner. Therefore, I think it is more interesting to relate the definiteness properties to the distinct LF configurations.

55. On the referential import of number and person see also Rizzi (1986: 543). According to the Visibility Hypothesis, the Case feature is also a prerequisite for a phrase to be argumental and referential; I do not discuss this issue here.

56. This hypothesis presupposes that PF rules can spell-out a substructure in the whole feature structure corresponding to the relevant DP category: see section 7.1. for more discussion. An alternative consistent with the raising analysis is the movement approach to (certain instances of) resumption advocated by Aoun and Choueiri (2000) and Aoun et al. (2001).

57. In type I languages, a resumptive pronoun is allowed in some apparently restrictive relative clauses with an indefinite head:

(i) Te imprestarò un pochi de libri che ti pol lezer(*li*) co ti vol.   (Venetian)
     (I) to-you will lend some books that you can read (them) when you want to

(ii) A 'l m'à cüntat sö ü segreto ca 'l gh' (*l'*) ìa mai cüntat sö a nesü.   (Bergamasco)
      he to-me has told a secret that he to-him (it) had never told to nobody

These data may be accounted for by Prince's suggestion that relative clauses with an indefinite head may be pseudo-restrictive: the indefinite head introduces a new discourse referent by itself, "the relative clause serving simply to predicate some property of that entity. . . . The appropriate file card has already been independently constructed/activated" (Prince 1990: 492).

58. One relevant case could be Lebanese Arabic, as described by Aoun et al. (2001): here "apparent resumption" chains allow for Q-binding of pronouns under reconstruction and show Principle C effects; the second property is assumed here to be restricted to nonspecific chains. The Lebanese Arabic data also feature resumptive epithets, which cannot be subsumed under the present approach; it is possible to assume the alternative movement derivation proposed by the authors, whereby apparently resumptive elements originate as appositive modifiers of the A' moved phrase and are stranded in the base position.

59. However, this claim has been called into question by Prince (1990: 485–486) and by Sharvit (1999: n. 5). The problem of the *de dicto* interpretation requires a much deeper investigation than I can undertake here.

60. The analysis proposed here only predicts the *possibility* of occurrence of optional resumptive pronouns in certain structures; what remains to be investigated is the factors that determine the actual realization of the resumptive pronoun. See Prince (1990) for a very interesting proposal from the perspective of discourse functions, and also Bernini (1989: 94) for some suggestions. According to Cennamo (1997), in some type I and type II dialects resumptive pronouns are actually obligatory in nonrestrictive relatives. I have no account for the obligatoriness versus optionality of spell-out in a given LF chain type.

61. In Brazilian Portuguese, there exists an alternative derivation in which the whole PP containing the relativization site undergoes unrecoverable deletion (the so-called *relativa cortadora*). For reasons of space, I cannot discuss this structure here.

62. Example (68a) is taken from Suñer (1998: 358). However, the dative clitic may be an instance of indirect object clitic doubling (see Suñer 1988: 394–395), rather than a true resumptive pronoun.

63. Borer (1984: 234) suggests that the clitic attached to the preposition is an instance of clitic doubling rather than a real resumptive pronoun. However, the contrast between direct object and prepositional object resumptive pronouns in free relatives is also found in Spanish and in Brazilian Portuguese, which have full pronouns as resumptives within PPs; in the discussion in this chapter, the two cases receive a unitary analysis.

64. Ur Shlonsky (personal communication) points out that if the resumptive pronoun is topicalized, the *de dicto* reading becomes impossible. In section 4.5, I analyzed the topicalized resumptive pronoun as the spell-out of a referential index on an intermediate chain link in Spec,TopP. Assume that the *de dicto* reading requires a nonspecific chain, in which all the chain links except for the lowest one are deleted: it follows that spell-out on the intermediate chain link in Spec,TopP will be only possible in a specific chain. However, the scope reconstruction data in Hebrew relatives are not entirely clear and require further investigation; see Sharvit (1999) for detailed discussion from a different viewpoint.

65. Pesetsky only provides examples with restrictive relatives.

66. As pointed out by R. Kayne (personal communication), (72) must be prevented from applying to Icelandic "quirky" PRO (cf. Sigurðhsson 1991). I have no concrete proposal on this point.

67. Their movement derivation also covers the case of resumptive epithets, unlike the present proposal (see also Safir 1999: n. 26 and 27 for relevant discussion). Apparently resumptive epithets and pronouns are analyzed as appositive modifiers of the raised DP; this assumption is plausible for epithets, but much less so for resumptive pronouns that have no descriptive content of their own. Also, appositive modifiers cannot usually be stranded by movement of the modified phrase. In any event, to me it is not obvious that intrusive pronouns and epithets are manifestations of a single phenomenon: in my own idiolect, relative clauses allow for intrusive pronouns but not for intrusive epithets (whereas these are allowed in the Hanging Topic structure).

68. See also Jackendoff (1997) for a thorough discussion and criticism of the T-model. My proposal could be made compatible with multiple spell-out at the phase level (Chomsky 2000, 2001) only if the relevant manipulations of the chain links (deletion of internal structure) could take place "along the way."

69. Although the term "feature structure" is systematically avoided in the minimalist literature, it seems to be implicitly assumed that the feature bundles have internal structure, so that a subset of the features of a given category can be targeted by an Agree/checking operation. Alternatively, Rouveret (1999) analyzes resumptive pronouns as the spell-out of φ-features that have fissioned from a lexical category.

70. I have not attempted to compare this approach to the alternative approach based on functional dependencies.

71. Pointed out by Frampton (1991).

72. From this perspective, weak islands are not selective by themselves: the selectivity is an effect of the possibility or impossibility of a resumptive pronoun in any given extraction.

73. See Bianchi (1993) for a thorough discussion.

References

Åfarli, T. A. (1994) "A Promotion Analysis of Restrictive Relative Clauses." *The Linguistic Review* 11, 81–100.

Aoun, J., and L. Choueiri (2000) "Epithets." *Natural Language and Linguistic Theory* 18, 1–39.

Aoun, J., L. Choueiri, and N. Hornstein (2001) "Resumption, Movement, and Derivational Economy." *Linguistic Inquiry* 32, 371–403.

Babby, L. H. (1987) "Case, Prequantifiers, and Discontinuous Agreement in Russian." *Natural Language and Linguistic Theory* 5.1, 91–138.

Barwise, J., and R. Cooper (1981) "Generalized Quantifiers and Natural Language." *Linguistics and Philosophy* 4, 159–219.

Bayer, J. (1984) "Comp in Bavarian Syntax." *The Linguistic Review* 3.3, 209–274.

Beghelli, F., and T. Stowell (1997) "Distributivity and Negation," in A. Szabolcsi (ed.) *Ways of Scope Taking*. Dordrecht: Kluwer, 71–107.

Benincà, P., and L. Vanelli (1982) "Appunti di sintassi veneta," in M. Cortelazzo (ed.) *Guida ai dialetti veneti 4*. Padua: CLEUP, 9–38.

Bernini, G. (1989) "Tipologia delle frasi relative italiane e romanze." *Atti della Società di Linguistica Italiana* 27. Rome: Bulzoni, 85–98.

Bhatt, R. (2000) "Adjectival Modifiers and the Raising Analysis of Relative Clauses." *North-Eastern Linguistic Society* 30, 55–67.

Bianchi, V. (1993) "An Empirical Contribution to the Study of Idiomatic Expressions." *Rivista di Linguistica* 5, 349–385.

————— (1999) *Consequences of Antisymmetry: Headed Relative Clauses*. Berlin: Mouton de Gruyter.

Borer, H. (1984) "Restrictive Relatives in Modern Hebrew." *Natural Language and Linguistic Theory* 2, 219–260.

Borsley, R. D. (1997) "Relative Clauses and the Theory of Phrase Structure." *Linguistic Inquiry* 28, 629–647.

Brody, M. (1995) *Lexico-logical Form: A Radically Minimalist Theory*. Cambridge, Mass.: MIT Press.

Broihier, K. (1995) "Optimality-theoretic Rankings with Tied Constraints: Slavic Relatives, Resumptive Pronouns and Learnability." Unpublished ms., Department of Brain and Cognitive Sciences, MIT. ROA-46.

Carlson, G. (1977) "Amount Relatives." *Language* 53, 520–542.

Cennamo, M. (1997) "Relative Clauses," in M. Maiden and M. Parry (eds.) *Dialects of Italy*. London; Routledge, 190–201.

Chomsky, N. (1993) "A Minimalist Program for Linguistic Theory," in K. Hale and S. J. Keyser (eds.) *The View from Building 20: Essays in Linguistics in Honor of Sylvain Bromberger*. Cambridge, Mass.: MIT Press; 1–52.

—————. (1995) *The Minimalist Program*. Cambridge, Mass: MIT Press.

—————. (1998) "Minimalist Inquiries: The Framework." *MIT Occasional Papers in Linguistics*, 15.

—————. (2000) "Minimalist inquiries: the framework," in R. Martin, D. Michaels, and J. Uriagereka (eds.) *Step by Step: Essays in minimalist Syntax in Honor of Howard Lasnik*. Cambridge, Mass.: MIT Press, 89–155.

—————. (2001) "Derivation by Phase," in M. Kenstowicz (ed.) *Ken Hale: A Life in Language*. Cambridge, Mass: MIT Press, 1–50.

Cinque, G. (1981) "On Keenan and Comrie's Primary Relativization Constraint." *Linguistic Inquiry* 12, 293–308.

—————. (1990) *Types of A' Dependencies*. Cambridge, Mass.: MIT Press.

Citko, B. (2000) "Deletion under Identity in Relative Clauses." *North-Eastern Linguistic Society* 31, 131–145.

Collins, C. (1997) *Local Economy*. Cambridge, Mass.: MIT Press.

Cresti, D. (2000) "Ellipsis and Reconstruction in Relative Clauses." *North-Eastern Linguistic Society* 30, 153–162.

Culicover, P. and R. Jackendoff (1995) "Something Else for the Binding Theory." *Linguistic Inquiry* 26, 249–275.

Demirdache, H. (1997) "Dislocation, Resumption, and Weakest Crossover," in E. Anagnostopoulou et al. (eds.), *Materials on Left Dislocation*. Amsterdam: John Benjamins, 193–231.

Diesing, M. (1992) *Indefinites*. Cambridge, Mass.: MIT Press.

Doron, E. (1982) "On the Syntax and Semantics of Resumptive Pronouns." *Texas Linguistic Forum* 19, 1–48.

Emonds, J. (1979) "Appositive Relatives Have No Properties." *Linguistic Inquiry* 10, 211–243.

Enç, M. (1991) "The Semantics of Specificity." *Linguistic Inquiry* 22, 1–25.

Epstein, S. D., E. M. Groat, R. Kawashima, and H. Kitahara (1998) *A Derivational Approach to Syntactic Relations*. New York: Oxford University Press.

Fiengo, R., and R. May (1994) *Indices and Identity*. Cambridge, Mass.: MIT Press.

Fox, D. (1999) "Reconstruction, Binding Theory, and the Interpretation of Chains." *Linguistic Inquiry* 30, 157–197.

——— (2000) *Economy and Semantic Interpretation*. Cambridge, Mass.: MIT Press.

Frampton, J. (1991) "Relativized Minimality: A Review." *Linguistic Review* 8, 1–46.

Groat, E., and J. O'Neil (1996) "Spell-Out at the LF Interface," in W. Abraham et al. (eds.) *Minimal Ideas*. Amsterdam: John Benjamins, 113–139.

Grosu, A. (2000) "Type-Resolution in Relative Constructions: Featural Marking and Dependency Encoding," in A. Alexiadou, P. Law, A. Meinunger, and C. Wilder (eds.) *The Syntax of Relative Clauses*. Amsterdam: John Benjamins, 83–119.

Grosu, A., and F. Landman (1998) "Strange Relatives of the Third Kind." *Natural Language Semantics* 6, 125–170.

Guéron, J. (1980) "On the Syntax and Semantics of PP Extraposition." *Linguistic Inquiry* 11, 637–677.

Harbert, W. (1982/3) "On the Nature of the Matching Parameter." *The Linguistic Review* 2, 237–284.

Heim, I. (1982) "The Semantics of Definite and Indefinite Noun Phrases," Ph.D. diss. University of Massachusetts at Amherst.

——— (1987) "Where Does the Definiteness Restriction Apply? Evidence from the Definiteness of Variables," in E. Reuland and A. ter Meulen (eds.) *The Representation of (In)definiteness*. Cambridge, Mass.: MIT Press, 21–42.

Heycock, C. (1995) "Asymmetries in Reconstruction." *Linguistic Inquiry* 26, 547–570.

Heycock, C., and A. Kroch (1999) "Pseudocleft Connectivity: Implications for the LF Interface." *Linguistic Inquiry* 30.3, 365–397.

Horvath, J. (1986) *Focus in the Theory of Grammar and the Syntax of Hungarian*. Dordrecht: Foris.

Jackendoff, R. (1992) "Mme. Tussaud Meets the Binding Theory." *Natural Language and Linguistic Theory* 10, 1–31.

——— (1997) *The Architecture of the Language Faculty*. Cambridge, Mass.: MIT Press.

Johnson, K., and S. Lappin (1997) "A Critique of the Minimalist Program." *Linguistics and Philosophy* 20, 273–333.

Kayne, R. S. (1994) *The Antisymmetry of Syntax*. Cambridge, Mass.: MIT Press.

Keenan, E., and B. Comrie (1977) "Noun Phrase Accessibility and Universal Grammar." *Linguistic Inquiry* 8, 63–99.

Kiss, K. (1993) "Wh-movement and Specificity." *Natural Language and Linguistic Theory* 11, 85–120.

Kroch, A. (1981) "On the Role of Resumptive Pronouns in Amnestying Island Constraint Violations." *Chicago Linguistic Society* 17, 125–135.

Lee, F. (2001) "Relative Clauses without Wh-Movement." *North-Eastern Linguistic Society* 31, 321–332.

Longobardi, G. (1986) "L'estrazione dalle isole e lo scope dei sintagmi quantificati," in *Parallela 2, Aspetti della sintassi dell'italiano contemporaneo*. Tuebingen: Gunter Narr.

McCloskey, J. (1990) "Resumptive Pronouns, A'-Binding, and Levels of Representation in Irish," in R. Hendrick (ed.) *Syntax and Semantics 23: The Syntax of Modern Celtic Languages*. New York: Academic Press, 199–248.

Milsark, G. (1977) "Toward an Explanation of Certain Peculiarities of the Existential Construction in English." *Linguistic Analysis* 3, 1–30.

Munn, A. (1994) "A Minimalist Account of Reconstruction Asymmetries." *North-Eastern Linguistic Society* 24, 397–410.

Pesetsky, D. (1998) "Some Optimality Principles of Sentence Pronounciation," in P. Barbosa et al. (eds.) *Is the Best Good Enough?* Cambridge, Mass.: MIT Press, 337–383.

Platzack, C. (2000) "A Complement-of-N° Account of Restrictive and Non-Restrictive Relatives: The Case of Swedish," in A. Alexiadou, P. Law, A. Meinunger, and C. Wilder (eds.) *The Syntax of Relative Clauses*. Amsterdam: John Benjamins, 265–308.

Pollard, C., and I. Sag. (1994) *Head-Driven Phrase Structure Grammar*. Stanford: CSLI Publications.

Postal, P. M. (1994) "Contrasting Extraction Types." *Journal of Linguistics* 30, 159–186.

——— (1998) *Three Investigations of Extraction*. Cambridge, Mass.: MIT Press.

Prince, E. (1990) "Syntax and Discourse: A Look at Resumptive Pronouns." *Berkeley Linguistic Society* 16, 482–497.

Reinhart, T. (1987) "Specifier and Operator Binding," in E. Reuland and A. ter Meulen (eds.) *The Representation of (In)definiteness*. Cambridge, Mass.: MIT Press, 130–167.

Reinhart, T., and E. Reuland (1993) "Reflexivity." *Linguistic Inquiry* 24, 657–720.

Rizzi, L. (1986) "Null Objects in Italian and the Theory of *pro*." *Linguistic Inquiry* 17, 501–557.

——— (1990) *Relativized Minimality*. Cambridge, Mass.: MIT Press.

——— (1997) "The Fine Structure of the Left Periphery," in L. Haegeman (ed.) *Elements of Grammar*. Dordrecht: Kluwer, 281–337.

——— (1999) "On the Position 'Int(errogative)' in the Left Periphery of the Clause." Unpublished ms., University of Siena. Available at http://www.ciscl.unisi.it/pubblicazioni.php

——— (2000) "Reconstruction, Weak Island Sensitivity, and Agreement." Unpublished ms., University of Siena. Available at http://www.ciscl.unisi.it/pubblicazioni.php

Rouveret, A. (1990) "X-bar Theory, Minimality, and Barrierhood in Welsh," in *Syntax and Semantics 23: The Syntax of Modern Celtic Languages*. New York: Academic Press, 27–79.

——— (1999) "A Derivational Analysis of Celtic Relatives." Conference handout.

Ruys, E. (2000) "Weak Crossover as a Scope Phenomenon." *Linguistic Inquiry* 31, 513–539.

Safir, K. (1986) "Relative Clauses in a Theory of Binding and Levels." *Linguistic Inquiry* 17, 663–689.

——— (1996) "Derivation, Representation, and the Domain of Weak Crossover." *Linguistic Inquiry* 27, 313–340.

——— (1999) "Vehicle Change and Reconstruction in A' chains." *Linguistic Inquiry* 30, 587–620.

Sauerland, U. (1998) "The Meaning of Chains." Ph.D. diss. MIT, Cambridge, Mass..

Schachter, P. (1973) "Focus and Relativization." *Language* 49, 19–46.

Sells, P. (1987a) "Binding Resumptive Pronouns." *Linguistics and Philosophy* 10, 261–298.

——— (1987b) "Aspects of Logophoricity." *Linguistic Inquiry* 18, 445–479.

Sharvit, Y. (1999) "Resumptive Pronouns in Relative Clauses." *Natural Language and Linguistic Theory* 17, 587–612.

Shlonsky, U. (1992) "Resumptive Pronouns as a Last Resort." *Linguistic Inquiry* 23, 443–468.

Sigurðsson, H. A. (1991) "Icelandic Case-marked PRO and the Licensing of Lexical Arguments." *Natural Language and Linguistic Theory* 9, 327–363.

Solan, L. (1984) "Focus and Levels of Representation." *Linguistic Inquiry* 15, 174–178.

Suñer, M. (1988) "The Role of Agreement in Clitic-Doubled Constructions." *Natural Language and Linguistic Theory* 6, 391–434.

—— (1992) "Subject Clitics in the Northern Italian Vernaculars and the Matching Hypothesis." *Natural Language and Linguistic Theory* 10, 641–672.

—— (1998) "Resumptive Restrictive Relatives: A Crosslinguistic Perspective." *Language* 74, 335–364.

Szabolcsi, A. (1994) "The Noun Phrase," in F. Kiefer & K. É. Kiss (eds.) Syntax and Semantics 27: *The Syntactic Structure of Hungarian*. New York: Academic Press.

Szamosi, M. (1976) "On a Surface Structure Constraint in Hungarian," in J. McCawley (ed.) *Syntax and Semantics 7: Notes from the Linguistic Underground*. New York: Academic Press, 409–425.

van Riemsdijk, H. (1989) "Swiss Relatives," in D. Jaspers et al. (eds.) *Sentential Complementation and the Lexicon*. Dordrecht: Foris, 343–354.

Vergnaud, J. R., and M. L. Zubizarreta (1992) "The Definite Determiner and the Inalienable Constructions in French and English." *Linguistic Inquiry* 23, 595–652.

Zamparelli, R. (1997) "Small Clauses: Modification and Predication." Paper presented at the *XXIII Incontro di Grammatica Generativa*. Pisa, Scuola Normale Superiore.

5

Toward a Cartography of Subject Positions

ANNA CARDINALETTI

This chapter aims to contribute to the current debate on clause structure by discussing the distribution of subjects. Starting from Chomsky (1981, 1986), the sentences in (1) have been assigned the basic clause structure in (2). The preverbal DP position accounts for the distribution of the thematic subject *a man* in (1a and b) and the expletive subject *there* in (1c). In (1c), the grammatical subject *a man* occupies the complement DP position of the unaccusative verb *come*:

(1) a. A man called (me).
     b. A man came.
     c. There came a man.

(2) $[_{IP}$ DP Infl $[_{VP}$ V DP$]$ $]$

Since then, much work on subjects has shown that this view is too simplistic. A thematic, VP-internal subject position has been argued for also in the case of transitive and intransitive verbs (Koopman and Sportiche 1991, among many others), and a middlefield subject position, specTP in a split Infl model, has been proposed to account for the intermediate placing of the subject in Transitive Expletive Constructions (TECs) in Icelandic (Bobaljik and Jonas 1996) (see (7a) below).

Comparative research indicates that this does not exhaust the distribution of subjects yet: natural languages dispose of other preverbal and postverbal subject positions. In this chapter I concentrate on the preverbal subject field, which seems to be rather homogeneous across languages. The discussion of the postverbal field will be rather sketchy; it displays massive language variation, which is still poorly understood and cannot be addressed here.

Two important conclusions are arrived at in this essay:

1. The preverbal subject field is more complex than usually thought, and more than one subject position should be assumed. The properties attributed to preverbal subjects (being the subject of predication, checking the EPP feature, checking ϕ-features, checking nominative case) can be distributed across discrete functional projections, each of which realizes a feature or a set of features. This work confirms the observation by McCloskey (1997: 197) that there is "a progressive deconstruction of the traditional category 'subject' so that the properties which are supposed to define it are distributed across a range of distinct (but derivationally linked) syntactic entities and positions."

2. The preverbal subject field has the same properties in null-subject (NSLs) and non-null-subject languages (non-NSLs). This conclusion is particularly important as it allows us to keep the difference between NSLs and non-NSLs to a minimum.

I reject the proposals according to which the preverbal subject of a NSL has a different status with respect to the subject in (1a and b), and I show that preverbal subject positions are necessary in NSLs for both null and overt subjects. The difference between the two types of languages reduces to the nature of the agreement head, which in the former languages, but not in the latter, is able to legitimate a null subject (Taraldsen 1978; Rizzi 1986). In turn, this has the advantage of restricting parametric variation to morphological properties of heads, as in the seminal proposal by Borer (1984).

The chapter is organized as follows. In section 1, an overview is provided of the postverbal subject positions. The thematic VP-internal subject position should be distinguished from higher, middlefield subject positions. In section 2, the preverbal subject field is introduced. Two subject positions are proposed: the higher one, which I call specSubjP, hosts the subject of predication; the lower one, which corresponds to the traditional specAgrSP, hosts the grammatical subject. In section 3, it is shown that XPs other than nominative DPs can occupy specSubjP, which independently argues for its existence. Since different features are checked in the two subject positions, it is expected that these positions host different types of subjects. This is shown in section 4, where the distribution of strong versus weak, null versus overt, referential versus nonreferential, and quantified versus nonquantified subjects is discussed. In section 5, the analysis is extended to account for the distribution of subjects in languages other than Italian. The properties of the two subject positions are discussed in detail in section 6, which also addresses the distribution of subjects in wh-questions and with respect to adverbs. Both subject positions are located in the Infl domain, and the subject-in-Comp hypothesis should be rejected. It is also shown that the preverbal subject field is homogeneous across languages and that NSLs do not display any peculiarities in the distribution of (preverbal) subjects with respect to non-NSLs. In section 7, some semantic issues are addressed. The interpretation of sentences without any subject of predication is said to occur at the semantic interface. The existence of three morphologically different subject pronouns in languages like Italian is accounted for in terms of the subject-of-predication feature. Finally, the subject-of-predication feature is compared with the EPP. The tentative conclusion is that these two properties should be expressed in two distinct functional projections.

1.   On the postverbal subject positions

1.1.   The VP-internal subject position

Since the earliest work on comparative syntax, the need for postulating another postverbal position in addition to the one in (1c) has arisen. In NSLs, any verb allows for the subject to stay postverbally:

(3)   a. (Mi) ha chiamato un uomo.
      b.*there called (me) a man

(4)   a. Ha comprato il giornale Gianni.
      b.*there bought the newspaper Gianni.

The position of the subject in the (a) sentences has been identified with a rightward VP-adjoined position (Rizzi 1982; Samek-Lodovici 1994), with a rightward specVP (Bonet 1990; Giorgi and Longobardi 1991; Saccon 1993), and with the rightward specifier of a Focus projection immediately above VP (Belletti and Shlonsky 1995). In all these proposals, such postverbal positions exist only in those languages that allow postverbal subjects. After the seminal work of Kayne (1994), which excludes rightward adjunctions and specifiers, a more restrictive approach has become possible. The position of the subject in (3a) and (4a) is simply the thematic position of the subject, or (leftward) specVP (Ordóñez 1997, 1998 for Spanish; Cornilescu 1997 for Romanian; Cardinaletti 1998 for Italian). Languages with postverbal subjects thus differ from those without in that in the former, but not in the latter, the subject remains in its thematic position.[1] These proposals make Romance languages very similar to those VSO languages whose subjects, assuming the VP-Internal Subject Hypothesis, have been claimed to occur VP-internally (cf. Koopman and Sportiche 1991 and McCloskey 1991, 1997 among others).

In (3a) and (4a), the linearly postverbal position of the subject is due to verb movement; in (4a), object movement across the subject must also be assumed. A postverbal subject can also occur in the word order in (5), where it is followed by a marginalized object (Antinucci and Cinque 1977)—that is, an object destressed in its base position (cf. Cardinaletti 1998).[2]

(5)   Ha letto GIANNI il giornale.
      has read Gianni the newspaper

A universal property of the thematic specVP position is that it cannot host weak pronouns—neither overt nor null (see Cardinaletti 1997a: §2 for discussion).

1.2.   The middlefield subject positions

In some languages, the subject can also occur in a "middlefield" (MF) subject position, which occurs to the left of other arguments of the verb. Example (6a) provides a Spanish example (taken from Ordóñez 1997:31); the sentences in (6b,c) show that the same word order is ungrammatical in Italian and Catalan (Catalan example from Bonet 1990: 6).[3]

(6)   a. Ayer ganó Juan la lotería.
         yesterday won Juan the lottery
      b.*Ha letto Gianni/lui il giornale.
         has read Gianni/he the newspaper
      c.*Va córrer en Lluís la marató.
         ran the Lluís the marathon

The reason for this language variation is still poorly understood. The characterization of the MF subject position is also unclear. Some scholars have proposed that it is an extra Case position (Belletti 1998: 15), while others assume that it lacks case. Ordóñez (1997: §3.4) takes the subject in (6a) to occur in specNeutP, a position hosting neutral subjects; Suñer (2000: 16) takes the subject position in (6a) to be specAspP.

It might be promising to look at (6a) as parallel to the Germanic Transitive Expletive Construction (TEC) in (7a) (Bobalijk and Jonas 1996; Chomsky 1995), and to the Hebrew construction in (7b) (Shlonsky 2000: 327).

(7)   a. Það luku sennilega einhverjir stúdentar alveg verkefninu.   (Icelandic)
         it finished probably some students completely the.assignment
      b. 'Eyn Rina mədaberet heitev rusit.   (Hebrew)
         not Rina speak-FS well Russian

Notice that in (6a)/(7a) on the one hand and (7b) on the other, the subject occupies a different location with respect to the verb and that in (7b), it is, strictly speaking, not postverbal. This difference can be due to the different scope of verb movement in Spanish and Icelandic on the one hand and Hebrew on the other, or it can be considered evidence for assuming the existence of more than one MF subject position. Adverb placement shows that the two possibilities are not incompatible. See Cinque (1999: §5.1) and Suñer (2000: 16), from which the following examples are taken (also see section 6.3).

(8)   a. Ya habían los estudiantes terminado todos el exámen cuando ...
         already had the students finished all the exam when ...
      b. El año pasado habían tres estudiantes terminado rápidamente todos les exámenes
         cuando ...
         the year past had three students finished rapidly all the exams when ...
      c. El año pasado habían terminado rápidamente tres estudiantes todos les exámenes
         cuando ...
         the year past had finished rapidly three students all the exams when ...

Understanding the function of each MF subject position must be left for future research. The only conclusion we are able to draw here, if the parallelism with TECs is on the right track, is that one of the MF projections could be the one responsible for nominative case checking. The subject position in TECs is taken to be a nominative case position (with the ancillary assumption that nominative case checking and φ-feature checking take place in two different heads) (Bobaljik and Jonas 1996: 228).

If this is correct, the reason of the language variation exemplified in (6) and (7) should be searched in the way DP movement takes place. In languages such as Spanish, overt checking of nominative case does not imply further movement to specAgrSP to check φ-features overtly, while in other languages—e.g., Italian—overt checking of case implies overt checking of φ-features as well. I do not pursue these issues here.

Although, as shown in in (6b), subjects cannot appear in the MF of finite clauses, Italian allows for pronominal subjects to occur in the MF of infinitival clauses:

(9)   a. Sperava [di intervenire *Giovanni/*lui* [a risolvere il problema]]. (Burzio 1986: 104f)
         hoped to intervene Giovanni/he to solve the problem
     b. [Andarci *Giovanni/*noi*] sarebbe un errore. (Burzio 1986: 114)
         go-there Giovanni/we would-be a mistake
     c. Vorrei chiederti se ti farebbe piacere [aprire *tu* il congressino]. (Vincent 1999)
         [I] would-like [to] ask-you if [it] you would please [[to] open you the workshop]

In Cardinaletti (1999), it is proposed that pronouns differ from DPs in that they can be intrinsically case-marked. Intrinsic case-marking can be understood as the capability of undergoing DP-internal case-checking (NP or DP moves to the highest projection in the noun phrase, which contains Case features and corresponds to CP in clauses; see Cardinaletti and Starke 1999: §5.2). This may dispense pronouns from undergoing DP-external case-checking—case-checking at the clausal level—and, consequently, it allows them to occur in contexts such as infinitivals, where external case-checking is not available.

The Italian-internal contrast between (6b) and (9) might also suggest that the MF subject positions are specialized to host different types of subjects (e.g., DPs versus pronouns). As discussed in section 4, this is a property of preverbal subject positions. The specialization of the MF subject positions is confirmed by the following data from Hebrew. Although both subject DPs and pronouns can follow the negative element *'eyn* (not), as shown in (10), in negative equative sentences only pronominal subjects are allowed, as shown in (11) (Shlonsky 2000: 342).

(10)   a. 'Eyn Rina mədaberet rusit.
         not Rina speaks Russian
     b. 'Eyn hi mədaberet rusit.
         not she speaks Russian
     c. 'Eyn ze kaše lə-daber rusit.
         not it difficult to-speak Russian

(11)   a.*'Eyn Rina gveret Levi.
         not Rina Mrs. Levi
     b. 'Eyn hi gveret Levi.
         not she Mrs. Levi
         'She is not Mrs. Levi.'

As suggested by Shlonsky, in (11) the MF subject position that hosts DPs is occupied by the predicative DP *gveret Levi*, which bans the occurrence of a DP subject. Since pronominal subjects are grammatical, they must occur in a position higher than DP subjects. As shown by the nonreferential pronoun *ze* in (10c), a pronoun following *'eyn* can be weak.

Spanish subjects have a similar distribution. An unstressed, weak pronoun necessarily precedes other complements of the verb, (12a and b), and differs in this respect from the strong counterpart found in, for example, contrastive focalization and coordination, (12c and d) (Ordóñez 1997: §2.4.4).

(12)   a. ¿Qué les compró él a sus hermanos?
          what to-them bought he to his siblings?
       b. ??¿Qué les compró a sus hermanos él?
       c. ¿Qué les compró a sus hermanos EL?
       d. ¿Qué les compró a sus hermanos él y su hermana?
          what to-them bought to his siblings he and his sister?

Furthermore, Hebrew provides evidence to distinguish between overt and null subject pronouns: the former can occur in the MF, as shown in (10b and c) and (11b), while the latter cannot, as shown in (13) (Shlonsky 2000: 328).

(13) *'Eyn kar.
       not cold
       'It isn't cold.'

Similar conclusions hold for Spanish. Although in (12a), an overt weak pronoun can occur in a MF subject position, *pro* seems to occur in the preverbal AgrSP subfield (see section 2). The arguments that *pro* is preverbal, discussed in Burzio (1986), Rizzi (1987), and Cardinaletti (1997a: §2) for Italian, hold for Spanish as well. In conclusion, weak pronouns must be case-licensed (Cardinaletti and Starke 1999), while null subjects undergo the further requirement that they must be licensed by a head realizing ϕ-features (Rizzi 1986).

Without attempting to provide the MF subject positions with a label, the following is a picture of the configurational space needed to account for the many postverbal subject positions individuated so far (the asterisk indicates that the ?P projection is recursive).

(14)	*spec??P*	*??°*	*spec?P*	*?°**	*specVP*	*V°*
	Weak pronouns		DPs		DPs	
	*pro		Strong pronouns		Strong pronouns	
			Predicative DPs			

2.   On the preverbal subject field

The preverbal subject position assumed in (2) must be split into a number of preverbal subject positions, specialized to host different subjects. The core of the proposal is summarized in (15):[4]

(15) [$_{SubjP}$ [$_{AgrSP}$* [$_{TP}$ . . . [. . . [$_{VP}$ . . .]]]]]

This makes two distinct, though related, claims:

- First, there exists more than one preverbal subject position. The two properties attributed to (preverbal) subjects—that is, being the grammatical subject according to morphosyntactic criteria and being the semantic subject—are attributed to two distinct functional projections: AgrSP and SubjP, respectively. AgrSP is the projection in which φ-features are checked on nominative DPs; this results in nominative case on the subject DP and verb agreement with the subject DP. SubjP is the projection in which the "subject-of-predication" feature is checked. In this way, the semantic property of subjects is encoded in the syntax through a morphosyntactic feature.[5] In turn, AgrSP can be split into discrete projections realizing different φ-features (see section 4.5).

- Second, the two projections superficially host different types of subjects: while specSubjP typically hosts strong subjects, SpecAgrSP typically hosts weak subjects ("strong" and "weak" in the sense of Cardinaletti and Starke 1999). Referentiality can also be a relevant feature, though interconnected with the weak/strong distinction. Nonreferential subjects, which are only weak, are restricted to the specAgrSP position. Referential subjects, which can be either weak or strong, can occur in either position.

The derivation of sentences containing preverbal subjects looks as follows. Weak subjects such as the Italian null subject *pro* only check nominative case and φ-features and occur in specAgrSP. Strong subjects such as DPs and Italian strong pronouns like *lui* continue their derivation to specSubjP since they also check the subject-of-predication feature (see section 7.1 for further discussion). For the peculiar properties of subject pronouns such as *egli*, which behave syntactically like weak pronouns, but pattern with DPs and strong pronouns with respect to the subject of predication property, see sections 4.2 and 7.2.

(16) a. [$_{SubjP}$ [$_{AgrSP}$ *pro*$_i$ Vfin [. . . [$_{VP}$ t$_i$]]]]
      b. [$_{SubjP}$ *Gianni$_i$/lui$_i$/egli$_i$* [$_{AgrSP}$ t$_i$ Vfin [. . . [$_{VP}$ t$_i$]]]]

The dissociation of the subject-of-predication feature and the nominative case feature has the advantage of denying that there is a semantic feature associated with nominative case. This complies with the idea that structural Case, contrary to inherent Case, has no semantic import.

Both subject positions are situated below the lowest Comp-projection FinP (Rizzi 1997) and thus occur in the Infl domain (see section 6.1). The articulation of the clause looks as follows:

(17)   ForceP TopP* FocusP FinP   SubjP AgrSP TP . . .   VP

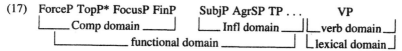

As will become clear in the following sections, the proposal in (15) holds for all languages and does not distinguish between NSLs and non-NSLs. The preverbal subject field looks more uniform across languages than the postverbal subject field. Although the difference between the preverbal and the postverbal subject fields in this respect is still mysterious, the conclusion that the preverbal subject field is cross-linguistically uniform has the advantage of minimizing the difference between NSLs and non-NSLs, in compliance with the poverty of stimulus paradox. The difference reduces to the nature of the agreement head, which in the former languages, but not in the latter, is able to license a null subject.

3. Evidence for the specSubjP position

If the two properties of subjects (checking nominative case and φ-features and being the subject of predication) are dissociated, we expect XPs to occur in the subject position without checking nominative case and φ-features. This is found in a number of constructions where a constituent different from the subject is fronted to what seems to be the subject position. These include dative fronting with a class of psych verbs, PP fronting with other unaccusative verbs, and inverse copular sentences.

3.1. Dative fronting with psych verbs

Psych verbs of the *piacere* class (*interessare* 'interest', *piacere* 'please', *venir voglia di* 'feel like', etc.) are unaccusative verbs that select a theme and a dative experiencer. Either the theme or the experiencer can be preposed to the preverbal position (Calabrese 1986; Belletti and Rizzi 1988):

(18)   a. La musica piaceva molto a Gianni.
            the music 'pleased' much to Gianni
        b. A Gianni piaceva molto la musica.
            to Gianni 'pleased' much the music
            'Gianni liked music a lot.'

The dative experiencer differs from other dative arguments and behaves like a subject. In Aux-to-Comp and complementizer-deletion (CD) constructions, which do not allow left-dislocated items, a dative experiencer is grammatical, but the dative argument of a transitive verb, which is necessarily left-dislocated, is not.[6]

(19)   a. Essendo a Gianni piaciuto molto il regalo, ...
            being to Gianni 'pleased' much the gift ...
        b.*Avendo(gli) {io}a Gianni {io}dato questi libri, ...
            having(to-him) (I) to Gianni (I) given these books ...
        c.*Avendo(gli) a Gianni dato questi libri, ...
            having(to-him) to Gianni [I] given these books ...

(20)   a. Credevo a Gianni piacessero queste storie.
            [I] believed to Gianni 'pleased' these stories
        b. ??Credevo a Gianni (gli) avesse dato questi libri.
            [I] believed to Gianni [she] (to-him) had given these books

The fronted dative can be taken to occur in the preverbal subject position (Belletti and Rizzi 1988), but it checks neither case nor φ-features. Its movement to the preverbal subject position looks unmotivated. The structure proposed in (15) circumvents this problem. The dative argument moves to the preverbal position specSubjP to check the subject-of-predication feature. Nominative case and φ-features are checked by the postverbal theme: via a chain with the expletive *pro* in specAgrSP (Chomsky 1986), via covert movement (Chomsky 1995), or long-distance agreement (Chomsky 1998, 1999):

(21) $[_{SubjP}$ a Gianni$_i$ $[_{AgrSP}$ *pro*$_{expl}$ piaceva$_k$ [molto [$_{VP}$ t$_i$ t$_k$ la musica]]]]

The preceding analysis is strenghtened by the cases in which a dative experiencer occurs with a referential null subject. Since *pro* occupies the preverbal subject position (see Burzio 1986; Rizzi 1987; Cardinaletti 1997a: §2), the dative must occupy a different position:

(22)   A Gianni *pro* piaceva molto.
       to Gianni   'pleased' much

Note that, as in the case of a postverbal subject in (19)–(20), the dative behaves like a subject in that it can occur in the constructions that disallow left-dislocation, such as Aux-to-Comp and CD:[7]

(23)   a. Essendo a Gianni piaciuto molto, ...
         being to Gianni [it] 'pleased' much . . .
     b. Credevo a Gianni piacessero.
         [I] believed to Gianni [they] 'pleased'

To reconcile the "subjecthood" of dative experiencers with the presence of a preverbal null subject, the more articulated clause structure proposed in section 2 can be used to account for these cases as well. The internal argument *pro* moves to specAgrSP, whereas the dative experiencer moves to specSubjP. Example (22) has the structure in (24):

(24)   [$_{SubjP}$ a Gianni$_i$ [$_{AgrSP}$ *pro*$_j$ piaceva$_k$ [molto [$_{VP}$ t$_i$ t$_k$ t$_j$]]]]

3.2. Dative fronting with other unaccusative verbs

Other unaccusative verbs behave like *piacere*: *capitare* (happen), *mancare* (be missing). The dative argument appears preverbally, whereas the grammatical subject, a theme, stays in situ in postverbal position (Belletti and Rizzi 1988: 341). The subjecthood tests used earlier can be repeated here: the preverbal dative is allowed in Aux-to Comp and CD constructions.

(25)   a. A Gianni è capitata una grande disgrazia.
         to Gianni is happened a big misfortune
     b. Essendo a Gianni capitata una grande disgrazia ...
         being to Gianni happened a big misfortune . . .
     c. Credo a Gianni sia capitata una grande disgrazia.
         [I] believe to Gianni is happened a big misfortune

As with *piacere*, a null subject is allowed in the structure, and the preposed PP still behaves like a subject, as shown in (26). As depicted in the structure in (27), the PP occurs in specSubjP, and the null subject occupies the lower of the two subject positions.

(26)   a. A Gianni capita spesso, ultimamente.
         to Gianni [it] happens often lately
     b. Essendo a Gianni capitata l'anno scorso, ...
         being to Gianni [it] happened last year . . .
     c. Credo a Gianni sia capitata l'anno scorso.
         [I] believe to Gianni [it] is happened last year

(27) a. [$_{SubjP}$ a Gianni$_i$ [$_{AgrSP}$ pro_{expl} è capitata   [$_{VP}$ t$_i$ una grande disgrazia]]]
      b. [$_{SubjP}$ a Gianni$_i$ [$_{AgrSP}$ pro_j capita spesso [$_{VP}$ t$_i$ t$_j$]]]

3.3. Dative fronting with unergative verbs

As pointed out to me by L. Rizzi, PP fronting is marginally possible with unergative verbs, as shown by the Aux-to-C test:

(28) ?Avendo a Gianni (già) parlato Maria, ...
      having to Gianni already spoken Maria . . .

In (28), PP fronting is not an instance of PP scrambling (note 14), since the PP competes with a preverbal subject.

(29) a.*Avendo a Gianni Maria (già) parlato, ...
      b.*Avendo Maria a Gianni (già) parlato, ...

Dative PPs differ from direct objects, which cannot be moved to SubjP. This holds for both theme and experiencer objects (Belletti and Rizzi 1988).

(30) a.*Avendo il mio libro letto Gianni, ...
      having the my book read Gianni . . .
      b.*Avendo Gianni preoccupato questo, ...
      having Gianni worried this . . .
      (cf. *Avendo questo preoccupato Gianni, ...*)

The constraint on the possible filler of SubjP can be formulated in terms of case. The difference between (28) and (30) concerns the type of case checked by the preposed XP, a structural and an inherent case, respectively. While DPs with inherent case (e.g., datives) can be fronted, DPs with structural case cannot. This hypothesis is confirmed by the fact that an experiencer marked with inherent accusative can be the subject of predication in, for example, German: cf. *Ihn dürstet* 'him is-thirsty' (He is thirsty). Notice that the accusative pronoun in sentence-initial position behaves like a subject and not as a topic; see Cardinaletti (1994a: 84–86) for discussion.

3.4. Locative fronting

Other unaccusative verbs allow their locative argument to be fronted to the subject position. The paradigms seen above with datives can be reproduced with locatives, as shown in (31) and (32). The relevant structures are provided in (33).[8]

(31) a. Su Gianni cadde una grande disgrazia.
      on Gianni fell a big misfortune
      b. Essendo su Gianni caduta una grande disgrazia, ...
      being on Gianni fallen a big misfortune . . .
      c. Credo su Gianni sia caduta una grande disgrazia, ...
      [I] believe on Gianni is fallen big misfortune . . .

(32) a. Su Gianni è caduta l'anno scorso.
      on Gianni [it] is fallen last year
      b. Essendo su Gianni caduta l'anno scorso, ...
      being on Gianni [it] fallen last year . . .

c. Credo su Gianni sia caduta l'anno scorso, ...
[I] believe on Gianni [it] is fallen last year

(33) a. [$_{SubjP}$ su Gianni$_i$ [$_{AgrSP}$ *pro*$_{expl}$ cadde   [$_{VP}$ t$_i$ una grande disgrazia]]]
      b. [$_{SubjP}$ su Gianni$_i$ [$_{AgrSP}$ *pro*$_j$ è caduta ... [$_{VP}$ t$_i$ t$_j$]]]

3.5. Predicate fronting in inverse copular sentences

In inverse copular sentences, a predicative DP moves to the preverbal position, and
the grammatical subject remains postverbally (cf. Moro 1993):

(34) La causa della rivolta sono Gianni e Maria.
      the cause of the riot are Gianni and Maria

The fronted predicate behaves like a preverbal subject: it occurs in Aux-to-Comp
and CD:

(35) a. Essendo la causa della rivolta Gianni e Maria, ...
         being the cause of the riot Gianni and Maria . . .
      b. Credevo la causa della rivolta fossero Gianni e Maria.
         [I] believed the cause of the riot were Gianni and Maria

Thus, inverse copular sentences can be assigned the structure in (15), as shown
in (36). The predicative DP moves to specSubjP, where it checks the subject-of-
predication feature. The grammatical subject remains in the postverbal position and
checks nominative case and φ-features covertly:

(36) [$_{SubjP}$ la causa della rivolta$_i$ [$_{AgrSP}$ *pro*$_{expl}$ sono [$_{SC}$ Gianni e Maria t$_i$]]]

This analysis can be extended to other languages, such as German, that have
expletive *pro* and allow the subject to remain postverbally, as shown in (37a). English differs in that the predicative DP checks both the subject-of-predication feature and case/φ-features, which results in verb agreement with the fronted predicate,
as shown in (37b):

(37) a. [$_{SubjP}$ die Ursache des Tumults$_i$ sind [$_{AgrSP}$ *pro*$_{expl}$ [$_{SC}$ Hans und Maria t$_i$]]]
      b. [$_{SubjP}$ the cause of the riot$_i$ [$_{AgrSP}$ t$_i$ is [$_{SC}$ Hans and Maria t$_i$]]]

The proposal in (36) and (37) is a reinterpretation of Moro's original analysis.
He suggested that the fronted predicate is adjoined to IP, while specIP is occupied
by an empty predicate:

(38) [$_{IP}$ la causa della rivolta [$_{IP}$ *pro*$_{pred}$ sono Gianni e Maria t$_{pred}$]]

Moro's proposal is motivated by the fact that in (34), the verb does not agree with
the singular preposed predicate but with the plural postverbal subject. To avoid the
assumption that the verb agrees directly with the postverbal subject and to ensure
instead that agreement always obtains in a configuration of spec-head agreement,
Moro suggested that an empty predicate is present (*pro* in specIP), which, sharing
the features of the postverbal subject, triggers agreement on the verb. He found independent evidence for the empty predicate in presentative sentences like *pro*$_{pred}$ *sono*
Gianni e Maria ([it] is Gianni and Maria), which display the same agreement pattern
as (34).

German provides one piece of evidence that is problematic for the empty-predicate approach to (34) but supports the analysis proposed in (36). In German, the overt predicate *es* is obligatory in presentative sentences but ungrammatical in inverse copular sentences with nominal predicates:

(39)   a.   ... , daß *(es) Hans und Maria sind.
             ... that it Hans and Maria are
       b.   Die Ursache des Tumults sind (*es) Hans und Maria.
             the cause of the riot are (*it) Hans and Maria

In (39a), *es* is the counterpart of the Italian empty predicate, *modulo* pro-drop. Its absence in (39b) indirectly indicates that no null predicate is present in Italian inverse copular sentences. Since in German, agreement patterns are the same as in Italian—in (39b) the verb is plural—this is evidence that in inverse copular sentences, agreement with the nonraised subject is not contingent on the presence of a null predicate. SpecAgrSP is filled with an expletive *pro*, and agreement with the subject takes place as in the other cases of postverbal/nonraised subjects in Italian and German (via checking after Spell-Out or long-distance agreement).

3.6.   Conclusions

Dative and locative PPs and predicative DPs do not agree with the verb and are not assigned nominative case. Therefore, their movement to specSubjP cannot be motivated by the need for checking φ-features and nominative case, and Subj° cannot be the locus of φ-features and case. Subj° must contain some feature that attracts this rather heterogenous set of elements: dative and locative PPs and predicative DPs, as well as subject DPs. The subject-of-predication feature represents what all these phrases have in common when they appear preverbally. The head Subj is thus the locus of the subject-of-predication feature. Another head is necessary for checking of case and φ-features by the grammatical subject present in the clause, and I take it to be AgrS.

4.   On the specialization hypothesis

I now turn to the second half of the proposal in (15): namely, the idea that different types of subjects check different features and therefore occupy different subject positions.

4.1.   Strong versus weak subjects

Consider the Italian pronoun *tu* (you) that occurs in subjunctive clauses, as in (40b). As shown by the ungrammaticality of the second-person singular interpretation in (40a), this is a case (in fact, the only case) in which Italian is non-pro-drop and requires an overt subject.[9]

(40)   a.   Crede che [*pro* sia ricco], ma non lo sono / *non lo sei / non lo è.
                                                         (*pro* = I / *you / he)
             [he] thinks that [I / he] am$_{SUBJ}$ / is$_{SUBJ}$ rich, but [I] am not / *[you] are not / [he] is not

    b. Crede che [tu sia ricco].
      [he] thinks that you are$_{SUBJ}$ rich

Tu is deficient: it cannot be moved long-distance to a Topic position, as shown in (41a), and it is weak, not clitic: it need not be adjacent to the verb, as shown in (41b).[10]

(41) a.*Tu crede che sia ricco.   (Cinque 1996: 81, n. 11)
       you [he] thinks that are$_{SUBJ}$ rich
    b. Crede che tu solitamente esca alle due.
       [he] thinks that you usually exit$_{SUBJ}$ at two

The contrasts in (42) show that the weak pronoun *tu* occurring in subjunctive clauses differs from subject DPs and strong pronouns. While the latter can precede a paren- thetical phrase, the former is very marginal before a parenthetical and preferably follows a parenthetical, (42b) versus (42c). Notice that (42b) has almost the same flavor as (42d), where the second-person singular pronoun does not occur, and *pro* cannot have a second-person singular interpretation.[11]

(42) a. il fatto che Gianni/lui, secondo noi, debba restare
       the fact that Gianni/he according to us must$_{SUBJ}$ remain
    b. ??il fatto che tu, secondo noi, debba restare
       the fact that you according to us must$_{SUBJ}$ remain
    c. il fatto che, secondo noi, tu debba restare
    d.*il fatto che, secondo noi, debba restare   (*pro* = you)
       the fact that according to us [you] must$_{SUBJ}$ remain

    The distribution of parentheticals is not free. Parentheticals cannot occur in con- texts where strict spec-head agreement is required (Cardinaletti 1997a). This is shown in Hungarian (43) and Gungbe (44) focus constructions. Parentheticals are also un- grammatical in Hungarian wh- and negative sentences, as shown in (45):

(43) a. János   ment ki.
    b.*János, öszerinte,   ment ki.
       'Janos, according to him, went away'

(44) a. Jan,   wè novi ce mo.
    b.*Jan, to Mari si ayixa   me, wè novi ce mo.
       J. at   M. of (poss) mind in FOC brother mine see
       'According to Mari, it is Jan that my brother saw.'

(45) a.*Senki, öszerinte,   nem ment el.
       nobody according to him not went PRT
    b.*Ki,   öszerinte,   (nem) ment el?
       who according to him (not) went PRT

In all these cases, spec-head agreement is taken to hold between the preposed XP and the verb or the focus particle (Brody 1990 and Puskàs 1992, 1997 for Hungarian; Aboh 1995 for Gungbe). The fact that a parenthetical cannot intervene between the XP and the head in (43)–(45) means that parentheticals cannot freely adjoin to X′.[12]
    Since a parenthetical can follow the subject in (42a), the subject must occupy a projection different from the one associated with the finite verb. In turn, since a par- enthetical cannot follow the weak subject in (42b), the weak subject must occupy a

lower position than the strong subject. Although the location of null subjects cannot be established directly, it can be deduced from that of *tu* in (42b), given that they both belong to the class of weak pronouns.

In conclusion, weak pronouns occur in a position lower than strong pronouns and DPs, as shown in the following structure:[13]

(46)   strong   weak
     [$_{SubjP}$ {*Gianni / lui* } [$_{XP}$ parenth. [$_{AgrSP}$ {*pro/tu*$_{weak}$} Vfin [...]]]]

4.1.1. Subjects in complementizer deletion

The different distribution of weak versus strong subjects is confirmed by CD contexts. Two groups of speakers are attested (also see Giorgi and Pianesi 1997: 234). The first group of speakers, represented by the judgments given so far in the paper, allows any type of subject to occur in CD. These speakers find a contrast in (47), where a subject cooccurs with a fronted PP:[14]

(47)   a. Credo a Gianni *pro* piaccia.
           [I] believe to Gianni [it] pleases$_{SUBJ}$
       b. Credo a Gianni tu piaccia.
           [I] believe that to Gianni you please$_{SUBJ}$
       c. *Credo a Gianni questo libro piaccia.
           [I] believe that to Gianni this book pleases$_{SUBJ}$

The grouping of *pro* and weak *tu* against strong subjects can be explained by the double subject hypothesis. Examples (47a and b) are accepted because the fronted dative and *pro/tu* occupy the two distinct subject positions in (46); (47c) is rejected because *a Gianni* and *Maria* compete for one and the same position, namely specSubjP.[15]

The second group of speakers also finds a difference between *pro/tu* and strong subjects. In CD, they accept the former and reject the latter:

(48)   a. Pensa [*pro* sia in grado di aiutarlo].   (*pro* = I/*you/he)
           [he] thinks [I/he] am$_{SUBJ}$/is$_{SUBJ}$ able to help-him
       b. Pensa [tu sia in grado di aiutarlo].
           [he] thinks you are$_{SUBJ}$ able to help-him
       c. *?Pensa [solo tu sia in grado di aiutarlo].
           [he] thinks only you are$_{SUBJ}$ able to help-him
       d. *?Pensa [Gianni/lui sia in grado di aiutarlo].
           [he] thinks Gianni/he is$_{SUBJ}$ able to help-him

(49)   a. Non sapevo [*pro* fosse malato].   (*pro* = he)
           [I] not knew [he] was$_{SUBJ}$ sick
       b. Non sapeva [tu fossi malato].
           [he] not knew you were$_{SUBJ}$ sick
       c. *?Non sapevo [tu e Maria foste malati].
           [I] not knew you and Maria were$_{SUBJ}$ sick
       d. *?Non sapevo [Gianni/lui fosse malato].
           [I] not knew Gianni/he was$_{SUBJ}$ sick

Once more, *pro* and weak *tu* pattern against strong subjects, a fact that can be explained straightforwardly by the double subject hypothesis. In the grammar of the most restrictive speakers, CD implies that the Subj projection is empty or non active (see 4.1.2). Strong subjects, which occur in specSubjP, are therefore ungrammatical. Only those subjects are possible that occur in specAgrSP: *pro* and, in subjunctive clauses, *tu*.[16]

4.1.2.   *Against verb movement in complementizer deletion*

The hypothesis that weak pronouns only occupy specAgrSP seems to be questioned by the proposal that in CD, the verb (subjunctive, conditional, or future indicative) moves to a modal head in the Comp domain (C° in Poletto 2000: §5.4.3.2, 2001; Mood°, i.e., a head between FocusP and FinP, in Damonte 2000). Consider the contrast between the a. and the b. sentences in (50) and (51).

(50)   a. *Credo sicuramente lo faccia.
      b. Credo lo faccia sicuramente.

(51)   a. *Credo tu sicuramente lo faccia.
      b. Credo tu lo faccia sicuramente.

Verb movement to a head of the Comp domain is meant to account for the ungrammaticality of (50a) and (51a) and the verb/adverb order in (50b) and (51b). If this is analysis is correct, the fact that *tu* precedes the verb in (51b) leads to the conclusion that it occurs in the Comp domain. This conclusion should be extended to the null subject *pro* in (50b).

In what follows, I show that my hypothesis concerning the position of weak subjects is not weakened by (50)–(51) since these data cannot be explained via verb movement to Comp.

If the verb movement hypothesis were correct, the grammaticality of (52b) and (53b) also displaying the verb–adverb order in the presence of the complementizer *che* (that) would be surprising.

(52)   a. Credo che sicuramente lo faccia.
         [I] believe that [he] surely it does$_{SUBJ}$
      b. Credo che lo faccia sicuramente.

(53)   a. Credo che tu sicuramente lo faccia.
         [I] believe that [you] surely it do$_{SUBJ}$
      b. Credo che tu lo faccia sicuramente.

Examples (52b) and (53b) show that the verb–adverb order found when the complementizer is absent, as in (50b) and (51b), is not necessarily due to verb movement. Furthermore, (54) shows that the verb can precede the adverb *sicuramente* even when the complementizer follows topics.[17]

(54)   ?Credo il libro a Maria che glielo dia sicuramente.
       I think the book to M. that [he] to-her it gives$_{SUBJ}$ certainly

In (54), *che* can only occupy Fin°, and the verb is still in a head higher than the adverb *sicuramente*. The hypothesis that in (52b) and (53b) *che* is merged in Force° and the verb is moved to the modal head should therefore be discarded. In conclusion, the postverbal position of the adverb in (50b) and (51b) does not say anything about the position of the verb (also see Giorgi and Pianesi 1997: 272, n. 54).

Furthermore, the two basic assumptions behind the verb-movement analysis can be questioned. First, the modal head is not in the Comp domain. According to Cinque (1999: 106), the irrealis Mood head and the future head occur in the IP domain, between the adverbs *probably* and *necessarily*.

(55)   ... > *probably* Mod$_{epistemic}$ > *once* T (Past) > *then* T (Future) > *perhaps* Mood$_{irrealis}$
       > *necessarily* Mod$_{necessity}$ > *possibly* Mod$_{possibility}$ > ...

Cinque's proposal complies with both the status of the subjunctive and the future heads and the superficial order of the morphemes realizing these heads. Subjunctive and future are inflectional heads realizing morphosyntactic features of the verb and should belong to the Infl domain (Rizzi 1997: 283). Subjunctive and future morphemes linearly precede agreement morphemes, which means that they realize heads that are structurally lower than the AgrS head, in accordance with the Mirror Principle (Chinellato 2001).[18]

Second, the verb does not move across the adverb in (50b) and (51b). Cinque (1999: 31, n. 80, and 214, n. 7) concludes that finite lexical verbs do not move across adverbs higher than habitual ones in the hierarchy illustrated in (56), as the data in (57) testify:

(56)   *onestamente/francamente * fortunatamente/purtroppo * evidentemente *
       probabilmente/sicuramente * ora/allora * forse * necessariamente * volentieri *
       obbligatoriamente * saggiamente/stupidamente * di solito/solitamente √ di nuovo √
       spesso/raramente √ rapidamente √ mica, etc.

(57)   a. Gianni lo merita di nuovo / raramente / Non lo merita mica.
           Gianni it deserves again / rarely / not it deserves not
       b. *Gianni lo merita francamente / fortunatamente / evidentemente / probabilmente /
           forse / ...
           Gianni it deserves frankly / luckily / evidently / probably / perhaps ...

Cinque suggests that in sentences like (50b) and (51b) there is a focusing usage of the realis mood adverb *sicuramente*, which is not possible with other adverbs (hence, (57b) is ungrammatical also assuming this analysis). This focusing usage of the adverb is also found in the presence of the complementizer in (52b), (53b), and (54).

The absence of verb-movement in (50) and (51) is confirmed by the paradigm in (58). Contrary to higher adverbs such as *sicuramente* in (50a) and (51a), lower adverbs can precede the verb, as shown in (58a–g). This is incompatible with the hypothesis that in CD, the verb necessarily moves across the higher adverbs. The judgments hold for both null subjects and the second-person singular weak pronoun *tu* (sentences built on Cinque 1999: 110f).

(58)   a. Crede pro/tu mica prenda il treno.
           [he] believes (you) not take$_{SUBJ}$ the train
       b. Crede pro/tu rapidamente abbia di nuovo alzato il braccio.
           [he] believes (you) quickly have$_{SUBJ}$ again raised the arm
       c. Crede pro/tu raramente faccia tutto bene.
           [he] believes (you) rarely does$_{SUBJ}$ everything well
       d. Crede pro/tu di nuovo faccia tardi a scuola.
           [he] believes (you) again be$_{SUBJ}$ late at school

e. Crede pro/tu solitamente esca alle due.
   [he] believes (you) usually exit$_{SUBJ}$ at two
f. Crede pro/tu stupidamente esca sempre senza ombrello.
   [he] believes (you) stupidly exit$_{SUBJ}$ always without umbrella
g. Crede pro/tu volentieri mi/ti/si sia offerto di aiutarlo.
   [he] believes (you) willingly REFL be$_{SUBJ}$ offered to help-him
h. ?Crede pro/tu non necessariamente sia pacifista.
   [he] believes (you) not necessarily be$_{SUBJ}$ pacifist
i. ??Crede pro/tu forse vada a trovarlo.
   [he] believes (you) perhaps go$_{SUBJ}$ to visit-him
j. ??Crede pro/tu allora fossi monarchico.
   [he] believes (you) then were$_{SUBJ}$ for the monarchy
k. ??Crede pro/tu probabilmente faccia sul serio.
   [he] believes (you) probably be$_{SUBJ}$ in earnest
l. ??Crede pro/tu evidentemente sia contento così.
   [he] believes (you) evidently be$_{SUBJ}$ happy with that
m. ??Crede pro/tu purtroppo abbia accettato.
   [he] believes (you) unfortunately have$_{SUBJ}$ acccepted
n. ??Crede pro/tu francamente abbia esagerato.
   [he] believes (you) frankly have$_{SUBJ}$ exaggerated

The marginal sentences do not ameliorate if the verb moves across the adverb, which confirms the conclusion that in CD, no verb-movement to the Comp domain takes place.

(58) i'. ??Crede pro/tu venga forse a trovarci.
      j'. ??Crede pro/tu fossi allora monarchico.
      k'. ??Crede pro/tu abbia probabilmente rinunciato.
      l'. ??Crede pro/tu sia evidentemente contento così.
      m'. ??Crede pro/tu abbia purtroppo accettato.
      n'. ??Crede pro/tu abbia francamente esagerato.

If the preceding considerations are correct, the ungrammaticality of (50a) and (51a) is not due to the lack of V-to-C movement. I take (50a) and (51a) to be ungrammatical because CD sentences have a reduced structure. The null complementizer found in CD differs from the overt complementizer *che* in that it realizes a different functional head. Suppose that the null complementizer is generated in the irrealis Mood head and moved to Force° to be properly governed by the matrix verb (Stowell 1981) or to cliticize to it (Pesetsky 1995: 8). If higher adverbs and topics are present in the clause, its movement to Force° is blocked by the intervening heads (see Rizzi 1997: 331, n. 22 and 332, n. 28 for similar ideas on the English empty complementizer). Preverbal subjects are treated on a par with higher adverbs and topics by the most restrictive speakers, whose judgments are provided in (48) and (49).

In conclusion, if in CD, the verb occurs in the Infl domain, the hypothesis can be safely maintained that null subjects and *tu* occur in specAgrSP.

4.1.3. *An aside on* pro

The structures assumed so far for sentences without overt subiects are clearly dependent on the assumption that *pro* exists. I take this to be the null hypothesis. A null pronominal is essentially like overt weak pronominals, such as English *it* and French *il*, minus phonological content. *Pro* shares with its overt counterparts all syntactic and semantic properties (see Cardinaletti and Starke 1999: §3.4) but has different phonological properties. It lacks both the suprasegmental specification (i.e., word accent), on a par with overt weak pronominals such as English *it* and French *il*, and the segmental specification, differently from *it* and *il*.

The hypothesis that *pro* exists complies with the Uniformity Principle of Chomsky (1999: 2):

(59)   In the absence of compelling evidence to the contrary, assume languages to be uniform, with variety restricted to easily detectable properties of utterances.

In the proposals that reject *pro*, either a null subject is understood as being a feature on the verb (Uriagereka 1999), or the verbal morphology is taken to have pronominal status (Alexiadou and Anagnastopoulou 1998). The verb itself checks subject-related features.

I do not see any advantage in denying the existence of a phonetically null pronoun. The alleged structural advantage of these proposals—namely, the hypothesis that NSLs do not possess a preverbal subject position so that checking can take place through verb-movement instead of DP merging—is denied by the necessity in Italian of a preverbal subject position to host the weak pronoun *tu* in subjunctive contexts. It is not obvious that a theory that says the subject position is there only when it is filled by some overt subject is superior to a theory that says the subject position is always there.

A corollary of these proposals is that in NSLs, preverbal subjects are always left-dislocated. Although this is not a necessary implication of the hypothesis that null pronouns do not exist (since a left-dislocated subject in specTopP can cooccur with a null subject in specAgrSP), there are empirical arguments against this assumption as well (see section 6.1).

See Suñer (2000) for further discussion of these issues and other arguments for the existence of null pronominals.

4.2.   Null versus overt weak subjects

The conclusion reached in 4.1 must be slightly refined after considering the Italian weak pronouns of the *egli/esso* series. Although syntactically weak, the distribution of *egli* and *esso* recalls that of strong pronouns and DPs.[19]

Contrary to subjunctive *tu*, *egli* can precede parentheticals. Compare (60a) with (42b). Furthermore, *egli* cannot cooccur with a fronted dative in Aux-to-Comp. This is expected if *egli* and the fronted dative argument compete for one and the same position, specSubjP—compare (60b) with (i) in note 15.

(60)   a. Il fatto che egli, secondo noi, debba restare ...
         the fact that he according to us must$_{SUBJ}$ remain . . .
        b.*Essendo a Gianni egli piaciuto molto, ...
         being to Gianni he 'pleased' much . . .

As for CD, the less restrictive speakers find a contrast between (47a and b) and (61), where *egli* cooccurs with a fronted dative and patterns similarly to the strong subject in (47c). The most restrictive speakers dislike *egli* in CD (62) on a par with the strong subjects in (48c and d) and (49c and d).

(61)　??Credo a Gianni egli piaccia.
　　　[I] think to Gianni he 'pleases'_SUBJ

(62)　a.*?Pensa [egli sia in grado di aiutarlo].
　　　　[he] thinks Gianni / he is_SUBJ able to help-him
　　　b.*?Non sapevo [egli fosse malato].
　　　　[I] not knew Gianni / he was_SUBJ sick

Although syntactically weak, pronouns of the *egli/esso* series have the same distribution as strong subjects: they occur in specSubjP. The following structure revises (46):[20]

(63)　　　　strong (and some weak)　　　　　　　　　weak
　　　[_SubjP　{*Gianni/lui/egli*}　[_XP parenth. [_AgrSP {*pro/tu*_weak} Vfin [. . .]]]]

The distribution of pronouns of the *egli/esso* series is correlated with the fact that they (a) have a null counterpart (whereas the second-person singular pronoun *tu* in subjunctive contexts does not) and (b) have distinct discourse properties with respect to their null counterpart (see section 7.2 for discussion).

4.3.　Referential versus nonreferential subjects

Weak pronouns of the *egli/esso* series are ungrammatical when used as nonreferential (expletive, quasi-argument, impersonal) subjects. A null subject must be used instead:

(64)　a.　*pro/*Esso* è chiaro che ha ragione.
　　　　　it is clear that [he] is right
　　　b.　*pro/*Esso* piove tanto qui.
　　　　　it rains much here
　　　c.　In quel negozio, *pro/*essi* mi hanno venduto un vecchio libro.
　　　　　in that shop they to-me have sold an old book

In this respect, the Italian overt weak pronouns *esso* and *essi* differ from their English and French counterparts, which can be used as nonreferential subjects.

(65)　a.　It is clear that he is right.
　　　b.　It rains a lot here.
　　　c.　In that shop, they have sold me an old book.

(66)　a.　Il est clair qu'il a raison.
　　　b.　Il pleut beaucoup ici.
　　　c.　Dans ce magasin, ils m'ont vendu un vieux livre.

The fact that a null pronoun is required in (64) cannot be due to a principle that makes explicit reference to the null versus overt opposition. First, there is never a preference of null over overt pronouns, all apparent cases falling in the more general choice principle that favors a clitic or a weak pronoun over a strong pronoun (Cardinaletti and Starke 1999: §3.3.2). Second, there are cases of referential subjects in which both the null and the overt form are allowed (see (134): *Esso/pro rappresenta dunque ...*).

Suppose that nonreferential subject pronouns are restricted to specAgrSP, while referential subjects are free to occur in either position. The rather obvious reason for this restriction is that nonreferential subjects cannot qualify as subjects of predication. Overt weak pronouns of the *egli/esso* series, which, as shown in section 4.2, occur in specSubjP, are thus excluded from nonreferential usages. Both *pro* and English and French weak pronouns fulfill the constraint by occurring in specAgrSP (for English and French, see section 5.2).

4.4.   Quantified subjects

A further factor that might be relevant in the individuation of subject positions is whether or not the subject is quantified.

In Tortora (1997: 67), evidence from Borgomanerese is discussed, with the conclusion that negative quantifiers occupy a different subject position with respect to nonquantified subject DPs. Consider the contrast in (67): whereas *nzün* (nobody) can cooccur with the locative clitic *ngh* (there), the subject DP *la Maria* (the Maria) cannot:

(67)   a. Nzün ngh è rivà-gghi.
          nobody LOC is arrived-LOC
       b. *La Maria ngh è rivà-gghi.
          the Maria LOC is arrived-LOC

The locative clitic *ngh* in AgrS requires a locative *pro* in specAgrSP. This prevents the nominative DP *la Maria* from checking φ-features. The negative quantifier can be taken to occur in a position higher than specAgrSP—that is, a position devoted to quantified subjects. This position cannot be specFocusP, however, as is sometimes proposed. Under the assumption that there is no language variation as far as the semantic component is concerned, it is natural to assume that quantified subjects have the same distribution across languages (cf. Beghelli 1995; Beghelli and Stowell 1997). On the basis of English, which shows that a quantified subject can follow the raised verb in questions, (68a), whereas topicalized and focalized phrases cannot, (68b–d), the conclusion can be drawn that negative quantifiers and focalized elements do not have one and the same distribution. Since in English, all quantifiers follow a raised auxiliary, all QP subject positions must be located lower than Fin°, the position reached by auxiliaries in I-to-C movement (Rizzi 1997: 303):

(68)   a. Whom does no one love?
       b. *Did yesterday John come?   (Rizzi 1997: 303)
       c. *Had yesterday John done that, . . .   (ibid.)
       d. *Did only in that occasion John come?

4.5.   Person features

Italian does not provide evidence to identify other preverbal subject positions in addition to specSubjP and specAgrSP (but see note 11 and section 7.4). Other languages, however, show that the agreement field must be split into distinct projections realizing different morphosyntactic features. Weak pronouns of different persons thus occupy different subject positions.

Poletto (2000) has shown that in Northern Italian dialects, distinct AgrS projections should be individuated to host subject clitics, which realize φ-features in the following way:

(69)   [$_{NumbP}$ 3rd SubjCl [$_{HearerP}$ 2nd SubjCl [$_{SpeakerP}$ Vfin [$_{TP}$ . . .]]]]

Hebrew also provides evidence for an articulated agreement field, but the order of the functional projections seems to be different. First- and second-person pronouns have the following two properties: (a) they cannot occur with the pronominal copula *hi*, and (b) they must occur above the inflected negation and cannot occur below the uninflected negation (Shlonsky 2000: 342).

(70)   'Ani (*hi) gveret Levi (lo gveret Cohen).
        I H-fs Mrs. Levi (not Mrs. Cohen)

(71)   a. 'Ani/'At 'eyn(ə)-ni/-ex gveret Levi.
           I/you-fs not-1s/-2fs Mrs. Levi
        b. ??'Eyn 'ani/'at gveret Levi.
           not I Mrs. Levi

In configurational terms, first- and second-person pronouns are too high in (70) and too low in (71b). They occur in a position between *hi* and *'eyn*. That *hi* is higher than inflected negation is supported by the word order found with DPs, where *hi* and the inflected negation can cooccur (Shlonsky 2000: 345).

(72)   Rina hi 'eyn-(ən)a gveret Levi.
        Rina H-fs not-3fs Mrs. Levi

French provides evidence that first-person pronouns are higher than second- and third-person pronouns. Lexical verbs cannot invert around a first-person singular pronoun, while auxiliary and modal verbs can. The contrast can be reduced to the different scope of verb movement in the two cases (De Crousaz and Shlonsky 2000). A lexical verb does not move higher than the head to which second- and third-person clitic pronouns adjoin. Auxiliary and modal verbs, which raise higher than lexical verbs (Pollock 1989), can precede first-person pronouns:[21]

(73) a.*Viens-je?   (74) a. Suis-je?   (75) a. Puis-je?
      b. Viens-tu?   b. Es-tu?   b. Peux-tu?
      c. Vient-il?   c. Est-il?   c. Peut-il?
      come(s)-I/-you/-he?   am-I?/are-you/is-he?   can-I/-you/-he?

Finally, consider the proposals by Tortora (1999) and Sigurðsson (2000), according to which the head responsible for number agreement (NumberP) is structurally higher than the one responsible for person agreement, (PersonP). For the opposite view (PersonP higher than NumberP), see Egerland (1996). For reasons of space, I cannot review their arguments here.

Although the internal articulation of the AgrS projection requires a more detailed study in comparative perspective, it seems correct to view AgrSP not as a unique projection but as a number of different projections, each realizing a φ-feature or a set of φ-features.

4.6. Conclusions

On the basis of the evidence surveyed in the previous sections, we end up with the following substructure concerning preverbal subjects:

(76)

SpecSubjP	Subj° <subject of predication>	specAgrSP	AgrS°* <φ-features>
DPs		Weak pronouns	
Strong pronouns		pro	
Weak pronouns			
(egli/esso)			

Combining (76) with the postverbal positions identified in section 1, the following cartography of subject positions is obtained:

SpecSubjP	Subj°	SpecAgrSP	AgrS°*	spec??P	??°	spec?P	?°*	SpecVP	V°
DPs		Weak pronouns		Weak pronouns		DPs		DPs	
Strong pronouns		pro				Strong pronouns		Strong pronouns	
Weak pronouns (egli/esso)						Predicate DPs			

5. Evidence from other languages

Other languages support the hypothesis that more than one preverbal subject position exists and that strong and weak subjects occur in designated positions where they check different features.

5.1. Two preverbal subject positions in Spanish and Portuguese

Our analysis can be extended to account for Spanish locative and dative arguments of unaccusative verbs, which, according to Fernández-Soriano (1999), occupy the preverbal subject position. I refer to her article for detailed discussion:

(77)   a. En esta casa falta café.
           in this house misses coffee
        b. Me falta café.
           to-me misses coffee

Galves (1991) uses the double-subject structure to account for a number of Brazilian Portuguese unaccusative constructions, in which DPs with various θ-roles (theme, as in (78a), locative, as in (78b,c)) cooccur with overt or null weak subject pronouns (see also Martins 1994 and Figueiredo Silva 1996):

(78) a. O café já descascado ele pode ser exportado assim.
          the coffee already peeled it can be exported this way
      b. Esta casa pro$_{expl}$ bate sol.
          this house [there] beats sun
          'The sun is beating down on this house.'
      c. A Belina pro$_{expl}$ cabe muita gente.
          the Belina [there] go-in-SG many people-SG.
          'There enter many people into the Belina.'

The subjecthood of the fronted DPs in (78) is confirmed by the agreement phenomena shown in (79). The verb agrees with the fronted theme in (79a) and the fronted locative in (79b):

(79) a. A pedra mineira ela esiste varias classificações.
          the stone from Minas she-SG exist-SG many classification-PL
          'There exist many classifications for the Minas stone.'
      b. Esses carros cabem muita gente.
          these car-PL enter-PL many people-SG

5.2. Weak versus strong subjects in English, French, and German

The evidence based on the distribution of parentheticals (see 4.1) can be reproduced in English, French (cf. Kayne 1983, 1984), and German. Whereas strong subjects can precede parentheticals, weak subjects cannot.

(80) a. John/He (as you know)   is a nice guy.
      b. It   (?*as you know)   costs too much / is too expensive.
      c. It   (*as you know)   rained the whole day.
      d. There   (*as you know)   was a man in the garden.

(81) a. Jean/Lui (je crois)   aime beaucoup la musique.
      b. Il   (*je crois)   aime beaucoup la musique.
          J./he   (I think)   likes much the music

(82) a. Hans/Er (soweit ich weiß) kommt morgen.
          Hans/he (as far as I know) comes tomorrow
      b. Es/Er   (*soweit ich weiß) kostet zuviel.
          it/it   (*as far as I know) costs too much
      c. Es   (*soweit ich weiß) hat viel geregnet.
          it   (*as far as I know) has much rained

As for English, the ungrammaticality of (80b–d) cannot be explained in terms of an adjacency restriction since adverbs can occur between the subject pronoun and the verb (section 6.3):

(83) a. There (surely)   was a man in the garden.
      b. It   (often)   rained the whole day.
      c. It   (probably)   costs too much.

The ungrammaticality of (81b) in French cannot be due to a phonological constraint that requires the weak subject pronoun to phonologically cliticize to some element of the clause. The cooccurrence of weak subjects and parentheticals is also banned in embedded clauses, where the weak pronoun *il* (he) could, in principle, attach to the complementizer:

(84)   Le fait qu'il (*selon toi) parle tres bien ...
         the fact that he (*according to you) speaks very well . . .

To account for (84) in phonological terms, the requirement should be formulated in such a way that weak subject pronouns have to form a phonological constituent with the verb. But no such requirement seems to exist independently of the very cases to be explained here. Nor can French *il* be marked as a proclitic rather than an enclitic pronoun. Toman (1992) has convincingly shown on the basis of Czech data that the direction of (phonological) cliticization cannot be stated univoquely but depends on the phonological environment. This implies that the variant of (84) with the parenthetical should satisfy phonological requirements and be grammatical, contrary to fact. Given these difficulties, it seems more promising to attribute the ungrammaticality of (84)—and of (81b)—to a syntactic constraint that relies on the distinction between weak and strong constituents.

Notice that in German (82), one and the same pronoun, *er*, has a different distribution depending on its interpretation: human versus nonhuman. The interpretation correlates with its strong versus weak status (see Cardinaletti and Starke 1996).

The strong versus weak distinction is also relevant to explain the following contrasts. Nonspecific indefinites are syntactically weak, while specific indefinites are strong. It is not clear how the ungrammaticality of (85) with a parenthetical could be accounted for in semantic terms:

(85)   a. One (*as you know) usually buys ice cream to calm down before exams.
         b. Man (*glaube ich) soll das nicht machen.
             one think I should this not do

(86)   a. One/Someone (as far as I know) has bought a house in the countryside.
         b. Einer (glaube ich) möchte ein Haus kaufen.
             one think I would-like a house buy

In sum, the asymmetries seen above can be attributed to the different distribution of weak and strong subjects. As in the structure proposed in (63) for Italian, parentheticals occur in a position between weak pronouns and strong subjects and can therefore not follow weak subjects.[22]

(87)   strong   weak
         a. [SubjP {John/he} Subj° [XP parenth. [AgrSP {it}   AgrS° [Vfin]]]]
         b. [SubjP {Jean/lui} Subj° [XP parenth. [AgrSP {il}   Vfin   [...]]]]
         c. [SubjP {Hans/er} Subj° [XP parenth. [AgrSP {es/er}   Vfin   [...]]]]

This proposal finds further support in a Spanish dialect—Dominican Spanish—that has overt expletives (Suñer 2000):

(88)   a. Juan/Él, a mi parecer, es muy simpático.
             'Juan/he, according to me, is very nice.'

b. Ello (*a mi parecer) no seria malo estudiar.
'It, according to me, wouldn't hurt to study.'

5.3. French Complex Inversion

In French Complex Inversion, DPs and strong pronouns behave differently from weak pronouns. The former can appear before the auxiliary, the latter cannot (Kayne 1984: chap. 10; Rizzi and Roberts 1989).

(89) a. Quand Pierre/lui a-t-il téléphoné?
      b.*Quand il a-t-il téléphoné?
         when Pierre/he has-he called

Suppose that Complex Inversion makes use of the structure proposed in (87b) in the following way: the clitic subject pronoun adjoins to Subj°, the verb adjoins to it (Kayne 1994: 139, n.15), and the strong subject occupies specSubjP, as shown in (90a). Example (90b) is ungrammatical because specSubjP is an illicit position for weak pronouns.[23]

(90) a. Quand [$_{SubjP}$ Pierre/lui a$_i$-t-il$_k$ [$_{AgrSP}$ t$_k$ t$_i$ [$_{VP}$ t$_k$ téléphoné?]]]
      b. *Quand [$_{SubjP}$ il   a$_i$-t-il$_k$ [$_{AgrSP}$ t$_k$ t$_i$ [$_{VP}$ t$_k$ téléphoné?]]]
         when   Pierre/he has-he   called

In varieties of popular French (Morin 1979) and Québec French (Vecchiato 2000), where the postverbal subject clitic is replaced by the invariable morpheme *ti* or *tu*, a preverbal weak subject pronoun is possible.

(91) a. Quand il a-ti téléphoné?
         when he has-TI called
      b. Je peux-ti ajouter quelque chose?
         I can-TI add some thing?

Here, the auxiliary verb adjoins to *ti*, which occupies a position lower than AgrS°. This allows the weak subject to precede the verb. Since the invariable morpheme *ti* does not have person distinctions, the proposal that it occurs in a head lower than AgrS° (or in the lowest of the AgrS heads; see section 4.5) is straightforward.

5.4. Hebrew copular constructions

An asymmetry between DPs and pronouns in preverbal position is also found in Hebrew. In predicational copular constructions such as (92) and in equative sentences such as (93), DPs and strong pronouns can cooccur with the pronominal copula, whereas weak pronouns cannot (Shlonsky 2000: 338, 340, 345).

(92) a. Rina hi zameret rok.
         Rina H-FS singer rock
         'Rina is a rock singer.'
      b. Hu (*hu) zamar rok.
         he H-MS singer rock

(93) a. Rina hi gveret Levi.
         Rina H-FS Mrs. Levi
         'Rina is Mrs. Levi.'

    b. Hi ve hu hem ha-Levim.
       she and he H-MPL the-Levis
    c. Hi (*hi) gveret Levi (lo gveret Cohen).
       she H-FS Mrs. Levi (not Mrs. Cohen)
    d. 'Ani (*hi) gveret Levi.
       I H-FS Mrs. Levi

It has often been proposed that *hi* is the lexicalization of a functional head (Shlonsky 2000 and the references cited there). Assuming the structure in (63), this functional head can be Subj°. A weak pronoun cannot precede *hi* because specSubjP (or higher specifier positions) cannot host weak pronouns.

6. On the properties of SubjP

In what follows, the properties of SubjP are discussed in detail. First, it is shown that SubjP belongs to the Infl domain and not to the Comp domain and that there is no language variation in the location of this projection. This conclusion is also valid for the distribution of subjects in interrogative clauses. Second, SubjP should not be identified either with the lowest projection of the Comp domain, FinP. Finally, the distribution of subjects with respect to adverbs shows that SubjP is a recursive phrase.

6.1. SubjP is in the Infl domain

It is very often proposed that preverbal subjects have a different status in NSLs and non-NSLs. In the latter they are "ordinary" subjects occurring in specAgrSP; in the former they are topicalized or left-dislocated in some sentence-peripheral A'-position (Beninca' and Cinque 1985; Contreras 1991; Dobrovie-Sorin 1994; Barbosa 1997; Picallo 1998; Alexiadou and Anagnastopoulou 1998; Cornilescu 1997; Pollock 1998; Manzini and Savoia 2002, among many others).

    In terms of the clause structure assumed in (17), this means that subjects occur in the Infl domain in non-NSLs and in the Comp domain in NSLs. Following Rizzi (1997: 283), I take the two domains to have different roles in the clause: the Infl domain is the locus of morphosyntactic features of the verb, while Comp is an interface between the propositional content (expressed by IP) and the superordinate structure or the previous discourse. In this view, the above-mentioned proposals imply that the subject has a deeply different status in the two types of languages.

    This conclusion is surprising, in particular for those cases in which preverbal subjects of transitive verbs occur in out-of-the-blue sentences or in answers to the question *What happened?* as in (94a). No topic analysis of the subject seems to be motivated for these cases, and no structural difference should hence be stipulated between Italian (94a) and, for instance, English (94b) (see section 7.4).

(94)   a. A: Che è successo? B: Gianni ha fatto piangere Maria.
       b. A: What happened? B: Gianni made Maria cry.

    Moreover, if in NSLs the subject is always left-dislocated, the proposals that do not assume null subjects (see 4.1.3) establish a fundamental difference between the left-dislocation of subjects (no resumptive pronoun) and the left-dislocation of objects and other categories (resumptive pronoun), a difference that is not motivated empirically.

Apart from conceptual arguments, there are empirical arguments against the hypothesis that in NSLs the preverbal subject is always left-dislocated. Suñer (2000 and 2001) responds to many of the alleged arguments discussed in the literature by showing that Spanish preverbal subjects have the same syntactic and semantic properties as English subjects. Her arguments are also valid for Italian.

Among the Italian-internal arguments discussed in Cardinaletti (1997a: §3), consider the fact that the weak pronoun *egli*, which cannot be left-dislocated (95a and b), can appear preverbally (95c) and the fact that subjects can appear in constructions such as Aux-to-Comp and CD where left-dislocated items cannot, (96)–(97) (see section 3):[24]

(95)   a. Gianni/*Egli la nostra causa non l'ha appoggiata.   (Left dislocation)
        Gianni/he the our cause [he] not it has supported
    b. Gianni/*Egli LA NOSTRA CAUSA ha appoggiato, non la loro.   (Left dislocation)
        Gianni/*he the our cause has supported not the theirs
    c. Gianni/Egli ha appoggiato la nostra causa.   (Subject position)
        Gianni/he has supported the our cause

(96)   a. Avendo Gianni/egli telefonato a Maria, ...   (Aux-to-Comp)
        having Gianni/he phoned to Maria . . .
    b.*Avendolo {io} il libro {io} dato a Gianni ieri, ...
        having it (I) the book (I) given to G. yesterday . . .
    c.*Avendolo il libro dato a Gianni ieri, ...
        having it the book [he] given to Gianni yesterday . . .

(97)   a. Credevo Gianni/egli avesse telefonato a Maria.   (CD)
        [I] believed Gianni/he had called to Maria
    b. ??Credevo il libro Maria lo avesse dato a Gianni.
        [I] believed the book Maria it had given to Gianni

In conclusion, Italian disposes of both preverbal subject positions, specSubjP and specAgrSP, on a par with, for example, English.

Another argument against the left-dislocation analysis of preverbal subjects in NSLs comes from Paduan, where the distribution of subject clitics allows the distinction between left-dislocated and non-left-dislocated subjects. A resumptive clitic pronoun is obligatory only when the subject precedes a left-dislocated object such as *mi* in (98a) and is therefore itself left-dislocated. When the subject is simply preverbal, as in (98b), the clitic is not present (Beninca' 2001: 56).[25]

(98)   a. Mario, mi, *(el) me vede volentiera.
        Mario me [he] me meets with-pleasure
    b. Mario me vede volentiera.

Similarly, the following data from Fiorentino show that the difference between preverbal and left-dislocated subjects is syntactically encoded, with *e* a kind of topic marker in the case of left-dislocated subjects (sentences and analysis from Brandi and Cordin 1989: 113–114). If the subject were left-dislocated in both the (a) and the (b) sentences, there would be no way to differentiate the two cases:

(99) a. La Maria la parla.
         the Maria she speaks
      b. La Maria, e la parla troppo.
         [as for] Maria TOP she speaks too much

(100) a. Te tu parli.
         you you speak
      b. Te, e tu parli troppo.
         [as for] you, TOP you speak
         too much

We can safely conclude that preverbal subjects are not left-dislocated in NSLs and that NSLs dispose of preverbal subject positions akin to what is found in, for example, English. No difference should be stipulated between the following set of sentences as far as the distribution of subjects is concerned:

(101) a. John loves Mary.   a' Gianni ama Maria.
      b. He loves Mary.   b' *Pro* ama Maria.
      c. He thinks that you are sick.   c' *Pro* crede che tu sia malato.

Although she rejects the left-dislocation analysis, Poletto (2000: chap. 6) nevertheless suggests that in NSLs, preverbal subjects occur in the Comp domain. Her arguments come from the distribution of subjects in Northern Italian dialects. A piece of evidence is provided by the fact that subjects precede complementizers in some varieties (Poletto 2000: 148f. and 165f.).

(102) a. A venta che gnun ch'a fasa bordel.
         it needs that nobody that SCL do$_{SUBJ}$ noise
         'It is necessary that nobody make noise.'
      b. Mario ch'a s presenta subit
         Mario that SCL go$_{SUBJ}$ immediately
         'Mario has to go immediately.'

In principle, data like these show that subjects *can* appear in the Comp domain, not that they *must*. If one considers the fact that the sentences in (102) contain subjunctive verbs, these sentences can be taken to show that the subject is not in the Comp domain but in the Infl domain. The "low" complementizer, underlined in (102), can be analyzed as the realization of the irrealis Mood head (as in Balkan languages, see n. 18). As discussed in section 4.1.2, this head seems to be located in the Infl domain. The subject in specSubjP precedes it.

Poletto (2000: 151) uses deictic clitics to make the same point. Since deictic clitics such as *a* in (103) are taken to occur in the Comp domain and strong subjects precede them, it follows that strong subjects occur in Comp.

(103) Mario a nol ven.
      Mario SCL not$_{SCL}$ comes
      'Mario is not coming.'

Here, it is the first assumption that can be called into question. In some Northern Italian and French dialects, vocalic subject clitics have the same properties as what Poletto calls deictic clitics, but they occur in the Infl domain (Cardinaletti and Repetti 2000; De Crousaz and Shlonsky 2000). Two possibilities come to mind: either these subject clitics constitute a further class, which has the same properties as deictic clitics apart from distribution, or the evidence that deictic clitics are in Comp must be reconsidered. With these questions in mind, it is not too unfair to conclude that (103) is not compelling evidence for the subject-in-Comp hypothesis.

Another argument often used to argue for the subject-in-Comp hypothesis is the distribution of subjects in wh-questions. Italian overt subjects cannot occur between wh-phrases and the verb, (104), and differ from English and German preverbal subjects, which can freely occur in wh-sentences, (105):

(104)   a.*Chi Gianni ha invitato?
           whom Gianni has invited
        b.*Chi egli ha invitato?

(105)   a. Who did John/he invite yesterday?
        b. Wen hat Hans/er gestern eingeladen?

Those who propose that preverbal subjects are left-dislocated in NSLs can easily explain the ungrammaticality of (104) in structural terms. Since it can be independently shown that left-dislocated items precede wh-phrases, (106a), they predict that the subject cannot follow a wh-item, as in (104), but must precede it, as in (106b):

(106)   a. Gianni quando l'hai visto?
           Gianni when [you] him have seen
        b. Gianni chi ha invitato?
           Gianni whom has invited

However, if the left-dislocation analysis were correct, the contrast between (95c) and (107) would remain unexplained:

(107)   *Egli chi ha invitato?
         he whom has invited

We take the subject pronoun *egli* to be left-dislocated in (107), which is structurally parallel to (106b), but not in (95c), where it occupies specSubjP.

The ungrammaticality of (107) and the contrast between (106b) and (107) also shows that in NSLs, the canonical position of the subject cannot be to the left of wh-phrases (*pace* Poletto 2000: 160). In (106b), the subject does not occupy its canonical specSubjP position, but is left-dislocated (in specTopP). In (107), *egli* is expectedly ungrammatical, as it is in (95a and b). Similarly, the quantified subject in (108) is ungrammatical because it occurs in a left-dislocated position:

(108)   *Nessuno chi ha invitato?
         nobody whom has invited

The structural approach to the ungrammaticality of strong subjects following wh-phrases in Italian can be discarded also on the basis of comparative evidence. Wh-questions do not seem to oppose NSLs against non-NSLs. French and Caribbean Spanish, which are non-NSLs, pattern like Italian in not allowing strong subjects in wh-questions, as shown in (109a) and (110a). They do allow weak subjects, however, as shown in (109b–d) and (110b) (data from Poletto and Pollock 1999 and Ordoñez and Olarrea 2000, respectively).

(109)   a. ??Quand Marie ira à MIT?
        b. Quand elle ira à MIT?
           when Maria/she will-go to MIT
        c. Quand tu pars?
           when you leave

    d. Qui il a vu?
       whom he has seen

(110) a. *Qué José quiere?
          what José wants
       b. Qué tú quieres?
          what you want

The French and Caribbean Spanish paradigms in (109) and (110) not only show that
a pro-drop parameter approach to (104) is incorrect. They also allow us to express
the distribution of subjects in wh-questions in a more fine-grained manner. Only those
subjects that occur in specSubjP (strong subjects and pronouns of the *egli/esso* series) are prevented from occurring between the wh-phrase and the verb, whereas
subjects in specAgrSP (weak pronouns) are ruled in. The occurrence of a null subject in Italian gives the same results as the occurrence of its overt counterparts in
(109b–d) and (110b): *Chi pro ha invitato?* (whom [he] has invited).
    Although the ungrammaticality of (104) and (109a)/(110a), as well as the contrast
with (105), is addressed in independent work (Cardinaletti 2001), the conclusion can
be drawn that wh-questions do not provide any support for the subject-in-Comp analysis
of preverbal subjects in NSLs.

6.2.   The subject of predication is not in specFin

Rizzi (1997) has introduced FinP as the lowest projection in the Comp domain. This
projection contains information about the finiteness of the clause. On the basis of the
observation that subject DPs can only occur in finite clauses, it might be tempting to
identify specSubjP with specFinP.
    To prevent a circular conclusion, the hypothesis can be checked with those XPs
that can be fronted to specSubjP (see section 3). Contrary to subject DPs, they can
marginally appear in infinitival clauses.

(111) a. ?un uomo che ritengo a Gianni piacere molto
          a man that [I] believe to Gianni [to] 'please' much
       b. ?una persona che ritengo a Gianni mancare molto
          a person that [I] believe to Gianni [to] 'miss' much
       c. ?le disgrazie che ritengo a Gianni capitare troppo spesso, negli ultimi tempi
          the misfortunes that [I] believe to Gianni [to] happen often lately

Consider the contrast between (111) and (112). Whereas a fronted dative can appear
in the infinitival complement of *ritenere*, a topic cannot (Rizzi 1997: 310):

(112) a. un uomo che ritengo (*a Gianni$_i$) potergli$_i$ parlare
          a man whom [I] believe to Gianni be-able-him [to] talk
       b. un uomo che ritengo (*Gianni$_i$) poterlo$_i$ assumere
          a man whom [I] believe Gianni be-able-him [to] hire

This contrast not only confirms the conclusions reached in sections 3.1 and 3.2 that
preverbal datives occurring with psych and unaccusative verbs are not topicalized
but occur in specSubjP. It also shows that specSubjP is not specFinP. Let's see why.

Example (112) has the structure in (113). Following Rizzi (1997: 310), (113a) is grammatical because the trace of the subject satisfies the ECP and is case-licensed by the matrix verb. Example (113b) is ungrammatical because the topic makes t' inaccessible to the matrix V for case licensing and satisfaction of the ECP:

(113) a. un uomo che ritengo [$_{FinP}$ t' -Fin [t potergli parlare ...]]
       b. *un uomo che ritengo [$_{TopP}$ a Gianni Top [$_{FinP}$ t' -Fin [t potergli parlare ...]]]

Since (111) is not ungrammatical, it cannot have the structure in (113b) but can have that in either (114a) or (114b):

(114) a. un uomo che ritengo [$_{FinP}$ a Gianni -Fin [t piacere molto ...]]
       b. un uomo che ritengo [$_{FinP}$ t' -Fin [$_{SubjP}$ a Gianni Subj [t piacere molto ...]]]

The hypothesis in (114a) must be discarded. The chain of the subject is case-less, since the Fin head intervenes between the matrix verb and the trace in subject position. This leaves (114b) as the structure of (111), where the matrix verb licenses the t' trace and the Subj head licenses the t trace. The marginality of (111) might be viewed as a subjacency effect (see Rizzi 1997: n. 30 and n. 32 for comparable cases).

In conclusion, specSubjP cannot be identified with specFinP, which complies with the hypothesis that SubjP is not in the Comp domain.

Notice that although SubjP is in principle available in infinitival clauses, it cannot host a fronted argument—as a dative—as shown by the fact that in (115a) the dative cannot follow the Fin element *di* (see n. 17). The dative PP must be topicalized, hence it precedes *di*, and SubjP must be empty or inactive, as shown in (115b):

(115) a. *Penso [$_{FinP}$ di [$_{SubjP}$ a Gianni [$_{AgrSP}$ PRO piacere molto]]].
          [I] think of to Gianni 'please' much
       b. Penso [$_{TopP}$ a Gianni [$_{FinP}$ di [$_{AgrSP}$ PRO piacergli molto]]].
          [I] think to Gianni of 'please'-to-him much

I take (115a) to be a Case violation. Under the hypothesis that PRO requires a null case (Chomsky and Lasnik 1991) and null case is sanctioned by [–fin] under government (Rizzi 1997: 305), the Subj head blocks government of PRO by Fin.

6.3. Subjects and adverbs

I have argued for the existence of a subject position responsible for the checking of φ-features on nominative DPs and a subject position responsible for the checking of the subject-of-predication feature. This proposal seems to be questioned by the evidence discussed by Cinque (1999: §5.1). An overt subject can occupy a number of positions above the adverb *mica* (not), as signaled by √ in (116). In (117)–(118), examples are provided with the highest and the lowest adverbs in Cinque's hierarchy.

(116) √ onestamente/francamente √ fortunatamente/purtroppo √ evidentemente √
       probabilmente/sicuramente √ ora/allora √ forse √ necessariamente √ volentieri √
       obbligatoriamente √ saggiamente/stupidamente √ di solito/solitamente √ di nuovo √
       spesso/raramente √ rapidamente √ mica * già * (non) più * ancora * sempre * etc.

(117)   a. Francamente Gianni ha esagerato.
      frankly Gianni has exaggerated
    b. Gianni francamente ha esagerato.

(118)   a. Maria mica prende il treno.
    b.*Mica Maria prende il treno.
      not takes Maria the train

Since the weak pronoun *egli* has the same distribution as the strong subject in (117)–(118) and is grammatical in all positions indicated in (116), subjects cannot be taken to occur in Topic positions when they precede high adverbs:

(119)   a. Francamente egli ha esagerato.
      frankly he has exaggerated
    b. Egli francamente ha esagerato.

(120)   a. Egli mica prende il treno.
      he not takes the train
    b.*Mica egli prende il treno.

Since *egli* can also precede the IP-edge adverb *domani*, the list of the Infl-domain adverbs in (116) can be slightly revised as in (122) (see note 18 for Romanian and note 25 for Paduan).

(121)   a. Gianni domani gli compra una casa.
      Gianni tomorrow to-him buys a house
    b. Egli domani gli compra una casa.
      he tomorrow to-him buys a house

(122)   √ domani √ onestamente/francamente √ fortunatamente/purtroppo, etc.

My proposal can be reconciled with Cinque's evidence by allowing a SubjP on top of each adverb-related XP above *già* or by allowing SubjP to be generated freely above any adverb of (122) above *già*. It is difficult to distinguish between the two alternatives, and the distribution of finite verbs does not help. Auxiliary verbs can follow the subject and IP-edge adverbs and precede *francamente* (frankly), or they can occur in any lower position without necessarily being adjacent to the subject (Cinque 1999: 49, 112):

(123)   a. *Gianni* ieri *si era* francamente purtroppo formato una pessima opinione di voi.
      Gianni yesterday REFL was frankly unfortunately formed a very bad opinion of you
    b. *Gianni* francamente *si era* purtroppo formato una pessima opinione di voi.
    c. *Gianni* francamente purtroppo *si era* formato una pessima opinione di voi.
    d. Francamente *Gianni si era* purtroppo formato una pessima opinione di voi.
    e. Francamente *Gianni* purtroppo *si era* formato una pessima opinione di voi.

The auxiliary verb can be taken to occur in one and the same projection as the subject only in (123d), where the verb and the subject are adjacent. In (123a, b, c, and e), the auxiliary verb occurs either in the heads of the adverb-related projections or in lower Subj heads with empty specifiers.

Comparative evidence confirms that subject placement is not directly correlated with verb movement. Italian and English subjects have the same distribution with respect to adverbs, but finite verbs occur in different positions (Kayne 1989; Pollock 1989; Cinque 1999: 112).

(124) a. John probably likes linguistics.
      b. Frankly he/John has exaggerated.
      c. John/He frankly has exaggerated.

Conversely, French finite verbs have a distribution similar to finite verbs in Italian, but no adverb can intervene between the subject and the verb (Belletti 1990: 44, 51, 55).[26]

(125) a.*Jean probablement aime la linguistique.
        Jean probably likes the linguistics
      b. Probablement que Jean lira ces livres.
        probably that Jean will-read these books
      c.*Jean probablement a fait plusieurs erreurs.
        Jean probably has made many mistakes
      d. Jean a probablement abordé le problème.
        Jean has probably faced the problem

The question as to whether we have a unique, freely generated SubjP or multiple SubjPs must remain open.[27] In either case, however, the highest SubjP occurs to the left of speech act adverbs (e.g., *francamente*). The speech act projection is taken by Cinque (1999: 84) to be the highest one in the Infl domain. Since IP-edge adverbs and SubjP can precede it (see (121) and (122)), SubjP is the highest projection of the Infl domain. This conclusion is supported by the distribution of the Hebrew pronominal copula, which I have taken to lexicalize Subj° (see section 5.4). It must precede all adverbs (Shlonsky 2000: 345 and personal communication).

(126) a.*Rina be-xenut/betax/kanir'e hi zameret rok.
        Rina honestly/certainly/apparently H-FS singer rock
      b. Rina hi be-xenut/betax/kanir'e zameret rok.
        Rina H-FS honestly/certainly/apparently singer rock

(127) a.*Rina betax/kanir'e hi gveret Levi.
        Rina certainly/apparently H-FS Mrs. Levi
      b. Rina hi betax/kanir'e gveret Levi.
        Rina H-FS certainly/apparently gveret Levi

Let's now see whether the location of AgrSP can be established. Since it is impossible to establish the position of null subjects directly, we check the distribution of subjunctive weak *tu* with respect to adverbs. Like strong subjects, *tu* cannot follow *mica* and can follow or precede any higher adverb (see the glosses in (58)).

(128) a. Crede che *mica tu / tu mica abbia preso il treno.
      b. Crede che rapidamente tu / tu rapidamente abbia di nuovo alzato il braccio.
      c. Crede che raramente tu / tu raramente faccia tutto bene.
      d. Crede che di nuovo tu / tu di nuovo faccia tardi a scuola.
      e. Crede che solitamente tu / tu solitamente esca alle due.
      f. Crede che stupidamente tu / tu stupidamente esca sempre senza ombrello.
      g. Crede che volentieri tu / tu volentieri ti sia offerto di aiutarci.
      h. Crede che non necessariamente tu / tu non necessariamente sia pacifista.
      i. Crede che forse tu / tu forse venga a trovarci.
      l. Crede che allora tu / tu allora fossi monarchico.

    m. Crede che probabilmente tu / tu probabilmente faccia sul serio.
    n. Crede che evidentemente tu / tu evidentemente sia contento così.
    o. Crede che purtroppo tu / tu purtroppo abbia accettato.
    p. Crede che francamente tu / tu francamente abbia esagerato.

Like SubjP, AgrSP is freely generated above any adverb-related projection higher than *mica*.[28] This also holds true for English, where a weak subject pronoun has the same distribution as strong subjects with respect to adverbs (see (124b and c)).

7. Some interpretive issues

Some semantic issues correlated with the subject-of-predication feature are discussed in this section.

7.1. On the absence of the subject of predication

If a sentence contains a weak pronoun in specAgrSP, nothing checks the subject-of-predication feature (see the derivation in (16a)). A sentence in which the subject-of-predication feature is not checked can be of two types: either it is a thetic sentence (see 7.4), or in the semantic component, the subject of predication is taken to be identical with the subject of predication of the previous clause, as in (129), or discourse, as in (130), about which the predicate says something new. (The predicate corresponds structurally to everything included in AgrSP.) The subject of predication can be a DP, such as *Carla* in (129a)/(130a), or an XP of the type discussed in section 3, such as *ad Andrea* in (129b)/(130b).

(129) a. Poiché Carla$_i$ ha dato un bacio a Mario, *pro*$_i$ è felice. (Calabrese 1986: 31)
       since Carla has given a kiss to Mario, [she] is happy
     b. Poiché ad Andrea$_i$ interessa l'iconografia, *pro*$_i$ abbandonerà con piacere la
       linguistica. (Ibid.: 28)
       since to Andrea interests the iconography [he] will-abandon with pleasure the
       linguistics

(130) a. Carla$_i$ ha incontrato Mario ieri per strada. Pur essendo vista da tutti, *pro*$_i$ non ha
       fatto nessun cenno di saluto. (Ibid.: 32)
       Carla has met Mario yesterday on the street although being seen by everyone
       [she] not has said hello
     b. Ad Andrea$_i$ interessa l'iconografia. Pur essendo un linguista affermato, *pro*$_i$
       abbandonerà con piacere la linguistica.
       to Andrea interests the iconography although being a famous linguist [he] will-
       abandon with pleasure the linguistics

If the subject of predication is different from the subject of predication of the previous clause or discourse, some element must move to specSubjP to check the relevant feature. This element can be a strong pronoun, such as *lui* in (131), or a fronted XP, such as the dative *a Gianni* in (132):

(131) a. Poiché Carla ha dato un bacio a Mario$_j$, lui$_i$ è felice.
       since Carla has given a kiss to Mario, he is happy

b. Carla ha incontrato Mario$_i$ ieri per strada. Pur essendo visto da tutti, lui$_i$ non ha fatto nessun cenno di saluto.

Carla has met Mario yesterday on the street although being seen by everyone he not has said hello

(132) Sebbene Carla$_i$ abbia sposato Mario, a Gianni *pro*$_i$ interessa ancora.
       although Carla has married Mario to Gianni [she] interests still

To account for (129) and (130), Calabrese (1986: 31) claims that "a pronominal in position of Thema is expected to have a referent of another Thema." Although the spirit of Calabrese's proposal is kept here, his proposal cannot be understood in structural terms. *Pro* occupies specAgrSP (and not "a position of Thema") in both (129a) and (132). SpecSubjP is either empty (as in (129a)) or filled (as in (132), where it is occupied by *a Gianni*). When it is empty, a semantic rule establishes that the subject of predication should be searched in the previous clause or discourse, as suggested above.

7.2. Why three third-person subject pronouns in Italian (*pro, egli, lui*)?

If a subject pronoun does not have a familiar antecedent or is focalized, coordinated, or modified, it is realized as a strong pronoun; if a subject pronoun has a familiar antecedent and is not focalized, coordinated, or modified, it is realized as a weak pronoun (in NSLs, this corresponds to the null subject *pro*) (see Cardinaletti and Starke 1999). But there are two contexts in Italian in which a null subject is replaced by an overt weak pronoun of the *egli/esso* series (see 4.2): when the subject pronoun refers to a DP that is familiar but nonprominent in the previous context (i.e., not a subject but, e.g., an object), as in (133), and when the antecedent of the pronoun is perceived as somehow too far away and needs to be mentioned again, as in (134). In (133) and (134), the antecedent of the pronoun is underlined.

(133) a. L'aspetto più interessante per noi europei è che, siccome per un indiano una società senza caste è semplicemente impensabile, *egli* ipotizza che in Europa le caste devono essere chiamate in un altro modo. (*Il Manifesto*, 5/11/1999: 23)
       'The aspect most interesting for us Europeans is that, since for an Indian a society without castes is simply unthinkable, he hypothesizes that in Europe the castes must be called in another way.'

   b. In verità, se i giornali d'oggi dovessero, come gli altri negozianti, mettere fuori un'insegna, *essa* dovrebbe portare la scritta: ... (A. Berardinelli, *L'eroe che pensa*, 1997: 43)
       'In truth, if the newspapers of today should, like the other shopkeepers, put up a sign, it should display the [following] writing: ...

(134) L'episodio Gide è un episodio tutto pubblico e in piena luce. *Pro* non contiene sfumature private, né accenti troppo personali. *Esso* rappresenta dunque, con altrettanta formale ufficialità, la rottura di un legame tattico ... (Ibid., 103)
       'The episode Gide is an episode all public and in full light. [It] does not contain private nuances, nor too personal accents. It represents, therefore, with as much formal official character, the severing of a tactical link.

In both (133) and (134), the overt subject pronoun can be analyzed as containing the subject-of-predication feature:

- In (133), the subject of predication needs to be explicitly mentioned through the overt pronoun, *egli* and *essa*, respectively. If nothing were to check the subject-of-predication feature, the subject of predication would be searched in the previous sentence (section 7.1)—that is, it would be *l'aspetto più interessante* and *i giornali d'oggi*, respectively, with a semantically odd result.[29]
- In (134), the subject of predication has not changed: it is the same as in the previous discourse (*l'episodio Gide*), and in principle it does not need to be repeated. The sentence is grammatical with a null subject: *né accenti troppo personali. Pro rappresenta dunque ...* The overt pronoun is used optionally as a stylistic mean in order to restate the subject of predication, presumably because it is perceived to be too far away. (The use of a pronoun is alternative to the repetition of the antecedent DP, which is also possible: *né accenti troppo personali. Questo episodio rappresenta dunque...*).

To sum up: Italian third-person subject pronouns realize a threefold distinction, for the expression of which the assumption of the subject-of predication feature looks unavoidable.[30]

(135)   a. *pro*$_{weak}$: {ϕ-features, case}
        b. *egli*$_{weak}$ / *esso*$_{weak}$: {ϕ-features, case, subject-of-predication}
        c. *lui*$_{strong}$ / *questo*$_{strong}$: {ϕ-features, case, subject-of-predication, (topic), (focus)}

The feature characterization in (135) complies with the structural conclusions reached in section 4.2. Since *pro* does not check the subject-of-predication feature, it cannot occur in specSubjP. Both *egli* and *lui* check this feature in specSubjP.

7.3.   Colloquial Italian

Pronouns of the *egli/esso* series belong to formal Italian. In colloquial Italian, *egli* is replaced by *lui*. Example (136) with *lui* sounds more colloquial than (133a), and (137b) with *egli* sounds more formal than (137a) with *lui*. As for the [–human] pronoun *essa* in (133b), it can be replaced by a demonstrative, as shown in (138):

(136)   L'aspetto più interessante per noi europei è che, siccome per <u>un indiano</u> una società senza caste è semplicemente impensabile, *lui* ipotizza che in Europa le caste devono essere chiamate in un altro modo.

(137)   a. Se un amico <u>gli</u> sollecitava la pratica di un familiare *lui* la trattava come le altre. (C. Piersanti, *L'amore degli adulti*, 1989: 77)
           if a friend to-him urged the case of a relative he it treated like the others
        b. Se un amico <u>gli</u> sollecitava la pratica di un familiare *egli* la trattava come le altre.

(138)   In verità, se i giornali d'oggi dovessero, come gli altri negozianti, mettere fuori <u>un'insegna</u>, *questa* dovrebbe portare la scritta: ...
           in truth, if the newspapers of today should, like the other shop-keepers, put up a sign, this should display the [following] writing: . . .

The counterpart of (135) for colloquial Italian is (139):[31]

(139)   a. *pro*$_{weak}$: {ϕ-features, case}
        b. *lui*$_{strong}$/*questo*$_{strong}$: {ϕ-features, case, subject-of-predication, (topic), (focus)}

7.4. Subject-of-predication versus EPP: some speculations

The movement of an XP to check the subject-of-predication feature should be kept distinct from the EPP requirement stipulating that every sentence must contain a subject (Chomsky 1981). The EPP essentially captures the necessity of expletives when no argument is raised to the preverbal subject position, as in (1c). Some attempts have been made to understand the EPP, yet it remains a rather mysterious property of grammar. The EPP has been expressed as a nominal feature D on AgrS (Chomsky 1995: 232), as a selectional feature that can be satisfied by an XP merged with the category it heads (Chomsky 1998), and as a feature P (suggesting *phonological*) (Holmberg 2000).

Although I will not try to understand the nature of the EPP-feature, I will show that (a) not all cases of preverbal subjects are to be analyzed in terms of the EPP, and (b) the EPP is an independent requirement with respect to the checking of the subject-of-predication feature. The main evidence is provided by the observation that sentences with a preverbal subject and sentences containing an expletive and a postverbal subject are different sentence types. If preverbal subjects and expletives were to check one and the same feature—either the EPP-feature or the subject-of-predication feature—no difference should be expected. Preverbal and postverbal subjects differ precisely with respect to the subject-of-predication feature. Only the former can check this feature, while the latter can never be subjects of predication. Consider the following sentences containing unaccusative verbs:

(140)   a. Gianni è arrivato.
            Gianni is arrived
        b. È arrivato GIANNI (non Maria).
            is arrived Gianni (not Maria)
        c. È arrivato Gianni.

Example (140a), with a preverbal subject, is a predication or categorical sentence. In categorical sentences, the predicate is "about" a prominent argument, here the subject *Gianni*. In addition to case and ϕ-features, the DP *Gianni* checks the subject-of-predication feature, as shown in (141) (to be revised below).

(141)   [$_{\text{SubjP}}$ Gianni$_k$ [$_{\text{AgrSP}}$ t$_k$ è ... [$_{\text{VP}}$ arrivato t$_k$]]].

In sentences with postverbal subjects, the grammatical subject can either be (contrastively) focused, as in (140b), or belong to the predicate, as in (140c). When the subject is focused, we get a categorical sentence in which the subject of predication is the one of the preceding context, which is negated by the contrasted element. When the postverbal subject is not focused, there is no subject of predication, and we get a presentation S or thetic sentence. A thetic sentence simply reports on an event, in which all the arguments of the verb are introduced as event participants. It is used in out-of-the blue contexts or as an answer to the question *What happened?* It is fair to assume that in thetic sentences, no XP in the clause checks the subject-of-predication feature, as shown in (142) (to be revised below).[32]

(142)   [$_{\text{SubjP}}$ [$_{\text{AgrSP}}$ è ... [$_{\text{VP}}$ arrivato Gianni]]].

The observations made so far can be visualized as in (143) (Lonzi 1986: 105). (A formal semantic characterization of the sentences in (140) is beyond the scope of this chapter.)

(143)   a. For X = Gianni, X has arrived.
        b. For X ≠ Maria and X = Gianni, X has arrived.
        c. For X = arrive Gianni, there happened X.

With transitive and intransitive verbs, things are slightly different. The difference concerns the thetic sentences. With these verb classes, thetic sentences display a preverbal subject, whereas unaccusative verbs have a postverbal subject. Compare (140c) with (144c) and (145c) (notice that the categorical sentences in (a) and (b) display the same word order with all verb classes):

(144)   a. Gianni ha chiamato Piero.
            'Gianni has called Piero.'
        b. Ha chiamato Piero GIANNI (non Maria).
            has called Piero Gianni (not Maria)
        c. Gianni ha chiamato Piero.

(145)   a. Gianni ha telefonato a Piero.
            Gianni has phoned to Piero
        b. Ha telefonato a Piero GIANNI (non Maria).
            has phoned to Piero Gianni (not Maria)
        c. Gianni ha telefonato a Piero.

The second issue raised by (in)transitive verbs is how to distinguish the (a) from the (c) sentences given that both word order and intonation are the same (whereas (140b) and (140c) differ with respect to intonation).

Extending the proposal made above for (140c) (see (142)), in the thetic sentences (144c) and (145c) the subject does not check the subject-of-predication feature. What forces its movement to the preverbal position? Checking of case and ϕ-features is not sufficient to trigger movement, since it can take place covertly (or long distance). Suppose that the trigger is the EPP. The highest argument moves to check the EPP feature (in addition to case and ϕ-features), as shown in (146a). The difference between (144c)/(145c) and (144a)/(145a) relies in the subject-of-predication feature. Extending the proposal made above for (140a) (see (141)), in (144a)/(145a) the subject-of-predication feature is checked by the subject *Gianni*, as shown in (146b). The two derivations are illustrated with the transitive verb of (144):

(146)   a. $[_{SubjP} \quad [_{EPPP} \text{Gianni}_k [_{AgrSP} t_k \text{ ha } \dots [_{VP} t_k \text{ chiamato Piero}]]]].$
        b. $[_{SubjP} \text{Gianni}_k [_{EPPP} t_k \quad [_{AgrSP} t_k \text{ ha } \dots [_{VP} t_k \text{ chiamato Piero}]]]].$

The structure in (146) is in compliance with the present enterprise of decomposing the subject properties into different morphosyntactic features and captures the semantic difference between (144a)/(145a) and (144c)/(145c) in structural terms.

Let's now go back to unaccusative verbs and consider (140c) again. Here, as mentioned, the EPP feature is considered to be the trigger for the insertion of an expletive subject (whereas case and ϕ-features are checked by the postverbal subject; Cardinaletti 1997b). In her detailed analysis of sentences like (140c), Tortora (1997) suggests that what occupies the preverbal position is not an expletive but a null location-goal argument of the unaccusative verb (parallel to the weak locative *there* found in the corresponding English sentence in (151)). Since this locative argument does not agree with the verb, it cannot check case and ϕ-features and cannot occupy specAgrS. I take it to occupy specEPPP. Example (147) revises (142):[33]

(147) $[_{SubjP} [_{EPPP} \emptyset_{Loc} [_{AgrSP} \grave{e} \ldots [_{VP} \text{arrivato Gianni}]]]]$.

In (140b), there is no such locative argument. The EPP position is filled with a true, nominal expletive, as shown in (148a). The locative argument is also absent in (140a), which has the structure in (148b) (which revises (141) in that it displays the EPPP projection):

(148)   a. $[_{SubjP} \quad\quad [_{EPPP} \emptyset_{NOM} [_{AgrSP} \grave{e} \ldots \quad [_{VP} \text{arrivato GIANNI}]]]]$.
          b. $[_{SubjP} \text{Gianni}_k [_{EPPP} t_k \quad [_{AgrSP} t_k \grave{e} \ldots [_{VP} \text{arrivato } t_k]]]]$.

The structural difference between (147) and (148) correlates with a different interpretation of the two sets of sentences. Tortora (1997: §4.2.1.2 and 2001) points out that in (140c), the goal of motion is necessarily speaker-oriented ("Gianni has arrived where the speaker is"), while it is free in reference in (140a) and (140b) ("Gianni has arrived somewhere, even if the speaker was not in that place at the time of arrival").

A true expletive is also found in the categorical sentences (144b) and (145b) containing unergative verbs with postverbal subjects. This null expletive is comparable to the overt nominal expletive found in Germanic TECs (e.g., *það* in Icelandic (7a)). The derivation is again illustrated with the transitive verb of (144):[34]

(149) $[_{SubjP} [_{EPPP} \emptyset_{NOM} [_{AgrSP} \text{ha [chiamato}_v [\text{Piero}_i [_{VP} \text{GIANNI } t_v t_i]]]]]]$.

Comparing NSLs and non-NSLs, it can easily be noticed that there is no difference between Italian and English, for example, with respect to the (a) and the (c) sentences of (144) and (145). Compare (150) with (146):

(150)   a. $[_{SubjP} \quad\quad [_{EPPP} \text{John}_k [_{AgrSP} t_k \text{ has} \ldots [_{VP} t_k \text{ called his friend}]]]]$.
          b. $[_{SubjP} \text{John}_k [_{EPPP} t_k \quad [_{AgrSP} t_k \text{ has} \ldots [_{VP} t_k \text{ called his friend}]]]]$.

The difference between NSLs and non-NSLs only concerns the (b) sentences of (144) and (145), whose counterparts are ungrammatical in non-NSLs. Differently from Italian, English does not allow for a true expletive to occur in specEPPP.

As for sentences containing the location-goal argument, the two types of languages do not differ: (151) is parallel to (147), *modulo* pro-drop.

(151)   a. There arrived three girls.
          b. $[_{SubjP} [_{EPPP} \text{there}_{Loc} [_{AgrSP} \ldots [_{VP} \text{arrived three girls}]]]]$.

But there remains an asymmetry in this case. English also allows for the subject of a thetic sentence to move to a preverbal position, as shown in (152). Example (152), with a rising intonation on *John*—signaled here by italics to distinguish it from contrastive focus—expectedly has the speaker-oriented interpretation of the location-goal (Tortora 1997: 175, n.110).[35]

(152)   *John* arrived.

Following Tortora, the speaker-oriented interpretation of the location-goal implies the presence of a locative argument. In her analysis, a phonologically null locative occurs in the subject position, while *John* occurs in a lower position. Similarly to *there* in (151b), I take the phonologically null locative to occupy the EPP-related position. Since in English, the overt movement of the subject to the preverbal position can only be triggered by the need to check nominative case and ϕ-features, I take *John* to occupy specAgrSP, which must therefore be located below the EPP-related position:[36]

(153)   [$_{SubjP}$ [$_{EPPP}$ $\emptyset_{LOC}$ [$_{AgrSP}$ *John*$_k$ . . . [$_{VP}$ arrived t$_k$]]]].

Italian does not allow a sentence like (154), parallel to (152)–(153), presumably because case and ϕ-features can be checked covertly (or long distance). In Italian, overt DP movement to the preverbal position can only be motivated by the need to check either the EPP or the subject-of-predication feature, as in (146) and (148b).

(154)   *[$_{SubjP}$ [$_{EPPP}$ $\emptyset_{LOC}$ [$_{AgrSP}$ *Gianni*$_k$ è . . . [$_{VP}$ arrivato t$_k$]]]].

In conclusion, we end up with the following preverbal subject positions:

(155)   specSubjP specEPPP specAgrSP*

The subject-of-predication feature and the EPP-feature are not identical, but there is a similarity between the two. Both features must universally be checked before Spell-Out, whereas other features, such as case and ϕ-features on the one hand and topic and focus features on the other, can be checked either before or after Spell-Out. This asymmetry is one of the many issues concerning subjecthood that are still open. For further open questions not addressed here, see McCloskey 1997: §9.

8.   Concluding remarks

Subjecthood has been split into different functional projections, each realizing a subject-related morphosyntactic feature. The following cartography of subject positions is obtained:

(156)   specSubjP specEPPP specAgrSP* . . . specVP

As said in section 4.5, the split of AgrSP requires further comparative work. Other subject positions are missing from (156), such as those hosting quantified subjects (see section 4.4) and the middlefield subject positions individuated in section 1.2.

Each subject position hosts a different type of subject. There are language-specific restrictions on the distribution of strong subjects. Weak subjects are instead universally restricted to projections in which nominative case and ϕ-features are checked. Expletive subject pronouns occur in either specAgrSP or specEPPP, according to whether or not they check nominative case and ϕ-features.

Notes

The audience of the Workshop on the Cartography of Syntactic Positions and Semantic Types, held in Siena on November 25–26, 1999, is kindly thanked for comments and suggestions. Thanks are also due to Paolo Chinellato, Manuela Schoenenberger, Luigi Rizzi, and an anonymous reviewer for comments on an earlier written version. The core ideas of the essay have circulated as Cardinaletti (1994b) and appeared as Cardinaletti (1997a).

1. In theories that allow covert raising (Chomsky 1995), the subject moves to specFocusP or specAgrSP, depending on whether or not it is focused.

2. Belletti's (1998, 1999) proposal differs minimally from ours: postverbal subjects occupy the (leftward) specifier of a Focus projection immediately above VP, while the object in (4a) and in (5) occurs in a Topic position above and below FocusP, respectively. Both proposals want to capture the fact that in (4a) and (5), the subject follows low adverbs such as *bene* (well) and *completamente* (completely). Notice that if the object is focused and the subject is destressed, as in (i), the object occurs in its VP-internal position and the subject is left-dislocated (Cardinaletti 1998). This means that the Topic position below FocusP in Belletti's terms cannot host subjects:

    (i)   Ha letto IL GIORNALE, Gianni.
         has read the newspaper Gianni

3. Example (6b) should be read with focus on the object. If the subject is focused and the object is destressed, the sentence is grammatical (see (5)). If both the subject and the object are focused, the sentence is also grammatical and gets a linked or paired focus reading. In this case, I take both the subject and the object to be VP-internal.

    (i)   Ha(nno) letto GIANNI IL GIORNALE, e MARIO I LIBRI.
         has/have read Gianni the newspaper and Mario the books

4. Example (15) is a refinement of the double Agr structure proposed in Cardinaletti and Roberts (2002). See Guasti and Rizzi (2002) for arguments that AgrSP exists as an independent projection, differently from what has been assumed since Chomsky (1995). See section 7.4 in this chapter for the discussion of the EPP.

5. "Subject of predication" is similar to the traditional notions of "psychological/notional subject" and "Theme," but differs from the notion "Topic." It pertains to the logical structure of the sentence (subject versus predicate), while Topic refers to the information structure of the sentence (given versus new). Two considerations support this. First, some DPs are subjects of predication from the semantic point of view without being Topics—for example, in out-of-the-blue sentences with transitive verbs (see sections 6.1 and 7.4). Second, almost any XP can be topicalized (in specTopicP; Rizzi 1997), while SpecSubjP is a position reserved for specific types of XPs (see section 3.). See Calabrese (1986), Salvi (1986), and Saccon (1993: 140ff) for related proposals.

6. In (19b) and throughout, different occurrences of curly brackets inside one and the same clause indicate alternative choices. The impossibility of left-dislocated items in Aux-to-Comp is due to the fact that the Top head blocks movement of the verb to Force° (cf. Rizzi 1997: 331,n. 22 for other cases of verb movement with the same restriction). For CD, see section 4.1.2.

7. From (i), it is safe to conclude that in (23a), the subject is *pro*:

    (i)   A proposito dello spettacolo, essendo a Gianni *pro* piaciuto molto, decidemmo
         di replicarlo anche i giorni seguenti.
         as for the performance being to Gianni [it] 'pleased' much [we] decided to
         repeat it also the next days

Gerunds thus seem to differ from the other Aux-to-Comp constructions, which do not allow referential *pro*s (see Rizzi 1982: chap. 4, §3 for the discussion of the types of *pro* licensed by nonfinite verbs when raised to C°).

    (ii)   a.*Ritengo essere *pro* piaciuta a Gianni.
         b.*Ritengo essere a Gianni *pro* piaciuta.
         [I] believe [to] be [it] 'pleased' to Gianni

8. Cases like (31a) and (32a) differ from English locative inversion, such as *Every Thursday at noon, into the saloon wander three drunken stevadores* (Branigan 1992: 78). Whereas English preposed locatives do not cooccur with A' movements, (i), and are only compatible with bridge verbs, (iii) (thanks to Ian Roberts and Chris Wilder for judgments), Italian preposed locatives, on a par with subject DPs, do not interfere with A' extraction, (ii), and can be embedded under any verb, (iv).

(i)   a. *the day when into the room ran John
      b. *the days when [John claimed [that on the wall hangs a huge portrait of the Maestro t]]

(ii) a. la disgrazia che su Gianni cadde l'anno scorso
         the misfortune that on Gianni fell last year
      b. l'anno in cui su Gianni cadde quella terribile disgrazia
         the year in which on Gianni fell that terrible misfortune

(iii) a. John claimed that on the wall hangs a huge portrait of the Maestro.
      b. ?Maria said that into the room ran John.
      c. *Everyone regrets that into the saloon wandered three drunken stevadores.

(iv) a. So che su Gianni è caduta quella terribile disgrazia.
         [I] know that on Gianni is fallen that terrible misfortune
      b. Mi dispiace che su Gianni sia caduta quella terribile disgrazia.
         [it] to-me 'displeases' that on Gianni is fallen that terrible misfortune

The Italian cases can thus be considered as "pure" cases of locative fronting, whereas English locative inversion seems to involve an extra step of the locative phrase to an A', topic position (see den Dikken 1992: 206f, n. 32; den Dikken and Naess 1993).

9. If the matrix verb is first person, *pro* can only be interpreted as third person.

(i)   Credo che sia ricco, ma *non lo sei / non lo è.   (*pro* = *you / he)
      [I] think that [he] is$_{SUBJ}$ rich, but *[you] are not / [he] is not

10. In indicative sentences, a homophonous strong pronoun is found that can be topicalized:

(i)   a. Dice che pro/tu sei ricco.
         [he] says that you are$_{IND}$ rich
      b. Tu dice che sei ricco.
         you [he] says that are$_{IND}$ rich

11. Some speakers do not dislike (42b) and do not find a clear contrast between (42b) and (42d). These speakers either allow *tu* to be a weak pronoun checking the subject-of-predication feature (cf. *egli* discussed in 4.2 and 7.2) or analyze *tu* as occurring in a position higher than the parenthetical, which I take to be higher than *pro* (see later). This would be the only evidence that in Italian, the overt second-person pronoun occurs in a different position with respect to (first- and third-person) null pronouns (see section 4.5).

12. Weak wh-phrases such as Italian *che* and French *que* cannot be followed by parentheticals, whereas strong wh-phrases such as *(che) cosa* and *qui* can (Cardinaletti 1994b: 71):

(i)   a. *Che, secondo te, deve fare?
      b. (Che) cosa, secondo te, deve fare?
         what, according to you, [he] must do

(ii) a. *Que, selon toi, doit-il faire?
         what according to you must-he do

     b. Qui, selon toi, doit-il inviter?
       who according to you must-he invite

The adjacency requirement between weak wh-phrases and the verb can be taken to be a reflex of the overt spec-head agreement necessary for weak elements (Cardinaletti and Starke 1999), whereas the possibility of parentheticals between strong wh-phrases and the verb suggests that the two do not need to occur in a spec-head configuration before Spell-Out. For a different analysis of the distribution of weak wh-phrases, see Munaro (1997, 1999) and Poletto and Pollock (1999).

13. In (46), XP can be either an adjunction to AgrSP or a designated functional projection between SubjP and AgrSP. Kayne's (1994) antisymmetry approach, which takes specifiers to be adjoined and bans double adjunctions, favors the latter analysis.

14. The following sentence is not a counterexample to the proposal that *tu* is lower than the dative argument as it is an instance of PP scrambling, available with other datives as well (Cinque 1999: 117, 214, n. 7).

  (i)   a. Credo che tu a Gianni piaccia.
        [I] believe that you to Gianni 'pleases'$_{SUBJ}$
      b. Credo che tu a Gianni abbia parlato ieri.
        [I] believe that you to Gianni had$_{SUBJ}$ spoken yesterday

15. Mutual exclusion of a preverbal strong subject and a dative experiencer is also found in Aux-to-C, as shown in (i). When the two constituents seem to cooccur, as in (ii), the left-most one is left-dislocated.

  (i)   *Essendo a Gianni questo libro piaciuto molto, ...
      being to Gianni this book 'pleased' much . . .

  (ii) a. A Gianni le patate piacciono molto.
        to Gianni the potatoes 'please' much
      b. Le patate a Gianni piacciono molto.
        the potatoes to Gianni 'please' much

Differently from fronted datives and similarly to other topics, the left-most constituent in (ii) preferably precedes a focalized constituent, as shown in (iii).

(iii)	a. ??	IN QUEL MODO,	a Gianni le patate piacciono, non fritte.	
		in that manner	to Gianni the potatoes 'please' not fried	
	b. ??	IN QUEL MODO,	le patate a Gianni piacciono, non fritte.	
	c. A Gianni,	IN QUEL MODO	le patate	piacciono, non fritte.
	d. Le patate,	IN QUEL MODO	a Gianni	piacciono, non fritte.

Differently from other topics, however, which are most naturally resumed by a clitic pronoun, the dative experiencer in (iia) and (iiic) does not need a resumptive clitic pronoun, a property still to be explained.

16. No speaker does the opposite—that is, accepts a strong subject without allowing weak subjects. This is explained by the hypothesis that SubjP is higher than AgrSP, combined with the reduced structure hypothesis formulated in 4.1.2. For a different analysis of the two groups of speakers in terms of syncretic categories, see Giorgi and Pianesi (1997: 239). They suggest that complementizer deletion features a syncretic category MOOD/AGR whose specifier can be analyzed either as an AGR specifier (by those speakers who allow a strong subject to occur) or as a MOOD specifier (by those speakers who don't). Since I do not share the assumption of syncretic categories, this analysis of the two grammars cannot be adopted here.

17. Differently from Rizzi (1997: 288), Beninca'(2001) points out that sentences like (54) and (ia) are not ungrammatical but only marginal. At least in the grammar behind (54) and (ia), the Italian finite complementizer *che* (that) can be generated either in Fin, as in (54) and (ia), or in Force, as in (ib) (while Rizzi takes *che* to be only a Force element).

    (i)   a. ?Credo il tuo libro, che loro lo apprezzerebbero molto.
           b. Credo che il tuo libro, loro lo apprezzerebbero molto.
             [I] believe that the your book they it would-appreciate a lot

Following Rizzi (1997: 288), the Italian infinitival complementizer *di* (of) in (ii) can only be a Fin element.

    (ii)   a. Credo il tuo libro, di apprezzarlo molto.
           b.*Credo di il tuo libro, apprezzarlo molto.
             [I] believe to the your book, appreciate-it a lot

18. This conclusion is supported by empirical evidence from Romanian. The finite verb, which is said to move to Mood°, moves above *acum* (now) but never crosses over epistemic adverbs such as *abia* (hardly) (Cornilescu 1997: 108):

    (i)   Ion apealează acum zilnic la părinţii lui.
         Ion resorts now daily to parents his

    (ii)   a. Ion abia îl aşteaptă pe Petru.
             Ion hardly him waits ACC Petru
           b.*Ion îl aşteaptă abia pe Petru.
             Ion him waits hardly ACC Petru

Similarly, both the finite verb and the particle *sa*, which realizes the Mood head, follow IP-edge adverbs (see section 6.3) such as *mîine* (tomorrow) (Cornilescu 1997: 106):

    (iii)   a. Ion mîine merge acolo.
             Ion tomorrow goes there
           b. Ion mîine să meargă acolo.
             Ion tomorrow sa go$_{SUBJ}$ there

Also see Rivero (1987, 1988, 1991) and Calabrese (1993) for the proposal that the complementizer found in subjunctive clauses in Balkan languages and Salentino is the realization of an IP-internal functional head.

19. The following contrasts show that the pronouns of the *egli/esso* series are weak. They cannot occur in contexts in which a strong pronoun is required—for example, when the subject is modified by a focalizing adverb. Compare (ia) with (ib). Conversely, in accordance with the choice principle (Cardinaletti and Starke 1999: §3.3.2), the strong pronoun *loro* is excluded if not needed, as shown in (id) (or it sounds colloquial, see 7.3):

    (i)   a. Temo che la generazione dei più giovani, e anche quella di mezzo, non abbia
             più la volontà di riprendere il testimone. Eppure, *solo loro* possono farci uscire
             da questo freddo letargo. (*Le Monde Diplomatique*, November 1999, p. 23)
             '[I] fear that the generation of-the most young, and also the one in the
             middle, does not have the will of taking over the baton again. And yet, only
             they can make us get out of this cold lethargy.'
           b.*... Eppure, *solo essi* possono farci uscire da questo freddo letargo.
           c. ... Eppure, *essi* possono farci uscire da questo freddo letargo.
           d.*... Eppure, *loro* possono farci uscire da questo freddo letargo.

20. As shown for DPs in n. 15, when a dative experiencer seems to cooccur with an overt weak subject pronoun, as in (i), it is left-dislocated. It preferably precedes a focalized constituent, as in (ii):

(i) A Gianni esse piacciono molto.
     to Gianni they 'please' much

(ii) a. ??   IN QUEL MODO, a Gianni esse piacciono, non fritte.
              in that manner to Gianni they 'please' not fried
     b. A Gianni, IN QUEL MODO esse   piacciono, non fritte.

21. De Crousaz and Shlonsky (2000) point out that "whereas *je suis* is ambiguous in French, meaning either 'I am' (>*être*) or 'I follow' (>*suivre*), the inverted form *suis-je* in (74a) can only mean 'am I?' (M. Starke personal communication). This is a clear indication that the relevant factor here is syntactic (i.e., the distinction between lexical and functional verbs) and not morphophonological."

22. The paradigm in (80) shows that in English a lower position of parentheticals, between specAgrSP and the verb, is disallowed.

23. See Vecchiato (2000) for the same analysis and a detailed discussion of the previous accounts. Sportiche (1999) suggests an analysis similar to ours, although it is different in many assumptions. The subject occupies specNomP, the specifier of a head which is higher than specAgrSP and where nominative case is checked, whereas the verb and the clitic pronoun—which is taken to be a morphological affix—are in AgrS. For similar assumptions, see Friedemann (1995).

24. Alexiadou and Anagnastopoulou (1998: 495, n. 4) exclude Italian from their analysis because of the arguments in Cardinaletti (1997a), which they treat as "complications."

25. The subject clitic is also not obligatory when the subject precedes the adverb *doman* (tomorrow), which is taken by Beninca' to be an IP-edge adverb (see section 6.3).

(i) Mario doman torna a casa.
     Mario tomorrow comes-back home

26. This fact cannot be captured in terms of strict adjacency between the subject and the verb (see (81a)). Rather, the movement of the subject and the movement of the verb are dependent on each other, with the result that the subject and the verb can either both precede (as in (125d)) or both follow (as in (125b)) sentential adverbs (while in the ungrammatical (125a) and (125c), only the subject precedes the adverb). For a similar connection in Italian, see note 28.

27. See also Cinque (1999: §5.1). The liberty exhibited by SubjP is also found with negative projections. A NegP can be generated on top of each adverb-related projection up to a certain height (below the epistemic Mod projection, which hosts the adverb *probabilmente*, probably) (Cinque 1999: 124).

28. In Italian, both strong and weak subjects undergo the following restriction: they can appear in any position above *mica*, provided that they precede the finite verb. For Cinque (1999: 111), this is due to the requirement that the verb be in a spec-head agreement relation with the subject or its trace.

29. For psycholinguistic evidence that a null subject always gets a prominent subject as its antecedent, see Carminati (2001). This work does not take *egli* into account.

30. This tripartition is not found with object pronouns, since objects do not check the subject-of-predication feature (section 3.3). In (135) *questo* is the strong counterpart of *esso*, which is [–human], while (strong) *lui* can only have [+human] referents.

31. Differently from what assumed in (139), we might hypothesize that colloquial Italian has both a strong and a weak subject *lui*. The hypothesis that *lui* can be weak in colloquial Italian could explain the fact that restrictive speakers who do not accept strong subjects in complementizer deletion (see (48c and d) and (49c and d)), can marginally accept *lui* if it is not modified or coordinated, as shown in (ia) and (ib–c), respectively. This contrast can be interpreted in the following way: these speakers accept weak *lui* but reject strong *lui* (the contrast between DPs and pronouns in complementizer deletion is also noted in Giorgi and Pianesi 1997: 234).

(i)   a. ?Pensa lui sia in grado di aiutarlo.
       [he] thinks he is$_{SUBJ}$ able to help-him
    b.*Pensa solo lui sia in grado di aiutarlo.
       [he] thinks only he is$_{SUBJ}$ able to help-him
    c.*Pensa lui e Maria siano in grado di aiutarlo.
       [he] thinks he and Maria are$_{SUBJ}$ able to help-him

32. The "predication" versus "presentation S" opposition stems from Guéron (1980). It can be rephrased in terms of the distinction between categorical and thetic (Kuroda 1972), recently used by Raposo and Uriagereka (1995) and others. The claim that in thetic sentences, no XP checks the subject-of-predication feature is consistent with Raposo and Uriagereka's proposal that in these sentences, it is the predicate itself that takes scope over the rest of the expression, which is about the predicate.

33. A French thetic sentence like (ia), in which the expletive *il* checks case and φ-features (Cardinaletti 1997b), has the structure in (ib):

(i)   a. Il est arrivé trois filles.
       it is arrived three girls
    b. [$_{SubjP}$ [$_{EPPP}$ Ø$_{Loc}$ [$_{AgrSP}$ il est ... [$_{VP}$ arrivè trois filles]]]].

34. The following mistaken English productions by a native speaker of Italian can be taken to confirm that in (140b), (144b), and (145b), the expletive is nominal:

(i)   a. *It* is astonishing the fact that no child ...
    b. *It* is more interesting the transformation that involves wh-movement ...

To get the VOS order in (149), the verb and the object move to VP-external positions (see section 1.1).

35. The optionality of subject placement shown in (151) and (152) is only apparent. First, (151) is only possible with indefinite subjects. A definite subject can only appear preverbally, as in (152). Second, (151) belongs to formal English. Examples (151) and (152) might be considered to be generated by different grammars. These are important issues, but they are not investigated here.

36. The assumption of a null locative in (153) is not an ad hoc device to account for (152). Tortora (1997: 174, n. 110) finds another instance of the null locative in locative inversion (see note 8), which also displays the speaker-oriented interpretation of the location-goal. Tortora does not address the question as to how licensing of the null locative in (153) takes place. Notice that in (153), *John* might also occupy one of the MF subject positions individuated in section 1.2. Since the properties of these positions are not well understood, the hypothesis that *John* checks case and φ-features in specAgrSP looks more cautious.

References

Aboh, E. (1995) "Notes on Focalization in Gungbe." *GenGenP* 3.1, 5–21.

Alexiadou, A., and E. Anagnostopoulou (1998) "Parametrizing Agr: Word Order, V-Movement and EPP-Checking." *Natural Language and Linguistic Theory* 16, 491–539.

Antinucci, F., and G. Cinque (1977) "Sull'ordine delle parole in italiano: l'emarginazione." *Studi di grammatica italiana* 6, 121–146.

Barbosa, P. (1997) "Subject Positions in the Null Subject Languages." *Seminarios de Linguística* 1, 39–63.

Beghelli, F. (1995) "The Phrase Structure of Quantifier Scope," Ph.D. diss., UCLA.

Beghelli, F., and T. Stowell (1997) "Distributivity and Negation: The Syntax of *each* and *every*," in A. Szabolcsi (ed.) *Ways of Scope Taking*. Dordrecht: Kluwer, 71–107.

Belletti, A. (1990). *Generalized Verb Movement*. Turin: Rosenberg and Sellier.

——— (1998). "'Inversion' as Focalization." Unpublished ms., University of Siena.

——— (1999). "Aspects of the Low IP Area." Paper presented at the Workshop on the Cartography of Syntactic Positions and Semantic Types, Certosa di Pontignano, November 1999.

Belletti, A., and L. Rizzi (1988) "Psych Verbs and θ-theory." *Natural Language and Linguistic Theory* 6, 291–352.

Belletti, A., and U. Shlonsky (1995) "The Order of Verbal Complements: A Comparative Study." *Natural Language and Linguistic Theory* 13.3, 489–526.

Beninca', P. (2001) "The Position of Topic and Focus in the Left Periphery," in G. Cinque and G. Salvi (eds.) *Current Studies in Italian Syntax: Essays Offered to Lorenzo Renzi*. Amsterdam: Elsevier, 39–64.

Beninca', P., and G. Cinque (1985) "Lexical Subjects in Italian and the pro-Drop Parameter." Paper presented at the Comparative Generative Grammar Fiesta, Salzburg, August 1985.

Bobaljik, J. D., and D. Jonas (1996) "Subject Positions and the Roles of TP." *Linguistic Inquiry* 27.2, 195–236.

Bonet, E. (1990) "Subjects in Catalan." *MIT Working Papers in Linguistics* 13, 1–26.

Borer, H. (1984). *Parametric Syntax*. Dordrecht: Foris.

Brandi, L., and P. Cordin (1989) "Two Italian Dialects and the Null Subject Parameter," in O. Jaeggli and K. J. Safir (eds.) *The Null Subject Parameter*. Dordrecht: Kluwer, 111–142.

Branigan, P. (1992) "Subjects and Complementizers," Ph.D. diss., MIT (distributed by *MIT Working Papers in Linguistics*).

Brody, M. (1990) "Some Remarks on the Focus Field in Hungarian." *UCL Working Papers in Linguistics* 2, 201–226.

Burzio, L. (1986) *Italian Syntax*. Dordrecht: Reidel.

Calabrese, A. (1986) "Some Properties of the Italian Pronominal System: An Analysis Based on the Notion of *Thema* as Subject of Predication," in H. Stammerjohann (ed.), *Tema-Rema in Italiano*. Tübingen: Gunter Narr Verlag, 25–36.

——— (1993) "The Sentential Complementation of Salentino: A Study of a Language without Infinitival Clauses," in A. Belletti (ed.) *Syntactic Theory and the Dialects of Italy*. Turin: Rosenberg and Sellier, 28–98.

Cardinaletti, A. (1994a) *La sintassi dei pronomi: uno studio comparativo delle lingue germaniche e romanze*. Bologna: Il Mulino.

——— (1994b) "Subject Positions." *GenGenP* 2.1, 64–78.

——— (1997a) "Subjects and Clause Structure," in L. Haegeman (ed.) *The New Comparative Syntax*. London: Longman, 33–63.

——— (1997b) "Agreement and Control in Expletive Constructions." *Linguistic Inquiry* 28.3, 521–533.

——— (1998) "A Second Thought on *emarginazione*: Destressing vs. 'Right Dislocation.'" *University of Venice Working Papers in Linguistics* 8.2, 1–28.

——— (1999) "Italian 'Emphatic' Pronouns Are Post-verbal Subjects." *University of Venice Working Papers in Linguistics* 9, 59–92.

———— (2001) "Subjects and wh-Questions. A Reply to Uriagereka (1999)." Unpublished ms., University of Bologna.

Cardinaletti, A., and L. Repetti (2000) "Phonology and Syntax of Piacentine Clitics." Unpublished ms., University of Bologna and SUNY at Stony Brook.

Cardinaletti, A., and I. Roberts (2002) "Clause Structure and X-second," in G. Cinque (ed.) *Functional Structure in DP and IP: The Cartography of Syntactic Structures, vol. 1.* New York: Oxford University Press, 123–166.

Cardinaletti, A., and M. Starke (1996) "Deficient Pronouns: A View from Germanic—A Study in the Unified Description of Germanic and Romance," in H. Thráinsson, S. D. Epstein, and S. Peter (eds.) *Studies in Comparative Germanic Syntax, Vol. II.* Dordrecht: Kluwer, 21–65.

———— (1999) "The Typology of Structural Deficiency. A Case Study of the Three Classes of Pronouns," in H. van Riemsdijk (ed.) *Clitics in the Languages of Europe.* Berlin: Mouton de Gruyter, 145–233.

Carminati, M. N. (2001) "The Processing of Italian Subject Pronouns," Ph.D. diss., University of Massachusetts at Amherst.

Chinellato, P. (2001) "L'interpretazione morfosemantica del modo congiuntivo in italiano e in tedesco." *Rivista di grammatica generativa*, 26, 3–20.

Chomsky, N. (1981) *Lectures on Government and Binding.* Dordrecht: Foris.

———— (1986) *Knowledge of Language.* New York: Praeger.

———— (1995) *The Minimalist Program.* Cambridge, Mass.: MIT Press.

———— (1998) *Minimalist Inquiries: The Framework.* MIT Occasional Papers in Linguistics 15. Cambridge, Mass.: MIT Press.

———— (1999) "Derivation by Phase." Unpublished ms., MIT, Cambridge, Mass.

Chomsky, N., and H. Lasnik (1991) "Principles and Parameters Theory," in J. Jacobs, A. von Stechow, W. Sternefeld, and T. Venneman (eds.) *Syntax: An International Handbook of Contemporary Research.* Berlin: De Gruyter, 506–569.

Cinque, G. (1996) "Genitivo e genitivi prenominali nel DP italiano," in P. Beninca', G. Cinque, T. de Mauro, and N. Vincent (eds.) *Italiano e dialetti nel tempo: saggi di grammatica per Giulio C. Lepschy.* Rome: Bulzoni, 67–84.

———— (1999) *Adverbs and Functional Heads: A Cross-Linguistic Perspective.* New York: Oxford University Press.

Cinque, G., and G. Salvi (eds.) (2001) *Current Studies in Italian Syntax: Essays Offered to Lorenzo Renzi.* Amsterdam: Elsevier.

Contreras, H. (1991) "On the Position of Subjects," in S. Rothstein (ed.) *Perspectives on Phrase Structure: Heads and Licensing.* Syntax and Semantics 25. San Diego: Academic Press, 63–79.

Cornilescu, A. (1997) "The Double Subject Construction in Romanian: Notes on the Syntax of the Subject." *Revue Roumaine de Linguistique* 42.3–4, 101–147.

Damonte, F. (2000) "Modality within the CP Domain." Unpublished ms., University of Padua.

De Crousaz, I., and U. Shlonsky (2000) "The Distribution of a Subject Clitic Pronoun in a Franco-Provençal Dialec." Unpublished ms., University of Geneva.

den Dikken, M. (1992) *Particles.* Holland Institute of Generative Linguistics.

den Dikken, M., and A. Naess (1993) "Case Dependencies: The Case of Predicate Inversion." *Linguistic Review* 10.4, 303–336.

Dobrovie-Sorin, C. (1994) *The Syntax of Romanian: Comparative Studies in Romance.* Berlin: Mouton de Gruyter.

Egerland, V. (1996) "On Pronoun Positions in Swedish and Italian, Antisymmetry, and the Person Phrase." *University of Venice Working Papers in Linguistics* 6.2, 65–104.

Fernández-Soriano, O. (1999) "Two Types of Impersonal Sentences in Spanish: Locative and Dative Subjects." *Syntax* 2.2, 101–140.

Figueiredo Silva, M. C. (1996) "La position sujet en Portugais Brésilien," Ph.D. diss., Université de Genève.

Friedemann, M.-A. (1995) "Sujets syntaxiques: positions, inversions et pro," Ph.D. diss., Université de Genève.

Galves, C. (1991) "Agreement and Subjects in Brazilian Portuguese." Unpublished ms., Universidade Estadual de Campinas, Brazil.

Giorgi, A., and G. Longobardi (1991) *The Syntax of Noun Phrases.* Cambridge: Cambridge University Press.

Giorgi, A., and F. Pianesi (1997) *Tense and Aspect: From Semantics to Morphosyntax.* New York: Oxford University Press.

Guasti, M. T., and L. Rizzi (2002). "Agreement and Tense as Distinct Syntactic Positions: Evidence from Acquisition," in G. Cinque (ed.) *Functional Structure in DP and IP: The Cartography of Syntactic Structures, Vol. 1.* New York: Oxford University Press, 167–194.

Guéron, J. (1980) "On the Syntax and Semantics of PP Extraposition." *Linguistic Inquiry* 11.4, 637–678.

Holmberg, A. (2000) "Scandinavian Stylistic Fronting: How Any Category Can Become an Expletive." *Linguistic Inquiry* 31.3, 445–483.

Kayne, R. S. (1983) "Chains, Categories External to S, and French Complex Inversion." *Natural Language and Linguistic Theory* 1, 107–139.

—— (1984) *Connectedness and Binary Branching.* Dordrecht: Foris.

—— (1989) *Notes on English Agreement. Bullettin* 1.2. Hyderabad, India: *CIEFL.*

—— (1994) *The Antisymmetry of Syntax.* Cambridge, Mass.: MIT Press.

Koopman, H., and D. Sportiche (1991) "The Position of Subjects." *Lingua* 85, 211–258.

Kuroda, S.-Y. (1972) "The Categorical and the Thetic Judgment: Evidence from Japanese Syntax." *Foundations of Language* 9, 153–185.

Lonzi, L. (1986) "Pertinenza della struttura Tema-Rema per l'analisi sintattica," in H. Stammer-johann (ed.) *Tema-Rema in Italiano.* Tübingen: Gunter Narr Verlag, 99–120.

Manzini, M. R., and L. M. Savoia (2002) "Parameters of Subject Inflection In Italian Dialects," in P. Svenonius (ed.) *Subjects, Expletives, and the EPP.* New York: Oxford University Press, 157–199.

Martins, A. M. (1994) "Clíticos na história do Português," Ph.D. diss., Universidade de Lisboa.

McCloskey, J. (1991) "Clause Structure, Ellipsis and Proper Government in Irish." *Lingua* 85, 259–302.

—— (1997) "Subjecthood and subject positions," in L. Haegeman (ed.) *Elements of Grammar.* Dordrecht: Kluwer, 197–235.

Morin, Y.-C. (1979) "There Is No Inversion of Subject Clitics in Modern French." Unpublished ms., Université de Montréal.

Moro, A. (1993) *I predicati nominali e la struttura della frase.* Padua: Unipress.

Munaro, N. (1997) "Proprietà strutturali e distribuzionali dei sintagmi interrogativi in alcuni dialetti italiani settentrionali," Ph.D. diss., Università di Padova e Venezia.

—— (1999) *Sintagmi interrogativi nei dialetti italiani settentrionali.* Padua: Unipress.

Ordóñez, F. (1997) "Word Order and Clause Structure in Spanish and Other Romance Languages," Ph.D. diss., CUNY.

—— (1998) "Postverbal Asymmetries in Spanish." *Natural Language and Linguistic Theory* 16, 313–346.

Ordóñez, F., and A. Olarrea (2000) "Weak Subject Pronoun in Caribbean Spanish and XP

Pied-Piping." Unpublished ms., University of Illinois at Urbana-Champaign and University of Arizona.

Pesetsky, D. (1995) *Zero Syntax*. Cambridge, Mass.: MIT Press.

Picallo, C. (1998) "On the Extended Projection Principle and Null Expletive Subjects." *Probus* 19, 219–241.

Poletto, C. (2000) *The Higher Functional Field: Evidence from Northern Italian Dialects*. New York: Oxford University Press.

——— (2001) "Complementizer Deletion and Verb Movement in Standard Italian," in G. Cinque and G. Salvi (eds.) *Current Studies in Italian Syntax: Essays Offered to Lorenzo Renzi*. Amsterdam: Elsevier, 265–286.

Poletto, C., and J.-Y. Pollock (1999) "On the Left Periphery of Romance Wh-Questions." Paper presented at the Workshop on the Cartography of Syntactic Positions and Semantic Types, Certosa di Pontignano, November 1999.

Pollock, J.-Y. (1989) "Verb-Movement, Universal Grammar, and the Structure of IP." *Linguistic Inquiry* 20, 365–424.

——— (1998) "On the Syntax of Subnominal Clitics: Cliticization and Ellipsis." *Syntax* 1.3, 300–330.

Puskàs, G. (1992) "The wh-Criterion in Hungarian." *Rivista di Grammatica Generativa* 17, 141–186.

——— (1997) "Focus and the CP Domain," in L. Haegeman (ed.) *The New Comparative Syntax*. London: Longman, 145–164.

Raposo, E., and J. Uriagereka (1995) "Two Types of Small Clauses (Toward a Syntax of Theme/Rheme Relations)," in A. Cardinaletti and M. T. Guasti (eds.) *Small Clauses*. Syntax and Semantics 28. New York: Academic Press, 179–206.

Rivero, M.-L. (1987) "Barriers and the Null Subject Parameter in Modern Greek," in J. Blevins and J. Carter (eds.) *Proceedings of NELS 18*, vol. 2, Amherst: University of Massachusetts.

——— (1988) "Barriers and Rumanian," in C. Kirschner and J. DeCesaris (eds.) *Studies in Romance Linguistics*. Amsterdam: John Benjamins, 271–294.

——— (1991) "Exceptional Case Marking Effects in Rumanian Subjunctive Complements," in D. Wanner and D. A. Kibbee (eds.) *New Analyses in Romance Linguistics*. Amsterdam: John Benjamins, 273–298.

Rizzi, L. (1982) *Issues in Italian Syntax*. Dordrecht: Foris.

——— (1986) "Null Objects in Italian and the Theory of *pro*." *Linguistic Inquiry* 17, 501–557.

——— (1987) "Three Issues in Romance Dialectology." Paper presented at the GLOW Workshop on Dialectology, Venice. [Published as ch. 3 of Rizzi 2000].

——— (1997) "The Fine Structure of the Left Periphery," in L. Haegeman (ed.) *Elements of Grammar*. Dordrecht: Kluwer, 281–337.

——— (2000) *Comparative Syntax and Language Acquisition*. London: Routledge.

Rizzi, L., and I. Roberts (1989) "Complex Inversion in French." *Probus* 1, 1–30.

Saccon, G. (1993) "Post-Verbal Subjects: A Study Based on Italian and Its Dialects," Ph.D. diss., Harvard University.

Salvi, G. (1986) "Asimmetrie soggetto/tema in italiano," in H. Stammerjohann (ed.) *Tema-Rema in Italiano*. Tübingen: Gunter Narr Verlag, 37–53.

Samek-Lodovici, V. (1994) "Structural Focusing and Subject Inversion in Italian." Paper presented at the 24th Symposium on Romance Languages, Los Angeles, March 1994; ms. available through Rutgers University.

Shlonsky, U. (2000) "Subject Positions and Copular Constructions," in H. Bennis, M. Everaert, and E. Reuland (eds.) *Interface Strategies*. Amsterdam: Royal Netherlands Academy of Arts and Sciences, 325–347.

Sigurðsson, H. A. (2000) "The Locus of Case and Agreement." *Working Papers in Scandinavian Syntax* 65, 65–108.

Sportiche, D. (1999) "Subject Clitics in French and Romance: Complex Inversion and Clitic Doubling," in K. Johnson and I. Roberts (eds.) *Beyond Principles and Parameters.* Dordrecht: Kluwer, 189–221.

Stowell, T. (1981) "Origins of Phrase Structure," Ph.D. diss., MIT.

Suñer, M. (2000) "On Null and Overt Subjects in Null Subject Languages and the EPP." Unpublished ms., Cornell University.

Suñer, M. (2001) "The Lexical Preverbal Subject in a Romance Null Subject Language: Where Art Thou?" Paper presented at *LSRL* 31, Chicago, April 2001.

Taraldsen, T. (1978) "On the NIC, Vacuous Application and the *That*-Trace Filter." Unpublished ms., MIT.

Toman, J. (1992) "A Note on Clitics and Prosody," in L. Hellan (ed.) *Clitics in Germanic and Slavic.* Eurotyp Working Papers, vol. 4. Tilbwig, 113–118.

Tortora, C. M. (1997) "The Syntax and Semantics of the Weak Locative," Ph.D. diss., University of Delaware, Newark.

——— (1999) "Agreement, Case, and i-Subjects," in P. Tamanji, M. Hirotani, and N. Hall (eds.) *Proceedings of the 29th Meeting of the North East Linguistic Society,* vol. 1. Amherst, Mass: GLSA, 397–408.

——— (2001) "Evidence for a Null Locative in Italian," in G. Cinque and G. Salvi (eds.) *Current Studies in Italian Syntax: Essays Offered to Lorenzo Renzi.* Amsterdam: Elsevier, 313–326.

Uriagereka, J. (1999) "Minimal Restrictions on Basque Movements." *Natural Language and Linguistic Theory* 17.2, 403–444.

Vecchiato, S. (2000) "The *ti/tu* Interrogative Morpheme in Québec French." *Generative Grammar in Geneva* 1, 141–164.

Vincent, N. (1999) "Il gerundio in napoletano antico e in toscano antico." Paper presented in Padua, February 1999.

6

Remnant Movement in the Theory of Phases

CARLO CECCHETTO

This chapter discusses the proper interpretation of the grammatical principle that states that a trace must be c-commanded by its antecedent. Assuming the most standard definition of c-command in terms of the first branching node (the complications that are necessary to treat head-adjunction are irrelevant for the problem addressed here) and also assuming that the landing site of movement must c-command the position that precedes movement, I focus on the configuration in (1), in which linear precedence indicates c-command:

(1) $[_z \ldots t_x \ldots] \ldots X \ldots t_z$

In (1), first the constituent X moves out of the constituent Z and reaches a position from which it c-commands its trace. However, in a later stage of the derivation the c-command configuration is destroyed because the constituent Z, which contains the trace of X, undergoes movement as well. The movement of Z in a configuration like (1) is commonly called "remnant movement." After remnant movement, the trace of X is not c-commanded anymore by its antecedent. The question I address here is whether (1) is a configuration allowed by Universal Grammar. Stated differently: Is the c-command requirement on the movement of a constituent X checked once and for all when X moves? Do later stages of the derivation that affect the position of the trace of X matter?

This question has been extensively investigated and, I think, the dominant answer used to be that (1) is, in fact, an ungrammatical configuration and remnant movement should not be allowed. This claim was based on the existence of a class of sentences that exemplify the configuration (1) and are ungrammatical. One such sentence is (2), in which Z corresponds to the wh-phrase "which picture of" while X corresponds to the wh-phrase "who":

(2)   *[Which picture of t_1]$_2$ do you wonder who$_1$ John likes t_2?

Since it is convenient to have a name for them, I will call Remnant Movement Effects cases like (2) that exemplify the configuration in (1) and are ungrammatical.

However, much recent research points to the conclusion that (1) is admitted by Universal Grammar and that Remnant Movement Effects, when present, are triggered by some independent condition. In particular, it has been suggested that what rules (2) out is a violation of a sophisticated version of Relativized Minimality.

My conclusion in this essay is that (1) is admitted in principle and that cases like (2) are excluded, not because they violate Relativized Minimality but because they do not obey the Phase Impenetrability Condition (PIC), an economy principle, distinct from Relativized Minimality, that dictates that the derivation, in order to overcome computational complexity, proceeds strictly by phases (cf. Chomsky 1999, 2000, and 2001 for a presentation of PIC).

Before entering the core of the essay, it is worth pointing out that the discussion concerning Remnant Movement Effects has important consequences for the current theoretical debate in at least two areas. First, in recent years, linguists adopting Kayne's (1994) framework, in which right adjunction and rightward movement are banned, have been increasingly using the type of derivation illustrated in (1) to derive word orders that prima facie instantiate right adjunction. These approaches capitalize on the fact that the category X seems to sit in the right edge in structures like (1), but this is an illusionary effect due to the remnant movement of the category Z that contains the trace of X. So the appearance of X to the right side can be explained without postulating any actual occurrence of right adjunction or rightward movement. In the same spirit, it has been argued that a wh-phrase that seems to be in situ actually occupies a slot in the CP area, because the IP from which it is extracted undergoes remnant movement and reaches a higher CP layer (cf. Poletto and Pollock, chapter 9 in this volume).

Koopman and Szabolcsi (2000) further exploit the strategy based on remnant movement in a variety of constructions. If configurations like (1) were not admitted, we would have an argument that shows that all these approaches, although very popular, cannot be on the right track. My position on this issue is somehow intermediate. As anticipated, I maintain that derivations like (1) are admitted in principle. However, as I show in this chapter, if the movement of X is not local enough (in a sense of local to be made precise below), the derivation in (1) violates PIC and is accordingly excluded. So, my conclusions, if correct, significantly narrow the number of cases in which derivations like (1) can be legitimately used, although they do *not* exclude this type of strategy altogether.

The second reason that makes Remnant Movement Effects particularly interesting for the current theoretical debate is the issue concerning the derivational or representational character of syntactic theory. This debate is notoriously difficult, and it is very hard—perhaps impossible—to find empirical arguments that can decide which approach is the best one. However, it seems fairly reasonable to say that the fact that the configuration in (1) is admitted in principle can be expressed more naturally in a derivational framework than in a representational one.[1] In fact, what one has to say in a derivational framework is simply that the c-command condition on the trace of X holds by the moment in which the movement of X takes place (later stages of the derivation do not count because the c-command condition on traces is checked cyclically). However, if the c-command condition on traces is checked on representations, there appears to be a problem with (1), since in this configuration the trace of X is not c-commanded. Arguably there are ways to formulate the requirement that traces be c-commanded to obtain the desired result in a representational model, but this might involve some technical complications that are not necessary in a derivational model. So, if empirical considerations matter on questions concerning the general design of the theory, the evidence discussed here favors the derivational model.

This chapter is organized as follows. In section 1, I present various examples of Remnant Movement Effects, and in section 2 I discuss the lack of Remnant Movement Effects in contexts in which they might be expected to arise. In section 3, I summarize previous accounts that reduce Remnant Movement Effects to Relativized Minimality, and in section 4 I argue against this line. In section 5, I outline the theory of phases proposed by Chomsky in his recent papers and present my account of Remnant Movement Effects, which is based on it. In section 6, I discuss some consequences of my analysis for long-distance movement in Japanese. In section 7, I suggest that a potential weakness of the theory of phases (the fact that it makes partially wrong predictions in the domain of wh-islands) can be overcome if the fine structure of the CP layer proposed by Rizzi (1997) is considered. Finally, section 8 is a conclusion.

1. Remnant Movement Effects

In many cases the configuration (1) seems to be responsible for an unacceptable output. One example that we already saw is (2). Moreover, (3) and (4) introduce two minimal pairs that involve wh-movement in English and Italian respectively:[2]

(3) a. *[How many chapters t_1]$_2$ do you remember [of which book]$_1$ you read?
     b. [Of which book]$_1$ do you remember [how many chapters t_1]$_2$ you read?

(4) a. *[Quanti capitoli t_1]$_2$ ricordi [di quale libro]$_1$ hai letto?
        how many chapters (you) remember of which book (you) have read
     b. [Di quale libro]$_1$ ricordi [quanti capitoli t_1]$_2$ hai letto?
        of which book (you) remember how many chapters (you) have read

One is tempted to conclude that the first member of each minimal pair is out because the trace t_1 is not c-commanded. This is the kind of explanation that was originally proposed for the ungrammaticality of (3a) (see Fiengo 1977). Various scholars have followed this line to explain minimal pairs that are structurally similar to (3) and (4). One famous case is scrambling in Japanese. As discussed by Saito (1985), the grammaticality of (6a) and the ungrammaticality of (6b) can be attributed to the fact that the trace t_1 is c-commanded in the former but not in the latter (both 6a and 6b are derived from 5):[3]

(5) Taroo-ga Hanako-ga sono hon-o yonda to itta (koto).[4]
     Taro-NOM Hanako-NOM that book-ACC read that said fact
     'Taro said that Hanako read that book.'

(6) a.*[Hanako-ga t_1 yonda to]$_2$ [sono hon-o]$_1$ Taroo-ga t_2 itta (koto).
        Hanako-NOM read that that book-ACC Taro-NOM said fact
     b. [Sono hon-o]$_1$ [Hanako-ga t_1 yonda to]$_2$ Taroo-ga t_2 itta (koto).
        that book-ACC Hanako-NOM read that Taro-NOM said fact

Cecchetto (1999a) discusses Remnant Movement Effects in Clitic Left Disloca-tion (CLLD). Example (7) is an Italian sentence that contains two sentential embed-dings; (8a) and (8b) are derived from (7). In (8b), which is acceptable, the dislocated constituent in the COMP area of the matrix clause is the direct object of the most embedded sentence, which, in turn, is dislocated in the intermediate COMP area.[5] Crucially, in (8b) the trace of the direct object *Maria* (t_1) is c-commanded. If the order of the two dislocated constituents is switched, the sentence becomes sharply ungram-matical, as shown by (8a). The relevant difference between (8a) and (8b) is that in the latter the DP *Maria* c-commands its trace t_1, whereas in the former it does not.[6]

(7) Non credo che Gianni sia convinto di conoscere Maria.
     (I) NEG believe that Gianni is convinced of knowing Maria
     'I don't think that Gianni is convinced that he knows Maria.'

(8) a.*[Di conoscerla t_1]$_2$ non credo che, Maria$_1$, Gianni ne sia convinto t_2.
        of knowing her (I) NEG believe that Maria Gianni of it is convinced
     b. Maria$_1$, non credo che, [di conoscerla t_1]$_2$, Gianni ne sia convinto t_2.
        Maria$_1$ (I) NEG believe that of knowing her Gianni of it is convinced

2.   Lack of Remnant Movement Effects

We have seen Remnant Movement Effects in English, Japanese, and Italian. Now we observe that Remnant Movement Effects are missing in contexts in which they are expected to arise.

In (9), assuming the VP internal subject hypothesis, the trace of *John* within the preposed VP is not c-commanded by its antecedent. Therefore, (9) exemplifies the configuration (1), but, contrary to what we have previously observed, the output is grammatical. The English sentence (10) and the Italian sentence (11) are even more problematic for the hypothesis that configuration (1) is unacceptable. They are struc-turally identical to (9) except that they exemplify unaccusative structures. There-fore, there must be a trace of the subject within the preposed VP, no matter whether the VP internal subject hypothesis is accepted, and this trace ends up being not c-commanded. Nonetheless, (10) and (11) are grammatical:

(9) [t_1 pass the exam]$_2$ John$_1$ indeed will t_2

(10) [fired t_1 by the company]$_2$ John$_1$ indeed was t_2

(11) [andato t_1 a casa]$_2$ Gianni$_1$ non è t_2
     gone to house Gianni NEG is

The acceptability of (9)–(11) is a serious problem for any theory that assumes that a trace must be c-commanded by its antecedent in *any* point of the derivation of a sentence. Furthermore, the problem is more general than (9)–(11) might suggest. Postulating some special device operating on the trace of the subject would not be sufficient because there are grammatical sentences that exemplify configuration (1) in which the trace that is not c-commanded is not a subject trace. An example is German remnant topicalization construction, illustrated by (12):

(12)   Gelesen hat Hans das Buch nicht.
        read has Hans the book NEG

Den Besten and Webelhuth (1990) discuss two possible derivations for (12). In the first derivation, the preposed constituent is the verb *gelesen*. This derivation violates the strict locality conditions on head movement. In particular, the alleged movement of the lexical verb *gelesen* should skip the auxiliary *hat* that is commonly taken to sit in COMP to satisfy the verb-second requirement that holds in German. Furthermore, the position that precedes the verb in German matrix sentences is occupied by maximal projections, and the lexical verb does not qualify as such. A more plausible derivation for (12), also discussed by den Besten and Webelhuth (1990) and much subsequent work, is given in (13).[7] In (13) the details that are not crucial for our purposes (including the trace of the subject) are omitted:

(13) $[_{CP} [_{VP} t_1 \text{ Gelesen}]_2$ hat $[_{IP}$ Hans ... [das Buch]$_1$ ... nicht ... t_2]].

In (13) first the direct object *das Buch* scrambles out of the VP and, second, the VP that contains the trace of the direct object moves to Spec,CP. Paradigm (13) is an example of configuration (1) in which the trace that ends up being not c-commanded is *not* a subject trace. Therefore, the problem introduced by the lack of Remnant Movement Effects is not limited to subject traces.

I take (9)–(12) to be conclusive evidence that configuration (1) is allowed by Universal Grammar. Of course, this opens the problem of explaining the ungrammaticality of the sentences discussed in section 1, which seem to show that configuration (1) is *not* allowed. The remaining part of this chapter is devoted to this problem.[8]

3.   Reducing Remnant Movement Effects to Relativized Minimality

The difference between the cases that display a Remnant Movement Effect and cases that do not can be traced back to a unique factor.[9] Let's go back to configuration (1), repeated as (14), to see what the source of the difference is:

(14) $[_Z \ldots t_X \ldots] \ldots X \ldots t_Z$

In all the ungrammatical cases of remnant movement, the movement out of X of Z and the later remnant movement of Z are of the same type. For example, in (3a) and (4a) there are two instances of wh-movement; in (6a) there are two instances of scrambling, and in (8a) there are two instances of Clitic Left Dislocation. In all the grammatical cases, however, the movement of X and the movement of Z are of different types. In

(9), (10), and (11) the movement of X is A-movement toward the subject position, whereas the movement of Z is a case of VP preposing (arguably an A-bar movement). In (12) the movement of X is scrambling, while the movement of Z is the kind of topicalization that moves a constituent in the initial position in V-2 languages.

Based on this observation, various authors, including Fox (1999), Fukui (1997), Müller (1998), Kitahara (1997), Koizumi (1995), Sauerland (1999), and Takano (1994), have suggested that Remnant Movement Effects (where they are attested) should be reduced to Relativized Minimality (in the sense of Rizzi 1990) or to the similar locality condition called Minimal Link Condition or Shortest Attract (Chomsky 1995). Although the implementation differs somewhat from author to author, the main idea can be summarized as follows. In classical cases of Relativized Minimality effects, the intervention effect is triggered by an element that c-commands the attractee but is c-commanded by the attractor. For example, in (15) the attractor, the interrogative COMP of the matrix clause, does not attract the closest element that can satisfy its requirements (the wh-phrase 'which book') but attracts a farther element (the wh-phrase 'why'). The sentence is out because Shortest Attract is violated:

(15)   *Why_1 do you wonder which book John read t_1?

The extension of the approach based on Relativized Minimality to Remnant Movement Effects consists in defining intervention in terms of containment (in addition to the classical definition in terms of c-command). For example, if Z contains X, Z acts as an intervener between X and any position outside Z. To illustrate, consider sentence (2), repeated as (16):

(16)   *[Which picture of t_1]$_2$ do you wonder who_1 John likes t_2?

Assume that the derivation is strictly cyclic and that it has reached a point in which the embedded interrogative COMP has been merged (cf. 17). At that point, potentially there are two attractees for C°: wh-phrase 1 ('who') and wh-phrase 2 ('which picture of who'). If intervention is defined as containment, only wh-phrase 2 can be attracted. If wh-phrase 1 is attracted instead, as in (16), a minimality effect is triggered because wh-phrase 2 is closer to the attractor than wh-phrase 1 (note that the classical version of Relativized Minimality based on c-command would not suffice here because wh-phrase 2 contains but does not c-command wh-phrase 1).

(17)   C° John likes [which picture of who_1]$_2$?

This account of (16) straightforwardly extends to the other cases of Remnant Movement Effects that we have observed. As the reader can easily verify, in all the relevant cases, the ungrammaticality can be attributed to the fact that a constituent X is extracted out of a constituent Z that should be attracted instead of X, because it is closer to the attractor. This account can also explain why (9)–(12) are grammatical. Take (10), repeated as (18), as an illustration:

(18)   [$_{VP}$ Fired t_1 by the company]$_2$ $John_1$ indeed was t_2.

The relevant step of the derivation is one in which the INFL node attracts an element that ends up filling Spec,IP. For obvious reasons, the VP does not qualify as a suitable attractee, and therefore the subject *John* can be attracted.

I conclude my summary of the theory that reduces Remnant Movement Effects to Relativized Minimality with the following observation, which turns out to be important for what I will say in the next section: to reduce the full set of Remnant Movement Effects to Relativized Minimality, it must be assumed that this locality condition blocks attraction of an element X from within an element Z only if X and Z share *exactly* the same feature that is attracted. For example, for cases of remnant topicalization like (12), it is necessary to assume that a constituent with a topicalization feature does *not* block the extraction of one with a scrambling feature. In (19) I indicate with F°, the head—whatever it is—that is the attractor for scrambling. This head can attract the DP *das Buch* even if the VP, which has a topicalization feature to check, intervenes (assuming the definition of intervention in terms of containment).

(19)   F° [$_{VP}$ Hans das Buch gelesen]

This way of conceiving Relativized Minimality is different from Rizzi's (1990) version in which any intervening A position blocks A movement and any intervening A-bar position blocks A-bar movement. Only Rizzi's version can explain why a negative operator blocks topicalization of one adverbial even if they do not share exactly the same feature. This is illustrated by (20), which does not have the reading in which the adverbial is interpreted within the scope of negation (the missing reading is present in sentence *John was not fired for this reason*, which can be true in a situation in which John was fired).

(20)   It is for this reason that John was not fired.

Summarizing, in order to maintain an explanation for the entire set of Remnant Movement Effects, including remnant topicalization in German, Relativized Minimality must be made feature-specific, but this forces us to abandon the explanation for the pattern in (20).

4.   Against reducing Remnant Movement Effects to Relativized Minimality

Here I discuss the problems that affect the analysis that reduces Remnant Movement Effects to Relativized Minimality. A first general concern is that, in order for the suggested analysis to work, scrambling must be equated to a feature-checking operation. This is not unnatural for scrambling in Western Germanic, since it can have a semantic import, but it is much more problematic for scrambling in Japanese, which it is known to be semantically vacuous (see Sauerland 1999 for a detailed comparison of Japanese and German scrambling in this respect).

However, there are more specific problems for the theory under consideration. I see three main difficulties. The first two arise from the expectation that if Remnant Movement Effects and classical cases of Relativized Minimality effects are equated, one should observe Relativized Minimality effects in all those contexts that trigger Remnant Movement Effects and, conversely, all the contexts that trigger Relativized Minimality effects should trigger Remnant Movement Effects as well. Unfortunately, neither of these predictions is borne out, as we will see in a moment. The third problem arises because the theory that reduces Remnant Movement Effects to Relativized Minimality requires that Relativized Minimality be made feature-specific (this is necessary to explain the possibility of remnant topicalization in German; cf. the discussion on (19)). This requirement makes the theory empirically inadequate in a set of cases.

Let us start from the expectation that Relativized Minimality effects ought to arise in all those contexts that trigger Remnant Movement Effects. This means that if extraction of X out of Z is blocked (cf. (21)), Z should also create an intervention effect whenever it c-commands the trace of X and is c-commanded by the landing site of X (cf. (22) in which liner precedence indicates c-command). So, whenever the configuration in (21) is out, the one in (22) should be out as well:

(21) $*X \ldots [_z \ldots t_X \ldots] \ldots$

(22) $*X \ldots Z \ldots t_X$

That this prediction is not borne out is shown by scrambling in Japanese and CLLD in Romance. Remnant Movement Effects do arise with scrambling and CLLD (cf. (6) for scrambling in Japanese and (8) for CLLD) but, as is well known, Relativized Minimality effects are *not* attested either in scrambling or in CLLD.[10] Therefore, in scrambling and CLLD, configuration (21) is out, whereas configuration (22) is acceptable. I take this to be the first serious problem for the theory that reduces Remnant Movement Effects to Relativized Minimality effects.

A second problem for this theory is raised by the fact that, as classical cases of Relativized Minimality effects show, a feature of the relevant type creates an intervention effect even if it has already been checked. For example, in (23) the interrogative phrase *when* and the embedded COMP enter into a checking configuration and, as a consequence, a wh-feature is checked. Nonetheless, the intervening wh-phrase creates a clear intervention effect in (23), which is ungrammatical (I use an aggressively non-D-linked wh-phrase like "what the hell" because this makes the judgment sharp).

(23) *[What the hell]$_i$ do you wonder when you bought t_i?

Since a checked feature creates a minimality effect when intervention is defined in terms of c-command (cf. (23)), the expectation is that it should also create a minimality effect when intervention is defined in terms of containment. The acceptability of the Italian sentence (24b) shows that this prediction is incorrect: (24a) is a control sentence that closely corresponds to the English sentence (23) and shows that also in Italian a checked feature creates a minimality effect when intervention is defined in terms of c-command:

(24) a.*[Cosa cavolo]$_i$ ti domandi quando hai comprato t_i?
       what the hell do you wonder when (you) have bought
      b. [Di quale cavolo di libro]$_i$ ti domandi [quanti capitoli t_i]$_2$ hai letto?
       of what the hell of a book do you wonder how many chapters (you) have read

Consider how (24b) can be derived. The derivation that obeys the cycle is one in which, after the movement of the interrogative phrase *quanti capitoli di quale cavolo di libro* (lit. 'how many chapters of what the hell of a book') to the embedded

COMP, the aggressively non-D-linked wh-phrase *di quale cavolo di libro* moves out of it toward the main COMP. However, if intervention is defined in terms of containment and an intervening feature creates a minimality effect even if it has already been checked, the movement of *di quale cavolo di libro* out of the superphrase *quanti capitoli di quale cavolo di libro* should be blocked because the superphrase is closer to the main COMP than is the wh-phrase contained in it. Furthermore, the intervention effect should be strong because the chain that is affected by the intervention is headed by an aggressively non-D-linked wh-phrase. To summarize, the second drawback of the theory that reduces Remnant Movement Effects to Relativized Minimality is that it incorrectly predicts that sentences like (24b) should be ungrammatical.[11]

The third problem is that the assumption that is required to explain remnant topicalization in German leads this theory to make wrong predictions in at least three unrelated contexts. The first one is the interaction between scrambling and Japanese Right Dislocation (JRD). I refer to Cecchetto (1999b) for a presentation of JRD. For our purposes, it suffices to focus on two features of this construction. First, JRD is not semantically vacuous. Although there is a discussion on the better way to characterize the pragmatics of JRD, there is a consensus that a right dislocation sentence requires a nonneutral informational pattern that is not required in the case of scrambling. An indication of this is the observation, originally due to Haraguchi (1973), that wh-elements cannot be right dislocated, even if they can be scrambled (Kuno 1978 relates the impossibility of right dislocating wh-elements to the fact that they have a character of an "afterthought"). The second relevant feature of JRD for our purpose is that it is a root phenomenon—that is, a constituent can only be dislocated to the right periphery of the main sentence (no right dislocation is possible to the periphery of the embedded sentence or to any other embedded position). To capture the root character of the construction, let us assume that a right-dislocated constituent is right-adjoined to the CP. With this background in mind, let us consider the following sentences (from Cecchetto 1999b):

(25)   a. John-ga Bill-ga kono mura-ni sundeiru to omotteiru.
          John-NOM Bill-NOM this village-in lives that thinks
          'John thinks that Bill lives in this village.'
       b. [Bill-ga t_1 sundeiru to]$_2$ John-ga omotteiru [kono mura-ni]$_1$
          Bill-NOM lives that John-NOM thinks this village-in
       c. *[kono mura-ni]$_1$ John-ga omotteiru [Bill-ga t_1 sundeiru to]$_2$
          this village-in John-NOM thinks Bill-NOM lives that

Both (25b) and (25c) are derived from (25a). In the grammatical case (25b), the embedded clause is scrambled and the PP *kono mura-ni,* which originates in the subordinate clause, is right-dislocated. Assuming that the right-dislocated PP sits in a position adjoined to the matrix CP and that the scrambled embedded clause sits in the periphery of the matrix IP, the trace of the PP is c-commanded by its antecedent. In (25c) the order of scrambling and right dislocation is switched: the embedded clause is right dislocated and the PP is scrambled. Therefore, the trace of the PP is not c-commanded, and the sentence is ungrammatical. The pattern in (25) is in all relevant respects similar to the other cases of Remnant Movement Effects that we have seen in this paper. Therefore, it's clearly desirable for the analysis of Remnant Movement Effects to be able to carry over to (25). However, this extension is not available if Relativized Minimality is feature specific. As a matter of fact, even if one makes the (dubious) assumption that Japanese scrambling and right dislocation are feature triggered, the conclusion is inevitable that they are triggered by two different features, since one operation is semantically vacuous while the other is not. Therefore, the analysis that reduces Remnant Movement Effects to Relativized Minimality wrongly predicts that a sentence like (25c) should be grammatical. In the relevant stage of the derivation of (25c), the PP *kono mura-ni* can be attracted by whatever head is responsible for scrambling because no closer attractee interposes (the embedded clause that contains the PP needs to check a "right-dislocation" feature, rather than a "scrambling feature"; therefore, it does not qualify as an intervener).

Two other cases, parallel to the Japanese one that I have just considered, confirm the problematic character of the requirement that only strict identity of features creates intervention effects. They are the following cases of interaction between wh-movement and topicalization in Italian and English, respectively ((26a) is discussed by Müller 1998, and (26b) is discussed by Longobardi 1985). The source of the ungrammaticality of (26a) and (26b) must be the fact that the wh-trace in the displaced constituent XP is not c-commanded. However, these sentences are predicted to be grammatical by the theory under consideration because the superphrase XP that contains the unbound wh-trace does not check a wh-feature and, consequently, does not count as an intervener.

(26)   a. *$[_{XP}$ Ready to marry $t_1]_2$ I wonder $[_{CP}$ [who]$_1$ C° John is $t_2]$
         b. *$[_{XP}$ A sposare $t_1]_2$ non so $[_{CP}$ [quale ragazza]$_1$ C° Gianni sarebbe disposto $t_2]$

It seems that either one assumes that only strict identity of features triggers a Remnant Movement Effect, in which case remnant topicalization in German is explained but the data in (25c), (26a), and (26b) remain mysterious, or one assumes that any intervening A' position blocks A' movement (much like in Rizzi's 1990 analysis) but in that case the explanation for remnant topicalization in German is missed, although the data in (25c), (26a), and (26b) can be explained. All in all, the theory that reduces Remnant Movement Effects to Relativized Minimality cannot cover the entire set of data concerning Remnant Movement Effects that we have observed.

5.   Remnant Movement Effects as Phase Impenetrability Condition Effects

The preceding section proposes that the theory that correlates Remnant Movement Effects and Relativized Minimality is inadequate in various ways. Given its shortcomings, in this section, I offer an alternative treatment for Remnant Movement Effects.

The empirical generalization that naturally suggests a treatment in terms of Relativized Minimality for Remnant Movement Effects is one that states that configuration (1) is unacceptable when the movement of X and the movement of Z are of the same type. However, there is another generalization that is descriptively more adequate and, as I am going to argue, can also lead us to a better explanation of the relevant facts. I will give a precise formulation of the alternative generalization at the end of this paragraph, after introducing the basic concepts of the theory of phases proposed in Chomsky (1999, 2000, and 2001). However, the following rough characterization can be preliminarily given: configuration (1) is unacceptable unless the movement of X is very local, where "very local" means that it can only target a position inside the first IP level that it encounters.

My summary of Chomsky's theory is much simplified in many aspects that are irrelevant for the problem of explaining Remnant Movement Effects. In particular, I use the neutral label "IP" to indicate the maximal projection that hosts the subject in its Spec and the label "VP" to indicate the complete verbal projection. Important issues—like whether agreement features head their own maximal projection or the internal structure of the VP shell—are irrelevant for our purposes and, accordingly, are put aside.

In Chomsky's theory, the access to the lexicon is a one-time selection of a lexical array LA. To reduce the computational burden, it is also assumed that the initial lexical array LA enters the derivation in different steps. In each step, a subarray of LA is put into active memory. Crucially, the derivation must exhaust one subarray, by forming a certain syntactic object, before returning to LA to extract another subarray (up to the moment in which LA is totally exhausted). The syntactic object formed when a subarray is exhausted is called by Chomsky "phase." As I understand them, the reasons that lead Chomsky to think that the derivations proceed in this way are mainly conceptual (the active memory at each step contains a very limited set of lexical items, and this is an advantage if computational complexity matters). However, he offers some empirical motivations, too. Take the fact that, since Merge is simpler than Move, the presence of an expletive in the initial lexical array should always block the movement of a subject from Spec,VP to Spec,IP (because merging the expletive in Spec,IP is more economical than moving the subject). This prediction is not fulfilled by sentences like (27) in which the embedded subject can move to the embedded Spec,IP:

(27)   There is a possibility that proofs will be discovered.

The problem is fixed if the expletive *there* and the subject *proofs* are located in two different subarrays and if the subarray that contains the former can only be accessed when the subarray that contains the latter is exhausted.

Obviously, the question that immediately arises is how a phase can de defined in a principled way. Chomsky's answer capitalizes on the fact that there are objects, roughly corresponding to VPs and CPs, that have a degree of independence, both on the phonetic side and on the meaning side. For example, VPs and CPs can be displaced, but this not true for IPs. Similarly on the "semantic" side, a VP is the space in which θ roles are assigned and a CP is the space in which tense and force of the sentence are determined. In this sense, VPs and CPs are propositional, but IPs are not propositional. This suggests that VPs and CPs, but not IPs, are phases.

The idea that derivations proceed by phases has potential widespread consequences, some of them directly relevant for our problem. For example, Chomsky assumes that Spell-Out is cyclic in a way that is determined by the interacting principles (28) and (29):

(28)   Evaluation for a phase is done at the level of the next highest strong phase.

(29)   Phase Impenetrability Condition (PIC)

The complement of a strong phase α is not accessible to operations at the level of the next highest strong phase β, but only the head and the edge of α are.

To understand (28) and (29), some terminological points must be clarified. For our limited purposes, we can take the term "evaluation" in (28) to indicate the moment in which Spell-Out takes place. The edge of a phase referred to in (29) is a position in periphery of the phase that is either a specifier or an adjoined position. Finally, weak phases are VPs lacking an external argument (passives, unaccusatives), while strong phases are all the other phases. (In this essay, the difference between strong and weak phases is not going to play any crucial role.)

It's worth illustrating how the system based on (28) and (29) works with a couple of examples. First, consider a case of wh-movement of the direct object as in (30):

(30)   [$_{CP}$ Who did [$_{IP}$ you [$_{VP}$ t'' [$_{VP}$ see t']]]]

Principle (28) dictates that the spell-out position of lexical items contained in the phase VP is determined at the level CP (remember that IP is not a phase, so the strong phase that is next highest with respect to VP is CP). Condition (29) states that the complement of the strong phase VP (that is, the complement of the verb *see*) is not accessible to operations at the level of the next highest strong phase CP. So, if the direct object remains in situ by the time in which the phase VP is completed, it cannot be attracted by the interrogative COMP. The only legitimate derivation, illustrated in (30), is one in which the wh-phrase moves to the edge of the VP phase and is therefore visible from the COMP position, in accordance with (29).[12]

Consider now the movement of the subject in unaccusative and passive constructions.

(31)   [$_{IP}$ John was [$_{VP}$ killed t]]

Note that in (31) the movement of the subject does not reach the strong phase CP, which is the next highest with respect to the phase VP in which the subject originates. Since (29) dictates that an element becomes invisible only at the level of the next highest strong phase, the subject *John* can be attracted by $I°$ even if it remains in the complement position of the passive verb. The consequence is that the traditional view that in unaccusative and passive constructions the subject never occupies Spec,VP can be maintained.

Even this sketchy presentation of the theory of phases is sufficient to see how it can be extended to the cases of Remnant Movement Effects. Take the two sentences in (3) repeated as (32) and (33) as representatives:

(32)   *[How many chapters t_1]$_2$ do you remember [of which book]$_1$ you read?

(33)   [Of which book]$_1$ do you remember [how many chapters t_1]$_2$ you read?

A derivation that, if possible, would have (32) as its output is given in (32a)–(32e). In my analysis, I do not consider the plausible assumption that also DPs are phases because the problem that leads the derivation to crash is independent from the possible phase nature of DPs. First the wh-phrase *of which book* moves to the periphery of the the embedded VP, which is a strong phase (32b). From this position, it can be attracted by the embedded interrogative COMP (32c). Then the derivation proceeds up to the moment in which the matrix interrogative COMP is merged (32e). This is the step of the putative derivation for (32) which is not legitimate: in (32e), if the matrix COMP attracts the wh-phrase *how many chapters*, PIC is violated.[13]

(32) a. [$_{IP}$ you I° [$_{VP}$ read [how many chapters [of which book]$_1$]$_2$]]
     b. [$_{IP}$ you I° [$_{VP}$ [of which book]$_1$ [$_{VP}$ read [how many chapters t$_1$]$_2$]]]
     c. [$_{CP}$ [of which book]$_1$ C° [$_{IP}$ you I° [$_{VP}$ t"$_1$ [$_{VP}$ read [how many chapters t'$_1$]$_2$]]]]
     d. [$_{IP}$ you I° [$_{VP}$ remember [$_{CP}$ [of which book]$_1$ C° [$_{IP}$ you I° [$_{VP}$ t"$_1$ [$_{VP}$ read [how many chapters t'$_1$]$_2$]]]]]]
     e. [$_{CP}$ C° [$_{IP}$ you I° [$_{VP}$ remember [$_{CP}$ [of which book]$_1$ C° [$_{IP}$ you I° [$_{VP}$ t"$_1$ [$_{VP}$ read [how many chapters t'$_1$]$_2$]]]]]]]]

The legitimate derivation of (33) is given in (33a)–(33f). As the reader can verify, at each step PIC is obeyed:

(33) a. [$_{IP}$ you I° [$_{VP}$ read [how many chapters [of which book]$_1$]$_2$]]
     b. [$_{IP}$ you I° [$_{VP}$ [how many chapters [of which book]$_1$]$_2$ [$_{VP}$ read t$_2$]]]
     c. [$_{CP}$ [how many chapters [of which book]$_1$]$_2$ C° [$_{IP}$ you I° [$_{VP}$ t"$_2$ [$_{VP}$ read t'$_2$]]]]
     d. [$_{IP}$ you I° [$_{VP}$ remember [$_{CP}$ [how many chapters [of which book]$_1$]$_2$ C° [$_{IP}$ you I° [$_{VP}$ t"$_2$ [$_{VP}$ read t'$_2$]]]]]]
     e. [$_{IP}$ you I° [$_{VP}$ [of which book]$_1$ [$_{VP}$ remember [$_{CP}$ [how many chapters t$_1$]$_2$ C° [$_{IP}$ you I° [$_{VP}$ t"$_2$ [$_{VP}$ read t'$_2$]]]]]]]
     f. [$_{CP}$ [of which book]$_1$ do [$_{IP}$ you I° [$_{VP}$ t"$_1$ [$_{VP}$ remember [$_{CP}$ [how many chapters t'$_1$]$_2$ C° [$_{IP}$ you I° [$_{VP}$ t"$_2$ [$_{VP}$ read t'$_2$]]]]]]]]

This explanation based on PIC straightforwardly extends to the cases of Remnant Movement Effects illustrated by (4b) and (8b). It can also extend to Remnant Movement Effects that are illustrated in (6a), (25c), (26a), and (26b). (Examples 25c, 26a, and 26b are particularly interesting because they are not explained by the theory that reduces Remnant Movement Effects to Relativized Minimality Effects.) Let us focus on (6a), repeated here as (34), (but the same reasoning applies to (25c), (26a), and (26b)).

(34) *[Hanako-ga t$_1$ yonda to]$_2$ [sono hon-o]$_1$ Taroo-ga t$_2$ itta (koto).
      Hanako-NOM read that that book-ACC T.-NOM said fact

Since long-distance scrambling in Japanese is known to have A-bar properties, like wh-movement, it's useful to compare a derivation in which long-distance wh-movement occurs and the one in which long-distance scrambling takes place.[14] Let us start from the former. A sentence like (35a) is derived as illustrated by (35b). PIC forces the wh-phrase to pass through the edge of the embedded VP, of the embedded CP and of the matrix VP:

(35) a. Who do you think that John saw?
     b. [$_{CP}$ Who$_1$ do [$_{IP}$ you [$_{VP}$ t'''$_1$ think [$_{CP}$ t"$_1$ that [$_{IP}$ John [$_{VP}$ t'$_1$ saw t$_1$]]]]]]

Given the similarities between wh-movement and long-distance scrambling, I assume that a long-distance scrambled constituent, like a wh-phrase in Spec,CP, sits at the edge of the strong phase XP (whatever its exact nature is) that is the next highest with respect to VP. This means that, in order to reach its final landing site in the left periphery of the matrix sentence, a long-distance scrambled constituent must pass through the edge of the matrix VP to become visible. With this in mind, let us look at the stage of the derivation of (34) in which the scrambled constituent *sono hon-o* has reached its position in the periphery of the matrix clause, while the embedded clause in which it originates is still in situ. (In (36) I have indicated only the traces of *sono hon-o* that are relevant for our discussion.)

(36) [[sono hon-o]$_1$ [$_{IP}$ Taroo-ga [$_{VP}$ t"$_1$ [$_{VP}$ ... [$_{CP}$ Hanako-ga t'$_1$ yonda to] itta]] I°]]

The final landing site of *sono hon-o,* like Spec,CP, marks the edge of the phase that is the next highest with respect to the matrix VP. Therefore *sono hon-o* must pass through the edge of the matrix VP to reach its final position. Note that, under PIC, the embedded clause is not visible in the configuration illustrated in (36) and is frozen in place. In fact, (34a) might only be derived if the embedded clause could use the edge of the matrix VP as an escape hatch to become visible. However, this position is not available because it is already occupied by the trace of *sono hon-o.* As for the derivation of (6b), repeated as (37), it is not problematic at all, since the embedded clause first moves to its scrambling position in the left periphery of the main clause (possibly passing through the edge of the matrix VP),[15] and only at this point does the direct object *sono hon-o* scramble out of the embedded clause:

(37) [Sono hon-o]$_1$ [Hanako-ga t$_1$ yonda to]$_2$ Taroo-ga t$_2$ itta
      that book-ACC Hanako-NOM read that Taro-NOM said

My explanation for the contrast between (34) and (37) presupposes that there is just one escape hatch from the VP that can be used by constituents that target a phase-external position—that is, a position outside IP. (If there were two edges, the explanation for the ungrammaticality of (34) would be missed because the embedded clause might use one of them to move to its surface position at the stage of the derivation illustrated in (36)). Now I turn to the consequences of this assumption.

I just claimed that the following empirical generalization can capture the selective distribution of Remnant Movement Effects: configuration (1) is permitted when X does not go as far as targeting the edge of the phase that is next highest with respect to the phase in which X originates. This generalization can be seen a theorem of the theory of phases.

6. Some consequences for Japanese

We saw that in Japanese there is just one VP edge that can be used by a constituent that moves from within the VP to a landing site outside the phase in which the VP is located. So only one constituent should be able to escape the VP to target an IP external position. Prima facie, this does not seem to be the case because instances of multiple long-distance scrambling out of the same VP (39), multiple right-dislocation out of the same VP (41), and multiple clefting[16] out of the same VP (43) are attested. In fact, in (39), (41), and (43) the two constituents that are displaced seem to have escaped the embedded CP and the matrix VP, as well. In each of the following pairs, the second sentence is derived from the first one.

(38) John-ga [$_{CP}$ Mary-ga sono hon-o Bill-ni watasita to] itta (koto).
John-NOM Mary-NOM that book-ACC Bill-to handed that said (fact)
'John said that Mary handed that book to Bill.'

(39) [$_{NP}$ sono hon-o] [$_{PP}$ Bill-ni] John-ga [$_{CP}$ Mary-ga t$_{NP}$ t$_{PP}$ watasita to] itta (koto).
that book-ACC Bill-to John-NOM Mary-NOM handed that said (fact)

(40) John-ga [$_{CP}$ Bill-ga sono mura-ni sundeiru to] omotteiru
John-NOM Bill-NOM that village-in lives that believes
'John believes that Bill lives in that village.'

(41) John-ga [$_{CP}$ t$_{NP}$ t$_{PP}$ sundeiru to] omotteiru [$_{PP}$ sono mura-ni] [$_{NP}$ Bill-ga].
J.-NOM lives that believes that village-in Bill-NOM

(42) John-ga [$_{CP}$ Mary-ga Bill-ni ringo-o 3-tu ageta to] itta.
John-NOM Mary-NOM Bill-to apple-ACC three(CLASS) gave that said
'John said that Mary gave three apples to Bill.'

(43) John-ga [$_{CP}$ Mary-ga t$_{PP}$ t$_{NP}$ ageta to] itta no-wa [$_{PP}$ Bill-ni] [$_{NP}$ ringo-o 3-tu] da.
John-NOM Mary-NOM gave that said NL-TOP Bill-to apple-ACC three(CLASS) be
Lit.: It is three apples to Bill that John said that Mary gave
NL = Nominalizer; CLASS = classifier; TOP = topic marker.

However, it would be too quick to conclude that what happens in (39), (41), and (43) is genuine multiple long-distance movement. An important observation is that the kind of movement illustrated by (39), (41), and (43) is possible only if the two (or more) constituents that undergo the movement are generated in the same clause. This clause-mate condition is shown by the ungrammaticality of (45) (derived from 44) for long-distance scrambling, by the ungrammaticality of (46) (derived from 40) for multiple right-dislocation and by the ungrammaticality of (48) (derived from 47) for multiple clefting.[17]

(44) [$_{IP}$ John-ga Bill-ni [$_{CP}$ Mary-ga sono mura-ni sundeiru to] itta].
John-NOM Bill-to Mary-NOM that village-in lives that said
'John told Bill that Mary lives in that village.'

(45) ?*[$_{PP}$ Bill-ni] [$_{PP}$ sono mura-ni] [$_{IP}$ John-ga [$_{VP}$ t$_{Bill-ni}$ [$_{CP}$ Mary-ga t$_{sono\ mura-ni}$ sundeiru to] itta]].
Bill-to that village-in John-NOM Mary-NOM lives that said

(46) *t $_{NP}$ [$_{CP}$ Bill-ga t$_{PP}$ sundeiru to] omotteiru, [$_{PP}$ sono mura-ni] [$_{NP}$ John-ga]
Bill-NOM lives that believes that village-in John-NOM

(47) Mary-ga Bill-ni [John-ga ringo-o 3-tu katta to] itta.
Mary-NOM Bill-to John-NOM apple-ACC three(CLASS) bought that said
'Mary said to Bill that John bought three apples.'

(48) *Katta to itta no-wa [Mary-ga Bill-ni John-ga ringo-o 3-tu] da.
bought that said NL-TOP Mary-NOM Bill-to John-NOM apple-ACC three(CLASS) be
Lit.: It is [Mary Bill John three apples] that said that bought

The clause mate condition illustrated by the ungrammaticality of (45), (46), and (48) has been explained in two different ways in the literature but, crucially, both explanations assume that genuine multiple long-distance movement of the kind that violates PIC does *not* exist, despite the appearances. In fact, both explanations have the idea that what moves is a superphrase that includes the constituents that seem to move separately, even if they diverge on the exact nature of this superphrase.

According to the first account, in (39), (41), and (43) there is remnant movement of the VP. Sentence (41), for example, would be attributed the derivation summarized in (49).[18] *Sono mura-ni* and *Bill-ga* do not move. Rather, what moves is the VP that contains them and the trace of the verb (a similar explanation can be applied to (39) and (43)).

(49)   John-ga [$_{CP}$ t$_{VP}$ sundeiru to] omotteiru, [$_{VP}$ sono mura-ni Bill-ga t$_{sundeiru}$].

Given the remnant movement account, the clause mate condition is easily derived.[19]

The second explanation for the clause-mate condition reanalyzes apparent long-distance multiple movement as "oblique" movement.[20] Oblique movement is the configuration independently attested in Japanese (see Sohn 1994 and Saito 1994) in which, instead of having X and Y moving separately out of a certain constituent Z, there is a single instance of movement out of Z of an element that is formed by the adjunction of X to Y.[21] For example, the oblique movement hypothesis takes (51) rather than (50) to be the configuration that underlies a case of apparent multiple long-distance right dislocation like (41):

(50)   [$_{CP}$ ... [$_{IP}$ ... [$_{VP}$ ... t$_Y$ ... t$_X$]] X ... Y]

(51)   [$_{CP}$ ... [$_{IP}$ ... [$_{VP}$ ... t$_{X+Y}$]] [X+Y]]

Crucially, oblique movement is known to be clause bound, so, if apparent multiple long-distance movement is oblique movement, the clause-mate condition comes for free.

We do not need to choose one of these two explanations for the clause-mate condition. The important point for us is that both of them have to assume that the proposed mechanism (remnant VP movement or oblique movement) is the only one that can generate the apparent cases of multiple long-distance movement. So they both presuppose that genuine multiple movement of the type that violates PIC is blocked. The analysis that I have proposed for Remnant Movement Effects, which is based on PIC, can *explain* why this type of movement does not occur (it can't occur because it would be a violation of PIC).

Summarizing: PIC turns out to make the right predictions in areas of Japanese syntax that are unrelated to the cases that initially motivated it. In particular, PIC correctly predicts that multiple long-distance scrambling, multiple long-distance right dislocation and multiple clefting are all impossible.[22]

7.   Weak islands, the theory of phases, and the structure of the CP

In this final section I propose some qualifications to the theory of phases, which allow the theory to cover some prima facie problematic cases of island extraction.

The assumption that there is just one edge for each strong phase proves to be valid for the Japanese constructions analyzed in sections 5 and 6. However, it appears to be too strong in other circumstances. One case is the interaction between topicalization and wh-movement. The Italian sentence (52) illustrates this. In (52), both the subject wh-phrase and the left-dislocated direct object originate in the embedded clause (an accusative clitic matches the dislocated direct object, as in other CLLD sentences). As a consequence, they must have somehow escaped the embedded CP in which they originate:

(52)   [Quel libro]$_1$, chi$_2$ [$_{IP}$ hai detto [$_{CP}$ che t$_2$ l'ha letto t$_1$]]?
       that book who (you) said that it has read
       'Who did you say read that book?'

If the embedded CP were a strong phase with a unique edge, (52) would be ungrammatical, contrary to fact. I see two ways to fix this problem. The first one is assuming that CLLD is the result of base-generation of the topic phrase, along the lines suggested by Cinque (1990). If this is assumed, (52) stops being problematic because the only constituent that has to escape the embedded CP is the wh-phrase. I won't adopt this strategy, though. I have argued elsewhere (Cecchetto 2000) that CLLD is a genuine case of movement of the topic phrase. More relevantly for my goals in this essay, in CLLD Remnant Movement Effects are observed (cf. (7) and (8)) and I have reduced them to PIC effects. Therefore, by assuming that a topic phrase is base-generated in its superficial position, I would miss the explanation for the pattern in (7)–(8). The second way out of the problem introduced by (52) is weakening the requirement that there is always a single edge for each phase. A possibility to do that in a way that is non–ad hoc is suggested by Rizzi's (1997) analysis of the left periphery. According to Rizzi, the COMP projection in Romance and English should be split into different maximal projections. One level of COMP hosts topic phrases (in Romance, Clitic Left Dislocated constituents) while another level hosts wh-elements. One obvious suggestion is that each of these maximal projections counts as an edge (that is, an escape hatch from the CP phase). Therefore, in (52) there would be two different CP edges: one used by *quel libro* and the other used by *chi*.

This analysis of (52) proves to be helpful in another respect. It is a well-known fact (see Cinque 1990, Rizzi 1990, and much subsequent work) that a wh-phrase can be marginally extracted from a wh-island if it is D(iscourse)-linked. So, there is a contrast between (53) and (54), due to the fact that *which book* can be D-linked but an adverbial like *why* cannot be:

(53)   ?Which book do you wonder who bought *t*?

(54)   *Why do you wonder who bought that book *t*?

From the point of view of the theory of phases, the ungrammaticality of (54) is expected. The adjunct *why* cannot use the edge of the embedded CP (because it is already occupied by *who*) and, under PIC, cannot be extracted from its base position either. However, this theory in its simplest form cannot explain why (53), although marginal, is better then (54).

I think that my proposal to explain the grammaticality of (52) can also take care of the contrast between (53) and (54). The first step to make sense of the difference between these two sentences within a theory based on PIC is capitalizing on the fact that the notion of D-linking (contextually given, or presupposed information) is reminiscent of the notion of "topichood" (a topic is a contextually given element that becomes a sort of "subject of predication"). Since, as the grammaticality of (52) suggests, the layer that hosts wh-phrases and the one that hosts topic phrases count as two distinct edges for extraction from the strong phase CP, it's only natural to think that the D-linked constituent *which book* can use, at least as a marked option, the CP layer that hosts topic phrases to escape from the embedded CP in (53).[23] This option is not available in (54) because an adverbial like *why* is inherently incompatible with topichood and can never sit in the COMP level that hosts topics.[24]

This account of the difference between (53) and (54) predicts that, if a topic phrase is extracted from a wh-island, the extraction of a D-linked wh-phrase from the same wh-island should be ungrammatical rather than marginal, because the two extracted phrases compete for the same CP edge. Although the data are delicate, because we are confronting two sentences that are both far from being perfect, this prediction seems to be borne out by a minimal pair like (55)–(56):

(55)   ?Quale dei tuoi libri non sai quando hai dato a quel ragazzo?
      which of your book NEG (you) know when (you) have given to that boy

(56)   *A quel ragazzo, quale dei tuoi libri non sai quando hai dato?
      to that boy which of your book NEG (you) know when (you) have given

Example (56), in which both the Clitic Left Dislocated phrase *a quel ragazzo* and the D-linked wh-phrase *quale dei tuoi libri* are extracted from the embedded question, is clearly worse than (55) in which the only extracted constituent is the D-linked wh-phrase.[25]

Summarizing: I propose that the theory of phases should be modified by taking into consideration Rizzi's (1997) proposal that the left periphery in English and Romance is internally organized in different layers. I claim that each of these layers can count as an escape edge for the XP that it is qualified to host.

8.   Conclusion

Although a trace must be c-commanded by its antecedent by the moment in which movement takes place, the c-command configuration can be later destroyed in the derivation. Remnant movement is possible in principle, and Remnant Movement Effects, when present, are due to violations of PIC. My analysis has other important consequences. First, it is not necessary to complicate the definition of Relativized Minimality to include both intervention in terms of c-command and intervention in terms of containment. Also, if the fine structure of the CP layer is taken into consideration, the pattern concerning wh-islands, which would be problematic for the theory of phases, can be explained.

Notes

For useful comments, I am indebted to the audience of *NELS 31* (Georgetown University, October 2000), of the 26th Incontro di Grammatica Generativa (University of Rome, March 2000) and of a seminar at Kanda University (Tokyo, September 1999). Thanks to Noam Chomsky, Luigi Rizzi, and an anonymous reviewer for helpful remarks. Two different preliminary versions of this essay are included in the proceedings of the 2nd Asian Glow Conference distributed by Nanzan University and in the proceedings of NELS 31 distributed by GLSA.

1. I came to this conclusion after attending a lively debate on this issue between Richard Kayne and Michael Brody at the University of Florence in summer 2001. What I say reflects my understanding of Kayne's position.

2. In English the choice between preposition stranding and pied piping introduces a complication. For some speakers the relevant minimal pair is (i) rather than (3):

> (i) a *[How many chapters of $t_1]_2$ do you remember [which book]$_1$ you read?
> b. [Which book]$_1$ do you remember [how many chapters of $t_1]_2$ you read?

However, no matter what the personal preference between preposition stranding and pied piping is, the sentence that exemplifies configuration (1) is much more degraded than the other member of the minimal pair.

3. As discussed by Sauerland (1999), German scrambling displays a pattern similar to the Japanese pattern in one respect, but with an important difference. Scrambling out a scrambled phrase, which is fully acceptable in Japanese, is very marginal in German, as shown by the degraded status of (ii). However, degraded as it is, (ii) is better than (i), which is totally out:

> (i) *Danny hat [t_1 zu putzen]$_2$ vergeblich [das Bad]$_1$ gestern t_2 versucht.
> Danny has to clean unsuccessfully the bathroom yesterday tried

> (ii) *?Danny hat [das Bad]$_1$ vergeblich [t_1 zu putzen]$_2$ gestern t_2 versucht.
> Danny has the bathroom unsuccessfully to clean yesterday tried

4. In the Japanese examples reported in the literature it is pretty common to add *koto* (the fact that) to avoid the unnaturalness resulting from the lack of topic in a matrix sentence.

5. In Italian CLLD constructions, CPs and DPs can be dislocated if they are matched by a clitic pronoun. In (8) the left dislocated sentence is a nonfinite CP, and the matching pronoun is the argumental clitic *ne* (literally 'of it'). The DP *Maria* is matched in (8) by the clitic *la* (her). The pattern illustrated by (8) does not change if a finite clause is substituted for a nonfinite one. See Cecchetto (2000) for a more precise analysis of the derivation of CLLD sentences.

6. Luigi Rizzi points out to me additional evidence that Remnant Movement Effects are observed in CLLD. Lets us start from (ii), which is derived from (i):

> (i) Piero crede [$_{CP}$ che Gianni abbia parlato [$_{PP}$ con Maria]].
> 'Piero believes that Gianni has(SUBJ) spoken with Maria.'

> (ii) [$_{CP}$ che Gianni le abbia parlato], [$_{PP}$ a Maria], Piero lo crede.
> that Gianni has(SUBJ) spoken with Maria Piero it believes

A priori there are two possible derivations for (ii). In the first derivation, after left dislocation of the PP *a Maria*, remnant movement of the CP occurs. In the second derivation, which is sketched in (iii), the PP sits in the right edge of the CP, which, in turn, is left dislocated (see Cecchetto 1999a for a discussion of clitic right dislocation in Italian).

> (iii) [$_{CP}$ che Gianni le abbia parlato [$_{PP}$ a Maria]] Piero lo crede

The one sketched in (iii) is the right analysis for (ii), as shown by the ungrammaticality of (iv). In (iv), the matrix subject interposes between the CP and the PP, therefore the latter cannot sit in the right edge of the former. The only possible derivation for (iv) is one in which the CP, the PP, and the matrix subject are all left dislocated in a independent fashion. In this derivation, the trace of the PP is not c-commanded, and a Remnant Movement Effect arises.

(iv) *[$_{CP}$ che Gianni le abbia parlato], [Piero], [$_{PP}$ a Maria], lo crede.
that Gianni has(SUBJ) spoken Piero with Maria it believes

7. However, see van Riemsdjik (1989) for a different treatment for sentences like (12).

8. Longobardi (1985) argues that the requirement that antecedents c-command the gaps associated with them is empirically inadequate. His arguments are based on multiple gap constructions in Italian. For example in (ii), which is derived from (i) via fronting of the adverbial clause, the parasitic gap *e* is not c-commanded by a suitable antecedent. Nevertheless, (ii) has the typical status of parasitic gaps constructions rather than being ungrammatical:

(i) ?Non so [quale ragazza]$_1$ Gianni sarebbe disposto a sposare t$_1$ [senza conoscere *e* bene].
(I) NEG know which girl Gianni would be ready to marry without knowing *e* well

(ii) ?[Senza conoscere *e* bene], non so [quale ragazza]$_1$ Gianni sarebbe disposto a sposare t$_1$.
Without knowing *e* well (I) NEG know which girl Gianni would be ready to marry

Longobardi proposes an account based on a modified version of Kayne's (1983) Connectedness Condition. In this chapter, I focus on the licensing conditions on traces, postponing investigating parasitic gaps to another occasion.

9. To the best of my knowledge, Müller (1993) and Takano (1993) are the first who (independently) proposed that Remnant Movement Effects, when present, depend on the fact that the movement of the superphrase Z and movement of the constituent X out of the superphrase Z are of the same type.

10. Examples that show that Japanese scrambling and Romance CLLD do not obey Relativized Minimality abound. One scrambling case is (i) in n. 17. CLLD sentences (i)–(iii) illustrate the same point; (ii) and (iii) are derived from (i). They are both grammatical even if the topic PP *con Gianni* has crossed over the topic DP *il libro* in (ii) and the other way around in (iii):

(i) Credo che dovremmo discutere il libro con Gianni.
(I) think that (we) should discuss the book with G.
'I think that we should talk about the book with Gianni.'

(ii) Con Gianni credo che il libro lo dovremmo discutere.
with Gianni (I) think that the book (we) it should discuss

(iii) Il libro credo che con Gianni lo dovremmo discutere.
the book (I) think that with Gianni (we) it should discuss

11. The proponents of the theory that reduces Remnant Movement Effects to Relativized Minimality discuss possible solutions for this problem (see Kitahara 1994, who suggests that a single violation of the Minimal Link Condition causes only a small degree of marginality, and Sauerland 1999, who proposes that an intervening checked and interpretable feature causes a smaller degree of markedness than an unchecked one). However, these treatments do not extend to cases like (24b), because the Remnant Movement Effect should be strong in this type of sentence, given the aggressively non-D-linked character of the relevant wh-chain.

12. A technical caveat: In the papers in which the theory of phases has been proposed, unlike in previous versions of the minimalist framework, the Accusative Case of the direct object can be checked in situ via an application of the operation Agree (that does not need to be associated with the operation Move). So, in (30) the direct object *who* moves to the edge of the VP in order to be allowed to further move to COMP, not for Case reason.

13. The derivation in (i)–(v) is not a possible derivation for (33) either, because in step (v) the sequence of words "how many chapters" that should move in order to produce the word order that is observed is not a constituent.

(i) [$_{IP}$ you I° [$_{VP}$ read [how many chapters [of which book]$_1$]$_2$]]

(ii) [$_{IP}$ you I° [$_{VP}$ [how many chapters [of which book]$_1$]$_2$ [$_{VP}$ read t$_2$]]]

(iii) [$_{CP}$ [how many chapters [of which book]$_1$]$_2$ C° [$_{IP}$ you I° [$_{VP}$ t"$_2$ [$_{VP}$ read t'$_2$]]]]]

(iv) [$_{CP}$ C° [$_{IP}$ you I° [$_{VP}$ remember [$_{CP}$ [how many chapters [of which book]$_1$]$_2$ C° [$_{IP}$ you I° [$_{VP}$ t"$_2$ [$_{VP}$ read t'$_2$]]]]]]]

(v) *[$_{CP}$ C° [$_{IP}$ you I° [$_{VP}$ remember [$_{CP}$ *how many chapters* [of which book]$_1$]$_2$ C° [$_{IP}$ you I° [$_{VP}$ t"$_2$ [$_{VP}$ read t'$_2$]]]]]]]

14. For the fact that short distance (roughly, clause-internal) scrambling can be A movement whereas long-distance scrambling must be A-bar, see Saito (1992) and references cited therein. One of Saito's arguments is that short-distance scrambling of a potential binder creates a configuration in which an anaphor is bound, as shown by the improvement of (ii) over (i), while long-distance scrambling of a potential binder does not alleviate the Principle A violation, as shown by the fact that (iv) does not improve over (iii):

(i) ?*[[Otagai$_i$-no sensei]-ga [karera$_i$-o hihansita]] (koto).
each other-GEN teacher-NOM they-ACC criticized (fact)
'Each other's teachers criticized them.'

(ii) ?[Karera$_i$-o [Otagai$_i$-no sensei]-ga [*t* hihansita]] (koto).
they-ACC each other-GEN teacher-NOM criticized (fact)
'Them, each other's teachers criticized.'

(iii) *[[Otagai$_i$-no sensei]-ga [$_{CP}$ [$_{IP}$ Hanako-ga karera$_i$-o hihansita] to] itta] (koto).
each other-GEN teacher-NOM Hanako-NOM they-ACC criticized that said (fact)
'Each other's teachers said that Hanako criticized them.'

(iv) *[Karera$_i$-o [otagai$_i$-no sensei]-ga [$_{CP}$ [$_{IP}$ Hanako-ga *t* hihansita] to] itta] (koto).
they-ACC each other-GEN teacher-NOM Hanako-NOM criticized that said (fact)
'Them, each other's teachers said that Hanako criticized.'

15. Actually, movement of the embedded clause might be an occurrence of short-distance scrambling. If this is the case, the embedded clause does not target a position outside the phase in which it originates.

16. On the surface, Japanese, unlike English, allows multiple foci, as (43) indicates. See the following discussion for possible analyses that reduce these cases of apparent multiple foci to the focalization of a single complex constituent. The focalized material is located between the topic marker *wa* and the copula *da*.

17. A sentence like (i), which is identical to (45) except for the switched order of the scrambled PPs, is grammatical. This difference between (i) and (45) can be explained by PIC, together with the assumption introduced in the text that the landing site of long-distance scrambling marks the edge of a strong phase. In (i), as in the ungrammatical case (45), both *sono mura-ni* and *Bill-ni* must escape the matrix VP to reach their superficial position. However, in (i) the movement of *Bill-ni*, which takes place before the movement of *sono mura-ni*, is a case of short-distance scrambling in which a constituent adjoins to the closest IP level that dominates its base position. Therefore it qualifies as a phase-internal movement and, under PIC, does not need to use the edge of the matrix VP, which can be used by *sono mura-ni*.

(i) [$_{PP}$ sono mura-ni] [$_{PP}$ Bill-ni] [$_{IP}$ John-ga [$_{VP}$ t$_{Bill-ni}$ [$_{CP}$ Mary-ga t$_{sono\ mura-ni}$
     sundeiru to] itta]]
     that village-in Bill-to John-NOM Mary-NOM lives that said

A similar derivation is blocked in (45) because the movement of *sono mura-ni*, which takes place before the movement of *Bill-ni*, is a case of long-distance scrambling and, as such, marks the edge of a strong phase. Therefore, the movement of *Bill-ni*, which targets a position higher than the one occupied by *sono mura-ni*, qualifies as phase-external movement as well. The result is that *sono mura-ni* and *Bill-ni* compete for the unique edge of the matrix VP.

18. The remnant movement account has been proposed by Koizumi (1995) and Kuwabara (1996) for multiple clefting and by Kitahara (1994) and Koizumi (1995) for multiple long-distance scrambling.

19. To be precise, the remnant movement account derives the clause mate condition from the fact that the largest constituent that can undergo remnant movement is IP. In turn, this follows from the fact that the verb cannot move outside IP.

20. This kind of explanation has been proposed by Takano (1999) for multiple foci and by Cecchetto (1999b) for multiple right dislocation.

21. Oblique movement has been proposed to explain cases like the following. In Japanese, a language that admits wh in situ, an adjunct wh-phrase as *naze* (why) cannot appear in a strong island:

(i) *John-wa [$_{NP}$ [$_{IP}$ sono hon-o naze katta] hito]-o sagasiteru no.
     J.-TOP that book-ACC why bought person-ACC looking-for Q
     'Why is John looking for the person who bought that book?'

The strong ungrammaticality of (i) is usually described as a case of ECP violation triggered by LF movement of the wh-phrase. Interestingly, the sentence significantly improves if the direct object *sono hon-o* (that book) is replaced by the wh-argument *nani-o* (what):

(ii) ??John-wa [$_{NP}$ [$_{IP}$ nani-o naze katta hito]-o sagasiteru no
      John-TOP what-ACC why bought person-ACC looking-for Q
      'Why is John looking for the person who bought what?'

Saito (1994) attributes the improvement of (ii) to the fact that the adjunct can be a free-rider of the argument. At LF, first the adjunct *naze* locally (=internally to the island) adjoins to the argument *nani-o*, and then the syntactic object created by this local adjunction escapes the island. The adjunction of *naze* to *nani-o* is an occurrence of oblique movement.

22. The discussion on multiple long-distance scrambling in Japanese might be reduplicated in the domain of multiple wh-extraction. For example, the theory of phases predicts that two wh-phrases should not be allowed to long-distance move out of an embedded clause to reach the COMP area in the matrix clause, since they would compete for the unique edge of the clause in which they originate. Data reported by Rudin (1988) shows that this prediction might be correct. In most Slavic languages that allow multiple wh-movement (including Serbo-Croatian, Polish, and Czech), although single wh-extraction from an embedded clause is allowed, multiple wh-extraction from an embedded clause is excluded (multiple wh-movement is allowed in these languages only if it is clause bound). So, these languages behave as the theory of phases in its strictest form dictates. Bulgarian and Romanian are different because they allow multiple wh-extraction, subject to various constraints. It is very tempting to extend to the Bulgarian and Romanian cases the oblique movement approach that has been proposed for Japanese. That this line of explanation is promising is shown by Rudin's observation that adverbs and parentheticals can split a sequence of wh-phrases in Serbo-Croatian, Polish, and Czech but cannot do that in Romanian and Bulgarian. As observed by Rudin, this

is clear evidence that in Romanian and Bulgarian (but not in Serbo-Croatian, Polish, and Czech) the sequence of wh-phrases is a unique constituent. In turn, this suggests to me that what takes place in Romanian and Bulgarian is oblique movement rather than genuine multiple wh-extraction.

23. See Grohmann (1998) and Rizzi (2001) for related proposals. Grohmann claims that an extracted wh-phrase can be a topic in multiple wh-constructions while Rizzi argues that the restriction of a D-linked wh-phrase is allowed to sit in the CP layer that hosts topic phrases.

24. Given my explanation for the ameliorating effect of (53) over (54), the complete ungrammaticality of sentence (2) (*Which picture of do you wonder who John likes?*) indicates that a wh-phrase like *which picture of who* can never be D-linked. The same must be true in general for wh-phrases that contain another wh-phrase. This is not only intuitively correct but also directly follows from the characterization according to which a wh-phrase is D-linked when it ranges over a known set of entities (for example, *which house of John's* is D-linked because it requires that the set of houses owned by John be familiar, either because it is given in the immediate discourse context or because it is shared knowledge). Obviously, the set over which a wh-phrase ranges cannot be known if its restriction contains another wh-phrase.

A related point is raised by a reviewer who asks what excludes the following derivation of (i). First, the superphrase *how many chapters of which book* raises to the embedded VP edge. Then, *which book* raises to the topic position at the embedded CP edge, and the remnant [*how many chapters of* t] raises to the wh-operator position at the embedded CP edge. Finally, when the ingredients of the matrix clause are merged, [*how many chapters of* t] raises to the root CP.

(i) *[How many chapters of t_1]$_2$ do you remember [which book]$_1$ you read?

My answer is that this derivation is excluded because the wh-phrase *which book* cannot check its wh-feature, since it never sits in a wh-operator position. Crucially, the derivation of (53) is different because the wh-phrase *which book* escapes from the embedded CP by using the layer that hosts topic phrases but later reaches a wh-operator position in which it can check its wh feature.

25. The degraded status of (56) cannot be attributed to a general ban against contemporary left dislocation and wh-movement. On the contrary, it is well known that left dislocation and wh-movement can naturally cooccur, as shown by the perfect acceptability of (i), in which there is no wh-island:

(i) A quel ragazzo, quale dei tuoi libri pensi di regalare?
to that boy which of your book (you) think to give
'Which of your books do you think you will give to that boy?'

References

Cecchetto, C. (1999a) "A Comparative Analysis of Left and Right Dislocation in Romance." *Studia Linguistica* 53.1, 40–67.

———— (1999b) "Optionality and Directionality: A View from Leftward and Rightward Scrambling in Japanese," in *Grant-in-Aid for COE*, Research Report No. 08CE1001. Kanda, Japan: Kanda University of International Study.

———— (2000) "Doubling Structures and Reconstruction." *Probus* 12.1, 1–34.

Chomsky, N. (1995) *The Minimalist Program.* Cambridge, Mass.: MIT Press.

———— (1999) "Derivation by Phase." *MIT Occasional Paper in Linguistics* 18.

———— (2000) "Minimalist Explorations," in R. Martin, D. Michaels, and J. Uriagereka (eds.) *Step by Step.* Cambridge, Mass.: MIT Press, 89–155.

———— (2001) "Beyond Explanatory Adequacy." Unpublished ms., MIT, Cambridge, Mass.

Cinque, G. (1990) *Types of A'-Dependencies*. Cambridge, Mass.: MIT Press.

den Besten, H., and G. Webelhuth (1990) "Stranding," in G. Grewendorf and W. Sternefeld (eds.) *Scrambling and Barriers*. Amsterdam: John Benjamins, 11–32.

Fiengo, R. (1997) "On Trace Theory." *Linguistic Inquiry* 8, 35–62.

Fox, D. (1999) *Economy and Semantic Interpretation*. Cambridge, Mass.: MIT Press.

Fukui, N. (1997) "Attract and the A-over-A Principle." In *UCI Working Papers in Linguistics* 3, 51–67.

Grohmann, K. (1998) "Syntactic Inquiries into Discourse Restrictions on Multiple Interrogatives." *Groninger Arbeiten zur germanistischen Linguistik* 42, 1–60.

Haraguchi, S. (1973) "Remarks on Dislocation in Japanese." Unpublished ms., MIT, Cambridge, Mass.

Kayne, R. (1983) "Connectedness." *Linguistic Inquiry* 14, 223–249.

——— (1994) *The Antisymmetry of the Syntax*. Cambridge, Mass.: MIT Press.

Kitahara, H. (1994) "Target α: A Unified Theory of Movement and Structure-Building," Ph.D. diss., Harvard University.

——— (1997) *Elementary Operations and Optimal Derivations*. Cambridge, Mass.: MIT Press.

Koizumi, M. (1995). "Phrase Structure in Minimalist Syntax," Ph.D. dissertation, MIT.

Koopman H., and A. Szabolcsi (2000). *Verbal Complexes*. Cambridge, Mass.: MIT Press.

Kuno, S. (1978) *Danwa-no Bunpoo* "Grammar of Discourse." Tokyo: Kuroshio Publishers.

Kuwabara, K. (1996). "Multiple Wh-Phrases in Elliptical Clauses and Some Aspects of Clefts with Multiple Foci," in M. Koizumi, M. Oishi, and U. Sauerland (eds.) *Formal Approaches to Japanese Linguistics 2. MIT Working Papers in Linguistics* 29.

Longobardi, G. (1985) "Connectedness, Scope and C-Command." *Linguistic Inquiry* 16, 163–192.

Müller, G. (1993) "On Deriving Movement Type Asymmetries," Ph.D. diss., University of Tübingen.

——— (1998) *Incomplete Category Fronting*. Dordrecht: Kluwer.

Rizzi, L. (1990) *Relativized Minimality*. Cambridge, Mass.: MIT Press.

——— (1997) "The Fine Structure of the Left Periphery," in Liliane Haegeman (ed.) *Elements of Grammar: Handbook of Generative Syntax*. Dordrecht: Kluwer, 281–337.

——— (2001) "Reconstruction, Weak Island Sensitivity, and Agreement," in C. Cecchetto, G. Chierchia, and M. T. Guasti (eds.) *Semantic Interfaces*. Stanford: CSLI, 145–176.

Rudin, C. (1988) "On Multiple Questions and Multiple wh-Fronting." *Natural Language and Linguistic Theory* 6, 445–501.

Saito, M. (1985) "Some Asymmetries in Japanese and Their Theoretical Implications," Ph.D. diss., MIT.

——— (1992) "Long Distance Scrambling in Japanese." *Journal of East Asian linguistics* 1, 69–118.

——— (1994) "Additional-WH Effects and the Adjunction Site Theory." *Journal of East Asian Linguistics* 3, 195–240.

Sauerland, U. (1999) "Erasability and Interpretation." *Syntax* 2.3, 161–188.

Sohn, K. (1994) "Adjunction to Argument, Free Ride and a Minimalist Program," in M. Koizumi and H. Ura (eds.) *Formal Approches to Japanese Linguistics 1. MIT Working Papers in Linguistics* 24.

Takano, Y. (1993) "Minimalism and Proper Binding." Unpublished ms., University of California, Irvine.

——— (1994) "Unbound Traces and Indeterminacy of Derivation," in M. Nakamura (ed.) *Current Topics in English and Japanese*. Tokyo: Hituzi Syobo, 229–253.

——— (1999) "Surprising Constituents." Unpublished ms., Kinjo Gakuin University.

van Riemsdijk, H. (1989) "Movement and Regeneration," in P. Beninca' (ed.) *Dialect Variation and the Theory of Grammar*. Dordrecht: Foris, 105–136.

7

Complementizer Deletion in Italian

ALESSANDRA GIORGI

AND FABIO PIANESI

The purpose of this chapter is to shed light on a phenomenon of Italian, which seems to have several interesting connections with issues in morphology, morphosyntax and semantics—namely, Complementizer Deletion.

Our main tenet is that so-called Complementizer "Deletion" is no deletion at all, nor is it movement of the verb to a complementizer position; it is simply an instance of the familiar V-to-Agr of Italian. More precisely, when CD is available Agr has peculiar properties due to the morphosyntactic environment in which it is realized, which license a structure with no overt complementizer.

This chapter is structured as follows. In section 1 we illustrate and discuss the basic data concerning complementizer deletion in Italian. In section 2 we present the theoretical background needed for a formal account; in section 3 we present and discuss our hypothesis and derive the empirical evidence previously illustrated.

We do not discuss cross-linguistic evidence here, but we'll try to make our point as clear as possible in claiming that Italian CD Italian is a language-specific phenomenon, due to the interplay of a set of cooccurring properties, and that it is very different from both English complementizer deletion and German embedded verb second.

1. The properties of CD contexts

Complementizer Deletion in Italian exhibits the following properties:

    a. It only occurs in subjunctive clauses and is optional (Scorretti 1994; Poletto 1995, 2000).

b. It is not available in factive complements, despite the presence of the subjunctive (Giorgi and Pianesi 1996, 1997).

c. It is not available in dislocated clauses, independently of the mood of the verb (Giorgi and Pianesi 1997).

d. Italian CD is different from *Aux-to-Comp* (Poletto 1995).

e. It is possible in non-embedded subjunctive contexts with a specific range of *modal* meanings.

f. It exhibits a strong correlation with the temporal interpretation of the embedded clause; in particular, a correlation with the so-called Double Access Reading (DAR) (Giorgi and Pianesi 1997, 2000).

g. CD clauses exhibit a peculiar distribution of the embedded subject (Giorgi and Pianesi 1996, 1997).

h. CD exhibits the *First-Person Effect.*

i. In CD contexts Topic and Focus have a very restricted distribution.

In other languages, such as for instance English or German, the properties of complementizer-less contexts are different from those found in Italian; at the same time, German and English differ from each other. This fact seems to suggest that the morphosyntactic properties of the various lexical items are involved, so that cross-linguistic differences obtain as a result of lexical differences.

Before attempting to provide a theoretical framework Italian CD, we discuss properties (a)–(i) in detail.

1.1.   Property (a): CD and mood choice

CD is available only when the mood of the embedded verb is the subjunctive:[1]

(1)   Mario crede (che) sia partito.
      'Mario believes (that) he left(SUBJ).'

(2)   Mario ha detto *(che) è partito.
      'Mario said that he left(IND).'

In standard Italian, the verb *credere* (believe) selects the subjunctive. In many substandard varieties, however, the indicative is often acceptable. As expected, in these cases, the complementizer cannot be dropped:

(3)   Gianni credeva *(che) aveva telefonato.
      'Gianni believed had(IND) called.'

Poletto (2000) points out that the same contexts in which clauses with the verb in the subjunctive mood admit CD—for example, the complements of *credere* (believe)—allow the omission of the complementizer even when the verb is in the conditional mood:

(4)   (?)?Gianni crede partirebbero, se potessero.
      'Gianni believes they would leave, if they could.'

To us (4) has more marked status than (1), even though it still neatly contrasts with (2).[2] In any case, for the purposes of this essay, the example in (4) can easily be assimilated to (1).

1.2.   Properties (b)–(c): CD in factive clauses, and dislocation contexts

It is not the case, however, that every subjunctive clause admits CD. Thus, the complement clause of factive predicates must be introduced by the complementizer:

(5)   Mario si rammarica *(che) sia partito.
      'Mario regrets that he left(SUBJ).'

(6)   Mario ha confessato *(che) è partito.
      'Mario confessed that he left(IND).'

In (5) we give an example with a factive predicate, *rimpiangere* (regret), which selects the subjunctive. With respect to CD, this case is on a par with (6), where the main predicate is a factive verb selecting the indicative, *confessare* (confess).[3]

Another environment where CD is disallowed is provided by clauses appearing at the left, or at the extreme right, periphery of the clause. In all these contexts, CD is not available, even when the verb is in the subjunctive mood:[4]

(7)   *Sia partito, Mario lo crede.
      'He left(SUBJ), Mario believes(SUBJ) it.'

(8)   *Sia partito, Mario lo ha detto.
      'He left(SUBJ), Mario said(IND) it.'

(9)   *SIA PARTITO, Mario crede (non che sia arrivato).
      'He left(SUBJ), Mario believes (not that he arrived).'

(10)   *SIA PARTITO, Mario ha detto (non che che è arrivato).
       'He left(IND), Mario said (not that he arrived).'[5]

(11)   *Sia malato, è un fatto noto da tempo.
       'He is(SUBJ) sick, is a well-known fact.'

(12)   *Sia malato, è stato riferito alla conferenza stampa.
       'He is(SUBJ) sick, has been reported to the press.'

In (7) and (8) the dislocated clause with the subjunctive is a topic; in (9) and (10) it is the sentence's (contrastive) focus. Finally in (11) and (12) we have sentences with subject clauses. As shown, CD is clearly ruled out, but when the dislocated clause is introduced by *che*, the sentence is fully grammatical.

A similar conclusion holds for right-dislocated clauses:

(13)   Mario lo crede, *(che) sia partito.
       'Mario believes(SUBJ) it, that he left(SUBJ).'

(14)   Mario ce lo ha detto, *(che) è partito.
       'Mario told(IND) it to us, that he left(IND).'

It is also true of right-dislocated, focused clauses:

(15)   Mario credeva *(CHE) GIANNI FOSSE PARTITO (non che Maria fosse tornata).
       'Mario believed (that) Gianni had(SUBJ) left (not that Maria had(SUBJ) arrived).'

1.3. Property (d): CD and Aux-to-Comp

As Poletto (1995) points out, in Italian there is a structure that has some superficial properties in common with CD—namely, the absence of the complementizer—but differs in relevant respects. Such a structure is *Aux-to-Comp* (Rizzi 1982):

(16) a. Essendo Mario/io arrivato, fummo tutti più contenti.
       'Having Mario/I arrived, we were much happier.'
    b.*Mario/io essendo arrivato, fummo tutti più contenti.
       'Mario/ I having arrived, we were much happier.'

In (16a) the auxiliary occupies a position to the left of the subject. This ordering, which is unavailable in Italian, significantly contrasts with the one reproduced in (16b), where the subject appears to the left of both the auxiliary and the main verb. This means that the nonfinite auxiliary is able to raise beyond a preverbal subject, which is licensed in the nominative form, cf. *io* (I) in (16a).[6]

The same pattern can be found in the following examples, where the auxiliary is in a finite tense (past subjunctive):[7]

(17) a. Fosse Mario arrivato in tempo, saremmo partiti prima.
       'Had(SUBJ) Mario arrived on time, we would have left earlier.'
    b. Fossi io arrivato in tempo, saremmo partiti prima.
       'Had(SUBJ) I arrived on time, we would have left earlier.'

(18) a.*Mario fosse arrivato in tempo, saremmo partiti prima.
       'Mario had(SUBJ) arrived on time, we would have left earlier.'
    b.*Io fossi arrivato in tempo, saremmo partiti prima.
       'I had(SUBJ) arrived on time, we would have left earlier.'

Another case in which this particular ordering can be found is the following:[8]

(19) a. La commissione ritiene aver Mario/io superato l'esame.
       'The committee believes to have Mario/I passed the examination.'
    b.*La commissione ritiene io/Mario avere superato l'esame.
       'The committee believes I/ Mario to have passed the examination.'

Observationally, there are two main differences between Aux-to-Comp and CD constructions. In the first place, in CD constructions a subject appearing between the auxiliary and the participle is ungrammatical:

(20) *Gianni credeva avesse Mario superato l'esame.
    'Gianni believed had(SUBJ) Mario passed the examination.'

The second difference—related to the first one—concerns the optionality of the absence of the complementizer given the relevant word order. In the contexts where it is available, CD is never obligatory:

(21) Gianni credeva (che) fosse partita Maria.
    'Gianni believed (that) she had(SUBJ) left Maria.'

In example (21), the subordinate clause with a postverbal subject—or even a preverbal one, for the speakers having this option—is acceptable either with or without a complementizer. In sentences with the word order typical of Aux-to-Comp, in contrast, the overt complementizer is always excluded:

(22) a. *Se fosse Mario arrivato in tempo, ...
         'If had(SUBJ) Mario arrived on time . . .'
      b. Se Mario fosse arrivato in tempo, ...
         Se fosse(SUBJ) arrivato Mario in tempo, . . .
         'If Mario had(SUBJ) arrived in time, ...'

(23) *La commissione ritiene di avere Mario superato l'esame.
       'The committee believes Mario to have passed the examination.'

Example (22a) shows that the order Aux-Subj-Participle is incompatible with the presence of the complementizer *se* (if), contrasting with sentences with the "normal" Subj-Aux-Part ordering, cf. (22b). Similarly, example (23) shows that the infinitival complementizer *di* is incompatible with the Aux-to-Comp word order and a nominative subject. Actually, *di* requires an empty controlled subject, as in the following example, where *Gianni* controls PRO:[9]

(24) Gianni ritiene di PRO aver superato l'esame.
      Lit.: Gianni believes to PRO have passed the examination.
      'Gianni believes that he has passed the examination.'

Given these two differences, we can conclude with Poletto (1995, 2000) that Aux-to-Comp is a different phenomenon than CD. The issue remains open concerning the status of Aux-to-comp exactly, in particular: Where has Aux moved to? Why only *Aux* and not a full verb? We put these questions aside.[10]

1.4.   Property (e): CD in matrix clauses

Let us turn now to investigate the status of CD in matrix subjunctive:

(25) a. (Che) parta!   (*Iussive*)
         '(That) he leaves(SUBJ).'
      b. (Che) partisse pure!   (*Concessive*)
         '(That) he left(SUBJ)!'
      c. (Che) ti pigli/pigliasse un colpo!   (*Desiderative*)
         '(That) you have/had(SUBJ) a stroke!'

In these sentences, which all have clear modal meanings, the verb is in the subjunctive and the complementizer can be dropped. Just to stress again the differences between CD and Aux-to-Comp, notice that the acceptability of (25a)–(25c) contrasts with unacceptability of the corresponding Aux-to-Comp cases:

(26) Oh, (*che) avesse la polizia arrestato Mario prima che commettesse quegli orrendi crimini!
      'Oh, (*that) had(SUBJ) the police arrested Mario before he committed those horrible crimes!'

1.5.   Property (f): CD and DAR

There are important correlations between CD and the temporal interpretation of embedded sentences. Consider the following examples:

(27)   Gianni ha detto che Maria è incinta.
       'Gianni said that Maria is(IND) pregnant.'

This example is the "classical" illustration of the DAR phenomenon: for an utterance of such a sentence to be true, it must be that (somehow) Maria's pregnancy overlaps both the utterance time and the time at which Gianni said what he did.[11] Similar facts obtain in English as well.[12] Notice that with the matrix verb *credere* (believe), which we know to select the subjunctive mood, a sentence corresponding to (27) is ungrammatical and the DAR is, a fortiori, not available:

(28)   *Gianni credeva che Maria sia incinta.
       'Gianni believed that Maria is(PRES SUBJ) pregnant.'

(29)   Gianni credeva che Maria fosse incinta.   (SIMUL)
       'Gianni believed that Maria was(PAST SUBJ) pregnant.'

This can be generalized: a verb in the present subjunctive can only appear under a matrix verb in the present tense. Analogously, a past form can only be dependent on a main past.[13]

These observations might suggest that the subjunctive is actually a *tenseless* verbal form, in that the presence of a certain "tense" is determined entirely by the tense of the matrix verb: if the latter is in the present, then the subordinate subjunctive verb is in the present as well; if it is a past tense, then a past tense shows up in the complement clause, and so on. In other words, subjunctive verbal forms, at least in these contexts, would be only the expression of a sort of morphological tense agreement between the matrix and the embedded forms. In the case of the main verb *believe*, such an analysis seems to be on the right track, given a paradigm such as the following:

(30)   Gianni credeva che Maria telefonasse ieri/oggi/domani.
       'Gianni believed that Maria called(PAST SUBJ) yesterday/today/tomorrow.'

Here, the embedded event can be temporally located anywhere. This is not the case with an embedded indicative:

(31)   Gianni ha detto che Maria telefonò ieri/*oggi/*domani.
       'Gianni said that Maria called(PAST IND) yesterday/today/tomorrow.'

We will put aside here the questions concerning SOT in Italian and focus on CD phenomena.

Consider now that, as is well known by now, CD is available with *credere*:

(32)   Gianni credeva (che) tu avessi telefonato.
       'Gianni believed that you had(SUBJ) called.'

It is not available with *dire* (say):

(33)   Gianni ha detto *(che) tu hai telefonato.
       'Gianni said (that) you have(IND) called.'

If we consider (32)–(33) together with (27)–(28) a pattern is emerging: the double access reading is available only in the environments that reject complementizer deletion.

An important confirmation to such a hypothesis comes from consideration of verbs such as *ipotizzare* (hypothesize). In Italian, these verbs select the subjunctive:

(34)   Gianni ha ipotizzato (che) Maria fosse incinta.   (SIMUL)
       'Gianni hypothesized that Maria is(PRES SUBJ) pregnant.'

Sentence (34), a case of a past tense embedded under a past, makes CD available. However, the following sentence is also possible:

(35)   Gianni ha ipotizzato *(che) Maria sia incinta.   (DAR)
       'Gianni hypothesized that Maria was(PAST SUBJ) pregnant.'

Here CD is not available, and the temporal reading and temporal reading is of the DAR sort.[14]

These observations provide important support to the preceding generalization: the DAR is present only when CD is not available.[15] In other words, no context allows both the DAR and CD:

(36)   +DAR → −CD

In Giorgi and Pianesi (2000) we provided additional arguments in favor of this generalization. We also observed that its scope is not limited to present-under-past sentences but extends to other tense combinations, falling under the rubric of generalized DAR.

1.6. Property (g): CD and the distribution of the embedded subject

Up to now, we have mainly exemplified CD by means of sentences with no overt subject in the complement clause. This is because an overt embedded subject in its "canonical" preverbal position is not acceptable to all speakers.

(37)   Gianni credeva che (Maria) avesse telefonato (Maria).
       'Gianni believed that (Maria) had(SUBJ) called (Maria).'

(38)   a. #Gianni credeva Maria avesse telefonato.
            'Gianni believed Maria had(SUBJ) called.'
        b. Gianni credeva avesse telefonato Maria.
            'Gianni believed had(SUBJ) called Maria.'

Normally, with an intransitive verb such as *telefonare* (to phone), both the preverbal and the postverbal positions are available for a lexical non-pronominal subject, cf. (37). When the embedded clause is not introduced by the complementizer, some speakers find the preverbal subject ungrammatical, cf. (38a). Postverbal subjects, in contrast, do not affect the acceptability of the sentence, as in (38b).

We split as to our judgments about (38a): one of us rejects lexical non-pronominal preverbal subjects, as well as preverbal strong pronouns—e.g., *lui* (he)—as ungrammatical, while accepting *pro* or the second-person weak pronoun *tu* (you). For the other, all subjects are equally acceptable in preverbal position. We also ascertained that this peculiarity hasn't a geographical basis and that the availability of a lexical preverbal subject in CD structures seems to uniformly distribute in the areas where the subjunctive is available.

1.7.   Property (h): CD and first-person reports

We turn now to consider an important property of CD structures. Sentences with the main verb in the first-person singular present tense are more amenable to CD than are sentences with the matrix predicate, taking on a different verbal form. Thus, if the subject of the ascribed attitude is the speaker—and the temporal location is *now*—the omission of the complementizer gives rise to grammatical sentences even in cases that would otherwise turn out to yield nonacceptable results. Consider the following examples:

(39)   a. #Gianni spera Mario abbia telefonato.
        'Gianni hopes Mario has(SUBJ) called.'
       b. Spero Mario abbia telefonato.
        'I hope Mario has(SUBJ) called.'

The "hash" sign on (39a) signals the fact that there are speakers who reject the sentence. That is, for some speakers preverbal lexical subjects in CD contexts are ungrammatical. Interestingly, the same speakers find a contrast between (39a) and (39b), the latter improving considerably.

To our judgment, the presence of a first person affects the acceptability of CD even in factive contexts. Example (40) reproduces the evidence already discussed to the effect that factive contexts, even when requiring a subjunctive verbal form, resist CD:

(40)   a.*Gianni rimpiange tu abbia perso il treno.
        'Gianni regrets you have(SUBJ) lost the train.'
       b.*A Gianni dispiace tu non abbia vinto.
        'Gianni regrets you didn't win(SUBJ).'

Shifting to first-person reports, however, dramatically changes things:[16]

(41)   a. (?)Rimpiango tu abbia perso il treno.
        'I regret you have(SUBJ) lost the train.'
       b. (?)Mi dispiace tu non abbia vinto.
        'I regret you didn't win(SUBJ).'

1.8.   Property (i): Topic and Focus distribution
in CD contexts

CD sentences are seriously degraded when a phrase in topic or in focus occurs. Consider the following cases:

(42)   a. Gianni crede che la mela Maria l'abbia mangiata.
        'Gianni believes that the apple Maria it has(SUBJ) eaten.'
       b. Gianni crede che LA MELA Maria abbia mangiato, non la pera.
        'Gianni believes that THE APPLE Maria has(SUBJ) eaten, not the pear.'

In (42a) a topic occurs on the right of the complementizer and on the left of the subject; (42b) features a phrase in focus position.[17] Compare now (42b) with (43):

(43)   a. ?*Gianni crede LA MELA tu abbia mangiato, non la pera.
        'Gianni believes THE APPLE you have(SUBJ) eaten, not the pear.'

      b. (?)Credo LA MELA tu abbia mangiato, non la pera.
         'I believe THE APPLE you have(SUBJ) eaten, not the pear.'

Sentence (43a) is a third-person CD sentence with a contrastive focus, and is very marginal. It clearly contrasts with (43b), a first-person report that, in line with the discussion above, is much more acceptable. Consider now topic cases:

(44)   a. (?)?Gianni crede la mela tu l'abbia mangiata.
         Gianni believes the apple you it have(SUBJ) eaten
      b. Credo la mela tu l'abbia mangiata.
         I believe the apple you it have(SUBJ) eaten

Sentence (44a), with an embedded topicalization, is better than cases with embedded focus, (43a), but it does not reach full acceptability. As before, a first-person report provides improved results, this time yielding full grammaticality, cf. (44b).[18]

    Notice that there is nothing in topicalization and focalization per se that is incompatible with CD, as exemplified by the full acceptability of complementizer deletion with right-dislocated topic and focus constituents:

(45)   a. Gianni crede tu l'abbia(SUBJ) mangiata, la mela.
         Gianni believes you it have eaten, the apple
      b. Gianni crede tu abbia(SUBJ) mangiato LA MELA, non la pera.
         'Gianni believes you have eaten THE APPLE, not the pear.'[19]

2. Our hypothesis

In this section we introduce and discuss our proposal to capture the facts mentioned in the previous section. We are going to argue that CD phenomena stem from the interaction between the morphosyntactic properties of the Italian subjunctive and the requirement of the embedded clause, in particular with respect to the aspects related to the temporal interpretation.

    Among the principles belonging to our theoretical background, we adopt Giorgi and Pianesi's (1997) proposal concerning the projection of features. In particular, let us mention here the Universal Ordering Constraint and the Feature Scattering Principle:

(46) Feature scattering (G&P 1997):
     (i) *Universal Ordering Constraint*: Features are ordered, so that given F1 > F2, the checking of F1 precedes the checking of F2.
    (ii) *Feature Scattering Principle*: Each feature can head a projection.

When heading a projection, a given morpheme can lexicalize more than one (formal) feature. We call this a case of *syncretic* heads. Under certain circumstances, the same feature bundles can be *scattered*, with one or more of them heading different projections. All the intermediate cases are also admitted, as shown in the example given earlier. Crucially, however, the ordering of the features remains unvaried. This is meant to account for the findings of Cinque (1999) and of other scholars working in frameworks similar to his. The proposal preserves these results and, at the same time, provides room for language variation along the "degree of syncretism" dimension.[20]

Returning to CD, we hypothesize that the subjunctive morphology is syncretic—that is, it lexicalizes both a modal feature (MOOD) and the usual φ-features that enter subject-verb agreement. Hence a typical CD sentence such as (47a) has the structure in (47b):

(47) a. Mario credeva fosse malata.
      b. [...[$_V$ credeva [$_{MOOD/Agr}$ fosse ...]]]

Sentences with the *che*+V configuration are cases in which scattering has obtained, *che* realizes the feature MOOD, and the φ-features are independently projected in Agr, as usual:

(48) a. Mario crede che Carlo sia partito
      b. [...[$_V$ credeva [$_{MOOD}$ che [$_{Agr}$ fosse ...]]]]

Therefore, CD configurations arise from the syncretic way, with both MOOD and the φ-features being projected through the same head, call it MOOD/Agr.[21] Importantly, CD is not the result of verb movement to some special position but it is simply the outcome of a particular realization of the morphological features of the verb. Complementizer deletion, in other words, is simply a case of syncretic realization of verbal features.

We want to strengthen this claim by proposing that the Italian verb moves no farther than Agr, primarily because the only trigger for verb movement in Italian is the φ-feature.[22]

Concerning the word *che* and the various roles it can play, we propose that:

1. In standard Italian *che* lexicalizes two different (sets of) features: those of the traditional complementizer C (which appears in indicative sentences and disallows CD) and the feature MOOD (which appears in subjunctive environment and allows CD through syncretism).

2. The relevant features of *che*/C in indicative contexts are temporal ones—namely, they are τ-features entering in relation with those of the embedded T head (see Giorgi and Pianesi 2000, 2001, and Higginbotham 2001).

3. *Che* can bear only one of those features at time—that is, either MOOD or the τ-features.

In the end, the word *che* lexicalizes one kind of verbal feature at a time, and this has important consequences on CD and the theory of Sequence of Tense.

The theory briefly outlined here provides an explanation for the absence of CD with indicative verbs. We have hypothesized, in fact, that V-to-C movement is not an option in standard Italian. Hence, for C omission with indicative verbs to be possible, resort should be made to the same mechanism proposed for subjunctive contexts—namely, the syncretic realization of the relevant features of *che*/C. It is possible to show, however, that such an option is not available to the features of *che*/C—that is, they cannot be syncretic with Agr—thus ruling out C omission in indicative embedded clauses.

The conclusion follows from the theory developed in Giorgi and Pianesi (2001) whereby it is proposed that (a) the complement clauses of propositional attitude verbs must feature a reference to the temporal coordinate of the attitude's subject—namely, the attitude's episode itself, and (b) the feature set of indicative tenses contains an indexical element that, upon evaluation, delivers the speaker's temporal coordinate. The joint effect of the two generalizations is to rule out LFs of embedded clauses with in situ indicative temporal features—that is, structures like $[. . .V . . .[_{CP} . . .[\tau\text{-ind} . . .]]]$. It was proposed that the τ-features are duplicated in *che*/C in such a way that the indexical component can be evaluated outside the clause and the in situ (in T) copy can contribute the required subject's temporal coordinate—that is: $[. . .V . . .[_{CP} . .C\text{-}\tau. . [T\text{-}\tau . . .]]]$. As discussed in Giorgi and Pianesi (2000, 2001), this proposal explains many interpretive facts (including the DAR). It also has the effect of making the presence of τ-features in *che*/C crucial for interface requirements, thus preventing their syncretic realisation any lower than C, at pain of incurring the same violation described earlier.

MOOD, the subjunctive-like complementizer, can be "deleted." Its syncretic realization, in fact, *is* an available option, given that MOOD does not enter the kind of relationships C does; in particular, there is no indexical component to the subjunctive. Hence, when MOOD is scattered, there is no movement of the verb to the corresponding position.

Before proceeding further, let us point out that the properties of Aux-to-Comp must be independently accounted for. As suggested in n. 10, we would like to argue that this structure has very different properties from the ones we are discussing. In fact, if we look at the cases where Aux-to-Comp is permitted, we see that they all have a peculiar semantic interpretation. The semantics of these structures seems to give rise to operator-variable structures.[23]

3.   Derivation of the properties of CD

Let us consider now how the properties discussed in section 1 can be derived within the framework presented in section 2.

Property (a) has it that CD is restricted to subjunctive clauses and that, even when available, it is not compulsory. These facts are derived as follows: our theory already explains why CD is possible with verbs in the subjunctive. This is because subjunctive morphology can realize both the ϕ-features and the feature MOOD. This possibility straightforwardly accounts for CD cases: they are such that the usual movement of the verb to Agr occurs, where such a head syncretically realizes both MOOD and ϕ-features. As we know by now, the possibility of having *che* signals that the scattered option has been taken, with the feature MOOD brought into the derivation by such an item. Hence, the optionality of *che* follows from the very way syncretic categories operate.

We have already discussed (in section 2) why the complementizer cannot be deleted with indicative verbs. Let us only recall that this is due to (a) the absence of the feature MOOD with such verbal forms and (b) the fact that indicative tenses have features that, for independent reasons, require the higher complementizer C.[24] As seen in section 2, no issue about syncretism arises in these case.[25]

Hence, in standard Italian we have the following options with respect to the realization of the embedded complementizer:

a. MOOD   AGR   V
   che   V+morph
b. C   AGR   V
   che   V+morph
c. MOOD/AGR   V
   V+morph
d. C   MOOD   AGR   V   (*ipotizzare*, factives, dislocations, etc.)

Option (a) is the *scattered* option with a subjunctive clause. Option (b) is the normal indicative complement clause. Option (c) corresponds to CD structures, and option (d) is the structure instantiated under such predicates such as *ipotizzare* (hypothesize)—that is, those verbs that both select the subjunctive and require a higher complementizer carrying *extra* specifications.

The latter possibility helps us explain property (b)—namely, the unavailability of Complementizer Deletion in the complements of factive predicates. Within our theory, the presence of the higher complementizer is due to the necessity of lexicalizing some particular feature. In the cases of indicative clauses, we saw that it was necessary to avoid a violation of the interface condition on the LF of the complement clause. In the case of factive clauses, we propose that a (selected) feature is needed, which we can call for simplicity +*factive*, and that such a feature cannot be syncretic with the verb and cannot be checked by it.[26]

This line of explanation extends naturally to property (c)—namely, the impossibility for dislocated sentences to undergo CD. It can be hypothesized that dislocation arises because of some feature (*focus, topic, . . .*) that plays a role in this process, and that such a feature is hosted in the higher C. As in previous cases, no issues of syncretism arise, under the hypothesis that these are not features the verb can check. Hence, there is no CD because there is an extra head.

Concluding, properties (a), (b), and (c) are a consequence of the possibility for Italian MOOD to be realized syncretically with Agr, and of the fact that the higher C hosts features for which issue of syncretism do not arise.

With respect to the fourth property, we already argued, following Poletto (1995, 2000) that Aux-to-Comp differs from CD. We suggest that Aux-to-Comp can be considered as movement—or perhaps base generation—of an auxiliary in a modal position. But we leave the question open for further investigation.[27]

The fifth property is a strong argument in favor of our hypothesis. The fact that these sentences have a modal meaning follows from the impossibility of assigning a temporal interpretation to an independent subjunctive (see the following argument), but the availability of CD shows that this property must be considered as characteristic of the subjunctive per se, and not of the context in which the subjunctive is embedded.

Property (f)—the complementary distribution of CD and the DAR—can be explained by resorting to the already mentioned theory developed in Giorgi and Pianesi (2000, 2001; see also Higginbotham 2001). Referring to our own work, the idea is that in DAR sentences C has temporal features that enter in relation (either by movement or by matching) with the τ-features of the embedded T. Moreover, C is the locus where the speaker's point of view (the speaker's temporal coordinate, in Giorgi and Pianesi's terms) is encoded. These two properties of the LF structure explain the double access reading in a straightforward way. The impossibility of DAR readings in CD contexts follows from the unavailability of higher C.

The peculiar distribution of the preverbal subject, property (g), is to be accounted for in terms of the alternative options available to the speakers. Notice that, in view of the discussion in section 1, the important point is to explain the *ungrammaticality* of a certain option—that is, the preverbal lexical subject—for a group of speakers, not the converse: namely, the availability of an additional position for a lexical subject, for some speakers. We think this is, in fact, the peculiarity of the phenomenon. Now, in the syncretic/CD case the head AGR/MOOD realizes two different sets of features, with different properties as to the status of the specifier in terms of the A/A' distinction. The ϕ-features would make it into an A position, whereas MOOD would make it into an A' one. If this is so, the split among speakers about the acceptability of preverbal lexical subjects in CD construction could reflect different ways to solve this tension—that is, two different categorizations of Spec,MOOD/Agr: as an A position for those who admit preverbal lexical subjects, and as an A' for those who don't.[28]

Concerning the availability for all speakers of a *pro* subject, or the weak pronoun *tu*, we suggest to resort to the idea of Cardinaletti and Roberts (1991) that there is an extra position for preverbal subjects—besides the *canonical* one—exhibiting exactly those properties. We therefore suggest that such a position, which has been shown by Cardinaletti and Roberts to be lower than the canonical one, is available even in these structures.

Concerning the unavailability of topic and focus in CD structures, property (i), Rizzi (1997; class lectures, UCLA 2000) shows that Topic and Focus are banned in positions preceding the complementizer. In this work, we have argued that topicalization is only (very) marginally possible in CD clauses, thus suggesting that the relevant positions are not available above MOOD/Agr. The residue could perhaps be explained as cases of adjunction or multiple-SPECS to MOOD/Agr, but this requires further investigation.

We conclude with some considerations concerning property (h). First, let us stress its heuristic importance: the greater liberality of first-person reports investigated in section 1 suggests that these sentences aren't a reliable basis for generalizations and claims about the acceptability of CD sentences (and other phenomena related to clausal structure).

On the explanatory side, we can recapitulate the scattered observations made in the previous sections by recalling that in first-person reports, (a) preverbal lexical subjects in CD contexts are more easily available, even to those speakers who tend to reject them in other cases, cf. (39); (b) CD is available with factive verbs (41) and with embedded future tenses, cf. (i) and (ii) in n. 2; (c) preverbal focus, (43), and topic, (44), dramatically improve in CD context; and (d) evaluative (and, in general, higher) adverbs are available, cf. (ii) in n. 19. In this connection, we also observed that, as far as non-first-person reports with a preverbal evaluative adverb are acceptable, the "evaluation" tends to be the speaker's rather than the subject's.

This last observation could provide a key to understand what is going on in first-person contexts. Suppose we analyze them in a different way than an "ordinary" embedded clause—(50) instead of (49):

(49) [...V...[$_{XP}$ ...]]

(50) [[$_{YP}$ [...credo...] Y [$_{XP}$ ...]]

Here, XP stands for the relevant clausal projection (be it CP, MOOD/AGR-P or others). In contrast, Y is a functional projection whose specifier hosts the first-person attitude predicate. In other words, we are suggesting that in a first-person report, what looks like a subordinate clause, XP in (50), actually is the main clause, and that what appears to be the main clause behaves as a sort of evaluative adverbial.

If an analysis along these lines proves tenable, the apparent liberality of first-person reports with respect to CD could turn out to be a mere epiphenomenon, in the sense that no complementation—hence, no CD—would be involved. What appears as a subordinate clause lacking the complementizer would actually be a "normal" matrix clause—hence, amenable to all the syntactic manipulation available with ordinary clauses. Thus, topic and focused constituents could find a place in the left periphery, preverbal lexical subjects would be obviously available, every kind of tenses could be used, and higher adverbs would easily be accommodated. At the same time, the difficulty for "real" complement clauses with CD to exhibit the same phenomena would be consistent with the hypothesis already made: complement clauses with CD are MOOD/AGR-P and do not make available any higher projection. In other words, MOOD/AGR-P is a boundary for clauses.

4. Conclusions

In this work we have shown that complementizer deletion in subordinate clauses, and the range of phenomena accompanying it, can be given an account that does not resort to V-to-C movement. This position is consistent with the more general claim that V-movement in standard Italian is limited to Agr. The explanation framework we adopted is the feature-theoretic one developed in Giorgi and Pianesi (1997), which exploits the possibility for a set of features to distribute over a varying number of functional projections. CD deletion is actually a case in which a set of features (MOOD and the φ-features) is introduced in the derivation through a unique functional category. Such a set can also be brought in by two distinct projections, MOOD (lexicalized by *che*) and Agr. In the end, complementizer deletion is no deletion at all.

We've also showed that CD has a stricter distribution than is often assumed in the literature. In particular, complementizer omission in first-person reports doesn't seem to pattern together with the corresponding phenomenon in non-first-person reports. Besides having a heuristic and methodological value, such a fact also suggests the possibility that first- and non-first-person reports instantiate different structures.

Notes

1. In certain cases, the complementizer can be dropped even in relative clauses. All instances of the phenomenon obey the relevant generalization—that is, the complementizer can be omitted only in relative clauses with the verb in the subjunctive mood:

(i)   Gianni vuole sposare qualsiasi ragazza (che) sia gentile con lui.
      'Gianni wants to marry any girl that is(SUBJ) nice with him.'

(ii) Gianni vuole sposare una ragazza *(che) è gentile con lui.
      'Gianni wants to marry a girl that is(IND) nice with him.'

The availability of CD in relative clauses is subject to a number of constraints; in particular, it requires the DP to be headed by quantifiers with universal force, such as *qualunque, qualsiasi* (whichever). We are not going to investigate further this phenomenon here, but only notice that it is consistent with our generalization.

2. Poletto (2000: 119, ex. 28) accepts the embedded future as well, on the basis of examples such as the following:

(i)   Credo sarà interessante ascoltarlo.
      'I believe it will be interesting to listen to him.'

We agree with her judgment about this sentence. It should be noticed, however, that the matrix verb is in the first-person singular and the acceptability of CD with the future tense decreases when we shift to third-person matrix verbs:

(ii) Gianni crede ?*(che) telefonerà.
      'Gianni believes (that) he will call.'

Given the claim to be discussed in this chapter, that sentences with the matrix verb in the first person are more liberal as to CD, we should be careful to conclude from (i) that the future tense is nothing more than compatible with CD. See also Giorgi and Pianesi (2000) for an analysis of these contexts as opposed to those where a future-in-the-past appears, like the following sentence:

(iii) Gianni credeva (che) avrebbe telefonato.
      'Gianni believed (that) he would call.'

3. There are other contexts with the subjunctive to be considered—namely, complements of adjectives and complements of nouns. It seems to us that complements of adjectives taking subjunctive admit CD, contrasting with the complements in the indicative mood. Consider the following examples:

(i)   E' possibile (che) abbia vinto la gara.
      'It is possible that he has(SUBJ) won the race.'

(ii) E' vero *(che) ha vinto la gara.
      'It is true that he has(IND) won the race.'

On the properties of the relevant kind of adjectives, see Cinque (1995).

With respect to nouns, our judgments are more uncertain, and the two authors differ from each other in being more or less liberal. However, a contrast between subjunctive and indicative is still clearly detectable:

(iii) La possibilità ??-?(che) tu abbia vinto la gara mi rallegra.
      'The possibility that you have(SUBJ) won the race makes me happy.'

(iv) L'affermazione *(che) tu hai vinto la gara mi sorprende.
      'The claim that you have(IND) won the race surprises me.'

Poletto (2000: 120, ex. 33b) considers an example similar to (iii) as fully grammatical.

4. Interestingly, in these contexts the subjunctive is possible even in cases that would disallow it in in situ clauses. Consider *verba dicendi*. A complement clause appearing in its basic position, on the right, rejects the subjunctive, as we know:

(i)   Gianni ha detto che Maria ha/*abbia telefonato.
       'Gianni said that Maria has(IND/*SUBJ) called.'

However, if the same clause is in topic position, then the subjunctive is (marginally) possible:

(ii)   ?Che sia partita, Gianni ce lo ha già detto.
       'That she had(SUBJ) left, Gianni it-to-us-said.'

(iii) ??CHE SIA PARTITA, Gianni ha detto.
       'That she had(SUBJ) left, Gianni said.'

In Giorgi and Pianesi (1997: chap. 5) we suggested that the contexts on the left, and analogously those on the extreme right, have a *quasi-factive* status. See also section 3 in this volume.
    5. In some cases *verba dicendi* can, more or less marginally, select the subjunctive in a subordinate clause—for example, under negation:

(i)   ?Gianni non ha detto che sia una stupida.
       'Gianni did not say that she is(SUBJ) silly.'

This can also occur when the *verbum dicendi* is used as an evidential, reporting about the source of belief, possibility, or other mood, expressed by the subordinate clause:

(ii)   Dicono che sia una stupida.
       'They say that she is(SUBJ) silly.'

While we leave aside the question of what licenses the subjunctive in these cases, let us point out that CD is routinely available in these examples:

(iii) ?Gianni non ha detto sia una stupida.
       'Gianni did not say she is(SUBJ) silly.'

(iv)   Dicono sia una stupida.
       'They say she is(SUBJ) silly.'

    6. Irrelevantly, the preverbal phrase in (16a) could be more acceptable if heavily stressed, as in *hanging topic* constructions.
    7. Even in these cases the subject cannot appear preverbally:

(i)   *Mario fosse arrivato in tempo, saremmo partiti prima.
       'Mario had(SUBJ) arrived on time, we would have left earlier.'

    8. The following order is ungrammatical:

(i)   *La commissione ritiene Mario/io aver superato l'esame.
       'The committee believes Mario/I to have passed the examination.'

    9. In PRO structures, the complementizer *di* is not "deletable":

(i)   Gianni crede *(di) aver superato l'esame.
       'Gianni believes that he passed the examination.'

We will not consider the status of infinitival clauses and their complementizers. See Pesetsky and Torrego (2000) for an attempt at unifying infinitival and finite clauses.
    10. We will not propose and discuss a solution to this problem here. Let us only point out that (a) presumably the position of the auxiliary verb in Aux-to-Comp clauses is higher than that of the verb in CD clauses—see section 3 for a suggestion in this direction, and (b) Aux-to-Comp structures seem to involve a (hidden) operator, hence they are amenable to be analyzed in terms of operator-variable configurations.

11. For theories about the DAR, see, among others, Giorgi and Pianesi (2000, 2001), Abusch (1997), Higginbotham (2001), and Ogihara (1996).

12. There are languages, however, such as Russian and Japanese, where the DAR is not available and in which a sentence like (27) would imply only that the pregnancy holds at the time of the *saying* and not at the present moment.

13. Irrelevantly, the following cases express anteriority of the embedded clause with respect to the matrix one:

> (i)   Gianni crede che Maria abbia telefonato.
>   'Gianni believes that Maria has(SUBJ) called.'
>
> (ii) Gianni credeva che Maria avesse telefonato.
>   'Gianni believed that Maria had(SUBJ) called.'

Anteriority is expressed by means of the perfect periphrasis, consisting, as usual, of the present or past form of the auxiliary and the past participle. The participle is responsible for the "past" interpretation; see Giorgi and Pianesi (1997).

In some contexts it is, indeed, possible to have a past subjunctive embedded under a matrix present form:

> (iii) Il testimone crede che la vittima alle 3 del mattino fosse a casa.
>   'The witness believes that the victim at 3 o'clock in the morning was(SUBJ) at home.'

Without going into detail here, let us simply point out that in these cases the acceptability of the embedded subjunctive depends on the availability of a temporal reference explicitly provided either by the sentence—as in (iii)—or by the extrasentential context. Compare (iii) with the following example, where such a temporal reference is not available:

> (iv) #Gianni crede che due più due facesse quattro.
>   'Gianni believes that two plus two was(SUBJ) four.'

We are not considering here the full theory of Sequence of Tense in Italian—the place where these facts should be accounted for—but only those phenomena that interact with CD. Therefore we do not pursue these matters any further here.

14. There is an important correlation between the availability of a sentence such as (35) and the meaning of the main predicate. A predicate like *believe*, which resists the DAR, refers to a mental state. A verb such as *say*, which admits the DAR, is a verb of communicative behavior. As it turns out, *ipotizzare* is ambiguous: it can refer to either a pure mental state or to a complex event that crucially involves an act of communication whereby the content of the mental state is manifested. In a way, such a predicate exhibits the same ambiguity of English *guess*. It seems to us that when the DAR reading is available with *ipotizzare*, as in (35), the only possible interpretation of the verb is one entailing a communicative act; nevertheless, the possibility of dropping the complementizer, as in (34), does not require the existence of a communicative behavior, but simply involves the mental state.

15. The other direction of the generalization does not hold: CD can be unavailable, for reasons that have nothing to do with the DAR. See later in this chapter.

16. First-person reports improve the status also of constructions that are not related to CD phenomena. For example, in previous work (Giorgi and Pianesi 2000) we showed that the future tense (indicative) is not available in the contexts created by *credere* (believe), as opposed to the so-called future-in-the-past which in Italian is realized by a non-indicative verbal form (perfect conditional):

> (i)   a.*Gianni credeva che Mario telefonerà.
>   'Gianni believed that Mario will call.'

    b. Gianni credeva che Mario avrebbe telefonato.
       'Gianni believed that Mario would call.'

Example (ia) improves if the main predicate is in the present tense, and it becomes nearly perfect if the attitude's subject is the speaker:

(ii)   a. ??Gianni crede che Mario telefonerà.
        'Gianni believes that Mario will call.'
      b. Credo che Mario telefonerà.
        'I believe that Mario will call.'

A borderline case, as to the relevance for CD, is the following example from Poletto (2000: 119, ex. 28), already discussed in n. 2:

(iii)   Credo sarà interessante ascoltarlo.
       'I believe it will be interesting to listen to him.'

This clearly is an improvement over the corresponding third-person report:

(iv)   ??Gianni crede sarà interessante ascoltarlo.
       'Gianni believes it will be interesting to listen to him.'

    17. Here, we assume Rizzi's (1997) arguments in favor of two distinct projections hosting topicalized and focused phrases.

    18. Speakers vary as to their judgments concerning the status of examples (43) and (44). The judgments given in the text correspond to the authors' intuitions. A sound generalization seems to be that all Italian speakers find CD sentences with preverbal topic and focus degraded with respect to the other cases. For some speakers, topic yields seriously ungrammatical results, and focus only milder ones—that is, the reverse of the authors' intuitions. Our theory captures the fact that topic and focus are sensitive to CD. The kind of suppletive strategies some speakers resort to (to partially rescue borderline cases) deserve further work.

    19. Poletto (2000: 119) discusses the position of the verb with respect to high adverbs, concluding that "When the complementizer is deleted, the verb cannot occur to the right of the higher adverbs, whereas it is possible when the complementizer is realized." This conclusion is questionable, though. Let us say that we substantially agree with her judgments concerning preverbal adverbs in CD contexts:

(i)   *Mario credeva fortunatamente tu ce la facessi.
      'Mario believed luckily you made(SUBJ) it.'

With respect to adverbs in postverbal position, Poletto finds them acceptable, taking this as evidence for a V-to-C analysis of CD in embedded clauses. However, the conclusion is based on data from first-person reports, and in this case, too, we find the same contrast between first- and non-first-person reports discussed in the text:

(ii)   a. Credo partano fortunatamente entro domani.
        think-1sing leave(SUBJ) luckily by tomorrow
      b. ??Maria crede partano fortunatamente entro domani.
        Maria thinks leave(SUBJ) luckily tomorrow

To us, (iib) sharply contrasts with (iia). Moreover, to the extent that (iib) is acceptable, the evaluative adverb *fortunatamente* does not seem to report on the subject's (Maria's) evaluation but on the utterer's. Furthermore, the contrasts Poletto reports are not always so sharp. For instance, we find the following two sentences equal on acceptability (Poletto's ex. 46, p. 126):

(iii)   a. Credo fortunatamente riesca a farcela.
        think luckily succeeds to do it
    b. Credo riesca fortunatamente a farcela.
        think succeeds luckily to do it

In other cases, one can question the acceptability of the subjunctive in the basic cases, those with the complementizer:

(iv)   Dicono che evidentemente ??abbia / ha lasciato la città.
      say that allegedly has(SUBJ)/has(IND) left the town

As a consequence, CD does not seem perfect (cf. Poletto's ex. 44d, p. 125):

(v)   a. Dicono evidentemente abbia la città.
       say allegedly has(SUBJ) left the town
    b. Dicono abbia evidentemente lasciato la città
       say has(SUBJ) allegedly left the town

So we conclude that there doesn't seem to be enough ground to state that the V+eval-adverb word order is acceptable in CD contexts. As a consequence, at least part of the evidence for a V-to-C analysis of the phenomenon is not available

20. In Giorgi and Pianesi (1997) we point out that features can be syncretic only if they can be acquired as such. This means that they must correspond to some lexical item overtly exhibiting syncretic properties. We think that subjunctive morphology can be a good example, and we briefly discussed this point in the mentioned work. This consideration is crucial in order to limit the power of a system that includes syncretism among its properties.

21. Alternatively, one might say that subjunctive morphology realizes MOOD plus *temporal* features (t-features), with agreement being a by-product of the presence of the latter. This view would be more in accord with recent developments within the minimalist program (Chomsky 1998, 1999). The scattered option, therefore, would project the modal feature as a separate head from the T feature. According to this view, the subject would be in Spec,T. This alternative, however, would not affect the core of our proposal.

22. Or, equivalently for our purposes, to T.

23. Rizzi (1982) judges the following sentences as grammatical:

(i)   Credevo aver tu telefonato a Maria.
    Lit.: I believed to have you called Maria
    'I believe you to have called Maria.'

To our ear, both sentences are very marginal, and, moreover, they are clearly degraded when a non–first-person subject is used.

(ii)   a.*Gianni credeva aver tu telefonato a Maria.
      Lit.: Gianni believed to have you called Maria
      'Gianni believed you to have called Maria.'
    b.*Gianni credeva avesse Piero telefonato a Maria.
      Gianni believed had(SUBJ) Piero called Maria

On why a structure such as (i) should exist at all, see n. 27.

We are not going to propose here a theory to account for Aux-to-Comp. Let us only suggest that it could be worth considering the possibility that the auxiliary is not *moved* to the leftmost position but is generated there. In other words, we could assimilate the position of the auxiliary to some very high modal positions (see Cinque 1999). Notice that auxiliaries can express a modal value in Italian, as in the following cases:

(iii) a. Non può uscire: oggi Gianni ha da lavorare.
        Lit.: he cannot go out today Gianni has to work
        'He cannot go out: today Gianni must work.'
      b. Questo libro è da leggere.
        Lit.: this book it to read
        'This book must be read.'

Therefore, it would not be surprising to find auxiliaries in modal positions preceding the subject. This consideration could also explain why these structures are available with auxiliaries and not with full lexical verbs.

24. The reasons we are alluding to in the text are related to SOT and DAR phenomena, and, ultimately, to the temporal interpretation of subordinate clauses. See Giorgi and Pianesi (2001) for more on this point.

25. Crucially, a system including this kind of syncretism would not be based on any morphological evidence. Therefore, we are discarding it on the basis of acquisition considerations.

26. The rationale behind the last property is that "factivity" is not a property of events or verbs but of whole clauses.

27. An anonymous reviewer correctly pointed out that the idea of the auxiliary in Aux-to-Comp structures being directly generated in a position to the left of Agr might entail a greater autonomy of this element with respect to the material lying below it. Hence, such a proposal might conflict with the observation that the *avere* (have) and *essere* (be) alternation is maintained even in these cases:

(i)   Essendo Gianni partito . . .
      Lit.: being Gianni left (having John left)

(ii) Avendo Gianni mangiato un panino . . .
      having Gianni eaten a sandwich . . .

However, let us point out that even when *avere* (have) and *essere* (be) play a modal role in modal periphrasis, some alternation can still be observed, as in the following cases:

(iii) Questo libro è da leggere.
       'This book is to be read.'

(iv)   Gianni ha da leggere questo libro.
       'Gianni has to read this book.'

Both (iii) and (iv) express obligation: (iii) is a passive-like structure and (iv) an active-like one, featuring *be* and *have*, respectively.

28. Attempting to cast these considerations in the minimalist jargon, one could say that the two sets of speakers differ as to whether or not the syncretic category MOOD/Agr can have an EPP feature.

References

Abusch, D. (1997) "Sequence of Tense and Temporal De Re." *Linguistics and Philosophy* 20, 1–50.

Cardinaletti, A., and I. Roberts (1991) "Clause Structure and X-Second," in W. Chao and G. Horrocks (eds.), *Levels of Representations*. Dordrecht: Foris.

Chomsky, N. (1998) *Minimalist Inquiries: The Framework.* MITOPL no. 15. Cambridge, Mass.: MIT.

────── (1999) *Derivation by Phases*. MITOPL no. 18. Cambridge, Mass.: MIT.

Cinque, G. (1995) *Italian Syntax and Universal Grammar*. Cambridge: Cambridge University Press.

────── (1999) *Adverbs and Functional Heads: A Crosslinguistic Perspective*. New York: Oxford University Press.

Giorgi, A., and F. Pianesi (1996) "Verb Movement in Italian and Syncretic Categories." *Probus* 8, 137–160.

────── (1997) *Tense and Aspect: From Semantics to Morphosyntax*. New York: Oxford University Press.

────── (2000) "Sequence of Tense Phenomena in Italian: A Morphosyntactic Analysis." *Probus* 12, 1–32.

────── (2001) "Tense, Attitudes and Subjects," iIn *Proceedings of* SALT 11. Ithaca: University of Cornell Press.

Higginbotham, J. T. (2001) "Why Is Sequence of Tense Obligatory?" in G. Preyer and G. Peter (eds.) *On Logical Form*. New York: Oxford University Press, 207–227.

Ogihara, T. (1996) *Tense, Attitudes and Scope*. Dordrecht: Kluwer Academic Press.

Pesetsky, D., and E. Torrego (2000) "T-to-C Movement: Causes and Consequences." Unpublished Ms., MIT and Boston University.

Poletto, C. (1995) *Complementizer Deletion and Verb Movement in Italian*. Working Papers in Linguistics. Venice: University of Venice.

────── (2000) *The Higher Functional Field*. New York: Oxford University Press.

Rizzi, L. (1982) *Issues in Italian Syntax*. Dordrecht: Foris.

────── (1997) "The Fine Structure of the Left Periphery," in L. Hageman (ed.) *Elements of Grammars*. Dordrecht: Kluwer, 281–387.

Scorretti, M. (1994) "Complementizer Deletion," Ph.D. diss., University of Amsterdam.

8

Clitics

Cooccurrence and Mutual
Exclusion Patterns

M. RITA MANZINI

AND LEONARDO M. SAVOIA

Our starting point for this discussion is a set of assumptions, motivated in section 1, which include the idea that clitics correspond to specialized categories and are inserted directly into the positions where they surface. Such categories are ordered in a universal hierarchy. In sections 2–5, we show that within such a framework, it is possible to account for some basic facts about the clitic string without having recourse to anything but a minimalist syntactic component. In particular, no use is made of a specialized morphological component or of optimality-type comparisons between derivations or representations. The main facts addressed include parametrization of the order of clitics (dative–accusative vs. accusative–dative), mutual exclusion of clitics (accusative and dative, object and subject), and the emergence of what are described in the literature as default clitics ("spurious" *se*) or as opaque forms.

1. Theoretical and empirical background

1.1. Previous theories

Broadly speaking, two approaches to cliticization—specifically in Romance languages—are present in the generative literature. The first approach holds that clitics are generated as (part of) full DPs in argumental position and moved to a position adjoined to V (Kayne 1975) or to a functional head of the sentence (Kayne 1989, 1991, 1994). However if clitics are generated under VP and adjoined, say to I, it is impossible or very hard to predict that they will appear in a fixed number, in a fixed order, with fixed cooccurrence (or mutual exclusion) patterns that do not necessarily correspond to the number, order, cooccurrence (or mutual exclusion) patterns of corresponding arguments and adjuncts. To be more precise, the theory described can derive the relevant properties of clitics in conjunction with a morphological component able to (re)order strings (Bonet 1995; Halle and Marantz 1993, 1994). Unfortunately, to the extent that the (re)ordering operations match those of the syntax (Merge and Move), the resulting system is highly redundant. Vice versa to the extent that the two sets of (re)ordering operations do not match, the resulting system is considerably more complex than one accounting for clitics in purely syntactic terms.

A second line of analysis holds instead that clitics are base-generated as functional heads (Sportiche 1996). We follow this second approach insofar as we assume that clitics are merged directly in the position where they surface and project their own specialized functional categories. We furthermore assume that the order of functional categories so defined is universal, much as hypothesized by Cinque (1999) for his adverbial hierarchies. Within such a theory, therefore, positions can be neither reordered (*contra* Ouhalla 1991) nor packed and unpacked (*contra* Giorgi and Pianesi 1998). This set of assumptions provides particularly stringent constraints when it comes to accounting for variation internal to the clitic string.

Contrary to Sportiche's (1996) characterization of clitic categories in terms of Case (Accusative Voice, etc.), we take the view that Case is not a viable syntactic category. One very general reason for this is that the grammar should be restricted to interpretable features (Brody 1997); a non-interpretable feature like Case is unrestricted or a mere diacritic for movement. Even if non-interpretable features are admitted in the grammar, Case would be the only example of a feature that is always non-interpretable (Chomsky 1995)—that is, it does not have an interpretable counterpart. Therefore we tentatively conclude that clitic positions cannot be characterized in terms of Case.

An alternative set of categories for clitics is potentially provided by the positions independently postulated to host arguments in a VP-shell conception of the predicate. In turn, the latter can reflect the idea that the VP-shell is articulated into primitive predicates such as CAUSE (Hale and Keyser 1993) or v (Chomsky 1995) or, alternatively, into aspectual categories such as Origin and Measure (Tenny 1994; Borer 1994). But primitive predicates cannot have a place outside the VP-shell, while aspectual categories can. The latter—in particular, the two categories Or for the Origin of the event and Meas for the Measure of the event, as in (1)—have been used to characterize the clitic shell by Manzini and Savoia (1998). In the simplest case— that of a transitive verb—Meas can be associated with the internal argument of the verb, while Or can be associated with the external argument.

(1)   Or = Origin of the event
      Meas = Measure of the event

If to the aspectual notions of Or(iginator) and Meas(ure) of the event we add a notion of Loc(ation), whose position in the clitic hierarchy intermediate between Or and Meas corresponds to that of Borer's (1994) Delimiter, we obtain the clitic string of Manzini and Savoia (1999) reproduced in (2):

(2)   [Or   [Loc   [Meas

While Or coincides with the initial point of the event and Meas with its extension up to the eventual final point, Loc, as opposed to Borer's (1994) Del, does not correspond to an aspectual property; rather, the idea is that the Loc category should be understood as providing a syntactic representation for one of the fundamental coordinates of discourse, the spatial one. Indeed, according to Enç (1987) the utterance time (*now*) is syntactically represented in a C-type position to which the temporal specifications of the event, represented in I, are anchored. Furthermore, following Manzini and Savoia (2001b), the speaker (*I*) and hearer (*you*) are syntactically represented by the specialized P category within the clitic string. In this perspective, the presence of a Loc category—that is, of a syntactic representation of the spatial location of the event—is a counterpart to the existence of a spatial coordinate (*here*) in the universe of discourse.

Beside the clitic positions in (2), clitic categories such as N, Q, D, and P(erson) are independently motivated for subject clitics by Manzini and Savoia (2001b). Following Manzini and Savoia (2001b), subject clitic categories corresponding to the features in (3) are hierarchically ordered as in (4):

(3)   P = Person, lexicalized by first- and second-person clitics
      N = Noun, lexicalized by third-person (singular) clitics
      Q = Quantifier, lexicalized by (third-person) plural clitics
      D = Definiteness, lexicalized by uninflected clitics

(4)   [D [Q [N [P

Assuming that the inflectional/denotational categories of subject clitics are ordered above the aspectual ones, we obtain the fragment of functional hierarchy in (5), used by Manzini and Savoia (1999, 2001a), Fici et al. (1999), and Cocchi (2000):

(5)   [D [Q [N [P [Or [Loc [Meas

Since clitics are generated directly in the position where they surface, there are clitic positions at least between I and C. At the same time, empirical evidence relating in particular to the doubling of clitics on either side of the verb strongly argues in favor of a conception in which the clitic string repeats itself identically in each of the three main verbal domains—that is, not only in the temporal domain immediately above I as in (5), but also immediately above V (in the basic predicative domain) and immediately above C (in the modal domain) (Manzini and Savoia 1999). This gives rise to the organization of the sentence in (6), where the dotted space is to be filled by the string in (5):

(6)   . . . [C . . . [I . . . [V

Despite the several empirical and theoretical advances that can be argued to accrue to the conception of the clitic string just illustrated, it becomes evident in close inspection that the analysis relies on assumptions that are themselves suspicious. In introducing the clitic hierarchy in (5), we said that it embeds two quite different sets of projections—namely, aspectual projections and inflectional projections. Such an internal asymmetry is not in itself problematic; what is more troubling is another asymmetry between the two sets of categories.

Aspectual specifications cannot be part of the lexical entry of a given clitic form, since they express the relation of the clitic form to the predicate and are therefore associated with the clitic by the process of lexical insertion. This situation contrasts with that of inflectional categories, that are associated with clitic forms as their intrinsic lexical property. In essence, inflectional categories correspond to a series of referentially relevant properties—in other words, properties that are crucial for fixing the denotation of the pronominal clitic. On the contrary, aspectual properties have no relevance for denotation but establish the relevant relations between the event denoted by the verb and whatever arguments are denoted by the clitics. This asymmetry entails a real conceptual problem: on the one hand, the inflectional hierarchy of clitics seems to organize properties that intrinsecally belong to lexical items (independently of whatever their interpretation may be); on the other hand, the aspectual hierarchy seems to provide an organization for categories that do not represent intrinsic lexical properties but, rather, properties of the interpretation of couples of lexical elements (verb and clitic). Thus, while the inflectional string can be created by simple Merge of lexical items and projection of their features, the aspectual string must have an existence independent from that of the lexical items inserted into it.

Now, given a strict model of minimalism (Chomsky 1995), we expect that the entire contribution to phrase structure made by two lexical items such as a(n inflected) verb and a clitic consists in the merger of those properties that are specified for them in the lexicon. If this is so, the merger of an N clitic with an inflected verb (conventionally an I category) produces exactly what the description says: an ordered set (N, I). Hence evidently, assuming minimalist Merge, the interpretation of the N clitic as the Meas or Or argument of the verb must be precisely that—the result of the application of some interpretive principle. We conclude that interpretive categories such as Meas and Or are to be eliminated from the clitic string in favor of the purely syntactic categories of inflection. This does not mean that Meas and Or are to be eliminated as interpretations available for the relevant syntactic structures at the LF interface; on the contrary, this is what we want Meas and Or to reduce to, that is, interpretations.

1.2.   Clitic categories and clitic hierarchies

As we saw, Manzini and Savoia (1999, 2001a) attribute the rough division observed between subject and object clitics (the former systematically preceding the latter when they cooccur) to a distinction between an inflectional string for subject clitics and an aspectual string for object clitics. In a conception in which all categories in the clitic string are denotational in nature, it seems correct neverthelesss to respect the basic demarcation found between object and subject clitics and to reserve the latter for the higher positions of the string. One natural option in this respect is to identify subject clitics with the D position of the string. As is well known from the work of Beninca' (1994) and Poletto (2000) an inflected subject clitic can cooccur with an uninflected subject clitic (typically *a*) in Northern Italian dialects. This is compatible with the existence of a single D position for subject clitics, if we assume that the doubling just described calls into play two clitic strings—that is, given the schema in (6), the clitic string immediately superordinate to I for the differentiated clitic and the string immediately superordinate to C for the nondifferentiated one.

In (5) we assumed that D is the highest position in the clitic hierarchy. In this connection, however, it is relevant to briefly consider the structure of DPs containing a partitive *di* 'of' like (7), which, according to Cardinaletti and Starke (1999), is identified with the highest functional projection of the DP. Similarly, Manzini and Savoia (forthcoming) propose that there is a position in the DP above the D position hosting the Determiner, characterized in terms of intensional Op properties, as D_{Op}; it is D_{Op} that hosts *di*.

(7) tre dei miei fratelli
     three of my brothers

On this basis, we establish at least for the DP a hierarchy in which the D projection is subordinated to a higher D_{Op} projection as in (8). As we discuss in section 1.3, there are reasons to extend the subhierarchy in (8) from the DP to the clitic string and, in general, to take the internal organization of the clitic string to reflect that of the DP, and vice versa. Therefore, (8) also represents the highest segment of the clitic string itself:

(8) $[D_{Op} [D \ldots$

If the D area of the string, enriched as indicated in (8), represents the canonical domain of subject clitics and of prepositions (hence of complementizers) the remaining projections in the hierarchy can be reserved for object clitics. Note that the original hierarchy in (5) already contained two positions (Q and N), which can host the third-person clitics of the object series. The relative order D . . . Q . . . N suggested by the scopal properties of D and Q, and also reflected by the internal structure of the DP, will remain unchanged with respect to (5). To these two positions we must add a Loc position, which we have already justified in section 1.1. If within the structure of the DP, Loc is identified with the position of demonstratives on the grounds of the locative properties of these elements, the Loc position turns out, like the demonstrative one, to be close to the N head—indeed, closer to it than the D . . . Q quantificational series (Bernstein 1997; Brugè 1996). We can further identify the P position, endowed with discourse reference properties similar to that of Loc, with a slot immediately above it; the P position will now be reserved for object P clitics. As one last refinement, it will prove useful to distinguish between the Q position for indefinite quantification from a higher R(eferential) position for specific elements. If so, the hierarchy takes the final shape in (9):

(9) $[D_{Op} [D [R [Q [P [Loc [N$

The set of object clitics that we consider in the empirical discussion in sections 2–5 includes, in particular, accusative and dative clitics; needless to say, given our earlier rejection of Case as an explanatory category in grammar, reference to Case categories such as accusative and dative is purely descriptive. If dative and accusative are characterized by the same inflectional (third-person) features, the question arises how they can be told apart at all. We identify the accusative with the lowest N position of the string, which therefore turns out to be the position associated with the internal argument (Meas) interpretation. As for the dative, one of the aims of our discussion is precisely to arrive at a satisfactory characterization of it. We shall furthermore make reference to the *si* clitic, which in Italian is associated with reflexives, impersonals, and passives. The only relevant point is that we take its insertion position to be normally Q, in virtue of its denotational properties, which are essentially those of a free variable (Manzini 1986). As detailed by Manzini and Savoia (1999, 2001a), an analysis along these lines derives the different construals for *si* as impersonal, passive, and reflexive.

Though other clitics are only indirectly relevant for the discussion to follow, we briefly note that the characterization of Loc in terms of spatial reference must be conceived in broad enough terms to include a whole series of possible interpretations associated with the locative clitic. Thus in a language like Italian, *ci* 'there' can have a strictly locative meaning, an instrumental one, a comitative one, and so on. Moreover, the purely locative interpretation can be seen to be internally articulated in several different meanings. Thus the locative can be associated with a stative interpretation or with a motion interpretation, under which the locative typically refers to the coordinates of the final point of the event. In general, as we have already seen, the Loc category does not correspond to a point on the aspectual contour of the event. Rather it must be understood in connection with other elements whose denotation is fixed by the universe of discourse—namely, the speaker ("I"), the hearer ("you"), and the temporal coordinates of the discouse ("now").

As for the partitive, on the basis of the analysis of the phrasal partitive di + D" in (7) as a D_{Op} constituent, we can assign the partitive clitic, *ne* in Italian, to the category D_{Op}. The property D_{Op} associated with *ne* is a denotational property, like D or Loc; in other words, it characterizes the way in which *ne* refers. Crucially, *ne* does not refer to a participant in the event associated with the verb, and it does not directly characterize a spatial, temporal, or other coordinate of the event itself. For instance, in (10) *ne* does not belong to the aspectual structure of "saw" or to the discourse specifications associated with it; on the contrary, the denotational content of *ne* enables us to fix the reference of the internal argument—that is, "three." In short, the partitive does not directly denote an argument in the event structure but allows us to establish the denotation of one such argument:

(10) Ne ho visti tre.
       of-them I-have seen three

Arguably, this property of *ne* accounts in a natural way for other contexts in which *ne* occurs—in particular, those in which *ne* establishes reference to a spatial coordinate of the event ("from there").

1.3.   The internal structure of clitics

As well as an analysis of the overall structure of the clitic string and of the categories it consists of, an account of cliticization in Romance dialects presupposes an analysis of the internal structure of clitics themselves. Previous approaches in the literature include both morphological and syntactic ones. Among the former is James Harris's (1994) account of the internal makeup of Spanish clitics, which recognizes for the third-person series a lexical basis *l-*, as well as nominal class morphemes such as *a* (traditionally the feminine) and a number suffix *-s*. A syntactic, rather than morphological, characterization of the internal structure of clitics is attempted in a few recent papers, including Kayne (2000) on first- and second-person clitics as opposed to third-person ones, and Cardinaletti and Starke (1999) on clitics compared to pronouns. The general idea of Cardinaletti and Starke (1999) is that clitics have the internal structure of a DP, albeit an impoverished one with respect to lexical DPs or even full pronouns. In their terms, the latter are associated with a full structure, equivalent to a sentential CP, whereas clitics are characterized by a deficient structure, reducing to the equivalent of a sentential IP projection. According to Kayne (2000), in turn, first- and second-person clitics and pronouns lack full DP structure, while the latter characterizes third-person clitics, as revealed by the presence of full agreement features.

The approach that we take to the internal structure of clitics retains the intuition, present already in the work of Abney (1986) and Szabolcsi (1994), that the structure of the noun phrase is organized along similar lines as the structure of the sentence. Thus the lowest nominal position in the noun phrase, like the lowest verbal position in the sentence, is associated with predicative content. As in the case of the sentence, we assume the existence of at least one I position in the noun phrase, whose generically inflectional properties will be specified in the course of the discussion. Furthermore, as the highest verbal position in the sentence—that is, the lowest C position in Rizzi's (1997) hierarchy—is associated with modal properties (hence, effectively with quantificational properties over possible worlds), we take it that the highest nominal position in the noun phrase is again C, associated with operator properties. We thus obtain the basic noun phrase skeleton in (11) built in parallel with the sentential skeleton in (6):

(11)   ... [C ... [I ... [N

In the present conception of the sentence, the fundamental positions for the insertion of the verb—that is, V, I, and C—each involve the projection of a clitic string, as schematized in (6). By analogy, we expect that each of the nominal positions individuated in the discussion that precedes—that is, N, I, and C—involves the insertion of its own clitic string. Thus as in (6), in (11) the dotted spaces are to be filled by the clitic string in (9).

As already noted in section 1.2, the clitic hierarchy in (9) includes many of the categories generally assumed for the internal structure of the DP. Indeed, D corresponds to the category of (definite) determiners and Q to the category of (weak) quantifiers; in turn, the ordering D–Q corresponds to the basic ordering of strong quantifiers (definites) over weak quantifiers (indefinites). Furthermore, D_{Op} has been argued for as a position for the preposition *di* 'of'. As for Loc, this position can be identified with the category of demonstratives, on the grounds not only of the general considerations of section 1.2 but, more specifically, of the fact that in Romance dialects they surface coupled with overtly locative pronouns (Bernstein 1997; Brugè 1996). This set of observations leads us to conclude that the determiners of the noun, including Ds, Qs, and demonstratives, do not require specialized projection, but are simply inserted into the D, Q, and Loc positions independently provided by the clitic string.

Going back to the basic skeleton in (11), we take it that the normal position of the head Noun within the Noun Phrase corresponds to I, exactly as the normal position of the Verb within the sentential skeleton. The lower N position corresponds to the predicative content of the Noun, while we take it that the head Noun is overtly lexicalized in the higher C position in cases where its associated functional material is enclitic rather than proclitic, or the head Noun itself suffices to fix the reference independently of the presence of Determiners or Quantifiers. In Romance dialects, this is the case in particular for kinship terms according to the discussion of Manzini and Savoia (forthcoming). The relatively high position of kinship Nouns in the DP with respect to that of other Nouns is already suggested by Longobardi (1994). If we assume, as it is reasonable to, that the lowest position in the Noun Phrase, N in (11), coincides with the lowest position in the nominal string in (9), then I and C in (11) are just labels for the N positions of the higher strings. In other words, the dotted spaces in (11) enclose just the functional subsequence D_{Op}–D–R–Q–P–Loc of the string in (9), and the structure of the Noun Phrase therefore results from the stacking of several of the sequences in (9) one above the other.

We are now in a position to turn to the analysis of clitic forms. Interpretive considerations tend to exclude Cardinaletti and Starke's (1999) conclusion that clitics are impoverished with respect to full pronouns, since definiteness properties, which are normally associated with the highest layer in the structure of noun phrases, are clearly lexicalized by clitics as well as by pronouns. To begin with, we can translate the morphological analysis of Romance clitics proposed in works such as James Harris (1994) into the present syntactic model by identifying gender morphemes such as o and a that accompany the l lexical base in many dialects with the I projection of a noun phrase. In other words, gender is not a functional specification of the noun but a nominal head itself. Indeed, gender does not add any referential specification to the predicative content of a Noun. Rather, as Di Domenico (1998) points out, there is a deep affinity between gender in the Indo-European languages we are considering and nominal inflection classes in other language families.

As for plural morphemes, a natural analysis within our framework identifies them with the Q category. This analysis applies in particular to number morphemes added to the nominal class (gender) morphemes, as is the case for -s in Spanish, but also in Sardinian, Friulan, and Romantsch dialects, yielding structures of the type in (12), which account for the -as and -os observed in the plural nominal inflections of typical Sardinian dialects. These proposals introduce an asymmetry between the conceptual status of traditional gender morphemes, which lexicalize the nominal category I, and that of number morphemes, which lexicalize the functional category Q in the clitic string.

(12) (Sardinia)
  a. $[_I \mathfrak{o} \, [_Q s \, [N] \,] \,]$
  b. $[_I a \, [_Q s \, [N] \,] \,]$

In (12) we only notated head-labels in our labeled bracketing representations, since we are only concerned with the position of head material. Within a conventional phrase structure theory, the I, Q, and N heads in (12) will nevertheless project their phrasal constituents—that is, IP, QP, and NP, respectively. The same applies to our representations throughout.

Inflections of the type in (12) can be added to adjectival or nominal bases, but what interests us directly here is that they can be added to the l morpheme of third-person clitics. Precisely the observation that inflectional series of the type in (12) have independent existence as nominal and adjectival agreement morphemes suggests that third-person clitics involve a nominal head *l*, which embeds a nominal constituent headed by the vocalic inflection morpheme. As illustrated in (13), we may take that *l* lexicalizes the normal inflectional position—that is, I—within the Noun Phrase.

(13) $[_I l \ldots [_I a [N]]]$

The internal structures of clitics are directly relevant to an important question concerning the hierarchy in (9). In rejecting in particular the morphological model of Halle and Marantz (1993), we have adopted the point of view of minimalist grammar of Chomsky (1995), where syntactic structures are directly projected by the insertion of lexical material. Thus there cannot be structures such as (9) produced by the syntactic component, to which lexical material is matched by lexical insertion. Rather, if hierarchies such as (9) hold, it must be because of independent constraints that, as suggested in section 6, can ultimately be thought of in Full Interpretation terms. This puts a heavy constraint on our grammar since we cannot simply insert a clitic in an already given position as a default lexicalization, not presenting any mismatch with the syntactic category. On the contrary, we must be able to show that in each case it is an internal category of the clitic that projects the relevant category of the sentential string.

The discussion that follows upholds this general conclusion; in many cases we are able to show that the category projected by the clitic on the sentential tree corresponds exactly to the category of the internal head of the clitic itself. Thus in the case of a clitic series such as (13), it will typically project N on the sentential tree. For pure ease of reading, exactly as we describe clitics in terms of accusative, dative, first person and second person, that is, of features that do not correspond to our actual categories, so we speak of their insertion points. In all cases, we understand by insertion point of a clitic, the category that the clitic itself projects on the basis of its internal constituency.

2.   Relative order of clitics

To show that the syntactic theory of clitics sketched in section 1 is empirically adequate, we shall consider the three main types of evidence from Romance languages quoted by Bonet (1995) in favor of her morphological analysis. The first such type of evidence concerns the fact that ordering of clitics can vary from language to language, though the underlying order of full lexical arguments remains apparently unchanging. One well-known case concerns the ordering of third dative and third accusative forms in languages such as Italian, where the dative precedes the accusative, and in languages such as French, where the accusative precedes the dative.

2.1.   Dative–accusative

In several Italian dialects, as in standard Italian, the dative form precedes the accusative form; this pattern is normally found in dialects of the Marche-Abruzzi-Molise area and emerges in the dialects of Lucania, as well as in Tuscan dialects, including Vagli di Sopra in (14). The (a) example displays the isolation form of the dative, the (b) example the isolation forms of the accusative. Note that the *ə* morpheme that surfaces in the feminine plural *lə* is a phonological alternant of e surfacing for instance in sentence-final position as in the enclitic *camə-le* 'call them!'; this yields an accusative clitic series *l/la/ʝi/le*. The (c) example shows the combination of dative and accusative, in this order; as shown in (d), other clitics, such as the P clitic, also precede the accusative, while the dative is also followed by other clitics, such as the partitive in (e). In general, the third dative form precedes all other object clitics that it can cooccur with. Conversely the third accusative clitic follows all clitics that it can cooccur with. To economize on glosses, we have given the basic meaning of *ʝi* as 'to him'. This is to be read as a shorthand for 'to him / to her/ to them' here and throughout the article.

(14)   *Vagli di Sopra* (Tuscany)
    a. i ʝi   ða   k'kwestɛ
       he to.him   gives this
    b. i l/la/ʝi/lə   've ðɛ
       he him/her/them-m./them-f. sees
    c. i ʝi   l/la/ʝi/lə   'ða
       he to.him it-m./it-f./them -m./them-f. gives
    d. i mə   l/la   'ða
       he to.me it-m./f. gives
    e. i ʝi   nə   ða   d'doi
       he to.him of.them   gives two

The theory of section 1 allows us to associate structural descriptions with the dative–accusative clusters found in languages like (14). Quite simply, in the languages under consideration the accusative form lexicalizes the category N, where it is preceded by the P clitic. The dative form is inserted in a higher position, which we can identify with the other third-person position—that is, Q; here it precedes the accusative, as illustrated in (15). Note that the linear format in (15), which we use for its readability, can be reduced to a more conventional tree or labeled bracketing representation. In particular, since we consider clitics to correspond to noun phrases, as illustrated in (12)–(13) above and below in (16) for Vagli itself, in terms of classical phrase structure the insertion of forms such as *ʝi* or *la* involves the Spec of Q or the Spec of N, respectively. The insertion under Q or N in linear representations of the type in (15) can be read as shorthand for this more conventional representation. The same general principles apply throughout this article.

(15)   *Vagli di Sopra*
    D_{Op} D R Q P Loc N   I
      | | | |
      i   ʝi   l/la/ʝi ða

Given a lexical parametrization model of the minimalist type adopted here, configurations such as (15) cannot but depend on the lexical entries associated with the clitic formatives. To begin with, we take *l* forms to correspond to a noun phrase structure. Because a head Noun normally occupies the I position within the Noun Phrase, we take *l* to occupy the I position within its nominal constituent following the schema in (13). As for the morphemes combining with *l*, *a* lexicalizes gender (that is, nominal class) in the I position of a separate nominal constituent, deriving the singular feminine form *la* as in (16b). In contrast, the feminine plural *le* appears to combine *l* with an *e* formative associated with the N position of a separate nominal constituent, as shown in (16d). We justify this latter conclusion by observing that *e* is the nominal morphology that turns up on the participle in the absence of person, number and gender agreement with the object or subject; in the terms of Manzini and Savoia (forthcoming) this means that *e* corresponds to a pure N form. The structure in (16d) implies that in the femininine, plurality is not lexicalized through a Q morpheme, but rather through the switch from the nominal inflection class *a*, to what we take to be a pure N morphology, i.e. *e*. In the masculine plural, we can assume that *fi* consists of a *i* morpheme lexicalizing plurality in Q, while *f* corresponds to the head of its own nominal constituent, as in (16c). As for *l* of the so-called masculine singular, it corresponds to uninflected *l*, as in (16a).

(16)   *Vagli di Sopra*
   a. $[_I\, l\ \ [\, N\,]\,]\,]$
   b. $[_I\, l\ \ldots \qquad\qquad [_I\, a\ [N]\,]\,]$
   c. $[_I\, f \ldots \qquad\qquad [_Q\, i\ [I\ \ \ [N]\,]\,]$
   d. $[_I\, l\ \ldots \qquad\qquad [I\ \ \ [_N\, e]\,]\,]$

According to our description, the language of Vagli also has a dative clitic, *fi*, invariant for number and gender. In fact, it is evident that *fi* is the very same form analyzed in (16c). More generally, the study of Italian dialects conducted by Manzini and Savoia (2002) reveals that what descriptive grammars treat as specialized dative forms generally coincide with accusative forms, typically masculine plural ones. We shall see more evidence for this in what follows (cf. also Manzini and Savoia 2002). In other words, Case distinctions, at least between accusative and dative, are in fact not registered by any specialized morphology in the pronominal system. This confirms our tentative conclusion that only inflectional features are relevant to the definition of such systems. The lexicon in (16) provides the basis for predicting structures of the type in (15). Indeed, in virtue of its properties, which include in all cases one or more nominal bases in I or N, the whole series of clitics in (16) can be inserted in the N position of the string in (15)—that is, descriptively the accusative position. In virtue of its Q properties on the other hand the *fi* clitic can equally insert in Q, i.e. descriptively the dative position. The insertion points of the Vagli clitics can therefore be summarized as in (16'); as before in conventional phrase structural terms N should be read as a shorthand for [Spec, N] and so on.

(16') (*Vagli di Sopra*)
   l, la, le → N
   ɟi   → N, Q

The Q point of insertion of the *fi* clitic goes hand in hand with an interpretation of the Q property different from plurality, since as we have seen so-called dative *fi* is ambiguous with respect to number as well as gender. In this connection, we note that the syntactic Q category is compatible with plurality, but it does not imply it; thus we expect plurality to be a possible interpretation of Q, but not a necessary one.

Next, we observe that in the case of an accusative *fi*, the Q specification is part of its internal structure but does not correspond to its position of insertion. Vice versa, in the case of a dative *fi*, Q represents both one of its internal specifications and its position of insertion in the clitic string. We propose that in the former case the internal Q specification of *fi* determines a plural reading. In the second case, however, the internal Q specification of *fi* is subsumed by the Q properties of the insertion position in the clitic string. Thus *fi* does not involve plurality, but only the interpretation that attaches to the Q position of the clitic string. As it turns out, the plural and the dative readings are mutually exclusive in the sense that the dative is not necessarily plural. We take this to be an effect of scope: either *i* has scope internal to the clitic, in which case its reading is plurality; or it takes scope in effect over the sentential string, in which case its reading is dativity. One scope excludes the other.

It is worth stopping a moment to consider what the interpretation of the Q position of the sentential string may be, given that it cannot simply be reduced to plurality. The Q–N order seems to imply that Q hosts elements taking scope over N. It is independently known from the literature that scopal phenomena are sensitive to the relative structural embedding of arguments. Thus Reinhart (1983) reads the relative scope of quantifiers off c-command relations in surface structure. While introducing the Quantifier Raising operation in abstract syntax, May (1985) notices further surface effects such as the possibility for a wh-quantifier to commute in scope with a subject but not with an object.

One scope phenomenon that involves dative and accusative in a particularly obvious way is distributivity; thus an appropriately quantified subject can distribute over an indefinite object and a dative over an accusative, while the reverse is not true. In essence, this is also the conclusion of Beghelli (1997). Exceptions involve the presence on the distributor of an *each* or *every* quantifier, or the presuppositional reading of the distributor; in the first case, there is no correspondence to surface argument hierarchies; in the second case, at least the indirect–direct object hierarchy breaks down. In both cases Beghelli (1997) argues that dedicated quantificational positions are involved. Some relevant examples of the normal case are provided in (17)–(18) from standard Italian:

(17)   a. Loro hanno visto un uomo ciascuno.
           they have seen a man each
       b.*Un uomo li ha visti ciascuno.
           a man them has seen each

(18)   a. Assegnai loro un compito ciascuno.
           I gave them an assignment each
       b.*Li assegnai a uno studente ciascuno.
           them I assigned to a student each

Putting together these observations with the hierarchy of argumental positions postulated in (9), it is natural to hypothesize that the accusative object does not have the properties of a distributor in that it corresponds to the purely nominal N category. Conversely, the set of possible distributors corresponds to the set of arguments—that is, datives or subjects—which have independently been motivated to occupy a position with quantificational properties, be it Q or D. In general, we agree with

Beghelli (1997) and Beghelli and Stowell (1997) that quantificational properties are syntactically encoded and that they do not necessarily belong to the high C domain of the sentence but can be found in the inflectional I domain. However, in our conception, there aren't two distinct series of argumental and quantifier positions, but a single series, that is partially defined in quantificational terms. Since the dative is associated with the Q position, we are led to conclude that the dative has quantificational properties, which can be construed as those of a distributor.

2.2.   Accusative–dative

In some languages, the third dative form precedes the third accusative form. This parametric possibility is illustrated by several dialects of Corsica and of Western Liguria, such as Olivetta S. Michele in (19) where third accusative precedes all other clitics that it can cooccur with, in particular the P clitic, as in (d). In turn, third dative also precedes all other clitics that it can cooccur with—for instance, the partitive in (e). Note that, as before, (a) illustrates the dative form in isolation, (c) the combination of accusative and dative, and (b) establishes that the accusative series is *u/a/ i/e*:

(19)   *Olivetta S. Michele* (Liguria)
    a. el   i   'duna a'ko
       he   to.him gives this
    b. u/ a/ i/ e   'tʃami
       him/her/them-m./them-f. I.call
    c. el u/ i/ a/e   i   'duna
       he it-m./it-f./ them-m./them-f. to.him gives
    d. el u/ a/ i/ e   mə   'duna
       he it-m./it-f./ them-m./them-f. to.me gives
    e el i   n   'duna 'dyi
       he to.him of.them gives two

On the basis of the discussion concerning Vagli, datives are associated with a high position in the sentential nominal string, and specifically with the Q position. This conclusion is confirmed by the empirical data of Olivetta, since, as shown in (19e), the dative clitic precedes the partitive in N. If the dative is inserted under Q, the accusative that precedes it has at its disposal only the R position, where it can be preceded, in turn, by the subject clitic in D, as indicated in (20); as before, subject clitics are not our concern here:

(20)   *Olivetta S. Michele*
    D_{Op} D R   Q P Loc N I
     | | | |
     el u/a/i/e i   *duna*

Explaining the parametrization between Vagli in (14) and Olivetta in (19) requires the lexicon of Olivetta to be accounted for. The *i* form (subsuming in descriptive terms the accusative masculine plural and the dative) has an internal structure comparable to that assigned to the *ʃi* clitic of Vagli in (16c); indeed, we propose that *i* lexicalizes a Q position within its phrase, as in (21c). As for the other forms of the accusative paradigm, we can assign *u*, *a*, and *e* to the I category, treating them as nominal class markers, as in (21a)–(21d). We note that the systematic lack of an *l* formative in the structures in (21) makes the clitics of Olivetta identical to the inflections observed on the nominal and adjectival system.

(21)   *Olivetta S. Michele*
    a. $[_I u \, [N] \,]$
    b. $[_I a \, [N] \,]$
    c. $[_Q i \, [I \quad [N] \,]$
    d. $[_I e \, [N] \,]$

What remains to be seen is how the lexicon in (21) relates to the structure in (20). To begin with, the Q specification of the *i* clitic makes it compatible with insertion in Q. What is more, the internal structure of all of the elements in (21) is evidently compatible with insertion in R; indeed, it is the general conclusion of Manzini and Savoia (2002) that R is a normal insertion position for all elements associated with specificity properties. Thus we obtain the basic observed order third Acc–third Dat. In fact, nothing in the lexical entries in (21) prevents the third-person clitics from inserting in N; we must assume that the fact that they take a scope position such as R, rather than the N position associated with the internal argument, is what the Olivetta child learns as a parameter of the language. Thus the insertion points for the dialect of Olivetta are as summarized in (21').

(21')   *Olivetta S. Michele*
    u, a, e $\rightarrow$ R
    i $\rightarrow$ R, Q

Saying that in Vagli the accusative clitic appears in the N position associated with the internal argument interpretation, while in Olivetta it appears in the scopal position R for specific elements, is similar to saying that the wh-phrase appears in its thematic position in a language like Chinese, while it appears in scope position in a language like English. One may object that the position of the wh-phrase in English is the result of movement, not of merger. In fact, in our view, the idea that lexical material merges directly in the position where it surfaces holds not only for clitics but for all elements in grammar; one possible instantiation of this idea is the representational model of Brody (1997). More precisely, wh-phrases can be inserted in argumental position in English as well, in appropriate contexts. There is therefore a particularly close match between the properties of wh-phrases in a language like English and the properties described in section 1 for clitic *ci* of standard Italian, which will either insert in Loc or in R according to the context. In general, we take it that the intrinsic denotational content of wh-phrases, as of clitics in the case at hand, determines their compatibility with positions in the syntactic tree; their actual position will depend on other properties. These are identified by Chomsky (1995, 1998, 1999) with noninterpretable or EPP properties of the landing site; but these are only notationally lexical properties, while in fact they correspond to a syntactic parameter that is fully comparable to the on given here for Vagli versus Olivetta.

The same high position, R, that hosts the *u, a, e* clitics associated with the internal argument interpretation can also host the *i* clitic, including when it is interpreted as a dative. This is shown by examples of the type in (22a), where the *i* clitic precedes the partitive *n* clitic and the impersonal *hə* clitic (corresponding to Italian *si*).

While the partitive can be associated with the N position, the impersonal is naturally associated with the Q position, in virtue of its generic quantificational interpretation. Therefore, the *i* clitic will itself appear in a position higher than Q—that is, R—as illustrated in (23a). The relevant contrast is with a dialect like Vagli, where the dative actually occurs after the impersonal; in this case, we must assume that the relative order of the two elements is the reverse, with *ɟi* keeping the quantificational Q position and *si* being allowed in R, as in (23b).

(22) a. *Olivetta S. Michele*
       i   hə n   'di 'katr
      to.him one of.them says four
      'One says a few things to him.'
   b. *Vagli di Sopra*
       i   si   ɟi   l'ðaɲi s'sɔldi
      they one to.him give the coins
      'One gives him money.'

(23) a. *Olivetta S. Michele*
      D_{Op} D R Q P Loc N I
         | | | |
        i hə   *n di*
   b. *Vagli di Sopra*
      D_{Op} D R Q P Loc N I
        | | | | |
        i si ɟi   *ðaɲ*

3. Mutual exclusion

Our general goal is to show that it is possible to maintain a purely syntactic theory of clitics based on a minimalist conception of both the computational component and parameters. The next major phenomenon to be explained in this perspective is the mutual exclusion between clitics, which does not have a counterpart in the mutual exclusion between the corresponding full arguments. This phenomenon is also parametrized. Thus in section 2 we considered two different types of languages in which clusters of dative and accusative are possible, in either order. In many Romance languages, however (possibly the majority of them), such a combination is unknown. Dative and accusative do not combine, and in the simplest case only one of the two clitics is lexicalized. In fact, before discussing the mutual exclusion of accusative and dative, we shall introduce and analyze a comparable case, involving Northern Italian dialects with subject clitics that do not allow for the combination of a third-person subject clitic with a third-person object clitic.

3.1. Object for subject

In the simplest case, mutual exclusion between accusative and subject clitics leads to the lexicalization of only one of the two clitics—namely, the accusative. Consider the dialect of Tavullia (Marche). This is a subject clitic language, giving rise in the third person to the *l/la/i/le* paradigm in (24a), which coincides with that of third-person object clitics illustrated in (24b). Crucially, in the dialect of Tavullia, the presence of a third-person object clitic excludes that of a third-person singular subject clitic, as in (25a); the presence of an additional P clitic does not interfere with this mutual exclusion, as in (25b). In contrast, the dialect allows for the combination of the third-person plural subject clitic *i* with the whole third-person series of object clitics, as in (24c); in this case the plural clitic takes on the denotation of both masculine and feminine.

There are several indications to the effect that the mutual exclusion between subject and object clitic in examples of the type in (25) is resolved in favor of the object. First, properties of the clitic such as masculine or feminine are interpreted as those of the object. Furthermore, in an example such as (25b), the third-person clitic follows the P clitic, as predicted if it is inserted in N like object clitics and not in D like subject clitics:

(24)   *Tavullia* (Marche)
   a. εl/la/i/le   te   'cɛma
       he/she/they-m./they-f. you call(s)
   b. t   εl/la/i/le   'cɛ:m
       you him/her/them-m./them-f. call
   c. i   l/la/i/le   'cɛma
       they him/her/ them-m./them-f. call

(25)   a. εl/la/i/le   'cɛma
       him/her/ them-m./them-f. calls
   b. m   εl/la 'da
       to.me it   gives

Though we essentially elicit from our native speakers positive data, rather than grammaticality judgments, it may be useful to indicate that what we do not find are crucially sentences of the type in (26) as opposed to (25):

(26)   *Tavullia*
   a. *εl la   'cɛma
       he her calls
   b. *εl m   la 'da
       he to.me it gives

We can exclude that the impossibility of combining object and subject clitics depends on a prohibition against repeating the same clitic in the string. On the one hand, it is clear that sequences such as those in (26) do not involve identical forms. On the other hand, there are several dialects which, contrary to those like Tavullia, allow for the combination of two identical third-person clitics as object and subject, respectively, as already discussed in section 2.1. Another example is provided by the dialect of Andràz (Veneto) in (27) where the relevant combination is possible in all cases, including those where there is identity between object and subject also from a purely phonological point of view, such as the feminine singular in (27b):

(27)   *Andràz* (Veneto)
   a. el   lo/la/ie/le   'veiga
       he him/her/them-m./them-f. sees

b. la   l/la/i/le   'veiga
she him/her/them-m./them-f. sees

Returning to Tavullia, the *l/la/i/le* clitics that we are concerned with are compatible both with insertion in the nominal N position of object clitics and with insertion in the D position of subject clitics. In the first case, they are preceded by the P clitic in subject position as in (28a); in the second case, they are followed by the object P clitic as in (28b):

(28) *Tavullia*

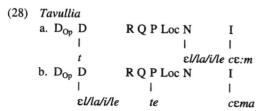

The fact to be explained about the dialect of Tavullia is that insertion of an *l/la/i/le* form in the N position of the clitic string blocks insertion of an *l* form in the D position, as in (29a), though the latter can host the *i* clitic as in (29b). From another perspective, we could equally say that insertion of an *l/la/i/le* clitic in N results in a form of partial *pro*-drop since third-person subject clitics are not lexicalized with the exception of the pure plural *i*.

(29) *Tavullia*

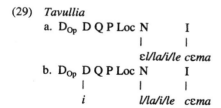

The lexical entries for third-person clitics provided so far for the dialects of Vagli and Olivetta treat the third-person clitics as noun phrases with an I head corresponding to an inflectional class (i.e., gender) morpheme in the Olivetta dialect, while in the Vagli dialect it corresponds to a definiteness specification *l*, which, in turn, can embed a nominal class morpheme. We propose that in the Tavullia dialect, the *l* clitics have the same type of structure, as indicated in (30). The *i* clitic has the familiar structure in (30c), which makes it coincide with a pure lexicalization of Q:

(30) *Tavullia*
   a. $[_I \ \varepsilon l \ [\ N \ ] \ ]$
   b. $[_I \ l \ ... \quad [_I \ a \ [\ N \ ] \ ] \ ]$
   c. $[_Q \ i \ [\ I \quad [\ N \ ] \ ] \ ]$
   d. $[_I \ l \ ... \quad [_I \ e \ [\ N \ ] \ ] \ ]$

We suggested that the object for subject phenomenon reduces to the fact that insertion of one of the clitic forms in (30) in the N position of the string causes the Tavullia dialect to display a partial *pro*-drop phenomenon. In terms of the present analysis non-null subject languages, as is Tavullia in the ordinary case, require the lexicalization of the Definiteness properties associated with the D position of the clitic string, through the insertion of a subject pronoun. Evidently in the cases under review, inserting one of the clitics in (30a), (30b), and (30d)—which by hypothesis is made up of a morpheme l intrinsecally associated with Definite reference and a nominal class morpheme—satisfies the requirement that Definiteness properties be lexicalized, no matter whether the clitic is inserted in D itself or in N. If it is inserted in D, it is interpreted as the subject of the verb, with whose inflection it agrees. Alternatively, however, the l clitic can be inserted in N, where its interpretation is that of the internal argument of the verb; the referential properties of the subject will be recovered in this case through the verb inflection. In either case, we assume that in a dialect like Tavullia the insertion of an l element results in the lexicalization of Definiteness for the whole string. Therefore, inserting one of the l forms in N excludes lexicalization of an l form in D. Generalizing this model we can assume that l lexicalizes all properties it is associated with for the whole string; in particular, then, the insertion of an l clitic prevents the re-lexicalization in the string of the nominal properties associated with the l morpheme, interpretively connected in our model to third-person reference.

The discussion that precedes does not yet take into account the peculiarity of i in the Tavullia dialect—namely, that insertion of i in D is compatible with the presence in the N position of clitics belonging to the series in (30). We note that while the other clitics in (30) coincide with the combination of the two nominal bases represented by l and the vocalic nominal class, the i clitic in (30c) consists entirely of a functional specification—that is, Q. The insertion of one of the forms in (30) in the N position of the string, while lexicalizing the Definiteness property, does not interfere with the lexicalization of purely functional properties such as Q; we can take it that the insertion of the Q form i in D is a consequence of this. In the same way, we can account for the fact that the clitics of the series in (30) can combine with clitics of the P series, as illustrated in (28). What P clitics have in common with the Q clitic is that they consist entirely of a functional specification. Because of this, P clitics, like i, do not interfere with the lexicalization of the Definiteness properties by one of the clitics in (30).

The discussion that precedes seems to predict that the insertion of the i clitic in N should also be compatible with the insertion of the whole series in (30) in the D position. In other words, we could expect that the Tavullia dialect, admitting of (24c), admits of (31) as well, which is instead ungrammatical:

(31)   *Tavullia*
　　　*la   i   'cɛma
　　　she them calls

Given the quantificational (plural) properties shared by subject and object instances of i, there is no reason to believe that different lexical entries are involved in (24a) and (31). Therefore it must be the point of insertion of the clitic that determines its different behavior. We may begin by considering what makes a Q clitic, like i in the Tavullia dialect, suitable for insertion in N. Remember that in the case in which an l clitic inserts in N or a Q clitic inserts in Q there is a straightforward match between the internal head of the clitic and the position in the clitic string. Furthermore, we have assumed that all clitics are compatible with certain positions, like D or R. Nevertheless, neither of these two general rules for insertion works for the case of lexicalization of N by *i*. We suggest that the insertion of *i* in N is possible only to the extent that *i* is interpreted as a Q specification of N itself; in other words, the insertion of *i* in N yields the equivalent of a clitic form including an N head together with the quantificational (plural) specification. We suggest that due to the general nature of nominal heads in the Tavullia dialects, the insertion of *i* in N works like that of any other clitic in the series in (30), lexicalizing the Definiteness properties of the whole string, with the consequences already noted for the lexicalization of the D position.

As noted in the presentation of the data, the *i* that appears in subject position when one of the clitics in (30) is inserted in N has a plural reference independent of nominal class (i.e., "gender" in traditional terms). As an object, and as a subject in contexts where N is not lexicalized by one of the clitics in (30), the *i* clitic has plural reference restricted to a particular nominal class (the so-called masculine). When it is inserted in N position, as in (24b), we have just theorized that *i* is interpreted as a Q specification of N itself. We can assume that its taking on properties of nominal class is connected to its syntactic N property; the plural properties depend, of course, on its intrinsic Q properties. When *i* is inserted in subject position, and the N properties of the string are independently lexicalized, the *i* clitic takes on the value of a pure plural. Finally, when *i* is inserted in subject position and N is not independently lexicalized, as in (24a), again it takes on nominal class (masculine) interpretation. This suggests that, in effect, in the Tavullia system, the lexicalization of plurality must in all cases be connected to a nominal property; in the contexts under consideration the latter surfaces precisely as a nominal class (i.e., masculine) property of *i* itself.

Interestingly, Tavullia patterns with Vagli and Olivetta in that in all of these dialects, the so-called third-person dative coincides with the (masculine) plural—that is, with *i* in the case of Tavullia. We should naturally like to extend to dative *i* the analysis in (30c), which associates the *i* morpheme with the Q functional specification within the clitic structure. If we do this, we predict that the dative clitic will be able to insert in Q, as in the Olivetta dialect, or in R as in the Vagli one. The evidence in (32a) suggests that this second possibility is the correct one because *i* precedes the *si*-type clitic *s*, which is itself inserted in Q. If we assume that *i* in R has the same properties as *i* inserted in D, we predict that it will combine with the accusative clitic series in (30), including *i* itself, and precede it, as is indeed the case in (32b):

(32)   *Tavullia*
    a. i   s   da   un 'libre
       to.him one gives a book
    b. i   ɛl/la   'da
       to.him it-m./it-f. he.gives

On this basis we can complete the picture of the insertion points for the clitics in (30) as indicated in (30'):

(30')   *Tavullia*
    ɛl, la, le → D, N
    i → D, R, N

In (32b), the presence of a clitic of the accusative series in N is sufficient to exclude the lexicalization of a subject clitic in D, while in the impersonal (32a) the problem does not arise. However, the exclusion of the subject clitic is determined also by the simple presence of the dative, as illustrated in (33):

(33)   *Tavullia*
    i   da   'kwest
    to.him he.gives this

The basis for this behavior is to be sought precisely in the characterization of the dative as a distributor over the N argument. Thus it can combine with a lexicalization of N by a clitic of the accusative series, as in (32b), in which case the accusative clitic can be assumed to exclude the subject clitic. Alternatively, it can combine with a lexical object (or an incorporated one for unergatives) as in (33); in any event, its nature as a distributor implies the lexicalization of N properties. Therefore, even the dative in isolation effectively amounts to a lexicalization of the combination of quantificational properties with N properties. This excludes lexicalization of the subject, on the usual grounds that in a dialect like Tavullia nominal definiteness is lexicalized only once in the clitic string.

Support for this analysis come from the comparison of the data in (24a)–(24b) and (25b) with (34). As already indicated, (24a)–(24b) show that a subject clitic of the P series can combine with an object clitic of the series in (30) and vice versa. As we expect, furthermore, the presence of an object clitic of the series in (30) prevents the lexicalization of the subject clitic in (25b) in the presence of a P clitic functioning as a dative. But as shown in (34), the subject clitic is optionally excluded also in cases where only the P clitic is lexicalized in the string, provided the latter functions as a distributor. We interpret this evidence along the same lines as (33); the optionality of the subject can be taken to be a result of the fact that only optionally is the P clitic computed as a distributor.

(34)   *Tavullia*
    (εl/la) me   da   'kwest
    he/she to.me gives this

Going back to the general solution that we have proposed to the mutual exclusion of subject and object clitic in the dialects of the type of Tavullia, we note that it has several interesting properties differentiating it from other approaches to mutual exclusion phenomena found in the literature. In particular, our analysis depends neither on the identity of the clitics that are in complementary distribution nor on the competition for a single position. Indeed, it is obvious not only that different clitics can be in complementary distribution as in (26) but also that different positions are available to the clitics in complementary distribution. Thus Tavullia has an N position to the right of P clitics for objects, as in (28a), and a separate subject D position to the left of P clitics, as in (28b). Moreover, the complementary distribution is not constrained by adjacency, as can be seen by the contrast between (25b) and (26b). All of these properties of the mutual exclusion phenomenon strongly point to the irrelevance of morphophonological considerations and to the purely (morpho)syntactic nature of the phenomenon itself.

In this perspective, we may consider what exactly is the parameter between Tavullia-like dialects and dialects like Andràz—that is, the information that the child learning the language must deduce from the data. We take it that in the case of Andràz in (27) the Definiteness properties lexicalized by the nominal head *l* cannot be computed separately from the nominal class properties they subcategorize, and that therefore they have to be lexicalized as many times in the string as there are interpreted arguments. In a dialect like Tavullia, in contrast, it appears that the Definiteness properties lexicalized by *l* can, in fact, be computed separately from the nominal class inflections they embed, and they can satisfy the Definiteness properties of the entire string. This produces the object for subject effect we are aiming to explain. Indeed, the insertion of an *l* clitic in object position lexicalizes the Definiteness properties of the string; at the same time, the referential properties of the subject are recoverable from the D position corresponding to the verbal inflection.

The most natural way to construe these different properties of *l* in the Tavullia and Andràz dialects is in terms of scope: in a dialect like Andràz *l* takes scope uniquely over its own constituent, while in a dialect like Tavullia the scope of *l* extends to the D position of the sentential string, even when the clitic is inserted lower. In turn, these different scopal properties are not specifically introduced here to account for mutual exclusion; rather, they represent an independently needed property of grammars. Furthermore, they have been invoked to account for clitics in connection with the fact that an *i* element (of Vagli, Olivetta, or Tavullia) can be interpreted both as taking scope within its own nominal N head, in which case it is a plural, or as taking scope over the whole string, in which case its interpretation is that of a distributor (dative). As it happens, in the dialects considered so far, the scopal properties of the distributor are overt, in the sense that they correspond to insertion in Q; however, Manzini and Savoia (2002) equally review cases where this reading corresponds to insertion of the relevant clitic in N. For an example of a specialized dative in N within this article, we refer to the Làconi case, in section 5.

3.2. Accusative for dative

With this much background, let's now return to the mutual exclusion of third-person accusative and dative clitics. In the simplest case, only one of two clitics survives. We begin by considering the case of mutual exclusion, with survival of the accusative only. This situation is found in a number of dialects of Apulia, Lucania, and Calabria, including Iacurso, as illustrated in (35). As before, (a) illustrates the dative in isolation, (b) the accusative in isolation, and (c) the survival of the sole accusative in dative–accusative contexts. In this dialect, the accusative clitic generally follows the clitics it combines with, as in (d); on the contrary, the dative precedes the clitics it cooccurs with, such as the partitive *nda* and the *si*-clitic in (e). The clitic repertory of a dialect like Iacurso includes three different forms for the accusative clitic: two for the singular (masculine and feminine), and one for the plural. The dative in isolation coincides with the descriptive accusative plural.

(35) *Iacurso* (Calabria)
    a. li   'ðuna 'kistu
        him   gives this
    b. lu/ la / li   'viju
        him/her/them I.see

c. lu/ la/ li   'ðuɲɲu
   him/her/them I.give
d. ti   lu/ la/ li   'ðuɲɲu
   to.you him/her/them I. give
e. li   si nda 'parra 'sɛmpʰɛ
   to.him one of.it talks always

The distribution of the accusative in a dialect like Iacurso follows usual lines, in that the accusative is preceded by all other clitics; (36a) illustrates the simple case in which the accusative follows the P clitic. However, the dative precedes both the partitive and the *si*-type clitic, leading us to conclude that it is inserted in R, as in (36b), where the *si*-clitic appears in Q and the partitive in N. Hence the mutual exclusion between two *l* clitics, one functioning as dative and one as the accusative, cannot simply be explained by the competition for the same position.

(36) *Iacurso*

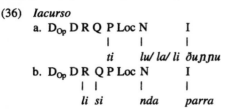

Following the analyses proposed here, we treat *l* as a nominal I head. The morpheme *a*, descriptively associated to feminine gender, is the lexicalization of a nominal class property I, as in (37b). As for the *u* morpheme, descriptively associated with the masculine, remember that Manzini and Savoia (2001b) theorize that what is normally described as the nonagreeing form of the verb is, in fact, a form agreeing with the subject with respect to the N property. Now, in the Iacurso dialect, the past participle ending in the N agreement (or descriptively nonagreement) contexts is *u*; this favors a treatment of *u* as pure N, of the type in (37a). Naturally the *i* morpheme showing up in the plural and in the dative is in present terms a Q element, as in (37c). The nominal properties of all these clitics make them compatible with insertion in N; the *li* clitic can furthermore be inserted in R, presumably in virtue of its quantificational properties, as in (37').

(37) *Iacurso*
      a. [$_I$ *l* ...   [I [$_N$ *u*]]]
      b. [$_I$ *l* ...   [$_I$ *a* [N]]]
      c. [$_I$ *l* ... [$_Q$ *i* [I [N]]]]

(37') *Iacurso*
       lu, la → N
       li   → R, N

To account for the mutual exclusion of accusative and dative in the Iacurso dialect, we take up again the line of explanation introduced for Tavullia. Specifically, we propose that when one of the forms in (37) is inserted into the N position of the clitic string, the properties associated with its *l* head are lexicalized for the string as a whole, preventing insertion of another *l* form. In particular, *l* is a nominal head establishing what is traditionally conceived of as the third-person reference. We can assume that insertion of an *l* form in the N position of the string lexicalizes this nominal property for the whole string, making it redundant and hence impossible to insert another *l* form—for instance, as the dative in R. The presence of an *l* form in N may therefore be interpreted as a straightforward lexicalization of the internal argument as in (35b); or it may interpretively imply reference to another third-person argument, such as the distributor in (35c).

Vice versa, the insertion of the *li* distributor in R is possible only if the N position is not independently lexicalized by an *l* clitic. Nevertheless, lexicalization of the dative, while excluding that of the accusative, is not able to subsume it; thus, the dative only surfaces in the presence of a lexical object (or an incorporated one in the case of unergatives). This asymmetry can be connected to the fact that lexicalization of the internal argument requires that of a nominal class property, such as *u* and *a* in (37a)–(37b), or of *i* itself interpreted as a plural specification of the *l* base. The dative alone does not suffice to lexicalize dative–accusative contexts in that it does not lexicalize a nominal class property. The scopal properties of dative, on the contrary, can be subsumed by the accusative, provided the *l* specification of the latter is interpreted with the relevant distributor scope.

Analogously, in the case of the Tavullia dialect, we have seen that insertion of a subject clitic of the *l* series excludes that of an object clitic but does not subsume it; thus, subject clitics only show up in intransitve contexts or with transitive verbs in the absence of an accusative clitic. Again the analysis proposed in section 3.1 predicts that this is is so, in that the scopal properties that we have imputed to *l* are sufficient to lexicalize the D properties of the string, even if belonging to a clitic inserted in the N position. In contrast, insertion of an *l* clitic in the D position cannot lexicalize the nominal class properties necessary to establish reference to the internal argument. We strengthen the empirical basis for connecting the internal argument to nominal class in section 4.

The preceding discussion is based on the idea that the two constituents of which an *l* clitic typically consists—i.e., *l* itself and the vocalic head corresponding to nominal class—may, in fact, behave to a large extent independently of one another. If this is so, we may expect to find mutual exclusion phenomena that instead of involving the whole clitic involve only the *l* subconstituent. This case is indeed found, for instance, in a dialect such as Gavoi in (38). Example (38a) illustrates the dative in isolation, (38b) the accusative in combination with a P clitic, and (38c) the combination of accusative and dative. While the clitics in (38a)–(38b) include an *l* morpheme, the cluster in (38c) has an *l* dative followed by an accusative including simply nominal class and eventually plural morphology:

(38) *Gavoi*
    a. li   'daða   'ʔustu
        to.him he.gives   this
    b. mi   lu/lɔr 'daða
        to.me it/them he.gives
    c. li   u/a/'r/ar   'daða
        to.him it-m./it-f./them-m./them-f. he.gives

The accusative paradigm of a dialect such as Gavoi can be analyzed along the same lines indicated in (12) for Sardinian dialects in general. The *l* morpheme corresponds as before to the I head of a nominal constituent, embedding a separate nominal constituent headed by a vocalic morpheme *u*, *a*, or *ɔ*. We treat *a* and *ɔ* as an I—that is, a nominal class (gender) morpheme—as in (39b)–(39d), while considerations pertaining in particular to past particple agreement lead us to analyze *u* as an N element in (39a). As suggested in (12), the plural morpheme *s* is a lexicalization of Q, as in (39c)–(39d); the *r* ending surfacing in the examples in (38) is simply a phonological alternant of *s*. Contrary to the other cases considered so far, the dative form does not coincide exactly with any of the accusative ones. We analyze the *l* morpheme again as for the accusative series, and we associate *i* with Q, as in (39e). This amounts to proposing that the Gavoi dialect, contrary to those considered so far, has a specialized lexicalization for distributivity (that is, *i*) distinct from the lexicalization of plurality (that is, *s*). Another example of this is provided by the dialect of Làconi in section 5.

(39) *Gavoi*
    a. $[_I (l) \ldots$ $[I$ $[_N u]]]$
    b. $[_I (l) \ldots$ $[_I a$ $[N]]]$
    c. $[_I (l) \ldots$ $[_I ɔ [_Q s [N]]]$
    d. $[_I (l) \ldots$ $[_I a [_Q s [N]]]$
    e. $[_I l$ $\ldots [_Q i [I$ $[N]]]]$

The nominal properties of accusative clitics require insertion in the N position of the clitic string. In virtue of its quantificational properties, we expect *li* to be inserted in a higher position as well, as it indeed is when it combines with accusatives. Since R alternates with N as a possible insertion point for *l* clitics in other dialects (Iacurso), we can identify the high position of datives with R. However R's nominal properties should also allow for insertion in N. We have direct evidence for this possibility in cases such as (40a), in which the dative is preceded by the partitive. If the dative were inserted in R, we could expect the partitive to normally insert in N and therefore to follow it, as it follows other clitics such as those of the P series in examples like (40b). We take it that the order observed in (40a) can only be explained by assuming that the partitive lexicalizes R, but it does so because the dative itself inserts in N.

(40) *Gavoi*
    a. nde   li   'daða   'duɔs
       of.them   to.him he.gives two
    b. ti   ndɛ   'daða   'duɔs
       to.you of.them   he.gives two

The points of insertion of the clitics in (39) are therefore as indicated in (39').

(39') *Gavoi*
    (l)u, (l)a, (l)ɔs, (l)as → N
    li → R, N

What is immediately relevant for present purposes is that the clustering of dative and accusative is impossible, with the dative and the accusative both lexicalized by *l* clitics, as indicated in (41). This is explained by our theory of mutual exclusions as due to the fact that the *l* head of the clitic lexicalizes nominal reference properties for the whole string. Therefore, once an *l* form is inserted, insertion of a second *l* form is excluded. At the same time, in analyzing the Iacurso dialect, we proposed that the insertion of the accusative for the dative, but not vice versa, is due to the fact that lexicalization of the internal argument requires that of nominal class properties present only on the accusative. The Gavoi dialect represents an even more transparent solution to the same set of requirements. Thus its morphology allows it to lexicalize only the nominal class properties for the accusative, while the dative lexicalizes distributivity and at the same time nominal *l* properties for the whole string.

(41)   *Gavoi*
　　　　*li　　　lu/la/lɔr/lar　　　　　　　　'daða
　　　to.him　it-m./it-f./them-m./them-f.　he.gives

4.   "Opaque" forms

In what precedes we have considered in some detail languages where the cluster subject and object is simplified to a single clitic, which would be described in traditional terms as the object; similarly the cluster of dative and accusative is simplified to the accusative. However, the literature on Romance languages typically considers cases in which the mutual exclusion between two clitics leads to either the replacement of one of the two by a different form (see section 5) or to the emergence of what Bonet (1995) calls an "opaque" form. In particular, James Harris (1994) and Bonet (1995) show that in the Catalan dialect of Barcelona (Barceloní) the cluster of accusative and dative (singular) does not surface as such, but as a single form *li* corresponding to the dative in isolation. In terms of the analysis of these authors, *li* is not simply the dative form in such a case but, rather, a single lexicalization for the complex of abstract morphosyntactic features associated with the whole dative–accusative cluster—what they call the opaque form. In what follows, we discuss cases of this kind in Italian dialects. As before, we begin by considering object for subject phenomena rather than dative–accusative clusters.

4.1.   Opaque forms in subject exclusion contexts

In dialects of the Lombardy region such as Castiglione d'Adda in (42) the third-person subject clitic is lexicalized in isolation or in combination with a P object clitic, as illustrated in (42a) for the singular and in (42b) for the plural. Furthermore, a P subject clitic is lexicalized when in combination with a third-person object clitic, as in (42c). However, Castiglione d'Adda excludes the combination of a third-person subject clitic with a third-person accusative, as in (43). The presence of an additional P clitic is irrelevant to the mutual exclusion, as in (44). The dialect of Castiglione d'Adda is different from that of Tavullia in that the mutual exclusion characterizes all third-person clitics, including the plural. But another difference that emerges from (42)–(44) is actually more striking. In particular, the data in (43a)–(43b) show that in contexts excluding the subject clitic, the singular object clitic takes the invariant form *la* whether it is interpreted as feminine or masculine. This contrasts with (42c) where the masculine and feminine forms are clearly distinguished in the context of a P subject clitic. In a framework such as Bonet's (1995), the *la* clitic in (43)–(44) could therefore be described as an opaque form. Similarly, the plural is apparently inflected by a final *a*, taking the form *ia* rather than the form *i* in (42b)–(42c).

(42)   *Castiglione d'Adda* (Lombardy)
    a. el/la me   'tʃama
      he/she me   calls
    b. i   me   'tʃamũ
      they me   call
    c. t   el/la/i   'tʃami
      you him/her/them call

(43)   a. la   'tʃama
      him/her he.calls
    b. la   'tʃamũ
      him/her they.call
    c. ia   'tʃama
      them he.calls
    d. ia   'tʃamũ
      them they.call

(44)   a. me la 'daŋ
      to.me it they.give
    b. m   ia   'daŋ
      to.me them they.give

In other words, the dialect of Castiglione d'Adda excludes the combination of two third-person forms of the type in (45), which do not appear in our data:

(45)   *Castiglione d'Adda*
    a.*el/la el/la/i   'tʃama
      he/she him/her/them calls
    b.*i   l/la/i   'tʃamũ
      they him/her/them call

The fact that *la* is restricted to the feminine in contexts without mutual exclusion, but ranges over all nominal classes in mutual exclusion contexts, is confirmed for instance by the data in (46). Thus in the mutual exclusion context in (46c) the *la* form can combine with an adjective agreeing in the masculine or in in the feminine, whereas in (46b) it can only combine with an adjective agreeing in the feminine:

(46)   *Castiglione d'Adda*
    a. t   el   'vedi   s'trak/*s'traka
      you him see   tired-m./tired-f.
    b. t   la   'vedi   s'traka/*s'trak
      you her see   tired-f./tired-m
    c. la   'ved   s'trak/ s'traka
      him/her he.sees   tired-m./tired-f.

The subject clitics that are lexicalized by Castiglione d'Adda in isolation or in combination with P clitics are *el* for the masculine singular, *la* for the feminine singular, and *i* for the plural, which also surface as object clitics in the presence of P subject clitics. The evidence at our disposal suggests that both singular and plural object clitics are inserted in N, while subject clitics appear in D position, since object clitics follow P clitics while subject clitics precede them, as in (47a). Furthermore, the conclusion that *la/ia* forms are inserted in N extends to examples of the type of (43)–(44). To begin, the number properties of such forms (singular or plural) are interpreted as attaching to the internal argument, not to the subject. What is more, such forms follow the P clitic in (44), indicating an N position for them, as in (47b):

(47)   *Castiglione d'Adda*
 a. D_{Op} D R Q P Loc N I
    | | |
   el/ la *me* *t∫ama*
 b. D_{Op} D R Q P Loc N I
        | | |
      me *la daŋ*

  The mutual exclusion of third-person clitics in (45) follows if the lexicon of Castiglione d'Adda is analogous in relevant respects to that of Tavullia; in other words, insertion of an *l* clitic in the N position lexicalizes Definiteness for the whole string preventing re-lexicalization of an *l* clitic in D. Because insertion of an *l* clitic in the N position satisfies the Definiteness requirement of the entire string, it induces what is in effect a null subject behavior. Vice versa, insertion of an *l* clitic in D excludes that of an *l* clitic in N but cannot subsume it. This is because *l* in D lexicalizes Definiteness for the whole string, but not nominal class properties, which, according to our hypotheses, must be independently lexicalized for the internal argument.

  We begin by considering the internal structure of the relevant clitics. In the plural, Castiglione d'Adda differentiates between *i* and *ia* for the mutual exclusion context. We identify the *i* morpheme with a Q category, as in (48c). The *ia* form is best analyzed as resulting from the combination of *i*, analyzed as before, and of the nominal class morpheme *a* lexicalizing the lower *l* in a biphrasal structure, as in (48d). Turning to the singular, the masculine *el* coincides with the pure nominal head without inflection, as in (48a). On the contrary, the feminine *la* results from the combination of the nominal base *l* with the inflectional base *a*; the latter is, of course, the same that appears in *ia* and is therefore to be construed as nominal class morpheme, rather than as a gender morpheme in the traditional sense of the term, as in (48b). Note that the majority of Northern Italian dialects do have a single nominal class inflection that is, *a*. Indeed, nouns and adjectives, as well as articles, have no inflection in the so-called masculine singular and the pure Q ending *i* in the plural, at least in some residual cases. This inflectional systems holds in the dialect of Castiglione at least for clitics.

(48)   *Castiglione d'Adda*
  a. $[_I \, el \, [\, N \,]\,]\,]$
  b. $[_I \, l \, \ldots \quad [_I \, a \, [\, N \,]\,]\,]$
  c. $[_Q \, i \, [I \quad [\, N \,]\,]\,]$
  d. $[_Q \, i \, [I \quad \ldots \quad [_I \, a \, [\, N \,]\,]\,]\,]$

  Consider (43a)–(43b) in which *la* is inserted in N as the singular object clitic in the presence of a third-person verb. In this case we have taken the *l* morpheme to lexicalize the D position of the string. We propose that the obligatory presence of the *a* morpheme reflects a requirement that a nominal class base, represented in this case by *a*, be lexicalized as well. This requirement is connected precisely to the fact that in mutual exclusion contexts the *l* head of the N clitic lexicalizes Definiteness properties of the whole string; the nominal class head—that is, *a*—therefore represents the dedicated lexicalization of the internal argument. Similarly, in the plural the two clitics *ia* and *i* differ in that the *i* clitic does not lexicalize a nominal head but only the functional Q specification, while *ia* has nominal content provided by the nominal class morpheme, *a*. We may assume that this is at the basis of the insertion of *ia* in the N position of mutual exclusion contexts. Insertion in this position requires the presence of a nominal class head in the internal structure of the clitic, which is provided by *a*.

In contexts where the D position is lexicalized by a subject clitic—for instance, a P clitic—the N position is normally filled by the *el/la/i* series; we shall return shortly to the fact that *la* in this case is restricted to the so-called feminine. Similarly the *el/la/i* series lexicalizes the D position, yielding the overall schema in (48') for the insertion of clitics:

(48')   *Castiglione d'Adda*
    el, la, i → D, N
    ia → N

As noted in the presentation of the data, *i* in the Castiglione d'Adda dialect is always in complementary distribution with the other clitics in (48), differing in this from *i* in the Tavullia dialect. We account for this, assuming that the pure Q morpheme *i*, insofar as it is interpreted as the plural specification of a nominal base, is treated as a nominal clitic, equivalent in all respects to clitics involving a nominal lexical base *l*. This correlates with the fact that the *i* clitic does not lexicalize the distributor (dative). In fact, there is no third-person lexicalization for the dative form in this dialect; rather, dative contexts present a locative form, as illustrated in (49). For an analysis of this and similar patterns, see Manzini and Savoia (2002).

(49)   *Castiglione d'Adda*
    a. i   ge   'daŋ   'kwɛst
        they there give this
    b. ge   'meti la 'sa:l
        there I.put the salt

One aspect of the analysis to be clarified concerns the treatment of *la*, which does not coincide with the traditional feminine gender specification in mutual exclusion contexts, though it does in other contexts. We argued in section 1.3 that there is no functional specification of gender to parallel categories such as Q for plurality or D for definiteness; this correlates with the fact that, while categories such as number or definiteness have denotational import, gender does not and can only be construed as a nominal class marker. In these terms, the problem regarding *la* is that in contexts where the presence of *a* is required by the verb as a lexicalization of nominal class content, it is not restricted to agree with nominal, adjectival, and other elements belonging to the nominal class traditionally labeled as feminine. On the contrary, when the presence of *a* is not required to mark nominal class content, it again agrees with nouns, adjectives, and other elements belonging to the traditional "feminine" class. We assume, therefore, that if the presence of a nominal class head *a* is required by the lexicalization conditions on N, as in mutual exclusion contexts, its reference is allowed to range on all nominal classes. In contrast, in contexts where no restriction is present on the lexicalization of N (or D), the range of *a* is restricted to one particular nominal class. These conclusions are consistent also with the appearence of *a* in the plural clitic form *ia*.

Our analysis explicitly eliminates a number of hypotheses that can potentially be entertained on the object for subject phenomenon and are, in fact, reflected by current descriptions of the data. In particular, some Lombardy dialects with substantial affinity to Castiglione d'Adda allow us to show that opaque object clitics emerge independently of the existence of subject clitics in the language. This shows that the phenomena of mutual exclusion and "opacity" cannot be analyzed in terms of the competition of morphologically similar forms or of the competition of such forms for the same position. Quite simply, an abstract syntactic solution is imposed by the fact that there is no subject clitic to compete with the object clitic or to fuse with it into an opaque form.

Consider, for instance, the dialect of Como. The interesting peculiarity of this dialect is that the lexicalization of the subject is subsumed by the verb inflection in the third-person plural as in (50b), though a subject clitic is inserted in the singular, as in (50a). On the contrary, object clitics in first- or second-person contexts present the *l/la/i* paradigm familiar from Castiglione d'Adda. Despite the absence of lexicalized subject clitics in (50b), the Como dialect—exactly as the Castiglione d'Adda dialect—restricts the lexicalization of the singular object clitic to the *la* form in any third-person context, not only in the singular as in (51a) and (52a) but also in the plural as in (51b) and (52b). Note that the plural object clitic in third-person contexts takes the form *ia* as in (51c)–(52d), even though, as we have seen, it is the *i* clitic that appears in first- and second-person contexts as in (50c). The lexical entries of the Como dialect are therefore as detailed in (48) for Castiglione d'Adda.

(50) *Como* (Lombardy)
    a. al/ la 'dɔrma
       he/she sleeps
    b. 'dɔrmaŋ
       they.sleep
    c. t al/la/i   'tʃamɐt
       you him-m./him-f./them call

(51) a. la   'tʃama
       him/her he.calls
    b. la   'tʃamaŋ
       him/her they.call
    c. ia   'tʃama
       them he.calls
    d. ia   'tʃamaŋ
       them they.call

(52) a. ma   la 'da
       to.me it he.gives
    b. ma   la 'daŋ
       to.me it they.give

To account for the Como data, it is necessary to provide a brief discussion of the exact nature of the null subject phenomenon, which we referred to informally in the preceding discussion. In particular, following intuitions of traditional grammar, developed by generative treatments from Taraldsen (1978) to Pollock (1996), we can think of the null subject phenomenon as strictly connected to the nature of the nominal inflection (i.e., the so-called agreement) of the verb. In section 1.1 we introduced the idea that the clitic string repeats itself identically in all of the different verbal domains, as schematically illustrated in (6). In particular, therefore, the D position will repeat itself to the left of the verb in I, in the position that we have associated with subject clitics, but also to the right of the verb in I, as illustrated in (53). Based on this structural hypothesis, Manzini and Savoia (forthcoming) associate the verb and eventually its temporal inflection with the I position of the sentence and assume that its nominal inflection lexicalizes the D position of the clitic string immediately to its right. In this perspective, the null subject or non-null subject nature of a given language appears to depend on properties relating to the lexicalization of a given clitic domain; thus, non-null subject languages require the lexicalization of D of the higher domain (the clitic domain proper), while a null subject language does not.

(53) $[D \dots [I \ [D_{Op} \ [D \dots [V$

In a language like Como, which is similar in this respect to many Northern Italian dialects, the null subject property concerns only some forms of the verbal paradigm. This suggests that the lexical properties of the relevant clitics are involved. To begin, we suggest that the -a ending of third-person singular is a pure N form. The -an ending of third-person plural has the same -a morpheme followed by an -ŋ morpheme specialized for plurality (in the third person) hence can be assigned in present terms to the category Q. It is natural to assume that in the third-person singular, an l clitic form lexicalizes domain-specific properties, which lead to its insertion. On the contrary, the i clitic corresponding to the third-person plural reference does not lexicalize any domain-specific properties—that is, properties not independently lexicalized by the –aŋ inflection of the verb.

We can now return to the lexicalization of la and ia accusative forms not only in mutual exclusion contexts proper, as in the third-person singular, but also in the third-person plural, which has the null subject property. This distribution supports our conclusion that while l or i respectively lexicalize Definiteness properties for the whole string, the presence of the a morpheme corresponds to a requirement on the lexicalization of nominal class properties that is specifically connected with the internal argument.

4.2.   Opaque forms in object exclusion contexts

As anticipated in the introduction to this section, in some languages, clusters of accusative and dative appear to reduce to the clitic form that also lexicalizes the dative in isolation. Languages of this type, known in the literature from Barceloní (Bonet 1995), also include some dialects of the Abruzzi such as Mascioni in (54)–(55). The clitic inventory of this language includes a lu/la/li/le series for masculine singular, feminine singular, masculine plural, and feminine plural, respectively, to which is added a *lo* form for the neuter, as illustrated in (55a)–(55b). Furthermore, the *li* clitic lexicalizes the dative as in (55c). Two *l* clitics cannot be combined, one as an accusative and the other as a dative; instead, we find the form *li* as in (55a). As in most other dialects considered so far, the accusative follows other clitics—for instance, P clitics—with which it normally combines, as in (55b). Interestingly, however, the dative can also be shown to follow the clitics it combines with, in particular the partitive as in (55c), whereas the partitive itself typically follows other clitics such as those of the P series as in (55d).

(54)   *Mascioni* (Abruzzi)
   a. lo 'iko
      it I.say
   b. lu/la/li/le   'camo
      him/her/them-m./them-f. I.call
   c. li   a   k'kweʃto
      to.him he.gives this

(55)   a. li   'a
      to.him.it he.gives
   b. me   lo 'a
      to.me it he.gives
   c. ne   li   a   d'du
      of.them to.him he.gives two
   d. me   ne   a   d'du
      to.me of.them he.gives two

The evidence in (55) points to the conclusion that both the accusative and the dative have N as their insertion position in the dialect of Mascioni. Thus the accusative follows all other clitics with which it cooccurs, including the P clitics, yielding structures of the type in (56a) that are analogous to those reviewed above for other Italian dialects. On the evidence of (55c), however, the dative also follows the clitics with which it cooccurs—in particular, the partitive. As suggested in connection with Gavoi, if the dative were inserted in Q we could expect the partitive to normally insert in N and therefore to follow it, as it indeed follows P, Loc, and *si*-type clitics. We take it that the order observed in (55c) can be explained by assuming that the partitive lexicalizes R, but it does so only because the dative is itself inserted in N, as illustrated in (56b):

(56)   *Mascioni*
   a. D_Op D R Q P Loc N I
             | | |
             me   lo a
   b. D_Op D R Q P Loc N I
          | | |
         ne   li a

As for the internal structure of the *lo/lu/la/li/le* series, following the analyses proposed throughout, we associate the *l* morpheme with the nominal head of a constituent, which in this dialect systematically embeds a vocalic inflection. The gender morpheme *a* is the lexicalization of I of its own nominal constituent as in (57c).

Furthermore Mascioni, like other dialects of Central Italy, specifically of the Abruzzi area, distinguishes in the singular between neuter and masculine. There is evidence that the *u* morpheme of the masculine fills the pure N specification, as in (57a); in particular, the past participle surfaces as a masculine in contexts traditionally described as nonagreeing but treated by Manzini and Savoia (2001b) as implying N agreement. The *o* morpheme of the neuter may therefore be treated as gender morpheme—that is, technically as a lexicalization of I, as in (57b). As for *le*, we treat *e* as yet another nominal class morpheme; thus for the feminine, plurality is denoted by a change in nominal class, as in (57e), rather than by a plural morpheme proper. On the contrary, *i* seems to be appropriately treated as a Q category, as in (57d), being associated either with plurality, as when it lexicalizes the descriptive accusative masculine plural, or with distributivity, when it lexicalizes the dative (for all numbers and genders).

(57) *Mascioni*
    a. $[_I l \ldots \quad [I \ [_N u]]]$
    b. $[_I l \ldots \quad [_I o \ [N]]]$
    c. $[_I l \ldots \quad [_I a \ [N]]]$
    d. $[_I l \ldots [_Q i \ [I \ [N]]]]$
    e. $[_I l \ldots \quad [_I e \ [N]]]$

In a dialect such as Mascioni the mutual exclusion of two clitics of the *l* series does not require any recourse to the idea that the insertion of one of these clitics lexicalizes properties of the whole string; indeed, the cooccurrence of dative and accusative is blocked by the simple fact that they insert in the same position (that is, N) for which they compete. In other words, there is a unique insertion point for the whole *l* series, as in (57'). This is not surprising in that, in general, we have seen that datives inserted in Q have either a pure *i* morphology (Olivetta, Tavullia) or a specialized consonantal head (*fi* of Vagli). Clitics comprising an *l* head and an *i* morpheme lexicalize N (Iacurso, Gavoi, Mascioni itself) and eventually R. The R alternative is open in the Gavoi and Iacurso dialects, but not in Mascioni.

(57') *Mascioni*
    lo, lu, la, li, le → N

The interesting point about Mascioni is the lexicalization of the *li* form in contexts implying a dative–accusative interpretation. The structure for *li* of Mascioni in (57d) includes a Q specification that can be associated with number or with distributivity (dativity), as well as a nominal *l* head associated with what is traditionally known as a third-person reference. Among the clitics in (57), however, *li* is the only one not to include a nominal class specification. Our idea is that, on the one hand, insertion of *li* in the N position entails lexicalization of the *l*—that is, third-person properties—for the whole string; on the other hand, it specifically lexicalizes through *i* the distributivity property. Thus *li* in a dialect like Mascioni is compatibile with the dative–accusative interpretation in that *l* can lexicalize multiple third-person referents, while *i* introduces the distributive interpretation that we have identified with dativity. On the contrary, insertion of a *lu/lo/la/le* form can only be interpreted as introducing reference to an accusative object, in that they lack the distributor in their internal structure.

It is particularly useful to compare the two dialects of Iacurso and Mascioni, which appear to make specular choices: Iacurso simplifies the cluster of dative and accusative to the accusative, while Mascioni simplifies it to the dative. In fact, in both dialects, the *l* head lexicalizes properties of the whole string and therefore gives rise to a potential third-person cluster reading. However, while Iacurso enforces the lexicalization of N properties through the nominal class morpheme, the Mascioni dialect enforces lexicalization of the distributor. This parametric choice is primitive and therefore learned.

5. "Spurious se"-type phenomena

So far, we have not touched on what is perhaps the best known instance of the dative–accusative mutual exclusion pattern in Romance languages: the fact that, in languages like Spanish, the incompatibility of accusative and dative leads to the apparent substitution of the dative with the *se* clitic, corresponding to Perlmutter's (1972) "spurious *se*" rule (see also Bonet 1995, and in an optimality framework Grimshaw 1997). If the discussion in sections 3–4 is correct, the mutual exclusion between accusative and dative is to be explained by the properties of certain clitics, or clitic subconstituents, to lexicalize properties of the whole string. Nevertheless, in sections 3–4 the mutual exclusion between two clitics is resolved in favor of one of them, or of a specialized lexicalization of one of them, as in the case of Castiglione d'Adda's or Como's *la/ia*. It remains for us to account for the apparent substitution of one clitic (the dative) by another one.

In this respect, the crucial observation is that the strings produced by this apparent substitution independently exist in the language with a different interpretive value; thus the *si*-clitic followed by an accusative will independently exist in Spanish with the value of a reflexive. Furthermore, though the substitution pattern systematically studied in the generative literature involves the *si*-type clitic, as in Spanish, the study of Italian dialects reveals additional possibilities analyzed in detail by Manzini and Savoia (2002). The most robustly attested substitution patterns involves the locative for the dative in combination with the accusative. A few dialects replace the dative in combination with the accusative with a *ne*-type partitive clitic, while others pattern with Spanish in replacing the dative with *si*.

The conclusion that mutual exclusion between accusative and dative is a phenomenon independent of the apparent substitution of the dative by other clitics is crucially supported by the observation that all of the clitics that apparently substitute for the dative in clusters with the accusative, in reality surface in other languages as the lexicalization of the dative in isolation as well. An example of an Italian dialect in which the dative does not have a third-person lexicalization, but surfaces in all cases as a locative is provided by Castiglione d'Adda in (49). Though this is the most frequently attested pattern, there are also several dialects in which the partitive or the *si*-type clitic surface in all contexts lexicalized in other languages by a third-person dative, as shown by Manzini and Savoia (2002).

Among Italian dialects, the spurious *se* pattern is attested by Sardininian ones. The essential data for the dialect of Làconi are reproduced in (58). The language has a specialized dative form which emerges in isolation, as in (58a), different from the accusative paradigm, illustrated in (58b). In combination with an accusative the dative interpretation is however conveyed by the *si* clitic, as in (58c). Both the accusative clitic and the dative clitic appear to follow all other clitics, such as the P clitic or the partitive in (58d)–(58e):

(58) *Làconi* (Sardinia)
    a. ḍḍi   a   k'kustu
       to.him he.gives this
    b. ḍḍu/ ḍḍa/ ḍḍuzu/ ḍḍaza b'biu
       it-m./it-f./ them-m./them-f. I.see
    c. si   ḍḍu 'aða
       to.self it   he.gives
       'He gives it to him'
    d. mi   ḍḍu 'aða
       to.me it   he.gives
    e. ndi   ḍḍi   a   d'duaza
       of.them to.him he.gives two

The analyses that precede provide us with a basis for the systematization of both the clitic inventory and the insertion positions involved in a dialect like Làconi. The evidence concerning the position of both accusative and dative clitics is compatible with the conclusion that the insertion point of both clitics is N. This explains the fact that they surface to the right of all other clitics, including P clitics that precede the accusative, as in (59a), and the partitive clitic that precedes the dative, as in (59b). In keeping with the conclusions regarding Gavoi, in (59b) the position of the partitive has been taken to be R; the argument that the dative is in N is particularly strong in cases of clusters such as (59b) since, if the dative could be inserted in a higher position in the string, we would expect the partitive itself to occur in N and thus to follow the dative. The *si*-accusative cluster can simply be assigned the structure in (59c) where *si* occupies the Q position, in consonance with the discussion in section 1.

(59) *Làconi*
    a. D_{Op} D R Q P Loc N   I
               | | |
               mi   *ḍḍu aða*
    b. D_{Op} D R Q P Loc N   I
        | | |
       ndi   *ḍḍi a*
    c. D_{Op} D R Q P Loc N   I
           | | |
        si   *ḍḍu aða*

As for the lexical entries of third-person clitics, we note that Sardinian dialects in general, and the Làconi one in particular, have a fully specified set of clitics corresponding to the accusative and dative paradigm. What is especially interesting is that as for Gavoi in section 3.2, there is no lexical overlapping of dative and accusative.

Let us begin with the accusative paradigm. The *ḍ* morpheme, which we analyze as an I head within the clitic constituent, combines with the *u* and *a* morphemes for the masculine and feminine singular, respectively, which we, in turn, analyze as heads of an embedded nominal. To da and du can be added the plural morpheme s; the latter will be identified with a lexicalization of Q, as in (60c)–(60d). The a morpheme is treated as an I, that is, as a nominal class (gender) morpheme, as in (60b), while considerations pertaining agreement (in particular, of the past participle) lead Manzini and Savoia (forthcoming) to analyze u as an N element, yielding (60a).

In the dative case as well, we find the I morpheme d followed by a morpheme i, which we may take to be specialized for distributivity. Because of this, we associate i with Q, as in (60e); the noteworthy property of the Làconi dialect in this respect is that it has two separate lexicalizations for plurality (i.e., s) and for distributivity (i.e., i). Nothing in principle prevents i and s from combining—and, indeed, they do combine in a dative plural clitic, which takes the form illustrated in (60f):

(60) *Làconi*
a. $[_I d \ldots \qquad\qquad [_N u]]$
b. $[_I d \ldots \quad [_I a \qquad [N]]]$
c. $[_I d \ldots \quad [_I u [_Q s [N]]]$
d. $[_I d \ldots \quad [_I a [_Q s [N]]]$
e. $[_I d \ldots [_Q i [I \qquad [N]]]]$
f. $[_I d \ldots [_Q i [I [_Q s [N]]]]$

The lexical properties of the clitics in (60)—in particular, the fact that they correspond to a full noun phrase, including a d nominal head—induce insertion into the N position. This holds also for the di/ dis forms which embed a Q specification, which evidently is not sufficient to induce insertion into Q. Remember that in discussing the Mascioni data in section 4.2, we suggested the tentative generalization that insertion in Q is limited to purely quantificational clitics (hence i of Olivetta, Tavullia, *fi* of Vagli). The high insertion point observed for l dative forms in dialects such as Iacurso and Gavoi coincides with R, but the availability of this latter insertion point for l clitics is independently parametrized (accounting for the position of the whole accusative series of Olivetta, among other things). Given the single insertion point N for the whole series in (60), as indicated in (60'), the mutual exclusion between accusative and dative can be attributed to the fact that they compete for the same position. Either one can be inserted into N, but if the accusative is inserted, then the dative is excluded, and vice versa.

(60') *Làconi*
du, dus, da, das, di, dis → N

What interests us here directly is that the mutual exclusion between accusative and dative results in the apparent substitution of the dative by the *si* clitic. To understand this phenomenon, we must go back to the fundamental characterization of *si*, in section 1, as a free variable. The categorization of *si* as a Q element straightforwardly predicts the existence of strings where *si* in Q is followed by the accusative inserted in N, as in (59c). Its semantic characterization as a quantificational variable furthermore implies the possibility of the impersonal interpretation—that is, a generic interpretation—as well as of the reflexive interpretation, whereby the reference of *si* is fixed by an antecedent. This interpretation is indeed systematically available in clusters with the accusative; thus a string like (58c) is potentially ambiguous between "he gives it to him" and the reflexive "he gives it to himself." The ambiguity between the reflexive interpretation of *si* and the nonreflexive dative is more evident in contexts such as (61), where both are equally salient:

(61) *Làconi*

    si   ɖɖaz a   ssamu'naðaza

    to.him/to.himself them he.has washed

    'He has washed them (e.g. his own/somebody else's hands)'

The remaining questions are how *si* also yields a distributive (dative) interpretation, and, furthermore, why the reflexive reading remains available in contexts where there is no accusative clitic, while the nonreflexive reading is impossible. That these questions are separate is shown precisely by existence of dialects, alluded to in what precedes, where the *si*-type clitic lexicalizes the third-person dative in all contexts. An example is provided by the dialect of S. Agata del Bianco in (62), discussed in detail by Manzini and Savoia (2002). While (62b)–(62c) show patterns coinciding with those of Làconi, (62a) shows that *si* lexicalizes the third-person dative also in isolation.

(62) *S. Agata del Bianco* (Calabria)

    a. si   'ðunanu 'kistu

        to.him they.give this

    b. s   u 'ðunanu

        to.him it they.give

    c. s   u k'kʰattʰa

        to.him/to.himself it he.buys

Faced with data such as (62a) for S. Agata del Bianco, we are led to propose that the quantificational properties of *si* can equally well receive a distributive reading—hence, conventionally a dative one. We can then go back to the question why this reading is restricted to combinations with the accusative in the Làconi dialect. From the present discussion of datives it emerges that the traditional third-person dative specification corresponds to the combination of two properties: the distributivity property and the property of third-person denotation, which is associated in a language like Làconi with the nominal base ɖ. Now, ɖi combines both properties, while *si* has distributivity, given its Q nature, but does not have definite denotation. Seen from this perspective, the third-person dative reading is available for purely quantificational *si* only in contexts in which third-person denotation, in the form of a ɖ clitic, is independently lexicalized in N. Once again, therefore, we are proposing that the ɖ subconstituent of the clitic inserted into N lexicalizes its referential properties for the whole string; this string lexicalization property ultimately makes it possible for *si* to have the nonreflexive distributor reading. In other contexts it remains perfectly possible to have *si*, but only with its reflexive/impersonal reading, which is different from that of a definite pronoun.

Crucially, if the preceding discussion is on the right track, the phenomena routinely described as substitution of a clitic for another in a cluster are nothing of the sort. Two independent accounts are involved, on the one hand, for the mutual exclusion of two clitics in a string such as accusative and dative and, on the other hand, for the emergence of some other combination such as *si*-accusative and the range of possible interpretations associated with it.

6. Concluding remarks

The approach presented here is profoundly different from the others found in the literature which effectively take the routine description of the phenomenon seriously and introduce therefore some form of comparison between derivations in the grammar to account for the "preference" of one clitic or another according to context. That comparison between derivations (or representations) is involved is particularly evident in the recent optimality treatment of Romance clitics by Grimshaw (1997, 1999). In essence, according to Grimshaw (1997, 1999) lexical insertion takes place on the basis of the need to safisfy the maximum possible amount of constraints defined by the grammar. This means that, in isolation, the closest match to a third-person dative is inserted—that is, in some languages a dedicated form. If for some reason that is unavailable, the grammar provides for the insertion of a severely underspecified element such as *se*, with other positively specified elements necessarily violating more constraints than it does. Essentially the same conceptual schema, based on the implicit or explicit comparison between derivations or representations, is in fact implied by morphological theories that use Elsewhere as the basic lexical insertion principle. This is effectively the main line of generative morphology down to current Distributed Morphology frameworks (Halle and Marantz 1993).

Our account of the relevant phenomena does not make use of the Elsewhere principle, with the allied notions of underspecification or default, and does not compare derivations or representations. It seems to us that to the extent that such notions represent an enrichment of the grammar, our account has an edge over its competitors. As for notions of comparisons of derivations or representations, recall that though they play some role in the earlier minimalist framework of Chomsky (1995) they have been shown not only to be unnecessary but also to effectively derive the wrong results in more recent statements of the theory (Chomsky 1998, 1999) where they are altogether abandoned. We note that the notions of Elsewhere, and the attending concepts of underspecification and default, have been discounted in the very phonological domain in which they have first arisen (cf. the government phonology literature, e.g., John Harris 1994).

The empirical discussion in sections 2–5 proves the thesis laid out in section 1, that clitic systems of the type found in Italian dialects, characterized both by internal complexity and by subtle parametrization, can be described by a minimalist syntax, which has no resort to comparisons between possible derivations or representations—or, indeed, to the choice between alternative lexical insertion patterns. This result is interesting in that current literature almost without exception assumes that accounting for phenomena such as Romance cliticization involves having recourse to specialized morphological components, mechanisms of underspecification and default, not to mention optimality schemas. Nevertheless, the theoretical proposals that we have advanced raise interesting questions of their own. We conclude our discussion by considering some of them.

We have so far adopted without any discussion the idea that clitics are ordered in rigid hierarchies; the hierarchy we proposed and used throughout specifically takes the form in (9). But whether hierarchies, of the present type or of the type discussed by Rizzi (1997) and Cinque (1999) among others, exist at all as part of the computational component is still an open question. The conceptual problem most often debated with respect to such hierarchies is that they seem to subsume under phrase structure a number of properties that ought to be dealt with (and could only adequately be dealt with) at the interpretive interface of LF.

Recent theoretical reconstructions of the minimalist framework (Freidin and Vergnaud 2000; Starke 2000) explicitly integrate functional hierarchies into the computational component. They assume that Merge is an operation of set-theoretical union, whose order of application defines an intrinsic order among constituents; the latter is constrained by hierarchies (constellations for Freidin and Vergnaud 2000; f-sequences for Starke 2000), which account for observed phrase structure configurations as opposed to nonexisting ones. A different approach is pursued by Manzini (1995, 1997, 1998) who explicitly proposes that the phrase structure building rule is constrained by an Interpretation Principle. The Interpretation Principle rules out any elementary constituent formed by the grammar that cannot be assigned an interpretation.

It is reasonable to think that relatively simple hierarchies, which are furthermore constant across categorial domains, can be derived on independent grounds. Now the clitic hierarchy provided in (9) is precisely of this type. In particular, we have emphasized the parallelism between the inflectional clitic hierarchy and the functional hierarchies within the DP; in essence, D–Q–N represents both the basic order of clitics in the sentence (nominative–dative–accusative) and the basic progression of categories in the noun phrase (definite determiner–numeral quantifier–noun). At the same time it is not difficult to find interpretive reasons for the order observed. Thus the ordering of Q and D with respect to N is motivated by their quantificational/ denotational nature, binding a variable in the argument structure of N (as originally proposed by Higginbotham 1985). The relative order of D with respect to Q is simply that of definite or strong quantifiers with respect to weak or existential ones, with which they can combine.

Notes

The research reported in this chapter has been financed partially through the Programma di Ricerca Cofinanziato of the MIUR "Categorie linguistiche: dalla mappatura strutturale all'architettura delle rappresentazioni mentali" for the years 2001–2003. The article is a result of the collaboration of the two authors in all respects. Nevertheless, for administrative purposes, Rita Manzini takes responsibility for sections 1, 3, and 5, and Leonardo Savoia for sections 2 and 4. The data relative to Vagli, Olivetta, and Làconi are also discussed by Manzini and Savoia (2002), though the emphasis of that article is entirely different from the present one since it is concerned with an exhaustive characterization of the possible lexicalizations of the dative.

References

Abney, S. (1986) "The English Noun Phrase in Its Sentential Aspect," Ph.D. diss., MIT.
Beghelli, F. (1997) "The Syntax of Distributivity and Pair-list Readings," in A. Szabolcsi (ed.) *Ways of Scope Taking.* Dordrecht: Kluwer, 349–408.
Beghelli, F., and T. Stowell (1997) "Distributivity and Negation: The Syntax of *each* and *every*," in A. Szabolcsi (ed.) *Ways of Scope Taking.* Dordrecht: Kluwer, 71–107.
Beninca', P. (1994) *La variazione sintattica.* Bologna: Il Mulino.

Bernstein, J. (1997) "Demonstratives and Reinforcers in Germanic and Romance Languages" *Lingua* 102, 87–113.

Bonet, E. (1995) "Feature Structure of Romance Clitics." *Natural Language and Linguistic Theory* 13, 607–647.

Borer, H. (1994) "The Projection of Arguments," in E. Benedicto and J. Runner (eds.) *Functional Projections*. Occasional Papers 17, Amherst: University of Massachusetts, 19–47.

Brody, M. (1997) "Towards Perfect Chains," in L. Haegeman (ed.) *Handbook of Syntax*. Dordrecht: Kluwer, 139–168.

Brugè, L. (1996) "Demonstrative Movement in Spanish: A Comparative Approach." *University of Venice Working Papers in Linguistics* 6.1, 1–53.

Cardinaletti, A., and M. Starke (1999) "The Typology of Structural Deficiency: A Case Study of Three Classes of Pronouns," in H. van Riemsdijk (ed.) *Clitics in the Languages of Europe*. Berlin: Mouton de Gruyter, 145–233.

Chomsky, N. (1995) *The Minimalist Program*. Cambridge, Mass.: MIT Press.

———— (1998) "Minimalist Inquiries: The Framework." Unpublished ms., MIT, Cambridge, Mass.

———— (1999) "Derivation by Phases." Unpublished ms., MIT, Cambridge, Mass.

Cinque, G. (1999) *Adverbs and Functional Heads: A Cross-Linguistic Perspective*. New York: Oxford University Press.

Cocchi, G. (2000) "Free Clitics and Bound Affixes," in B. Gerlach and J. Grijzenhout (eds.) *Clitics in Phonology, Morphology, and Syntax*. Amsterdam: John Benjamins, 85–119.

Di Domenico, E. (1998) *Per una teoria del genere grammaticale*. Padua: UniPress.

Enç, M. (1987) "Anchoring Conditions for Tense." *Linguistic Inquiry* 18, 633–657.

Fici, F., M. R. Manzini, and L. M. Savoia (1999) "Clitics in Macedonian." *Quaderni del Dipartimento di Linguistica dell'Università di Firenze* 9, 13–30.

Freidin, R., and J.-R. Vergnaud (2000) "A Presentation of Minimalism." Unpublished ms., University of Southern California and Princeton University.

Giorgi, A., and F. Pianesi (1998) *Tense and Aspect: From Semantics to Morphosyntax*. New York: Oxford University Press.

Grimshaw, J. (1997) "The Best Clitic: Constraint Conflict in Morphosyntax," in L. Haegeman (ed.) *Elements of Grammar*. Dordrecht: Kluwer, 169–196.

———— (1999) "Optimal Clitic Positions and the Lexicon in Romance Clitic Systems." Unpublished ms., Rutgers University

Hale, K., and S. J. Keyser (1993) "On Argument Structure and the Lexical Expression of Syntactic Relations," in K. Hale and S. J. Keyser (eds.) *The View from Building 20*. Cambridge, Mass.: MIT Press, 53–110.

Halle, M., and A. Marantz (1993) "Distributed Morphology and the Pieces of Inflection," in K. Hale and S. J. Keyser (eds.) *The View from Building 20*. Cambridge, Mass.: MIT Press, 111–176.

———— (1994) "Some Key Features of Distributed Morphology," in A. Carnie, H. Harley, and T. Bures (eds.) *Papers on Phonology and Morphology*. Working Papers in Linguistics, no. 21. Cambridge, Mass.: MIT, 275–288.

Harris, James (1994) "The Syntax-Phonology Mapping in Catalan and Spanish Clitics," in A. Carnie, H. Harley, and T. Bures (eds.) *Papers on Phonology and Morphology*. Working Papers in Linguistics no. 21. Cambridge, Mass.: MIT.

Harris, John (1994) *English Sound Structure*. Oxford: Blackwell.

Higginbotham, J. (1985) "On Semantics." *Linguistic Inquiry* 16, 547–593.

Kayne, R. (1975) *French Syntax: The Transformational Cycle*. Cambridge, Mass.: MIT Press.

———— (1989) "Null Subjects and Clitic Climbing," in O. Jaeggli and K. Safir (eds.) *The Null Subject Parameter*. Dordrecht: Kluwer, 239–262.

———— (1991) "Romance Clitics, Verb Movement and PRO." *Linguistic Inquiry* 22, 647–686.

———— (1994) *The Antisymmetry of Syntax.* Cambridge, Mass.: MIT Press.

———— (2000) *Parameters and Universals.* New York: Oxford University Press.

Longobardi, G. (1994) "Reference and Proper Names: A Theory of N-Movement in Syntax and Logical Form." *Linguistic Inquiry* 25, 609–665.

Manzini, M. R. (1986) "On Italian *si*," in H. Borer (ed.) *The Syntax of Pronominal Clitics.* Syntax and Semantics, no. 18. New York: Academic Press, 241–262.

———— (1995) "From Merge and Move to Form Dependency." *UCL Working Papers in Linguistics* 7, 323–345.

———— (1997) "Adjuncts and the Theory of Phrase Structure," in D. Berrman, D. Leblanc, and H. van Riemsdijk (eds.) *Rightward Movement.* Amsterdam: John Benjamins,   –   .

———— (1998) "Dependencies, Phrase Structure and Extractions," in D. Adger et al. (eds.) *Specifiers.* Oxford: Clarendon Press, 188–205.

Manzini, M. R., and L. M. Savoia (1998) "Clitics and Auxiliary Choice in Italian Dialects: Their Relevance for the Person Ergativity Split." *Recherches Linguistiques de Vincennes* 27, 115–128.

———— (1999) The syntax of middle-reflexive and object clitics: a case of parametrization in arbëresh dialects. In *Studi in onore di Luigi Marlekaj*, ed. M. Mandalà. Bari: Adriatica, 283–328.

———— (2001a) "The Syntax of Object Clitics: *si* in Italian Dialects," in Guglielmo Cinque and Giampaolo Salvi (eds.) *Current Studies in Italian Syntax: Essays to Honour Lorenzo Renzi.* Amsterdam: North Holland, 234–269.

———— (2001b) "Parameters of Subject Inflection," in P. Svenonius (ed.) *Subjects, Expletives and the EPP.* Oxford: Oxford University Press.

———— (2002) "Clitics: Lexicalization Patterns of the So-called Third Person Dative." *Catalan Journal of Linguistics* 1, 117–155.

———— (Forthcoming) *I dialetti italiani: morfosintassi.* Bologna: Il Mulino.

May, R. (1985) *Logical Form.* Cambridge, Mass.: MIT Press.

Ouhalla, J. (1991) *Functional Categories and Parametric Variation.* London: Routledge.

Perlmutter, D. (1972) *Deep and Surface Constraints in Syntax.* New York: Holt, Rinehart and Winston.

Poletto C. (2000) *The Higher Functional Field.* New York: Oxford University Press.

Pollock, J.-Y. (1996) *Language et cognition: introduction au programme minimaliste de la grammaire generative.* Paris: Presses Universitaires de France.

Reinhart, T. (1983) *Anaphora and Semantic Interpretation.* London: Croom Helm.

Rizzi L. (1997) "The Fine Structure of the Left Periphery," in L. Haegeman (ed.) *Elements of Grammar.* Dordrecht: Kluwer, 281–337.

Sportiche, D. (1996) "Clitic Constructions," in J. Rooryck and L. Zaring (eds.) *Phrase Structure and the Lexicon.* Dordrecht: Kluwer, 213–276.

Starke, M. (2000) "Move Dissolves into Merge: A Theory of Locality," Ph.D. diss., University of Geneva.

Szabolcsi, A. (1994) "The Noun Phrase," in K. Kiss and F. Kiefer (eds.) *The Syntactic Structure of Hungarian.* Syntax and Semantics 27. New York: Academic Press, 179–274.

Taraldsen, T. (1978) "On the NIC, Vacuous Application, and the that-t Filter." Unpublished ms., MIT, Cambridge, Mass.

Tenny, C. (1994) *Aspectual Roles and the Syntax-Semantics Interface.* Dordrecht: Kluwer.

9

On the Left Periphery of Some Romance Wh-Questions

CECILIA POLETTO

AND JEAN-YVES POLLOCK

This chapter sketches out the fine structure of the left periphery of questions as it emerges from our ongoing research on French, Bellunese, and Italian wh-questions (see Pollock et al. 1999; Poletto and Pollock 1999, 2000; Pollock 2000).

The two basic principles that have guided our inquiry are simply stated. The first is standard in comparative work in generative grammar; it claims that the considerable variation in spell-out sequences exhibited by the wh-configurations across (those three) languages is not random; rather, it can be profitably (re)analyzed as reflecting the interplay of the invariant structure of the complementizer domain (in Romance) and a small number of morphologically based differences that are part of the primary linguistic data to which the language learners are necessarily exposed. The second principle is more controversial; it claims, in line with Kayne's (1998) "radical" interpretation of Chomsky's (1995, 1998) minimalist guidelines, that UG does not allow for any *covert* syntactic displacement, be it phrasal or feature movement.

When that radical tack is taken, Remnant Movement operations are put to crucial use and replace not only much covert movement but also (many) head movement analyses in the Government and Binding tradition; postulating such Remnant Movement operations leads, we shall see, to illuminating comparative analyses of the syntax of wh-questions in the three languages under study; furthermore the remnant phrases that move to the left periphery of questions will be shown to be attracted to semantically motivated layers in the fixed hierarchy of categories that make up the "split" complementizer area—cf. Rizzi (1997)—of questions in the Romance languages.

1. Bellunese versus French (first pass)

As is well known, French has a variety of apparent (see Pollock et al. 1999),[1] wh–in situ questions like (1a, b, and c); bare *que*, on the other hand, cannot occur in such contexts, as the sharp ungrammaticality of (1d) shows:

(1)   a. Tu vas où?
         you go where
         'Where are you going?'
      b. Tu as parlé à qui?
         you've spoken to whom
         'To whom did you speak?'
      c. Tu pars quand?
         you leave when
         'When are you leaving?'
      d. *Jean a acheté que?
         Jean has bought what
         'What did Jean buy?'

In that respect Bellunese behaves quite unexpectedly: *che*, the counterpart of *que*, and the other bare wh-words—*andé* 'where', *chi* 'who', and *come* 'how'—*must* occur in sentence-final position (cf. Munaro 1999):

(2)   a. Ha-tu magnà che?
         have you eaten what
         'What did you eat?'
      b. *Che ha-tu magnà?
         what have you eaten
      c. Se-tu 'ndat andé?
         are you gone where
         'Where did you go?'
      d. *Andé se-tu 'ndat?
         where are you gone

Sentences like (2) in Bellunese must be carefully distinguished from (1) since they show obligatory subject verb inversion, which (apparent) wh–in situ in French bans totally:

(3) *Vas-tu où?
      go you where
      'Where are you going?'

Modulo that important difference—to which we return at length in sections 6 and 7—the distribution of *che* and *que* with respect to "sentence internal/final" positions is extremely puzzling; if one took Bellunese *che* to be in a position within IP, one would be hard put to explain why its French counterpart *que*, which does not appear to be any more or less "defective" morphologically or semantically than *che*,[2] has to move to the left periphery; in short, the morphological similarity of *que* and *che* should lead one to expect similar syntactic behavior that reasonable expectation pairs like (1d) versus (2a) seem to falsify, unexpectedly.

As Pollock et al. (1999) showed, appearences are (fortunately) deceptive; one can begin to reconcile Bellunese and French wh-syntax by positing that *che* in (2a) and *andé* in (2c) have indeed moved to the left periphery of the clause, just as French *que* visibly has in sentences like (4):

(4) a. Qu'a acheté Jean?
         what has bought Jean
         'What did Jean buy?'
     b. Qu'a-t-il acheté?
         what has-t-he bought
         'What did he buy?'

In a theory that does not countenance covert (feature) movement, this conclusion is independently required by the fact noted and analyzed in Munaro (1999) that (apparent) wh–in situ configurations like (2a and c) and (5) in Bellunese are sensitive to strong and weak island effects, as (6) from Munaro (1999: chap. 1, 50–56, 74) shows:

(5) a. Ha-tu parecià che?
         have you prepared what
         'What did you prepare?'
     b. Va-lo 'ndé?
         goes he where
         'Where is he going?'
     c. Se ciame-lo comé?
         himself call-he how
         'What's his name?'

(6) Strong island effects:
     a. *Te ha-li dit che i clienti de chi no i-ha pagà?
        to you have they told that the customers of whom not they have paid
        'Who have they told you the customers of haven't paid?'
     b. *Ho-e da telefonarte prima de 'ndar andé?
        have I to phone you before of going where
        'Where have I to phone you before going?'

     Weak island effects:
     c. ??Te despiàse-lo de aver desmentegà ché?
        to you displeases-it to have forgotten what
        'What are you sorry you have forgottten?'

That Bellunese *che* in (5a) is *not* in its IP internal argument position is also suggested by the following data:

(7) a. Al ghe ha dat al libro a so fradel.
         he to him has given the book to his brother
         'He gave the book to his brother.'
     b. *Ghe halo dat che a so fradel?
         to him has he given what to his brother
         'What did he give to his brother?'
     c. Ghe halo dat che, a so fradel?
         to him has he given what to this brother

Example (7) shows that the dative complement *a so fradel* is necessarily "emarginated" in Bellunese *che, ande, come,* and *chi* questions like (7b and c), though not in statements like (7a). If *che* were in the ordinary sentence internal-object position in which *el libro* in (7a) is presumably standing, such facts would be difficult to understand; (7) thus gives added support to an *overt* movement analysis of all wh-questions in Bellunese.

Accepting the (desirable) conclusion that *che, ande, come,* and *chi* in (5) have indeed moved to the CP field, we are evidently forced to adopt the idea that the rest of the clause has itself moved past the "low" Comp position in which the bare wh-words are standing to a higher layer of the left periphery; such sentences therefore involve wh-movement of the expected variety and Remnant Movement of (some layer(s) of) IP; this conclusion goes in the direction of much recent work in Generative Grammar—for example, Koopman and Szabolczi (2000), Kayne and Pollock (2001), Pollock et al. (1999), and Pollock (2000). The much simplified derivation of a sentence like (5) in Bellunese must thus look something like (8):

(8)   Input: [IP tu ha parecià che]
   a. Wh-movement → [$_{XP}$ che $_i$ X° [$_{IP}$ tu ha parecia t$_i$]]
   b. Remnant IP Movement → [$_{YP}$ [$_{IP}$ ha-tu parecia t$_i$]$_j$ Y [$_{XP}$ che $_i$ X° t$_j$]]

Step (8b) is clearly lumping together computations that must be teased apart and analyzed. That we proceed to do now.

2.   SCLI in French and Bellunese

If the preceding discussion is correct, Bellunese seems to allow one type of Remnant Movement to the left periphery that French does not; compare (9) versus (10) again:

(9)   Se-tu 'ndat andé?
   are you gone where
   'Where did you go?'

(10)   *Es-tu allé où?
   are you gone where

We believe that appearances are again deceptive; putting aside for the moment the low position of *andé* in (9) versus the high position of *où* in (10)—to which we return in section 7—(9) displays the subject/verb inversion pattern known as "subject clitic inversion" (SCLI) that is common to many Romance languages; the null hypothesis then, is that such sequences should be analyzed like their French counterparts in (11):[3]

(11)   Où est-il allé?
   where is he gone
   'Where did he go?'

This is strongly suggested by the fact that both SCLI in French and (apparent) wh–in situ sentences like (9) in Bellunese are restricted to root contexts:

(12)   a. *Je ne sais pas (ce) qu'a-t-il acheté.
   I don't know what has he bought[4]
   'I do not know what he bought.'

b. *Je ne sais pas où est-il allé.
   I don't know where went-he
   'I do not know where he went.'

(13) a. *No so (che) ha-lo comprà che.
         neg I know that has-he bought what
         'I do not know what he bought.'
      b. *No so (che) se-tu 'ndat andé.
         neg I know that are you gone where
         'I do not know where he went.'

(14) a. No so *che* che l'ha comprà.
         neg I know what that he has brought
         'I do not know what he bought.'
      b. No so andé che te se ndat.
         neg I know where that you are gone
         'I do not know where he went.'

It thus seems highly desirable, perhaps mandatory, to suppose that the same computations to the left periphery, all restricted to root contexts, are at work in (9) and (11) in the two languages.

We adopt this view and now show, first, that SCLI in Bellunese and French is the reflex of *overt* (pre-spell-out) computations[5] and, second, that SCLI cannot be analyzed in terms of head movement, as the surface form it has in Bellunese would in itself suggest.

3. SCLI is overt movement

SCLI is a widespread phenomenon in the Northern Italian Dialects (henceforth NIDs), as discussed extensively by Poletto (2000: chap. 1, section 3.2); (15) gives examples from two varieties:

(15) a. Cossa fa-lo?   (Paduan)
         what does-he
         'What does he do?'
      b. Ce fas-tu?   (Friulian)
         what do-you
         'What are you doing?'

In Monnese, SCLI obligatorily triggers "fà-support" (see Beninca' and Poletto 1997) in contexts in which English triggers "do-support":

(16) a. Ngo fa-l ndà?
         where does-he go
         'Where is he going?'
      b. Ngo fè-t ndà?
         where do you-SING. go
         'Where are you going?'
      c. Ngo fè-f ndà?
         where do you-PL. go
         'Where are you going?'

English do-support and Monnese fa-support are strikingly similar in that they occur only in root contexts when no auxiliary or modal verbs are present, and both are banned when the subject is questioned (Beninca' and Poletto 1997). Fa-support, unlike do-support, does not occur in negative clauses, but that difference can be shown to be a consequence of an orthogonal difference between English and Romance: in Monnese, in particular, and Romance, in general, main verbs cross over the negation position (which is, in fact, defined by Zanuttini 1997 as postverbal) while Modern English main verbs do not (Pollock 1989).

As should be clear even from this cursory summary, fa-support and do-support cry out for a uniform analysis. Beninca' and Poletto (1997) provide one and show that fa-support is indeed to be analyzed in the same terms as English do-support. Despite the fact that there have been many different views on do-support in the literature over the last fifty years or so, no one to our knowledge has ever suggested that it should be analyzed as an instance of covert LF movement. If so, the shape SCLI takes in Monnese is an instance of *overt* movement to the Comp domain; it is therefore highly desirable to also view SCLI in the more usual varieties of Romance as a case of pre-spell-out movement to the left periphery.

The NIDs provide at least two other arguments in favor of overt movement in SCLI. First, in the dialect of Rodoretto di Prali, it is possible to coordinate SCLI constructions and wh-structures with an overt complementizer, as in (17) (Poletto 2000: chap. 3 (21)):

(17)   L'achatte-tu ou qu' tu l'achatte pa?
       it buy-you or that you it buy not
       'Are you going to buy it or not?'

On the well-supported assumption that coordination is always coordination of two identical phrases, *l'acheta-tu* must have activated the Comp field whose presence in the second conjunct is overtly signaled by *qu-*; therefore, SCLI in Rodoretto di Pralese must involve overt computation to the CP field.

Second, Fassano—the dialects spoken in the Fassa valley—SCLI is only possible when the verb has crossed the position of a "new information" particle that has been shown to be a CP particle (Poletto and Zanuttini 2000; Poletto 2000: 46–49):

(18)   a. Olà vas-t pa?
          where go you PARTICLE
          'Where are you going?'
       b. Olà pa tu vas?
          where PARTICLE you go
       c. *Olà pa vas-t?
          where PARTICLE go you
       d. *Olà tu vas pa?
          where you go PARTICLE

In (18a) SCLI has taken place, and both the verb *vas* and the subject clitc -*t* precede the Comp particle *pa*; in (18b) SCLI inversion has not taken place—as is possible in many varieties, including colloquial French (cf. *Où tu vas? = where you go*)–and *pa* precedes the subject clitic and the verb; (18c) shows that *pa* cannot precede the verb and the clitic when SCLI has taken place, and (18d) shows that the particle cannot follow them when it has not. Evidently, (18) can be explained neatly if SCLI is a computation that *overtly* displaces the verb and the subject clitic to the Comp field—more precisely, to a position higher than *pa*.[6]

4. SCLI is not head movement

Since French SCLI constructions share crucial properties with their counterparts in the NIDs, we conclude, fairly reasonably, that they also involve overt computations to the CP field. At the same time, SCLI can be shown *not* to be amenable to a I°/V° head movement analysis; this somewhat paradoxical conclusion follows from Kayne's (1994) and Sportiche's (1993) analyses of the various types of non-nominative clitics as heading a number of functional projections distinct from the verb's; under such analyses, SCLI questions as, for example, *te l'as-t-il donné?* 'to you it has he given', clearly cannot arise as a consequence of I°/V° movement. The same extends to the equivalent clitic-verb sequences in the NIDs.

As Kayne (1991) argues, the view that non-nominative clitics need not be analyzed as adjoined to V is almost certainly imposed on one by examples like (19a) in literary French; in (19b, c, and d)—from Madame de Sévigné's *Lettres*—in classical French; and in (19e and f) in Modern Triestino and Calabrian in which the clitics are separated from the verb by various (maximal) adverbial phrases:

(19) a. Il a dû en fort bien parler.
       he must have of it very well spoken
       'He must have spoken very well of it.'

   b. Elle dit qu'elle lui doit tout son bonheur, par le soin qu'elle a eu de la bien élever
      she says she owes her her happiness because of the care she has had to her well bring up
      'She says she owes her her happiness because she brought her up so well.'

   c. . . . ils ont été affligés de ne vous point voir.
      they were sorry to *ne* you not see
      'They were sorry not to have seen you.'

   d. Nous faisons une vie si réglée qu'il n'est quasi pas possible de se mal porter.
      we lead one life so orderly that it is almost impossible to *se* ill bear
      'We lead such an orderly life that it is almost impossible to be in poor health.'

   e. Nol se gnanca vedi. (Modern Triestino)
      not-it REFL not-even see
      'You cannot even see it.'

   f. El me sempre disi...
      he to-me always says
      'He always says to me . . .'

   g. Un ti manco canusciu. (Modern Calabrian)
      not you at all know
      'I do not know you at all.'

   h. Ci propiu volia.
      LOC-cl really want
      'It was really necessary.'

Such examples show beyond any doubt that French, Triestino, and Calabrian clitics need not and have not always adjoin(ed) to the verb. Now, if the clitics in (20) also head a projection different from that of the verb—the null hypothesis—we clearly cannot analyze the *overt* (recall section 3) computation(s) to the left periphery at work in (21) as instances of $I°/V°$ movement:

(20) a. Pierre me l'a donné.
        Pierre to me it has given
        'Pierre gave it to me.'
      b. Pierre ne lui a pas parlé.
        Pierre *ne* to him has not spoken
        'Pierre did not speak to him.'
      c. Il ne m'en donnera pas.
        he *ne* to me of it will-give not
        'He will not give it to me.'
      d. Elle m'y conduira.
        she me there will-take
        'She will take me there.'

(21) a. Pierre me l'a-t-il donné?
        Pierre to me it has-he given
        'Did Pierre give it to me?'
      b. Pierre ne lui a-t-il pas parlé?
        Pierre *ne* to him hashe not spoken
        'Didn't Pierre speak to him?'
      c. Ne m'en donnera-t-il pas?
        ne to me of it will-he give not
        'Won't he give it to me?'
      d. M'y conduira-t-elle?
        me there will-she take
        'Will she take me there?'

Additional arguments against the traditional $I°/V°$ head movement analysis of (21) have been given in the literature. For example, Kayne (1994) notes that claiming that clitics adjoin to the verb leaves us without an account for the fact that referential expressions are typically banned from appearing within words: compare OK *a self hater* with **a(n)* {*it, her, you*} *hater*. Hulk (1993: 3.3), Kayne (1994: 45), and Terzi (1999: section 2) note that on the standard assumption that in Romance imperatives the verb *does* move to some "high" (see Terzi 1999) head position in the CP field, the fact that in (22a) the clitics are obligatorily stranded by the verb is in itself an argument that no verb movement has applied in SCLI sentences like (22c):

(22) a. Donne le lui!
        give it to him
        'Give it to him!'
      b.*Le lui donne!
        it to him give
      c. Le lui donnera-t-il?
        it to him will-give you
        'Will he give it to her?'

Hulk (1993)—and also Terzi (1999)—observes further that the negative head *ne* blocks head movement in imperatives, as (23) shows:

(23) a. *Ne donne le lui pas.
          ne give it to him not
      b. Ne le lui donne pas.
          ne it to him give not
          'Don't give it to him.'

She points out that if head movement was involved in (22b and c), one would expect, everything else being equal, perfectly fine SCLI sentences like (24) to be ungrammatical:

(24) Ne le lui donnera-t-il pas?
      ne it to him will-give you not
      'Won't he give it to him?'

We conclude, then, like Hulk (1993), Kayne (1994), and Sportiche (1993), that SCLI does *not* involve Infl°/Verb° movement to some head position in the CP field. But our section 3 arguments prevent us from concluding that SCLI results from *covert*, post-spell-out computations, as these scholars claimed.

5. SCLI is Remnant Phrasal Movement

To solve this apparent paradox we need only conclude that SCLI is derived via overt *phrasal* movement to the Comp domain. *Le lui donnera-t-il?* can now be derived, as it must, if the string 'le+lui+donnera' is a constituent and moves as one to the left periphery. However, XP in (25), and object clitic + finite verb strings in general are typically *not* constituents.

(25) $[_{XP}$ le $[_{YP}$ lui $[_{ZP}$ donnera . . .]]]

They are not in (26) for example:

(26) a. Il ne le lui donnera pas.
          he NEG it to-him will-give not
          'He will not give it to him.'
      b. Il ne m'a pas parlé.
          he NEG to-me has not spoken
          'He did not speak to me.'
      c. Je n'y suis pas allé.
          I NEG there am not gone
          'I did not go there.'

It appears, then, that a phrasal movement analysis of SCLI—forced on us by the facts and arguments in section 4—entails that XP in (25) and the like can only move as a constituent because the elements included in the ellipses have vacated their input position at some earlier stage in the derivation; in short, any overt phrasal movement analysis of SCLI in French has to be a *Remnant* Movement analysis, as the spell-out string of Bellunese wh-questions like (9)—*Se-tu 'ndat andé?* 'are you gone where'—would in itself suggest. The derivations that have to be posited to yield the French sentences in (27), thus involve previous displacement of the negative phrase *pas* in (27a), of the infinitival clause *lui prêter un livre* in (27b), and of the participial phrase *envoyé un livre à Paul* in (27c) followed by Remnant Movement, as sketched in the much simplified derivations of (28):

(27)   a. Ne le lui donnera-t-il pas?
           neg it to-him will-give him not
           'Won't he give it to him?'
       b. Va-t-elle lui prêter un livre?
           will she to-him lend a book
           'Will she lend him the book?'
       c. Avez-vous envoyé un livre à Paul?
           have you sent a book to Paul
           'Did you send a book to P.?'

(28)   a. Il ne le lui donera$_i$ [pas [t$_i$]] → Il [pas [t$_i$]]$_j$ [ne le lui donera t$_j$] → [ne le lui donera t$_j$]$_k$ il [pas [t$_i$]$_j$ t$_k$]
       b. Elle [va [lui prêter un livre]] → Elle [lui prêter un livre]$_i$ [va t$_i$] → [va t$_i$]$_j$ elle [lui prêter un livre] t$_j$
       c. Vous [avez [envoyé un livre à Paul]] → Vous [envoyé un livre à Paul]$_i$ [avez t$_i$] → [avez t$_i$]$_j$ vous [envoyé un livre à Paul]$_i$ t$_j$

6.   Characterizing SCLI: French and Bellunese (second pass)

Let us try to be more precise about derivations like (28) and the various layers of the left periphery that we need if we are to give formal status to the conclusions we have just reached.

The first point to make is that our "split" Comp domain will have to contain (at least) two different positions for the (various types of) wh-phrases; this follows from our discussion of Bellunese versus French pairs like (29):

(29)   a. Se-tu 'ndat andé?
           are you gone where
           'Where have you gone?'
       b. Où est-il allé?
           where is-he gone

If, as concluded in the preceding section, both sentences involve Remnant Movement of *se-tu 'ndat* and *est-il allé* to some (ideally) identical layer(s) of the left periphery, then the chief difference between Bellunese and French will have to lie in the fact that *andé* in (29a) is standing low in the structure while *où* has crossed over the position(s) to which *est-il allé* has been attracted on its way to a higher layer of the Comp area.

That there should be (at least) two such positions is overtly manifested in various NIDs; in Bellunese, in particular, in addition to (30) and the like, one can also have "doubling structures" like (31), under semantic conditions described precisely in Munaro and Obenauer (1999):

(30)   Ha-lo fat che?
       has he done what
       'What did he do?'

(31)   Cossa ha-lo fat che?
       what has he done what

Similarly, Monnese "doubling" wh-questions like (32) alternate with non-doubling ones like (33):[7]

(32)   Ch'et fat què?
       what have you done what
       'What have you done?'

(33)   Ch'et fat?
       what have-you done

Bellunese (31) and Monnese (33) thus display at spell-out the two wh-positions that we shall posit are part of the left periphery of the wh-questions of *all* the Romance languages under study; more precisely, we say that (30) is an invisible instance of doubling with a null version of *cossa*, which we call "Rest(rictor)," standing in the uppermost layer of the Comp field:

(34)   Rest ha-lo fat che?
       what has he done what
       'What has he done?'

We say furthermore that in Bellunese null "Rest" is a nonlexical NP in a complex wh-phrase that has the structure in (35), parallel to that of standard Italian *che cosa*:

(35)   [che {cossa, Rest.}]

The two wh-positions in the Comp area overtly manifested in (30), (32), and (34), we shall call Op1 and Op2, respectively.

In addition to those two positions, it can be argued that SCLI crucially involves (the more traditional) "ForceP"; this is because, as emphasized in the preceding discussion, SCLI is restricted to root contexts. On the usual view that in embedded contexts the feature checking done via (Remnant IP) movement to ForceP in root sentences is unnecessary—hence, impossible by economy—because the matrix verb or predicate suffices to identify the sentence type (its "force"), the nonexistence of SCLI in embedded contexts follows if it targets Spec Force°. We thus conclude that in *Où est-il allé?* and *À qui parles-tu?* the remnant phrase, including the finite verb, is indeed attracted by the [+question] feature of (root) Force°.

French SCLI questions like *Où est-il allé?* are evidence that the Remnant phrase checking the [+question] feature has had all its lower portion removed, as indicated in (28). As for that lower portion itself, we claim that it moves to yet another layer of the Comp domain and that the nominative subject clitic does, too, to yet another one. To make things slightly more perspicuous, we give those two extra layers the somewhat arbitrary, though fairly transparent, labels "TopP" and "GroundP," respectively.

Adding up and ordering the five layers we have now introduced, we obtain the full(er) structure in (36):

(36)   [$_{Op2P}$ Op2° [$_{ForceP}$ Force°] [$_{GroundP}$ G° [$_{TopP}$ Top°[$_{Op1P}$ Op1° IP]]]]

We shall come back to the independent syntactic justification for TopP and GroundP in the next section; and we will discuss the semantics associated with each of the five layers in (36) as we proceed and come back to them in the concluding section of this chapter.

To illustrate how the system works in French, consider the derivation of *Où est-il allé?* 'Where is he gone?'; it would go as follows:

(37) Input: [il est allé où]

    a. Merge Op1° and IP and attract 'où' to spec Op1P $\rightarrow$ [$_{Op1P}$ où$_i$ Op1° [il est allé t$_i$]]

    b. Merge TopP and Op1P and attract the participial phrase[8] [allé t$_i$] to spec Top $\rightarrow$ [$_{TopP}$ [allé t$_i$]$_j$ Top° [$_{Op1P}$ où$_i$ Op1° [il est t$_j$]]]

    c. Merge G° and TopP and attract 'il'[9] to spec G $\rightarrow$ [$_{GP}$ il$_k$ G° [$_{TopP}$ [allé t$_i$]$_j$ Top° [$_{Op1P}$ où$_i$ Op1° [t$_k$ est t$_j$]]]]

    d. Merge Force and GP and attract IP to spec Force° $\rightarrow$ [$_{ForceP}$ [t$_k$ est t$_j$]$_l$ F° [$_{GP}$ il k G° [$_{TopP}$ [allé t$_i$]$_j$ Top° [$_{Op1P}$ où$_i$ Op1° t$_l$]]]]

    e. Merge Op2P and ForceP and attract 'où' to Spec Op2° $\rightarrow$ [$_{Op2P}$ où$_i$ Op2° [$_{ForceP}$ [t$_k$ est t$_j$]$_l$ F° [$_{GP}$ il$_k$ G° [$_{TopP}$ [allé t$_i$]$_j$ Top° [$_{Op1P}$ t$_i$ Op1° t$_l$]]]]]

A major property of (37) is that it has no head movement at all; as noted, we analyze the root versus nonroot asymmetry of SCLI (which in much current work is taken to be a reflex of (I° to C°) head movement) as a consequence of the fact that the [+question] feature of Force° is checked "lexically" by the main predicate in embedded contexts. The main sentence predicate "types" the subordinate interrogative clause.

Going back to Bellunese, we can advantageously say that the derivation of apparent wh–in situ SCLI sentences like (29)—*Se-tu 'ndat andé?*—is identical to that shown in (37), with one essential difference and one minor one. The essential difference lies in the fact that Bellunese, unlike French, has "doubling wh-phrases," such as [andé Rest] and [che Rest], parallel to [che cos(s)a];[10] we say that in Bellunese Spec Op2P attracts the null Rest., just as *cosa* is so attracted in Standard Italian or as Bellunese *cossa* is in doubling structures like (38)

(38) Cossa ha-lo fat che?
    what has he done what
    'What has he done?'

In that perspective, then, (29) is derived as shown in (39), which is identical in all relevant respects to the derivation of (38) or of its null Rest. variant *ha-lo fat che?*[11]

(39) Input: [tu sé 'ndat [andé Rest.]]

    (a) Merge Op1° and IP and attract [andé Rest.] to spec Op1P $\rightarrow$ [$_{Op1P}$ [andé Rest.]$_i$ Op1° [tu sé 'ndat t$_i$]]

    (b) Merge TopP and Op1P and attract the participial phrase [ndat t$_i$] to spec Top $\rightarrow$ [$_{TopP}$ [ndat t$_i$]$_j$ Top° [$_{Op1P}$ [andé Rest.]$_i$ Op1° [tu sè t$_j$]]]

    (c) Merge G° and TopP and attract 'tu' to spec G[12] $\rightarrow$ [$_{GP}$ tu$_k$ G° [TopP [ndat t$_i$]$_j$ Top° [$_{Op1P}$ [andé Rest.]$_i$ Op1° [t$_k$ sèt t$_j$]]]]

    (d) Merge Force and GP and attract IP to spec F° $\rightarrow$ [$_{ForceP}$ [t$_k$ sè t$_j$]$_l$ F° [$_{GP}$ tu$_k$ G° [$_{TopP}$ [ndat t$_i$]$_j$ Top° [$_{Op1P}$ [andé Rest]$_i$ Op1° t$_l$]]]]

    (e) Merge Op2P and ForceP and attract Rest. to Spec Op2° $\rightarrow$ [$_{Op2P}$ Rest.$_m$ Op2 [$_{ForceP}$ [t$_k$ sè t$_j$]$_l$ F° [$_{GP}$ tu$_k$ G° [$_{TopP}$ [ndat t$_i$]$_j$ Top° [$_{Op1P}$ [andé t$_m$]$_i$ Op1° t$_l$]]]]]

The "minor" difference has to do with the fact that Bellunese, unlike French, has a special class of nonassertive clitics that differ morphologically and distributionally from assertive clitics across the verbal paradigm. Table 9.1 gives the morphology of the two classes of clitics.

Let us capitalize on the fact that the nonassertive paradigm is morphologically somewhat "heavier" than the assertive one, and let us claim that the former are merged in the specifier of Agrs, while the latter are the spell-outs of Agrs°—that is, "real" clitic heads, as in many other NIDs. We say further that nonassertive clitics are necessarily [+ground] in the lexicon. When the GroundP layer is merged in the left periphery, it will have to attract a [+ground] element; if it fails to, the derivation crashes. This will ultimately require that the numerations yielding (SCLI) questions in Bellunese merge the nonassertive clitics. Even if assertive clitics were also optionally [+ground] in the numeration, they would still fail to be attracted to GroundP on the view that heads *never* move to the Comp field. Conversely, if nonassertive weak pronouns are part of a numeration and the GroundP is not merged in the left periphery, as it presumably is not in (many) noninterrogative sentences, the [+ground] feature of nonassertive clitics will fail to be checked, also causing the derivation to crash, thus banning them in assertive contexts, as Bellunese requires.

(Standard) French, in contrast, has a single set of (weak) nominative pronouns that may optionally bear [+ground]. When GP is merged, some [+ground] element must be attracted to SpecGround to delete an uninterpretable feature. French nominative pronouns will then have to be [+ground] in precisely those cases.[13]

Let us now consider SCLI sentences with D-linked wh-phrases in Bellunese; (40) gives the relevant paradigm:

(40)   a. Quanti libri à-tu ledest?
          how many books have-you read
          'How many books did you read?'
       b. Che vestito à-la comprà?
          what dress has she bought
          'Which dress did she buy?'
       c. Con che tozàt à-tu parlà?
          with what boy have you spoken
          'Which boy did you talk to?'
       d. *Ha-tu ledest quanti libri?
          have-you read how many books
       e. *Ha-la comprà che vestito?
          has she bought what dress

Example (40) does not differ from (41) in French:

(41)   a. Combien de livres as-tu lus?
          how many books have-you read
          'How many books did you read?'

Table 9.1.   Morphology of Assertive and Nonassertive Clitics

	1 pers.	2 pers.	3 pers.	1 plur.	2 plur.	3 plur.
Assertive clitics	/	te	al/la	/	/	i/le
Nonassertive clitics	/	tu	lo/la	e	o	li/le

    b. Quelle robe a-t-elle achetée?
       what dress has she bought
       'Which dress did she buy?'
    c. Avec quel garçon as-tu parlé?
       with what boy have you spoken
       'Which boy did you talk to?'
    d.*As-tu lu combien de livres?
       have-you read how many books
    e.*A-t-elle acheté quelle robe?
       has she bought what dress

The null hypothesis should be that all such sentences are derived in the same way. Granted the invariant left periphery in (36) and the computations it triggers, one can arrive at that desirable conclusion fairly easily: the derivation of the sentences in (40) is identical to (37), *modulo* the lexical choices. That of (40a), for example, goes as follows:

(42)   Input: [tu ha ledest [quanti libri]]
    a. Merge $Op1°$ and IP and attract [quanti libri] to spec Op1P $\rightarrow$ $[_{Op1P}$ [Quanti libri]$_i$ $Op1°$ [tu ha ledest t_i]]
    b. Merge TopP and Op1P and attract the participial phrase [ledest t_i] to spec Top $\rightarrow$ $[_{TopP}$ [ledest t_i]$_j$ Top° $[_{Op1P}$ [quanti libri]$_i$ Op1° [tu ha t_j]]]
    c. Merge G° and TopP and attract 'tu' to spec G $\rightarrow$ $[_{GP}$ tu$_k$ G° $[_{TopP}$ [ledest t_i]$_j$ Top° $[_{Op1P}$ [quanti libri]$_i$ Op1° [t_k ha t_j]]]]
    d. Merge Force and GP and attract IP to spec F° $\rightarrow$ $[_{ForceP}$ [t_k ha t_j]$_l$ F° $[_{GP}$ tu$_k$ G° $[_{TopP}$ [ledest$_i$]$_j$ Top° $[_{Op1P}$ [quanti libri]$_i$ Op1° t_l]]]
    e. Merge Op2P and ForceP and attract Wh-phrase to Spec Op2° $\rightarrow$ $[_{Op2P}$ $_{Op1P}$ [Quanti libri]$_i$ Op2 $[_{ForceP}$ [t_k ha t_j]$_l$ F° $[_{GP}$ tu$_k$ G° $[_{TopP}$ [ledest t_i]$_j$ Top° $[_{Op1P}$ t_i Op1° t_l]]]]]

At step (e) no (null) 'Rest(rictor)' attraction to Spec Op2P is possible since the wh-phrase *quanti* has a lexical complement *libri*; one might still ask why *libri* or *vestito* in (39) couldn't move to Op2P the way the null Rest. or its lexical counterpart *cossa* in (31) does, yielding totally ungrammatical sentences like (43):

(43)   a.*Libri ha-tu ledest quanti?
      books have you read how many
      'How many books did you read?'
    b.*Vestito ha-la comprà che?
      dress have you bought what
      'Which dress did she buy?'

Example (43) would be excluded if Op2P only attracted "abstract" domain restrictors. Let us say, as a first approximation, that the nonlexical "Rest." and its "deficient"—see Munaro and Obenauer (1999)—opposite number *cossa* qualify unlike fully specified lexical items like *libri*. We claim, a little more precisely, that what counts as the appropriate restrictor in the displaced *quanti libri* in (40a) is a (nonlexical) "quantity phrase"; in short *quanti libri* = Wh-quantity (book); similarly, in *che vestito* in (40b) we say that the restrictor is a nonlexical "token phrase": *che vestito* = wh-(token)vestito, and so on.[14]

Following this line, let us now raise the further question of why such syntactic functional positions couldn't host a nonlexical "Restrictor" of the required type the way the null counterpart of *cos(s)a* does; if, furthermore, such null restrictors were attracted to Op2P the way they are in (39), the ungrammatical (40d and e)—*à-tu ledest quanti libri?* and *à-la comprà che vestito?*—would be incorrectly derived.

Derivations of this type would obtain if the null Q or D restrictors were extractable from within a structure in which they have a *lexical* complement; but pied piping is obligatory in all such cases: under certain conditions only the "tail" of a syntactic constituent can be extracted from that constituent without pied-piping the rest. This will suffice to account for the ungrammaticality of (40d and e) under the hypothetical derivation entertained here. Put another way, although constituents can be discontinuous, they cannot be "scattered."

One might still ask why the complex "null restrictor+{libri, vestito}" couldn't itself be extracted from within the wh-phrase, yielding once again ungrammatical strings like *libri à-tu ledest quanti?* and *vestito à-la comprà che?* Certainly Bellunese does have sentences that it is very tempting to analyze along such lines; in that dialect bare wh-phrases like *qual* (which) and *quanti* (how many) can appear in sentence-initial position or in (apparent) sentence-internal position (cf. Pollock et al. 1999: (47); Munaro 1999). This is illustrated in (44):

(44) a. Qual avé-o ciot?
         which have you taken
         'Which one did you take?'
      b. Avé-o ciot qual?
         have you taken which
      c. Quant avé-o laorà?
         how much have you worked
         How long did you work?
      d. Avé-o laorà quant?
         have you worked how much

In our terms, this means that *qual* and *quant* can behave like full DPs of the *quanti libri* type or like the bare wh-words *che, ande, chi,* and *come.* If this is correct, then (44b) and (44d) must have two nonlexical "Restrictors" in the highest layer of their left periphery, as the spell-out parses in (45) indicate:

(45) a. $[_{Op2P}$ Rest$_m$ Op2° $[_{ForceP}$ $[t_k$ avé $t_j]_l$ F° $[_{GroundP}$ o$_k$ G° $[_{TopP}$ [ciot $t_i]_j$ Top° $[_{Op1P}$ [qual $t_m]_i$ Op1° $t_l]$]]]]
      b. $[_{Op2P}$ Rest$_m$ Op2° $[_{ForceP}$ $[t_k$ avé $t_j]_l$ F° $[_{GroundP}$ o$_k$ G° $[_{TopP}$ [laora $t_i]_j$ Top° $[_{Op1P}$ [quant $t_m]_i$ Op1° $t_l]$]]]]

"Rest.$_m$" in (45a and b) must be a "token" phrase and a "quantity" phrase, respectively, rather than the invisible *cossa* restrictor of strings like *ha-lo fat che?*

We believe that this may optionally obtain in (45a) because the final consonant in *qual* is an (optionally) incorporated definite determiner. When this takes place, *qual* is comparable to French *(le)quel* and functions like a pronominal binding a null $[_{NP}$ pro] variable that provides the "token" restrictor needed by *qual*—our (informal) "Rest." in (45a). When no such definite determiner incorporation takes place, *qual* should be analyzed as $[_{QP}$ Qu(a)- $[_{DP}$l $[_{NP}$ Rest.]]] and pied piping of the null restrictor to Op2P is then required, yielding (44a). We claim that this is because (some minimalist version of) subjacency makes it impossible to extract Rest. across DP and QP. We note in passing that what this says of -*l* agrees fairly well with Vanelli (1992) and Kayne (2000) in the context of a wider discussion of pronouns and determiners in French and Italian—which shows that the definite article in standard and Northern Italian is (our optionally incorporated) -*l* whose vocalic neucleus in other contexts is epenthetic.

As for (44d), we posit that in such cases *quant* can optionally take a null (measure) PP complement, as it does quasi-overtly in *de'sti libri, ghen'avé-o ledest quanti?* 'of these books of them have you read how many?' It is that null PP that counts as the null quantity Restrictor in "*quant* in situ" derivations like (45b). When that reanalysis fails to obtain, however, the whole [$_{QP}$quant [$_{NumP}$ ø [$_{NP}$ Rest.]]] must be pied piped to SpecOp2P, as in (44a and c). Again, this is because extracting Rest. alone would violate (some minimalist version of) subjacency.

Before we can conclude our analysis of (44), we still have to say why a derivation in which the constituent [$_{NumP}$ ø [$_{NP}$ Rest.]], headed by a (null) head—sometimes overtly manifested, as in *quanti*—would be extracted from within the wh-phrase is excluded. What we have said so far isn't enough since an appeal to (some form of) subjacency could not be made. Our view is that such a derivation would yield an incorrect input to the PF component, just as the corresponding displacement of [$_{DP}$ l [$_{NP}$ Rest.]] in (44b) would; the string **lavé-o ciot qua?* is ungrammatical.

If this is on the right track, we can say that PF convergence and (some minimalist version of) subjacency converge to require pied piping of the whole wh-phrase to Op2P in (40a, b, and c) in Bellunese. Wh-"stranding" as in (44b and d) seems restricted to cases in which the complement of *qual* and *quant(i)* are phonetically null.

This analysis of (44) forces us to go back to (30) and (38) and be a little more precise than we have been so far. We are now forced to assume that *che, andè, comè,* and *chi* in Bellunese can take a bare NP complement: should null or lexical *cossa* be analyzed as a string of the form "null determiner+(non)lexical *cossa*," a PF violation would be incurred if the whole string stranded the wh-phrase (as in **lavé-o ciot qua?*), or subjacency would be violated if NP were extracted from within a QP of the form [QP wh-[DPø NP]]. If this is correct, it is tempting to say that the wh-phrases of Bellunese that allow apparent wh–in situ are (re)analyzed as "truncated" [QP che NP] DP structures. This should ultimately be tied to other properties of Bellunese, although we are not in a position to do so here (see Poletto and Pollock (in prep).

Nevertheless, we can now conclude that Bellunese speakers analyze wh-questions like (40) exactly as French speakers analyze (41), and this is surely the best analysis. In neither language can attraction of a restrictor to Op2P yield a well-formed output unless pied piping of the rest of the wh-phrase takes place. It appears, then, that the massive spell-out differences between French and Bellunese with which we started follow as a consequence of our invariant (36) and the existence of "doubling" wh-phrases like (38) in Bellunese and their nonexistence in French.[15]

7. Another instance of Remnant Movement: French Stylistic Inversion

Before we can deal with Italian wh-questions, we need to introduce and briefly discuss another type of construction, "Stylistic Inversion" (SI) sentences like (46) in French:

(46)   a. Où est allé Jean?
          where has gone Jean
          'Where has Jean gone?'
       b. À qui a téléphoné Jean?
          to whom has phoned Jean
          'Who did Jean phone?'

SI sentences share with SCLI the fundamental property that their subjects occur in a noncanonical, displaced posititarion. In SI, though not in SCLI, that noncanonical position is made licit by (certain types of (local)) wh-phrases (see Kayne and Pollock 1979, 2001); thus, for instance, (46) contrasts sharply with (47):

(47)   a.*A Paris est allé Jean?
          to Paris is gone Jean
          'Did Jean go to Paris?'
       b.*A téléphoné Jean?
          has telephoned Jean
          'Has Jean phoned?'
       c. Y est-il allé?
          there-is-he gone
          'Did he go there?'
       d. A-t-il téléphoné?
          has he telephoned
          'Has he phoned?'

SCLI and SI contrast in many other respects (Kayne 1972). To mention just two other well-known differences, SI is not restricted to root contexts, unlike SCLI, as the pair in (48) shows, and the postverbal subject of SI sentences must occur in postparticipial or postinfinitival position, which the postverbal subject clitic in SCLI cannot do ((49)–(50)):

(48)   a. Je ne sais pas quand partira Jean.
          I know not when will-leave Jean
          'I do not know when Jean will leave.'
       b.*Je ne sais pas quand partira-t-il.
          I know not when will-leave-t-he
          'I do not know when he will leave.'

(49)   a. Où croit-il être?
          where thinks-he (to) be
          'Where does he think he is?'
       b.*Où croit Jean être?
          where thinks Jean (to) be
          'Where does Jean think he is?'
       c. Où a-t-il été?
          where has he been
          'Where has he been?'
       d.*Où a Jean été?
          where has Jean been
          'Where has John been?'

(50)   a.*Où croit être il?
          where thinks (to) be he

    b. Où croit être Jean?
       where thinks (to) be Jean
       'Where does Jean think he is?'
    c.*Où a Jean été?
       where has Jean been
    d. Où a été Jean?
       where has been Jean
       'Where has Jean been?'

Despite these major differences, SI and SCLI share one important property: they are both instances of Remnant phrasal movement to the IP field. That that is how SI should be analyzed has been argued at length in Kayne and Pollock (2001)—henceforth K&P—in ways that we cannot go into in any detail here. We shall be content to mention two important properties of SI and its spell-out structure. On K&P's analysis, the postverbal subject of SI has been attracted to the left periphery and is thus structurally "high" rather than "low," as hypothesized in many past analyses, including Kayne and Pollock (1979). Furthermore that high position is a topic-like position. These two claims are supported by a number of facts, among which are the following four:

1. Like preverbal subjects, but unlike direct objects, *de NP* 'of NP', postverbal subjects are excluded in SI—compare, for example, *Peu de linguistes nous ont critiqués* (few linguists have criticized us) and **de linguistes nous ont peu critiqué* (of linguists us have few criticized) with **le jour où nous ont peu critiqués de linguistes* (the day when us have few criticized of linguists) and *J'ai peu critiqué de linguistes* (I have few criticized of linguists).
2. Postverbal subjects in SI, like preverbal subjects and unlike objects, cannot give rise to subnominal *en* extraction (on which, see Pollock 1998—compare, for example, *J'en ai critiqué trois* (I have criticized three) with **Le linguiste qu'en ont critiqué trois* (the linguist that of them have criticized three) and **trois en ont critiqué ce linguiste* (three of them-have criticized this linguist).
3. Postverbal subjects in SI resist long-distance *pas* (neg) quantification, unlike objects and like preverbal subjects—compare, for example, **Quel livre n'ont pas lu de linguistes?* (what book NEG. have not read of linguists) and **De linguistes n'ont pas lu ce livre* (of linguists have not read this book) with *Je n'ai pas vu de linguiste* (I NEG have not seen of linguist).
4. The "high" subject position of the postverbal subjects is shown to be a Topic-like position by the anti-indefiniteness effect at work in SI, first noted by Cornulier (1974)—compare, for example, **Quel gâteau a mangé quelqu'un?* (what cake has eaten someone) with **Quel article critiquera quelqu'un?* (what article will-criticize someone). Since the postverbal subject in SI is by hypothesis in (a topic position in) the left periphery, this anti-indefiniteness effect can be seen in same light as the unfelicitousness of, say, **Quelqu'un il a critiqué mon article* (someone he has criticized my article), **Quelqu'un il a mangé le gâteau* (*someone he has eaten the cake), although the CLLD position of such sentences cannot be equated with that of SI subjects. SI subjects, unlike CLLD subjects, can be quantified subjects like *personne*—

compare, for example, *La personne à qui n'a parlé personne c'est Jean* (the person to whom has spoken no one) with **Personne, il n'a parlé à Jean* (No one, he NEG has spoken to Jean).

Summarizing: the DP subject in SI is attracted by a topic feature to the left periphery; the (remnant) IP crosses over TopP on its way to a higher position in the CP field; it is *not* targeting ForceP, however, unlike SCLI. This is shown, as already stressed, by the fact that SI is optional in subordinate clauses. Furthermore, IP in SI does not "strand" its infinitival or participial phrases, as pairs like (48) and (49) show.

In part, taking advantage of the homophony between the GroundP introduced in the previous sections and K&P's (more abstract) GP, we now attempt to tie some of the respective properties of Remnant IP movement in SCLI and SI to a difference in the positions that IP and their subjects target in the two constructions. In our section 6 analysis of French and Bellunese SCLI, the nominative weak pronouns target the GroundP layer of the left periphery and the participial, infinitival complements of the finite verb (see note 8), target a Topic layer; in SI, in contrast, we say with K&P that the DP subject targets a topic layer while the IP itself targets the Ground layer.

If this is so, 'ForceP' plays no part in SI Remnant IP movement. Assuming it is obligatorily present in main root questions, as the invariant structure of the left periphery in (51) (= (36) above) would lead one to assume, we conclude that in French the wh-phrases themselves can—and therefore must—check the interrogative force feature in root SI questions.

(51) $[_{Op2P}$ Op2° $[_{ForceP}$ Force°$]$ $[_{GroundP}$ G° $[_{TopP}$ Top°$[_{Op1P}$ Op1° IP$]$ $]$ $]$ $]$

On this analysis, then, the derivation of sentences like (46a) is (52):

(52)   Input: [IP Jean est allé où]
   a. Merge Op1° and IP and *où* movement to Op1P → $[_{Op1P}$ où$_i$ Op1° $[_{IP}$ Jean est allé t$_i]$ $]$
   b. Merge Top° and Op1° and attract *Jean* to TopP → $[_{TopP}$ [Jean]$_j$ Top° $[_{Op1P}$ où$_i$ Op1° $[_{IP}$ t$_j$ est allé t$_i]$ $]$ $]$
   c. Merge Ground and TopP and attract (Remnant) IP movement to GroundP → $[_{GroundP}$ $[_{IP}$ t$_j$ est allé t$_i]_k$ G° $[_{TopP}$ [Jean]$_j$ Top° $[_{Op1P}$ où$_i$ Op1° $[_{IP}$ t$_k]$ $]$ $]$ $]$
   d. Merge Force° and GroundP and attract *où* to Spec Force → $[_{ForceP}$ Où$_i$ Force° $[_{GroundP}$ $[_{IP}$ t$_j$ est allé t$_i]_k$ Ground° $[_{TopP}$ [Jean]$_j$ Top° $[_{Op1PP}$ t$_i$ Op1° $[_{IP}$ t$_k]$ $]$ $]$ $]$ $]$
   e. Merge Op2 and Force and attract *où* to Spec Op2P → $[_{Op2P}$ Où$_i$ Op2° $[_{ForceP}$ t$_i$ Force° $[_{GroundP}$ $[_{IP}$ t$_j$ est allé t$_i]_k$ Ground° $[_{TopP}$ [Jean]$_j$ Top° $[_{Op1PP}$ t$_i$ Op1° $[_{IP}$ t$_k]$ $]$ $]$ $]$ $]$ $]$

Although we cannot even begin to do justice to the extremely complex empirical properties of SI sentences here, three remarks are nevertheless in order. First, if the fully acceptable wh-less cases of subjunctive triggered SI and the (far) more marginal indicative ones dealt with in part II and III of K&P can be integrated into this general perpective, this analysis would give us an immediate and principled account, different from K&P's, of why SI, but not SCLI, is typically "triggered" by (local) wh-phrases: only when a Force checking phrase is present can the requirements of checking theory be met in the CP field of questions; wh-phrases have that ability, unlike topicalized elements; this immediately accounts for (53) versus (54) (= (46)–(47) above):[16]

(53)   a. Où est allé Jean?
          where has gone Jean
          'Where has Jean gone?'
       b. À qui a téléphoné Jean?
          to whom has phoned Jean
          'Who did Jean phone?'

(54)   a. *À Paris est allé Jean?
          to Paris is gone Jean
          'Did Jean go to Paris?'
       b. *A téléphoné Jean?
          has telephoned Jean
          'Has Jean phoned?'

Since, on the other hand, Remnant IP movement accomplishes that task in SCLI, no such additional checking of the force feature need to take place, whence the acceptability of (55):[17]

(55)   a. Est-il allé à Paris?
          is he gone to Paris
          'Has he gone to Paris?'
       b. A-t-il téléphoné?
          has he telephoned
          "Has he phoned?"

Second, derivations like (52) claim that (Remnant) IP is checking a Ground feature. Suppose, reasonably enough, that for an IP to have that ability, all its constituents must also be [+ground]. Assuming only clitic pronouns,[18] variables, quantifiers, quantified DPs and idioms can be so characterized, we could begin to give some intuitive content to the notion of lexical argument of K&P's principle (169)—from Koopman and Szabolcsi (in press)—repeated in (56):

(56)   IP preposing results in a violation if IP contains a lexical argument.

This would account for the following facts and contrasts (all from K&P):

(57)   a. Depuis quelle heure ont faim les enfants?
          since what time have hunger the kids
          'Since when are the kids hungry?'
       b. À quelle pièce donne accès cette clé?
          to what room gives access this key
          'Which room does this key give access to?'
       c. Quand ont pris langue Paul et Marie?
          when have taken tongue Paul and Marie
          'When did Paul and Marie discuss the issue?'

(58)   À qui l'a montré Jean-Jacques?
       to whom it has shown Jean-Jacques
       'To whom did Jean-Jacques show it?'

(59)   Qu'a dit Jean?
       what has said Jean
       'What did Jean say?'

(60)   a. la fille à qui a tout dit Jean-Jacques
          the girl to whom has everything told Jean-Jacques
          'the girl to whom Jean-Jacque said everything'
       b. la fille à qui n'a rien laissé sa grand'mère
          the girl to whom NEG. has nothing left her grandmother
          'the girl to whom her grandmother left nothing'
       c. la fille à qui laissera sûrement quelque chose sa grand'mère
          the girl to whom will-leave surely something her grandmother
          'the girl to whom her grandmother will surely leave something'

(61)   *À qui a donné ce livre Jean?
       to whom has given that book Jean
       'To whom did Jean give this book?'

In (61) the R-expression *ce livre* is by hypothesis *not* [+ground], so IP cannot be either and it fails to check the ground feature of the left periphery, causing the derivation to crash. In (57) through (60), on the contrary, IP does contain only (lexical) [+ground] elements, so the derivations converge.[19]

Third, wh-phrases like *où* on our analysis are 'wild cards' in that they not only check Op1 and Op2 features but also a [+question] Force feature. Granted this, a natural expectation is that not all wh-phrases have that ability; the unacceptability of (62), first noted by Cornulier (1974), and discussed at length in a different perspective in K&P's section 13, could now be seen as stemming from the inability of *pourquoi* and *en quel sens* to check an interrogative Force feature:

(62)   a. ?*Pourquoi parle Pierre?
          why speaks Pierre
          'Why does Pierre speak?'
       f. ?*Pourquoi travaillent les linguistes?
          why work the linguists
          'Why do linguists work?'
       g. ?* En quel sens parlent les fleurs?
          in what sense speak the flowers[20]
          'In which sense do flowers speak?'

More generally, depending on the partly idiosyncratic syntactic and morphological makeup of their wh-phrases, one would expect closely related languages to differ with respect to this "extra" ability, which should yield interesting minimal differences. We shall see in the next section that French and Italian meet that expectation.

8.   Italian

In our general perspective, the structure of interrogative clauses is invariant across the Romance languages. Because each of them has to check the same set of features in the left periphery, the computations at work in French should be present elsewhere as well, although orthogonal differences between them might make them "opaque" at spell-out. If this is on the right track, standard Italian might be expected to have two different types of interrogative constructions: one should correspond to SCLI, be restricted to main contexts, and occur in both wh- and yes/no questions; the other should be the counterpart of French SI and should thus be licit in both main and embedded contexts, although it should be banned in yes/no questions and can be expected to be restricted to certain types of wh-items, just as it is in French.

In this section, we try to show that Italian indeed has both SCLI and SI, a property that has remained undetected up to now because standard Italian is a null subject language. In addition, we suggest that the SI phenomenology in the two languages has a partly different distribution because Italian non-D-linked wh-phrases are unable to check the Force feature, unlike (most of) their French analog (see (62)).

8.1.   SCLI and the main versus embedded asymmetry

Standard Italian does not have lexical subject clitics, although it has a corresponding null pronoun, pro.[21] As a consequence, the only way to distinguish *Italian* SCLI configurations corresponding to French sentences like *Qu'a-t-il fait, Jean?* (What has he done, Jean?) and Italian SI of the type *Qu'a fait Jean?* (What has Jean done?), if such exists, should be intonation.

French sentences like *Qu'a-t-il fait, Jean?* are derived via SCLI and display an obligatory intonation break before the sentence-final "subject" since such subjects are moved to, or merged in, a (very high) CLLD position. If SCLI of this type exists in Italian as well, the same should hold true.[22] In contrast, in SI like *Qu'a fait Jean?* the postverbal subject has moved (leftward) to a position in the left periphery before Remnant IP movement; it is thus standing much lower in the clause structure and is not—in fact, cannot be—separated from the rest of the clause by any pause. If Italian has configurations to be analyzed in terms of SI, non-emarginated subjects should surface, just as they do in French, for exactly the same reasons.

With those remarks in mind, we note that, everything else being equal, the intonational pattern of Italian main questions like (63b) does correspond to that of French SCLI cases like (63a):

(63)   a.   Qu'a-t-il fait, Jean?
             what has-he done Jean
             'What has Jean done?'
        b.   Cosa ha fatto, Gianni?
             what has-he done, Gianni.

We take our lead from this and now claim that (63b) should indeed be analyzed as in (64):

(64)   Cosa ha-pro fatto, Gianni?
        what has *pro* done Gianni

This says that (63b) has a *pro* subject, the null counterpart of French *il* and that *pro*, like *il*, occurs immediately to the right of the auxiliary; the derivation of (63b) is thus exactly the same as that proposed for its French analogs in section 6; the "*pro* inversion" version of SCLI at work in Italian is also a consequence of remnant IP movement to the Spec Force, as sketched in (65):

(65)   Input: [pro è andato dove]

    a. Merge $Op1°$ and IP and attract dove to spec Op1P → $[_{Op1P}$ dove$_i$ $Op1°$ [pro è andato t_i]]

    b. Merge TopP and Op1P and attract the participial phrase [andato t_i] to spec Top → $[_{TopP}$ [andato $t_i]_j$ $Top°$ $[_{Op1P}$ dove$_i$ $Op1°$ [pro è t_j]]]

    c. Merge $G°$ and TopP and attract 'pro' to spec G → $[_{GP}$ pro$_k$ $G°$ $[_{TopP}$ [andato ti]$_j$ $Top°$ $[_{Op1P}$ dove$_i$ $Op1°$ $[t_k$ è $t_j]$]]]

    d. Merge $Force°$ and GP and attract IP to spec $Force°$ → $[_{ForceP}$ $[t_k$ è $t_j]_l$ $F°$ $[_{GP}$ pro$_k$ $G°$ $[_{TopP}$ [andato $t_i]_j$ $Top°$ $[_{Op1P}$ dove$_i$ $Op1°$ $t_l]$]]]

    e. Merge $Op2P°$ and ForceP and attract dove to Spec $Op2°$ → $[_{Op2P}$ dove$_i$ $Op2°$ $[_{ForceP}$ $[t_k$ è $t_j]_l$ $F°$ $[_{GP}$ pro$_k$ $G°$ $[_{TopP}$ [andato $t_i]_j$ $Top°$ $[_{Op1P}$ t_i $Op1°$ $t_l]$]]]]

In that derivation *pro* moves to the SpecGround position just as *il* does in French SCLI, and Remnant IP movement shifts the (IP constituent containing the) finite auxiliary to *pro*'s left; nominative weak pronouns move because they have a [+ground] feature in the numeration and are attracted to the relevant layer of the Comp domain to check an uninterpretable feature; if Italian *pro* is a weak pronoun, the extension is automatic.

Of course, standard Italian is similar to French and different from Bellunese in not having the wh-doubling structure that results in (apparent) wh–in situ and SCLI in that language. With no doubling mechanism, no null or lexical Restrictor can move alone to the higher OpP layer, and the full wh- phrase must therefore move to SpecOp2.

If French SCLI (63a) and Italian *pro* inversion in (63b) are derived by one and the same computation, they should obey the same restrictions; in particular, they should be banned in embedded questions. We believe that this is true and that the well-formed (66a) is the counterpart of the noninverted French configuration in (66b):

(66)   a. Mi hanno chiesto cosa pro ha fatto, Gianni.
        to me have asked what *pro* has done Gianni
        'They asked me what Gianni has done.'

    b. Ils m'ont demandè ce qu'il a fait, Jean
        they to me have asked what he has done Jean
        'They've asked me what Jean has done.'

    c.*Ils m'ont demandé (ce) qu'a-t-il fait, Jean
        they to me have asked what has-he done Jean

Because *pro* is phonetically null, (66a) and (63b) are deceptively identical; but in (66a) there can't have been any more Remnant IP movement than in (66c) in French, for reasons stated above; so only wh-movement has applied and *pro* is in its usual preverbal IP position.[23]

This sketch ties together a number of facts and makes interesting predictions. First, it explains the ungrammaticality of (67) in the same terms as it does its French analogs in (68):

(67)   a.*Cosa pro (non) ha letto, nessuno?
        what *pro* (not) has read nobody

b.*Nessuno, cosa pro (non) ha letto?
nobody, what *pro* not has read?
'What did nobody read?'

(68) a.*Que n'a-t-il pas lu, personne? (same as (67a))
b.*Personne, que n'a-t-il pas lu? (same as (67b))

This simply follows from the fact that no (negative) quantifier can be merged in or attracted to a (Clitic) left-dislocated position.

Second, if our SCLI analysis of non-D-linked wh-questions in main contexts can be shown to be the only available option in Italian, we will have a simple account of the necessary "emargination" of subjects in such contexts, a well-known—though, to our knowledge, still-unexplained—fact. Compare:

(69) a. Cosa ha fatto, Gianni?
what has done Gianni
b.*Cosa ha fatto Gianni?
what has done Gianni
'What did Gianni do?'

The next sections will show that this is the correct tack; (69b) will thus follow from our analysis of *pro* inversion and the unavailability of SI in Italian main questions with non-D-linked wh-phrases.

Third, if (63b) is really a case of "invisible" SCLI unavailable in embedded questions, we expect Italian questions to be able to surface with a preverbal subject only in subordinate clauses; (69) and (70) show the expected contrast:

(70) a. Mi hanno chiesto dove Gianni fosse andato.
to me have asked where Gianni were gone
'They asked me where Gianni went.'
b. Mi hanno chiesto dove Gianni è andato ieri.
to me have asked where Gianni is gone yesterday
'They asked me where Gianni went yesterday.'
c.*Dove Gianni è andato (ieri)?
where Gianni is gone (yesterday)
'Where did Gianni go (yesterday)?'

As is well known, preverbal subjects are fine when the verb is in the subjunctive, as in (70a); when it is in the indicative, the sentence is fine, provided the VP contains an object or an adverb, as in (70b). In contrast, their counterparts in main clauses like (69) are unacceptable, as expected.[24]

8.2. Italian non-D-linked wh-phrases and Stylistic Inversion

We know from section 6 that SI is a case of remnant movement to the Ground layer of the invariant left periphery in (71):

(71) $[_{Op2P}$ Op2° $[_{ForceP}$ Force°] $[_{GroundP}$ G° $[_{TopP}$ Top°$[_{Op1P}$ Op1° IP]]]]

Granted this, SI requires that the Force and OP2 features be checked by some other means. The only acceptable candidates seem to be the wh-phrases themselves, which thus have to have the ability to check three different features in the left periphery, Op1 and Op2—as discussed in section 7—but also [+Question] in Force. This does not hold for SCLI, in which Force is checked by remnant IP movement itself. As already noted, this may well suffice to account for minimal pairs, as, for example, *Est-il parti?* (Is he gone?) versus **Est parti Jean?* (Is Jean gone?) in French. In SCLI, in contrast, only the OP2 feature is checked by the wh-item.[25] We now capitalize on this difference to account for the distribution of SI in standard Italian.

We interpret the contrast in (72) as showing that SI is fine in embedded contexts but excluded in main ones:

(72) a. *Cosa ha fatto Gianni?
         what has done Gianni
         'What did Gianni do?'
      b. Mi hanno chiesto cosa ha fatto Gianni.
         to me have asked what has done Gianni
         'They asked me what Gianni did.'

If so, Italian contrasts with French, where SI is *not* limited to embedded questions:

(73) a. Qu'a fait Jean?
         what has done Jean
         'What did Jean do?'
      b. Ils m'ont demandè ce qu'a fait Jean
         they to me have asked what has done Jean
         'They asked me what Jean did.'

The SI derivation of (73) would be as in (74):

(74) Input : [IP Gianni è andato dove]
      a. Merge Op1° and IP and *dove* movement to Op1P → [$_{Op1P}$ dove$_i$ Op1° [$_{IP}$ Gianni è andato t$_i$]]
      b. Merge Top° and Op1° and attract *Gianni* to TopP → [$_{TopP}$ [Gianni]$_j$ Top° [$_{Op1P}$ dove$_i$ Op1° [$_{IP}$ t$_j$ è andato t$_i$]]]
      c. Merge Ground and TopP and attract (Remnant) IP movement to GroundP → [$_{GroundP}$ [$_{IP}$ t$_j$ è andato t$_i$]$_k$ G° [$_{ToPP}$ [Gianni]$_j$ Top° [$_{Op1P}$ dove$_i$ Op1° [$_{IP}$ t$_k$]]]]
      d. Merge Force°and GroundP and attract *dove* to Spec Force → [$_{ForceP}$ Dove$_i$ Force° [$_{GroundP}$ [$_{IP}$ t$_j$ è andato t$_i$]$_k$ Ground° [$_{TopP}$ [Gianni]$_j$ Top° [$_{Op1PP}$ t$_i$ Op1° [$_{IP}$ t$_k$]]]]]
      e. Merge Op2 and Force and attract *dove* to Spec Op2P → [$_{Op2P}$ Dove$_i$ Op2° [$_{ForceP}$ t$_i$ Force° [$_{GroundP}$ [$_{IP}$ t$_j$ è andato t$_i$]$_k$ Ground° [$_{TopP}$ [Gianni]$_j$ Top° [$_{Op1PP}$ t$_i$ Op1° [$_{IP}$ t$_k$]]]]]]

Example (74) yields a converging derivation only in embedded questions in Italian; there is a consensus that the main versus embedded contrast is a consequence of some form of lexical checking by the matrix verb of the Force feature in embedded clauses, which is unavailable in root sentences and requires XP movement to Force. We conclude that Italian wh-words like *cosa*, *dove*, and *a chi* can only check their "ordinary" OP1 and Op2 features: (non D-linked) bare wh-words cannot bear a [+question] force feature.

That [+question] feature must therefore be checked some other way; it can only be via remnant IP movement in main contexts, which requires (obligatory) SCLI in its *pro*-inversion version, or by lexical checking by a selecting verb in embedded contexts; this gives us an account of the mysterious contrasts in (75), which we see as parallel to those in (76) in French:[26]

(75) a. Cosa ha fatto, Gianni?
          what has *pro* done Gianni
          'What did Gianni do?'
      b.*Cosa ha fatto Gianni?
          what has *pro* done Gianni
      c. Mi hanno chiesto cosa ha fatto Gianni.
          to me have asked what has done Gianni
          'They asked me what Gianni did.'

(76) a. Pourquoi avait-il téléphoné, (Jean)?
          why had he phoned Jean
          'Why had Jean phoned?'
      b.*Pourquoi avait téléphoné Jean?
          why had phoned Jean
      c. Ils m'ont demandé pourquoi avait téléphoné Jean.
          they to me have asked why had phoned Jean
          'They asked me why Jean had phoned.'

In (75b) and (776b) a [+question] force feature has remained unchecked, giving rise to an uninterpretable LF; in (75a) and (76a), Remnant IP movement to Force checks the [+question] force feature, thus relieving *cosa* and *pourquoi* of an impossible task. Lexical checking of [+question] by *chiesto* and *demandé* in (75c) and (76c) does the same, with the same (fortunate) consequences.

8.3.   D-linked wh-words and SI

Our analysis so far has crucially relied on the idea that Italian wh-phrases are deficient in a way that their French analogs are not. If this is correct, one might expect Italian to have other types of wh-items behaving differently. With this in mind, let us turn to D-linked wh-phrases; they show strikingly different behavior in root SI contexts, as (77) shows:

(77) a. Quale libro ha letto Gianni?
          which book has read Gianni
          'Which book did Gianni read?'
      b.*Cosa ha letto Gianni.
          what has read Gianni
          'What did Gianni read?'
      c. Mi hanno chiesto quale libro ha letto Gianni.
          to me have asked which book has read Gianni
          'They asked me which book Gianni read.'

They thus provide strong support for our view that the explanation for why SI is excluded in matrix contexts like (75b) crucially hinges on the properties of the wh-element.

In our terms, examples like (77) establish that D-linked wh-items make SI structures licit in questions, both in root and embedded contexts; if this is so, (77) should be seen in the same light as (78) in French:

(78) a. Dans quel but a téléphoné Jean?
          in what goal has phoned Jean
          'What has Jean phoned for?'
     b.*Pourquoi a téléphoné Jean?
          why has phoned Jean
          'Why has Jean phoned?'
     c. Ils m'ont demandé dans quel but avait téléphoné Jean
          they to me have asked in what goal had phoned Jean
          'They asked me why Jean had phoned.'

Both will follow from our invariant structure of the left periphery if D-linked wh-phrases like *quale libro* and *dans quel but* can check the [+question] feature of the Force layer, unlike non D-linked wh-items like *cosa* in Italian or *pourquoi* in French.

In brief, in both French and Italian those wh-phrases that cannot check the [+question] feature can only occur in embedded cases of SI, where [+question] is checked by means of the selecting verb; chosing such wh-phrases in the numeration of a main question will thus force SCLI. However, those wh-phrases that can type their clause as a question—that is, check [+question] in ForceP—make it possible for SI to occur in main contexts as well.

That the checking of the [+question] feature is achieved by two different means in main and embedded clauses is also shown by contrasts like the following:

(79) a. Quale libro non ha letto nessuno?
          which book not has read nobody
          'Which book did nobody read?'
     b.*Cosa non ha letto nessuno?
          what not has read nobody[27]
          'What did nobody read?'
     c. Mi hanno chiesto quale libro non ha letto nessuno.
          to me have asked which book has read nobody
          'They asked me which book nobody read.'
     d. Mi hanno chiesto cosa non ha letto nessuno.
          to me have asked what has read nobody
          'They asked me what nobody read.'

Such examples show that there is a main versus embedded asymmetry with SI as well, but it reverses what is at work in V2 structures and SCLI. SI is *unrestricted* in embedded clauses *because* Force is checked by something other than the wh-phrase itself, which erases all surface differences concerning the checking capabilities of the various types of wh-items.

One additional argument in favor of a parallel between French SI and its Italian counterpart is given by the ungrammaticality of sentences like the following:

(80) a.*Quale libro ha letto qualcuno?
          which book has read someone
          'Which book has someone read?'
     b.*Quale politico vota qualcuno?
          which politician votes someone
          'Which politician does somebody vote for?'

In our perspective, this should be seen as the exact counterparts of (81) in French:

(81)   a. *Quel gateau a mangé quelqu'un?
          what cake has eaten someone
          'Which cake did someone eat?'
       b. *Quel article critiquera quelqu'un?
          what article will-criticize someone
          'Which article will someone criticize?'

Both violate the anti-indefiniteness effect described in section 7 and in Kayne and Pollock (2001: section 6).

The picture we have just drawn is somewhat simplified in that the judgments concerning *quale* wh-phrases in (80a) can be reproduced even with bare wh-words, provided a suitable intonation is adopted, as in (82):

(82)   a. COSA non ha fatto nessuno?
          what *non* has done nobody
          'What has nobody done?'
       b. A CHI non ha parlato nessuno?
          to whom not has spoken nobody
          'Whom did nobody talk to?'

In (82) there is high pitch on *COsa* or *A CHI* and then a low level tone on the rest of the sentence. In such cases, *cosa* and *a chi* are interpreted as D-linked, and, as a consequence, a SI configuration can be licitly produced.

8.4.   D-linked wh-items and noninverted structures

D-linked wh-items can of course also be found in SCLI contexts like (83):

(83)   Quale libro ha letto, Gianni?
       which book has read Gianni
       'Which book has Gianni read?'

These show that D-linked wh-items are only *optional* [+question] checkers.

That more is involved in the syntax of Italian D-linked wh-phrase questions, however, is shown by minimal pairs like (84a) versus (84b):

(84)   a. ?(?)Quale ragazzo Gianni ha visto ieri?
          which boy Gianni has seen yesterday
          'Which boy did Gianni see yesterday?'
       b. *Cosa Gianni ha visto ieri?
          what Gianni has seen yesterday
          'What did Gianni see yesterday?'

Keeping to our strategy so far, we shall try to make sense of such (somewhat marginal but clear) pairs by aligning them with French noninverted interrogatives like (85) and viewing (84a) versus (84b) in the same light as (85) versus (86):[28]

(85)   a. Quel livre Marie n'a pas lu?
          which book Marie *ne* has not read
          'Which book didn't Marie read?'

b. Quel livre seul Jean a lu?
which book only Jean has read
'Which book did only Jean read?'

c. Quel linguiste seul Jean supporte?
which linguist only Jean (can) stand
'Which linguist can only Jean stand?'

(86) a.*Que Marie n'a pas lu?
what Marie *ne* has not read
'What didn't Marie read?'

b. ?*Où seul Jean part?
where only Jean goes
'Where did only Jean go?'

c. ?*Qui seul Jean supporte?
who only Jean (can) stand
'Who can only Jean stand?'

Since no inversion at all is seen in (85), we claim, as in Pollock et al. (1999), that French complex wh-phrases like *quel livre* can in and of themselves check all the features of the invariant left periphery of interrogative sentences. When that option is chosen, the complex wh-phrases in the numeration bear [+ground] and [+question] features in addition to their usual Op1 and Op2 features. If this is so, nothing need—hence can—happen in the IP field, which is what we see in (84a) and (85). Assuming bare wh-phrases like *que, où,* and *qui* fail to have the ability to bear a [+ground] feature, another phrase must. We know from K&P and section 7 that IP itself can be [+ground]; we also know, however, that in Remnant IP movement to Spec GP subject topicalization must apply in the derivation of sentences like (84a) and (85). Since neither have moved in (84b) and (86), such sentences are excluded because the (strong) features of the French CP field of interrogatives have failed to be checked by a licit checker in overt syntax.[29] The (84a) versus (84b) pair will follow likewise if in Italian too-complex wh-phrases like *quale libro* can move from their IP internal argument position to the Op2 position in the CP field, thus checking all four Op1, G, Force, and Op2 features on their way. If this occurs, there is no remnant IP movement at all in (84a), and the preverbal subjects in those sentences are standing in their usual preverbal position. That explains why QPs like *nessuno* and *solo qualcuno* occur where they do in (87):

(87) a. A quale politico nessuno ha dato il proprio voto?
to which politician nobody has given his vote
'Which politician did nobody vote for?'

b. A quale politico solo qualcuno ha dato il proprio voto?
to which politician only someone has given his vote
'Which politician did only someone vote for?'

c. A quale politico solo Gianni ha dato il proprio voto?
to which politician only Gianni has given his vote
'Which politician did only Gianni vote for?'

In (88), however, since bare *a chi* cannot check the [+ground] feature—or, for that matter, the [+question] force feature, see above—Remnant IP movement should take place:

(88)   a.   ??A chi nessuno ha dato il proprio voto?
            to whom nobody has given his vote
            'Whom did nobody vote for?'
       b.   ??A chi solo qualcuno ha dato il proprio voto?
            to whom only someone has given his vote
            'Whom did only someone vote for?'
       c.   ?? A chi solo Gianni ha dato il proprio voto?
            to whom only Gianni has given his vote
            'Whom did only Gianni vote for?'

This suffices to exclude all such examples. If Remnant IP movement to [+ground] did apply, *nessuno* would have to first move out of IP, but there would still be a [+question] feature to check, which no element in the structure could do.

The facts concerning the acceptability of preverbal subjects in Italian wh-questions with complex wh-phrases are somewhat more fuzzy than this sketch indicates. Many speakers find (89) (much) worse than (87a):

(89)   ??Quale libro nessuno legge?
       which book nobody reads
       'Which book does nobody read?'

Descriptively, it seems that the perfect acceptability of preverbal DP or QP subjects in wh-questions with (complex) D-linked wh-phrases is contingent on the presence of an object in VP or an adverbial in postverbal position. When there is one, as in (87a), a postverbal position for the subject is degraded and the preverbal position is correspondingly perfect. When no such object or adverb is present, Italian speakers seem to prefer a Remnant IP movement strategy.[30]

Contrasts of that type are not restricted to wh-questions, as the following examples show:

(90)   A.   Gianni ha dato il libro a Maria.
            'Gianni has given the book to Maria.'
       B.   (a)   No, NESSUNO ha dato il libro a Maria.
                  'No, nobody has given the book to Maria.'
            (b) *No, non ha dato il libro a Maria NESSUNO.
                  no not has given the book to Maria nobody
            (c)   No, a Maria, il libro non l'ha dato NESSUNO.
                  no to Maria the book not it-has given nobody

(91)   A.   Gianni vuole dare il proprio voto a Berlusconi.
            'Gianni wants to give his vote to Berlusconi.'
       B.   (a)   No, NESSUNO vuole dare il proprio voto a Berlusconi.
                  'No, nobody wants to give his vote to Berlusconi.'
            (b) *No, non vuole dare il proprio voto a Berlusconi NESSUNO.
                  no *non* wants to give his vote to Berlusconi nobody
            (c)   No, il proprio voto a Berlusconi non lo vuole dare NESSUNO.
                  no his vote to Berlusconi *non* it-wants to give nobody

(92)   A.   Gianni è arrivato ieri (Gianni is arrived yesterday)
       B.   (a)   ??No, NESSUNO è arrivato ieri (no nobody is arrived yesterday)
            (b)   No non è arrivato NESSUNO ieri (no *non* is arrived nobody yesterday)

Such examples show that the optimal position for contrastively stressed subject QPs in Italian depends on what there is in the VP. If, as in (89) and (91), an argument fills the object position, the contrastively stressed preverbal QP subject is fine; if an object is not present in the VP, the subject seems to require a postverbal position, as in (92).

On this basis, it seems fair to say that a finer-grained study of (89) would have to carry over to (90), (91), and (92); such a study would be at least in part orthogonal to the syntax of wh-questions and is beyond the scope of our work here.[31]

In sum, the general picture concerning the difference between D-linked and non-D-linked wh-items emerging from this discussion is the following: D-linked wh-phrases are in general "more liberal" than non-D-linked ones in allowing for a greater variety of interrogative constructions. In our account, this observation translates in terms of different checking abilities. French and Italian D-linked wh-phrases can check all the (strong) features activated in the different layers of invariant interrogative left periphery repeated in (93)— Op1, Ground, Force, and Op2:

(93) $[_{Op2P}$ Op2° $[_{ForceP}$ Force°] $[_{GroundP}$ G° $[_{TopP}$ Top°$[_{Op1P}$ Op1° IP]]]]

When this obtains, noninverted structures are derived where no displacement other than "pure" wh-movement can take place. In Italian or French, D-linked wh-phrases need not check the [+ground] feature; when that obtains, Remnant IP movement to GroundP must take place, resulting in main clause SI configurations. Non-D-linked wh-items like *cosa* and *a chi* only check Op2 and Op1 in Italian, which excludes them from acceptable root SI structures; in that respect, they are like French *pourquoi*, which shows the same distribution. As a consequence, Italian *cosa* and *a chi* and French *pourquoi* are only compatible with SI in embedded contexts, in which some form of lexical checking of the [+question] feature of ForceP takes place. In root contexts they thus force the *pro*-inversion and SCLI strategies.[32]

This analysis of the various wh-configurations in French and Italian thus relies on two differences between the two languages: (a) the (noncontroversial) fact that Italian is a *pro*-drop language, and (b) the deficient character of non-D-linked, bare wh-phrases in Italian, which prevents them from checking [+question] in Root clauses, thereby obligatorily triggering (nonlexical though overt) SCLI configurations at spell-out.

9.   Conclusion: on characterizing the left periphery of questions

The five functional projections—ForceP, GP, Op1P, Op2P, and TopP—that this work, capitalizing on previous research by Kayne and Pollock (2001), Pollock et al. (1999), and Poletto and Pollock (1999), has added to the standard interrogative ForceP of (wh-)questions (in Romance) have so far been motivated only syntactically. Consequently, the labels that we have given them have remained essentially mnemonic. This is a perfectly legitimate move, which we share with most work on the fine structure of the IP and CP fields conducted over the last fifteen years or so (see, e.g., Pollock 1989; Cinque 1999). The logic that leads to the identification of five different positions in the left periphery, as expressed in the hierarchy of functional projections in

(93), should be familiar, although we have kept it implicit so far. We have been claiming, in effect, that without (93), it would be very difficult to account in a unitary and principled fashion for the syntax of (subject positions in) wh-questions in French, Italian, and Bellunese. More precisely, we have been arguing that (93) allows for a natural account of the apparently idiosyncratic behavior and location of the (bare) wh-words in the three languages and the various properties of postverbal subjects in different types of wh-questions. Without (93), no such explanatorily satisfying account would be possible. This is because (93) has five different sites in the left periphery of questions to which various phrases can be attracted, in accordance with the usual requirements of checking theory, which gives just the leeway that the word order phenomena studied here[33] seem to require if they are to be integrated in the explanatory framework for comparative syntax developed in generative grammar over the last twenty five years or so.[34]

Let us summarize and highlight the chief properties of, and motivations for, the different positions of (93) as they emerge from the preceding discussion.

Starting with the lowest and highest layers, Op1 and Op2, in Bellunese these features attract different types of wh-elements or, in the case of pied piping, different features in the same wh-phrase. 'OpP1' is the spell-out position in which all bare wh-words in Bellunese obligatorily stand in sentences like (94):

(94) a. Ha-tu magnà chè?
          have you eaten what
          'What did you eat?'
      b. Se-tu 'ndat andè?
          are you gone where
          'Where did you go?'

Through this, all wh-words move on their way to ForceP and Op2P in French and Italian. Op2 is the position that attracts phonetically overt elements like *cos(s)a* or their null counterparts Rest., as discussed in section 6. Postulating those two positions is virtually forced on one by the "doubling" configurations in Bellunese and various other NIDs (see examples (30)–(32)). On this basis, we have made what we take to be the null hypothesis and claimed that the two positions exist as well in the other Romance languages examined here. If this is correct, the high position in which all the French and Italian wh-phrases surface at spell-out is the Restrictor position, not the wh-(operator) position. Wh-items reach it for the same reason complex wh-phrases in Bellunese do in sentences like, for example, *Che vestito à-la comprà?* (what dress has she bought), namely because UG makes it impossible in such cases to attract only the restrictor of the variable bound by *che* (see also discussion of (40), (43), and (44)).

What this is saying, then, is that the familiar distinction between binding and strong binding (see, e.g., Chomsky 1986: 85) is syntactically encoded in the left periphery of questions in (some of) the Romance languages. That that distinction should be expressed syntactically is not particularly surprising. What is a little more surprising, perhaps, is the ordering and hierarchy of the two functional layers that express it: the domain restrictor is specified (checked) later in the derivation; hence it is structurally higher than the variable binding by the wh-operator.[35] But then our surprise may well only be due to our incorrectly expecting languages to mimic the formulas of familiar logic in too direct a way.

Our TopicP and Force P are more familiar. TopP is the position to which the subject of SI and the various participial and infinitival complements of the finite verb in SCLI are attracted. That the postverbal subject of French (and Italian) SI constructions stands in such a (high) position in the left periphery is argued for at length in Kayne and Pollock (2001: part 1), and we have repeated some of their basic arguments in section 7. In addition, the label 'TopP' plays an important role in explaining the anti-indefiniteness effect of postverbal subjects in SI. As for our "ForceP," it is the layer made familiar by recent literature on the left periphery, and the use we have made of it is fairly standard. Our only major innovation is the claim that Remnant IP movement to Spec Force°, rather than head movement to Force°, is at work in French SCLI and its (covert) variants in Bellunese and Italian (see examples 2–5).

If this is on the right track, *all* question-related verb movements in Romance are cases of Remnant movement; in particular Remnant IP movement in SI only differs from Remnant IP movement in SCLI—and CI (see Pollock 2000)—in targeting a different layer of the Comp domain: Kayne and Pollock's (2001) 'GP' rather than ForceP. We believe that this unitary approach to the verb-related displacements to Comp should be regarded as a step forward, especially if we are correct in our tentative account of why Remnant IP movement to GP crucially forces the subject to vacate its SpecIP position while in SCLI—and, more obviously so, in CI—no such requirement holds (see section 7). Our analysis of this major difference has banked on the fortunate homophony between K&P's (abstract) "GP" and our own "GroundP"; it states, fairly naturally, that *all* elements in a [+ground] IP must also be [+ground]. On the assumption that nonpronominal DPs in Romance can never be [+ground],[36] we expect them to move out of IP, which is what we see in SI.[37] In SCLI and CI, on the other hand, Remnant IP movement is triggered by a [+question] feature and a sentence can be so characterized regardless of its having a [+ground] subject or not. Certainly, in viewing K&P's "GP" and our "GroundP" as one element, we have been exploiting a general view of the left periphery also developed in Poletto (2000) and Beninca' and Poletto (1999) in which the left periphery (of questions) divides fundamentally into two subparts: a lower half in which "new" information is located, and a higher half in which the "known" information stands, a hierarchy which our (93) respects.

The present work has made very crucial use of GroundP since it has claimed it is obligatorily present in the left periphery of Romance (wh-)questions; it must therefore attract a constituent appropriately marked to its specifier. When that is impossible, a nonconverging derivation obtains; in our analysis a variety of constituents can be so displaced:

1. D-linked (complex) wh-phrases, as in French *Combien de linguistes Marie a rencontrés?* (how many linguists Mary has met) and Italian *Quanti linguisti Maria ha incontrato* (same).
2. (Remnant) IP, yielding French and Italian SI (see sections 8.1 and 8.2), like *A qui a téléhoné Marie?* (to whom has telephoned Marie) and *A quale ragazzo ha telefonato Maria?* (to which boy has telephoned Maria).[38]

3. Overt or covert subject clitics in French, Bellunese, and Italian SCLI configurations like *A qui a-t-elle parlé?* (To whom has she spoken?).

Consider Remnant IP movement to GroundP first. The idea that the non-wh-part of IP somehow denotes presupposed knowledge has been taken for granted by most work on the syntax and semantics of wh-questions in generative grammar since at least Katz and Postal (1964). Put in very informal terms, this is saying that 'who did you see' should be analyzed as 'presupposition (you saw someone) and wh-(someone)'; 'who saw you?' should be analyzed as 'presupposition (someone saw you) and wh-(someone)'; 'when did you leave?' should be analyzed as 'presupposition (you left at some time, and wh-(some time),' and so on. On that view, a [+ground] IP is attracted to the syntactic layer of the left periphery that is cross-linguistically devoted to the expression of shared or presupposed information. We may note in passing that this (re)interpretation of Remnant IP movement in SI may well offer an account of the well-known fact that the interrogative *si* complementizer of French, unlike *pourquoi*, does not allow for SI in embedded interrogatives and for the fact that root yes/no questions ban SI altogether:

(95)   a.*Je ne sais pas si a téléphoné Marie.
          I know not if has phoned Marie
          'I do not know if Marie has phoned.'
       b.*A téléphoné Marie?
          has telephoned Marie
          'Has Marie phoned?'

If *si* lexicalizes Force°, as commonly assumed (see, e.g., Kayne 2000; chap. 4), and checks the [+question] feature of the embedded sentence, we can—probably must—impute the ungrammaticality of (95) to the fact that IP is *not* "presupposed" in yes/no questions in general and in *si* subordinates in particular. If this is correct, the attracting IP to the GroundP layer in yes/no questions like (95) cannot yield a converging derivation.

Going back to the other two ways of checking [+ground], the fact that D-linked (complex) wh-phrases should be able to do so is natural. D-linked wh-phrases do contain information shared by the speaker and hearer since the domain over which the variable bound by *lequel, quale,* and *combien* can range in sentences like *Lequel de tes amis Marie va épouser?* and *Quale libro ha letto Gianni?* is known to both hearer and speaker at the relevant stage in discourse. Thus, nothing precludes taking the relevant part of the wh-phrase as [+ground], allowing it to move to SpecGroundP. That *non*-D-linked wh-phrases should on the contrary be incapable of so moving also follows from the same consideration since the range of the variable bound by bare wh-phrases like *qui, que, où,* and *comment* is typically unknown to the speaker.[39] That other [+ground] elements like (nonassertive) nominative clitic pronouns should be similarly attracted in SCLI also seems fairly natural.

The left periphery of SCLI (and French CI) and SI share a ground layer, but they differ crucially in their sensitivity to the root versus embedded asymmetry. French and Italian SCLI only obtain in root contexts; Italian has a less well known though equally interesting pattern of facts, which reverses the root versus embedded asymmetry: its SI is unrestricted in embedded contexts and restricted—in fact, impossible, with non-D-linked wh-phrases—in main wh-questions, as pairs like (96) show:

(96)   a. *Dove va Maria?
          where goes Maria
          'Where is Maria going?'
       b. Dimmi dove va Maria.
          tell me where goes Maria
          'Tell me where Maria is going.'

The root versus embedded contrast exhibited by SCLI structures will follow, as standardly assumed, if the Comp domain targeted by Remnant IP movement in root SCLI has its feature checked by the matrix verb in embedded contexts.[40]

Italian pairs like (96) we have interpreted as showing that the [+question] Force feature cannot be checked by remnant IP movement. If this is so, (96a) shows that Italian bare wh-phrases cannot check the [+question] feature; (96b) now follows since embedded questions have their force feature checked by the matrix verb.

In sum, the five basic projections of the left periphery of some of the Romance wh-questions trigger the following computations:

1. OP1 and OP2 features are checked by the wh-item, or by their restrictor, in doubling constructions.
2. The topic feature can be checked either by a DP subject in SI sentences or by the lower portion of IP corresponding to AspP (see note 8) in SCLI contexts.
3. [+ground] can be checked either by remnant IP movement, by the wh-item if its internal structure contains a [+ground] feature (as in D-linked wh-phrases), or by lexical or nonlexical subject clitics.
4. [+question] Force can be checked by the wh-items themselves in SI sentences, unless they are "defective" like French *pourquoi* and Italian non-D-linked wh-items. Remnant IP movement can also check that feature, as in SCLI contexts; lexical checking by a selecting verb plays the same part in embedded contexts.

Although our semantic characterization of the various layers of (93) has remained very informal, we feel it has some good first approximation plausibility. The unified treatment of SCLI, SI, Bellunese wh–in situ, and wh-doubling in French, Bellunese, and Italian that (93)—our highly "split" complementizer area—makes possible is an indirect but cogent argument that at least that level of complexity is required if a truly explanatory account of the syntax of questions in Romance is to be ultimately developed.

Notes

We thank Manuela Amber, Nicole Munero, Hans-Georg Obeneuer, Richard Kayne, and two anonymous reviewers for their comments. For the concerns of the Italian academy Cecilia Poletto takes responsibility for sections 1 to 6 and Jean-Yves Pollock for sections 7 to 10.

1. That article provides an analysis of French wh–in situ capitalizing on the idea that the left periphery of these sentences is defective or "truncated," thereby sharing most of its

properties with that of declarative clauses. On the contrary, Bellunese wh–in situ has a fully fledged interrogative left periphery: this accounts for the differences between the two languages (see also Poletto and Pollock (in prep)). Cheng and Rooryck (2000) propose a different analysis of such configurations relying on covert movement of a Q-feature. We will not focus our attention on wh–in situ here because our main goal is to shed light on the left periphery of moved-wh structures in French and standard Italian.

2. On "defective" wh-words, see Munaro and Obenauer (1999), and Poletto and Pollock (in prep).

3. The inversion pattern of (9) and (11) is also present in another type of inversion construction specific to French (and Valdôtain), the so-called Complex Inversion (CI) of (i):

> (i) a. Où Jean est-il allé?
>   where Jean is-he gone
>   'Where has Jean gone?'
> b. Quand tout est-il tombé?
>   when all is-it fallen
>   'When has everything fallen?'
> c. Martin mindze-të de seuppa?   (Valdôtain, Aosta)
>   Martin eats he the soup
>   'Does Martin eat the soup?'
> b. Pequè lo mèinô medze-t-i la pomma?   (Valdôtain, St. Nicholas)
>   why the child eats-t-he the apple
>   'Why does the child eat the apple?'

Example (i) only differs from (9) and (11) in having an additional preverbal DP subject; in particular, CI is also restricted to root clauses. On the analysis developed in this chapter, this must mean that CI also involves Remnant IP movement to ForceP, as Pollock (2000) argues in detail. See note 21; on CI (and SCLI) in French and Valdôtain, see also Kayne (1972, 1975), Roberts (1993), and Laenzlinger (1998).

4. On the orthogonal question of why *que* surfaces as *ce que* in French embedded questions, see Poletto and Pollock (2000, in prep).

5. Contra Sportiche (1993), Kayne (1994), and Friedemann (1997).

6. That *pa* is a Comp particle—more precisely, the specifier of a (low) Focus layer in the Comp field (see. Poletto and Zanuttini 2000)—is shown by a variety of facts. First, *pa* occurs after the inflected verb, which is expected given the fact that Central Rhaetoromance is a V2 language but it stands higher than all the adverbials in the IP field in Cinque's (1999) hierarchy. This is shown in (i):

> (i) a. Al a *pa d sigy* mangé.   (S. Leonardo)
>   SCL have *pa* of sure eaten
>   'He has surely eaten.'
> b. *Al a *d sigy pa* mangé.
>   SCL has of sure *pa* eaten
> c. Al a *pa magari* bel mangé.
>   SCL has *pa* perhaps already eaten
>   'Maybe he has already eaten'
> d. *Al a *magari pa* bel mangé

Second, *pa* stands higher than inverted subjects as (ii) shows:

> (ii) Inier a *pa* Giani mangé la ciara.
>   yesterday has *pa* John eaten the meat
>   'Yesterday John ate meat.'

Finally, *pa* is incompatible with lower complementizers like the interrogative *s* in embedded questions; this is shown by the ungrammaticality of (iii):

(iii) *A i m a domané *s* al n fus *pa* bel.
     SCL SCL me asked if SCL neg was *pa* nice
     'He asked me whether it was nice.'

7. In questions without an auxiliary, Monnese shows "fà-support," for independent reasons; see section 3 in the text and the references given there.

8. It is not just participial phrases that are attracted to TopP in SCLI constructions but all the elements following the main finite verb. Taking our clue from the hierarchy of functional projections in Cinque (1999) we arrive at the idea that what is moving to TopP in SCLI is a habitual aspectual phrase (see Cinque 1999: 130). An anonymous reviewer points out that movement of the past particle to SpecTop has to be made obligatory for this derivation to work, although it cannot be obligatory in SI constructions since there the whole IP moves to SpecGroundP, which leads to an apparent paradox. The solution, we believe, lies in the fact that OP2, Force, Ground, Top, and Op1 features do need to be checked before spell-out but that various elements can do the job, depending on the features they have in particular numerations. In SCLI structures like the one above, the feature in SpecTop is checked by AspP movement, while in SI subject movement does the checking. Hence, the requirement we propose here is not obligatory movement of the AspP to SpecTop, but obligatory movement to SpecTop of a phrase that has a Top feature. This can be the past participle (thus yielding a SCLI structure) of a DP subject (yielding SI). In SCLI structures, the subject clitic cannot move to SpecTop because, in our terms, clitics can only be [+ground], not [+topic].

9. Note that *il* is moving as a phrase here; if nominative clitics are heads in the sense of Cardinaletti and Starke (1999)—contrary to what they say concerning nominative clitics—this may mean that what is attracted to GP is a Kaynian or Sporticheian clitic phrase (cf. Kayne 1972; Sportiche 1993) whose head is *il* and whose specifier is phrasal *pro*; if nominative clitics are phrases, then *il* moves as one, evidently.

10. By analyzing 'where' and 'how(many)' as taking a null restrictor complement, we are following Munaro (1999: n. 14, 227–229).

11. The conditions ruling the *cossa* versus null Rest. alternation still have to be fully worked out. Munaro and Obenauer (1999) show that *cossa* must be used when the question is not "neutral," in some relevant dimension—for example, when some form of "surprise" is intended or when the wh-item has the special interpretation that they call "why-like," which is restricted to *cossa*. If the special interpretations found when *cossa* is used are a reflex of a higher position of the wh-item, as Munaro and Obernauer (1999) claim, the distinction between *cossa* and our null Rest. could be tied to the different movement path of the two elements and, ultimately, to the fact that *cossa*, though not Rest., can check "higher" features in the Comp domain.

12. An anonymous reviewer points out that this derivation would fail if another element could be attracted to SpecGround. The only possible candidate here would be the AspP containing the past participle. However, the Topic layer must also have its feature checked before spell-out; hence, AspP movement to SpecTop is obligatory, given that, in our terms, subject clitics cannot be Topics (see n. 8). Hence, attracting AspP to Ground instead of the subject clitic would yield an illicit derivation since the Topic feature would remain unchecked.

13. We are saying here that nominative clitic heads, like clitics in general, never move out of their head positions: they are "frozen in place" once they have reached them. As a consequence, they can only be displaced further up in the structure as part of a bigger phrase, as object clitics are in Remnant IP Movement. Put slightly differently, clitic movement to the CP domain is never possible because clitic movement can only be the syntactic analog of

morphological processes that concern only IP internal functional projections like AGR, Tense, neg, (clitic) voice, and so on.

French and Valdôtain SCLI and CI differ from Bellunese SCLI in having an obligatory -*t*- morpheme precede third-person clitics, as in (i):

    (i) a. Où (Marie) va *(-t-) elle aller?
              where (Marie) will-t-she go?
              'Where will she/Marie go?'
        b. Où va *(-t-) il aller?
              where will-t-he go
              'Where will he go?'

As Poletto (2000) and Pollock (2000) show, the standard analysis of -*t* as an epenthetic consonant is falsified by the data in (ii), from Morgeux, a Provençal dialect. In that dialect, standard French -*t*- surfaces as –*lo*, but its insertion cannot be a purely PF phenomenon since neither -*li* (they) nor -*lou* (she) is in need of an epenthetic consonant.

    (ii) a. Ven-lo-li? (Morgeux, Provençal)
             come-INTERR MARKER-they
             'Are they coming?'
        b. Ven-lo-lou? (Morgeux, Provençal)
             come-INTERR MARKER-she
             'Is she coming?'

Like Pollock (2000) we hypothesize that -*t*- in French and -*lo* in Morgeux have syntactic import and are interrogative morphemes in main clause questions. More precisely, we follow much traditional work in claiming that French -*t*- and Morgeux -*lo* are "conjugaison interrogative" markers, or [+interrogative] morphemes merged as heads in Force°. On our derivations, -*t*- will thus end up to the immediate left of the subject clitics and the immediate right of the finite verb. Since those "conjugaison interrrogative" morphemes play no part in the rest of this essay, we ignore that important aspect of the SCLI phenomenology here.

14. This is tantamount to saying, as Katz and Postal (1964) did years ago, that 'what book' is really 'Wh–some book', 'which book', 'Wh–the book', etc., on the assumption that what we informally call "quantity" and "token" in the text are syntactically encoded in functional projections in the DP, as a (specifier of) Q(P), as Det(P), or as other functional layers in the DP.

15. Next to that of Bellunese, Monnese examples like (i) (=(32)–(33) in the text) show that another doubling pattern exists:

    (i) a. Ch'et fat què?
              what have you done what
              'What did you do?'
        b. Ch'et fat?

In (1b), as in standard Italian *Cosa* questions like (iiia), the element that has no phonetic shape at spellout is the qu- element in Op1 rather than the restrictor in Op2. It thus seems clear that some Romance varieties may fail to lexically express one of the two elements in (ii):

    (ii) [Ch- NP]

Bellunese lexically realizes *ch*- and may fail to realize NP; Italian, Friulian, and Paduan in sentences like (iii) fail to lexicalize *ch*- but always lexicalize the NP restrictor, just as Monnese does:

(iii)   a. Cosa ha fatto?
            what has done
            'What did he do?'

        b. Cossa fa-lo?   (Paduan)
            what does-he
            'What does he do?'

        c. Ce mangia-l?   (Friulian)
            what eats-he
            'What does he eat?'

Written Italian differs from Monnese and Bellunese in that when both *ch-* and NP are lexically expressed, they obligatorily move as a unit to Op2P: *che cosa ha fatto?* versus **Cosa ha fatto che*. In Monnese, sentences like (ia) and Bellunese (38), in contrast, no such pied piping is obligatory (see text); in fact, one could posit that standard Italian, Friulian, and Paduan "strand" their nonlexical *ch-*. Therefore, (iiia) should be analyzed as in (iv):

(iv)   [$_{NP}$ Cosa]$_i$ ha pro fatto [$_{QP}$ ⌀ t$_i$]

Here ⌀ = null *ch-*. If this is correct, one would want to explain why the "truncated" DPs discussed in connection with Bellunese (43b and d) are only available in standard Italian, Friulian, and Paduan when the QP layer of *ch-*phrases is phonetically null. Alternatively, one might want to stick to a more conventional analysis in which no stranding of the null *ch-*phrase is involved in such sentences and where the restrictor movement to Op2P pied-pipes the whole *ch-*phrase in all cases. The spell-out parse of (iiia), for example, would then be (v):

(v)   [$_{QP}$ ⌀ [$_{NP}$ Cosa]]$_i$ [ha pro fatto t$_i$]

    The question of the status of *ce que* questions like (vi) in French might be reconsidered in this light:

(vi)   Je ne sais pas ce qu'il fera.
       I know not *ce* that he will do
       'I do not know what he will do.'

One might claim, for example, that *ce que* consists of *ce*, the French counterpart to *ch'* in Monnese and *cos(s)a* in Italian/Bellunese followed by *que*, the lexicalization of Force°. If this is correct, then an exclamative like (vii) or (viii) might be analyzed as containing a lexical or nonlexical *ch'/cosa/ce*:

(vii)   Ce qu'il est bête!
        ce that he is silly
        'How silly he is!'

(viii)   Qu'il est bête!
         that he is silly
         'How silly he is!'

Alternatively, *ce que* in (vi) and (vii) could be viewed as the counterpart of *che cossa* plus additional movement of *ce* to some slot in the left periphery of the DP, followed by pied piping of the whole constituent to Comp, again because of (some refined version of) subjacency. Under the first alternative, French—like Bellunese, Monnese, and Italian—would also have the option not to lexicalize *ch-* or *qu-*; under the second, it would always lexicalize *qu-*. In any case, French only allows fleeting manifestations of a lexical restrictor of the *cos(s)a* variety, as in (vi) and (vii). On how best to analyze *que* in *Que fait-il?* and the ungrammaticality of **qu'il fait?* see Poletto and Pollock (in prep).

16. As pointed out to us by an anonymous reviewer, one might wonder why in SCLI cases the remnant IP can check Force, while in yes/no question it must be prevented from doing so or else illicit cases of SI like, say, *A téléphoné Marie? 'Has phoned Marie?' would be derived. We observe, first that the left periphery of yes/no questions may well turn out to be different from that of wh-questions, in particular if—*pace* Rizzi (1997)—no null counterpart of the wh-element exists in yes/no questions. Assuming so, the remnant IP in wh-questions contains the variable left by the wh-phrase, while none would be present in its yes/no counterpart. It is tempting, then, to speculate that the remnant IP's ability to check interrogative force rests on the presence of that wh-variable in ways that we shall not try to spell out here (see Poletto and Pollock (in prep)). Also, Force here is only Interrogative Force, and the Force projection of declarative clauses is located much higher in the Comp field, as shown by the fact that a declarative complementizer occurs higher than Left Dislocation, while interrogative complementizers in those languages that have overtly realized ones occur lower than Left Dislocation—on this, see Poletto (2000). Moreover, declarative clauses do not seem to have any Operator-Ground-Topic split, which should evidently be tied to the semantics of interrogative wh-clauses, where part of the sentence is presupposed and part isn't (see section 9). This would also explain why SI is not found in ordinary main declaratives.

17. This analysis of pairs like (54) and (55) presupposes that no (subpart of the remnant) IP in Spec,Ground in SI can be attracted further up to check the Force feature in SI; we hold that remnant phrases are "frozen in place" once they have reached their target.

18. Only *nonassertive* clitics in Bellunese. See discussion of Table 9.1.

19. In acceptable cases of SI, like (i) [-ground] constituents like *à Paul* or *à Marie* are extracted—either pied piped by wh-movement to Op1P, or topicalized (cf. K&P)—previous to IP movement to GP:

    (i)   a. Quel livre a donné Jean à Paul?
            which book has given Jean to Paul
            'Which book did Jean give to Paul?'
        b. Qu'a donné à Marie cet homme?
            what has given to Marie this man
            'What did this man give to Marie?'

As K&P show, direct objects like *ce livre* cannot undergo either wh–pied piping or topicalization, whence (61). Note that our reinterpretation of (56) also provides an account of why the [-ground] DP subject *must* topicalize out of IP in SI.

See Pollock's (2000) analysis of French Complex Inversion sentences like (i):

    (i)   Quand Pierre a-t-il téléphoné à Marie?
         when Pierre has he phoned to Marie
         'When did Pierre phone Marie?'

Remnant movement has taken place, carrying along the [-ground] subject *Pierre* and the finite verb *a* to the left periphery. Since in such cases, just as in SCLI, IP is moving to SpecForce, *NOT* to SpecGround, no violation of our reinterpretation of (56) is incurred, although its literal phrasing would be violated, incorrectly.

20. K&P point out in their note 59 that, when argumental, *en quel sens* is compatible with SI, as in (i):

    (i)   En quel sens a tourné la voiture?
         in what direction has turned the car
         'Which direction did the car turn?'

21. See all the literature on the null subject parameter and Cardinaletti and Starke (1999). On Alexiadou and Anagnostopoulou's (1998) reanalysis of the null subject parameter, no null

pronoun needs to be posited in the Romance type null subject languages; such a view would make our very direct assimilation of Italian pro inversion and French SCLI more difficult to express.

22. For the sake of execution, we say that cases of Clitic Right dislocations like (63) are derived from the corresponding Clitic Left dislocations configurations via (further) CP movement to the left periphery. Recall that the "very high" CLLD position in which *Jean* is standing in *Qu'a-t-il fait, Jean* should be carefully distinguished from the "lower" Comp position in which *Jean* is standing in SI sentences like *Qu'a fait Jean*. Although the DPs standing in both positions show an anti-indefiniteness effect (see section 7), the lower position, unlike the higher one, can host quantifiers; compare *À qui n'a parlé personne?* (To whom has spoken no one?) vs **À qui n'a-t-il parlé, personne* (To whom has he spoken, no one?) is sharply ungrammatical.

As is well-known—see Kayne (1972)—sentences like (i) should also be carefully distinguished from complex inversion cases like (ii):

(i) À qui a-t-il parlé, Jean?
     to whom has he spoken Jean
     'Who did Jean talk to?'

(ii) À qui Jean a-t-il parlé?
     to whom Jean has he spoken

In the latter, though not in the former, the subject *Jean* has been merged in Spec IP and has moved to Spec Force along with the remainder of IP. For reasons discussed in Pollock (2000), CI is not available in Italian or in the NIDs, even though the NIDs often show SCLI; this is because full DPs in Italian move further up than they do in French and can thus never be dragged along by Remnant IP movement, which suffices to exclude derivations like (iii):

(iii) * $[_{OpP}$ Cosa Op° $[_{ForceP}$ $[_{IP}$ [Gianni t_i] ha $t_j]_k$ Force° $[_{Agrs°}$ pro$_i$ Agrs°] [fatto . . .]$_j$ $t_k]$]

This should arguably be tied to Italian and the NIDs being null subject languages, unlike French. In Pollock (2000), this link is expressed as follows: Romance SCLI and CI inversion are really instances of Remnant *TP* movement; in non-pro-drop languages, full DPs—and, more exceptionally, nominative clitics in the -*ti* dialects of French and Valdôtain—can stand in SpecTP; in the null subject languages, in contrast, they can't and must at least move to Spec AgrS. It follows that (i) can never obtain in Italian.

23. IP here stands for AgrsP, if the nonexistence of CI in Italian is analyzed, as sketched in note 20.

24. We come back in section 8.3 to the fact that (i) and the like are often judged to be degraded:

(i) ??Mi hanno chiesto dove Gianni è andato
     to me have asked where Gianni is gone
     They asked me where Gianni has gone

Moreover, bare wh-phrases like *dove* and *cosa*, when contrastively stressed under D-linking, to a varying degree allow noninverted questions like (ii):

(ii) ? DOVE Gianni è andato?
     where Gianni is gone
     'Where has Gianni gone?'

25. Our analysis of yes/no questions has no need for null wh-phrases; in our perspective, Op2P and Op1P are only required to be merged in (72) when the numeration contains wh-phrases—that is, items whose Op1 and Op2 features must be checked. When none are

present, the Op1 and Op2 layers need not—in fact, cannot—be merged since there won't be any element in the structure to erase their noninterpretable features.

26. Pairs like (76b) and (76c) were pointed out to Jean-Yves Pollock and Richard Kayne by Paul Hirschbühler about twenty-five years ago but had so far remained without any explanation. For unclear reasons in the text perspective, there is no main versus embedded contrast with *en quel sens*, and the embedded version of (62) remains unacceptable.

27. Example (79b) is ungrammatical only when the wh-word is interpreted as non D-linked. See (82).

28. Example (86a) is sharply ungrammatical, but (86b and c) are less so, probably because they can be rescued on a marked intonation that would stress *où, qui*, etc., and give a low-level tone to the rest of the sentence, not unlike that of Italian in examples like (82). Because *que* cannot be stressed in this way, that strategy remains unavailable to (82a). Without that marked intonation, (86b and c) strike the native speaker of French among us as rather sharply deviant.

29. An IP with a [-ground] subject cannot check a [+ground] feature in the left periphery; see section 7 and references cited there.

30. On our analysis, Italian postverbal subjects in wh-questions are always derived via remnant IP movement to the left periphery. *Pace* Belletti (2001), it would seem natural to extend the same type of approach to *all* postverbal subjects in declarative clauses, as this formulation implies. We will not develop this any further here, as the task is clearly beyond the scope and topic of this essay; We simply note that any such analysis will have to account for the well-known fact—see Belletti (1988) and (1999) and much previous work—that Italian and French have at least two different types of postverbal subjects: those of inaccusatives tolerate *ne/en*-extraction, while those of (in)transitives (typically) don't. See Poletto and Pollock (in prep). Rather than relying on the idea that in the former case the subjects are generated low—thus allowing for acceptable *ne* cliticization to some c-commanding Clitic Phrase head—while in the latter they are generated too high for that to take place, a uniform Remnant IP movement to the left periphery will have to claim that *ne/en* cliticization can apply before Remnant movement takes place when IP contains an inaccusative, though typically not when it contains intransitives (see Kayne and Pollock 2001: n. 9).

31. Examples (90B(a)) and (91B(a)) are not the most natural sentences in the dialogue. Most speakers would probably prefer to left-dislocate the constituent inside the VP and have a postverbal contrastively stressed QP, as in (90B(c)) or (91B(c)).

32. Contrasts like (i) and (ii) might conceivably be viewed in the same terms, with the subjunctive making a groundP layer fully available in noninterrogative subordinates, which indicatives would typically ban:

(i)   ??Je crois qu'est parti Jean.
      I think that is left Jean
      'I think Jean has left.'

(ii) Je doute que soit parti Jean
      I doubt that be left Jean
      'I doubt that Jean has left.'

On the nonavailability of SI in yes/no questions and *si* subordinates, see later. See Kayne and Pollock (2001: part 2) for an analysis of such contrasts relying on subject extraction from the subordinate and Remnant movement to the Comp domain of the *matrix* clause rather than on Remnant movement to the left periphery of the *embedded* sentence.

33. See Poletto (2000) and Obenauer and Poletto (1999) for arguments that other higher positions must be added to (94) when rhetorical questions are taken into account.

34. The assumption is that anything does *not* go in the variation among languages: more precisely, that surface differences in the syntax of languages as closely related as French, Bellunese, the Northern Italian dialects, and Italian, however bizarre in appearance, like the respective surface distribution of *que* and *che* in French and Bellunese (see section 2), should follow from the interplay of general UG principles and a limited set of parameters, often tied to the morphology of each language. The analysis developed here fits into that general picture fairly well, although, of course, the fact that it does doesn't suffice to make it right.

35. What this formulation implies is that (wh-)quantification is read—or fed to the Conceptual/intensional systems—'on line'; the question of whether non-wh-operators can also stand in or move through Op1/2P cannot be discussed here. In the likely event that they don't—despite French sentences like *Il faut tous qu'ils partent* (they must all that they go = 'They must all go')—our 'OpP' label will remain apt if UG regulates the choice of the different operator positions to which different types of operators are attracted and from which they (weakly) bind their variables. This is the tacit assumption concerning the position to which QPs like *beaucoup* move in French QAD (quantification at a distance) constructions like (i)—on which see Obenauer (1984, 1994):

(i)   Il a beaucoup lu de livres.
      he has many read of books
      'He read a lot of books.'

Beaucoup in (i) is presumably standing in an IP internal operator position, but that position cannot host wh-phrases—cf. (ii):

(ii)   *Il a combien lu de livres?
       he has how many read of books
       'Did he read lot of books?'

36. If English in particular and the Germanic languages in general didn't share that restriction, we might consider that sentences like *Who has John rung up?* are derived via exactly the same Remnant IP movement to Force as its French counterpart *Qui a-t-il appelé?* On this, see Poletto and Pollock (in prep).

37. This formulation implies that there should be cases of (concealed) stylistic inversion with a [+ground] pronominal subject; Poletto and Pollock (1999, in prep) do, in fact, claim that pairs like (i) and (ii) in French follow from the fact that in (i) (string vacuous remnant) IP movement to GP is possible, though it is not in (ii), for the reason just stated in the text:

(i)   a. Où il va?
          where he goes
          'Where is he going?'
       b. Qui t'as vu
          who you've seen
          'Whom did you see?'

(ii)   a. ?*Où Yves va
          where Yves goes
          'Where is Yves going?'
       b. ?* Qui Paul a vu
          who Paul has seen
          'Whom has Paul seen?'

38. This is also in possibly apparent noninverted sentences like *Où il va?* (where he goes) and *Quand elle a téléphoné?* (when she has phoned). (See previous note), as well as

subject extraction sentences like *Qui est venu*? (Who came?) in which it is very tempting to say that string vacuous Remnant IP movement has (obligatorily) applied. See Poletto and Pollock (in prep).

39. But see the discussion of (82) on D-linked *COsa*. The fact that Remnant IP movement and SCLI are still possible options in sentences like (i) containing D-linked wh-phrases, we take to follow from a possible option in the assignment of the ground feature either to IP or to the D-linked (complex) wh-phrase:

(i) a. Lequel de tes amis ont rencontré Marie et Jean
        which of your friends have met Marie and Jean
        Which of your friend did Marie and Jean meet?
     b. Quale libro ha letto, Gianni?
        which book has read, Gianni
        Which book did Gianni read?

The numerations of (i) and (ii) are thus crucially different:

(ii) a. Lequel de tes amis Marie et Jean ont rencontré?
        which of your friends Marie and Jean have met
        'Which of your friends did Marie and Jean meet?'
     b. Quale libro ha letto Gianni?
        which book has read Gianni
        'Which book did Gianni read?'

This is because in (ii) (*lequel de*) *tes amis* and *Quale libro* are [+ground] while I(P) is in (i); this should most probably be tied to the "salience" of what counts as Ground in the discourse.

40. We have remained vague as to the precise mechanism that allows this (lexical) checking; see Poletto and Pollock (in prep).

References

Alexiadou, A., and E. Anagnostopoulou (1998) "Parametrizing Agr: Word Order, V-Movement, and EPP-Checking." *Natural Language and Linguistic Theory* 16, 491–539.

Belletti, A. (1988) "The Case of Unaccusatives." *Linguistic Inquiry* 19, 1–34.

———— (2001) "Inversion as Focalization," in A. Hulk and J-Y. Pollock (eds.) *Inversion in Romance and the Theory of Universal Grammar*. New York: Oxford University Press, 60–90.

Beninca', P., and C. Poletto (1997) *Quaderni di lavoro dell' ASIS,* 1. Padua: Centro Stampa Maldura.

———— (1999) "Topic, Focus and V2: Defining the CP Sublayers." Unpublished ms., university of Padua. Also chapter 3 in this volume.

Cardinaletti, A., and M. Starke (1999) "The Typology of Structural Deficiency: On the Three Grammatical Classes," in H. van Riemsdijk (ed.) *Clitics in the Languages of Europe*, vol. 8 of *Empirical Approaches to Language Typology*. Berlin: Mouton de Gruyter, 145–234.

Cheng, L. S., and J. Rooryck (2000) "Licensing Wh-in-Situ." *Syntax* 3.1, 1–19.

Chomsky, N. (1986) *Barriers*. Cambridge, Mass.: MIT Press.

———— (1995) *The Minimalist Program*. Cambridge, Mass.: MIT Press.

———— (1998) "Minimalist Inquiries: The Framework." MIT Occasional Papers in Linguistics, no. 15. Cambridge, Mass.: MIT.

———— (1999) *Adverbs and Functional Heads: A Cross-Linguistic Perspective*. New York: Oxford University Press.

Cornulier, B. de (1974) *"Pourquoi* et l'inversion du sujet non clitique," in C. Rohrer and N. Ruwet (eds.) *Actes du Colloque Franco-Allemand de Grammaire Transformationnelle.* Tübingen: Niemeyer, vol. 1, 139–163.

Friedemann, M.-A. (1997) *Sujets syntaxiques, positions, inversion et pro.* Berlin: Peter Lang.

Hulk, A. (1993) "Residual Verb-Second and the Licensing of Functional Features." *Probus* 5, 127–154.

Katz, J. J., and P. Postal (1964) *An Integrated Theory of Linguistic Descriptions.* Cambridge, Mass.: MIT Press.

Kayne, R. S. (1972) "Subject Inversion in French Interrogatives," in J. Casagrande and B. Saciuk (eds.), *Generative Studies in Romance Languages.* Rowley, Mass.: Newbury House, 70–126.

——— (1975) *French Syntax: The Transformational cycle.* Cambridge, Mass.: MIT Press.

——— (1991) "Romance Clitics, Verb Movement, and PRO." *Linguistic Inquiry* 22, 647–686.

——— (1994) *The Antisymmetry of Syntax.* Linguistic Inquiry Monographs no. 25. Cambridge, Mass.: MIT Press.

——— (1998) "Overt vs Covert Movement." *Syntax* 1.2, 128–191.

——— (2000) *Parameters and Universals.* New York: Oxford University Press.

Kayne, R. S., and J.-Y. Pollock (1979) "Stylistic Inversion, Successive Cyclicity and Move NP in French." *Linguistic Inquiry* 9, 595–621.

——— (2001) "New Thoughts on Stylistic Inversion," in A. Hulk and J.-Y. Pollock (eds.) *Inversion in Romance and the Theory of Universal Grammar.* New York: Oxford University Press, 107–162.

Koopman, H., and A. Szabolcsi (2000) *The Hungarian Verbal Complex: Incorporation as XP-Movement.* Cambridge, Mass.: MIT Press.

Laenzlinger, C. (1998) *Comparative Studies in Word Order Variation: Adverbs, Pronouns and Clause Structure in Romance and Germanic.* Amsterdam: John Benjamins.

Munaro, N. (1999) *Sintagmi interrogativi nei dialetti italiani settentrionali.* Padua: Unipress.

Munaro, N., and H.-G. Obenauer (1999) "Underspecified *wh*-Phrases in Pseudo-interrogatives." Unpublished ms., CNRS Paris-St. Denis / CNR Padua.

Obenauer, H.-G. (1984) "On the Identification of Empty Categories." *Linguistic Review* 4, 153–202.

——— (1994) "Aspects de la syntaxe A-barre: effets d'intervention et mouvements des quantifieurs." Thèse d'Etat, Université de Paris VIII.

Obenauer, H.-G., and C. Poletto (1999) *Rhetorical Wh-Phrases in the Left Periphery of the Sentence.* Venice Working Papers in Linguistics. Venice: CLI.

Poletto, C. (2000) *The Higher Functional Field: Evidence from the Northern Italian Dialects.* New York Oxford University Press.

Poletto, C., and J.-Y. Pollock (1999) "On the Left Periphery of Romance *Wh*-Questions." Talk delivered at the Workshop on the Cartography of Functional Projections, Pontignano, November 1999.

——— (2000) "Remnant Movement and Deficient *wh*-words in some Romance Languages." Talk delivered at the Workshop on the Antysimmetry of Syntax. Cortona, May 15–17, 2000.

——— (in prep) "On Romance Interrogatives," (Unpublished ms.).

Poletto, C., and R. Zanuttini (2000) "Marking New Information in the Left Periphery: The Case of *pa* in Central Rhaetoromance." Talk delivered at the 6th Giornata di Dialettologia Padua, June 8, 2000.

Pollock, J.-Y. (1989) "Verb Movement, Universal Grammar and the Structure of IP." *Linguistic Inquiry* 20, 365–424.

—— (1998) "On the Syntax of Subnominal Clitics: Cliticization and Ellipsis." *Syntax* 1.3, 300–330.

—— (2000) "Subject Clitics, Subject Clitic Inversion and Complex Inversion: Generalizing Remnant Movement to the Comp Area." Unpublished manuscript, Amiens.

Pollock, J.-Y., N. Munaro, and C. Poletto (1999) "Eppur si Muove! On comparing French, Portuguese and Bellunese *Wh*-movement." In the electronic *Festchrift for Noam Chomsky's 70th birthday,* available at http://mitpress.mit.edu/celebration.

Rizzi, L. (1997) "The Fine Structure of the Left Periphery," in L. Haegeman (ed.) *Elements of Grammar.* Dordrecht: Kluwer, 281–337.

Roberts, I. (1993) "The Nature of Subject Clitics in Franco-Provençal Valdôtain," in A. Belletti (ed.) *Syntactic Theory and the Dialects of Italian.* Turin: Rosenberg and Sellier, 319–353.

Sportiche, D. (1993) "Subject Clitics in French and Romance: Complex Inversion and Clitic Doubling." Unpublished ms., UCLA.

Terzi, A. (1999) "Clitic Combinations, Their Hosts and Their Ordering." *Natural Language and Linguistic Theory* 17, 85–121.

Vanelli, L. (1992) "Da lo a il: la storia dell'articolo definito maschile singolare in italiano e nei dialetti settentrionali." *Rivista Italiana di Dialettologia* 16, 29–66.

Zanuttini, R. (1997) *Negation and Clausal Structure: A Comparative Study of Romance Languages.* New York: Oxford University Press.

10

The C-System in Brythonic Celtic Languages, V2, and the EPP

IAN ROBERTS

The basic empirical goal of this chapter is to examine the nature and structure of the C-system in Welsh and in at least some of the other Celtic languages. (I leave aside Scots Gaelic and Modern Irish; for some remarks on the latter, see McCloskey 2000). The theoretical issue behind the discussion is to consider whether we can maintain that the Extended Projection Principle (EPP) holds at the CP-level in these languages, and, if so, in what form. Doing this entails a discussion of Germanic verb second (V2), since it has been proposed that the obligatory XP-movement into the C-system that makes up part of this phenomenon is a consequence of the EPP (cf. Chomsky 2000, 2001; Haegeman 1996; Laenzlinger 1998; Roberts 1993; and Roberts and Roussou 2002).

Section 1 looks at the Welsh particle system and compares it with the V2 system of Germanic languages. At the relevant level of abstraction, the two systems are alike, as we shall see. Section 2 deals with the Breton particle system. This system differs from Welsh in one crucial respect, which appears to be connected to the existence of long V-movement in Breton. Following Borsley et al. (1996) and Roberts (2000), I will show that this construction is a genuine violation of the standard Head Movement Constraint, and also show how the version of Relativized Minimality in Rizzi (2000) can account for this and for the constraints on long V-movement that have been observed. In both of these systems we observe variants of a default "filled-Fin" requirement that is reminiscent in significant respects of the Germanic V2 property. In section 3 I attempt to account for this observation in terms of the EPP.

1. Welsh particles

The "sentential particles" of Welsh are illustrated in (1):[1]

(1) a. Root affirmative *fe, mi, y*:
        Fe/mi welais i John.
        PRT saw I John
        'I saw John.'
     b. Direct relative:
        y dynion a ddarllenodd y llyfr
        the men PRT read-3SG the book
        'the men who read the book'
     c. Indirect relative:
        y dynion y dywedodd Wyn y byddant yn darllen y llyfr
        the men PRT said Wyn that will-be-3PL ASP read the book
        'the men who Wyn said will read the book'
     d. Root negative:
        Ni ddarllenodd Emrys y llyfr.
        NEG read Emrys the book
        'Emrys didn't read the book.'
     e. Subordinate negative:
        Dan ni 'n gobeithio nad ydach chi yn siomedig.
        are we ASP hope *nad* are you PRED disappointed
        'We hope that you're not disappointed.'

Let us look at these one by one.

The root affirmative particles, like most of the other particles, are natural candidates for membership of the C-system. This is apparent from the fact that these elements must be adjacent to the finite verb (only an "infixed pronoun" can intervene, such as *mi'ch gwelais i* 'I saw you(PL)'; we treat these pronouns as Romance-style proclitics on the finite verb that are moved with the finite verb to the highest head position inside IP and so show up immediately adjacent to C).[2] In particular, adverbs cannot intervene between these particles and the finite verb:

(2) a. Bore 'ma, *fe/mi* glywes i'r newyddion ar y radio.
        morning this PRT heard I the news on the radio
        'This morning, I heard the news on the radio.'
     b.*Fe/mi   bore 'ma glywes i 'r newyddion ar y radio.
        PRT morning this heard I the news on the radio

The "direct" and "indirect" relative particles illustrated in (1b and c) have very interesting properties. They appear in relatives, as in (1b and c); in wh-questions, as in (3a); and in focused clauses and in abnormal sentences, which, following Tallerman (1996), I analyze as topicalization (3c):[3]

(3) a. Pa ddynion *a* werthodd y ci?   (wh-question)
        which men PRT sold the dog
        'Which men sold the dog?'
     b. Y dynion *a* werthodd y ci.   (Focussed clause)
        the men PRT sold-3SG the dog
        'It's the men who have sold the dog.'

   c. Y dynion *a* werthasant y ci.   (Abnormal sentence)
      the man PRT sold-3PL the dog
      'The men, they sold the dog.'

They thus appear to mark a Wh-dependency in C. For this reason, I will refer to them as Wh-particles henceforth. The "direct" particle appears when an object, subject, or VP is fronted; otherwise, the "indirect" particle appears.[4] These particles are in complementary distribution with *fe/mi*, can host an "infixed pronoun," and cannot be separated from V by anything else. All of these properties can be accounted for if we say they occupy the same position as *fe/mi*—namely, C. I discuss the focus construction of (3b) in more detail later.

    I do not intend to propose an analysis of the Welsh negation system here (cf. Borsley and Jones 2000), and so I do not have much to say regarding the negative particles. In a simple finite clause, *ni(d)* appears to occupy the same position as *fe/mi* and the Wh-particles—although, as we shall see below, *ni(d)* is not in full complementary distribution with the Wh-particles:

(4) Ni redodd Siôn i ffwrdd.   (Rouveret 1994: 127)
    NEG ran John away
    'John didn't run away.'

The "subordinating" negative particle *nad* introduces negative clauses containing the auxiliary *bod* (be) in either the present or the imperfect tense, as seen in (1e) where the form of the auxiliary is suppletive *ydach*. (On these clauses, which have very interesting properties, see Rouveret 1996; Tallerman 1998; and Roberts (to appear)). This particle also appears in negated focused clauses:

(5) a. Mi wn i nad y dyn a ddaeth.   (Tallerman 1996: 119)
      PRT know I NEG the man PRT came
      'I know it was not the man who came.'
    b. Nid y dyn na ddaeth.   (Watkins 1991: 332, cited in Tallerman 1996: 119)
      NEG the man NEG came
      'It's not the man who didn't come.'

So *na(d)* seems to occupy the same position as the other particles here.

    It seems clear that the particles just discussed occupy C. However, if we adopt a split-C system—for example, that proposed by Rizzi (1997)—the question arises as to which position these elements occupy. In this connection, the data and analysis in McCloskey (1996) are relevant. On the basis of the relative positions of sentential adverbs and complementizers, McCloskey argues that C lowers to I in Irish. The argument is based on the observation that, in general across languages, sentential adverbs don't adjoin to CP:

(6) a. In general, he understands what's going on.
    b. It's probable that in general he understands what's going on.
    c.*It's probable [CP in general [CP that he understands what's going on]].
    d.*[In general [that he understands what's going on]] is surprising.

In (6c and d) the bracketing is meant to indicate that the adverb should be interpreted as modifying the *that*-clause. These readings are impossible in English. McCloskey calls this general ban on the adjunction of adverbs to CP the Adjunction Prohibition.

Irish shows the opposite distribution of adverbs in relation to CPs:

(7)   Is doíche [faoi cheann cúpla   lá [go bhféadfaí imeacht]]
      is probable at-the-end-of couple day that   could leave
                     ADV   C   I

McCloskey also shows that we cannot maintain that Irish simply lacks the Adjunction Prohibition (however exactly this idea might be formulated). The evidence against
this idea is that the order *adverb–WH-phrase* is bad:

(8)   *Ní bhfuair siad amach ariamh an bhliain sin cé a bhí ag goid a gcuid móna.
      NEG found they out ever the year that who PRT was stealing their turf

McCloskey proposes (i) that sentential adverbs adjoin to IP in Irish just as in
English (and other languages), and (ii) that Irish has a rule that lowers C to I. The C-
to-I lowering rule derives orders like that in (7) and, since it is obligatory, it explains
the ungrammaticality of (8). Schematically, the relevant parts of (7) have the following structure:

(9)   t [$_{IP}$ Adv [$_{IP}$ C+I . . .

A system like Rizzi's offers a simple way of handling McCloskey's data without having recourse to the C-to-I lowering operation. The basic idea is to capitalize
on the overall similarity between the structure of McCloskey's argument and the
structure of Pollock's (1989) arguments for V-to-I raising in French and I-to-V lowering in English. Pollock observed, among others, the following contrast between
French and English:

(10)   a. *French:* V+Infl Adv   direct object
       b. *English:* Adv   V+Infl direct object

Pollock concluded that V raises to Infl in French but that Infl lowers to V in English.
The Irish-English contrast that we saw in (6) and (7) can be handled in the same way.
Here what we have is the following:

(11)   a. *Irish:*   Adv C IP
       b. *English:* C Adv   IP

As Rizzi (1997) points out, complementizers like English *that* and Irish *go* mark
two things: that the clause they introduce is declarative and that it is finite. In this
respect, they are each associated with features of two heads, Force and Fin, just as a
finite verb is associated with properties of V (thematic structure) and T (tense). So
we might expect that cross-linguistically, some complementizers are overtly realized
in Force and others in Fin. Looking again at (11), we can see that in these terms, *that*
can be analyzed as appearing in Force and *go* as appearing in Fin. So it may be that
English Force overtly attracts Fin (see Rizzi 1997 and later in this discussion for some
qualification of this idea), while in Irish this is not the case. We need only add that
sentential adverbs either appear in a TopP between Force and Fin or occupy specifier positions reserved for them (along the lines proposed in Cinque 1999), and we
derive the different distributions of adverbs and complementisers without recourse
to a lowering rule. Example (12) summarizes the proposal:

(12)   [_ForceP [_Force *that*] . . . [_TopP Adv . . . [_FinP [_Fin *go*] IP]]]

The fact that sentential adverbs cannot precede Wh-phrases in Irish, illustrated in (8), can be accounted for if we assume that Wh-phrases in Irish move to a Specifier position higher than TopP; Rizzi argues that Italian interrogative Wh-phrases occupy Spec,FocP (FocP is situated in between ForceP and TopP). In that case, we can account straightforwardly for (8).[5]

Let us now return to Welsh. In terms of the schema for the difference between English and Irish given in (11), we can observe that Welsh has the order *C–Adv–C*. In other words, adverbs can appear after certain complementizers but not others, as shown in Tallerman (1996). They cannot intervene between the particle *y*, which introduces finite clauses, and the verb:

(13)   *Dywedodd ef y yfory bydd yn gadael.
       said he PRT tomorrow he-will-be ASP leave

By parity of reasoning with what I said about Irish *go*, we could take (13) as evidence that *y* is in Fin. I also observed in (2) that adverbs cannot intervene between *fe/mi* and the verb. Again, I can apply the analysis of McCloskey's Irish data and take it that *fe/mi* are in Fin.

Most interestingly, focused clauses like (3b) can be embedded under another complementizer, as in (14) (examples again from Tallerman 1996: 108,117,119):

(14)   a. Dywedais i *mai* ['r dynion *a* fuasai'n gwerthu'r ci].
          said I *mai* the men PRT would-ASP sell-the dog
          I said that it's the men who would sell the dog.
       b. *Ai* [ceffyl *a* fuasai hi'n gwerthu]?
          ai horse PRT would she-ASP sell
          'Is it the horse that she'd sell?'
          Nid can also precede the focused clause:

(15)   *Nid* [y dyn *a* ddaeth].
       NEG the man PRT came
       'It wasn't the man who came.'

In this case, the complementary distribution between *nid* and the wh-particles breaks down. The natural way to account for this is to say that *nid* is able to occupy two different positions in the C-system: Fin and Force.[6] Recall that *nid* can introduce a focused clause with the negative particle *nad*, and that *nad* introduces embedded negative focused clauses, as shown in (5), repeated here:

(5)   a. Mi wn i *nad* y dyn a ddaeth.   (Tallerman 1996: 119)
          PRT know I NEG the man PRT came
          'I know it was not the man who came.'
       b. Nid y dyn *na* ddaeth.   (Watkins 1991: 332, cited in Tallerman 1996: 119)
          NEG the man NEG came
          'It's not the man who didn't come.'

Rouveret (1994) and Tallerman (1996) both treat these structures as involving "CP-recursion." Now, the interesting observation, due to Tallerman, is that adverbs can appear between *mai* and the focused constituent, but not—with embedded scope—before *mai*:

(16)   a. Dywedais i *mai* fel arfer y dynion *a* fuasai'n gwerthu'r ci.
            said I *mai* as usual the men PRT would ASP sell-the dog
            'I said that it's, as usual, the men who would sell the dog.'
        b.*Dywedais i fel arfer *mai* 'r dynion *a* fuasai'n gwerthu'r ci.
            said I as usual *mai* the men PRT would ASP sell-the dog

However, it is also possible to separate a focused constituent from the focus particle with an adverb, as (17) shows:

(17)   Dywedais i *mai*'r dynion fel arfer *a* fuasai'n gwerthu'r ci.
        said I *mai* the men as usual PRT would-ASP sell-the dog
        'I said that it's the men, as usual, who will sell the dog.'

It seems reasonable to situate the focused XP in SpecFoc; this implies that the adverb in (17) occupies a position between Foc and Fin (possibly SpecFinP or a special position for adverbial specifiers), and so the position for *a* must be Fin. This accords with the observed complementary distribution of *a/y* with *fe/mi*. We consider *mai* and the other elements that introduce "CP-recursion" illustrated in (14) and (15) to be in Force. Hence the intervening adverb in (16a) can be thought of as occupying a specifier position in between Force and FocP.[7]

So, I propose that the sentence-initial particles of Welsh fit into Rizzi's (1997) split-C system in the following way:

(18)   *Force*   *Fin*
        mai/ai/nad/nid   *a/y/fe/mi/bod*(Pres/imperf)

With these points in mind, let us now compare the Welsh particle system with the V2 system of the Germanic languages.

The obvious similarity lies in the fact that full V2 is characteristic of root affirmative clauses:

(19)   a. Yesterday John danced.
        b. Gestern hat Johann getanzt.
        c.*Gestern Johann hat getanzt.

Taking the movement here to be V-movement to Fin, it is natural to see this V-movement as directly analogous to the merger of the root affirmative particles in Welsh. If, following Roberts (2001), we consider parameterization to be a question of PF-realization (or not) of functional categories, with movement triggered just where the lexicon makes available no lexical item which can satisfy the realization requirement by merger, then we can understand this similarity as a manifestation of the fact that Welsh actually has the same parametric property as German: namely, that Fin must have a lexical realization at some stage in the derivation (Fin* in the notation of Roberts 2001). This idea is very close to Chomsky's (2000, 2001) "strong EPP-feature," but I keep the two notions distinct here, reserving the term "EPP-feature" for the requirement for movement to a Specifier position as in Chomsky's system—see section 3.2). Welsh differs from German in having particles that can be inserted into root Fin, preempting movement of the finite verb. Like V-movement to Fin in German, the particles appear only in finite clauses. This can be stated simply: Fin requires a PF-realization when +finite. Nonfinite Fin is subject to different PF-realization conditions (which, unsurprisingly, are not quite the same in the two languages; see Tallerman (1998) on infinitival *i* in Welsh). On why V+T-movement to Fin is accompanied by obligatory XP-fronting in Germanic, see section 3.2.

The proposals just made for the difference between English and Welsh/Irish complementizers point the way to an account of Germanic-style root-embedded asymmetries in verb-movement. Following Rizzi and Roberts (1989), I assume that the generalization has to do with selection. Let us suppose, then, that a selected Force position has features in virtue precisely of being selected by a higher predicate. The fact that typical complementizers like English *that* raise from Fin to Force must then be attributed to the fact that selected Force triggers overt Fin-movement (presumably because it requires PF-realization). Let us suppose that the verb-movement part of V2 is a reflex of the fact that Fin requires a PF-realization, so in this case we have Fin*. In these terms, we can see that complementizers are able to satisfy this requirement in embedded clauses, even if they subsequently raise to Force. So all the Germanic languages, including English, have Fin-to-Force movement where Force is selected (i.e., in embedded clauses). This blocks V-movement to Fin in embedded clauses as a general case of Merge preempting Move; exploiting the presence of complementizers in C as a way of blocking V2 is an idea that goes back to den Besten (1983).

The claim that all the Germanic V2 languages have Fin* predicts that, in all these languages, the presence of a complementizer is required in finite embedded declaratives. English and the Mainland Scandinavian languages allow for complementizer deletion in certain environments. (See Stowell 1981 for a discussion of the English environments; an anonymous reviewer points out that they are the same in the Mainland Scandinavian languages.) German diverges somewhat from the general pattern in that it requires embedded V2 exactly where the complementizer is missing:

(20) Ich glaube, *gestern habe* Maria dieses Buch gelesen.
      I believe yesterday has Maria this book read
      'I believe Maria read this book yesterday.'

But of course this is consistent with the general proposal for Fin* (where there is no complementizer deletion).

A further refinement is required to account for the presence of *that* in "CP-recursion" contexts in English like (21) (and the comparable situation in the Scandinavian languages; see Vikner 1994):

(21) a. I said that never in my life had I seen a place like Bangor.
      b. Vi ved at denne bog har Bo ikke læst.   (Danish: Vikner 1994: 67)
         we know that this book has Bo not read
         'We know that Bo has not read this book.'

Assuming V is in Foc and the negative constituent in SpecFocP in (21a), *that* cannot have raised to Force from Fin. To account for this, I assume that *that* is merged in Force in the complements to bridge verbs, again presumably to satisfy the requirement that embedded Force has a lexical realization. In these cases in V2 languages, as for example in (21b), Fin* is satisfied by V-movement (Fin* is satisfied by V-movement passing through it in (21a)). The ability to directly select a complementizer in Force is a property of bridge verbs in the languages in question (this is presumably connected to the observation that these embedded clauses have assertive illocutionary force; see Hooper and Thompson 1973); German presumably does not allow this but instead selects the subjunctive in examples like (20) (see also Penner and Bader 1995 on further properties of this construction). Non-bridge verbs (canonically factives like *regret*, etc.) are unable to directly select a complementizer in this position.[8]

In wh-complements where no overt complementizer is present, something more must be said. Here I can capitalize on an observation by Stowell (1981: 422) to the effect that selection for +WH neutralizes selection for Fin. This can be illustrated by paradigms such as the following:

(22) a. I explained how to fix the sink.   [+WH, −Fin]
      b. I explained how we should fix the sink.   [+WH, +Fin]
      c. I explained that we should fix the sink.   [−WH, +Fin]
      d.*I explained to fix the sink.   [−WH, −Fin]

In Rizzi's system, this is straightforwardly accounted for by the local nature of selection (see Chomsky 1965) and the fact that both Force and Foc are structurally higher than Fin. In that case, it follows that selection for Force as Interrogative or for Foc as +WH[9] blocks selection for a feature of Fin. Hence the requirement for a finite complement (i.e., selection for Fin), violated in (22d), is inoperative where a feature of Foc is selected, as in (22a and b). The crucial assumption here is that local selection can take place "across" a head that lacks features relevant for selection; in other words, (23a) and (23b) are possible selection configurations, but not (23c) (where ". . ." contains no heads and each head asymmetrically c-commands the next from left to right):

(23) a. A[+F] . . . B[+F]   (Local selection)
      b. A[+F] . . . B . . . C[+F]   (Non-local selection across an inert head)
      c. A[+F] . . . B[+F] . . . C[+F]   (Impossible for A to directly select C)

The parallels between selection so construed and the Agree relation of Chomsky (2000), as well as certain versions of relativized minimality are clear, but I will not pursue them here.

What we observe in (22), then, are the following selection relations (and nonrelations):

(22a,b):   V selects Force[+Q]; Force [+Q] selects Foc[+WH]; Foc[+WH] *does not* select any property of Fin

(22c):   V directly selects finite Fin; Force and Foc are inert (see (23b)); this requirement is violated in (22d) (assuming *explain* requires finite Fin where it is structurally able to select a property of Fin).

In matrix clauses, we observe essentially the same situation. Force[+Q] can select a [+WH] Foc, in which case Fin is not selected for. In contrast, if Foc is inactive (i.e., [−WH]), then Fin must be finite. These facts are illustrated by the following paradigm:

(24)   a. What to do?   (Force[+Q], Foc[+WH], Fin not selected)
      b. What should we do?   (Force[+Q], Foc[+WH], Fin not selected)
      c. Should we leave?   (Force[+Q] selects finite Fin where Foc is inactive)
      d. *Whether/if to leave?   (Violation of selection property of Force[+Q])

If Fin is active, it is Fin*; as (24) shows, where Foc is [+WH], Fin may be either active or not, but where Foc is inactive, Fin* is selected by Force[+Q], and must be active.[10]

What about Fin in (22)? Why does it not trigger movement in V2 languages if it is not selected? Clearly, the reason is that this is not an inherently declarative Fin. Suppose then that Fin (and therefore the clause it heads) is interpreted as declarative just when no higher position in the C-system is active. This is very natural, since it amounts to saying that +finite Fin is interpreted as declarative when it is in a clear intuitive sense the head of CP. It also entails that Force is inactive in (root) declarative clauses, and so declarative is the unmarked clause type. So, nonselected declarative Fin is equivalent to root, finite Fin. Nonselected declarative Fin is in principle distinct from selected, declarative Fin; the former is a kind of default, while the latter is a selected C-head, entering into selection relations like other heads. Selected, nondeclarative Fin is different again. We thus arrive at the following general picture of the varieties of Fin (here the asterisk means that the relevant type of Fin needs a PF-realization in the language in question, not that it is ungrammatical):

(25)   a. +selected, +declarative   (* in Germanic)
      b. −selected, +declarative   (* in Germanic, not in English (full V2))
      c. +selected, −declarative   (*in Germanic, *in English (residual V2))
      d. −selected, −declarative   (not found, as declarative is a default)

Both German V-movement and Welsh *fe/mi*-merger are root phenomena, as I have mentioned. Let us suppose that root declarative Force has no feature content, such clauses being interpreted as declarative by default. In fact, we can go a step further and assume that selection for a +finite Fin automatically implies a declarative clause, and thus that there is no declarative feature. This is directly supported by Stowell's (1981: 422) observation that selection for a wh-feature preempts selection for finiteness (see the paradigm in (22)). Hence, the generalization about languages like German and Welsh is that unselected Fin requires PF-realization. In German, unselected Fin has no lexical realization and so V-movement is triggered. In Welsh, unselected Fin can be realized by *fe/mi*.

It is clear from (1) that the Welsh interrogative, negative, and relative particles manifest substantially the same features as those that are manifested by residual V2. These features are naturally treated as associated with Force (interrogative, negation) or Focus (wh, negation). Although most of the Welsh particles are in Fin, as we have seen, negative *ni(d)/na(d)* can be in Force.[11] The particles that clearly occur in Fin are root *fe/mi*, embedded *y*, and the wh-particles *a* and *y*. None of these is inherently associated with a marked clause type; *fe/mi* and *y* are declarative, and *a/y* can mark a focused or a relativized constituent, hence a wh-dependency in an otherwise declarative clause. However, the *a/y* particles can also appear in indirect questions; I account for this by saying that these particles may be—but do not have to be—selected by a Q-morpheme in Force. Evidence that the *a/y* particles can be associated with different features in Force comes from focused clauses embedded under a negative and an interrogative Force, exemplified in (14b) and (15).

To conclude, in this section I have looked at the particle system of Welsh and shown how, at the relevant level of abstraction, it can be seen as a manifestation of the same parameter value as that which gives rise to full V2 in the Germanic languages. In these terms, I gave an account of the root nature of both the affirmative *fe/mi* particles and of V2. This account relies on the idea that declarative clauses are the unmarked clause type, in the sense that there is no distinct declarative feature, [+finite] Fin being interpreted as declarative. From this, an important observation regarding full V2 emerges. If the Welsh particles manifest a default value of Fin*, and so does the V-movement component of V2, then it follows that the XP-movement component of V2, since it takes place where there is V-movement but not where there is merger of a particle, must be systematically related to the V-movement operation. To put it more succinctly, the Welsh data lead to the following observation about V2 (this observation was anticipated in Roberts and Roussou 2002):

(26)   Observation I:
       The second-position effect only arises where Fin is realized by Move.

2.   Breton

I now turn to a consideration of the Breton data, which will lead to a confirmation of observation I in (26) and a refinement of what I have said about declarative Fin.

Breton has a very similar particle system to that of Welsh, with one very significant difference that emerges immediately upon inspection of the list in (27) and a comparison with (1):

(27)   Subordinating: *e*
       Interrogative: *hag-en*
       Negative: *ne*
       "Direct" relative: *a*
       "Indirect" relative: *e*

The difference with Welsh is that Breton has no root affirmative particles (see Borsley and Roberts 1996: 26). The significance of this observation will emerge later in this discussion.

As observed by Borsley et al. (1996), Breton, although a VSO language (as we saw in chapter 1), does not allow simple verb-first clauses with an initial main verb:

(28)   *Lenn Anna al levr.
       reads Anna the book

Instead, the equivalent of the Welsh focus construction must be used, as illustrated in (29):

(29)   Al levr a lenn Anna.
       the book PRT reads Anna
       'Anna reads the book.'

Example (29) is equivalent to a Welsh example like (3b) (in fact, (29) probably corresponds to the Middle/Biblical Welsh abnormal sentence; following Willis 1998, I take this to be the same construction as the Modern Welsh focus construction of (3b)—see note 3). In neutral clauses, Breton makes use of "long V-movement" (LVM),[12] illustrated in (30):

(30) a. Lenn a ra Anna al levr.
          read-INF PRT does Anna the book
          'Anna reads the book.'
      b. Lennet en deus Anna al levr.
          read-PPRT has Anna the book
          'Anna has read the book.'

In (30a) the infinitive has been fronted, and the finite auxiliary is a form of *ober* 'do'. In (30b) the past participle has been fronted and the finite auxiliary—the compound element *en deus* here—is a form of 'have'.[13]

At first sight, examples like (30b) resemble the German remnant-topicalization construction (see den Besten and Webelhuth 1990; Müller 1998), as in (31):

(31) Gelesen hat Anna das Buch nicht.
      read-PPRT has Anna the book not
      'Anna has not read the book.'

However, the two constructions can be shown to be quite distinct (much of the argumentation and many of the examples in what follows are from Borsley et al. 1996; henceforth BRS). The standard analysis of the German construction in (31) involves the postulation of scrambling of the object *das Buch* and topicalization of the ("remnant") VP containing the trace of scrambling. The postulated structure of (31) is thus (31'):

(31') [$_{VP}$ Gelesen t$_{das\ Buch}$] hat Anna das Buch nicht t$_{VP}$

There are several reasons why this analysis does not carry over to Breton examples like those in (30).

First, Breton has a VP-fronting operation, which has quite different properties from the LVM construction in (30). Comparing these two constructions, we see that VP-fronting can occur across clause boundaries, while LVM is clause-bounded:

(32) a. [$_{VP}$ O lenn al levr] a ouian emañ Yann. (VP-fronting[14])
          PROG read the book PRT know-1SG is Yann
          'I know Yann is reading the book.'
      b.*Desket am eus klevet he deus Anna he c'hentelioù. (LVM)
          learned 1SG have heard 3SGF has Anna her lessons
          'I have heard that Anna has learned her lessons.'

In (32a), the VP (or larger category; see note 14) has been fronted from the complement clause into the C-system of the main clause, and the example is fully grammatical. In (32b), in contrast, the participle of the lower clause is unable to be fronted to the initial position in the main clause.

A second important difference between VP-fronting and LVM is that VP-fronting is possible in negative clauses, while LVM is impossible in this context:

(33) a. [$_{VP}$ O lenn al levr] n'emañ ket Yann.   (VP-fronting)
      PROG read the book NEG is NEG Yann
      'Yann isn't reading the book.'
    b.*Lennet n'en deus ket Tom al levr.   (LVM)
      read NEG.3SGM has NEG Tom the book
      'Tom hasn't read the book.'

Third, the two constructions differ as to which auxiliaries they may occur with. In particular, LVM is impossible with progressive *bezañ*:

(34) *O lenn emañ Yann al levr.
      PROG read is Yann the book

VP-fronting of the complement to progressive *bezañ* is possible, however, as shown in (35a). But stranding of the object is not allowed here, as shown in (35b):

(35) a. [$_{VP}$ O voueta ar moc'h] e oa Helen.
      PROG feed the pigs PRT was Helen
      'Helen was feeding the pigs.'
    b. *O voueta e oa Helen ar moc'h.   (Schafer 1994: 2)

This straightforwardly shows that German-style remnant VP-fronting is unavailable in Breton.[15] From the data in (32–35), we can conclude that the LVM construction is not a case of remnant VP-fronting.

A third difference between German VP-fronting and Breton LVM has been brought to light by Borsley and Kathol (2000). In German, certain types of infinitival complements (so-called coherent infinitives) can be fronted either separately from their selecting verb or together with that verb, but the selecting verb cannot front separately from the infinitival complement:

(36) a. ... daß Peter das Buch wird finden können.
      ... that Peter the book will find can
      '... that Peter will be able to find the book.'
    b. [Finden] wird Peter das Buch können.
      find will Peter the book can
      'Peter will be able to find the book.'
    c.*Können wird Peter das Buch finden.
      can will Peter the book find
    d. [Finden können] wird Peter das Buch.
      find can will Peter the book
      'Peter will be able to find the book.'

These data can be straightforwardly accounted for by assuming that the fronting operation is VP-fronting in every case and that *können* does not form a VP that excludes *finden* (see Wurmbrand 1998 for a recent analysis of coherent infinitives, which argues that such complements are in fact VPs associated with no T- or C-level).

Breton allows structures containing a nonfinite auxiliary and a nonfinite main verb, a kind of *temps surcomposé* shown in (37) (with a PP in initial position and an agreement proclitic occupying the particle position; see note 13):

(37) Er gegin am eus bet kavet al levr.
      in-the kitchen 1SG have had found the book
      'I have found the book in the kitchen.'

What we find here as regards verb and VP-fronting is precisely the opposite of the German facts seen in (36), in that either nonfinite form may undergo movement, but not both together:

(38) a. Kavet am eus bet al levr.
          found 1SG have had the book
          'I have found the book.'
    b. Bet am eus kavet al levr.
          had 1SG have found the book
          'I have found the book.'
    c.*Bet kavet am eus al levr.
          had found 1SG have the book

The contrast with German can be simply accounted for if we analyze the Breton construction as V–, and not VP–, movement.

In addition to what we have seen in contrasting the construction with (remnant) VP-fronting, LVM has a number of interesting properties that are compatible with the fact that it involves movement into the C-system. First, LVM is a root phenomenon (this was first pointed out by Stephens 1982, and then by Schafer 1994 and BRS):

(39) *Lavaret he deus Anna [lennet en deus Tom al levr].
      said 3SGF has Anna read 3SGM has Tom the book
      'Anna said Tom had read the book.'

As mentioned, LVM is subject to what Schafer calls "strict locality": unlike VP-fronting, it cannot take place out of an embedded clause into a main clause (see also (32)). Here I illustrate with an infinitival embedded clause:

(40) a. Gellout a reont goro ar saout.
          be-able(INFIN) PRT do-3SG milk the cows
          'They can milk the cows.'
    b.*Goro a c'hellont ober a saout. (Schafer 1994: 145)
          milk PRT can-3SG do the cows

(An anonymous reviewer points out that the contrast between (38a) and (40b) implies that the complement to a modal is distinct to an aspectual; in the absence of evidence to the contrary, I will assume that the infinitival complements to modals are full infinitival clauses; the ban on LVM in (40b) therefore is a case of the clause-boundedness of LVM.)

Second, LVM cannot take place in negative clauses. Since negation is partly indicated by a negative particle in C (*ne*; see (27) and (33)), we can see this as a case of sensitivity to properties of C. Third, LVM is impossible where some XP is fronted:

(41) *Al levr lennet en deus Tom.
      the book read 3SG has Tom

This can clearly be seen as a further case of sensitivity to a property of C.

Two other properties of LVM are relevant here. First, nothing can intervene between the fronted nonfinite verb and the particle/auxiliary, not even a pronoun (Schafer 1994: 141–142):

(42) a. Plijout a ra din eo tomm an heol.
        please-INFIN PRT do to-me be warm the sun
        'I am happy the sun is warm.'
      b.*Plijout din a ra eo tomm an heol.
        please-INFIN to-me PRT do be warm the sun

(43) a. Gwardet deus he breur gant aked.
        looked-after has-3SGF her brother with care
        'She looked after her brother with care.'
      b.*Gwardet gant aked deus he breur.
        looked-after with care has-3SGF her brother

Second, Schafer (1994: 146f.) shows in detail that the construction is discourse-neutral; it is associated neither with topic nor with focus interpretations.

From all of the preceding arguments, we can conclude that Breton LVM is a genuine case of long head-movement of a nonfinite verb. It appears to move the verb into the C-system, to a position immediately preceding the *a* particle or a form of the 'have'-auxiliary. More precisely, I propose that this is a case of movement of the nonfinite verb to Fin. The verb left-adjoins to the particle or auxiliary in this position, creating the structure in (44) for an example like (30a):

(44)

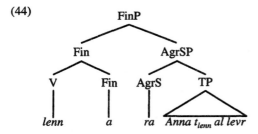

Here movement of the nonfinite verb clearly crosses AgrS (i.e., its constituent heads) and presumably at least also T. In fact, this is allowed by the version of relativized minimality (see Roberts 2000):

(45) $(A_1, \ldots A_n)$ is a chain iff, for $1, i < n$:
      (i) $A_i = A_{i+1}$
      (ii) A_i c-commands A_{i+1}
      (iii) A_{i+1} is in a minimal configuration with A_i

(46) Y is in a minimal configuration with X iff there is no Z such that:
      (i)   Z is nondistinct in structural and featural type from X, and
      (ii) Z c-commands Y and Z does not c-command X.

If we take Fin to be of a distinct featural type from (the heads that make up) AgrS and T, then it will be possible for the moved V in (44) to form a minimal configuration (MC) with its trace according to the definition in (46) (the moved V is Y, its trace is X, and the intervening heads fail to count as Z owing to the fact that they are of a different type). Hence, the moved V can form a well-formed chain with its trace according to the definition in (45). What is the basis for saying that Fin is of a distinct featural type from AgrS and T? Suppose that heads (and, indeed, categories of all types) can, in general, be divided into operators and nonoperators and that this property is relevant for the creation of intervention effects and, hence, for the definition of MC in (45) (see Rizzi 1990, 2000). More generally, as a first approximation we can propose the following partition of heads:[16]

(47) a. Operator heads: Force, Topic, Focus, Fin, Neg ...
      b. Non-operator heads: Agr, T, Asp ...

It certainly seems very natural to propose that Agr-heads are not operators; for T this is perhaps less obvious, although Roberts and Roussou (2002) propose that T contains a variable that is bound by an operator in Fin as a way of accounting for the well-known observation that there is an inherent link between the temporal properties of the C-system and those of the I-system: in this they follow a long line of analysis going back through, among others, Holmberg and Platzack (1995), Pollock (1989), den Besten (1983), Pesetsky (1982), and Stowell (1981). Assuming Roberts and Roussou's approach, then, T is not an operator and the preliminary classification in (47) can be maintained. In turn, this means that we can postulate long-movement of the nonfinite verb in structures like (44) with no violation of relativized minimality.

The proposed account of Breton LVM gets the locality facts just right. In addition to allowing long movement where it is needed—in core cases like (44)—it also accounts for the "strict locality" of LVM, discussed by Schafer and BRS, who observed that LVM can never cross a C-position, and so is strictly clause-bounded. Now we see that this follows from relativized minimality: an intervening Fin (or any element of the C-system; see note 16) blocks the formation of a minimal configuration between the moved head and its trace in examples like (32b) and (33b). Also, I can account for the possibility of long movement of either of a sequence of nonfinite verbs, as illustrated in (38a and b). The formulation of relativized minimality just given combined with (47) means that, if the entire structure is contained within a single IP, neither nonfinite verb will block long-movement of the other.

More generally, the approach to the locality of head movement embodied in (45)–(47) implies that head movement will always be local except in one context, which I can schematize as follows:

(48) $[_{Fin}$ V [-fin] Fin$]$ ... $[_I$ Aux[+fin] $]$ ... t_V ...

In other words, a nonfinite V can move into Fin without violating relativized minimality in cases where Fin has some property that triggers head movement, a finite auxiliary checks the relevant tense and agreement features in the I-system, and some property of Fin or the auxiliary prevents the auxiliary from raising to Fin (see latter in this essay for more on this). Within the I-system (possibly modulo "low" negative markers; see note 16), within the C-system and, trivially, between the highest position in the I-system and the lowest position in the C-system, head movement is always strictly local; that is, the traditional Head Movement Constraint of Travis (1984) and Baker (1988) holds. The contention here is that this is an artefact of the nature of the heads involved and relativized minimality; the locality system allows for a very limited and precisely defined range of cases of long head movement. Other cases that appear to fall under the general schema in (48) have been discussed in the literature: see BRS for a range of Slavic and Romance languages, Čavar and Wilder (1992) on Croatian, and Rivero (1991, 1994).[17]

Given the preceding analysis of Breton, I now need to relate the LVM construction to what was said in the previous section regarding Welsh and German. It seems clear, given the almost minimal difference between the Breton particle system and that of Welsh (basically just the absence of neutral *fe/mi*-type particles in Breton), and given the discourse-neutrality, declarative, root nature of the LVM construction, that this construction is a way to fill a nonselected Fin* (see also Schafer 1994 for a similar proposal). In this respect it is in a sense the functional equivalent of the *fe/mi* particles and therefore of full V2. So I ascribe the same parameter value to Breton as to Welsh and German. The Breton construction differs from the Welsh one in that the presence of *fe/mi* in Welsh means that merger of these elements preempts movement in Welsh, while merger of *a* causes it in Breton (consistent with the fact that Breton *a* is always associated with movement). The availability of particles also distinguishes Breton from German; the Breton particles are such that they allow Breton to satisfy Fin* with one movement, whereas German requires two, so we can see that the LVM possibility preempts full V2.

Diachronic evidence from the history of Welsh confirms the minimal nature of the difference between Breton and Welsh. According to Willis (1996, 1997, 1998), Welsh had the LVM construction until the Early Modern Welsh period (1400–1600):

(49)   Gwyssyaw a oruc Arthur milwyr yr ynys honn.   (CO 922–923: Willis 1997: 17)
       summon PRT did Arthur soldiers the island this
       'Arthur summoned the soldiers of this island.'

Interestingly, at this period the *fe/mi* particles did not exist. These elements developed out of fronted pronouns soon after the Early Modern period (the earliest written examples are from the mid-eighteenth century and are documented in detail by Willis 1998: 225f.). The following are examples of the historical antecedents of *fe* and *mi* cooccurring with particles (note that *ef* is an expletive in (50a); as in Modern German, overt expletives only appeared in the fronted position in Middle Welsh):[18]

(50)   a. Ef a doeth makwyueit a gueisson ieueinc y diarchenu.   (PKM 4.8–9: Willis
          1998: 154)
          it PRT came squires and lads young to-him disrobe
          'There came squires and young lads to disrobe him.'
       b. Mi a rodaf Pryderi a Riannon it.   (PKM 64.18–20: Willis 1997:13–14)
          I PRT will-give Pryderi and Rhiannon to-you
          'I shall give Pryderi and Rhiannon to you.'

It seems then that the loss of LVM in Welsh is connected to the development of the *fe/mi* particles as true Fin-elements from topicalized pronouns.[19]

So, if LVM has the structure in (44) and is the functional equivalent of *fe/mi* and full V2, I can make the following further observation about V2, in addition to the one already given in (26):

(51)   Observation II:
       The second-position requirement can be satisfied by long head-movement.

Putting together this observation and observation I in (26), we can see the following range of properties of nonselected declarative Fin*:

(52) a. Merger of a head: Welsh
      b. Adjunction to a head: Breton.
      c. Creation of a Spec-head relation: full V2.
      d. No morphophonological realization: English, etc.

Example (52c) subsumes observation I in (26), in that V-movement to Fin does not seem to be tolerated on its own: in just this case an XP must be fronted.[20]

The main goal of this section was to analyze the particle system of Breton. We have seen that this system is very similar to that of Welsh, with the sole difference that long V-movement applies to license root declarative Fin, "neutral" particles analogous to Welsh *fe/mi* not being available. Putting this together with the discussion of full V2 in the previous section, we see that there are several ways to license root declarative Fin. In Welsh this is achieved by merger of *fe/mi* (Fin* satisfied by Merge); in German it is achieved by movement of the finite verb (Fin* satisfied by Move), and in Breton it is achieved by merger of *a* and the associated XP-fronting (Fin* satisfied by merger of an element which further triggers movement).

3.   Second Position and the EPP

It is now time to consider the results discussed and to attempt to arrive at a definitive picture both of the nature of the V2 phenomenon and of the EPP.

3.1.   The status of the declarative feature

Let us begin our investigation of the relation between second-position phenomena and the EPP by looking again at the question of the status of the declarative feature. I suggested in the account of the nature of root-embedded asymmetries put forward in the preceding sections that there is no such feature, declarative clauses being interpreted as such in the absence of any feature specification on Force. In this case, Fin remains simply unselected in root declarative clauses (where no higher position is activated). In this section, I want to give a general argument that there is no declarative feature in UG.

The argument is based on the following two candidate implicational universals for finite clauses:

(53) a. If a language has V2 in declarative clauses, then it has V2 in nondeclarative clauses.
      b. If a language has declarative particles, then it has nondeclarative particles.

As far as I am aware, these two generalizations hold across languages. Example (53a) states that languages may be fully V2, like German and most of the other Germanic languages, or they may be V2 in interrogative and other marked clause types but not in declaratives (like English, French, etc), but rules out the existence of a residual V2 language with V2 in declarative clauses but not in, for example, interrogative clauses. Roughly speaking, such a language would have the pattern in (54) (using English words to represent words in the language):

(54) a. Yesterday danced John.
      b.*Yesterday John danced.

c. Which song John sang?

I know of no example of such a language.[21]

Paradigm (53b) states that, while there may be languages with interrogative (etc.) particles and declarative particles (Welsh is an example of such a language, in fact, but certainly not the only one), and languages with interrogative particles and no declarative particles, there are no languages with declarative particles and no interrogative particles. Again, this claim is empirically correct as far as I am aware.

The two generalizations in (53) are really a single generalization, with (53a) referring to Move and (53b) to Merge. We can thus restate (53) as follows:

(53')   If Fin requires PF-realization in declarative clauses, then it requires it in nondeclarative clauses.

It is possible to account for (53') by assuming that selected features of a head may be subfeatures of that head. In general, then, suppose that functional heads, as features F, G, H, . . . , can come with various further feature specifications $f, g, h, \ldots$ (I write the selected subfeatures in lowercase italics and the labels of autonomous functional categories with initial uppercase).

We can then treat the autonomous functional feature F as simply the unmarked value of the functional head in question, while the marked value will have a further subfeature, giving F+f. Now suppose that unspecified Force means "declarative," while Force+f, where f is a clause-type feature, means nondeclarative. The same is true of Fin (where the subfeature is the feature selected by Force). On this view, [+/-declarative] does not exist and a clause is interpreted as declarative in the absence of clause-type features. What exist are other clause-type features: Question, Exclamative, Imperative, and so on. These are all subfeatures of Force that may be selected on Fin. In other words, instead of saying that we have Force with the two values [±declarative], we have Force = Declarative by default and Force = *Imperative, Interrogative* (etc.) as marked subfeatures.

I mentioned in section 1 that one way to construe parameterization is very simply in terms of the idea that any functional feature F may or may not be associated with a diacritic requiring it to have a PF-realization. This realization may be obtained by Merge or Move, with Merge standardly preempting Move if appropriate lexical material is available. So we can think that the (functional) lexicon of every language contains a parameterization operator, which randomly assigns the diacritic to functional features. Now, if we assume that the parameterization operator applies equally well both to autonomous functional features and to selected subfeatures in the sense in which these were described in the previous paragraph, then we can see that F+f will have two chances of PF-realization, while F will only have one. Thus, marked feature values are more likely to be overtly realized than unmarked ones, and we derive implicational statements of the form in (53') from the fact that where F* must be realized, then so must all subfeatures of F* (this follows directly if we think of the subfeatures in terms of feature geometry). From this it follows that, to the extent that (53') is correct, there is no declarative feature.

A further important point in this connection is that root nonfinite Fin is never declarative:

(55) a. Oh! to be in England, now that April's here!   (Optative)
      b. Ne pas cracher par terre.   (Imperative)
         NEG not to-spit on ground
         'Do not spit on the ground.'
      c. Tornare a casa? Mai!   (Exclamative/interrogative)
         to-return to home never
         'Go back home? Never!'

Given the marked clause type of these examples, we must conclude that Force se-lects Fin (despite the fact that neither has an apparent overt realization in these ex-amples). So, wherever Fin is not selected, it is finite. Embedded nonfinite Fin does not have to be nondeclarative, but here it seems most natural to say that embedded infinitivals very often have no specific clause type of their own, implying that Force is inert in such cases.

We can thus conclude that, since there is no declarative feature, the operations in (52), including full V2, cannot be triggered by this feature. Instead, as already suggested at the end of the previous section, they seem to simply be different ways of realizing unmarked, finite, root Fin. This makes sense for (52a, b, and d) in terms of Roberts's (2001) system of lexicalization parameters: (52a) is the lexical realization of Fin* by merger; (52b) is the realization of Fin* by merger and movement together (as merged *a* triggers further movement), and (52d) is the opposite parametric value. But what of (52c)? If it is simply the realization of Fin* by movement, why is not move-ment of the finite verb or auxiliary alone sufficient for grammaticality? As mentioned, it seems that simple verb movement is not tolerated on its own. In fact, there is a clear cross-linguistic generalization here (which emerges from the study of the Celtic languages since they are VSO and have fairly rich C-systems):

(56) Independent V1 in C is not allowed in root declaratives.[22]

Generalization (56) combines with the Fin* parameter in its Move manifestation to give V2. It also has the flavor of the EPP.

3.2.   The EPP and second-position effects

In this section I focus on the link between the EPP and V2. The core V2 phenom-enon of the Germanic languages has four main components:[23]

(57) a. V-movement to Fin
      b. XP-movement to SpecFinP
      c. The restriction to just one XP
      d. (The root-embedded asymmetry)

Component (57d) was discussed in section 1, and I have nothing further to add here.

Component (57a) follows from the fact that (finite) Fin has the parametric prop-erty of requiring a PF-realization in V2 languages, and that these languages lack par-ticles like Welsh *fe/mi* which can be merged into Fin. Hence Fin attracts a head that it selects. This head is T, assuming that Fin selects directly for T (there is abundant cross-linguistic evidence for this, and the Agr-heads arguably do not intervene for the Fin-T probe-goal relation, which depends on an Agreement relation in temporal features). V clearly moves to T in Icelandic (Platzack 1987; Vikner 1994). Following Sabel (1999), I assume that it does so also in German, and, following Haegeman (2001), I take it that in the Continental West Germanic languages the complement of T moves into a specifier position higher than T, creating the effect of verb-final order. Finally, following Roberts (1993), I take it that V moves to T in Mainland Scandinavian. Thus T, containing V, raises to Fin where we have Fin*.[24]

Component (57b) can be accounted for by the EPP. Crucially, the EPP applies where we have both V-movement to Fin (caused by Fin* and the lack of relevant particles) and no feature in Fin (other than [+finite]). Although V-movement to Fin satisfies the lexical-realization requirement, this clearly is not enough to license Fin under these conditions, as (56) implies. V2 arises in languages with rather poor agreement systems, no root declarative C-particles and Fin*.[25] It seems to be the case, then, that Fin which lacks features and exponents (i.e., particles) to this extent must have an EPP-feature and, hence, triggers movement of an XP.

These characterizations of the relation between V2 and the EPP have analogues in the Agr system. Like Agr, Fin has an EPP-feature when it has no other substantive feature. We can note that the "pure" EPP-effects involving Agr, where expletives are required (as in *For there to be a riot would be a disgrace*), are characteristic of languages with poor agreement marking. In languages where agreement features are more fully realized by morphology, the requirement to fill SpecAgr (or some position in the Agr-field; see note 2) does not hold in the same way. However, the way in which Fin realizes EPP-features is unlike Agr in one important respect: unlike Agr, Fin does not require a DP to occupy its Spec. This can be attributed to the fact that Agr is a D-element but Fin is not.

So I propose that (56) is an observation about feature content: Fin* with so little content (no selected features, just [+finite]) is not allowed. Such an element seems to be too impoverished to survive. This tells us something about the restrictions on the feature content of categories. Of course, the parametric asterisk (*) is crucial here, as we can certainly leave root declarative Fin empty and, indeed, the entire C-system. This suggests that, since the EPP-feature and the asterisk are both PF-sensitive features, one PF-feature entails the other (where substantive features are absent).

Concerning (57c), the question is: Why is V exactly second under the conditions of full V2 as just described? I have proposed that the finite verb occupies Fin and the fronted XP SpecFinP in V2 constructions. This leaves a range of higher positions, which in V2 clauses are unavailable. Given the discussion of long head movement in section 2, it should be clear why no head movement to higher positions is available: all the heads in the C-system are Operator heads, like Fin, and so Fin blocks movement to all those positions. The only thing that could move into a higher head position is Fin itself, but this can only happen if one of the higher heads is activated, that is, not in an unmarked declarative clause. Concerning the ban on XP-movement to higher Specifier positions, I would like to reason, following a suggestion by Luigi Rizzi (personal communication), along the following lines. XP-movement to SpecFin in full V2 clauses is movement caused only by Fin's EPP-feature, as we have just seen. The moved XP is thus of no particular type in terms of the typology of potential interveners, and so is able to block any type of movement. Thus, since Fin has the null featural specification, XP-movement to value it "blocks off" all higher head and specifier positions in the clause. The fact that the verb is second where we have Fin*, poor agreement, and no particles, even in an elaborately structured left periphery, thus follows straightforwardly from the statement of relativized minimality given in (45) and (46). This also underlies the "last resort" effect of full V2: once XP-fronting for V2 takes place, no more movement operations are available in that CP.

We can extend the same account to Breton-style LVM, but with one major difficulty. Here we want the movement of the nonfinite verb to block off all movement to higher positions, creating the second-position effect and the last-resort effect. This can apparently only be achieved with the statement of relativized minimality in (45) and (46) if the fronted verb is treated like an XP for relativized minimality (Rizzi 2000). In that case, the long-moved head will thus act like the topicalized XP in V2, or in the manner just described. This can be achieved if (46i) is altered to make reference only to the "featural type" of potential interveners, rather than to both structural and featural type, as stated earlier (see Roberts 2000 on this).

However, this account of the second-position effect does not prevent merger into higher positions. Merger of into SpecTopP gives rise to a V2 construction with a D-pronoun in German (e.g., *Den Mann, den habe ich gesehen* 'The man, him have I seen'; see Grohmann 2000 for discussion and analysis). Merger into SpecFocP is not allowed, as elements in this position must enter into A'-dependencies (see Rizzi 1997), which I assume can only be created by movement. However, this is what we find in embedded V2 of both the symmetric and nonsymmetric varieties. Also, this analysis correctly predicts that embedded V2 clauses are islands; see Müller and Sternefeld (1993):

(58)   a.*Radios glaube ich [$_{CP}$ gestern hat [Fritz t$_{gestern}$ t$_{Radios}$ repariert]].
       radios believe I yesterday has Fritz repaired
       b.*Was glaubst du [$_{CP}$ gestern hat [Fritz t$_{gestern}$ t$_{was}$ repariert]].
       radios believe I yesterday has Fritz repaired

The analysis does not predict the strength of the island directly (note that the examples in (58) involve long object-movement), but we can clearly see how relativized minimality, construed as above, accounts for the intervention effect of V2 topics here.[26]

We might also need the option of merger into C-positions above Fin for the "abnormal sentences" of Welsh, if these are to be reduced to a V2–like system featuring obligatory topicalization; see Willis (1996, 1998) for arguments that in cases of apparent multiple fronting in this construction all XPs but one are merged in the C-system, and the one that is not merged there but moved there "counts" for determining the form of the particle as *a* or *y*. It is also consistent with this analysis that material can be moved to positions higher than *fe/mi*:

(59)   Yfory fe fydd Ifan yn mynd adref.   (Willis 1998: 202, (30b))
       tomorrow PRT will-be Ifan ASP go home
       'Tomorrow Ifan will be going home.'

Modal adverbs cannot appear in the pre-*fe* position, presumably because Fin has modal feature-content here and so is incompatible with merger of *fe*:

(60)   *Hwyrach fe fydd Ifan yn mynd adref yfory.   (Willis 1998: 203, (31b))
       probably PRT will-be Ifan ASP go home tomorrow

Finally, I need to say something about cases of embedded V2 again, as in German examples like (20), repeated here:

(61)   Ich glaube, *gestern habe* Maria dieses Buch gelesen.
        I believe yesterday has Maria this book read
        'I believe Maria read this book yesterday.'

To account for V2 here we have to say that Fin* acts as if it were in a root context. It seems that Force in this type of case imposes no requirement on Fin and, at the same time, structurally protects Fin from outside selection. I have no proposal for what happens in symmetric V2 languages beyond what was mentioned in note 8.[27]

4. Conclusion

In this chapter I have developed an account of parametric variation in the C-system or, more precisely, involving nonselected, root, finite Fin, which covers two of the Celtic languages (Welsh and Breton), as well as the V2 Germanic languages. The account also extends in a straightforward way to selected Fin and to residual V2 (which in fact I treat as a case of selected root Fin).

I was also able to account for the main features of V2, as listed in (57). The most important of these is (57b), the fact that moving V+T into Fin as a consequence of the Fin* parameter combined with the absence of Celtic-style particles causes XP-fronting exactly in root declaratives. I accounted for this by saying that a category that is so impoverished in feature content requires an EPP-feature, triggering XP-movement of any XP. This can be thought of as analogous to expletive-insertion in the agreement system of a language with impoverished agreement morphology—this is always third-person agreement (which may represent the absence of features in an underspecified system of agreement features). In that case, it comes as no surprise that the fronted XP can be an expletive in V2 languages, as well-known examples such as the following show:

(62)   a. Es wurde getanzt. (German)
        b. Það verið dansað. (Icelandic)
            'It/there was danced.'

My analysis of V2 led to the conjecture that a head has an EPP-feature when it is in some sense defective in substantive features. I noted that this may carry over to Agr systems. Although this idea still needs to be made more precise, it certainly points in the direction of further investigation of the feature structures that may be associated with heads. I also need to explicate the relation between the EPP-feature, the lexical-realization requirement I have indicated as F* and head movement. This is important, since the V2 effect does not arise in the absence of head movement. This suggests that the EPP feature must be sensitive to head movement,[28] a matter which requires further investigation in the light of Chomsky's (2001) proposal that head movement is not part of narrow syntax. This point is developed further in Roberts (2004, chap. 5), but will be left open here.

Notes

This chapter is a revised version of chapter 4 of Roberts (2004). My thanks to the audience at Pontignano, Luigi Rizzi, and an anonymous reviewer for Oxford University Press.

1. The particles are frequently not pronounced, but their mutation effects remain. This implies that the particles are subject to a low-level PF-deletion rule and, as such, are present in the syntax. (See also Willis 1998: 3, n. 1.)

Willis (2000: 551) argues that colloquial Welsh has a zero-particle that triggers soft mutation.

Willis (1998: 194f.) argues that "true" VSO orders arise fairly suddenly in Early Modern Welsh, treating this as a consequence of the loss of V2. In these examples, the initial V does not undergo soft mutation:

(i) Gellwch wybod yn hysbys am bob peth y fo kyfiownys na wnaf i yn erbyn ych wllys.   (*TWRP, Yr Enaid a'r Corff*, 139–141 (MS sixteenth century); Willis 1998: 196, (20b))

you-can know publicly about every thing PRT be-SUBJ just *nad* will-do I against your will

'You may know publicly that, regarding everything that is just, I shall not act against your will.'

The mutated form of *gallu* (to be able) would lack initial /g/. In contemporary Welsh root affirmative declaratives, neither a particle nor a soft mutation is obligatory. We must conclude that either the particle or the mutation is optional. On the grounds of general consistency, I assume movement is optional and a particle is always syntactically present.

2. As this remark implies, I assume that VSO order in finite clauses where there is no auxiliary is derived by V-movement to the highest position in IP, with the subject occupying the immediately subjacent specifier. This is by now the consensual analysis among linguists working on Celtic: see, in particular, McCloskey (1996) for arguments for this structure in Irish, and Rouveret (1994) and Roberts (2000) on Welsh. Roberts argues that the verb occupies Pers(on), while the subject appears in SpecNumP.

3. The striking characteristic of the abnormal construction is that the verb agrees with a fronted subject. Generally in Welsh, as in many other VSO languages, the verb does not fully agree with the subject. The contrast in agreement between an abnormal sentence and a focused sentence is illustrated in (i):

(i) Myfi a gef*ais* anrheg.   (Abnormal sentence, agreement)
me PRT got-1SG present
'I got a gift.'

(ii) Myfi a gaf*odd* anrheg.   (Focused sentence, no agreement)
me PRT got-3SG present
'It was me who got a gift.' (Tallerman (1996: 98))

The abnormal construction is somewhat archaic, having been very productive in Middle and Biblical Welsh, but rarely found in this century. Tallerman argues that this construction is different from the focus construction—in particular, in that it does not involve movement but, rather, a resumption strategy. Tallerman treats the fronted constituent as adjoined to CP; it may be that it occupies Rizzi's (1997) TopP, since (a) it has a topic (as opposed to focus) reading and (b) more than one constituent can be "fronted" in this construction but not in the focus construction.

On the other hand, Willis (1998: 6) argues that this construction was not syntactically distinct from the focus construction in Middle Welsh and that it was, in fact, a V2 construction. Willis (1998: 51f.) analyzes apparent multiple-fronting cases as involving base-generation of adverbs in the C-system, or left dislocation, thus maintaining a general V2 analysis of this construction for Middle Welsh.

4. The situation is more complex and interesting than these brief comments imply. In particular, *y* appears, along with "resumption" (presence of overt agreement and an optional echo pronoun), in long-distance subject and object extractions (where "long-distance" is defined as crossing two bounding nodes):

(i)   y dyn *yr* hoffwn iddo ddod   (Subject of infinitive)
      the man PRT I-would-like to-3SG come
      'the man who I would like to come'

(ii) y dynion y dywedodd Wyn y byddant yn darllen y llyfr   (Subject of finite clause)
      the man PRT said Wyn PRT will-be-3PL ASP read the book
      'the men that Wyn said will read the book'

(iii) y dyn y gwelai Wyn ef   (Object of finite verb)
      the man PRT saw Wyn he
      'the man Wyn saw'

The echo pronoun is obligatory in (iii), but there is no agreement possibility (although Welsh has prepositional agreement, as (i) shows, it lacks object agreement). Moreover, in (iii) the two bounding nodes are not crossed, so (iii) is not a true instance of long-distance movement. The interesting question then is, why do long-distance extractions behave as indirect extractions (i.e., requiring particle *y* and resumption)? As is well known, Irish allows long-distance "direct" extraction, with the relevant particle (*aL*, leniting *a*—in fact identical to Welsh *a*, which also lenites) showing up in all intervening Cs (see McCloskey 1979, 2000, forthcoming):

(iv) rud a gheall tú a dhéanfa
      thing a-L promised you a-L you-would-do
      'something that you promised you would do'

In Welsh, the exact equivalent of (iv) is grammatical at least for some speakers (*contra* the judgment reported in Rouveret 1994: 398):

(v)   y dynion a wn i a ddaeth
      the men PRT know I PRT came-3SG
      'the men that I know came'

If we carry over the analysis of the Irish relative particles proposed by McCloskey (2000), we might be able to treat Welsh *a* as triggered by Move to its Specifier and *y* as triggered in other cases (Merge into its specifier or nothing in its specifier). I will not pursue this here, however. See Awbery (1977), Sadler (1988), and Rouveret (1994) on direct and indirect relatives in Literary Welsh and Willis (2000) on long-distance extraction in Colloquial Welsh.

5. McCloskey argues that C-to-I lowering takes place at PF on the basis of the distribution of negative-polarity items (NPIs). Assuming standardly that NPIs must be c-commanded by a negative element that licenses them at S-structure, McCloskey points out that Irish NPIs can be fronted by a process known as Narrative Fronting to a position that does not appear to be c-commanded by a negative element (the elements in question must be NPIs, since Irish lacks negative quantifiers of all kinds—see Acquaviva 1996):

(i)   Neach ar bith dínn ní bheidh beo.
      being any of-us NEG will-be alive
      'Not one of us will be alive.'

McCloskey reconciles this fact with the general condition on NPIs by assuming that the NPI
is c-commanded by *ní* at S-structure, with lowering of *ní* in PF.

   To fully deal with this point would take us quite far afield, into a detailed consideration
of how NPIs are licensed. However, I would like to briefly sketch an alternative approach to
these data. The requirement that NPIs be licensed by a c-commanding negation is motivated
by data such as the following (see Ladusaw 1979; Laka 1990; Zanuttini 1991; and the references given there):

(ii) a. He didn't speak to anybody.
      b. *Anybody didn't speak to him.

Example (iib) shows that NPIs in subject position are bad; this is standardly attributed that
NPIs must be c-commanded by the category that licenses them. In English, NPIs are systematically bad in SpecCP, as McCloskey observes (his (109), p. 43):

(iii) a. *Ever haven't I seen such a sight.
      b. *Under any circumstances wouldn't I do that.

Suppose that the c-command condition derives from the fact that the Neg head must
license NPIs. In English, the Neg head is found either in the position of the finite auxiliary
where there is no inversion, or in C—more precisely, in Foc, according to Rizzi (1997).
The subject cannot form a chain whose head is the Neg-element in the noninverted auxiliary position, but can if the Neg element is in the Foc position. Features of a complement
are c-commanded by the auxiliary position. In this way, the data in (ii) and (iii) can be
accounted for.

   But what of the Irish example in (i)? Here the crucial observation is that the Irish negative elements are part of the C-system. Suppose, then, that in line with my analysis of *go*, *ní*
occupies Fin in (i) and raises covertly to Force. We must regard the condition on NPIs as an
LF condition, since one of the tenets of minimalism is that independent S-structure well-
formedness conditions do not exist. Hence at LF, *ní* will be in a position that c-commands the
fronted constituent. (I am assuming that the fronted negative constituent in (i) is in SpecFoc
or SpecTop.) The essential difference between Irish and English lies in the fact that (a) Force
does not overtly attract Fin in Irish, as we have already seen, and (b) Fin is inherently able to
contain negative material—that is, the simple observation that Irish has negative complementizers. An important feature of this analysis is that the negative head in English cannot be
supposed to raise into the C-system covertly, and when it does raise to Foc, as in the well-
formed counterparts of (iii), it does not raise further to Force.

   6. In the negatives of "abnormal sentences" of Biblical Welsh (see note 3), the negative
element *ny* must follow the topicalized constituent:

(i)   Y dyn ny daeth.
      the man NEG came
      'The man didn't come.'

It is not clear what is going on here; see Tallerman (1996: 119) for discussion.

   7. To make this consistent with the account of (8), we have to assume that in Irish the
interrogative Wh-phrases are in SpecForceP.

   8. This account also leaves open the possibility that there may be languages in which
all predicates are like English bridge verbs in directly selecting complementizers merged in

Force, but like Irish in that Force does not trigger movement of Fin. If such a language also has the Fin* property, V+T should be able to freely raise to Fin, giving rise to the absence of root-embedded asymmetries. This may well be the situation in the "symmetric" V2 languages Yiddish and Icelandic.

9. If Force is noninterrogative, Foc may still be +WH. This can account for semi-questions and exclamatives like (I) and (ii):

(i)   It's amazing how many people were there.

(ii) We found out who did it.

See McCloskey (1992).

10. Following Roberts (2001: 103), Foc* triggers movement to both specifier and head since the head which moves there has no feature which is capable of licensing the content of Foc, although it can morphologically realize it.

11. Roberts (2004) also provides evidence that interrogative *a* is in Force. This builds on an analysis of the auxiliary *bod*, which treats this element as moving to Fin, unlike main verbs (one piece of evidence for this is that *bod* is in complementary distribution with *fe/mi* and *a/y*). The observation then is simply that interrogative *a* can cooccur with *bod*:

(i)   A ydych chi yn mynd?
      PRT are you ASP go
      'Are you going?'

12 Strictly speaking, LVM is misnomer. Other predicative heads can appear in this construction:

(i)   Sioul eo ar mor.   (Schafer 1994: 2)
      calm is the sea
      'The sea is calm.'

The analysis I propose carries over to this type of case.

13. The auxiliary 'have' in Breton is formed from the combination of an agreement proclitic and *bezañ* 'be'. These forms are in complementary distribution with particles, while *bezañ* alone apparently is not. It appears, then, that 'have' (or perhaps just the proclitic particle) raises to Fin in Breton in examples like (i):

(i)   Al levr en deus lennet Anna.
      the book 3SG is read Anna
      'Anna has read the book.'

14. Given the the fact that *o* in (32a) is an aspectual particle, it is likely that the fronted constituent here is larger than VP; in fact, it is probably AspP. This does not affect the contrast that these examples establish in the text discussion. One could try to claim that, since the fronted category in (32a) and other relevant examples is larger than VP, LVM is true VP-fronting of a VP that is obligatorily emptied of everything except the verb. However, it is hard to see why such VP-fronting would be so local and sensitive to properties of C—features of LVM that come out naturally on the analysis being defended here.

For expository simplicity, I continue to call the clearly phrasal category that undergoes fronting in examples like (32a) VP.

15. In fact, Breton allows nominal object shift, as Schafer (1994: 37–49) shows, as in:

(i)   a. Breman e wel Maia an treñ.
         now PRT sees Maia the train
         'Now Maia sees the train.'

b. Breman e wel an treñ Maia.
now PRT sees the train Maia
'Now Maia sees the train.'

Schafer shows that object shift in Breton has the same properties as object shift in the Scandinavian languages as described by Holmberg (1986), Vikner (1994), and the references given there.

16. This classification is extremely close to the structural division between the C-system (operator heads) and the I-system (non-operator heads). However, Rizzi (1997) argues that topics are non-quantificational, but I nevertheless tentatively list Topic under the operator heads as an element in its Specifier forms an A'-type dependency with its trace (which, like typical A'-traces, requires Case and obeys Principle C in GB terms). In many languages Neg is part of the I-system. In the Celtic languages, where Neg is frequently part of the C-system, the structural division corresponds more closely to the functional one, although perhaps still not exactly given the *pas*-like negative elements found in Welsh and Breton.

17. Another construction that may be connected to (48) is Scandinavian Stylistic Fronting. This construction is best known in Icelandic, although it is attested in Faroese (Holmberg 2000), in older stages of Swedish (Platzack 1987), and in Middle English (Trips 2001). Originally discussed by Maling (1990), this construction has given rise to a considerable literature (see the overview in Trips 2001). An Icelandic example is:

(i)   Það fór að rigna, þegar farið var af stað.   (Maling 1990: 78)
      it began to rain when gone was from place

Stylistic Fronting shows a number of properties that are highly reminiscent of Breton LVM, and which can be analyzed as in the text. First, it is strictly clause-bound, unlike V2 topicalization:

(ii)   *menn sem lesa reyna að þessar bækur   (Sigurðsson 1989)
       people who read try to these books

Second, it is subject to an "accessibility hierarchy," which basically states that negation blocks fronting of VP-internal material, as in (iii):

(iii)   a. Þetta er glæpamaðurinn sem ekki hefur verið dæmdur.
           this is the-criminal that not had been convicted
        b.*Þetta er glæpamaðurinn sem dæmdur hefur ekki verið.
        c.*Þetta er glæpamaðurinn sem verið hefur ekki dæmdur.

This is exactly parallel to (33b), except that the "low" negative element fronts in Icelandic but not in Breton, a fact we can readily attribute to the presence of a negative marker merged in the C-system in Breton but not in Icelandic. Stylistic Fronting differs from Breton LVM in that, where there is both a nonfinite auxiliary and a nonfinite main verb, only the main verb may front. Compare (iv) with (38a and b):

(iv)   a. Verðbólgan varð verri en búist hafð verið við.   (Maling 1990: 82)
          inflation became worse than counted had been on
       b. *Verðbólgan varð verri en verið hafð búist við.
          inflation became worse than been had counted on.

The fact that predicative adjectives and particles like *við* in (iv) can be fronted suggests that stylistic fronting does not allow auxiliary material to be fronted. Otherwise, the locality facts are as in Breton.

However, Stylistic Fronting presents a number of further puzzles. Foremost among these is the "subject-gap" condition: the construction can only take place where there is a subject gap. But, since subjects occupy a lower position in Breton than in Icelandic (see Roberts 2004, chap. 1) we can regard this condition as always satisfied in Breton. It is also plausible that this condition is connected to the EPP, as Holmberg (2000) has suggested. Furthermore, Stylistic Fronting can apply to DPs and PPs, which is clearly not the case for the Breton construction. It remains to be seen whether this last property can be connected to the fact that Icelandic is a true full V2 language, unlike Breton. See also Holmberg (2000).

18. These examples, certainly (50a) with a fronted expletive, cannot involve focus. Recall that Middle Welsh had both the abnormal and the focus construction productively (if they were distinct; see Willis 1998); see Tallerman (1996) and Willis (1996, 1998) on the abnormal construction.

19. Compare the development of the vocalic clitics in many Northern Italian dialects, discussed in Poletto (2000).

20. Verb-initial clauses are allowed in the V2 Germanic languages in contexts where they can be interpreted as "lively narrative style," as in:

>   (i)   *Kommt* eine Frau herein und...
>   'There comes in a woman, and . . .'

Here I assume that the particular discourse context is connected to feature in Force, and so Fin is selected by Force just like in residual V2 cases. Some languages appear to mark this feature overtly, as Old English *þa*, and Old French *si*.

21. Poletto (2000, chap. 4) shows that in Rhaeto-Romansch left-dislocation is impossible in declarative V2 clauses but allowed in interrogative clauses with Wh-movement:

>   (i)   a. Gonoot va-i a tʃ aza sya.
>   often go I at home his
>   'I often go to his house.'
>   b.*Gonoot i vad a tʃ aza sya.
>   often I go to house his
>   c. Gonoot ula va-al pa?
>   often where goes-he Q
>   'Where does he often go?'

The important thing about these examples in the present context is that we can see I-to-C movement in the form of subject-clitic inversion in both cases. The difference between declaratives and interrogatives has to do with the possibilities of XP-fronting rather than head-movement. (In terms of the analysis to be proposed here, we expect that declarative V2 tolerates no further fronting operations, while Wh-movement may in principle tolerate nonoperator fronting.)

22. Old Irish is an exception to this generalization, but interestingly has a very rich agreement system which shows sensitivity to clause type (see Carnie et al. 2000; Doherty 1999, 2000; Roberts 2004). In Modern Irish V is radically initial but does not appear in C, see McCloskey (1996) (the same may also be true of collquial Welsh—see Willis 1998, 2000).

23. Zwart (1993, 1997), following Travis (1984), proposed that subject-initial V2 clauses do not involve the CP-level. Roberts and Roussou (2002) argue against this on the grounds that (a) it involves essentially a Topic Criterion, or topic-feature checking, but topics do not behave in such a way as to justify this idea (they can be iterated [Rizzi 1997], they are never in situ), and (b) an approach like Zwart's cannot explain why there are no languages with strong Top-features, but weak wh-features, in other words why we might not find a language of the type in (54).

24. The fact that auxiliaries but not main verbs move into the C-system in residual V2 contexts in English shows that T raises and that V does not move to T in this language, as is well known. It is possible that Fin* in various marked root clauses (induced by selection from Force) is responsible for the appearance of *do* when no other auxiliary is available.

25. V2 is also found in languages with agreement rich enough to license null subjects, at least under certain conditions. The best-known example of this is Old French (Roberts 1993; Vance 1997). In such languages, null subjects show up just when we have V2:

    (i)   Si firent grant joie la nuit.   (Clark and Roberts 1993: 320)
           so made (they) great joy the night.
           'So they made great joy that night.'

We can account for the impossibility of verb-first orders with null subjects at the Fin-level if we assume that there is no *pro* able to appear in SpecFin and satisfy the EPP. Then the EPP will inevitably be violated. However, it remains unclear why null subjects are allowed just when the verb moves to Fin.

26. Note that relativized minimality doesn't predict the strength of the islands created by A-interveners, either. In fact, the correct statement regarding island strength is that certain movement types, notably argument Wh-movement, are exempted in virtue of their inherent properties from sensitivity to interveners in the way defined by relativized minimality.

27. Yiddish in fact allows extraction from embedded V2 clauses, while Icelandic does not. See Vikner (1994: 108f.) for discussion and examples. Besides the obvious observation that this fact indicates that the two systems are different in some way, I have nothing to say about this here.

28. However, in the Agr-system, expletive insertion is entirely independent of V-movement to Agr (i.e., of Agr*), as English shows. But, as (56) attests, the statement in the text is true at the C-level. Clearly more research is needed here.

References

Acquaviva, P. (1996) "Negation in Irish and the Representation of Monotone Decreasing Quantifiers," in R. Borsley and I. Roberts (eds.) *The Syntax of the Celtic Languages.* Cambridge: Cambridge University Press, 284–313.

Awbery, G. (1977) *The Syntax of Welsh: A Transformational Study of the Passive.* Cambridge: Cambridge University Press.

Baker, M. (1988) *Incorporation: A Theory of Grammatical-Function Changing.* Chicago: Chicago University Press.

Borsley, R. D., and R. M. Jones (2000) "The Syntax of Welsh Negation." *Transactions of the Philological Society* 98:1, 15–47.

Borsley, R. D., and A. Kathol (2000) "Breton as a V2 language." *Linguistics* 38, 665–710.

Borsley, R. D., and I. Roberts (1996) *The Syntax of the Celtic Languages.* Cambridge: Cambridge University Press.

Borsley, R. D., M.-L. Rivero, and J. Stephens (1996) "Long Head Movement in Breton," in R. Borsley and I. Roberts (eds.) *The Syntax of the Celtic Languages.* Cambridge: Cambridge University Press, 53–74.

Carnie, A., E. Pyatt, and H. Harley (2000) "VSO Order as Raising Out of IP? Some Evidence from Old Irish," in A. Carnie and E. Guilfoyle (eds.) *The Syntax of Verb-Initial Languages.* New York: Oxford University Press, 39–60.

Čavar, D., and C. Wilder (1992) *Long Head Movement? Verb Movement and Cliticization in Croatian.* Arbeitspapier No. 7. Frankfurt am Main: Institut für Deutsche Sprache und Literatur II, Johann-Wolfgang-von-Goethe Universität.

Chomsky, N. (1965) *Aspects of the Theory of Syntax.* Cambridge, Mass: MIT Press.

——— (2000) "Minimalist Inquiries: The Framework," in R. Martin, D. Michael, and J. Uriagereka (eds.) *Step by Step: Essays in Honor of Howard Lasnik.* Cambridge, Mass.: MIT Press, 89–155.

——— (2001) "Derivation by Phase," in M. Kenstowicz (ed.) *Ken Hale: A Life in Language.* Cambridge, Mass.: MIT Press, 1–52.

Cinque, G. (1999) *Adverbs and Functional Projections.* New York: Oxford University Press.

Clark, R., and I. Roberts (1993) "A Computational Approach to Language Learnability and Language Change." *Linguistic Inquiry* 24, 299–345.

den Besten, H. (1983) "On the Interaction of Root Transformations and Lexical Deletive Rules," in W. Abraham (ed.) *On the Formal Syntax of the Westgermania.* Amsterdam: John Benjamins, 47–138.

den Besten, H., and G. Webelhuth (1990) "Stranding," in G. Grewendorf and W. Sternefeld (eds.) *Scrambling and Barriers.* Amsterdam: John Benjamins, 77–92.

Doherty, C. (1999) "The Syntax of Old Irish Clause Structure." Unpublished ms., University College Dublin.

——— (2000) "Residual Verb Second in Early Irish: On the Nature of Bergin's Construction." *Diachronica* 17.1, 5–38.

Grohmann, K. (2000) "Prolific Peripheries: A Radical View from the Left," Ph.D. diss. University of Maryland.

Haegeman, L. (1996) "Verb Second, the Split CP and Null Subjects in Early Dutch Finite Clauses." *GenGenP* 4.2, 133–175.

——— (2001) "Antisymmetry and Word Order in West Flemish." *Journal of Comparative Germanic Syntax* 3.3, 207–232.

Holmberg, A. (1986) "Word Order and Syntactic Features in the Scandinavian Languages," Ph.D. diss. University of Stockholm.

——— (2000) "Scandinavian Stylistic Fronting: How Any Category Can Become an Expletive." *Linguistic Inquiry* 31, 445–484.

Holmberg, A., and C. Platzack (1995) *The Role of Inflection in Scandinavian Syntax.* New York: Oxford University Press.

Hooper, J., and S. Thompson (1973) "On the Applicability of Root Transformations." *Linguistic Inquiry* 4, 465–497.

Ladusaw, W. (1979) "Polarity Sensitivity as Inherent Scope Relations," Ph.D. diss. University of Texas, Austin.

Laenzlinger, C. (1998) *Comparative Studies in Word Order Variation.* Amsterdam: John Benja.tziar (1990) "Negation in Syntax: On the Nature of Functional Categories and Projections," Ph.D. diss. MIT, Cambridge, Mass.

Maling, J. (1990) "Inversion in Embedded Clauses in Modern Icelandic," in J. Maling and A. Zaenen (eds.) *Syntax and Semantics XXIV: Modern Icelandic Syntax.* San Diego: Academic Press, 71–91.

McCloskey, J. (1979) *Transformational Syntax and Model-Theoretic Semantics.* Dordrecht: Kluwer.

——— (1992) "Adjunction, Selection and Embedded Verb Second." Unpublished ms., University of California at Santa Cruz.

——— (1996) "The Scope of Verb-Movement in Irish." *Natural Language and Linguistic Theory* 14, 46–104.

——— (2000) "Resumption, Successive Cyclicity and the Locality of Operations." Unpublished ms., University of California at Santa Cruz.

——— (forthcoming) "On the Morphosyntax of Wh-Movement in Irish." *Journal of Linguistics.*

Müller, G. (1998) *Incomplete Category Fronting.* Dordrecht: Kluwer.

Müller, G., and G. Sternefeld (1993) "Improper Movement and Unambiguous Binding." *Linguistic Inquiry* 24, 461–507.

Penner, Z., and T. Bader (1995) *Topics in Swiss German Syntax.* Bern: Peter Lang.

Pesetsky, D. (1982) "Paths and Categories," Ph.D. diss., MIT, Cambridge, Mass.

Platzack, C. (1987) "The Scandinavian Languages and the Null Subject Parameter." *Natural Language and Linguistic Theory* 5, 377–401.

Poletto, C. (2000) *The Higher Functional Field in the Northern Italian Dialects.* New York: Oxford University Press.

Pollock, J. Y. (1989) "Verb Movement, Universal Grammar, and the Structure of IP." *Linguistic Inquiry* 20, 365–424.

Rivero, M.-L. (1991) "Patterns of V-raising in Long Head Movement, and Negation: Serbo-Croatian vs. Slovak." *Linguistic Review* 8, 319–352.

———— (1994) "The Structure of the Clause and V-movement in the Languages of the Balkans." *Natural Language and Linguistic Theory* 12, 63–120.

Rizzi, L. (1990) *Relativized Minimality.* Cambridge, Mass.: MIT Press.

———— (1997) "The Fine Structure of the Left Periphery," in L. Haegeman (ed.) *Elements of Grammar.* Dordrecht: Kluwer, 281–337.

———— (2000) "Relativized Minimality Effects," in M. Baltin and C. Collins (eds.) *Handbook of Syntactic Theory.* Oxford: Blackwell, 89–110.

Rizzi, L., and I. Roberts (1989) "Complex Inversion in French." *Probus* 1, 1–39.

Roberts, I. (1993) *Verbs and Diachronic Syntax: A Comparative History of English and French.* Dordrecht: Kluwer.

———— (2000) "Head Movement," in M. Baltin and C. Collins (eds.) *Handbook of Syntactic Theory.* Oxford: Blackwell, 113–147.

———— (2001) "Language Change and Learnability," in S. Bertolo (ed.) *Language Acquisition and Learnability.* Cambridge: Cambridge University Press, 81–125.

———— (2004) *Principles and Parameters in a VSO Language: A Case Study in Welsh.* New York: Oxford University Press.

Roberts, I., and A. Roussou (2002) "The Extended Projection Principle as a Condition on the Tense Dependency," in P. Svenonius (ed.) *Subjects, Expletives, and the EPP.* New York: Oxford University Press, 125–155.

Rouveret, A. (1994) *Syntaxe du gallois: principes généraux et typologie.* Paris: CNRS Editions.

———— (1996) "*Bod* in the Present Tense and in Other Tenses," in R. D. Borsley and I. Roberts (eds.) *The Syntax of the Celtic Languages: A Comparative Perspective.* Cambridge: Cambridge University Press, 125–171.

Sabel, J. (1999) "On V-to-I Movement in German." Talk given at the University of Stuttgart.

Sadler, L. (1988) *Welsh Syntax: A Government-Binding Approach.* London: Croom Helm.

Schafer, R. (1994) "Nonfinite Predicate Initial Constructions in Modern Breton," Ph.D. diss., University of California, Santa Cruz.

Sigurðsson, H. (1989) "Verbal Syntax and Case in Icelandic," Ph.D. diss., University of Lund.

Stephens, J. (1982) "Word Order in Breton," Ph.D. diss., University College London.

Stowell, T. (1981) "The Origins of Phrase Structure," Ph.D. diss., MIT, Cambridge, Mass.

Tallerman, M. (1996) "Fronting Constructions in Welsh," in R. Borsley, and I. Roberts (eds.) *The Syntax of the Celtic Languages.* Cambridge: Cambridge University Press, 97–124.

Tallerman, M. (1998) "On the Uniform Case-Licensing of Subjects in Welsh." *Linguistic Review* 15, 69–133.

Travis, L. (1984) "Parameters and Effects of Word Order Variation," Ph.D. diss., MIT, Cambridge, Mass.

Trips, C. (2001) "From OV to VO in Early Middle English," Ph.D. diss., University of Stuttgart.

Vance, B. (1997) *Syntactic Change in Medieval French.* Dordrecht: Kluwer.

Vikner, S. (1994) *Verb Movement and Expletive Subjects in the Germanic Languages.* New York: Oxford University Press.

Watkins, T. A. (1991) "The Function of the Cleft and Non-cleft Constituent Orders in Modern Welsh," in J. Fife and E. Poppe (eds.) *Studies in Brythonic Word Order.* Amsterdam: John Benjamins, 329–351.

Willis, D. (1996) "Syntactic Change in Welsh: A Study of the Loss of Verb Second," Ph.D. diss., University of Oxford.

———— (1997) "P-Celtic." Unpubished ms., University of Oxford.

———— (1998) *Syntactic Change in Welsh: A Study of the Loss of Verb Second.* Oxford: Clarendon Press.

———— (2000) "On the Distribution of Resumptive Pronouns and wh-Trace in Welsh." *Journal of Linguistics* 36, 531–573.

Wurmbrand, S. (1998) "Infinitives, " Ph.D. diss., MIT, Cambridge, Mass.

Zanuttini, R. (1991) "Syntactic Properties of Sentential Negation: A Comparative Study of Romance Languages," Ph.D. diss., University of Pennsylvania.

Zwart, J.-W. (1993) "Dutch Syntax," Ph.D. diss., University of Groningen.

———— (1997) *The Morphosyntax of Verb Movement: A Minimalist Approach to the Syntax of Dutch.* Dordrecht: Kluwer.

11

Enclisis and Proclisis

UR SHLONSKY

1. The relation of proclisis to enclisis

Imperatives aside, pronominal clitics in Catalan, Spanish, and Italian (CASPIT) are realized as proclitics on finite verbs and as enclitics on nonfinite ones. From a descriptive perspective, the factor determining the choice between proclisis and enclisis in CASPIT is finiteness.

Finiteness also plays a role in the choice between enclisis and proclisis in European Portuguese, Galician, and some other Iberian varieties (GALPORT). However, the role of finiteness in GALPORT is partly obscured by other factors, such as whether the clause is affirmative or negative, whether the infinitive is inflected for subject agreement, and whether the infinitive appears in a prepositional or adverbial adjunct clause. *Enclisis* is the rule in (affirmative) nonfinite subject and complement clauses, and *proclisis* is possible in negated infinitival clauses, as well as in adverbial clauses that contain an inflected infinitive. Finally, both proclisis and enclisis are possible in adverbial clauses that contain an uninflected infinitive (see Raposo 2001 for a recent discussion.)

In finite clauses, the situation is as follows: Only enclisis is possible in root affirmative clauses, while proclisis is required in negative and in subordinate clauses, as well as in sentences in which the left periphery is activated by wh-expressions or by contrastive or emphatic topics.

If we factor out the impact of negation, complementizers, and clause-peripheral affective operators, the directionality of clisis in CASPIT and GALPORT has a common core: in both language types, enclisis is manifested in subject and complement affirmative nonfinite clauses.

The theoretical challenge lies in formulating the principles that govern Romance clitic placement so as to express this common core and to explain why these two branches of Romance differ. The question is all the more intriguing since the patterns of clisis found in GALPORT are not unique. With minor differences, the pattern found with finite verbs is manifested in all varieties of Berber and in some varieties of Greek (both lack Romance-type infinitives so the comparison must be restricted to finite forms). These cross-linguistically disparate but consistent patterns should be treated by the same set of principles. The purpose of this chapter is to see how far we can go in pursuing this goal.

I put aside the question of why clitics exist in the first place—namely, what it is about such pronominal elements that forces them to be placed in positions other than those filled by nonclitics. (See, e.g., Cardinaletti and Starke 1999 for a recent comprehensive discussion.) Although it is fairly clear that clitics are related via a movement chain to the base position of the constituent they pronominalize, it is not obvious whether the clitic itself is moved (as argued in Kayne 1975, 1989, 1991; Belletti 1999; and much other work), or whether the clitic lexicalizes a head position, the null specifier of which is the moved element (as in Sportiche 1998).

Both accounts of cliticization are compatible with the view that I endorse here: that enclisis obtains when, at a given point in the syntactic derivation, the clitic is sitting in a functional head position or is adjoined to one, and V^0 or $F^0_{[+V]}$ is adjoined to it. This derivation is schematized in (1):[1]

(1)

V^0 or $F^0_{[+V]}$+cl.

Proclisis should be thought of not as a simple alternative to enclisis but as a mechanism appealed to whenever enclisis—as diagrammed in (1)—leads to a derivational crash. Unlike enclisis, proclisis is not a unitary phenomenon but, rather, a cover term for a family of language-specific rules, the output of which display a clitic to the left of its host. A common form of proclisis is manifested when the clitic is itself adjoined to V^0 or to $F^0_{[+V]}$. This situation can come about when, for example, the clitic is the head of an XP in specifier position at the point in the derivation at which the verb moves above it to F and movement of V to F is followed by extraction of the clitic head and its incorporation to the c-commanding head. This kind of proclisis is a strict inversion of enclisis: instead of the host adjoining to the clitic, as in (1), the clitic adjoins to the host. An analysis of this sort is developed in Belletti (1999) and Hegarty (1999), for example. It is schematized in (2), where the numbers indicate the steps in the derivation:

(2)   FP

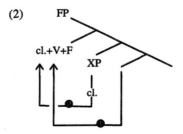

cl.+V+F

XP

cl.

Proclisis can take other forms as well. For example, when the clitic precedes the host but is not, strictly speaking, incorporated to it. Cases like this abound: proclitics to nonfinite verbs in (literary) French which are separated from their host by an adverb, (3a), discussed in Kayne (1989, 1991); Galician object clitics that precede the subject, (3b), from Uriagereka (1995b); and (literary) European Portuguese clitics that can precede a coordination of verbs, (3c), from Rouveret (1999). In these three cases of proclisis, the nexus between the clitic and its host is looser than in (2):[2]

(3) a. Pour *le* bien faire...
        to 3MS well to do
        'In order to do it well . . .'
     b. Cántas veces *a* Pedro veu?
        how many times 3FS Pedro saw
        'How many times did Pedro see her?'
     c. Alguém *o* viu e assustou.
        Someone 3MS saw and helped
        'Someone saw him and helped him.'

It is important to stress here that enclisis is a well-defined syntactic configuration in which a host is adjoined to a clitic, while proclisis is a cover term for a number of distinct phenomena. This should be understood not merely as a terminological but also as a substantive hypothesis: proclisis only obtains when enclisis is ruled out.

1.1. Enclisis in CASPIT

The following Italian examples illustrate proclisis and enclisis in CASPIT. Example (4) contains examples of proclisis on finite verbs in the indicative, subjunctive, and conditional moods, and the sentences in (5) exemplify enclisis on infinitives, gerunds, and past participles.

(4) a. La canto.
        3FS (I) sing-IND
        'I sing it.'
     b. che *la* canti
        that 3FS (I) sing-SUBJ
        'that I sing it'
     c. La canterei.
        3FS (I) sing-COND
        'I would sing it.'

(5) a. cantar*la*
        to sing-3FS
        'to sing it'
     b. cantando*la*
        singing-3FS
        'singing it'
     c. cantato*la*
        (having) sung-3FS
        'having sung it'

The question that arises is why enclisis is possible only in nonfinite clauses, or, conversely, why it is ruled out in finite ones. Although the salient difference between the verbal forms in (4) and (5) is the value of the feature [±finite], it is not conceptually clear why finiteness should be a factor in determining clitic placement. Finiteness is an interpretive notion, relevant in Logical Form, while clitic placement constraints are morphosyntactic.

But even if principles were devised to relate the feature [±finite] to the position of the clitic with respect to its host, they would lack in generality and would not, ceteris paribus, carry over to the GALPORT system, nor to that of Berber, discussed later in this chapter. Whereas (affirmative) nonfinite verbs in GALPORT complement clauses manifest enclisis exactly as in CASPIT—consider (6)—proclisis is not manifested in [+finite] clauses. On the contrary, enclisis is the rule in root clauses, as shown by the contrast in (7) (data from Madeira 1993 and Rouveret 1989).

(6) a. A Ana espera ver-*te* esta tarde.
        the Ana hopes to see-2s this afternoon
        'Ana hopes to see you this afternoon.'
     b. Despediu o Pedro, julgando-*o* incapaz disso.
        sent away the Pedro judging-ACC3MS incapable of that
        'She sent Pedro away, judging him incapable of that.'

(7) a. O João deu-*lhe* esse livro ontem.
        the João gave-DAT3s this book yesterday
        'João gave him/her this book yesterday.'
     b.*O João *lhe* deu esse livro ontem.
        the João DAT3s gave this book yesterday
        'João gave him/her this book yesterday.'

A different tack is taken by Kayne (1991, 1994) and developed, with important modifications, by Rizzi (1993). The leading idea, shared by both Kayne and Rizzi, is that the choice between enclisis and proclisis in CASPIT does not depend on the value of the feature [±finite] as such, but on the different morphological makeup of finite and nonfinite verb forms and their relative position in the functional hierarchy. Neither approach makes claims with respect to GALPORT.

Example (8) slightly rephrases Rizzi's generalization:

(8) We have enclisis when
     a. the verb is *inflectionally complete* under the cliticization site
        and
     b. the verb moves at least as far as the cliticization site.

The case of (8b) holds by definition, as argued above in (1). The case of (8a) embodies the idea that nonfinite morphology is associated with a functional head $Infin^0$, which is lower than the cliticization site, while finite morphology is associated with a higher head (Pollock 1989). It needs to also be assumed, and I take this to be the null hypothesis, that the cliticization site or sites are the same in finite and nonfinite clauses. Putting these ideas together, it transpires that the cliticization site lies hierarchcally between T—where finite inflection is checked—and $Infin^0$, the syntactic head associated with nonfinite morphology (or a part of it).

Although nonfinite verbs in Italian raise at least as high as finite verbs (Belletti 1990), or even higher in non-wh contexts (Cinque 1999), movement above $Infin^0$ does not result in the addition of any inflection. Nonfinite verbs are *inflectionally complete* under the cliticization site, and movement to or above the clitic has no inflectional consequences. Finite inflection, in contrast, is checked higher and, hence, finite verbs are incomplete inflectionally at the point at which they raise to or above the clitic.

Why is inflectional completeness relevant to clitic placement? Assume that inflectional feature checking is subject to a rigid version of the Head Movement Constraint (HMC), disallowing excorporation. In other words, a ϕ-feature on a verb can only be checked against ϕ on a functional head F when V is directly adjoined to F. If V is first adjoined to the clitic or to the head to which the clitic is adjoined, then, on the following cycle of head movement, the X^0 adjoining to F will not be V but, instead, Cl_{+V} (or $X_{+[cl.+[V]]}$). It is reasonable to suppose that the features of V are too deeply embedded in the multimorphemic X^0 to be accessible to the checking head F.[3] Thus, whenever the clitic head intervenes in the path of verb movement, the inflectional features of the verb remain unchecked.

In the derivation of nonfinite verbs, all the inflectional features of V are checked against functional heads *below* the clitic position; hence, V can adjoin to the clitic, and the result is enclisis. Further movement of the verbal complex (adjoined to the clitic) may take place since whatever other features are checked, they are not features of the verb itself.

The derivation of finite verbs cannot properly proceed if V adjoins to the clitic because V's features need to be checked against functional heads, which are *higher* than the clitic. In such a state of affairs, encliticization as in (1) cannot take place. The consequence is that proclisis applies.

1.2. Enclisis in GALPORT

Now let us consider the GALPORT pattern, starting with the question of why enclisis is not blocked in root affirmative finite clauses. The analysis developed in the preceding paragraphs can naturally answer this question: enclisis is possible in GALPORT because the functional heads associated with finite morphology are lower than the cliticization site.

It has been argued—for example, by Madeira (1992, 1993), Martins (1994a), Raposo (2000, 2001), and Uriagereka (1995a,b)—that GALPORT clitics are associated with a peripheral position in the Comp domain. If this were indeed the case, then the cliticization site would perforce be located higher than finite morphology, which is within IP, and generalized enclisis on finite verbs would be fully expected. However, a number of considerations militate against the view that clitics are in Comp in GALPORT.

If the cliticization site in (9) is in Comp, then the adverb and the subject that both precede the verb *must* also be in Comp, in topic or topic-like positions. But, as Rouveret (1999) points out, this word order is independent of enclisis: it is found in contexts of proclisis, as in (9b) and when there is no clitic at all, as in (9c). Moreover, the clause-initial subject may be a (non-left-dislocable) quantifier, (9d). Hence, although the subject *may* be a topic in (9a), there is no reason why it *must* be a topic. If the subject *may* occupy Spec/AgrS, then, since the cliticization site is lower than Spec/AgrS, it *must* be in IP and not in CP.[4]

(9)   a. O João provavelmente deu-*o* à Maria ontem.
          the João probably gave-3MS to Maria yesterday
          'João probably gave it to Maria yesterday.'
      b. Eu digo que o João provavelmente *o* deu à Maria ontem.
          I say that the João probably 3MS gave to Maria yesterday
          'I say that João probably gave it to Maria yesterday.'
      c. O João provavelmente deu esse livro à Maria ontem.
          the João probably gave this book to Maria yesterday
          'João probably gave the book to Maria yesterday.'
      d. Ninguém provavelmente errara.
          Nobody probably fail-fut
          'Nobody will probably fail.'

In the same spirit, the null subject in (10) cannot be a topic since it is not lexical, and there does not seem to be any motivation for obligatorily raising the inflected verb to C:

(10) Deu-*lhe* esse livro ontem.
      gave DAT-3s this book yesterday
      'She/he gave him/her this book yesterday.'

Furthermore, clitics can appear in reduced or small clause complements to perception verbs. Such clausal chunks are characterized by an impoverished left-periphery incapable of hosting wh-words, fronted foci, fronted adverbs or (clitic) left-dislocated arguments. There is thus very little if any configurational space in the left periphery of the embedded small clauses in (11) to host Uriagereka's (1995a,b) F position.

(11) a. Eu ouvi a Maria falar-lhe.
          I heard Maria speak-DAT3MS
          'I heard Maria speaking to him.'
      b. Eu vi João come-lo.
          I saw João eat-3ms
          'I saw João eating it.'

Related to this is the fact that (en)clitics appear on affirmative inflected infinitival complements to emotive (factive) verbs, which Raposo (1987) argues to be IPs and not CPs; consider (12), noting the presence of a preverbal pronominal subject, a good indication that the verb and its clitic are internal to IP:

(12) Lamento eles ter-em *na* visto / a ter-em visto.
      (I) regret they to have-3PL 3FS seen 3FS / to have-3PL seen

Finally, European Portuguese mesoclisis, exemplified in (13), should be understood as enclisis—that is, V→cl.—followed by cl_{+v} adjunction to a higher, lexicalized (future tense) head. But this presupposes that enclisis applies *lower* than the position of the future tense morpheme. (Mesoclisis is further discussed later in this chapter.)

(13) a. Ele ver –*te* -a.
          he see 2s FUT-3s
          'He will see you.'
      b. Conduzi –*lo* -ei.
          (I) conduct 3s FUT-1s
          'I will conduct him.'

A comparative consideration might also be adduced as an argument against the peripherality thesis of clitic placement in GALPORT. The pattern of clitic placement in the Cypriot Greek dialect described by Terzi (1999a) is remarkably similar to the GALPORT pattern: enclisis is the rule on both finite and nonfinite verbs in affirmative clauses, whereas proclisis is manifested in negative and interrogative clauses and in clauses containing focalized constituents. Where Cypriot Greek differs from GALPORT, however, is in embedded clauses. Whereas in GALPORT enclisis gives way to proclisis in both indicative and subjunctive embedded clauses, proclisis is only manifested in Cypriot Greek subjunctive clauses; in clauses embedded under the indicative complementizer *oti* (and optionally under *pos*), enclisis is enforced. Compare the switch from enclisis to proclisis in GALPORT (14) with the pattern of consistent enclisis in Cypriot Greek in (15):

(14) a. O João leu-*o* ontem.
          the João read-3MS yesterday
          'João read it yesterday.'
      b. Disseram-me que o João *o* leu ontem.
          (they) told-1s that the João 3MS read yesterday
          'They told me that João read it yesterday.'

(15) a. I Maria edhkiavasen *to*.
          the Maria read 3MS
          'Maria read it.'
      b. Ksero oti i Maria edhkiavasen *to*.
          (I) know that the Maria read 3MS
          'I know that Maria read it.'

I come back to proclisis and its triggers later. The point to bear in mind here is only that Cypriot Greek provides overt evidence for a process that is partially obscured in GALPORT: namely, that cliticization takes place below the complementizer.[5]

In summary, the evidence to the effect that cliticization in GALPORT avails itself of a clitic position in the left periphery, unavailable or unused in CASPIT, is inconclusive. Let us therefore put this hypothesis aside and assume, essentially following Rouveret (1989), that the cliticization site in GALPORT is a functional head internal to IP. Indeed, the strongest hypothesis we can make is that the cliticization site or sites in GALPORT are the same as in CASPIT.

Now consider the following reasoning: if the cliticization site in GALPORT is not higher than in CASPIT, then the difference between these two sets of languages must lie with the position of finite inflection. The idea is that enclisis is conditioned in GALPORT by the possibility of checking or of assigning finite inflection in positions that are lower than in CASPIT. Moreover, we expect this to correlate to some extent with the domain of inflectionally driven verb movement.

There is some prima facie evidence to this effect based on the position of the finite verb relative to various adverbs. Rouveret (1989) discusses the fact that the unmarked position for adverbs like *provavilmente* (as well as *frequentemente* and *cuidadosamente*) in European Portuguese is to the left of the tensed verb. In addition, the finite verb must follow *quase*. In Italian, in contrast, the unmarked position for the verb is to the left of *quasi*, as Cinque (1999) shows. In Cinque's approach, this difference signals a difference in the position of the verb, which can be taken to be lower in European Portuguese than in Italian. Belletti (1990) argued that when Italian *probabilmente* appears between the subject and the verb, the subject is topicalized. Costa (1999) shows that this is not the case in Portuguese, citing sentence (16), which contains an untopicalizable negative quantifier subject:

(16)   Ninguém provavelmente leu o livre.
       Nobody probably read the book
       'Probably nobody read the book.'

Costa also shows that the inflected perfect auxiliary *ter* occurs below *já*, whereas Cinque has demonstrated that Italian *avere* must raise above *gia*. These differences suggest that obligatory verb movement in European Portuguese systematically targets a position that is lower than what is targeted in Italian. This difference can be interpreted to mean that the heads responsible for morphological feature-checking are *lower* in Portuguese than in Italian.[6]

GALPORT differs from CASPIT in yet another respect. In the former, the auxiliary employed in the complex tenses is *ter* and not *haber* or *avere*.[7] Suppose, now, that there is a correlation between the lexical form of the auxiliary (i.e., *ter* or *haber*) and the position of finite inflection such that Infl is located in a higher position in the clause in *haber* systems than it is in *ter* systems.[8]

The correlation between enclisis and the form of the auxiliary is confirmed by Raposo (2000), who cites the sentences in (17), commenting that despite the absence of *haber* from Modern Portuguese, speakers express a firm judgment: enclisis is impossible in finite clauses in the context of *haber*; only proclisis is tolerated.

(17)   a. ?*Hei-*lhe* dado muita coisa.
           (I) have DAT3MS given many things
           'I have given him many things.'
       b. Muita coisa *lhe* hei dado.
           many things DAT3MS (I) have given

Ter differs from *haber* in yet another sense: it licenses VP-ellipsis (see, in particular, Martins 1994b; Rouveret 1989, 1999). Compare the sentences in French and Italian in (18a and b), in which VP ellipsis is not possible, with the European Portuguese example in (18c), where it is (note also the difference in the relative positions of the auxiliary and the adverb meaning 'also'):

(18) a.*Gianni ha comprato i romanzi di Faulkner e Pietro ha anche.
      b.*Jean a acheté les romans de Faulkner et Pierre a aussi.
      c. O João tem comprado as novelas de Faulkner e o Pedro também tem.
      John has bought the novels of Faulkner and Peter has also / also has

One influential view of VP-ellipsis—elaborated in, for example, Lobeck (1987, 1995) and Zagona (1988a,b)—holds that ellipted VPs must be head-governed by a lexically-filled functional head. This is why English VP ellipsis is only possible under an auxiliary or a modal. Zagona attributes the difference between English (where VP ellipsis is possible) and CASPIT (where it is not) to the S-structure position of the auxililiaries in the two language types. (For Lobeck, the difference is stated in terms of the strength of the inflectional features.) Although Zagona's claim that English auxiliaries do not move is surely overstated (as Martins 1994b points out), it is reasonable to adhere to a weaker version of her hypothesis and associate null VP licensing with the lexicalization of a relatively low functional head. English auxiliaries move, this much is certain, but they presumably do not move as high as their CASPIT counterparts. Similarly, European Portuguese *ter* targets a lower position than CASPIT *haber*, low enough to license the null VP.

The putative positional difference between *ter* and *haber* can be exploited to sketch an account for European Portuguese mesoclisis, as illustrated in (13). Descriptively, clitics are lodged between the verbal stem and the morphemes that represent the future tense or the conditional mood. These morphemes are etymologically descended from Vulgar Latin *haber*. Suppose that they are vestiges of the "high" Infl. It is this Infl, positioned higher than the cliticization site, which is active and which feature-attracts the verb in the modern, *haber*-based systems, such as CASPIT. In CASPIT, indeed, the future and the conditional forms are inflectional suffixes that are no different in status from the preterit or imperfect ones. In European Portuguese, however, the "high" Infl no longer attracts the verbal stem; it does not check any of its features. Checking the features of the verbal stem is effected by the lower inflectional head which, it must be assumed, is active even in the presence of the higher Infl. Hence, the verb is inflectionally complete under the cliticization site, and enclisis does not impede adjunction of the verbal stem (adjoined to the clitic) to the future or conditional morphemes (or movement to M(ood)^0, as in Terzi 1999b and Petinou and Terzi 2002).[9]

Before moving on to an investigation of proclisis, let us summarize the discussion up to this point. I have tried to defend two related theses: namely, that enclisis applies whenever possible and that the mechanism that enforces enclisis in CASPIT and GALPORT is one and the same. The latter hypothesis is called into question by the existence of different patterns of enclisis in CASPIT and in GALPORT. Further investigation, however, confirms the original thesis: the "parametric" difference between these two sets of languages does not govern cliticization directly; rather, it concerns the position of the active finite Infl. In GALPORT, this Infl is configured lower than in CASPIT. The ban on encliticization in CASPIT finite clauses is a direct consquence of the relative position of its finite Infl. It remains to be established whether the parameter in question in fact determines the relative position of the head(s) checking finite morphology or whether it marks one (of several) such heads as active or inactive in a particular grammar.

2. Proclisis

Proclisis obtains when enclisis is ruled out. In CASPIT, the presence of an active Infl above the cliticization site rules out enclisis in finite clauses and triggers proclisis. In GALPORT, finite inflection does not interfere in the way of enclisis. Negation, however, does: compare the affirmative (7a), repeated below as (19a), with its negative counterpart in (19b):

(19) a. O João deu-*lhe* esse livro ontem.
          the João gave-DAT3s this book yesterday
          'João gave him/her this book yesterday.'
      b. O João não *lhe*-deu esse livro ontem.
          the João NEG DAT3s gave this book yesterday
          'João di not give him/her this book yesterday.'

The contrast in (19) should be taken to mean that the negative head is positioned higher than the cliticization site *and* that it attracts a feature of the pre-cliticization verbal complex. In other words, the relation between the verb and negation is similar to that of an inflectional head and the verb.[10] The morphosyntactic dependency between negation and a tensed verb is overtly represented in Berber. I therefore turn to a discussion of cliticization in Berber before returning to proclisis in GALPORT.

2.1.   Cliticization in Berber and the impact of negation

The sentences in (20), taken from Guerssel's (1985) description of Ait Seghrouchen Tamazight, are representative of a pervasive pattern in Berber (see also Boukhris 1998 on the Tamazight of Zemmour; Sadiqi 1997, 1998 on Ait Hassan Tamazight; Ouhalla 1989 on Tarifit; and Meziani 1997 on Tashawit). We see that the clitic appears to the right of the verb in an affirmative sentence and to its left in a negative one.

(20) a. Yuzn -*as-tt* Moñ.
          sent-3MS DAT3s-ACC3FS Moñ
          'Moñ sent it to her.'
      b. Ur -*as-tt* yuzin Moñ.
          NEG DAT3s-ACC3FS sent-3MS Moñ
          'Moñ didn't send it to her.'
      c. *Ur yuzin -*as-tt* Moñ.
          NEG sent-3MS DAT3s-ACC3FS Moñ
          'Moñ didn't send it to her.'

Berber is generally described as manifesting only enclitics. The difference between (20a) and (20b) is taken to show that the hosts of enclisis can vary: it is the verb in (20a) and the negative particle *ur* in (20b).

As Boukhris (1998) notes, however, the sentences in (20) provide information as to the *phonological* attachment of Berber clitics, not necessarily about their syntax. The fact is that Berber clitics are prosodically associated with the prosodic word on their left. These prosodic supports should not be thought of as *syntactic* hosts, since they do not constitute a syntactic or categorial natural class. Thus, an X^0 such as the negative head *ur*, as in (20b), a (perhaps left-dislocated) subject, as in Boukhris's

(1998: 75, n. 19) example in (21a) or a wh-word in Spec/C, in (21b), from Guerssel (1985) can prosodically host clitics:[11]

(21)   a. Nkk as tinix hða, nta itazayað.
     I DAT3s say-1s this he continues-3MS
     'Me, I say this to him while he, he continues.'
   b. Maymi *as-tt* yuzn Moħ?
     why DAT3s-ACC3FS sent Moħ
     'Why did Moħ send it to her?

    In the framework developed in this essay, we have syntactic enclisis only when (1) is manifested. This comes about only when the host raises and adjoins to the clitic—namely, in (20a): only verbs can be syntactic hosts for enclisis. Thus, (20b), as well as (21a and b) should be considered cases of syntactic proclisis, which, in the terms of this essay means nonenclisis. Proclisis can take a myriad forms, none of which involve attachment of the host to the left of the clitic.

    Prosodically, Berber clitics are enclitics, and this is encoded as a phonological feature on the clitic. In the component where prosodic rules apply, presumably PF, this feature is interpreted by associating the clitic with the preceding adjacent prosodic word, independently of whether this word is syntactically adjoined to the clitic, as the verb is in (20a), or whether it is not, as in (20b).[12]

    Aside from this phonological difference, Berber resembles GALPORT and, in line with the earlier discussion of enclisis, I assume that the cliticization site in Berber is higher than the position(s) of the heads that check tense and agreement.

    The cliticization site, however, is lower than negation in all Berber dialects—with the possible exception of Imdlawn Tashelhiyt (Dell and Elmedlaoui 1989), which is discussed at length in Ouhalla (2002). Not only does negation "trigger" proclisis, but, in addition, the verb undergoes an internal vowel change. Looking at (20), we see *yuzn* 'he sent' and *ur yuzin* 'he did not send'. In a similar vein, in (22) it is not the presence of the negative word *ur* as such that triggers the ablaut on the verb but the appearance of negation, in the form of a negative head or a negative adverb (perhaps associated with a phonetically unexpressed head):

(22)   a. T-swa.
     3FS-drank
     'She drank.'
   b. Ur t-swi / *t-swa.
     NEG 3FS-drank / 3FS drank
     She did not drink.'
   c. Ursar t-swi / *t-swa.
     never 3FS-drank / 3FS drank
     'She never drank.'

    Suppose, with Boukhris (1998), that the vowel [i] in, for example, (22b and c), is the phonetic realization of a quasi-inflectional negative feature on the verb. Being a morphosyntactic feature, it has to enter a checking relationship with the negative head *ur* in (22b and c). Let us assume that this feature is attracted to the negative head, its attraction being signaled phonologically (cf. note 10 on English negative auxiliaries.) Now, if V were to adjoin to the clitic before the negative inflection is checked, the negative feature would be too deeply embedded to be accessible to Neg; it would remain unchecked, and the derivation would crash. To avert a crash, adjunction of V to the clitic, namely enclisis, is abandoned in favor of proclisis.[13] Formally speaking, then, negation in Berber has the same impact on clisis and for the same reasons as finite inflection in CASPIT.

Negation also determines a vowel change on the imperfective or present tense modal *la*, transforming it to *lli* when it appears between the negative head the verb. The main verb, however, is not modified; compare (23a) and (23b):[14]

(23)   a. La iddu.
　　　　　PRES 3MS-leave
　　　　　'He is leaving.'
　　　 b. Ur lli iddu.
　　　　　NEG PRES 3MS-leave
　　　　　'He is not leaving.'

The verb in (23) is in the "imperfective" form, which, in many dialects, is preceded by one of several modal or aspectual particles, such as *la*. In this respect, the imperfective form resembles an Indo-European participle and the *la* + imperfect construction is a form of periphrasis (see Boukhris 1998 and Sadiqi 1997 for further discussion).

When a clitic appears, it is intercalated between the modal and the main verb (and is prosodically attached to the modal). This is shown in (24):

(24)   La *as* itari.
　　　　PRES DAT-3S 3MS-write
　　　　'He is writing to him.'

One way of deriving this word order consists of assuming that the cliticization site is above the modal. Then, pursuing the similarity with Indo-European periphrasis, it comes as no surprise that in the presence of *la*, the main verb does not raise above the clitic. Rather, the modal does, adjoining to the clitic.

However, as it stands, the preceding analysis engenders a false prediction. When *la* is preceded by negation, which, as (23) indicates, attracts a feature on the modal, adjunction of the modal to the clitic ought to be blocked, for exactly the same reason that it is blocked when negation precedes—and attracts a feature of—the main verb. Alongside (20b), we expect (25a), but we get (25b):

(25)   a.*Ur *as* lli itari.
　　　　　NEG DAT-3S PRES 3MS-write
　　　　　'He is not writing to him.'
　　　 b. Ur lli *as* itari.
　　　　　NEG PRES DAT-3S 3MS-write
　　　　　'He is writing to him.'

This should lead us to reject the idea that the cliticization site is above the modal. Let us assume, instead, that it is below it but above the position of the verb. Thus, the verb does not move to or above the clitic in (24), but remains below it, as it is a participle of sorts. The negative feature on the modal does not encounter any barrier in its movement path to the negative head, and (25b) is the only possible output. While (20a) is a case of enclisis, there is no enclisis in (24) since condition (8b) is not satisfied, independently of the presence of negation. Both (24) and (25b) are cases of proclisis.

In conclusion, the heads that check the more familiar kinds of verbal morphology (e.g., tense, agreement, and aspect) are configured lower than the cliticization site in Berber, which is why we find generalized enclisis on finite verbs. NegP, however, lies above the cliticization site. This partial ordering of functional categories is arrayed in (26):

(26)   Neg > Modal > Clitic > Tense/AGR > V

2.2.   Triggers for proclisis

The difference between the traditional inflectional categories and negation is that the former are typically incorporation hosts that attract the verbal stem. It is quite conceivable, nonetheless, that a head will attract a feature on a lower head without actually attracting or incorporating the lower head itself—that is, without pied-piping it. This is the case of negation in Berber, but clearly the same holds for the GALPORT contrast in (19) and for the Cypriot Greek pattern, illustrated by the contrast between the affirmative (15a), repeated here as (27a), and the negative (27b):

(27)   a. I Maria edhkiavasen *to*.
           the Maria read 3MS
           'Maria read it.'
       b. En *ton* iksero.
           NEG 3MS (I) know
           'I don't know him.'

Aside from negation, left-peripheral focus and overt wh-movement exercise a blocking effect on enclisis in Berber (28), Cypriot Greek (29) and GALPORT (30). This is evidenced by the obligatory manifestation of proclisis in these examples:

(28)   a. Maymi-*as-tt* yuzn Moħ?
           why DAT3s-ACC3FS sent Moħ
           'Why did Moħ send it to her?'
       a'. M ay tsɣu terbatt?
           What that bought girl
           'What did the girl buy?'
       b. Moħ ay-*as-tt* yuzn.
           Moħ that DAT3s-ACC3FS sent
           'It is Moħ who sent it to her.'

(29)   a. Pjos *ton* idhe?
           Who 3MS saw
           'Who saw him?'
       b. Tuto to vivlio *su* edhoken i Maria
           this the book 2s gave the Maria
           'This book, Maria gave you.'

(30)   a. O que *lhe* deu a Maria ontem?
           the what DAT3s gave the Maria yesterday
           'What did Maria give him/her yesterday?'

b. ISSE *lhe* disse eu.
This DAT3s said I
'This is what I told him/her.'

In sentences (28a and a'), (29a), and (30a), there is a wh-expression in Comp. Assume it is sitting in the specifier of a dedicated functional head. Assume further, as seems natural, that the [+wh]-marked head of the category housing the wh-expression attracts a lower head. This is surely the morphosyntactic driving force behind I to C movement, which is cross-linguistically very common in interrogatives and can be taken to pied-pipe $V_{[+wh]}$ or, more likely, $I_{[+wh]}$, to the relevant functional head. But, as with negation, the [+wh]-feature can be attracted without pied piping. This is systematically the case in Berber. The head of the wh-comp is either null, as in (28a), or filled by the focus complementizer *ay*, as in (28a'). In both cases and for the same reasons, enclisis is blocked: the source of the attracted feature is below the cliticization site, and adjunction of the verb to the clitic would render the feature inaccessible to checking by the wh-head in Comp, as already argued.[15]

The same reasoning carries over to the focalization cases in (28b)–(30b). Not only in Berber, where it is manifest, but in general, wh-movement *is* a form of (left-peripheral) focalization, in which the wh-word is in focus. (For a recent treatment, see Rizzi 1997.) Focalization, like wh-movement, triggers I to C movement in many grammatical systems, and this indicates that there is an attracting feature in Comp.

Grammatical systems in which I to C movement systematically applies in focalization or wh-movement just as systematically disallow I to C movement in topicalization or clitic left-dislocation structures. Admittedly, this is no accident and should be taken to indicate that the head of TopicP does not attract an IP-internal feature or, perhaps, no feature at all.[16] The absence of proclisis in clitic left-dislocation constructions in GALPORT (Rouveret 1999), Berber (Shlonsky 1987), and Cypriot Greek (Terzi 1999a) is a direct consequence of this.[17]

While yes/no questions in GALPORT do not block enclisis, as shown by the grammaticality of (31a) and hence differ from their wh-counterparts, Berber interrogatives invariably trigger proclisis, as illustrated in (31b).

(31) a. O Pedro encontrou-*a* no cinema?
         the Pedro met-ACC3FS in-the cinema
         'Did Pedro meet her in the cinema?'
      b. Is-*tt* yzra Aħmd?
         Q 3FS saw Ahmd
         'Did Ahmed see her?'

This difference is surely related to the fact that Berber has an overt question morpheme in Comp, whereas GALPORT does not. Berber *is* attracts a feature on the inflected verb, while in GALPORT, the Q position in Comp does not contain any lexical material and, hence, no feature that needs to be checked. In other words, it is not the presence of a Q operator as such that is relevant to the choice between enclisis and proclisis, but of a head that attracts features.

Similarly, interrogatives with a (non-echo) wh–in situ are possible in European Portuguese, but they do not trigger proclisis, as in (32), from Rouveret (1999). This is due to the absence of an attracting element in Comp at the level at which the choice between enclisis and proclisis is taken (for similar reasons, wh–in situ does not trigger I to C movement in French, as Rizzi (1996) argues).

(32)   A Maria deu-*lhe* o quê?
       the Maria gave-DAT3s the what
       'Maria gave him/her what?'

2.3.   Proclisis in embedded clauses

One of the arguments adduced against the peripherality thesis of clitic placement in GALPORT is based on the observation that subordination is a trigger for proclisis in GALPORT but not in Cypriot Greek. Contrast the GALPORT example in (33a) with the Cypriot Greek sentence in (33b).

(33)   a. Disseram-me que o João *o* leu ontem.
           (they) told-1s that the João 3MS read yesterday
           'They told me that João read it yesterday.'
       b. Ksero oti i Maria edhkiavasen *to*.
           (I) know that the Maria read 3MS
           'I know that Maria read it.'

It is, however, not the case that proclisis is never triggered in Cypriot Greek embedded clauses. Terzi (1999a) shows that the factor relevant for the choice between enclisis and proclisis is not embedding as such, but rather the mood of the embedded clause: enclisis is preserved in indicative clauses while proclisis is forced in subjunctive clauses, introduced by the overt subjunctive mood marker *na*. Compare (33b) and (34):

(34)   Thelo na *ton* dho.
       (I) want SUBJ 3MS (I) see
       'I want to see him.'

Putting aside Salentino and similar varieties (see Calabrese 1993) as well as Romanian, subjunctive mood in Romance is represented as a component of verbal inflection and not by a choice of complementizer. It makes sense, however, to consider this mood inflection as containing a feature which is attracted by a mood or a low comp head (see note 5). This mood head is overt in Greek, attracting T or V over the cliticization site, whence enclisis.

To explain why the indicative complementizer does not force proclisis in Greek while it does so in GALPORT, let us once again consider the situation in Berber. Within Berber, there are dialects like Tarifit, Tachawit, and some varieties of Tamazight, where the indicative complementizer does not effect enclisis and (at least one) variety of Tamazight where enclisis is blocked in embedded clauses and gives way to proclisis. In other words, we find the Greek ~ GALPORT alternation manifested internally to Berber. Consider the sentences in (35), from Tarifit (Ouhalla 1989), and those in (36), from Guerssel's (1985) Tamazight:[18]

(35) a. *Tnna qa-*t* yarzm sg tynjayt.
          (she) said that 3MS (he) opened with spoon
          'She said that he opened it with a spoon.'
      b. tnna qa yarzm -*t* sg tynjayt.
          (she) said that (he) opened 3MS with spoon
          'She said that he opened it with a spoon.'

(36) a. Ssnx is -*as-tt* yuzn Moħ.
          (I) know that DAT3S-ACC3FS sent Moħ.
          'I know that Moħ sent it to her.'
      b. *Ssnx is yuzn-*as-tt* Moħ.
          (I) know that sent DAT3S-ACC3FS Moħ

Tarifit *qa* does not attract a feature from under the cliticzation site, while Tamazight *is* does.[19] Note, now, that this difference correlates with the position of a proleptic or dislocated object in the two varieties. In Tamazight, the natural position of a topic is to the left of the complementizer, as in (37) with *Moħ* as a (clitic left-dislocated) topic. Such a word order is impossible in Tarifit, J. Ouhalla informs me (personal communication):

(37) Ssnx Moħ is *t* tssudm Tifa.
          (I) know Moħ that 3MS kissed Tifa
          'I know that Moħ, Tifa kissed him.'

Thinking of Irish 'it is probable in the next few days that he will leave' (McCloskey 1996) and of Italian *penso a Gianni di doverlo parlare* (Rizzi 1997), let us hypothesize that *is* occupies a lower position in the Comp system than *qa*, since it follows, rather than precedes, a topic. Concretely, suppose that Tamazight *is* sits in Fin^0, while Tarifit *qa* (and similarly Tachawit *bǝlli*; cf. Meziani 1997) are in $Force^0$, above the highest topic position. Fin^0 contains tense or tense-related features (cf., in this respect, Cottell's 1995 study of Irish tense). Suppose that its "interfacing'" with IP, in Rizzi's (1997) sense, means that it attracts a feature from the inflectional domain, from below the cliticization site in Berber. Hence, enclisis under *is* is blocked and proclisis is manifested. In Tarifit, only $Force^0$ contains morphosyntactic features, but $Force^0$ does not interface with IP and attracts no IP-internal feature. Fin^0 is not lexicalized in this Berber variety and does not attract any morphosyntactic features from inside IP. Hence, enclisis is unperturbed under *qa*.

I would like to suggest, now, that in GALPORT, Fin^0 is always active in embedded clauses and systematically attracts a feature from T. Since the cliticization site is configured between T and Fin, enclisis is predictably blocked and we have proclisis. Uriagereka (1995a) takes what he terms the "sandwiched dislocation" illustrated in (38) to be a hallmark of the languages that display the GALPORT pattern of cliticization. It makes sense to identify the higher *que* in (38) with $Force^0$ and the lower one with Fin^0. Suppose, further, that even when the lower *que* is sometimes unpronounced, it is always active from a morphosyntactic point of view and attracts a feature. (It differs, in this respect, from Tarifit Fin^0, which is never lexically realized.)

(38) Dixeron que a este home que non *o* maltratemos.
          (they) said that a this man that NEG ACC3MS maltreat
          'They said of this man that we should not treat him badly.'

3.   Some remaining issues

In the course of this essay, I have developed a general theory of clitic placement which takes enclisis (i.e., V to cl.) to apply whenever possible and proclisis only as a last resort. This theory is combined with a hypothesis concerning cross-linguistic differences in the postion of the cliticization site relative to finite inflection, negation, and feature-attracting morphemes in the Comp domain. The empirical result is a unified explanation of clisis from Rabat to Rome and from Lisbon to Larnaca.

Rhetoric aside, there remain a certain number of unanswered questions that I would like to briefly address in the guise of a conclusion.

One issue is how to best state the difference between French infinitives (in which proclisis is enforced) and CASPIT ones. The approach developed in this essay leads me to follow Kayne (1989) and suggest that the cliticization site in French infinitives is lower than the one in CASPIT infinitives. In particular, it is lower than Infin^0, so that enclisis is systematically blocked. In other respects, French is exactly like CASPIT.

There is some evidence for the low clitic position in French. Zubizarreta (1985) shows that the French clitic *se* can remain on the infinitival verbal complement of causative *faire*, contrasting sharply, though in different ways, with Spanish and Italian. Rouveret and Vergnaud (1980), as well as Kayne (1975), report similar facts for locative *y* and adnominal *en*. These observations might be interpreted to mean that in French—though neither in Spanish nor in Italian—there is a cliticization site internal to the reduced infinitival complement to the causative verb.

The French/Italian contrasts in cliticization options under *tough movement* also point to the presence of a lower clitcization site in French. In both languages, clitics are possible on infinitival complements to adjectives such as 'difficult'—see (39a and b) and (40a and b)—but only French allows the clitic to remain on the infinitive when *tough movement* applies. Compare (41a) and (42a) with (41b) and (42b). If the infinitival complement to the adjective in (41) and (42) is a "reduced" clause (lacking, e.g., a position for negation; viz. Rizzi 1993), then the contrast can be taken to show that the lowest cliticization site in French is lower than in Italian:

(39)   a.   È difficile spiegar*gli* questo teorema (agli studenti).
             is difficult explain-DAT3 this theorem (to the students)
       b.   Il est difficile à *leur* expliquer ce théorème (aux étudiants).
             it is difficult to DAT2PL explain this theorem (to the students)
             'It is difficult to explain the theorem to them (to the students).'

(40)   a.   È difficile appender*vi* questo quadro (al muro).
             Is difficult to hand-LOC this painting (on the wall)
       b.   Il est difficile à *y* accrocher ce tableau (au mur).
             It is difficult to LOC hang this painting (on the wall)
             'It is difficult to hang this painting there (on the wall).'

(41)   a. *Questo teorema è difficile da spiegar*gli*.
             This theorem is difficult to explain-DAT3
       b.   Ce théorème est difficile à *leur* expliquer.
             This theorem is difficult to DAT2PL explain
             'This theorem is difficult to explain to them.'

(42) a. *Questo quadro è difficile da appender*vi*.
         This painting is difficult to to hang-LOC
      b. ?Ce tableau à est difficile à *y* accrocher.
         This painting to is difficult to LOC hang
         'It is difficult to hang this painting there.'

Another question is whether the proclisis-triggering effect of the "high" heads, such as negation, has any traces in CASPIT. Let us consider a possible CASPIT candidate for what we might call the *GALPORT effect*. The empirical domain in which this effect is visible is that of cliticization in imperatives. The discussion here is limited to French.

In French, enclisis is manifested in affirmative imperatives, as shown in (43):

(43) Mange-*la*!
      eat-3FS
      'Eat it!'

I assume that (true) imperative clauses are truncated and do not project a CP. This is why they cannot be embedded, host a wh-element or a topic, and so on. I further assume that the imperative morphology is associated with a very low head, lower than the cliticization site.[20] Formally speaking, French imperatives are therefore like CASPIT infinitives: the imperative form is inflectionally complete under the cliticization site. Enclisis is therefore possible.

Now, although they are structurally reduced clauses, there must be a position for negation in imperatives, and negation is surely configured higher than the cliticization site. In other words, negative imperatives are formally similar to negative GALPORT finite clauses. Indeed, when negation appears in a French imperative, enclisis is blocked and only proclisis is possible:

(44) a. Ne *la* mange pas!
         NEG 3FS eat NEG
         'Don't eat it!'
      b. *Ne mange *la* pas!
         NEG eat 3FS NEG
         'Don't eat it!'

Sentence (44) reflects the situation in the variety of (Standard) French in which the preverbal negative head *ne* is present. Alongside this pattern of negation in imperatives, there exists another, in which *ne* is impossible. In this variety, enclisis is preserved. Contrast the grammatical (45a) with the ungrammatical (45b):

(45) a. *La* mange pas!
         3FS eat NEG
         'Don't eat it!'
      b. *Ne mange *la* pas!
         NEG eat 3FS NEG
         'Don't eat it!'

We can make sense out of this pattern by assuming that in the variety in which *ne* is impossible, we are dealing with a different NegP, one that is crucially lower than the cliticization site (viz., Zanuttini 1997 on multiple negation positions in Romance). Enclisis in (45) is possible because the imperative form is inflectionally complete under the cliticization site, where inflection now includes a (sometimes null) negative feature. When enclisis is possible, proclisis cannot apply.

Just as intriguing is the question of why CASPIT infinitives, participles, and so on do not revert to proclisis under negation (or wh-movement), since they do so in GALPORT, and the relative positions of Infin^0 or Part^0, Neg^0, and the cliticization site are presumably the same in both language types. The logic of the analysis pursued in this chapter should lead us to explore the idea that negation does not attract (a feature of) the head responsible for infinitival morphology—neither in GALPORT nor in CASPIT—but that of another functional head situated below the cliticization site in GALPORT and above it in CASPIT. Further research is needed to determine the nature of this head: whether it is related to the nominal characteristics of nonfinite verbs, or alternatively, to their value for [±realis], but note that its position relative to the cliticization site in the two language types mirrors the relative position of the active finite Infl.

Notes

Parts of this essay or earlier versions were presented at the Universities of Geneva, Fes, Venice, Padua, Paris VII, and CUNY and at the Cartography of Syntactic Structures Workshop in Siena. I am grateful to the audiences at these venues for their questions and comments. Particular thanks to I. Roberts, A. Terzi, and R. Kayne and to two anonymous reviewers for written comments. This work has also benefited from suggestions and comments from A. Cardinaletti, G. Cinque, H. Koopman, A. Ledgeway, A. Belletti, A. Rouveret, C. Poletto, L. Rizzi, J. Gueron, M. Starke, D. Sportiche, M. Ennaji, F. Sadiqi, J. Lowenstamm, G. Rigau, and C. Picallo. I acknowledge the generous assistance of E. Raposo with the Portuguese data and that of J. Ouhalla, F. Sadiqi, and N. Omari for help with Berber.

1. This derivation departs from Kayne's (1994) proposal, according to which enclisis obtains when the verb moves to a higher head position than that occupied by the clitic; see also Terzi (1999b). Kayne's analysis does not square well with the strict adjacency requirement that is characteristic of the verb-clitic nexus; see. Beninca' and Cinque (1993).

2. See Martins (1994a) for a study of "interpolation effects" in Old Iberian dialects, Barbosa (1996), and Raposo (2000), who also writes that "One intriguing aspect of interpolation is that there are no attested cases where the clitic is separated from the verb, but with the positions . . . reversed, i.e. with the verb . . . higher than the clitic" (27a). If enclisis is defined as adjunction of V to cl., then the absence of interpolation is expected (cf. note 1).

3. Alternatively, if head movement pied-pipes features (Chomsky 1995), then the conditions of accessibility of these features might resemble those which hold of wh–pied piping in many languages (see Webelhuth 1992).

4. See Cardinaletti (chapter 5 this volume) who argues against the view that subject in null subject languages are invariably dislocated.

5. Moreover, the fact that (pro)clitics appear to the right of the subjunctive (mood) particle *na* is an indication that they are within IP not in CP since *na* is either an IP-internal Mood head (Rivero 1994) or Modal head (Tsimpli 1990) or, as Roussou (2001) argues, a realization of Rizzi's (1997) Fin^0—that is, a "low" head in the CP domain, directly interfacing with IP.

6. In and of itself, this argument is inconclusive since Spanish appears to pattern with European Portuguese and not with Italian insofar as adverb interpolation is concerned, and yet Spanish eschews enclisis in finite clauses. This matter requires further investigation.

7. The auxiliary *ter* and its equivalents are found in some (Modern) CASPIT varieties, notably in certain Italian dialects from the upper south (see Rohlfs 1996 and Loporcaro 1988), as well as in some local varieties of Spanish (see Cartagena 1999 and Yllera 1999). Portuguese *ter* gradually replaced *haber* over the fifteenth and sixteenth centuries, passing through a stage in which it expressed the possessive, as it continues to do in Modern Spanish (see Bourciez 1967: §387 and Diez 1876: 261). Raposo (2000) writes that the change from *haber* to *ter* was not complete until the early nineteenth century.

In this context, the Modern Spanish periphrastic complex *haber + participle* evolved from vulgar Latin *habeo factum*, which was a resultative/adjectival construction in pre-Classical Spanish, of the sort that would be expressed nowadays by means of, for example, *tener*, as in (i); cf. Loporcaro (1999). See Harre (1991) for further discussion.

> (i) Tengo escritos cinco capítulos del libro.
> 'I have five chapters of this book (already) written.'
> Compare: 'I have written five chapters of this book.'

8. Giorgi and Pianesi (1997: §3.3.3) point out that the Portuguese periphrastic present perfect (with *ter*) encodes an iterative interpretation, unlike both its Italian counterpart (with *avere*) and the Portuguese simple past. See (Schmitt 2001) for in-depth discussion. This should correlate with the position of *ter* in the clausal hierarchy, although it is not clear to me how. The iterative interepretation is only associated with the present perfect—that is, with *ter* in the present tense. The pluperfect, formed with *ter* in the past tense, has the same intereprecation as its CASPIT counterparts.

9. As for the drive for this movement step, one might entertain the idea that the semi-auxiliaries in the high Infl enter into a checking relationship with features of the clitic head itself, which, then, must be present even when there is no clitic. Cardinaletti and Shlonsky (2003) argue that the clitic head is syntactically represented even in the absence of a clitic. Whatever is correct, it is clear that movement of a head can continue beyond the cliticization site. The point is simply that such movement does not implicate any features of the pre-cliticization head.

In this context, note that verbal agreement is a suffix on the future or conditional morpheme. This might be taken to mean that Agr—if represented as an independent head—attracts T and not V (see Shlonsky 1997: chap. 3). This is indirectly supported by the fact that enclisis is preserved in European Portuguese infinitives whether or not they are inflected for subject agreement. For example, compare (ia) and (ib) from Madeira (1993). If Agr attracted V, we would expect proclisis in (ib):

> (i) a. Penso convidá-la. / *a convidar.
>   (I) think to invite-3FS / 3FS to invite
>   'I consider inviting her.'
>   b. Penso ter-em-na / *a ter-em convidado.
>   (I) think to have-3PL-3FS / *-3FS to have-3PL invited
>   'I think they have invited her.'

In adjunct (preositional) infinitival CPs containing uninflected infinitives, proclisis and enclisis are in free variation (see the discussion in Raposo 2001). This might be due to whether the preposition is merged in CP (e.g., in Fin°, like Italian *di*; cf. Rizzi 1997) or above it, inducing proclisis only in the fomer case. Raposo shows that inflected infinitives in the same context only allow proclisis, a fact which suggests that person inflection on infinitivals is lower than the cliticization site, while being higher in finite clauses.

10. See Roberts (1999) for the view that English *don't*, *can't*, and *won't* are negative auxiliaries—that is, auxiliaries with negative features.

11. Imagine that Italian clitics had the same property. Then, clitics would never occur in first position, so that, for example, (4a) would be ungrammatical, and the clitic *lo* in (i) would be attached in the surface string to the subject *Gianni* and not to the verb *spiega*. Clitic systems with these characteristics are not uncommon (particularly in Slavic and Old Romance; see, e.g., Beninca' 1995; Cardinaletti and Roberts 2002; Halpern 1995; and Wanner 1987).

    (i)   Gianni-lo spiega agli studenti.
          Gianni-3MS explains to-the students
          'Gianni explains it to the students.'

12. However, see Ouhalla (2002), who argues that clitics left-adjoin to a functional head, which is then inverted around it in PF. See Halpern (1995) and many of the papers in Halpern and Zwicky (1996) for discussion of this sort of prosodic inversion.

13. I stay aloof, here and throughout, of any specific implementation of proclisis. Recalling the discussion surrounding (2) and taking inspiration from Belletti's (1999) treatment of CASPIT proclisis (see also Laenzlinger 1994), one might conceive of it as involving two steps. First, the verb "skips" the clitic head on its way up, thereby circumventing a potential crash. Second, the clitic head is itself adjoined to the functional head above it (which hosts the verb). Although the first step violates the HMC derivationally, the second step corrects or undoes the violation representationally since the traces of all the heads below the surface position of the verb can form a representational chain. For such a derivation to be acceptable (it is modeled on Belletti's 1990 analysis of the cliticization of the negative head), the principle of strict cyclicity must be relaxed and this, perhaps, is undesirable for other reasons. Another option, which revives and adapts Ouhalla's (1989) original treatment of Berber cliticization, is that a verb (or a modal) simply fail to raise above the clitic when it is preceded by negation or some other proclisis trigger.

14. The geminate *l* of the negative form of the modal is a vestige of its underlying form, derived from 'be' and which is realized as *lla* in the closely related Ait Seghrouchen dialect; see Guerssel (1985).

15. Proclisis should not disturb feature attraction if the feature does not adjoin to either the clitic or to the head of which the clitic is a specifier. See note 13.

16. In this context, see, Rizzi's (1997) point to the effect that there is no Top to Force movement. If Top is never directly attracted to Force, and if it never attracts, then Rizzi's point follows.

17. Rouveret (1999) argues that proclisis is optional in *embedded* topicalization. His examples (50) and (51) contain fronted PPs. It is possible that these sentences are structurally ambiguous between focalization and topicalization, since topicalized PPs, unlike topicalized DPs, are only optionally associated with a clitic in Romance, as Cinque (1990) and Rizzi (1997) have shown. The different interpretations of focalization and topicalization are presumably masked in the context of subordination. Enclisis would then be retained under topicalization but give way to proclisis under focalization.

18. For further discussion of Tamazight complementizers, see Shlonsky (1987), Shlonsky and Sigler (1986) written under different assumptions and, especially Ouhalla (2002).

19. This *is* should be distinguished from the homophonous [+Q] *is* in Tamazight; see (31b). See Ouhalla (2002) for the view that the two are related.

20. The imperative head must be lower than (French) Infin°, which, in turn, is higher than the cliticization site. See Laenzlinger (1994), Rizzi (1997), Rooryck (1992), Rivero and Terzi (1995) among others, for the view that the imperative head is in Comp.

References

Barbosa, P. (1996) "Clitic Placement in European Portuguese and the Position of Subjects," in A. Halpern and A. Zwicky (eds.) *Approaching Second: Second Position Clitics and Related Phenomena.* Stanford: CSLI Publications, 1–40.

Belletti, A. (1990) *Generalized Verb Movement.* Rosenberg and Sellier, Turin: Rosenberg and Sellier.

——— (1999) "Italian/Romance Clitics: Structure and Derivation," in H. van Riemsdijk (ed.) *Clitics in the Languages of Europe.* Berlin: Mouton de Gruyter, 543–579.

Beninca', P. (1995) "Complement Clitics in Medieval Romance: The Tobler-Mussafia Law," in A. Battaye and I. G. Roberts (eds.) *Clause Structure and Language Change.* New York: Oxford University Press, 325–344.

Beninca', P., and Cinque, G. (1993) "Su alcune differenze tra enclisi e proclisi," in *Omaggio a Gianfranco Folena.* Editoriale Programma, Padua: Editoriale Programma, 2313–2326.

Boukhris, F. (1998) "Les clitiques en Berbère tamazighte; parler Zemmour, Khémisset," Ph.D. diss., Université Mohamed V, Rabat.

Bourciez, E. (1967) *Eléments de linguistique romane.* Paris: C. Klincksieck.

Calabrese, A. (1993) "The Sentential Complementation of Salentino: A Study of a Language without Infinitival Clauses," in A. Belletti (ed.) *Syntactic Theory and the Dialects of Italy.* Rosenberg & Sellier, Turin: Rosenberg and Sellier, 28–98.

Cardinaletti, A., and Roberts, I. (2002) "Clause Structure and X-Second," in G. Cinque (ed.) *Functional Structure in DP and IP.* New York: Oxford University Press, 123–166.

Cardinaletti, A., and Shlonsky, U. (2003) "Clitic Positions and Restructuring in Italian," Unpublished ms., Universities of Venice and Geneva. http://www.unige.ch/lettres/limge/syntaxe/shlonsky/lectures/Restructuring.pdf.

Cardinaletti, A., and Starke, M. (1999) "The Typology of Structural Deficiency: On the Three Grammatical Classes," in H. van Riemsdijk (ed.) *Clitics in the Languages of Europe.* Berlin: Mouton de Gruyter, 145–233.

Cartagena, N. (1999) "Los Tiempos Compuestos," in I. Bosque and V. Demonte (eds.) *Gramática descriptiva de la lengua española.* Madrid: Real Academia Española, 2935–2943.

Chomsky, N. (1995) *The Minimalist Program.* Cambridge: MIT Press.

Cinque, G. (1990) *Types of A' Dependencies.* Cambridge: MIT Press.

——— (1999) *Adverbs and Functional Heads: A Cross-Linguistic Perspective.* New York: Oxford University Press.

Costa, J. (1999) "Adverbs as Adjuncts to Non-Universal Functional Categories: Evidence from Portuguese," in A. Alexiadou and P. Svenonius (eds.) *Adverbs and Adjunction.* Potsdam: 19–32.

Cottell, S. (1995) "The Representation of Tense in Modern Irish." *Geneva Generative Papers* 3, 105–124.

Dell, F., and Elmedlaoui, M. (1989) "Clitic Ordering, Morphology and Phonology in the Verbal Complex of Imdlawn Tashelhiyt Berber." *Langues Orientales Anciennes: Philologie et Linguistique,* 165–194.

Diez, F. (1876) *Grammaire des langues romanes.* Trans. Alfred Morel-Fatio and Gaston Paris. Geneva: Slatkine.

Giorgi, A., and F. Pianesi (1997) *Tense and Aspect.* New York: Oxford University Press.

Guerssel, M. (1985) "Some Notes on the Structure of Berber." Unpublished ms., Massachusetts Institute of Technology.

Halpern, A. (1995) *On the Placement and Morphology of Clitics.* Stanford: CSLI Publications.

Halpern, A., and Zwicky, A. L. (eds.) (1996) *Approaching Second: Second Position Clitics and Related Phenomena.* Stanford: CSLI Publications.

Harre, C. E. (1991) *"Tener"* + *Participle: A Case Study in Linguistic Description.* London: Routledge.

Hegarty, M. (1999) "Clitic Placement and the Projection of Functional Categories," in A. Alexiadou, G. Horrocks and M. Stavrou (eds.) *Studies in Greek Syntax.* Dordrecht: Kluwer, 135–152.

Kayne, R. (1975) *French Syntax.* Cambridge: MIT Press.

———— (1989) "Null Subjects and Clitic Climbing," in O. Jaeggli and K. J. Safir (eds.) *The Null Subject Parameter.*, Dordrecht: Kluwer, 239–261.

———— (1991) "Romance Clitics, Verb Movement and PRO." *Linguistic Inquiry* 22, 647–686.

———— (1994) *The Antisymmetry of Syntax.* Cambridge: MIT Press.

Laenzlinger, C. (1994) "Enclitic Clustering: The Case of French Positive Imperatives." *Rivista di Grammatica Generativa* 19, 71–104.

Lobeck, A. (1987) *Syntactic Constraints on VP Ellipsis.* Bloomington, Indi.: University Linguistics Club.

———— (1995) *Ellipsis.* New York: Oxford University Press.

Loporcaro, M. (1988) *Gramatica storica del dialetto di Altamura.* Pisa: Giardini.

———— (1999) "Il futuro cantare-habeo nell'Italia meridionale." *Archivio Glottologico Italiano* 53, 67–114.

Madeira, A-M. (1992) "On Clitic Placement in European Portuguese." *UCL Working Papers in Linguistics* 95–122.

———— (1993) "Clitic-Second in European Portuguese." *Probus* 5, 155–174.

Martins, A.-M. (1994a) "Clíticos na História do Português," Ph.D. diss., Universidade de Lisboa.

———— (1994b) "Enclisis, VP-Deletion and the Nature of Sigma." *Probus* 6, 173–205.

McCloskey, J. (1996) "On the Scope of Verb Movement in Irish." *Natural Language and Linguistic Theory* 14, 47–104.

Meziani, M. (1997) *Les clitiques en Tachawit.* Mémoire DEA. Geneva: Université de Genève.

Ouhalla, J. (1989) "Clitic Movement and the ECP: Evidence from Berber and Romance Languages." *Lingua* 79, 165–215.

———— (2002) "Clitics, Functional Categories and Prosody in Berber." Unpublished ms., University College Dublin.

Petinou, K., and Terzi, A. (2002) "Clitic Misplacement among Normally Developing Children and Children with Specific Language Impairment and the Status of Infl Heads." *Language Acquisition,* 10, 1–28.

Pollock, J.-Y. (1989) "Verb Movement, Universal Grammar and the Structure of IP." *Linguistic Inquiry* 20, 365–424.

Raposo, E. (1987) "Case Theory and Infl-to-Comp: The Inflected Infinitive in European Portuguese." *Linguistic Inquiry* 18, 85–109.

———— (2000) "Clitic Positions and Verb Movement," in J. Costa (ed.) *Portuguese Syntax: New Comparative Studies.* New York: Oxford University Press, 266–298.

———— (2001) "Some Notes on Clitic Placement in European Portuguese," in M.-J. Kim and U. Strauss (eds.) *Proceedings of the Thirty-first Annual North Eastern Linguistic Society Meeting (NELS).* GLSA.

Rivero, M. L. (1994) "Clause Structure and V-Movement in the Languages of the Balkans." *Natural Language and Linguistic Theory* 12, 63–120.

Rivero, M. L., and Terzi, A. (1995) "Imperatives, V-Movement, and Logical Mood." *Journal of Linguistics* 31, 301–332.

Rizzi, L. (1993) "Some Notes on Romance Cliticization." Paper presented at the Durham meeting of the 'Clitics' group, EuroType Project, October 1993, published in Rizzi (2000), Ch. 4.

———— (1996) "Residual Verb Second and the *Wh*-Criterion," in A. Belletti and L. Rizzi (eds.) *Parameters and Functional Heads.* New York: Oxford University Press, 63–90.

———— (1997) "The Fine Structure of the Left Periphery," in L. Haegeman (ed.) *Elements of Grammar: A Handbook of Generative Syntax.* Dordrecht: Kluwer, 281–337.

———— (2000) *Comparative Syntax and Language Acqusition.* London and New York: Routledge.

Roberts, I. (1999) "Have/Be Raising, Move F and Procrastinate." *Linguistic Inquiry* 29, 113–125.

Rohlfs, G. (1996) *Grammatica storica della lingua italiana e dei suoi dialetti.* Einaudi, Turin: Einaudi.

Rooryck, J. (1992) "Romance Enclitic Ordering and Universal Grammar." *Linguistic Review* 9, 219–250.

Roussou, A. (2001) "On the Left Periphery: Modal Particles and Complementizers." *Journal of Greek Linguistics* 1, 65–94.

Rouveret, A. (1989) "Clitisation et temps en portugais européen." *Revue des Langues Romanes* 93, 337–371.

———— (1999) "Clitics, Subjects and Tense in European Portuguese," in H. van Riemsdijk (ed.) *Clitics in the Languages of Europe.* Berlin: Mouten de Gruyter, 639–677.

Rouveret, A., and Vergnaud, J.-R. (1980) "Specifiying Reference to the Subject: French Causatives and Conditions on Representations." *Linguistic Inquiry* 11, 97–102.

Sadiqi, F. (1997) *Grammaire du Berbère.* Paris: L'Harmattan.

———— (1998) "The Syntactic Nature and Position of Object Clitics in Berber." *Languages and Linguistics* 1, 25–47.

Schmitt, C. (2001) "Cross-Linguistic Variation and the Present Perfect: The Case of Portuguese." *Natural Language and Linguistic Theory* 19, 403–453.

Shlonsky, U. (1987) "Focus Constructions in Berber," in M. Guerssel and K. Hale (eds.) *Studies in Berber Syntax.* Lexicon Project Working Papers, Vol. 14. Cambridge: Center for Cognitive Science, Massachusetts Institute of Technology, 1–20.

———— (1997) *Clause Structure and Word Order in Hebrew and Arabic: An Essay in Comparative Semitic Syntax.* New York: Oxford University Press,.

Shlonsky, U., and Sigler, M. (1986) "Unexceptional Exceptional Case-Marking," in S. Berman, J.-W. Choe, and J. McDonough (eds.) *Proceedings of the Sixteenth Annual Meeting of the North Eastern Linguistic Society (NELS).* Amherst, Mass.: GLSA, 447–461.

Sportiche, D. (1998) *Partitions and Atoms of Clause Structure.* London: Routledge.

Terzi, A. (1999a) "Cypriot Greek Clitics and Their Positioning Restrictions," in A. Alexiadou, G. Horrocks, and M. Stavrou (eds.) *Studies in Greek Syntax.* Dordrecht: Kluwer, 227–240.

———— (1999b) "Clitic Combinations, Their Hosts and Their Ordering." *Natural Language and Linguistic Theory* 17, 85–121.

Tsimpli, I. M. (1990) "The Clause Structure and Word Order in Modern Greek." *UCL Working Papers in Linguistics* 2, 226–255.

Uriagereka, J. (1995a) "An F Position in Western Romance," in K. É. Kiss. (ed.) *Discourse Configurational Languages.* New York: Oxford University Press, 153–175.

———— (1995b) "Aspects of the Syntax of Clitic Placement in Western Romance." *Linguistic Inquiry* 26, 79–123.

Wanner, D. (1987) *The Development of Romance Clitic Pronouns: From Latin to Old Romance*. Berlin: Mouton de Gruyter.

Webelhuth, G. (1992) *Principles and Parameters of Syntactic Saturation*. New York: Oxford University Press.

Yllera, A. (1999) "Las perífrasis verbales de gerundio participio," in I. Bosque and V. Demonte (eds.) *Gramática descriptiva de la lengua española*. Madrid: Real Academia Española, 3431–3435.

Zagona, K. (1988a) "Government and Proper Government of Antecedentless VP in English and Spanish." *Natural Language and Linguistic Theory* 6, 95–128.

———— (1988b) *Verb Phrase Syntax*. Dordrecht: Kluwer.

Zanuttini, R. (1997) *Negation and Clausal Structure*. New York: Oxford University Press.

Zubizarreta, M. L. (1985) "The Relation Between Morphophonology and Morphosyntax: The Case of Romance Causatives." *Linguistic Inquiry* 16, 267–289.

Subject Index

Language Index

Name Index

364